Lecture Notes in Artificial Intelligence 1761

Subseries of Lecture Notes in Computer Science
Edited by J. G. Carbonell and J. Siekmann

Lecture Notes in Computer Science
Edited by G. Goos, J. Hartmanis and J. van Leeuwen

Springer
Berlin
Heidelberg
New York
Barcelona
Hong Kong
London
Milan
Paris
Singapore
Tokyo

Ricardo Caferra Gernot Salzer (Eds.)

Automated Deduction in Classical and Non-Classical Logics

Selected Papers

Springer

Series Editors
Jaime G. Carbonell, Carnegie Mellon University, Pittsburgh, PA, USA
Jörg Siekmann, University of Saarland, Saarbrücken, Germany

Volume Editors

Ricardo Caferra
Leibniz-IMAG
46 Avenue Felix Viallet, 38031 Grenoble cedex, France
E-mail: Ricardo.Caferra@imag.fr

Gernot Salzer
Technical University of Vienna
Favoritenstraße 9-11/E185-2, 1040 Vienna, Austria
E-mail: salzer@logic.at

Cataloging-in-Publication Data applied for

Die Deutsche Bibliothek - CIP-Einheitsaufnahme

Automated deduction in classical and non-classical logics /
Ricardo Caferra ; Gernot Salzer (ed.). - Berlin ; Heidelberg ; New
York ; Barcelona ; Hong Kong ; London ; Milan ; Paris ; Singapore ;
Tokyo : Springer, 2000
(Lecture notes in computer science ; Vol. 1761 : Lecture notes in
artificial intelligence)
ISBN 3-540-67190-0

CR Subject Classification (1998): I.2.3, F.4.1, F.3.1

ISBN 3-540-67190-0 Springer-Verlag Berlin Heidelberg New York

Springer-Verlag is a company in the specialist publishing group BertelsmannSpringer

Printed in Germany

Typesetting: Camera-ready by author
Printed on acid-free paper SPIN: 10719651 06/3142 5 4 3 2 1 0

Preface

This volume is a collection of papers on automated deduction in classical, modal, and many-valued logics, with an emphasis on first-order theories. Some authors bridge the gap to higher-order logic by dealing with simple type theory in a first-order setting, or by resolving shortcomings of first-order logic with the help of higher-order notions. Most papers rely on resolution or tableaux methods, with a few exceptions choosing the equational paradigm.

In its entirety the volume is a mirror of contemporary research in first-order theorem proving. One trend to be observed is the interest in effective decision procedures. The main aim of first-order theorem proving was and still is to demonstrate the validity or unsatisfiability of formulas, by more and more sophisticated methods. Within the last years, however, the other side of the medal – falsifiability and satisfiability – has received growing attention. Though in general non-terminating, theorem provers sometimes act as decision procedures on subclasses of first-order logic. In particular cases their output can even be used to extract finite representations of models or counter-examples. Another development is the extension of deduction techniques from classical logic to many-valued and modal logics. By suitably generalizing classical concepts many results carry over to non-classical logics. This line of research is stimulated by artificial intelligence with its need for more expressive logics capable of modeling real-world reasoning.

From a formal point of view this volume comprises two types of papers, invited and contributed ones. Gilles Dowek, Melvin Fitting, Deepak Kapur, Alexander Leitsch, and David Plaisted accepted our invitation to present recent developments in and their view of the field. Contributed papers on the other hand underwent a two-staged selection process. The first selection took place when choosing extended abstracts for presentation at *FTP'98 – International Workshop on First-Order Theorem Proving* held in November 1998 in Vienna. Authors of accepted abstracts were invited to submit full versions, which were again thoroughly refereed. Therefore this volume owes much to those people who helped evaluating the submissions. In particular we would like to thank Maria Paola Bonacina, Adel Bouhoula, Anatoli Degtyarev, Jürgen Dix, Uwe Egly, Christian G. Fermüller, Ulrich Furbach, Fausto Giunchiglia, Rajeev Gore, Bernhard Gramlich, Miki Hermann, Jieh Hsiang, Florent Jacquemard, Alexander Leitsch, Reinhold Letz, Georg Moser, Hans Jürgen Ohlbach, David Plaisted, Michael Rusinowitch, Rolf Socher-Ambrosius, Jane Spurr, Mark Stickel, Andrei Voronkov, and Hantao Zhang for their efforts and support.

August 1999 Ricardo Caferra and Gernot Salzer

Table of Contents

Invited Papers

Contributed Papers

Automated Theorem Proving in First-Order Logic Modulo: On the Difference between Type Theory and Set Theory

Gilles Dowek

INRIA-Rocquencourt, B.P. 105, 78153 Le Chesnay Cedex, France
Gilles.Dowek@inria.fr
http://coq.inria.fr/~dowek

Abstract. *Resolution modulo* is a first-order theorem proving method that can be applied both to first-order presentations of simple type theory (also called higher-order logic) and to set theory. When it is applied to some first-order presentations of type theory, it simulates exactly higher-order resolution. In this note, we compare how it behaves on type theory and on set theory.

Higher-order theorem proving (e.g. higher-order resolution [1, 17, 18]) is different from first-order theorem proving in several respects. First, the first-order unification algorithm has to be replaced by the higher-order one [19, 20]. Even then, the resolution rule alone is not complete but another rule called *the splitting rule* has to be added. At last, the skolemization rule is more complicated [24, 25].

On the other hand, higher-order logic, also called simple type theory, can be expressed as a first-order theory [7], and first-order theorem proving methods, such as first-order resolution, can be used for this theory. Of course, first-order resolution with the axioms of this theory is much less efficient than higher-order resolution. However, we can try to understand higher-order resolution as a special automated theorem proving method designed for this theory. A motivation for this project is that it is very unlikely that such a method applies only to this theory, but it should also apply to similar theories such as extensions of type theory with primitive recursion or set theory.

In [11], together with Th. Hardin and C. Kirchner, we have proposed a theorem proving method for first-order logic, called *resolution modulo*, that when applied to a first-order presentation of type theory simulates exactly higher-order resolution. Proving the completeness of this method has required to introduce a new presentation of first-order logic, called *deduction modulo* that separates clearly computation steps and deduction steps.

Resolution modulo can be applied both to type theory and to set theory. The goal of this note is to compare how resolution modulo works for one theory and the other. In order to remain self contained, we will first present shortly the ideas of deduction modulo and resolution modulo.

R. Caferra and G. Salzer (Eds.): Automated Deduction, LNAI 1761, pp. 1–22, 2000.

1 Resolution Modulo

1.1 Deduction Modulo

In deduction modulo, the notions of language, term and proposition are that of (many sorted) first-order logic. But, a theory is formed with a set of axioms Γ *and a congruence* $\equiv$ defined on propositions. In this paper, all congruences will be defined by confluent rewrite systems (as these rewrite systems are defined on propositions and propositions contain binders, these rewrite systems are in fact *combinatory reduction systems* [23]). Propositions are supposed to be identified modulo the congruence $\equiv$. Hence, the deduction rules must take into account this equivalence. For instance, the *modus ponens* cannot be stated as usual

$$\frac{A \Rightarrow B \quad A}{B}$$

but, as the two occurrences of A need not be identical, but need only to be congruent, it must be stated

$$\frac{A' \Rightarrow B \quad A}{B} \text{ if } A \equiv A'$$

In fact, as the congruence may identify implications with other propositions, a slightly more general formulation is needed

$$\frac{C \quad A}{B} \text{ if } C \equiv A \Rightarrow B$$

All the rules of natural deduction or sequent calculus may be stated in a similar way, see [11,13] for more details.

As an example, in arithmetic, in natural deduction modulo, we can prove that 4 is an even number:

$$\cfrac{\cfrac{\cfrac{}{\forall x \; x = x}\text{ axiom}}{2 \times 2 = 4}\,(x, x = x, 4)\;\forall\text{-elim}}{\exists x \; 2 \times x = 4}\,(x, 2 \times x = 4, 2)\;\exists\text{-intro}$$

Substituting the variable x by the term 2 in the proposition $2 \times x = 4$ yields the proposition $2 \times 2 = 4$, that is congruent to $4 = 4$. The transformation of one proposition into the other, that requires several proof steps in natural deduction, is dropped from the proof in deduction modulo. It is just a computation that need not be written, because everybody can re-do it by him/herself.

In this case, the congruence can be defined by a rewriting system defined on terms

$$0 + y \longrightarrow y$$

$$S(x) + y \longrightarrow S(x + y)$$

$$0 \times y \longrightarrow 0$$

$$S(x) \times y \longrightarrow x \times y + y$$

Notice that, in the proof above, we do not need the axioms of addition and multiplication. Indeed, these axioms are now redundant: since the terms $0 + y$ and y are congruents, the axiom $\forall y\ 0+y = y$ is congruent to the equality axiom $\forall y\ y = y$. Hence, it can be dropped. In other words, this axiom has been built-in the congruence [26, 1, 30].

The originality of deduction modulo is that we have introduced the possibility to define the congruence directly on propositions with rules rewriting atomic propositions to arbitrary ones. For instance, in the theory of integral rings, we can take the rule

$$x \times y = 0 \longrightarrow x = 0 \vee y = 0$$

that rewrites an atomic proposition to a disjunction.

Notice, at last, that deduction modulo is not a true extension of first-order logic. Indeed, it is proved in [11] that for every congruence $\equiv$, we can find a theory $\mathcal{T}$ such that $\Gamma \vdash P$ is provable modulo $\equiv$ if and only if $\mathcal{T}\Gamma \vdash P$ is provable in ordinary first-order logic. Of course, the provable propositions are the same, but the proofs are very different.

1.2 Resolution Modulo

When the congruence on propositions is induced by a congruence on terms, automated theorem proving can be performed like in first-order logic, for instance with the resolution method, provided the unification algorithm is replaced by an *equational unification* algorithm modulo this congruence. Equational unification problems can be solved by the *narrowing* method [15, 21, 22]. The method obtained this way, called *equational resolution* [26, 30], is complete.

The situation is different when the congruence identifies atomic propositions with non atomic ones. For instance, in the theory of integral rings, the proposition

$$a \times a = 0 \Rightarrow a = 0$$

is provable because it reduces to

$$(a = 0 \vee a = 0) \Rightarrow a = 0$$

Hence the proposition

$$\exists y\ (a \times a = y \Rightarrow a = y)$$

is also provable. But, with the clausal form of its negation

$$a \times a = Y$$

$$\neg a = Z$$

we cannot apply the resolution rule successfully, because the terms $a \times a$ and a do not unify.

Hence, we need to introduce a new rule that detects that the literal $a \times a = Y$ has an instance that is reducible by the rewrite rule

$$x \times y = 0 \longrightarrow x = 0 \vee y = 0$$

instantiates it, reduces it and puts it in clausal form again. We get this way the clause

$$a = 0$$

that can be resolved with the clause $\neg a = Z$.

Hence, the rewrite rules have to be divided into two sets: the set $\mathcal{E}$ of rules rewriting terms to terms that are used by the equational unification algorithm and the set of rule $\mathcal{R}$ rewriting atomic propositions to arbitrary ones and that are used by this new rule called *extended narrowing*. The system obtained this way is called *extended narrowing and resolution* or simply *resolution modulo*. Figure 1 gives a formulation of this method where unification problems are postponed as constraints. A proposition is said to be provable with this method when, from

Extended resolution:

$$\frac{\{A_1,\ldots,A_n,B_1,\ldots,B_m\}/E_1 \quad \{\neg C_1,\ldots,\neg C_p,D_1,\ldots,D_q\}/E_2}{\{B_1,\ldots,B_m,D_1,\ldots,D_q\}/E_1 \cup E_2 \cup \{A_1 =_{\mathcal{E}} \ldots A_n =_{\mathcal{E}} C_1 =_{\mathcal{E}} \ldots C_p\}}$$

Extended narrowing:

$$\frac{C/E}{cl(C[r]_p)/(E \cup \{C_{|p} =_{\mathcal{E}} l\})} \text{ if } l \longrightarrow r \in \mathcal{R}$$

Fig. 1. Resolution modulo

the clausal form of its negation, we can deduce an empty clause constrained by a $\mathcal{E}$-unifiable set of equations.

Transforming axioms into rewrite rules enhances the efficiency of automated theorem proving as shown by this very simple example.

Example. To refute the theory $P_1 \Leftrightarrow (Q_2 \vee P_2)$, ..., $P_i \Leftrightarrow (Q_{i+1} \vee P_{i+1})$, ..., $P_n \Leftrightarrow (Q_{n+1} \vee P_{n+1})$, P_1, $Q_2 \Leftrightarrow \bot$, ..., $Q_{n+1} \Leftrightarrow \bot$, $P_{n+1} \Leftrightarrow \bot$, resolution yields $4n+2$ clauses

$$\neg P_1, Q_2, P_2$$

$$\neg Q_2, P_1$$

$$\neg P_2, P_1$$

$$\ldots$$

$$\neg P_i, Q_{i+1}, P_{i+1}$$

$$\neg Q_{i+1}, P_i$$

$$\neg P_{i+1}, P_i$$

$$\ldots$$

$$\neg P_n, Q_{n+1}, P_{n+1}$$

$$\neg Q_{n+1}, P_{n+1}$$

$$\neg P_{n+1}, P_{n+1}$$

$$P_1$$

$$\neg Q_2$$

$$\ldots$$

$$\neg Q_{n+1}$$

$$\neg P_{n+1}$$

While, in resolution modulo, the propositions $P_i \Leftrightarrow (Q_{i+1} \vee P_{i+1})$, $Q_i \Leftrightarrow \bot$ and $P_{n+1} \Leftrightarrow \bot$ can be transformed into rewrite rules

$$P_i \longrightarrow Q_{i+1} \vee P_{i+1}$$

$$Q_i \longrightarrow \bot$$

$$P_{n+1} \longrightarrow \bot$$

The only proposition left is P_1. It reduces to $\bot \vee \ldots \vee \bot$ and its clausal form is hence the empty clause.

Of course, reducing the proposition P_1 has a cost, but this cost is much lower than that of the non deterministic search of a refutation resolution with the clauses above. Indeed, the reduction process is deterministic because the rewrite system is confluent.

1.3 Cut Elimination and Completeness

Resolution modulo is not complete for all congruences. For instance, take the congruence induced by the rewrite rule

$$A \longrightarrow A \Rightarrow B$$

The proposition B has a proof in sequent calculus modulo

$$\begin{prooftree}
\AxiomC{}
\RightLabel{axiom}
\UnaryInfC{$A \vdash A$}
\AxiomC{}
\RightLabel{axiom}
\UnaryInfC{$B \vdash B$}
\RightLabel{weak.-left}
\UnaryInfC{$A, B \vdash B$}
\RightLabel{$\Rightarrow$-left}
\BinaryInfC{$A, A \vdash B$}
\RightLabel{contr.-left}
\UnaryInfC{$A \vdash B$}
\RightLabel{$\Rightarrow$-right}
\UnaryInfC{$\vdash A$}
\AxiomC{}
\RightLabel{axiom}
\UnaryInfC{$A \vdash A$}
\AxiomC{}
\RightLabel{axiom}
\UnaryInfC{$B \vdash B$}
\RightLabel{weak.-left}
\UnaryInfC{$A, B \vdash B$}
\RightLabel{$\Rightarrow$-left}
\BinaryInfC{$A, A \vdash B$}
\RightLabel{contr.-left}
\UnaryInfC{$A \vdash B$}
\RightLabel{cut}
\BinaryInfC{$\vdash B$}
\end{prooftree}$$

but it is not provable by resolution modulo. Indeed, the clausal form of the negation of the proposition B is the clause

$$\neg B$$

and neither the extended resolution rule nor the extended narrowing rule can be applied successfully.

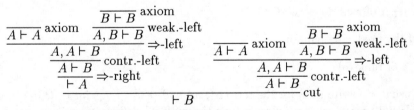

However, it may be noticed that the proposition B has no cut free proof in sequent calculus modulo. Hence sequent calculus modulo this congruence does not have the cut elimination property. We have proved in [11] that resolution modulo is complete for all congruences $\equiv$ such that the sequent calculus modulo $\equiv$ has the cut elimination property. Together with B. Werner, we have proved in [13] that cut elimination holds modulo a large class of congruences and conjectured that it holds modulo all congruences that can be defined by a confluent and terminating rewrite system.

When cut elimination does not hold, only propositions that have a cut free proof are proved by resolution modulo.

2 Simple Type Theory and Set Theory

2.1 Simple Type Theory

Simple type theory is a many-sorted first-order theory. The sorts of simple type theory, called *simple types*, are defined inductively as follows.

- ι and o are simple types,
- if T and U are simple types then $T \rightarrow U$ is a simple type.

As usual, we write $T_1 \rightarrow ... \rightarrow T_n \rightarrow U$ for the type $T_1 \rightarrow ... (T_n \rightarrow U)$.

The language of simple type theory contains the individual symbols

- $S_{T,U,V}$ of sort $(T \rightarrow U \rightarrow V) \rightarrow (T \rightarrow U) \rightarrow T \rightarrow V$,
- $K_{T,U}$ of sort $T \rightarrow U \rightarrow T$,
- $\dot{\vee}$ of sort $o \rightarrow o \rightarrow o$,
- $\dot{\neg}$ of sort $o \rightarrow o$,
- $\dot{\forall}_T$ of sort $(T \rightarrow o) \rightarrow o$,

the function symbols

- $\alpha_{T,U}$ of rank $(T \rightarrow U, T, U)$,

and the predicate symbol

- ε of rank (o).

As usual, we write $(t\ u)$ for the term $\alpha(t, u)$ and $(t\ u_1\ ...\ u_n)$ for $(...(t\ u_1)\ ...\ u_n)$.

Usual presentations of simple-type theory [6, 2] define propositions as terms of type o. But, as we want type theory to be a first-order theory, we introduce a predicate symbol ε that transforms a term of type o into a genuine proposition. Then, we need an axiom relating the proposition $\varepsilon(\alpha(\alpha(\dot{\vee}, x), y))$ and the proposition $\varepsilon(x) \vee \varepsilon(y)$. For instance, the axiom

$$\forall x\ \forall y\ (\varepsilon(\dot{\vee}\ x\ y) \Leftrightarrow (\varepsilon(x) \vee \varepsilon(y)))$$

$$(S\ x\ y\ z) \longrightarrow (x\ z\ (y\ z))$$
$$(K\ x\ y) \longrightarrow x$$
$$\varepsilon(\dot{\neg}\ x) \longrightarrow \neg\varepsilon(x)$$
$$\varepsilon(\dot{\vee}\ x\ y) \longrightarrow \varepsilon(x) \vee \varepsilon(y)$$
$$\varepsilon(\dot{\forall}\ x) \longrightarrow \forall y\ \varepsilon(x\ y)$$

Fig. 2. Rewriting rules for simple type theory

This axiom can be built in the congruence, if we take the rewrite rule

$$\varepsilon(\dot{\vee}\ x\ y) \longrightarrow \varepsilon(x) \vee \varepsilon(y)$$

This leads to the rewrite system of the figure 2. This rewrite system is confluent because it is orthogonal and we prove in [10] that it is strongly normalizing. Hence, the congruence is decidable.

It is proved in [13] that deduction modulo this congruence has the cut elimination property, i.e. every proposition provable in sequent calculus modulo this congruence has a cut free proof.

2.2 Set Theory

The language of Zermelo's set theory is formed with the binary predicate symbols $\in$ and $=$. This theory contains the axioms of equality and the following axioms.
pair:

$$\forall x\ \forall y\ \exists z\ \forall w\ (w \in z \Leftrightarrow (w = x \vee w = y))$$

union:

$$\forall x\ \exists y\ \forall w\ (w \in y \Leftrightarrow \exists z\ (w \in z \wedge z \in x))$$

power set:

$$\forall x\ \exists y\ \forall w\ (w \in y \Leftrightarrow \forall z\ (z \in w \Rightarrow z \in x))$$

subset scheme:

$$\forall x_1 ... \forall x_n\ \forall y\ \exists z\ \forall w\ (w \in z \Leftrightarrow (w \in y \wedge P))$$

where $x_1, ..., x_n$ are the free variables of P minus w.
To these axioms, we may add the extensionality axiom, the foundation axiom, the axiom of infinity, the replacement scheme and the axiom of choice.

To have a language for the objects of the theory we may skolemize these axioms introducing the function symbols $\{\}$, $\bigcup$, $\mathcal{P}$ and $f_{x_1,\dots,x_n,w,P}$. We then get the axioms

$$\forall x\ \forall y\ \forall w\ (w \in \{\}(x,y) \Leftrightarrow (w = x \vee w = y))$$

$$\forall x\ \forall w\ (w \in \bigcup(x) \Leftrightarrow \exists z\ (w \in z \wedge z \in x))$$

$$\forall x\ \forall w\ (w \in \mathcal{P}(x) \Leftrightarrow \forall z\ (z \in w \Rightarrow z \in x))$$

$$\forall x_1 ... \forall x_n\ \forall y\ \forall w\ (w \in f_{x_1,...,x_n,w,P}(x_1, ..., x_n, y) \Leftrightarrow (w \in y \wedge P))$$

Then, these axioms may be built in the congruence with the rewrite system of figure 3. This rewrite system is confluent because it is orthogonal. But it does

$$w \in \{\}(x, y) \longrightarrow w = x \vee w = y$$

$$w \in \bigcup(x) \longrightarrow \exists z\ (w \in z \wedge z \in x)$$

$$w \in \mathcal{P}(x) \longrightarrow \forall z\ (z \in w \Rightarrow z \in x)$$

$$v \in f_{x_1,...,x_n,w,P}(y_1, ..., y_n, z) \longrightarrow v \in z \wedge [y_1/x_1, ..., y_n/x_n, v/w]P$$

Fig. 3. Rewriting rules for set theory

not terminate. A counter-example is M. Crabbé's proposition. Let C be the term $\{x \in a \mid \neg x \in x\}$ i.e. $f_{w,\neg w \in w}(a)$. We have

$$x \in C \longrightarrow x \in a \wedge \neg x \in x$$

Hence, writing A for the proposition $C \in C$ and B for the proposition $C \in a$ we have

$$A \longrightarrow B \wedge \neg A$$

This permits to construct the infinite reduction sequence

$$A \longrightarrow B \wedge \neg A \longrightarrow B \wedge \neg(B \wedge \neg A) \longrightarrow ...$$

Up to our knowledge, the decidability of this congruence is open.

Deduction modulo this congruence does not have the cut elimination property. A counter example is again Crabbé's proposition (see [16, 14] for a discussion). As we have seen, this proposition A rewrites to a proposition of the form $B \wedge \neg A$. Hence, the proposition $\neg B$ has the following proof

$$\dfrac{\dfrac{\dfrac{\dfrac{}{B \vdash B}\,\text{axiom} \quad \dfrac{\dfrac{\dfrac{\dfrac{\dfrac{\dfrac{\dfrac{}{A \vdash A}\,\text{axiom}}{A, B \vdash A}\,\text{weakening-left}}{A, B, \neg A \vdash}\,\neg\text{-left}}{A, A \vdash}\,\wedge\text{-left}}{A \vdash}\,\text{contraction-left}}{\vdash \neg A}\,\neg\text{-right}}{B \vdash \neg A}\,\text{weakening-left}}{B \vdash A}\,\wedge\text{-right} \quad \dfrac{\dfrac{\dfrac{\dfrac{\dfrac{}{A \vdash A}\,\text{axiom}}{A, B \vdash A}\,\text{weakening-left}}{A, B, \neg A \vdash}\,\neg\text{-left}}{A, A \vdash}\,\wedge\text{-left}}{A \vdash}\,\text{contraction-left}}{B \vdash}\,\text{cut}}{\vdash \neg B}\,\neg\text{-right}$$

but it is easy to check that the proposition $\neg B$, i.e. $\neg f_{w,\neg w \in w}(a) \in a$, has no cut free proof.

3 Resolution Modulo in Type Theory and in Set Theory

3.1 Resolution Modulo in Type Theory

In the rewrite system of figure 2, the first two rules

$$(S\ x\ y\ z) \longrightarrow (x\ z\ (y\ z))$$

$$(K\ x\ y) \longrightarrow x$$

rewrite terms to terms and are used by the unification algorithm. The three others

$$\varepsilon(\dot{\neg}\ x) \longrightarrow \neg\varepsilon(x)$$

$$\varepsilon(\dot{\vee}\ x\ y) \longrightarrow \varepsilon(x) \vee \varepsilon(y)$$

$$\varepsilon(\dot{\forall}\ x) \longrightarrow \forall y\ \varepsilon(x\ y)$$

rewrite propositions to propositions and are used by the extended narrowing rule.

Equational unification modulo the rules S and K is related to higher-order unification. Actually since the reduction of combinators is slightly weaker than the reduction of λ-calculus, unification modulo this reduction is slightly weaker than higher-order unification [8]. To have genuine higher-order unification, we have to take another formulation of type theory using explicit substitutions instead of combinators (see section 5).

The extended narrowing modulo the rules $\dot{\neg}$, $\dot{\vee}$ and $\dot{\forall}$ is exactly the splitting rule of higher-order resolution. A normal literal unifies with the left member of such a rule if and only if its head symbol is a variable.

The skolemization rule in this language is related to the skolemization rule of type theory. When we skolemize a proposition of the form

$$\forall x\ \exists y\ P$$

we introduce a function symbol f of rank (T, U) where T is the type of x and U the type of y (not an individual symbol of type $T \rightarrow U$) and the axiom

$$\forall x\ [f(x)/y]P$$

Hence, the Skolem symbol f alone is not a term, but it permits to build a term of type U when we apply it to a term of type T. This is, in essence, the higher-order skolemization rule, but formulated for the language of combinators and not for λ-calculus. Again, we have the genuine higher-order skolemization rule if we use the formulation of type theory using explicit substitutions instead of combinators (see section 5).

3.2 Resolution Modulo in Set Theory

In set theory, there is no rule rewriting terms to terms. Hence, unification in set theory is simply first-order unification. Conversselly, all the rules of figure 3 rewrite propositions to propositions and thus the extended narrowing is performed modulo all theses rules.

In set theory, resolution modulo is incomplete. We have seen that the proposition

$$\neg f_{w,\neg w \in w}(a) \in a$$

has a proof in set theory, but it cannot be proved by the resolution modulo method. Indeed, from the clausal form of its negation

$$f_{w,\neg w \in w}(a) \in a$$

we can apply neither the resolution rule nor the extended narrowing rule successfully.

4 On the Differences between Set Theory and Type Theory

4.1 Termination

The first difference between resolution modulo in type theory and in set theory is that the rewrite system is terminating in type theory and hence all propositions have a normal form, while some propositions, e.g. Crabbé's proposition, have no normal form in set theory.

Hence, during proof search, we can normalize all the clauses while this is impossible in set theory. Formally, the method modified this way requires a completeness proof.

4.2 Completeness

Another difference is that, as type theory verifies the cut elimination property, resolution modulo this congruence is complete, while it is incomplete modulo the congruence of set theory.

A solution to recover completeness may be to use an automated theorem proving method that searches for proofs containing cuts. For instance if we add a rule allowing to refute the set of clauses S by refuting both the set $S \cup \{\neg P\}$ and the set $\{P\}$ then we can refute the proposition B above.

Another direction is to search for another presentation of set theory or for a restriction of this theory that enjoys termination and cut elimination. We conjecture that if we restrict the subset scheme to *stratifiable* propositions in the sense of W.V.O. Quine [27], we get a restriction of set theory that is sufficient to express most mathematics, that terminates and that verifies the cut elimination property. The cut elimination and completeness results obtained by S.C. Bailin [4, 5] for his formulation of set theory let this conjecture be plausible.

4.3 Typing Literals

A minor difference is that when we try to prove a theorem of the form "for all natural numbers x, $P(x)$", we have to formalize this theorem by the proposition

$$\forall x\ (x \in \mathbb{N} \Rightarrow P(x))$$

in set theory. In contrast, in type theory, we can choose to take ι for the type of natural numbers and state the theorem

$$\forall x\ P(x)$$

During the search, in set theory, extra literals of the form $x \in \mathbb{N}$ appear and have to be resolved.

4.4 The Role of Unification and Extended Narrowing

In resolution modulo, like in most other methods, the main difficulty is to construct the terms that have to be substituted to the variables. In resolution modulo, these terms are constructed by two processes: the unification algorithm and the extended narrowing rule.

The main difference between resolution modulo in type theory and in set theory is the division of work between the unification and the extended narrowing. In type theory, unification is quite powerful and the extended narrowing is rarely used. In contrast, in set theory, unification is simply first-order unification and all the work is done by the extended narrowing rule.

This difference reflects a deep difference on how mathematics are formalized in a theory and the other. Indeed, the unification in type theory is rich because there are rules that rewrite terms to terms and these rules are there because the notion of function is primitive in type theory. When we have a function f and an object a we can form the term $(f\ a)$ and start rewriting this term to a normal form. In set theory, there is no such term and a term alone can never be reduced. Instead of forming the term $(f\ a)$ we can form a proposition expressing that b is the image of a by the function f, $< a, b >\in f$, that then can be rewritten.

For example, in the proof of Cantor's theorem we have a function f from a set B to its power set and we want to form Cantor's set of objects that do not belong to their image.

If x is an element of B, in type theory we can express its image $(f\ x)$, then the term of type o reflecting the proposition expressing that x belongs to its image $(f\ x\ x)$, the term of type o reflecting its negation $\dot{\neg}(f\ x\ x)$ and then Cantor's set $\lambda x\ \dot{\neg}(f\ x\ x)$ that, with combinators, is expressed by the term

$$C = (S\ (K\ \dot{\neg})\ (S\ (S\ (K\ f)\ (S\ K\ K))\ (S\ K\ K)))$$

In contrast, in set theory, we cannot form a term expressing the image of x by the function f. Instead of saying that x does not belong to its image we have to say that it does not belong to any object that happens to be its image.

$$C = \{x \in B \mid \forall y\ (< x, y >\in f \Rightarrow \neg x \in y)\}$$

This requires to introduce two more logical symbols $\Rightarrow$ and $\forall$. These symbols cannot be generated by the unification algorithm and are generated by the extended narrowing rule.

It is not completely clear what is the best division of work between unification and extended narrowing. Experiences with type theory show that the unification algorithm is usually well controlled while the splitting rule is very productive. Loading the unification and unloading the extended narrowing seems to improve efficiency.

However, two remarks moderate this point of view. First, in type theory, the functions that can be expressed by a term are very few. For instance, if we take the type ι for the natural numbers and introduce two symbols O and $Succ$ for zero and the successor function, we can only express by a term the constant functions and the functions adding a constant to their argument. The other functions are usually expressed with the description operator (or the choice operator) and hence as relations. We may enrich the language of combinators and the rewrite system, for instance with primitive recursion, but then it is not obvious that unification is still so well controlled.

Another remark is that having a decidable and unitary unification (such as first-order unification) permits to solve unification problems on the fly instead of keeping them as constraints. This permits to restrict the use of the extended narrowing rule. For instance, in type theory, when we have a literal $\varepsilon(P\ x)$ and we apply the extended narrowing rule yielding two literals $\varepsilon(A)$ and $\varepsilon(B)$ and a constraint

$$\varepsilon(P\ x) = \varepsilon(A \dot{\vee} B)$$

we keep this constraint frozen and we may need to apply the extended narrowing rule to other literals starting with the variable P. In contrast, in set theory, if we have a literal $x \in P$ and we apply the extended narrowing rule yielding two literals $y = a$ and $y = b$ and a constraint $(x \in P) = (y \in \{a, b\})$. The substitution $\{a, b\}/P$ can be immediately propagated to all the occurrences of P initiating reductions that let the extended narrowing steps be useless.

5 Advanced Formulations of Type Theory and Set Theory

As an illustration of this discussion, we want to compare resolution modulo proofs of Cantor's theorem in type theory and in set theory. However, the presentations of type theory and set theory above are a little too rough to be really practicable. In both cases, we shall use a more sophisticated presentation where the language contains a full binding operator.

Indeed, in type theory, we want to express Cantor's set by the term

$$C = \lambda x\ \dot{\neg}(f\ x\ x)$$

and not by the term

$$C = (S\ (K\ \dot{\neg})\ (S\ (S\ (K\ f)\ (S\ K\ K))\ (S\ K\ K)))$$

Similarly, in set theory we want to express this set as

$$C = \{x \in B \mid \forall y\ (< x, y > \in R \Rightarrow \neg x \in y)\}$$

where $< x, y >$ is a notation for the set $\{\{x, y\}, \{x\}\}$ i.e. $\{\}(\{\}(x, y), \{\}(x, x))$, and not by the term

$$C = \{x \in B \mid \forall y\ (\forall u\ ((\forall v\ (v \in u \Leftrightarrow (\forall w\ (w \in v \Leftrightarrow (w = x \vee w = y)) \vee \forall w\ (w \in v \Leftrightarrow w = x)))) \Rightarrow u \in R) \Rightarrow \neg x \in y)\}$$[1]

For type theory, such a first-order presentation with a general binding operator has been proposed in [12]. It uses an expression of λ-calculus as a first-order language based on de Bruijn indices and explicit substitutions. In this presentation, the sorts are of the form $\Gamma \vdash T$ or $\Gamma \vdash \Delta$ where T is a simple type and Γ and Δ are finite sequences of simple types. The language contains the following symbols

- 1_A^Γ of sort $A\Gamma \vdash A$,
- $\alpha_{A,B}^\Gamma$ of rank $(\Gamma \vdash A \rightarrow B, \Gamma \vdash A, \Gamma \vdash B)$,
- $\lambda_{A,B}^\Gamma$ of rank $(A\Gamma \vdash B, \Gamma \vdash A \rightarrow B)$,
- $[]_A^{\Gamma,\Gamma'}$ of rank $\Gamma' \vdash A, \Gamma \vdash \Gamma', \Gamma \vdash A)$,
- id^Γ of sort $\Gamma \vdash \Gamma$,
- $\uparrow_A^\Gamma$ of sort $A\Gamma \vdash \Gamma$,
- $\cdot_A^{\Gamma,\Gamma'}$ of rank $(\Gamma \vdash A, \Gamma \vdash \Gamma', \Gamma \vdash A\Gamma')$,
- $\circ^{\Gamma,\Gamma',\Gamma''}$ of rank $(\Gamma \vdash \Gamma'', \Gamma'' \vdash \Gamma', \Gamma \vdash \Gamma')$,
- $\dot{\vee}$ of sort $\vdash o \rightarrow o \rightarrow o$,
- $\dot{\neg}$ of sort $\vdash o \rightarrow o$,
- $\dot{\forall}_T$ of sort $\vdash (T \rightarrow o) \rightarrow o$,
- ε of rank $(\vdash o)$.

And the rewrite system is that of figure 4.

A formulation of set theory with a general binder has been given in [9]. But it is not expressed in a first-order setting yet. Waiting for such a theory, for the example of Cantor's theorem, we add a constant C and an *ad hoc* rewrite rule

$$x \in C \longrightarrow x \in B \wedge \forall y\ (< x, y > \in R \Rightarrow \neg x \in y)$$

---

[1] In the presentation of set theory above, there is no instance of the subset scheme for the proposition

$$\forall y\ (< x, y > \in R \Rightarrow \neg x \in y)$$

because it contains Skolem symbols. Hence, we replace the proposition $< x, y > \in R$ by the equivalent one

$$\forall u\ ((\forall v\ (v \in u \Leftrightarrow (\forall w\ (w \in v \Leftrightarrow (w = x \vee w = y)) \vee \forall w\ (w \in v \Leftrightarrow w = x)))) \Rightarrow u \in R)$$

Then we can build the set C with the function symbol introduced by the skolemization of this instance of the scheme. The proposition $x \in C$ is then provably equivalent to $x \in B \wedge \forall y\ (< x, y > \in R \Rightarrow \neg x \in y)$ but it does not reduce to it.

β-reduction and η-reduction:

$$(\lambda a)b \longrightarrow a[b.id]$$

$$\lambda(a\ 1) \longrightarrow b \text{ if } a =_\sigma b[\uparrow]$$

σ-reduction:

$$(a\ b)[s] \longrightarrow (a[s]\ b[s])$$

$$1[a.s] \longrightarrow a$$

$$a[id] \longrightarrow a$$

$$(\lambda a)[s] \longrightarrow \lambda(a[1.(s \circ \uparrow)])$$

$$(a[s])[t] \longrightarrow a[s \circ t]$$

$$id \circ s \longrightarrow s$$

$$\uparrow \circ (a.s) \longrightarrow s$$

$$(s_1 \circ s_2) \circ s_3 \longrightarrow s_1 \circ (s_2 \circ s_3)$$

$$(a.s) \circ t \longrightarrow a[t].(s \circ t)$$

$$s \circ id \longrightarrow s$$

$$1.\uparrow \longrightarrow id$$

$$1[s].(\uparrow \circ s) \longrightarrow s$$

reduction of propositions:

$$\varepsilon(\dot{\vee}\ x\ y) \longrightarrow \varepsilon(x) \vee \varepsilon(y)$$

$$\varepsilon(\dot{\neg}\ x) \longrightarrow \neg\varepsilon(x)$$

$$\varepsilon(\dot{\forall}_T\ x) \longrightarrow \forall y\ \varepsilon(x\ y)$$

Fig. 4. The rewrite rules of type theory with explicit substitutions

6 Three Proofs of Cantor's Theorem

We now give three resolution modulo proofs of Cantor's theorem that there is no surjection from a set to its power set. The first is in type theory with a function expressing the potential surjection from a set to its power set. The second is also in type theory, but this potential surjection is expressed by a relation. The last one is in set theory and the surjection is, of course, expressed by a relation.

Automated theorem proving for Cantor's theorem in type theory is discussed in [17,18,3].

6.1 In Type Theory with a Function

In type theory, a set is expressed by a term of type $T \rightarrow o$. Here, we choose to consider only the set of all objects of type ι. Its power set is the set of all objects of type $\iota \to o$. Hence we want to prove that there is no surjection from the type ι to $\iota \to o$. The first solution is to represent this potential surjection by a function f of type $\iota \to \iota \to o$. The surjectivity of this function can be expressed by the existence of a right-inverse g to this function, i.e. a function of type $(\iota \to o) \to \iota$ such that for all x, $(f\ (g\ x)) = x$. Using Leibniz' definition of equality this proposition is written

$$\forall x\ \forall p\ (\varepsilon(p\ (f\ (g\ x))) \Leftrightarrow \varepsilon(p\ x))$$

Putting this proposition in clausal form yields the clauses

$$\neg\varepsilon(P\ (f\ (g\ X))), \varepsilon(P\ X)$$

$$\varepsilon(Q\ (f\ (g\ Y))), \neg\varepsilon(Q\ Y)$$

The search is described on figure 5. It returns the empty clause constrained by

1		$\neg\varepsilon(P\ (f\ (g\ X))), \varepsilon(P\ X)$
2		$\varepsilon(Q\ (f\ (g\ Y))), \neg\varepsilon(Q\ Y)$
3	narr. (1)	$\neg\varepsilon(P\ (f\ (g\ X))), \neg\varepsilon(R)/c_1$
4	narr. (2)	$\varepsilon(Q\ (f\ (g\ Y))), \varepsilon(S)/c_2$
5	res. (3, 4)	$\Box/c_1, c_2, c_3, c_4, c_5$

with

$$\begin{array}{ll} c_1 & (P\ X) = \dot{\neg}R \\ c_2 & (Q\ Y) = \dot{\neg}S \\ c_3 & (P\ (f\ (g\ X))) = R \\ c_4 & (Q\ (f\ (g\ Y))) = S \\ c_5 & (P\ (f\ (g\ X))) = (Q\ (f\ (g\ Y))) \end{array}$$

Fig. 5. Cantor's theorem in type theory with a function

the equations

$$\begin{array}{l} (P\ X) = \dot{\neg}R \\ (Q\ Y) = \dot{\neg}S \\ (P\ (f\ (g\ X))) = R \\ (Q\ (f\ (g\ Y))) = S \\ (P\ (f\ (g\ X))) = (Q\ (f\ (g\ Y))) \end{array}$$

that have the solution

$$\begin{array}{l} X = Y = \lambda\dot{\neg}[\uparrow](f[\uparrow]\ 1\ 1) \\ P = Q = \lambda(1\ (g[\uparrow]\ \lambda\dot{\neg}[\uparrow^2](f[\uparrow^2]\ 1\ 1))) \\ R = S = (f\ (g\ \lambda\dot{\neg}[\uparrow](f[\uparrow]\ 1\ 1))\ (g\ \lambda\dot{\neg}[\uparrow](f[\uparrow]\ 1\ 1))) \end{array}$$

6.2 In Type Theory with a Relation

Instead of using the primitive notion of function of set theory, we can code the functions as functional relations R of type $\iota \rightarrow (\iota \rightarrow o) \rightarrow o$. The surjectivity and functionality of this relation are expressed by the propositions

$$E : \forall y\ \exists x\ \varepsilon(R\ x\ y)$$

and

$$F : \forall x\ \forall y\ \forall z\ (\varepsilon(R\ x\ y) \Rightarrow \varepsilon(R\ x\ z) \Rightarrow \forall p\ (\varepsilon(p\ y) \Leftrightarrow \varepsilon(p\ z)))$$

Putting these propositions in clausal form yields the clauses

$$\varepsilon(R\ g(U)\ U)$$

$$\neg\varepsilon(R\ X\ Y), \neg\varepsilon(R\ X\ Z), \neg\varepsilon(P\ Y), \varepsilon(P\ Z)$$

$$\neg\varepsilon(R\ X\ Y), \neg\varepsilon(R\ X\ Z), \neg\varepsilon(P\ Z), \varepsilon(P\ Y)$$

The search is then described on figure 6 where we simplify the constraints and substitute the solved constraints at each step. It returns the empty clause constrained by the equations

$$\begin{aligned}
&(P\ Y) = \dot\neg\dot\forall G_1\\
&(G_1\ W_1) = \dot\neg(R\ g(U_1)\ U_1)\dot\vee\dot\neg\dot\forall G_2\\
&(G_2\ y_1) = \dot\neg A_2\dot\vee\dot\neg B_2\\
&(G_1\ W_1') = \dot\neg A_2\dot\vee\dot\neg B_2\\
&(P\ Y) = \dot\neg\dot\forall G_3\\
&(G_3\ y_2) = \dot\neg(R\ g(Y')\ Z')\dot\vee\dot\neg B_3\\
&(P\ Z') = \dot\neg B_3\\
&(P\ Y') = \dot\neg\dot\forall G_4\\
&(G_4\ W_2) = \dot\neg(R\ g(U_2)\ U_2)\dot\vee\dot\neg\dot\forall G_5\\
&(G_5\ y_3) = \dot\neg A_5\dot\vee\dot\neg B_5\\
&(G_4\ W_2') = \dot\neg A_5\dot\vee\dot\neg B_5
\end{aligned}$$

that have the solution

$$\begin{aligned}
&P = \lambda\dot\neg[\uparrow](1\ (g(C)[\uparrow]))\\
&G_1 = G_2 = G_3 = G_4 = G_5 = \lambda(\dot\neg[\uparrow](R[\uparrow]\ g(C)[\uparrow]\ 1)\dot\vee[\uparrow]\dot\neg[\uparrow](1\ g(C)[\uparrow]))\\
&Y = W_1 = U_1 = Y' = W_2 = U_2 = C\\
&W_1' = y_1\\
&Z' = y_2\\
&W_2' = y_3\\
&A_2 = (R\ g(C)\ y_1)\\
&B_2 = (y_1\ g(C))\\
&B_3 = (y_2\ g(C))\\
&A_5 = (R\ g(C)\ y_3)\\
&B_5 = (y_3\ g(C))
\end{aligned}$$

where $C = \lambda x\ \dot\forall\lambda y\ (\dot\neg(R\ x\ y)\dot\vee\dot\neg(y\ x))$,
i.e. $\lambda\ \dot\forall[\uparrow]\lambda\ (\dot\neg[\uparrow^2](R[\uparrow^2]\ 2\ 1)\dot\vee[\uparrow^2]\dot\neg[\uparrow^2](1\ 2))$.

1	$\varepsilon(R\ g(U)\ U)$
2	$\neg\varepsilon(R\ X\ Y), \neg\varepsilon(R\ X\ Z), \neg\varepsilon(P\ Y), \varepsilon(P\ Z)$
3	$\neg\varepsilon(R\ X\ Y), \neg\varepsilon(R\ X\ Z), \neg\varepsilon(P\ Z), \varepsilon(P\ Y)$
4 res. (1, 2)	$\neg\varepsilon(R\ g(Y)\ Z), \neg\varepsilon(P\ Y), \varepsilon(P\ Z)$
5 res. (1, 4)	$\neg\varepsilon(P\ Y), \varepsilon(P\ Y)$
6 five narr. (5)	$\neg\varepsilon(A_1), \neg\varepsilon(B_1), \varepsilon(P\ Y)/c_1, c_2$
7 res. (6, 1)	$\neg\varepsilon(B_1), \varepsilon(P\ Y)/c_1, c_2'$
8 four narr. (7)	$\varepsilon(A_2), \varepsilon(P\ Y)/c_1, c_2'', c_3$
9	$\varepsilon(B_2), \varepsilon(P\ Y)/c_1, c_2'', c_3$
10 renaming (6)	$\neg\varepsilon(A_1'), \neg\varepsilon(B_1'), \varepsilon(P\ Y)/c_1, c_4$
11 res. (10, 8)	$\neg\varepsilon(B_1'), \varepsilon(P\ Y)/c_1, c_2'', c_3, c_4'$
12 res. (11, 9)	$\varepsilon(P\ Y)/c_1, c_2'', c_3, c_4''$
13 five narr. (12)	$\varepsilon(A_3)/c_1, c_2'', c_3, c_4'', c_5, c_6$
14	$\varepsilon(B_3)/c_1, c_2'', c_3, c_4'', c_5, c_6$
15 renaming (4)	$\neg\varepsilon(R\ g(Y')\ Z'), \neg\varepsilon(P\ Y'), \varepsilon(P\ Z')$
16 res. (15, 13)	$\neg\varepsilon(P\ Y'), \varepsilon(P\ Z')/c_1, c_2'', c_3, c_4'', c_5, c_6'$
17 narr. (16)	$\neg\varepsilon(P\ Y'), \neg\varepsilon(Q)/c_1, c_2'', c_3, c_4'', c_5, c_6', c_7$
18 res. (17, 14)	$\neg\varepsilon(P\ Y')/c_1, c_2'', c_3, c_4'', c_5, c_6', c_7'$
19 five narr. (18)	$\neg\varepsilon(A_4), \neg\varepsilon(B_4)/c_1, c_2'', c_3, c_4'', c_5, c_6', c_7', c_8, c_9$
20 res. (19, 1)	$\neg\varepsilon(B_4)/c_1, c_2'', c_3, c_4'', c_5, c_6', c_7', c_8, c_9'$
21 four narr. (20)	$\varepsilon(A_5)/c_1, c_2'', c_3, c_4'', c_5, c_6', c_7', c_8, c_9'', c_{10}$
22	$\varepsilon(B_5)/c_1, c_2'', c_3, c_4'', c_5, c_6', c_7', c_8, c_9'', c_{10}$
23 renaming (19)	$\neg\varepsilon(A_4'), \neg\varepsilon(B_4')/c_1, c_2'', c_3, c_4'', c_5, c_6', c_7', c_8, c_{11}$
24 res. (23, 21)	$\neg\varepsilon(B_4')/c_1, c_2'', c_3, c_4'', c_5, c_6', c_7', c_8, c_9'', c_{10}, c_{11}'$
25 res. (24, 22)	$\Box/c_1, c_2'', c_3, c_4'', c_5, c_6', c_7', c_8, c_9'', c_{10}, c_{11}''$

with

$$
\begin{array}{ll}
c_1 & (P\ Y) = \dot{\neg}\dot{\forall}G_1 \\
c_2 & (G_1\ W_1) = \dot{\neg}A_1\dot{\vee}\dot{\neg}B_1 \\
c_2' & (G_1\ W_1) = \dot{\neg}(R\ g(U_1)\ U_1)\dot{\vee}\dot{\neg}B_1 \\
c_2'' & (G_1\ W_1) = \dot{\neg}(R\ g(U_1)\ U_1)\dot{\vee}\dot{\neg}\dot{\forall}G_2 \\
c_3 & (G_2\ y_1) = \dot{\neg}A_2\dot{\vee}\dot{\neg}B_2 \\
c_4 & (G_1\ W_1') = \dot{\neg}A_1'\dot{\vee}\dot{\neg}B_1' \\
c_4' & (G_1\ W_1') = \dot{\neg}A_2\dot{\vee}\dot{\neg}B_1' \\
c_4'' & (G_1\ W_1') = \dot{\neg}A_2\dot{\vee}\dot{\neg}B_2 \\
c_5 & (P\ Y) = \dot{\neg}\dot{\forall}G_3 \\
c_6 & (G_3\ y_2) = \dot{\neg}A_3\dot{\vee}\dot{\neg}B_3 \\
c_6' & (G_3\ y_2) = \dot{\neg}(R\ g(Y')\ Z')\dot{\vee}\dot{\neg}B_3 \\
c_7 & (P\ Z') = \dot{\neg}Q \\
c_7' & (P\ Z') = \dot{\neg}B_3 \\
c_8 & (P\ Y') = \dot{\neg}\dot{\forall}G_4 \\
c_9 & (G_4\ W_2) = \dot{\neg}A_4\dot{\vee}\dot{\neg}B_4 \\
c_9' & (G_4\ W_2) = \dot{\neg}(R\ g(U_2)\ U_2)\dot{\vee}\dot{\neg}B_4 \\
c_9'' & (G_4\ W_2) = \dot{\neg}(R\ g(U_2)\ U_2)\dot{\vee}\dot{\neg}\dot{\forall}G_5 \\
c_{10} & (G_5\ y_3) = \dot{\neg}A_5\dot{\vee}\dot{\neg}B_5 \\
c_{11} & (G_4\ W_2') = \dot{\neg}A_4'\dot{\vee}\dot{\neg}B_4' \\
c_{11}' & (G_4\ W_2') = \dot{\neg}A_5\dot{\vee}\dot{\neg}B_4' \\
c_{11}'' & (G_4\ W_2') = \dot{\neg}A_5\dot{\vee}\dot{\neg}B_5
\end{array}
$$

Fig. 6. Cantor's theorem in type theory with a relation

6.3 In Set Theory

We consider a set B and a potential surjection from this set to its power set. We express this potential surjection by a set R. The surjectivity and functionality of this set are expressed by the propositions

$$E : \forall y\ (y \in \mathcal{P}(B) \Rightarrow \exists x\ (x \in B \wedge <x, y> \in R))$$

$$F : \forall x\ \forall y\ \forall z\ (<x, y> \in R \Rightarrow <x, z> \in R \Rightarrow y = z)$$

We use also the axiom of equality

$$L : \forall z\ \forall x\ \forall y\ (x = y \Rightarrow \neg z \in x \Rightarrow \neg z \in y)$$

The proposition E reduces to the proposition

$$\forall u\ (\forall y\ (y \in u \Rightarrow y \in B)) \Rightarrow \exists x\ (x \in B \wedge <x, u> \in R))$$

Putting this proposition in clausal form yields the clauses

$$y(U) \in U, <g(U), U> \in R$$

$$\neg y(U) \in B, <g(U), U> \in R$$

$$y(U) \in U, g(U) \in B$$

$$\neg y(U) \in B, g(U) \in B$$

The two other propositions yield the clauses

$$\neg <X, Y> \in R, \neg <X, Z> \in R, Y = Z$$

$$\neg X = Y, Z \in X, \neg Z \in Y$$

The search is described on figure 7 where we simplify the constraints and substitute the solved constraints at each step. Propagating the solved constraints may lead to new reductions that require to put the proposition in clausal form again. This explains that some resolution steps yield several clauses. It returns the empty clause.

6.4 Remarks

The termination and completeness issues are not addressed by these examples because, even in set theory, Cantor's theorem has a cut free proof and the search involves only terminating propositions.

The proof in set theory is longer because several steps are dedicated to the treatment of typing literals that are repeatedly resolved with the clause (12).

In type theory with a function, only two extended narrowing steps are needed to generate the symbol $\dot\neg$ in the term $\lambda\ \dot\neg[\uparrow](f[\uparrow]\ 1\ 1)$ (i.e. $\lambda x\ \dot\neg(f\ x\ x)$) that expresses Cantor's set. In type theory with a relation, four extended narrowing steps are needed to generate the term $\lambda\ \dot\forall[\uparrow]\lambda\ (\dot\neg[\uparrow^2](R[\uparrow^2]\ 2\ 1)\dot\vee[\uparrow^2]\dot\neg[\uparrow^2](1\ 2))$

1	$y(U) \in U, < g(U), U > \in R$
2	$\neg y(U) \in B, < g(U), U > \in R$
3	$y(U) \in U, g(U) \in B$
4	$\neg y(U) \in B, g(U) \in B$
5	$\neg < X, Y > \in R, \neg < X, Z > \in R, Y = Z$
6	$\neg X = Y, Z \in X, \neg Z \in Y$
7 narr. (1)	$y(C) \in B, < g(C), C > \in R$
8	$\neg < y(C), W > \in R, \neg y(C) \in W, < g(C), C > \in R$
9 res. (7, 2)	$< g(C), C > \in R$
10 narr. (3)	$y(C) \in B, g(C) \in B$
11	$\neg < y(C), W > \in R, \neg y(C) \in W, g(C) \in B$
12 res. (10, 4)	$g(C) \in B$
13 res. (9, 5)	$\neg < g(C), Z > \in R, C = Z$
14 res. (9, 13)	$C = C$
15 res.(14, 6)	$Z \in B, \neg Z \in B, < Z, y_1(Z) > \in R$
16	$Z \in B, \neg Z \in B, Z \in y_1(Z)$
17	$\neg < Z, W_1 > \in R, \neg Z \in W_1, \neg Z \in B, < Z, y_1(Z) > \in R$
18	$\neg < Z, W_1 > \in R, \neg Z \in W_1, \neg Z \in B, Z \in y_1(Z)$
19 res. (17, 9)	$\neg g(C) \in B, < g(C), y_2 > \in R, < g(C), y_1(g(C)) > \in R$
20	$\neg g(C) \in B, g(C) \in y_2, < g(C), y_1(g(C)) > \in R$
21 res. (19, 12)	$< g(C), y_2 > \in R, < g(C), y_1(g(C)) > \in R$
22 res. (20, 12)	$g(C) \in y_2, < g(C), y_1(g(C)) > \in R$
23 res. (18, 9)	$\neg g(C) \in B, < g(C), y_3 > \in R, g(C) \in y_1(g(C))$
24	$\neg g(C) \in B, g(C) \in y_3, g(C) \in y_1(g(C))$
25 res. (23, 12)	$< g(C), y_3 > \in R, g(C) \in y_1(g(C))$
26 res. (24, 12)	$g(C) \in y_3, g(C) \in y_1(g(C))$
27 res. (17, 21)	$\neg g(C) \in y_2, \neg g(C) \in B, < g(C), y_1(g(C)) > \in R$
28 res. (27, 12)	$\neg g(C) \in y_2, < g(C), y_1(g(C)) > \in R$
29 res. (28, 22)	$< g(C), y_1(g(C)) > \in R$
30 res. (18, 25)	$\neg g(C) \in y_3, \neg g(C) \in B, g(C) \in y_1(g(C))$
31 res. (30, 12)	$\neg g(C) \in y_3, g(C) \in y_1(g(C))$
32 res. (31, 26)	$g(C) \in y_1(g(C))$
33 res. (29, 13)	$C = y_1(g(C))$
34 res. (33, 6)	$Z \in B, \neg Z \in y_1(g(C))$
35	$\neg < Z, W_2 > \in R, \neg Z \in W_2, \neg Z \in y_1(g(C))$
36 res. (35, 32)	$\neg < g(C), W_2 > \in R, \neg g(C) \in W_2$
37 res. (36, 9)	$\neg g(C) \in B, < g(C), y_4 > \in R$
38	$\neg g(C) \in B, g(C) \in y_4$
39 res. (37, 12)	$< g(C), y_4 > \in R$
40 res. (38, 12)	$g(C) \in y_4$
41 res. (36, 39)	$\neg g(C) \in y_4$
42 res. (41, 40)	$\square$

Fig. 7. Cantor's theorem in set theory

(i.e. $\lambda x\ \dot{\forall}\lambda y\ (\dot{\neg}(R\ x\ y)\dot{\vee}\dot{\neg}(y\ x)))$ that expresses Cantor's set. The term expressing Cantor set is thus mostly constructed by the unification algorithm in the first case and mostly constructed by the extended narrowing rule in the second. In set theory, like in type theory with a relation, the term expressing Cantor's set is mostly constructed by the extended narrowing rule.

In this case, a single step is needed because we have taken the *ad hoc* rule

$$x \in C \longrightarrow x \in B \wedge \forall y\ (< x, y > \in R \Rightarrow \neg x \in y)$$

But in a reasonable formulation of set theory several steps would be needed.

Notice, at last, that in the proof in type theory with a relation, the term expressing Cantor's set is constructed several times, because the constraints are frozen while in set theory, because the constraints are solved on the fly, this term is constructed only twice and propagated. To avoid this redundancy in type theory with a relation, it would be a good idea to solve as soon as possible the constraints c_1 and c_2.

7 Conclusion

Using a single automated theorem proving method for type theory and for set theory permits a comparison.

Although the use of a typed (many-sorted) language can be criticized, type theory has several advantages for automated theorem proving: typing permits to avoid typing literals, it enjoys termination and cut elimination, and the possibility to form a term $(f\ a)$ expressing the image of an object by a function avoids indirect definitions.

This motivates the search of a type-free formalization of mathematics, that also enjoys termination and cut elimination and where functions are primitive.

References

1. P.B. Andrews. Resolution in type theory. *The Journal of Symbolic Logic*, 36, 3 (1971), pp. 414-432.
2. P.B. Andrews, An introduction to mathematical logic and type theory: to truth through proof, *Academic Press* (1986).
3. P.B. Andrews, D.A. Miller, E. Longini Cohen, and F. Pfenning, Automating higher-order logic, W.W. Bledsoe and D.W. Loveland (Eds.), *Automated theorem proving: after 25 years*, Contemporary Mathematics Series 29, American Mathematical Society (1984), pp. 169-192.
4. S.C. Bailin, A normalization theorem for set theory, *The Journal of Symbolic Logic*, 53, 3 (1988), pp. 673-695.
5. S.C. Bailin, A λ-unifiability test for set theory, *Journal of Automated Reasoning*, 4 (1988), pp. 269-286.
6. A. Church, A formulation of the simple theory of types, *The Journal of Symbolic Logic*, 5 (1940), pp. 56-68.

7. M. Davis, Invited commentary to [28], A.J.H. Morrell (Ed.) *Proceedings of the International Federation for Information Processing Congress*, 1968, North Holland (1969) pp. 67-68.
8. D.J. Dougherty, Higher-order unification via combinators, *Theoretical Computer Science*, 114 (1993), pp. 273-298.
9. G. Dowek, Lambda-calculus, combinators and the comprehension scheme, M. Dezani-Ciancaglini and G. Plotkin (Eds.), *Typed Lambda Calculi and Applications*, Lecture notes in computer science 902, Springer-Verlag (1995), pp. 154-170. *Rapport de Recherche* 2565, INRIA (1995).
10. G. Dowek, Proof normalization for a first-order formulation of higher-order logic, E.L. Gunter and A. Felty (Eds.), *Theorem Proving in Higher-order Logics*, Lecture notes in computer science 1275, Springer-Verlag (1997), pp. 105-119. *Rapport de Recherche* 3383, INRIA (1998).
11. G. Dowek, Th. Hardin, and C. Kirchner, Theorem proving modulo, *Rapport de Recherche* 3400, INRIA (1998).
12. G. Dowek, Th. Hardin, and C. Kirchner, HOL-$\lambda\sigma$: an intentional first-order expression of higher-order logic, to appear in *Rewriting Techniques and Applications* (1999). *Rapport de Recherche* 3556, INRIA (1998).
13. G. Dowek and B. Werner, Proof normalization modulo, *Rapport de Recherche* 3542, INRIA (1998).
14. J. Ekman, Normal proofs in set theory, *Doctoral thesis*, Chalmers University of Technology and University of Göteborg (1994).
15. M. Fay, First-order unification in an equational theory, *Fourth Workshop on Automated Deduction* (1979), pp. 161-167.
16. L. Hallnäs, On normalization of proofs in set theory, *Doctoral thesis*, University of Stockholm (1983).
17. G. Huet, Constrained resolution: a complete method for higher order logic, *Ph.D.*, Case Western Reserve University (1972).
18. G. Huet, A mechanization of type theory, *International Joint Conference on Artificial Intelligence* (1973), pp. 139-146.
19. G. Huet, A unification algorithm for typed lambda calculus, *Theoretical Computer Science*, 1,1 (1975), pp. 27–57.
20. G. Huet, Résolution d'équations dans les Langages d'Ordre 1,2, ..., ω, *Thèse d'État*, Université de Paris VII (1976).
21. J.-M. Hullot, Canonical forms and unification, W. Bibel and R. Kowalski (Eds.) *Conference on Automated Deduction*, Lecture Notes in Computer Science 87, Springer-Verlag (1980), pp. 318-334.
22. J.-P. Jouannaud and C. Kirchner, Solving equations in abstract algebras: a rule-based survey of unification, J.-L. Lassez and G. Plotkin (Eds.) *Computational logic. Essays in honor of Alan Robinson*, MIT press (1991), pp. 257–321.
23. J.W. Klop, V. van Oostrom, and F. van Raamsdonk, Combinatory reduction systems: introduction and survey, *Theoretical Computer Science*, 121 (1993), pp. 279-308.
24. D.A. Miller, Proofs in higher order logic, *Ph.D.*, Carnegie Mellon University (1983).
25. D.A. Miller, A compact representation of proofs, *Studia Logica*, 46, 4 (1987).
26. G. Plotkin, Building-in equational theories, *Machine Intelligence*, 7 (1972), pp. 73-90.

27. W.V.O. Quine, Set theory and its logic, *Belknap press* (1969).
28. J.A. Robinson. New directions in mechanical theorem proving. A.J.H. Morrell (Ed.) *Proceedings of the International Federation for Information Processing Congress*, 1968, North Holland (1969), pp. 63-67.
29. J.A. Robinson. A note on mechanizing higher order logic. *Machine Intelligence* 5, Edinburgh university press (1970), pp. 123-133.
30. M. Stickel, Automated deduction by theory resolution, *Journal of Automated Reasoning*, 4, 1 (1985), pp. 285-289.

Higher-Order Modal Logic—A Sketch

Melvin Fitting

Dept. Mathematics and Computer Science
Lehman College (CUNY), Bronx, NY 10468, USA,
fitting@alpha.lehman.cuny.edu
WWW home page: http://math240.lehman.cuny.edu/fitting

Abstract. First-order modal logic, in the usual formulations, is not sufficiently expressive, and as a consequence problems like Frege's morning star/evening star puzzle arise. The introduction of predicate abstraction machinery provides a natural extension in which such difficulties can be addressed. But this machinery can also be thought of as part of a move to a full higher-order modal logic. In this paper we present a sketch of just such a higher-order modal logic: its formal semantics, and a proof procedure using tableaus. Naturally the tableau rules are not complete, but they are with respect to a Henkinization of the "true" semantics. We demonstrate the use of the tableau rules by proving one of the theorems involved in Gödel's ontological argument, one of the rare instances in the literature where higher-order modal constructs have appeared. A fuller treatment of the material presented here is in preparation.

1 Introduction

Standard first-order classical logic is so well behaved that concentration on it lulls the mind. The behavior of terms provides an instructive example. For one thing, classical terms are always defined—in every classical model all terms have values. But it is well-known that this convention leads to difficulties when definite descriptions are involved since, considered as terms, they don't always denote. As Bertrand Russell noted, "The King of France is not bald" has two quite different, but equally plausible readings. First, it could mean that the King of France has the non-baldness property. This is false since non-existents don't have properties—they don't even have the non-existence property. Second, it could deny the assertion that the King of France has the baldness property. This is true because no bald King of France can be produced. The single string of English words has two possible logical formulations, and conventional first-order syntax cannot distinguish them.

Russell's solution to the problem was to introduce a scoping mechanism—it appears fully developed in *Principia Mathematica.* While he thought of it only in the context of definite descriptions, it is more generally applicable. Using more modern notation, we distinguish between a *formula* Φ and a *predicate abstract* $\langle\lambda x.\Phi\rangle$ drawn from it. Thinking of $B(x)$ as "x is bald," and k as "King of France," we can symbolize the two possible readings mentioned in the previous paragraph as $\langle\lambda x.\neg B(x)\rangle(k)$ and $\neg\langle\lambda x.B(x)\rangle(k)$. It can be shown that, with a reasonable

R. Caferra and G. Salzer (Eds.): Automated Deduction, LNAI 1761, pp. 23–38, 2000.

semantics, these two are equivalent exactly when k denotes, so it is non-denoting terms that force us to use such machinery classically.

Frege noted an analogous problem with intentional contexts, and introduced the notions of "sense" and "denotation" to deal with it. Roughly, this gives terms two kinds of values, what they denote, and what they mean. Of course this is loose. But the introduction of a scoping mechanism also turns out to be of considerable use here. This was done first in [7,9]. My colleague Richard Mendelsohn and I developed the idea quite fully in [3], and a highly condensed version is available in [2]. But suffice it to say that the notion of predicate abstraction supplies an essential missing ingredient for formal treatments of intentional logics, modal in particular, as well as for cases where terms can lack designations.

Thinking further on the matter, I came to realize that even with predicate abstraction machinery added as outlined above, first-order modal logic is still not as expressive as one would like. And an informal illustration is easy to present.

Assume the word "tall" has a definite meaning—say everybody gets together and votes on which people are tall. The key point is that the meaning of "tall," even though precise, drifts with time. Someone who once was considered tall might not be considered so today.

Now suppose I say, "Someday everybody will be tall." There is more than one ambiguity here. On the one hand I might mean that at some point in the future, everybody alive will be a tall person. On the other hand I might mean that everybody now alive will grow, and so at some point everybody now alive will be a tall person. Let us read modal operators temporally, so that $\Box X$ informally means that X is true and will remain true, and $\Diamond X$ means that X either is true or will be true at some point in the future. Also, let us use $T(x)$ as a tallness predicate symbol. Then the two readings of our sentence are easily expressed in conventional notation as follows.

$$(\forall x)\Diamond T(x) \tag{1}$$
$$\Diamond(\forall x)T(x) \tag{2}$$

Formula (1) refers to those alive now, and says at some point they will all be tall. Formula (2) refers to those alive at some point in the future, and asserts of them that they will be tall. All this is standard, and is not the ambiguity that matters here. The problem is with the adjective "tall." Do we mean that at some point in the future everybody (read either way) will be tall as *they* use the word in the future, or as *we* use the word now? Standard possible world semantics for first-order modal logic is constrained to interpret formulas involving T at a world according to that world's meaning of T. In fact, there is no way of formalizing, using standard first-order modal machinery, the assertion that, at some point in the future, everybody will be tall as *we* understand the term. But this is what is most likely meant if someone says, "Someday everybody will be tall."

The missing piece of machinery to disambiguate the sentence "Someday everybody will be tall," is abstraction, applied at the level of relation symbols, rather than at the level of terms. We get the following *six* versions.

$$(\forall x)\langle\lambda X.\Diamond X(x)\rangle(T) \tag{3}$$

$$(\forall x)\Diamond\langle\lambda X.X(x)\rangle(T) \tag{4}$$

$$\langle\lambda X.\Diamond(\forall x)X(x)\rangle(T) \tag{5}$$

$$\Diamond(\forall x)\langle\lambda X.X(x)\rangle(T) \tag{6}$$

$$\langle\lambda X.(\forall x)\Diamond X(x)\rangle(T) \tag{7}$$

$$\Diamond\langle\lambda X.(\forall x)X(x)\rangle(T) \tag{8}$$

We will introduce semantics for interpreting these shortly, but for the time being we can provide informal readings. Once semantics have been introduced, it can be shown that item (7) is equivalent to (3), and item (8) is equivalent to (6), so we omit readings for them.

It is true of everybody currently alive that they will be tall, as we understand the word. (3)

It is true of everybody currently alive that they will be tall, as the word is understood in the future. (4)

At some point in the future everybody then alive will be tall, as we understand the word. (5)

At some point in the future everybody will be tall, as the word is understood at that time. (6)

Essentially, in first-order modal logic as it has usually been formulated, all relation symbols are read as if they had narrow scope, and all constants as if they had broad scope. Thus it is as if (4) and (6) were meant by (1) and (2) respectively. There is no way of representing (3) or (5). The machinery for this representation makes for complicated looking formulas. But we point out, in everyday discourse all this machinery is hidden—we infer it from our knowledge of what must have been meant.

Now, why not go the whole way? If we are going to introduce abstraction syntax for terms and for relation symbols, why not treat relation symbols as terms of a higher order. And then why not introduce the whole mechanism of higher-order logic, and do things uniformally all the way up. In fact, this is what we do. The following is a very brief sketch—a much fuller development is in preparation.

2 Syntax

In first-order logic, relation symbols have an *arity*. In higher-order logic this gets replaced by a *typing* mechanism. There are several ways this can be done: logical connectives can be considered primitive, or as constants of the language; a boolean type can be introduced, or not. We adopt a straightforward approach similar to the usual treatments of first-order logic.

Definition 1 (Type). *0 is a type. If $t_1, \ldots, t_n$ are types, $\langle t_1, \ldots, t_n \rangle$ is a type. We systematically use t, t_1, t_2, t', etc. to represent types.*

For each type t we assume we have infinitely many constant and variable symbols of that type. We generally use letters from the beginning of the Greek alphabet to represent variables, with the type written as a superscript: α^t, β^t, γ^t, ... Likewise we generally use letters from the beginning of the Latin alphabet as constant symbols, again with the type written as a superscript: A^t, B^t, C^t, ... We take equality as primitive, so for each type t we assume we have a constant symbol $=^{\langle t,t \rangle}$ of type $\langle t, t \rangle$. Generally types can be inferred from context, and so superscripts will be omitted where possible, in the interests of uncluttered notation.

Sometimes it is helpful to refer to the *order* of a term or formula—first-order, second-order, and so on. Types will play the fundamental role, but order provides a convenient way of referring to the maximum complexity of some construct.

Definition 2 (Order). *The type 0 is of* order *0. And if each of $t_1, \ldots, t_n$ is of order $\leq k$, with at least one of them being of order k itself, we say $\langle t_1, \ldots, t_n \rangle$ is of* order $k+1$.

When we talk about the order of a constant or variable, we mean the order of its type. Likewise, once formulas are defined, we may refer to the order of the formula, by which we mean the highest order of a typed part of it.

Next we define the class of formulas, and their free variables. Unlike in the first-order version, the notion of term cannot be defined first; both term and formula must be defined together. And to define both, we need the auxiliary notion of predicate abstract which is, itself, part of the mutual recursion.

Definition 3 (Predicate Abstract). *Suppose Φ is a formula and $\alpha_1, \ldots, \alpha_n$ is a sequence of distinct variables of types $t_1, \ldots, t_n$ respectively. We call $\langle \lambda \alpha_1, \ldots, \alpha_n . \Phi \rangle$ a* predicate abstract. *Its type is $\langle t_1, \ldots, t_n \rangle$, and its free variable occurrences are the free variable occurrences in the formula Φ, except for occurrences of the variables $\alpha_1, \ldots, \alpha_n$.*

Definition 4 (Term). *Terms of each type are characterized as follows.*

1. *A constant symbol or variable is a term. If it is a constant symbol, it has no free variable occurrences. If it is a variable, it has one free variable occurrence, itself.*
2. *A predicate abstract is a term. Its free variable occurrences were defined above.*

We use τ, with and without subscripts, to stand for terms.

Definition 5 (Formula). *The notion of* formula *is given as follows.*

1. *If τ is a term of type $t = \langle t_1, \ldots, t_n \rangle$, and $\tau_1, \ldots, \tau_n$ is a sequence of terms of types $t_1, \ldots, t_n$ respectively, then $\tau(\tau_1, \ldots, \tau_n)$ is a formula. The free variable occurrences in it are the free variable occurrences of τ, $\tau_1, \ldots, \tau_n$.*

2. *If Φ is a formula so is $\neg\Phi$. The free variable occurrences of $\neg\Phi$ are those of Φ.*
3. *If Φ and Ψ are formulas so is $(\Phi \wedge \Psi)$. The free variable occurrences of $(\Phi \wedge \Psi)$ are those of Φ together with those of Ψ.*
4. *If Φ is a formula and α is a variable then $(\forall\alpha)\Phi$ is a formula. The free variable occurrences of $(\forall\alpha)\Phi$ are those of Φ, except for occurrences of α.*
5. *If Φ is a formula so is $\Box\Phi$. The free variable occurrences of $\Box\Phi$ are those of Φ.*

We use $\vee$, $\supset$, $\Diamond$, $\exists$ as defined symbols, with their usual definitions. Also we use square and curly parentheses, in addition to the official round ones, to aid readability. In addition, since equality plays a fundamental role, we introduce a standard abbreviation for it.

Definition 6 (Equality). *Suppose τ_1 and τ_2 are variables of type t, and $=$ is the equality constant symbol of type $\langle t, t\rangle$. We write $(\tau_1 = \tau_2)$ as an abbreviation for $=(\tau_1, \tau_2)$.*

Example 1. For this example we give explicit type information (in superscripts), until the end of the example. In the future we will generally omit the superscripts, and say in English what is needed to fill them in.

Suppose x^0, $X^{\langle 0\rangle}$, and $\mathcal{X}^{\langle\langle 0\rangle\rangle}$ are variables (the first is of order 0, the second is of order 1, and the third is of order 2). Also suppose $\mathcal{P}^{\langle\langle 0\rangle\rangle}$ and g^0 are constant symbols (the first is of order 2 and the second is of order 0).

1. Both $\mathcal{X}^{\langle\langle 0\rangle\rangle}(X^{\langle 0\rangle})$ and $X^{\langle 0\rangle}(x^0)$ are atomic formulas. All variables present have free occurrences.
2. $\langle\lambda\mathcal{X}^{\langle\langle 0\rangle\rangle}.\mathcal{X}^{\langle\langle 0\rangle\rangle}(X^{\langle 0\rangle})\rangle$ is a predicate abstract, of type $\langle\langle\langle 0\rangle\rangle\rangle$. Only the occurrence of $X^{\langle 0\rangle}$ is free.
3. Since $\mathcal{P}^{\langle\langle 0\rangle\rangle}$ is of type $\langle\langle 0\rangle\rangle$, $\langle\lambda\mathcal{X}^{\langle\langle 0\rangle\rangle}.\mathcal{X}^{\langle\langle 0\rangle\rangle}(X^{\langle 0\rangle})\rangle(\mathcal{P}^{\langle\langle 0\rangle\rangle})$ is a formula. Only $X^{\langle 0\rangle}$ is free.
4. $[\langle\lambda\mathcal{X}^{\langle\langle 0\rangle\rangle}.\mathcal{X}^{\langle\langle 0\rangle\rangle}(X^{\langle 0\rangle})\rangle(\mathcal{P}^{\langle\langle 0\rangle\rangle}) \supset X^{\langle 0\rangle}(x^0)]$ is a formula. The only free variable occurrences are those of $X^{\langle 0\rangle}$ and x^0.
5. $(\forall X^{\langle 0\rangle})[\langle\lambda\mathcal{X}^{\langle\langle 0\rangle\rangle}.\mathcal{X}^{\langle\langle 0\rangle\rangle}(X^{\langle 0\rangle})\rangle(\mathcal{P}^{\langle\langle 0\rangle\rangle}) \supset X^{\langle 0\rangle}(x^0)]$ is a formula. The only free variable occurrence is that of x^0.
6. $\langle\lambda x^0.(\forall X^{\langle 0\rangle})[\langle\lambda\mathcal{X}^{\langle\langle 0\rangle\rangle}.\mathcal{X}^{\langle\langle 0\rangle\rangle}(X^{\langle 0\rangle})\rangle(\mathcal{P}^{\langle\langle 0\rangle\rangle}) \supset X^{\langle 0\rangle}(x^0)]\rangle$ is a predicate abstract. It has no free variable occurrences, and is of type $\langle 0\rangle$.

We need the type machinery to guarantee that what we write is well-formed. Now that we have gone through the exercise above, we can display the predicate abstract without superscripts, as

$$\langle\lambda x.(\forall X)[\langle\lambda\mathcal{X}.\mathcal{X}(X)\rangle(\mathcal{P}) \supset X(x)]\rangle,$$

leaving types to be inferred, or explained in words, as necessary.

3 Models

Just as in the classical setting there are standard higher-order modal models and non-standard ones. Because of space limitations I'll only sketch the standard version, and say a few words later on about the non-standard one.

A higher-order modal model is a structure $\mathcal{M} = \langle \mathcal{G}, \mathcal{R}, \mathcal{D}, \mathcal{I} \rangle$, and we spend much of the rest of the section saying what each component is.

The pair $\langle \mathcal{G}, \mathcal{R} \rangle$ is a *frame*. In it, $\mathcal{G}$ is a non-empty set of possible worlds, and $\mathcal{R}$ is an accessibility relation on $\mathcal{G}$. This much is familiar from propositional modal logic treatments, and we do not elaborate on it. As usual, different restrictions on $\mathcal{R}$ give rise to different modal logics.

Domains of (ground level) objects are introduced into a modal model, just as in a classical one. There are two different ways of doing this. Each possible world in $\mathcal{G}$ can have its own domain, in which case we take $\mathcal{D}$ to be a *domain function*, mapping worlds to non-empty sets. Or, all possible worlds can have the same domain, in which case we take $\mathcal{D}$ to be just a set, the common domain for all worlds. In [5] and [3] reasons are presented as to why either version can be taken as basic in the first-order case—essentially each can simulate the other. In the interests of simplicity we adopt the constant domain version in the higher-order setting. Philosophically, this amounts to a possibilist approach to quantification, rather than an actualist one.

Formally, we take $\mathcal{D}$ to be a single non-empty set, called the *domain* of the model $\mathcal{M}$.

Definition 7 (Relation Types). *Let S be a non-empty set. For each type t we define the collection $[\![t, S]\!]$ of* relations of type t over S.

1. $[\![0, S]\!] = S$.
2. $[\![\langle t_1, \ldots, t_n \rangle, S]\!]$ *is the collection of all subsets of* $[\![t_1, S]\!] \times \cdots \times [\![t_n, S]\!]$.

We say O is an object of type t over S *if* $O \in [\![t, S]\!]$.

At last we can characterize $\mathcal{I}$, the *interpretation* of the model. Note that it is world-dependent.

Definition 8 (Interpretation). *$\mathcal{I}$ is a mapping from constant symbols and worlds meeting the following conditions. For each world $\Gamma \in \mathcal{G}$:*

1. *If A^t is a constant symbol of type t, $\mathcal{I}(A^t, \Gamma) \in [\![t, \mathcal{D}]\!]$.*
2. *If $=^{\langle t,t \rangle}$ is an equality constant symbol, $\mathcal{I}(=^{\langle t,t \rangle}, \Gamma)$ is the equality relation on $[\![t, \mathcal{D}]\!]$.*

This completes the specification for each component of $\mathcal{M} = \langle \mathcal{G}, \mathcal{R}, \mathcal{D}, \mathcal{I} \rangle$. If all the conditions given above are met, we say $\mathcal{M}$ is a *higher-order modal model.*

4 Truth

Assume $\mathcal{M} = \langle \mathcal{G}, \mathcal{R}, \mathcal{D}, \mathcal{I} \rangle$ is a higher-order modal model. We give meaning to $\mathcal{M}, \Gamma \Vdash_v \Phi$, which is read: the formula Φ is true at the world Γ of the model $\mathcal{M}$, with respect to the valuation v which assigns meanings to free variables. To do this we have to assign denotations to terms in general—the denotation of a term of type t will be an object of type t over $\mathcal{D}$. And this can not be done independently. The assignment of denotations to terms, and the determination of formula truth at worlds constitutes a mutually recursive pair of definitions, as was the case for the syntactic notions of term and formula in Section 2.

Definition 9 (Valuation). *We say v is a* valuation *in model $\mathcal{M} = \langle \mathcal{G}, \mathcal{R}, \mathcal{D}, \mathcal{I} \rangle$ if v assigns to each variable α^t of type t some member of $[\![t, \mathcal{D}]\!]$, that is, $v(\alpha^t) \in [\![t, \mathcal{D}]\!]$.*

Note that, unlike interpretations, valuations are not world dependent.

Definition 10 (Variant). *We say a valuation w is an α-*variant *of a valuation v if v and w agree on all variables except possibly α. More generally, we say w is an $\alpha_1, \ldots, \alpha_n$-*variant *if v and w agree on all variables except possibly $\alpha_1, \ldots, \alpha_n$.*

Definition 11 (Denotation of a Term). *Let $\mathcal{M} = \langle \mathcal{G}, \mathcal{R}, \mathcal{D}, \mathcal{I} \rangle$ be a higher-order modal model, and let v be a valuation in it. We define a mapping $(v * \mathcal{I})$, assigning to each term and each world a denotation for that term, at that world.*

1. *If A is a constant symbol then $(v * \mathcal{I})(A, \Gamma) = \mathcal{I}(A, \Gamma)$.*
2. *If α is a variable then $(v * \mathcal{I})(\alpha, \Gamma) = v(\alpha)$.*
3. *If $\langle \lambda\alpha_1, \ldots, \alpha_n.\Phi \rangle$ is a predicate abstract of type t, then $(v * \mathcal{I})(\langle \lambda\alpha_1, \ldots, \alpha_n.\Phi \rangle, \Gamma)$ is the following member of $[\![t, \mathcal{D}]\!]$:*

$$\{\langle w(\alpha_1), \ldots, w(\alpha_n) \rangle \mid w \text{ is an } \alpha_1, \ldots, \alpha_n \text{ variant of } v \text{ and } \mathcal{M}, \Gamma \Vdash_w \Phi\}$$

Definition 12 (Truth of a Formula). *Again let $\mathcal{M} = \langle \mathcal{G}, \mathcal{R}, \mathcal{D}, \mathcal{I} \rangle$ be a higher-order modal model, and let v be a valuation in it. The notion $\mathcal{M}, \Gamma \Vdash_v \Phi$, is characterized as follows.*

1. *For an atomic formula, $\mathcal{M}, \Gamma \Vdash_v \tau(\tau_1, \ldots, \tau_n)$ provided $\langle (v * \mathcal{I})(\tau_1, \Gamma), \ldots, (v * \mathcal{I})(\tau_n, \Gamma) \rangle \in (v * \mathcal{I})(\tau, \Gamma)$.*
2. *$\mathcal{M}, \Gamma \Vdash_v \neg\Phi$ if it is not the case that $\mathcal{M}, \Gamma \Vdash_v \Phi$.*
3. *$\mathcal{M}, \Gamma \Vdash_v \Phi \wedge \Psi$ if $\mathcal{M}, \Gamma \Vdash_v \Phi$ and $\mathcal{M}, \Gamma \Vdash_v \Psi$.*
4. *$\mathcal{M}, \Gamma \Vdash_v \Box\Phi$ if $\mathcal{M}, \Delta \Vdash_v \Phi$ for all $\Delta \in \mathcal{G}$ such that $\Gamma \mathcal{R} \Delta$.*
5. *$\mathcal{M}, \Gamma \Vdash_v (\forall\alpha)\Phi$ if $\mathcal{M}, \Gamma \Vdash_{v'} \Phi$ for every α-variant v' of v.*

Here are a few examples on which you can test your understanding of the definitions above. We are assuming our models are constant domain, so not surprisingly, the Barcan formula is valid. But one must be careful. If Φ is a formula, the following is certainly valid.

$$\Diamond(\exists x)\Phi \supset (\exists x)\Diamond\Phi.$$

But, the following formula is *not* valid, even though it has a Barcan-like quantifier/modality permutation.

$$\Diamond(\exists x)\langle\lambda X.X(x)\rangle(P) \supset (\exists x)\langle\lambda X.\Diamond X(x)\rangle(P).$$

The shift of variable binding for X changes things; in the antecedent it is narrow scope, but in the consequent it is not.

As another slightly surprising example, the following formula is valid.

$$\langle\lambda X.\Diamond(\exists x)X(x)\rangle(P) \supset \langle\lambda X.(\exists x)X(x)\rangle(P) \tag{9}$$

In this example the symbol P is given broad scope in both the antecedent and the consequent of the implication. This essentially says its meaning in alternative worlds will be the same as in the present world. Under these circumstances, existence of something falling under P in an alternate world is equivalent to existence of something falling under P in the present world. (Don't forget, we are assuming constant domains.) This is just a formal variation on the old observation that, in conventional first-order Kripke models, if relation symbols could not vary their interpretation from world to world, modal operators would have no effect. It is also something that can't be said without the use of abstraction notation.

5 Non-standard Models

Just as in the classical case, there can be no proof procedure that is complete with respect to the semantics presented in the previous two sections. And just as in the classical case, one can introduce a modal version of *Henkin models*. Essentially, at each type level of a model we take *some* of the relations available in principle, but not necessarily all of them. We do not have the space here to give details, but they are direct analogs of the classical version.

The important thing to note, for our purposes, is that the most natural higher-order modal tableau rules do *not* give completeness with respect to modal Henkin models. Instead we need a broader notion of model yet—*non-extensional* Henkin models. These can be characterized, and are natural things to study, though knowledge of them is not widespread even though Henkin himself mentioned them. After all, it seems reasonable to have a notion of model in which the properties of being the morning star and being the evening star are different even though they have the same extension.

Space does not permit a formulation of modal higher-order non-extensional Henkin models here. But when formulated, tableau rules given below turn out to be complete with respect to them. Then extensionality can be imposed by adopting extensionality axioms, in the usual way. The completeness proof has considerable complexity, but ultimately is based on constructions of [6, 8].

6 Tableaus

We present a version of *prefixed* tableaus, which incorporate a kind of naming mechanism for possible worlds in such a way that syntactic features of prefixes—world names—reflect semantic features of models, or of candidates for them. Prefixed tableau systems exist for most standard modal logics. Here we only give a version for **S5**, *without equality and without extensionality.* We refer you to the literature for modifications appropriate for other modal logics—the same modifications that work at the propositional level work in our setting too.

Definition 13 (Prefix). *An* **S5** prefix *is a single positive integer.*

Prefixes have two uses in tableau proofs. The first gives them their name.

Definition 14 (Prefixed Formula). *A* prefixed formula *is an expression of the form $\sigma\,\Phi$, where σ is a prefix and Φ is a formula.*

Think of a prefix as a name for a possible world of some model. And think of $\sigma\,\Phi$ as saying that formula Φ is true at the world that σ names.

All tableau proofs are proofs of *sentences*—closed formulas. A tableau proof of Φ is a tree that has $1\,\neg\Phi$ at its root, is constructed according to certain *branch extension* rules to be given below, and is *closed*, which essentially means it embodies an obvious syntactic contradiction. This intuitively says $\neg\Phi$ cannot happen at an arbitrary world, and so Φ is valid.

The branch extension rules for the propositional connectives are all straightforward. We give them here, including rules for various defined connectives, for convenience. In these, and throughout, we use σ, σ', σ_1, and the like as standing for prefixes.

Definition 15 (Conjunctive Rules). *For any prefix σ,*

$$\frac{\sigma\, X \wedge Y}{\begin{array}{c}\sigma\, X\\ \sigma\, Y\end{array}} \quad \frac{\sigma\,\neg(X \vee Y)}{\begin{array}{c}\sigma\,\neg X\\ \sigma\,\neg Y\end{array}} \quad \frac{\sigma\,\neg(X \supset Y)}{\begin{array}{c}\sigma\, X\\ \sigma\,\neg Y\end{array}} \quad \frac{\sigma\, X \equiv Y}{\begin{array}{c}\sigma\, X \supset Y\\ \sigma\, Y \supset X\end{array}}$$

For the conjunctive rules, if the prefixed formula above the line appears on a branch of a tableau, the items below the line may be added to the end of the branch. The rule for double negation is of the same nature, except that only a single added item is involved.

Definition 16 (Double Negation Rule). *For any prefix σ,*

$$\frac{\sigma\,\neg\neg X}{\sigma\, X}$$

Next we have the disjunctive rules. For these, if the prefixed formula above the line appears on a tableau branch, the end node can have two children added, labeled with the two items shown below the line in the rule. In this case we say there is tableau branching.

Definition 17 (Disjunctive Rules). *For any prefix σ,*

$$\frac{\sigma X \vee Y}{\sigma X \mid \sigma Y} \qquad \frac{\sigma \neg(X \wedge Y)}{\sigma \neg X \mid \sigma \neg Y}$$

$$\frac{\sigma X \supset Y}{\sigma \neg X \mid \sigma Y} \quad \frac{\sigma \neg(X \equiv Y)}{\sigma \neg(X \supset Y) \mid \sigma \neg(Y \supset X)}$$

Next we give the modal rules. It is here that the structure of prefixes plays a role. For **S5**, each world is accessible from each world.

Definition 18 (Possibility Rules). *If the positive integer n is new to the branch,*

$$\frac{\sigma \Diamond X}{n\, X} \quad \frac{\sigma \neg \Box X}{n \neg X}$$

This implicitly treats $\Diamond$ as a kind of existential quantifier. Correspondingly, the following rules treat $\Box$ as a version of the universal quantifier.

Definition 19 (Necessity Rules). *For any positive integer n,*

$$\frac{\sigma \Box X}{n\, X} \quad \frac{\sigma \neg \Diamond X}{n \neg X}$$

Many examples of the application of these propositional rules can be found in [3]. We do not give any here.

Next, for quantifiers. For the existential quantifier we do the usual thing: if an existentially quantified formula is true (at some world), we introduce a new name into the language and say in effect, let that be the thing of which the formula is true. For this it is convenient to enhance the collection of free variables available. We add a second kind, called parameters.

Definition 20 (Parameters). *We have assumed that for each type t we had an infinite collection of free variables of that type. We now assume we also have a second, disjoint, list of free variables of type t, called* parameters. *They may appear in formulas in the same way as the original list of free variables* but we never quantify them. *Also* we never λ bind them. *We use letters like p, q, P, Q, ... to represent parameters.*

Technically, parameters are free variables. When interpreting a formula with parameters in a model, a valuation must provide values for parameters as well as for the standard free variables. But since parameters are never quantified or used in λ bindings, any occurrence of a parameter must be a free occurrence. (Consequently they cannot appear in sentences.) We will never need to substitute a term for a parameter, though we will need to substitute terms for free occurrences of variables that are not parameters. For this, and other reasons, we adopt the following convention.

Definition 21 (Variable Convention). *Occurrences of parameters in a formula are not counted as free occurrences. Further, if we refer to a* variable, *it is assumed it is not a parameter. If we need to speak about a parameter, we will explicitly say so.*

To state the existential tableau rules, we use the following convention. Suppose $\Phi(\alpha^t)$ is a formula in which the variable α^t, of type t, may have free occurrences. And suppose p^t is a parameter of type t. Then $\Phi(p^t)$ is the result of replacing all free occurrences of α^t with occurrences of p^t. Since our convention is that parameters are never bound, we don't have to worry about accidental variable capture. Now, here are the existential quantifier rules.

Definition 22 (Existential Rules). *In the following, p^t is a parameter of type t that is* new to the tableau branch.

$$\frac{\sigma\,(\exists\alpha^t)\Phi(\alpha^t)}{\sigma\,\Phi(p^t)} \quad \frac{\sigma\,\neg(\forall\alpha^t)\Phi(\alpha^t)}{\sigma\,\neg\Phi(p^t)}$$

The rules above embody the familiar notion of existential instantiation. As noted, the use of parameters instead of conventional variables avoids complications due to conflicts between free and bound occurrences.

We said prefixes had two roles. We have seen one: formulas are prefixed. The other use of prefixes is to qualify *terms.* Loosely, think of a term τ with σ as prefix as representing the value taken on by the term τ at the world designated by σ. However, writing prefixes in front of terms makes formulas even more unreadable than they already are. Instead, in an abuse of language, we have chosen to write them as subscripts, τ_σ though, of course, the intention is the same, and we still refer to them as prefixes.

Formally, we broaden the notion of term (and consequently of formula) to allow for prefixes/subscripts. Constant symbols may have prefixes—they are non-rigid and can have different values at different worlds, so a prefix plays a significant role, fixing the world at which its value is determined. Similarly for predicate abstracts. But variables and parameters are thought of as ranging over objects directly, and are not world-dependent. Consequently they are not given prefixes.

Definition 23 (Extended Term). *An* extended term *is like a term except that some subterms have prefixes attached (as subscripts). Prefixes may appear as subscripts on constant symbols and predicate abstracts; they may not appear on variables or parameters. It is allowed that no prefixes occur, in which case we have a term in the conventional sense. The* type *of an extended term is the same as the type of the underlying term, that is, of the expression resulting from dropping all prefixes.*

Extended terms are allowed to occur in the formulas appearing in tableaus. Next we need an analog of the notion of closed term, as used in classical first-order tableaus.

Definition 24 (Grounded). *A parameter is a grounded term. A prefixed constant symbol is a grounded term. A prefixed predicate abstract containing no free variables (parameters are allowed) is a grounded term. Also, if $\tau_0(\tau_1, \ldots, \tau_n)$ is an atomic formula and τ_0, τ_1, ..., τ_n are grounded terms, we refer to the formula as grounded.*

Example 2. $\langle \lambda x.(\forall X)[\langle \lambda \mathcal{X}.\mathcal{X}(X)\rangle(\mathcal{P}) \supset X(x)]\rangle$ is a predicate abstract, hence a term. Then, $\langle \lambda x.(\forall X)[\langle \lambda \mathcal{X}.\mathcal{X}(X)\rangle_2(\mathcal{P}_1) \supset X(x)]\rangle$ is an extended term. It is not grounded, but $\langle \lambda x.(\forall X)[\langle \lambda \mathcal{X}.\mathcal{X}(X)\rangle_2(\mathcal{P}_1) \supset X(x)]\rangle_3$ is.

The presence of a prefix σ on a subterm is intended to indicate that we are thinking about the object the subterm denotes at the world that σ denotes. Since not all subterms may have been intuitively evaluated at a particular stage of a proof, there might be subterms that have not been prefixed.

Definition 25 (Universal Rules). *In the following, τ^t is any grounded term of type t.*

$$\frac{\sigma\ (\forall \alpha^t)\Phi(\alpha^t)}{\sigma\, \Phi(\tau^t)} \quad \frac{\sigma\, \neg(\exists \alpha^t)\Phi(\alpha^t)}{\sigma\, \neg\Phi(\tau^t)}$$

Now we give the rules for predicate abstracts and atomic formulas. And to do this, we first define an auxiliary notion. The intuition is that $\tau@\sigma$ plays the role of the object the extended term τ designates at world σ. Note that $\tau@\sigma$ must be grounded.

Definition 26 (Evaluation at a Prefix). *Let σ be a prefix. If τ is an extended term without free variables, $\tau@\sigma$ is defined as follows.*

1. *If τ is a parameter, $\tau@\sigma = \tau$.*
2. *If τ is an unsubscripted constant symbol or predicate abstract, $\tau@\sigma = \tau_\sigma$.*
3. *If τ is a subscripted constant symbol or predicate abstract, $\tau@\sigma = \tau$.*

Also, if $\tau_0(\tau_1, \ldots, \tau_n)$ is atomic, where each τ_i is an extended term without free variables, we set

$$[\tau_0(\tau_1, \ldots, \tau_n)]@\sigma = [\tau_0@\sigma(\tau_1@\sigma, \ldots, \tau_n@\sigma)]$$

The next rule says that determining the truth of an atomic formula at a world requires we evaluate its constituents at that world.

Definition 27 (Atomic Evaluation Rules). *Let X be an atomic formula.*

$$\frac{\sigma\, X}{\sigma\, X@\sigma} \qquad \frac{\sigma\, \neg X}{\sigma\, \neg X@\sigma}$$

If a term is grounded, its meaning is fixed across worlds. If I say "the President of the United States," it means different people at different times, but if I say "the President of the United States in 1812," it designates the same person at all times. This motivates the following rule.

Definition 28 (World Shift Rules). *Let X be a* grounded *atomic formula.*

$$\frac{\sigma\, X}{\sigma'\, X} \qquad \frac{\sigma \neg X}{\sigma' \neg X}$$

Finally, a rule intended to capture the meaning of predicate abstracts. Note the respective roles of σ and σ'. Also, we extend earlier notation so that, if $\Phi(\alpha_1, \ldots, \alpha_n)$ is a formula, $\alpha_1, \ldots, \alpha_n$ are free variables, and $\tau_1, \ldots, \tau_n$ are extended terms of the same respective types as $\alpha_1, \ldots, \alpha_n$, then $\Phi(\tau_1, \ldots, \tau_n)$ is the result of simultaneously substituting each τ_i for all free occurrences of α_i in Φ.

Definition 29 (Predicate Abstract Rules). *In the following, $\tau_1, \ldots, \tau_n$ are all* grounded *terms*

$$\frac{\sigma' \langle \lambda \alpha_1, \ldots, \alpha_n.\Phi(\alpha_1, \ldots, \alpha_n)\rangle_\sigma(\tau_1, \ldots, \tau_n)}{\sigma\, \Phi(\tau_1, \ldots, \tau_n)}$$

$$\frac{\sigma' \neg\langle \lambda \alpha_1, \ldots, \alpha_n.\Phi(\alpha_1, \ldots, \alpha_n)\rangle_\sigma(\tau_1, \ldots, \tau_n)}{\sigma \neg\Phi(\tau_1, \ldots, \tau_n)}$$

Finally what, exactly, constitutes a proof.

Definition 30 (Closure). *A tableau branch is* closed *if it contains $\sigma\, \Psi$ and $\sigma \neg\Psi$, for some formula Ψ.*

Definition 31 (Tableau Proof). *For a sentence Φ, a closed tableau beginning with $1 \neg\Phi$ is a* proof *of Φ.*

This concludes the presentation of the basic tableau rules. We have not given rules for equality or extensionality. In fact, extensionality is not provable without further rules. In the next section we give a few examples of tableau proofs using the rules above.

7 Tableau Examples

Tableaus for classical logic are well-known, and even for propositional modal logics they are rather familiar. The abstraction rules of the previous section are new, and we give two examples illustrating their uses, one easy, one harder.

Example 3. Here is a proof of (9), $\langle \lambda X.\Diamond(\exists x)X(x)\rangle(P) \supset \langle \lambda X.(\exists x)X(x)\rangle(P)$, which we earlier noted was valid.

$1 \neg [\langle \lambda X.\Diamond(\exists x)X(x)\rangle(P) \supset \langle \lambda X.(\exists x)X(x)\rangle(P)]$ 1.
$1\ \langle \lambda X.\Diamond(\exists x)X(x)\rangle(P)$ 2.
$1 \neg\langle \lambda X.(\exists x)X(x)\rangle(P)$ 3.
$1\ \langle \lambda X.\Diamond(\exists x)X(x)\rangle_1(P_1)$ 4.
$1 \neg\langle \lambda X.(\exists x)X(x)\rangle_1(P_1)$ 5.
$1\ \Diamond(\exists x)P_1(x)$ 6.
$1 \neg(\exists x)P_1(x)$ 7.
$2\ (\exists x)P_1(x)$ 8.
$2\ P_1(p)$ 9.
$1 \neg P_1(p)$ 10.
$1\ P_1(p)$ 11.

In this, 2 and 3 are from 1 by a conjunctive rule; 4 is from 2 and 5 is from 3 by atomic evaluation; 6 and 7 are from 4 and 5 respectively by predicate abstract rules; 8 is from 6 by a possibility rule; 9 is from 8 by an existential rule (p is a new parameter); 10 is from 7 by a universal rule; and 11 is from 9 by a world shift rule.

Example 4. Our next example is from Gödel's ontological argument for the existence of God [4]. We don't need all the details—think of it simply as a technical issue. Essentially, Gödel modified an earlier argument due to Leibniz. Part of what Gödel did was replace a somewhat intuitive notion of *perfection* with the notion of a *positive* property. This notion was not analyzed, but certain features were assumed for it—axioms, in effect.

Positive Property. We have a constant symbol $\mathcal{P}$ of type $\langle\langle 0\rangle\rangle$ (think of it as "positiveness"). We assume

$$(\forall X)[\neg\mathcal{P}(X) \supset \mathcal{P}(\neg X)]$$

where, for X of type $\langle 0\rangle$, $\neg X$ abbreviates $\langle\lambda x.\neg X(x)\rangle$.

Next, Gödel takes *being God* to mean having all positive properties.

Being God. We use G to abbreviate the type $\langle 0\rangle$ term

$$\langle\lambda x.(\forall X)[\mathcal{P}(X) \supset X(x)]\rangle.$$

Finally as far as our example is concerned, Gödel characterizes a notion of *essence.* Roughly speaking, a property X is the essence of an object x if every property of x is a necessary consequence of X.

Essence. We use $\mathcal{E}$ to abbreviate the type $\langle\langle 0\rangle, 0\rangle$ term

$$\langle\lambda X, x.(\forall Y)[Y(x) \supset \Box(\forall y)[X(y) \supset Y(y)]]\rangle$$

Now we show one step of Gödel's argument: $(\forall x)[G(x) \supset \mathcal{E}(G, x)]$. That is, being God is the essence of anything that is, in fact, God. We give a tableau derivation of it from the assumption about positive properties.

$$
\begin{array}{l}
1\,\neg(\forall x)[G(x) \supset \mathcal{E}(G,x)] \quad 1.\\
1\,\neg[G(g) \supset \mathcal{E}(G,g)] \quad 2.\\
1\;\; G(g) \quad 3.\\
1\,\neg\mathcal{E}(G,g) \quad 4.\\
1\;\; G_1(g) \quad 5.\\
1\,\neg\langle\lambda X, x.(\forall Y)[Y(x) \supset \Box(\forall y)[X(y) \supset Y(y)]]\rangle(G,g) \quad 6.\\
1\,\neg\langle\lambda X, x.(\forall Y)[Y(x) \supset \Box(\forall y)[X(y) \supset Y(y)]]\rangle_1(G_1,g) \quad 7.\\
1\,\neg(\forall Y)[Y(g) \supset \Box(\forall y)[G_1(y) \supset Y(y)]] \quad 8.\\
1\,\neg[Q(g) \supset \Box(\forall y)[G_1(y) \supset Q(y)]] \quad 9.\\
1\;\; Q(g) \quad 10.\\
1\,\neg\Box(\forall y)[G_1(y) \supset Q(y)] \quad 11.\\
1\;\; (\forall X)[\neg\mathcal{P}(X) \supset \mathcal{P}(\neg X)] \quad 12.\\
1\,\neg\mathcal{P}(Q) \supset \mathcal{P}(\neg Q) \quad 13.
\end{array}
$$

In this, 2 is from 1 by an existential rule (g is a new parameter); 3 and 4 are from 2 by a conjunctive rule; 5 is from 3 by an atomic evaluation rule; 6 is 4 unabbreviated; 7 is from 6 by an atomic evaluation rule; 8 is from 7 by a predicate abstract rule; 9 is from 8 by an existential rule (Q is a new parameter); 10 and 11 are from 9 by a conjunctive rule; 12 is our assumption about positiveness; 13 is from 12 by a universal rule.

At this point the tableau branches, using item 13. We first present the *right* branch, then the left.

$$1\,\mathcal{P}(\neg Q) \quad 14.$$
$$1\,\langle\lambda x.(\forall X)[\mathcal{P}(X) \supset X(x)]\rangle(g) \quad 15.$$
$$1\,\langle\lambda x.(\forall X)[\mathcal{P}(X) \supset X(x)]\rangle_1(g) \quad 16.$$
$$1\,(\forall X)[\mathcal{P}(X) \supset X(g)] \quad 17.$$
$$1\,\mathcal{P}(\neg Q) \supset (\neg Q)(g) \quad 18.$$

Left: $1\,\neg\mathcal{P}(\neg Q) \quad 19.$

Right:

$$1\;\;(\neg Q)(g) \quad 20.$$
$$1\;\;\langle\lambda x.\neg Q(x)\rangle(g) \quad 21.$$
$$1\;\;\langle\lambda x.\neg Q(x)\rangle_1(g) \quad 22.$$
$$1\,\neg Q(g) \quad 23.$$

Item 14 is from 13 by a disjunctive rule; 15 is 3 unabbreviated; 16 is from 15 by an atomic evaluation rule; 17 is from 16 by a predicate abstract rule; 18 is from 17 using a universal rule; 19 and 20 are from 18 by a disjunctive rule; 21 is 20 unabbreviated; 22 is from 21 an atomic evaluation rule; 23 is from 22 by a predicate abstract rule. Closure is by 14 and 19, and 10 and 23.

Now we display the *left* branch.

$$1\,\neg\neg\mathcal{P}(Q) \quad 24.$$
$$1\;\;\mathcal{P}(Q) \quad 25.$$
$$2\,\neg(\forall y)[G_1(y) \supset Q(y)] \quad 26.$$
$$2\,\neg[G_1(q) \supset Q(q)] \quad 27.$$
$$2\;\;G_1(q) \quad 28.$$
$$2\,\neg Q(q) \quad 29.$$
$$2\;\;\langle\lambda x.(\forall X)[\mathcal{P}(X) \supset X(x)]\rangle_1(q) \quad 30.$$
$$1\;\;(\forall X)[\mathcal{P}(X) \supset X(q)] \quad 31.$$
$$1\;\;\mathcal{P}(Q) \supset Q(q) \quad 32.$$

Left: $1\,\neg\mathcal{P}(Q) \quad 33.$ Right: $1\,Q(q) \quad 34.$

Item 24 is from 13 by a disjunctive rule; 25 is from 24 by double negation; 26 is from 11 by a possibility rule; 27 is from 26 by an existential rule (q is a new parameter); 28 and 29 are from 27 by a conjunctive rule; 30 is 28 unabbreviated; 31 is from 30 by a predicate abstract rule; 32 is from 31 by a universal rule; 33 and 34 are from 32 by a disjunctive rule. Closure is by 25 and 33, and 29 and 34.

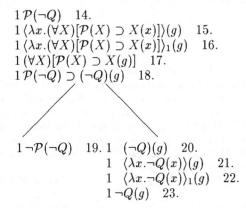

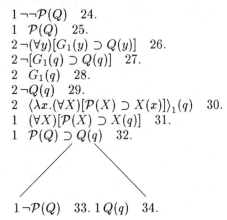

8 Conclusion

Higher-order modal logic is inherently complex. Just a sketch was possible here. There was no room to present Henkin-modal models, let alone non-extensional versions, though they are extremely natural to work with. Tableau completeness arguments are especially elaborate. A much longer treatment is in preparation. We hope this brief sketch is enough to raise interest in an issue that has rarely been looked at in modal logic ([1] is a rare but noteworthy instance).

References

1. A. Bressan. *A General Interpreted Modal Calculus.* Yale University Press, 1972.
2. M. C. Fitting. Bertrand Russell, Herbrand's theorem, and the assignment statement. In J. Calmet and J. Plaza, editors, *Artificial Intelligence and Symbolic Computation*, pages 14–28. Springer Lecture Notes in Artificial Intelligence, 1476, 1998.
3. M. C. Fitting and R. Mendelsohn. *First-Order Modal Logic.* Kluwer, 1998.
4. K. Gödel. Ontological proof. In S. Feferman, J. W. Dawson, Jr., W. Goldfarb, C. Parsons, and R. M. Solovay, editors, *Kurt Gödel Collected Works*, volume III, pages 403–404. Oxford, Oxford, 1995.
5. G. E. Hughes and M. J. Cresswell. *A New Introduction to Modal Logic.* Routledge, London, 1996.
6. D. Prawitz. Hauptsatz for higher order logic. *Journal of Symbolic Logic*, 33:452–457, 1968.
7. R. Stalnaker and R. Thomason. Abstraction in first-order modal logic. *Theoria*, 34:203–207, 1968.
8. M. Takahashi. A proof of cut-elimination theorem in simple type theory. *J. Math. Soc. Japan*, 19:399–410, 1967.
9. R. Thomason and R. Stalnaker. Modality and reference. *Nous*, 2:359–372, 1968.

Proving Associative-Commutative Termination Using RPO-Compatible Orderings*

Deepak Kapur[1] and G. Sivakumar[2]

[1] Department of Computer Science, University of New Mexico
kapur@cs.unm.edu
[2] Computer Science Department, Indian Institute of Technology, Bombay, India
siva@cse.iitb.ernet.in

Abstract. Developing path orderings for associative-commutative (AC) rewrite systems has been quite a challenge at least for a decade. Compatibility with the recursive path ordering (RPO) schemes is desirable, and this property helps in orienting the commonly encountered distributivity axiom as desired. For applications in theorem proving and constraint solving, a total ordering on ground terms involving AC operators is often required. It is shown how the main solutions proposed so far ([7],[13]) with the desired properties can be viewed as arising from a common framework. A general scheme that works for non-ground (general) terms also is proposed. The proposed definition allows flexibility (using different *abstractions*) in the way the candidates of a term with respect to an associative-commutative function symbol are compared, thus leading to at least two distinct orderings on terms (from the same precedence relation on function symbols).

1 Introduction

Rewrite systems provide a useful model of computation based on the simple inference rule of "replacing equals by equals." Rewrite techniques have proved successful in many areas including equational programming, theorem proving, specification and verification, and proof by induction.

Rewriting techniques particularly are effective in reducing the search space for finding proofs because of the ability to orient equations into one-directional rewrite rules. Rewrite rules are used for "simplifying" expressions by repeatedly replacing instances of left-hand sides by the corresponding right-hand sides. For example, the rules below express addition and multiplication over natural numbers.

* This paper is a revised version of an earlier draft entitled *A recursive path ordering for proving associative-commutative termination* [8] by the authors which was published as a technical report of the Department of Computer Science, State University of New York, Albany, NY 12222, May 1998. This research has been partially supported by the National Science Foundation Grant nos. CCR-9712366, CCR-9712396, and CDA-9503064.

R. Caferra and G. Salzer (Eds.): Automated Deduction, LNAI 1761, pp. 39–61, 2000.

$$\begin{array}{|rcl|} 0+x & \rightarrow & x \\ s(x)+y & \rightarrow & s(x+y) \\ 0*x & \rightarrow & 0 \\ s(x)*y & \rightarrow & y+(x*y) \end{array}$$

A sample derivation chain is $s(0)*s(0) \rightarrow s(0)+(0*s(0)) \rightarrow s(0)+0 \rightarrow s(0+0) \rightarrow s(0)$.

Termination of such derivations is crucial for using rewriting in proofs and computations, as well as for mechanizing proofs by induction. One approach to prove termination is to design *well-founded orderings* on terms which include the *rewrite* relation. Several syntactic *path orderings* based on extending a precedence relation $\succ$ on function symbols to terms have been developed [4].

The Recursive Path Orderings (RPO) [4] are the most commonly used orderings in rewrite-based theorem provers . When $\succ$ is a total precedence relation on function symbols, RPO is total (up to equivalence) on ground terms (terms without variables). That is, given two distinct ground terms, either they are equivalent under the ordering, or one of them is bigger. Total orderings on ground terms have been found useful in theorem proving and constraint solving.

Many interesting and useful theories use operators (such as $+, *, \vee, \wedge, \oplus$) which are *associative* and *commutative*. We refer to such operators as AC-operators and terms using these operators as AC-terms in the rest of the paper. Developing well-founded orderings on AC-terms which are useful for proving termination of AC-rewrite systems has been quite a challenge. A number of attempts have been reported in [1, 15, 3]; see also [11, 2] for polynomial orderings as well as [5] for other approaches.

Two properties can be used to distinguish between most of the related previous work and to motivate the work done in this paper. The first property is *RPO-compatibility.* That is, whether an AC-ordering behaves exactly like RPO on non-AC terms as well as allows (like RPO) the orientation of the distributivity axiom $(x*(y+z) \rightarrow (x*y)+(x*z)$ as desired by making $* \succ +$, even though both $+$ and $*$ are AC-operators. The second property is the *ground totality.* That is, whether the proposed ordering is total on ground terms when the precedence relation on function symbols is total.

In 1990, Kapur, Sivakumar and Zhang proposed a general ordering scheme based on recursive path ordering with status (rpos) without any restrictions on the precedence relation between function symbols [9]. Their ordering scheme however has a weakness: it is not total on equivalence classes of AC ground terms even when the precedence relation on function symbols is total. A total ordering on AC-ground terms was first proposed by Narendran and Rusinowitch [12] based on polynomial interpretations (hence, it is not RPO-compatible). That ordering does not orient distributivity appropriately.

Rubio and Nieuwenhuis introduced a total ordering on ground terms for a total precedence relation on function symbols [14] which uses both interpretations similar to [1], and the idea of *elevation* used in [9]. They showed how their ordering can be lifted to non-ground terms. The main weakness of their ordering is that it does not orient distributivity properly. In particular, even if $* > +$, $x * (y + z) < (x * y) + (x * z)$, so that ordering is not RPO-compatible either.

In [7], we proposed a path ordering based on rpos that is total on AC ground terms, and orients the distributivity law properly by making $a * (b + c) > (a * b) + (a * c)$ if $* > +$. However, we could not give a natural extension of the definition to non-ground terms, and had to resort to approximations and constraint solving for extending the ordering to general terms. Using ideas similar to [7], Rubio proposed an ordering using a bottom-up construction [13]. He defined an interpretation associated with a term (with respect to an AC symbol) as a multiset of sequences. This ordering has all the desired properties on ground terms, but does not lift to non-ground terms. In [13], Rubio stated "the ordering we have defined on ground terms ... cannot be used directly on terms with variables." He instead gave two approximations to extend his interpretations to non-ground terms. While the first approximation is not as complex, it is unable to handle comparisons of simple terms such as $f(i(i(x)), x)$ with $f(i(x), i(x))$ with $f \succ i$. The second approximation is quite complex.

In this paper, we show how the main ideas used in the earlier approaches can be cast in a uniform framework. The proposed scheme simplifies the definitions in our earlier paper [7] even though the basic concepts of candidates and constructions for generating candidates in the two papers are related. More importantly, it is possible to extend the definition directly to non-ground (general) terms. This scheme also allows us to identify the main parameter— the *abstraction* used to compare contributions from function symbols ignored during *elevation*— that allows variants (two are given in this paper) of the basic ordering.

The rest of this paper is organized as follows. In Section 2, we give the relevant definitions and background for proving termination using RPO. In Section 3, we explain the major issues in designing a RPO-compatible ordering for AC-terms using illustrative examples to bring out the key ideas that have been proposed. In Section 4, we define an ordering scheme for comparing AC-terms. It is parameterized by an *abstraction* function, giving at least two distinct orderings for the same precedence relation on function symbols. Sections 5 and 6 discuss proofs, focusing on irreflexivity, transitivity, subterm, replacement and stability properties. It is also shown that the ordering is total on nonequivalent ground terms. We conclude in Section 7 with discussion of related work and suggestions for future work.

2 Rewrite Systems and Simplification Orderings

Let $T(F, X)$ be a set of terms constructed from a (finite) set F of function symbols and a (countable) set X of variables. We normally use the letters a through h for function symbols; s, t, and u through w for arbitrary terms; x, y, and z for variables. Each function symbol $f \in F$ has an *arity* $n \geq 0$; *constants* are function symbols of arity zero. Variable-free terms are called *ground* .

A term t in $T(F, X)$ may be viewed as a finite ordered tree. Internal nodes are labeled with function symbols (from F) of arity greater than 0. The out-degree of an internal node is the same as the arity of the label. Leaves are labeled with either variables (from X) or constants. We use $root(t)$ to denote the symbol labeled at the root of the tree corresponding to t. A subterm of t is called *proper* if it is distinct from t. By $t\mid_\pi$, we denote the *subterm* of t rooted at *position* π. Let u be a term and π a position in u. We use $u[\cdot]_\pi$ to denote the *context* for position π in u. Loosely speaking, the context is the tree obtained by deleting the subterm at position π leaving a "hole" in the term. We use $u[t]_\pi$ to denote a term that has t plugged in as a subterm at the "hole" in the context $u[\cdot]_\pi$.

A substitution σ is a mapping from variables to terms such that $x\sigma \neq x$ for a finite number of variables. The depth of a substitution σ is the maximum of the depths of the terms used in this mapping. A substitution can be extended to be a mapping from terms to terms. We use $t\sigma$ to denote the term obtained by applying a substitution σ to a term t. For example, the ground substitution $\sigma = \{x \mapsto k(a), y \mapsto d\}$ when applied to the term $t = f(x, y)$ gives the ground term $t\sigma = f(k(a), d)$.

A rewrite *rule* over a set $T(F, X)$ of terms is an ordered pair (l, r) of terms such that the variables in r also appear in l, and is written $l \rightarrow r$. A *rewrite system* (or *term rewriting system*) R is a set of such rules. Rules can be used to replace instances of l by corresponding instances of r.

One approach to proving termination of rewrite systems is to use simplification orderings [4]. A simplification ordering has the following properties.

1. **Subterm Property**: $u[t] \succ t$ for any term t and a non-empty context $u[\cdot]$.
2. **Monotonicity**: $s \succ t$ implies that $u[s]_\pi \succ u[t]_\pi$, for all contexts $u[\cdot]$, terms s and t, and positions π.

We have omitted the deletion property which is needed only if there are function symbols with varying arity. Any simplification ordering $\succ$ on terms is well-founded, that is, there is no infinite descending chain of terms $t_1 \succ t_2 \succ t_3 \cdots$.

A simplification ordering that also has the following property

- **Stability**: for all terms s and t, $s \succ t$ implies that for all substitutions σ, $s\sigma \succ t\sigma$.

can be used for proving termination of rewrite systems. If for every rule $l \rightarrow r$ in R, $l \succ r$ in a simplification ordering $\succ$ which is stable under substitutions, then $\rightarrow$ is terminating.

2.1 Recursive Path Ordering

Let $\succ$ be a well-founded precedence relation on a set of function symbols F. For simplicity and without loss of generality, we assume in the rest of the paper that $\succ$ is *total*, i.e., any two distinct function symbols f, g are comparable using $\succ$ (i.e. they are equivalent or one is bigger). Also without loss of generality, we assume that there is at least one constant symbol in F, and we denote the smallest constant in F by a. The recursive path ordering extends $\succ$ on function symbols to a well-founded ordering on terms [4]. For convenience we do not use left-to-right or right-to-left status for any operator as in LRPO although all results in this paper easily extends to this also.

Definition 1. Two terms t and s are *equivalent* ($t \sim s$) if they are either the same variable, or both are non-variables i.e. $t = f(t_1, \ldots, t_n)$, $s = g(s_1, \ldots, s_m)$ and $f = g$, $n = m$, and there is a permutation p of $(1, \ldots, n)$ such that $t_i \sim s_{p(i)}$.

Definition 2 (RPO[4]). $s = f(s_1, \ldots, s_n) \succ g(t_1, \ldots, t_m) = t$ iff one of the following holds.

1. $f \succ g$, and $s \succ t_j$ for all j $(1 \leq j \leq m)$.
2. $f = g$, and $\{s_1, \ldots, s_n\} \succ^{mul} \{t_1, \ldots, t_m\}$.
3. $f \not\succeq g$, and for some i $(1 \leq i \leq n)$, either $s_i \sim t$ or $s_i \succ t$.

The ordering $\succ$ is a simplification ordering [4]. Also, when the precedence relation on F is total, two distinct ground terms are either equivalent or comparable under $\succ$.

2.2 AC-Rewriting and Its Termination

With operators that are associative and commutative, the definition of rewriting needs to be modified to include the consequences of these two properties which are not explicitly added as rules (since $x * y = y * x$ cannot be oriented). Let F_{AC} denote the set of such operators.

Consider a rule $a * b \rightarrow c$, where $* \in F_{AC}$. The term $t = (b * c) * a$ cannot be rewritten directly if we use the definition of $\rightarrow$ given earlier, as no subterm of t is of the form $a * b$. But t is equivalent to the term $s = (a * b) * c$ (using the AC properties of $*$) and $s \rightarrow c * c$. AC-rewriting ($\rightarrow_{AC}$) is defined to cover such cases as follows.

Definition 3 (AC-Rewriting). $u[t] \rightarrow_{AC} u[s']$ if $t \leftrightarrow_{AC} \cdots \leftrightarrow_{AC} s$ (re-arranging arguments of AC-operators) and $s \rightarrow s'$ using $l \rightarrow r$ in R.

With this definition of rewriting, we need to ensure that any simplification ordering also has the following property to ensure its usefulness in proving termination of AC-rewriting.

Definition 4 (AC-Compatibility). A simplification ordering $\succ$ is AC-compatible if, for any terms t, t_1, s, and s_1, if $t \sim^* t_1$, $s \sim^* s_1$, and $t \succ s$, then $t_1 \succ s_1$.

2.3 Flattening

A key idea that figures in many approaches to AC-rewriting is to treat AC-operators not as strictly binary functions (arity = 2) but to let them be vary-adic and use *flattening* (of AC-operators) to convert terms like $(a * b) * c$ to $*(a, b, c)$. We use $\bar{t}$ to denote the flattened form of a term t.

Definition 5. The flattened form $\overline{t}$ of a term t is defined below.

$$\overline{t} = \begin{cases} x & \text{if } t = x, \text{ a variable} \\ f(\overline{t_1}, \ldots, \overline{t_n}) & \text{if } t = f(t_1, \ldots, t_n) \text{ and } f \notin F_{AC} \\ f(T_1 \cup \cdots \cup T_n) & \text{if } t = f(t_1, \ldots, t_n), f \in F_{AC} \text{ and} \\ & T_i = \begin{cases} \{s_1, \ldots, s_m\} \text{ if } \overline{t_i} = f(s_1, \ldots, s_m) \\ \{\overline{t_i}\} \quad \text{otherwise} \end{cases} \end{cases}$$

The important question that arises is, whether the termination of $\rightarrow_{AC}$ can be proved using $\succ$ and treating AC-operators just like other function symbols (except that they have variable arity), and using flattened terms always. That is, we may attempt to define an ordering $\succ$ on AC-terms using $s \succ t$ iff $\overline{s} \succ \overline{t}$.

3 Issues in Extending RPO to AC-Terms

It is well known that defining RPO on flattened terms does not give a simplification ordering on AC terms. We show through a series of examples, first with ground terms and then with terms containing variables, the difficulties encountered in adapting RPO to terms with AC-operators. We then introduce the notion of *candidates* for a term, taking into consideration how different subterms with an outermost symbol smaller than an AC-operator are elevated; this concept of elevation was first used in [9]. We motivate possible *abstractions* that can be used when comparing candidates. This leads to several versions of AC-RPO including an ordering similar to [7] and an ordering in [13].

In all examples henceforth, we use $g \succ f \succ j \succ i \succ c \succ b \succ a$ with $f \in F_{AC}$ as the precedence relation.

Using RPO, $g(a) \succ f(a,a) \succ i(a)$. By *monotonicity*, the following chain must hold. The second inequality does not hold under RPO since $\{i(a), a\} \succ \{a, a, a\}$.

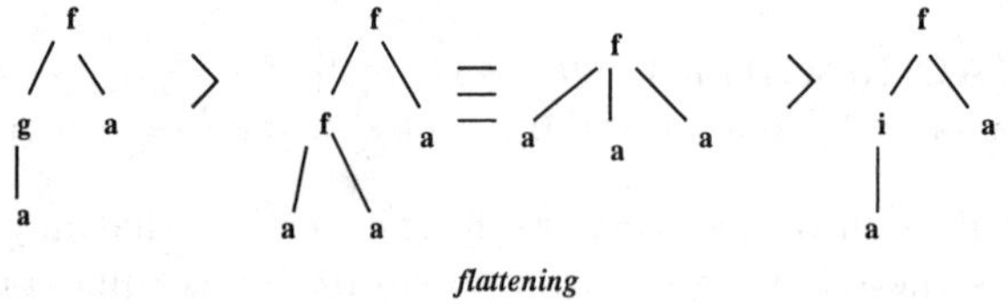

This shows that when comparing two terms having the same AC-operator as root symbol, the arguments cannot be compared simply as multisets (or sequences) as in RPO. A more nuanced comparison of arguments is needed to prove $f(a,a,a) \succ f(i(a),a)$.

The number of arguments (referred to as *fcount* later) below the AC-operator has a role to play to account for the effect of flattening. A similar example is $f(a,a,a) \succ f(c,c)$. A useful idea that helps is to compare *small* terms (no symbol bigger than f) first by number of such terms and then only the actual terms themselves, is to abstract such terms by a (the smallest constant) first.

It may be useful to observe that when operators bigger than f are involved, the situation is somewhat different. That is, since $g(a) \succ f(c, \ldots, c)$ (any number of c's since $g \succ f$), we have that $f(g(a), a) \succ f(c, \ldots, c)$. So, the number of arguments becomes a factor only when the *big* arguments (those with root symbol bigger than f) do not play any role in the strict comparison.

To summarize, to maintain the monotonicity property, in comparing two ground terms, an argument of f with a symbol bigger than f can take care of many smaller arguments of f (which do not have any occurrence of a symbol bigger than f), but otherwise, the number of arguments to f becomes relevant.

A second interesting observation is that since $f(b, c) \succ i(f(a, c))$ by RPO, we should make $f(b, c, b, c) \succ f(i(f(a, c)), i(f(a, c)))$. That is, the role of the smaller operator i in between nested $f's$, that can be **elevated**, is less important than that of the actual arguments b, c below the AC-operator, even though i is bigger than b and c.

The following example shows a third dimension–how the arguments of an AC-operator are partitioned. The first comparison is because we have simply

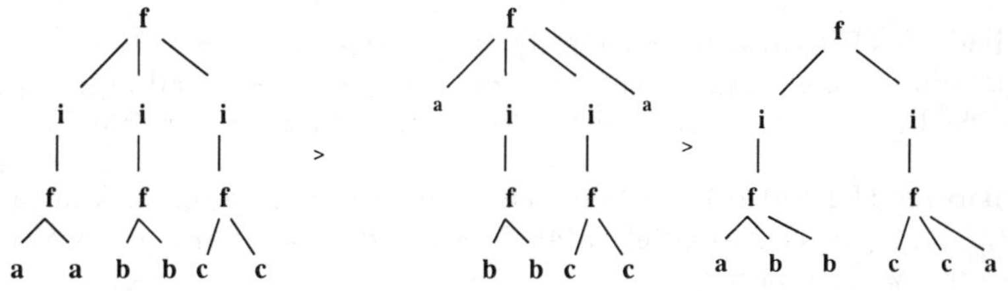

replaced $i(f(a, a))$ by its subterm $f(a, a)$ and flattened. The second follows once we note that $f(a, i(f(c, c))) \succ i(f(a, c, c))$ by RPO.

In the examples above, the requirements of any *simplification* ordering such as the subterm and monotonicity properties, forced the outcome of the comparison. Whatever method of comparing AC-terms we provide must preserve the order in these examples.

In the following example we have persevered the arguments below the AC-

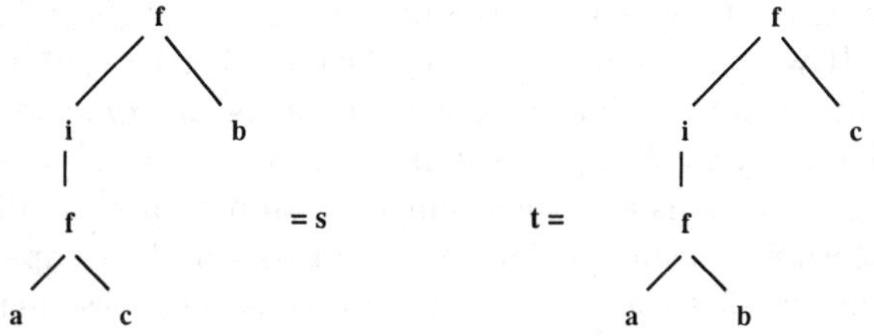

operator and kept the partition sizes the same. Then, different ways of defining

comparison of AC-terms could orient these differently. Using [7], $t \succ s$, whereas using [13] as well as the orderings proposed in this paper, $s \succ t$.

3.1 Candidates

The main approaches for developing RPO-compatible orderings for AC-terms ([9],[7],[13]) have tackled the problems identified above in slightly different ways. All of them change RPO only in the case when we compare $s = f(S)$ with $t = f(T)$ with $f \in F_{AC}$. They give different ways to compare S and T.

A unifying framework can be developed using the common threads. Some useful definitions are given first.

Definition 6 (Big Terms). A term t is called *big* with respect to an AC-operator f, if $t = g(t_1, \ldots, t_m)$ with $g \succ f$.

Definition 7 (Small Terms). A term t is called *small* with respect to an AC-operator f, if t is a ground term with all function symbols and constants in t smaller than f.

If a non-variable term is neither Big nor Small, then it is said to be *elevatable.*

Definition 8 (Elevatable Position). A position λ in $t = i(t_1, \ldots, t_n)$ with $f \succ i$ is said to be elevatable with respect to $f \in F_{AC}$, if for all proper prefixes λ' of λ, we have $f \succ top(t|_{\lambda'})$ and $top(t|_\lambda) \geq f$, or $t|_\lambda = x$ a variable.

Definition 9 (Elevatable Subterm). A subterm t' at position λ in the term $t = i(t_1, \ldots, t_n)$ is said to be elevatable with respect to f if λ is an elevatable position in t with respect to f.

For example, in the term $j(g(x), i(f(x, a)))$, we have two elevatable subterms $g(x)$ and $f(x, a)$ with respect to f. In the term $t = j(x, j(g(a), i(y)))$, we can elevate x, $g(a)$ or y; in $f(a, j(f(b, c), g(a)))$, $f(b, c)$ as well as $g(a)$ can be elevated.

Definition 10 (Elevation). We can derive s from t by *elevation* (denoted $t \Rightarrow s$) if $t = f(\ldots, i(t_1, \ldots, t_n), \ldots)$ with $f \succ i$, and $s = f(\ldots, t', \ldots)$ for some term t' elevatable from $i(t_1, \ldots, t_n)$ with respect to f. We say that t elevates to s.

For example, $f(a, j(f(b, c), g(a)))$ elevates to either $f(a, g(a))$ or $f(a, b, c)$ depending on which subterm is used in the elevation.

We say that a term $t = f(T)$ is in elevation normal form (*enf*) iff $T = B \cup V \cup S$ where B is a multiset of big term, V is a multiset of variables and S is a multiset of small terms. If we further require that each small term $s \in S$ is only a the smallest constant, then we call such a term as being in *argument normal form.* We can convert a term $s = f(S)$ to argument normal form $s' = anf(s)$, by first doing all possible elevations and then replacing all maximal small terms by a.

Comparing terms in argument normal form by simply comparing the arguments as multisets is safe to do. This has been used as a subcase in many previous approaches to designing AC-RPO.

With this comparison of terms, a sufficient condition for $s = f(S) \succ f(T) = t$ can be stated.

Definition 11 (ACRPO-1). $s = f(S) \succ f(T) = t$ if for every $t' \in anf(t)$, there is a $s' \in anf(s)$ such that $s' \succ t'$.

Note that this definition is sufficient to handle some of the problem cases described earlier. For example, we can show $f(a,a,a) \succ f(i(a),a)$.

ACRPO-1, though sound, is not enough to ensure that we have a simplification ordering since it cannot show, for example, that
$f(i(f(a,a)), i(f(a,a)), i(f(a,a))) \succ f(i(f(a,a,a)), i(f(a,a,a)))$.

It is essential to give some way to compare terms whose biggest anf-forms are identical as in the case above. It becomes necessary, therefore, to build up another view (called *Context* in [7]) while deriving the enf-form (called *Arguments* in [7]). The role of *context* is to bring back the actual values of the Small terms (replaced by a), the smaller operators (such as i) lost during the elevation, and the role they play in partitioning the arguments.
Consider the example shown in the figure.

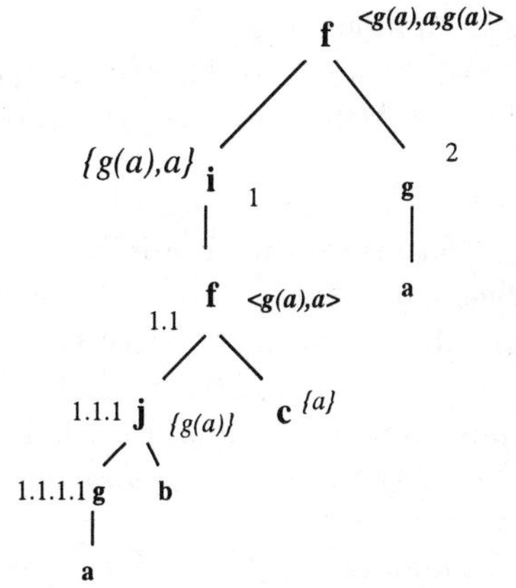

The view as *Arguments* is $\{g(a), a, g(a)\}$ (the anf-form) with the elevations happening at position 1 and later at the subterm $j(g(a), b)$ at position 1.1.1. We can define the context of this view as the multiset of pairs $\{\langle\{g(a)\}, j(g(a),b)\rangle, \}$ $\{\langle\{g(a),a\}, i(f(j(g(a),b),c))\rangle, \langle\{a\}, c\rangle\}$ which is the collection of the subterms in which elevations occurred and by the contribution of this elevated subterm to the view as Arguments, and also the Small Terms in the elevation normal form that were replaced by a.

This leads to the idea of *candidates*. A candidate for a term $s = f(S)$ (with $f \in F_{AC}$) is obtained by taking from each $s_i \in S$, its contribution to two different "views" of S– **Arguments** and **Contexts**. When comparing two terms $f(S_1)$ and $f(S_2)$, the views as Arguments are compared first, and only if they are equivalent, the contexts are compared. The interesting issue is how contexts should be compared.[1]

3.2 Context Comparison

We go back to the example shown earlier for partitioning to illustrate some im-

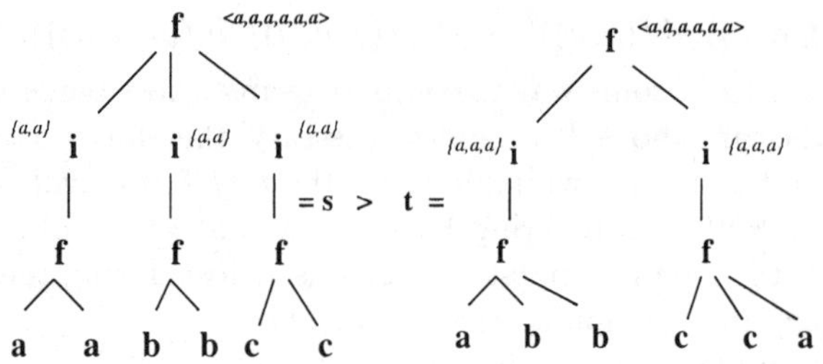

portant issues in context comparison. The view as Arguments is the same for both terms: $(\{a, a, a, a, a, a\})$. So, we have to consider the role of the contexts C_s and C_t where dropping common pairs,
$C_s - C_t = \{\langle\{a, a\}, i(f(a, a))\rangle\langle\{a, a\}, i(f(b, b))\rangle\langle\{a, a\}, i(f(c, c))\rangle\}$ and
$C_t - C_s = \{\langle\{a, a, a\}, i(f(a, b, b))\rangle\langle\{a, a, a\}, i(f(a, c, c))\rangle\}$ and we must have $C_s \succ C_t$.

Since the Arguments are overall the same on both sides, if an elevated subterm has contributed less, that means that it appears in a bigger context (more contribution from the other arguments), and it should be given more weight. This suggests that the contribution of the elevated subterms to the Arguments play an *inverse* role in the comparison.

Pairs in contexts are thus compared by first using union of contributions from other subterms to this view (Arguments) first, and then going to the elevated subterms themselves.

That is, if $f(S)$ has a candidate $\langle A_s, C_s\rangle$ and $f(T)$ has a candidate $\langle A_t, C_t\rangle$ and we need to compare C_s with C_t (since $A_s = A_t$), then for every pair $\langle A, tt\rangle \in C_t - C_s$, we look for a pair $\langle B, ss\rangle \in C_s - C_t$ such that either $A_s - B$, the context of ss, takes care of $A_t - A$, the context of tt, or the two contexts are equivalent and $ss \succ tt$.

In the example above, we compare
$C'_s = \{\langle\{a, a, a, a\}, i(f(a, a))\rangle\langle\{a, a, a, a\}, i(f(b, b))\rangle\langle\{a, a, a, a\}, i(f(c, c))\rangle\}$ and $C'_t = \{\langle\{a, a, a\}, i(f(a, b, b))\rangle\langle\{a, a, a\}, i(f(a, c, c))\rangle\}$ and as desired we get $C_s \succ C_t$.

For comparing the contexts themselves ($A_s - B$ with $A_t - A$), variations are possible. One is to compare them just as multiset of terms (the *term abstraction*)

[1] Definitions of [7] have been simplified here. The context in a candidate as defined in [7] is a multiset of pairs of terms corresponding to the order in which elevatable subterms are elevated; the first component in the pair is the rest of the term obtained after deleting the elevated argument, and the second component is the elevated argument itself.

using the same ordering. This leads to a definition similar, but not exactly the same, as the one in [7]. Another approach is to simply compare their lengths (number of terms in $A_s - B$ with the number in $A_t - A$) since this is a measure of how the views of Arguments are partitioned.

An example that distinguishes the two orderings is given: $s = f(i(g(b)), g(c))$, $t = f(i(g(c)), g(b))$. The Arguments for both s and t are the same: $\{g(b), g(c)\}$. In s, $g(b)$ is elevatable, whereas in t, $g(c)$ is elevatable. The context of the candidate of s is $\{\langle\{g(b)\}, i(g(b))\rangle\}$; the context of the candidate of t is $\{\langle\{g(c)\}, i(g(c))\rangle\}$; If we use the *fcount* abstraction, then $t \succ s$. Using the *term* abstraction, we get $s \succ t$.

4 Definition of AC-RPO ($\succ_{ac}$)

As indicated in the previous section, a *candidate* for a term t is a pair $\langle A, C\rangle$ where A is the view as arguments, and C is the context for this view. The multiset of candidates of any term t with respect to an AC-operator f is defined formally below as $cands(t, f)$.

Definition 12 (Candidates).

1.	$cands(x, f) \Rightarrow \{\langle\{x\}, \phi\rangle\}$	
2.	$cands(t = g(t_1, \ldots, t_n), f) \Rightarrow \{\langle\{t\}, \phi\rangle\}$	if $g \succ f$.
3.	$cands(t, f) \Rightarrow \{\langle\{a\}, \{\langle\{a\}, t\rangle\}\rangle\}$	if t is a Small term wrt f.
4.	$cands(f(t_1, \ldots, t_n), f) \Rightarrow \{\biguplus_i c_{t_i} \in cands(t_i, f)\}$	
5.	$cands(t = i(t_1, \ldots, t_n), f) \Rightarrow \bigcup\{\langle A', C' \cup \{\langle A', t\rangle\}\rangle \mid \langle A', C'\rangle \in cands(t', f)\}$	if $f \succ i$ and t' is elevatable from t.

The first three rules are the base cases. A term t which is a variable, or whose top symbol is bigger than f (i.e. a Big term), contributes itself to Arguments and nothing to the Context. A Small term contributes a to arguments (the smallest constant) and $\langle\{a\}, t\rangle$ to context.

Rule 4 defines the candidates of $f(t_1, \ldots, t_n)$ to be union of candidates obtained by the component-wise union of one candidate from each of the arguments $t_1, \ldots, t_n$. Note that if t_j has n_j candidates, then the number of candidates of $f(t_1, \ldots, t_n)$ is the **product** of the n_j-s.

Finally, Rule 5 defines the interesting case when $i < f$ is the top symbol of $t = i(t_1, \ldots, t_n)$ and t has some elevatable subterm t'. A candidate $c_t = \langle A_t, C_t\rangle$ for t is obtained from each candidate $c_{t'} = \langle A'C'\rangle$ of t' by not changing the view in Arguments (i.e. $A_t = A'$), and adding to the view as Context the pair $\langle A', t\rangle$ (i.e. $C_t = C' \cup \langle A', t\rangle$). In this case, if each elevatable t' has n_j candidates, the number of candidates is the **sum** of the n_j-s.

A few illustrative examples of candidates is given below. In all these examples $g \succ f \succ j \succ i \succ c \succ b \succ a$ is the precedence relation, as before.

Example 1. $s_1 = f(i(i(i(a))), b)$ has only one candidate:
$\langle\{a, a\}, \{\langle\{a\}, b\rangle, \langle\{a\}, i(i(i(a)))\rangle\}\rangle$. Notice that both small terms have contributed only a to the Argument view.

Example 2. $s_2 = f(i(g(b)), c)$ has only one candidate:
$\langle\{g(b), a\}, \{\langle\{g(b)\}, i(g(b))\rangle\langle\{a\}, c\rangle\}\rangle$

Example 3. $s_3 = f(i(f(b, c)), c, c)$ also has only one candidate:
$\langle\{a, a, a, a\}, \{\langle\{a\}, b\rangle, \langle\{a\}, c\rangle, \langle\{a\}, c\rangle, \langle\{a\}, c\rangle, \langle\{a, a\}, i(f(b, c))\rangle\}\rangle$. Notice that $i(f(b, c))$ contributes $\{a, a\}$ to Arguments.

Example 4. $s_4 = f(j(g(x), g(c)), g(z))$ has two candidates:
$\langle\{g(x), g(z)\}, \{\langle\{g(x)\}, j(g(x), g(c))\rangle\}\rangle$ and $\langle\{g(c), g(z)\}, \{\langle\{g(c)\}, j(g(x), g(c))\rangle\}\rangle$ depending on which argument of $j(g(x), g(c))$ is elevated.

Example 5. $s_5 = f(i(c), j(f(b, b), y))$ also has two candidates:
$\langle\{a, a, a\}, \{\langle\{a\}, i(c)\rangle, \langle\{a\}, b\rangle, \langle\{a\}, b\rangle, \langle\{a, a\}, j(f(b, b), y)\rangle\}\rangle$ if $f(b, b)$ is elevated from $j(f(b, b), y)$. Or,
$\langle\{a, y\}, \{\langle\{a\}, i(c)\rangle, \langle\{y\}, j(f(b, b), y)\rangle\}\rangle$ if y is elevated from $j(f(b, b), y)$ which then gets $\{y\}$ as its contribution to the Arguments.

Example 6. $s_6 = f(i(f(x, i(f(b, y)))), c)$ has only one candidate:
$\langle\{x, a, y, a\}, \{\langle\{a\}, b\rangle, \langle\{y, a\}, i(f(b, y))\rangle, \langle\{x, y, a\}, i(f(x, i(f(b, y))))\rangle\langle\{a\}, c\rangle\}\rangle$
Note that the repeated elevation from $i(f(x, i(f(b, y))))$ adds one pair to the context each time with its contribution to the Arguments.

4.1 Properties of Candidates

Definition 13 (f-blocked). A term t is said to be f-blocked if it is a variable, a Big term, or the smallest constant a.

Property 14. Let $\langle A_t, C_t\rangle \in cands(t, f)$. Then,

1. Every term in A_t is an f-blocked term. That is A_t contains only big terms, variables, or a (smallest constant).
2. $A_t = \{t\}$ or A_t is a multiset of proper subterms of t. So, if $\succ$ is any ordering with the subterm property, then $\{t\} \geq A_t$.
3. In every pair $\langle A, tt\rangle \in C_t$,
   (a) A contains only f-blocked terms.
   (b) tt is never a variable. It is either Small (ground) term or has an elevatable subterm with respect to f.
   (c) $A \subseteq A_t$. If $top(t) = f$, then $A \subset A_t$ (strict subset) and tt is a proper subterm of t.

Property 15 (Equivalent Candidates). If $s \sim t$ and $f \in F_{AC}$, then for every candidate $\langle A_t, C_t\rangle \in cands(t, f)$, there is a candidate $\langle A_s, C_s\rangle \in cands(s, f)$ (1-1 correspondence) which is component-wise equivalent. That is, $cands(s, f) = cands(t, f)$ (= is modulo $\sim$).

Proof. Since $s \sim t$, we can map the positions used in t to derive any $\langle A_t, C_t\rangle$ to an appropriate set of positions (arguments can be permuted) in s and use it to derive the corresponding $\langle A_s, C_s\rangle$.

Property 16 (Distinct Candidate Sets). If $s \not\sim t$ and $f \in F_{AC}$, then $cands(s, f) \neq cands(t, f)$.

4.2 Comparing Terms

Definition 17 (AC-RPO). A non-variable term $s \succ_{ac} x$ for any variable x in s. Otherwise, $s = f(s_1, \ldots, s_n) \succ_{ac} g(t_1, \ldots, t_m) = t$, if one of the following holds.

1. $f \succ g$, and $s \succ_{ac} t_j$ for all j $(1 \leq j \leq m)$.
2. $f = g \notin F_{AC}$, and $\{s_1, \ldots, s_n\} \succ_{ac}^{mul} \{t_1, \ldots, t_m\}$.
3. $f = g \in F_{AC}$, and $cands(s, f) \succ_c^{mul} cands(t, f)$.
   (That is, for every candidate $c_t \in cand(t, f) - cands(s, f)$, there is a candidate $c_s \in cands(s, f) - cands(t, f)$ such that $c_s \succ_c c_t$.)
4. $f \not\succeq g$ and for some i $(1 \leq i \leq n)$, either $s_i \sim t$ or $s_i \succ_{ac} t$.

Note that if x is a variable, $x \not\succ_{ac} t$ for any t. Also, $x \succeq_{ac} a$, given that a is the smallest constant.

The comparison $\succ_c$ of candidates used above is defined as follows. Let $c_s = \langle A_s, C_s \rangle \in cands(s, f)$ and $c_t = \langle A_t, C_t \rangle \in cands(t, f)$. $c_s \succ_c c_t$ if $A_s \succeq_{ac}{}^{mul} A_t$ and and one of the following holds.

1. $A_s \succ_{ac}^{mul} A_t$. Or,
2. $A_s \succeq_{ac}{}^{mul} A_t$, and $C_s \succ C_t$ as defined below:
   $(C_s - C_t) \neq \phi$ and for every pair $\langle A, tt \rangle \in C_t - C_s$, there is a pair $\langle B, ss \rangle \in C_s - C_t$ such that
   (a) $abs(A_s - B, f) > abs(A_t - A, f)$, or
   (b) $abs(A_s - B, f) \geq abs(A_t - A, f)$ and $ss \succ_{ac} tt$

The function $abs(M, f)$ where M is a multiset of f-blocked terms is a suitable *abstraction* of the contribution of M to the Argument view. This abstraction can be defined in different ways yielding different orderings provided that the orderings on abstractions satisfy properties such as *irreflexivity*, *transitivity*, *monotonicity*, *stability*, and *totality* on ground cases. These properties will be mentioned as needed in the proofs.

4.2.1 Abstractions for Contexts.

Different *abs*'s are motivated and illustrated using the comparison of $s = f(i(f(a,a)), i(f(b,b)), i(f(c,c)))$ with $t = f(i(f(a,b,b)), i(f(a,c,c)))$. Recall from previous section that any RPO-compatible simplification ordering must make $s \succ_{ac} t$.

There is only one candidate for each side—$c_s = \langle A_s, C_s \rangle$ and $c_t = \langle A_t, C_t \rangle$ where $A_s = A_t = \{a, a, a, a, a, a\}$. But,

$$C_s - C_t = \{\langle \{a,a\}, i(f(a,a)) \rangle, \langle \{a,a\}, i(f(b,b)) \rangle, \langle \{a,a\}, i(f(c,c)) \rangle\},$$

whereas

$$C_t - C_s = \{\langle \{a,a,a\}, i(f(a,b,b)) \rangle, \langle \{a,a,a\}, i(f(a,c,c)) \rangle\}.$$

For defining candidate comparison, we compare the contexts of the elevated subterms by comparing the measures of the multiset differences $A_s - B$ and $A_t - A$ above.

4.2.1.1 fcount. One way to define a measure of the contribution of a subterm is by using $fcount$ on f-blocked terms as defined below.

Definition 18.

$$fcount(t, f) = \begin{cases} x \text{ if } t = x, \text{ a variable}, \\ 1 \text{ if } top(t) = g \succ f, \\ 1 \text{ if } t \text{ is a Small term w.r.t. } f. \end{cases}$$

For a multiset A of f-blocked terms,

$$fcount(A, f) = \sum_{t_i \in A} fcount(t_i, f).$$

For example, $fcount(\{g(x), x, a, y, x\}, f) = 2 * x + y + 2$; $fcount(\phi, f) = 0$.

The measure for any non-variable f-simple term is 1. A variable's measure depends on what is substituted for it. If $\sigma(x)$ has no elevatable f-subterm, then $\sigma(x)$ contributes 1. Otherwise, it may contribute more due to elevation and flattening. So, the variables in the measure only take values > 0 (i.e. $x, y \geq 1$ above). Given two measures, which are linear polynomials p and q, we compare them by checking if $p - q > 0$ for all non-zero positive integers for the variables. For example, $(3x + 4) > (2x + 3)$, and $(x + 1) \geq 2$, but $(x + 1) \not> 2$.

4.2.1.2 Term. Another abstraction can be defined by considering f-blocked terms themselves instead of abstracting out how many f arguments they contribute. So $abs(M, f)$ is defined as $f(M)$ which is compared using the same underlying ordering since terms serving as indices are smaller in size. This leads to a different ordering since $fcount$ does not distinguish between the contributions of f-blocked terms such as $g(a)$ and $g(c)$ (both have $fcount$ of 1).

An example which distinguishes this abstraction from $fcount$ is to compare $s = f(i(f(g(a), g(b))), g(c))$ with $t = f(i(f(g(a), g(c))), g(b))$. Using $fcount$, $t \succ_{ac} s$, but using the term abstraction, $s \succ_{ac} t$.

In contrast to the above abstraction functions, in [7], the context in a candidate is a multiset of pairs, but the first component in a pair is the term obtained after deleting the subterm being elevated. For the example below, $t \succ s$, since

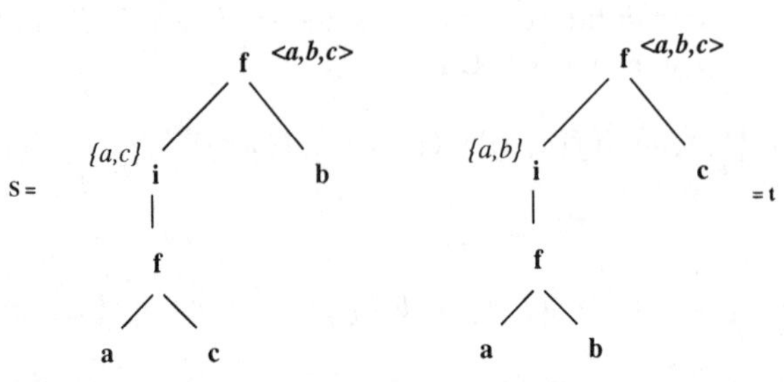

$c \succ b$, whereas using $fcount$ or $term$ abstractions, $s \succ t$ since $i(f(a, c)) \succ i(f(a, b))$.

4.3 Examples

We will use the *fcount* abstraction in all the examples below. We assume $f \in F_{AC}$ and $g > f > i > c > b > a$.

Example 7. $s = f(i(b), b) \succ_{ac} i(f(b, b)) = t$ because $f \succ i$, and $f(i(b), b) \succ_{ac} f(b, b)$ due to the Context component using $\langle\{a\}, i(b)\rangle \succ \langle\{a\}, b\rangle$.

Example 8. $s = f(i(b), b, i(b), b) \succ_{ac} f(i(f(b, b)), i(f(b, b))) = t$
Both sides have only one candidate each with Arguments component $A_s = A_t = \{a, a, a, a\}$, but $C_s - C_t = \{\langle\{a\}, i(b)\rangle, \langle\{a\}, i(b)\rangle\}$ whereas
$C_t - C_s = \{\langle\{a\}, b\rangle, \langle\{a, a\}, i(f(b, b))\rangle, \langle\{a\}, b\rangle, \langle\{a, a\}, i(f(b, b))\rangle\}$.
The pair $\langle\{a\}, i(b)\rangle \succ \langle\{a, a\}, i(f(b, b))\rangle$ because $abs(A_s - \{a\}) = 3 > 2 = abs(A_t - \{a, a\})$. Hence $C_s > C_t$.

Example 9. $s = f(i(f(a, c)), b) \succ_{ac} f(i(f(a, b)), c) = t$. Arguments are the same, but $C_s - C_t = \{\langle\{a, a\}, i(f(a, c))\rangle\}$ and $C_t - C_s = \{\langle\{a, a\}, i(f(a, b))\rangle\}$. Since $i(f(a, c)) \succ_{ac} i(f(a, b))$, we have $C_s \succ C_t$.

Example 10. $s = f(x, x, x) \succ_{ac} f(a, b) = t$. Since $\{x, x, x\} \succ_{ac} \{a, a\}$.

Example 11. $s = f(a, i(x)) \succ_{ac} f(a, b) = t$. Using $x \geq a$, $A_s = \{a, x\} \geq \{a, a\} = A_t$. We also have $\langle\{x\}, i(x)\rangle \succ \langle\{a\}, b\rangle$ since $abs(A_s - \{x\}) = 1 = abs(A_t - \{a\})$ and $i(x) \succ_{ac} b$.

It is quite easy to verify that with $* \succ +$, $x * (y + z) \succ_{ac} (x * z) + (y * z)$. Further, $s = x * y * (u + v) \succ_{ac} x * ((y * u) + (y * v))$ with $* \succ +$.

5 Proofs

We prove the properties of $\succ_{ac}$ in the following order: irreflexivity, subterm property, transitivity, replacement, totality on ground terms. In the next section, we prove that $\succ_{ac}$ is stable under substitutions. Most proofs are done using induction on the size of the term, or the sum of sizes of terms being compared. Except for the replacement and stability properties, the proofs are similar to proofs for RPO [4].

Property 19 (Irreflexivity). For every term t, we have $t \not\succ_{ac} t$.

Proof. By induction on $|t|$. If $t = f(t_1, \ldots, t_n)$, then if $f \notin F_{AC}$, by induction since $\{t_1, \ldots, t_n\} \not\succ \{t_1, \ldots, t_n\}$, we have the desired result. If $f \in F_{AC}$, we have similarly $cands(t, f) \not\succ_c^{mul} cands(t, f)$.

Property 20 (Subterm). If $s \succeq_{ac} t$, then $s \succ_{ac} t_j$ for any proper subterm t_j of t and also $h(\ldots s \ldots) \succ_{ac} t$ for any proper superterm of s.

Proof. As in [4], we can prove these two simultaneously by induction on $\langle |t|, |s| \rangle$ and case analysis.

Property 21 (Transitivity). Given $s = f(s_1, \ldots, s_n), t = g(t_1, \ldots, t_m)$ and $u = h(u_1, \ldots, u_k)$, if $s \succ_{ac} t$ and $t \succ_{ac} u$, then $s \succ_{ac} u$.

Proof. By induction on $|s| + |t| + |u|$. All cases except $f = g = h \in F_{AC}$ are very similar to [4]. In this case also (i.e., $f = g = h \in F_{AC}$), since all terms in any component of $cands(s, f), cands(t, f), cands(u, f)$ are strictly smaller in size than s, t, u, respectively, and since the comparison of abstraction function $(abs(M, f))$ is also transitive, we have the desired result by induction.

To show the replacement property, we first prove a useful lemma.

Lemma 1 (Candidates Property). *$s \succ_{ac} t$ and $f \in F_{AC}$ implies $cands(s, f) \succ_c^{mul} cands(t, f)$.*

Proof. By induction on $\langle |t|, |s| \rangle$. The base case when t is a constant or a variable is simple. Otherwise, let $s = g(s_1, \ldots, s_m)$ and $t = h(t_1, \ldots, t_n)$. We now do case analysis on the relation between g and f.

1. $g \succ f$: In this case s has only one candidate $c_s = \langle \{s\}, \phi \rangle$. In any candidate $c_t = \langle A_t, C_t \rangle \in cands(t, f)$, we have by Property 14, $\{t\} \geq A_t$. By transitivity, we have $\{s\} \succ_{ac}^{mul} A_t$. Thus $c_s \succ_c c_t$ for any c_t which means $cands(s, f) \succ_c^{mul} cands(t, f)$.
2. $g = f$: Consider the cases for h.
   (a) $h \succ f$: Since $s \succ_{ac} t$ and $h \succ f = g$, for some i, either $s_i \succ_{ac} t$ in which case, by induction, $cands(s_i, f) \succ_c^{mul} cands(t, f)$, or $s_i \sim t$ in which case by Property 15, $cands(s_i, f) = cands(t, f)$.
   Since $top(s) = f$, for every $\langle A_{s_i}, C_{s_i} \rangle \in cands(s_i, f)$, there is a $\langle A_s, C_s \rangle \in cands(s, f)$ with $A_{s_i} \subset A_s$ and $C_{s_i} \subset C_s$, by the definition of candidate construction. Hence, $cands(s, f) \succ_c^{mul} cands(t, f)$.
   (b) $h = f$: In this case since $f = h = g$ and $s \succ_{ac} t$, by the definition of $\succ_{ac}$, $cands(s, f) \succ_c^{mul} cands(t, f)$.
   (c) $f \succ h$: If $t = h(t_1, \ldots, t_n)$ is a Small Term, then the only candidate c_t of t is $\langle \{a\}, \{\langle \{a\}, t \rangle\} \rangle$. Since $top(s) = f$, in any candidate $c_s = \langle A_s, C_s \rangle \in cands(s, f)$ we must have $|A_s| \geq 2$ and hence $A_s \succ_{ac}^{mul} \{a\}$. So, $c_s \succ_c c_t$.
   Otherwise if t is not a Small Term, t must have at least one proper elevatable subterm t'. Since $s \succ_{ac} t$, $s \succ_{ac} t'$ for each subterm t' of t using the subterm and transitivity properties. By induction, $cands(s, f) \succ_c^{mul} cands(t', f)$ for every elevatable subterm t' of t, that is, for every $c_{t'} = \langle A', C' \rangle \in cands(t', f)$ there is a $c_s = \langle A_s, C_s \rangle$ with $c_s \succ_c c_{t'}$.
   Also, by the definition of $cands(t, f)$, since $f \succ top(t)$, every candidate c_t of t can be written as $c_t = \langle A', C' \cup \{\langle A', t \rangle\} \rangle$ where $\langle A', C' \rangle \in cands(t', f)$, meaning there is one extra pair $\langle A', t \rangle$ in C_t than in $C_{t'}$. We must show that c_s can take care of this pair also.
   Consider the cases used to show $c_s \succ_c c_{t'}$. If $A_s \succ_{ac}^{mul} A'$ then we also have that $c_s \succ_c c_t$. Otherwise, we must have $A_s \succeq_{ac}^{mul} A'$ and $C_s \succ C'$. We must show that there is at least one $\langle B, ss \rangle \in C_s - C'$ that can take care of $\langle A', t \rangle$ also as follows. Since $top(s) = f$, by Property 14, $B \subset A_s$. Hence $abs((A_s - B) \neq \phi) > abs((A' - A') = \phi)$. This implies $C_s \succ C_t$ also. Hence $c_s \succ_c c_t$ also and $cands(s, f) \succ_c^{mul} cands(t, f)$.

3. $f \succ g$: Consider the cases for h.
   (a) $h \succ f$ or $h = f$: Since $top(t) \succ top(s)$ and $s \succ_{ac} t$, by the definition of $\succ_{ac}$, either there is some $s_i \succ_{ac} t$ (then by induction, $cands(s_i, f) \succ_c^{mul} cands(t, f)$) or $s_i \sim t$ (in which case $cands(s_i, f) = cands(t, f)$). Since $f \succ top(s)$, for every candidate $\langle A_{s_i}, C_{s_i}\rangle \in cands(s_i, f)$, we have $\langle A_{s_i}, C_{s_i} \cup \langle A_{s_i}, s\rangle\rangle \in cands(s, f)$. So, in the either case above, $cands(s, f) \succ_c^{mul} cands(t, f)$.
   (b) $f \succ h$: If $t = h(t_1, \ldots, t_n)$ is a Small Term, then the only candidate c_t of t is $\langle\{a\}, \{\langle\{a\}, t\rangle\}\rangle$. If s is also small then its candidate $c_s = \langle\{a\}, \{\langle\{a\}, s\rangle\}\rangle$ is clearly bigger than c_t. Otherwise, let s have an elevatable subterm s' and let $c_s = \langle A_s, C_s\rangle$ be the candidate obtained by elevating s' from s. If s' is Big or $top(s') = f$, then $A_s \succ_{ac}^{mul} \{a\}$ and hence $c_s \succ_c c_t$. Finally, if $s' = x$, a variable, then $A_s = \{x\} \succeq_{ac}{}^{mul} \{a\} = A_t$ and $\langle\{x\}, s\rangle \succ \langle\{a\}, t\rangle$ since $abs(\{x\} - \{x\}) = abs(\{a\} - \{a\})$ and $s \succ_{ac} t$. Otherwise if t is not a Small Term, t must have at least one proper elevatable subterm t'. Since $s \succ_{ac} t$, $s \succ_{ac} t'$ for each subterm t' of t using the subterm and transitivity properties. For every elevatable subterm t' of t, by induction, $cands(s, f) \succ_c^{mul} cands(t', f)$, i.e., for every $c_{t'} = \langle A', C'\rangle \in cands(t', f)$ there is a $c_s = \langle A_s, C_s\rangle$ with $c_s \succ_c c_{t'}$.
   By the definition of $cands(t, f)$, every candidate c_t of t can be written as $c_t = \langle A_t, C_t\rangle = \langle A', C' \cup \{\langle A', t\rangle\}\rangle$ where $c_{t'} = \langle A', C'\rangle \in cands(t', f)$ for some elevatable t'. As before, there is only one extra pair in the context. Since $cands(s, f) \succ_c{}^{mul} cands(t', f)$, there is some $c_s = \langle A_s, C_s\rangle \in cands(s, f)$ with $c_s \succ_c c_{t'}$.
   If $A_S \succ^{mul} A'$ then $c_s \succ_c c_t$. Otherwise, $A_s \geq A'$ and $C_s \succ C'$. Since $f \succ g = top(s)$, $\langle A_s, s\rangle$ is in C_s. Also, this tuple cannot be in C' since $s \succ_{ac} t$ and s, therefore, cannot be a subterm of t. Also $\langle A_s, s\rangle \succ \langle A_t, t\rangle$ since $s \succ_{ac} t$.
   Thus $cands(s, f) \succ_c^{mul} cands(t, f)$ in this case also.

Using the above lemma, it is easy show the replacement property.

Property 22 (Replacement). $s \succ_{ac} t$ and $f \in F$ implies $s' = f(\ldots, s, \ldots) \succ_{ac} f(\ldots, t, \ldots) = t'$.

Proof. If $f \notin F_{AC}$, then this follows directly from the multiset comparison.

If $f \in F_{AC}$, then by the previous lemma $cands(s, f) \succ_c^{mul} cands(t, f)$. Since every argument in s' and t' other than s and t is the same, and $cands(s', f)$ (similarly $cands(t', f)$) is simply a component-wise summation of contributions from each argument, we have that $cands(s', f) \succ_c^{mul} cands(t', f)$ and hence $s' \succ_{ac} t'$.

Monotonicity is a direct corollary of the replacement property.

Property 23 (Ground Totality). Let $s = f(S) = f(s_1, \ldots, s_n)$ and $t = g(T) = g(t_1, \ldots, t_m)$ be ground terms, and $\succ$ be any total precedence relation on F. Then s and t are comparable. That is, $s \sim t$, or $s \succ_{ac} t$, or $t \succ_{ac} s$.

Proof. By induction on $|s| + |t|$. The basis case is when s and t are constant symbols, and this follows from the totality of $\succ$. Further, when $f \neq g$ or f, g

are not in F_{AC}, the proof that s and t are comparable, is the same as in the proof of totality of RPO on ground terms.

When, $f = g \in F_{AC}$, then by Property 16, $cands(s,f) \neq_{ac} cands(t,f)$. Since terms in a candidate of s (t) are strictly smaller in size than s (t, respectively), and abs used to compare the first component in the pairs in contexts is total for ground terms, s and t are comparable in this case also.

From the ground totality, we have the following property used later in proving that $\succ_{ac}$ is *stable* under substitutions.

Property 24 (Maximum Candidate). Let s be a ground term. Then s has a maximum candidate, i.e. there is $c_m \in cands(s,f)$ such that $c_m \succ_c c_s$ for any $c_s \in cands(s,f)$ with $c_s \neq_{ac} c_m$.

6 Stability of $\succ_{ac}$

We first analyze the effect of application of a ground substitution σ to a term s and the relationship between candidates of s and $s\sigma$ using an example. We show how the biggest candidate from a ground substitution of each variable can be used to construct the biggest candidate for $\sigma(s)$. To prove that the ordering $\succ_{ac}$ is preserved under a ground substitution σ, we compare $\sigma(s)$ with $\sigma(t)$ by comparing their biggest candidates constructed using the biggest candidates of substitutions. Later, we sketch a proof of stability of $\succ_{ac}$ for an arbitrary substitution.

Consider the term $s = i(f(x,x)$ with $f \in F_{AC}$ and the ground substitution $\sigma = \{x \mapsto gt\}$ where $gt = j(g(a), f(b,c))$.

The term s has only one candidate $\langle\{x,x\},\{\langle\{x,x\},i(f(x,x))\rangle\}\rangle$. The term gt has two candidates $c^1_{gt} = \langle\{g(a)\},\{\langle\{g(a)\},j(g(a),f(b,c))\rangle\}\rangle$ and $c^2_{gt} = \langle\{a,a\},\{\langle\{a\},b\rangle,\langle\{a\},c\rangle,\langle\{a,a\},j(g(a),f(b,c))\rangle\}\rangle$. Note that $c^1_{gt} \succ_c c^2_{gt}$.

$s\sigma = i(f(j(g(a),f(b,c)),j(g(a),f(b,c))))$ has the following four candidates (only 3 are distinct).

$c_1 = \langle\{g(a),g(a)\}, \{\langle\{g(a)\},j(g(a),f(b,c))\rangle,\langle\{g(a)\},j(g(a),f(b,c))\rangle,$
$\langle\{g(a),g(a)\},i(f(j(g(a),f(b,c)),j(g(a),f(b,c))))\rangle\}\rangle$ $c_2 = \langle\{g(a),a,a\},$
$\{\langle\{g(a)\},j(g(a),f(b,c))\rangle,\langle\{a\},b\rangle,\langle\{a\},c\rangle,\langle\{a,a\},j(g(a),f(b,c))\rangle,$
$\langle\{g(a),a,a\},i(f(j(g(a),f(b,c)),j(g(a),f(b,c))))\rangle\}\rangle$ $c_3 = \langle\{a,a,g(a)\},$
$\{\langle\{g(a)\},j(g(a),f(b,c))\rangle,\langle\{a\},b\rangle,\langle\{a\},c\rangle,\langle\{a,a\},j(g(a),f(b,c))\rangle,$
$\langle\{a,a,g(a)\},i(f(j(g(a),f(b,c)),j(g(a),f(b,c))))\rangle\}\rangle$ $c_4 = \langle\{a,a,a,a\},$
$\{\langle\{a,a\},j(g(a),f(b,c))\rangle,\langle\{a\},b\rangle,\langle\{a\},c\rangle,\langle\{a\},b\rangle,\langle\{a\},c\rangle,$
$\langle\{a,a\},j(g(a),f(b,c))\rangle,\langle\{a,a,a,a\},i(f(j(g(a),f(b,c)),j(g(a),f(b,c))))\rangle\}\rangle$

Of these four, we say that c_1 and c_4 are obtained by *uniform replacement* since they always use the same candidate of gt when handling different occurrences of x, while c_2 and c_3 have been obtained by non-uniform replacement. Note also that c_1 is the biggest candidate of $s\sigma$, and c_1 uses the biggest candidate c^1_{gt} of the term substituted for x. We formalize this notion below.

Definition 25 (Parent Candidate). Let s be any term, $f \in F_{AC}$, σ be any ground substitution, and $c_{s\sigma} = \langle A_{s\sigma}, C_{s\sigma}\rangle \in cands(s\sigma, f)$. Let $\mathcal{P}_{s\sigma}$ be the positions in $s\sigma$ used (where elevations are done) in the derivation of $c_{s\sigma}$. Let $\mathcal{P}_s$ be the restriction of $\mathcal{P}_{s\sigma}$ to positions in s (i.e. omit any positions not in s). We call $c_s = \langle A_s, C_s \rangle$ derived using $\mathcal{P}_s$ as the *parent candidate* of $c_{s\sigma}$ in s.

Definition 26 (Uniform Replacement). Let $f \in F_{AC}$ and A be any multiset of f-blocked terms, i.e., A has only variables, small terms, and terms with top symbol bigger than f. Let $\sigma = \{x_i \mapsto gt_i\}$ be a ground substitution. Let $c_{gt_i} = \langle A_{gt_i}, C_{gt_i} \rangle \in cands(gt_i, f)$. The multiset A_σ is obtained by uniform replacement by candidates (denoted $A_\sigma = urep(A, \{x_i \mapsto A_{gt_i}\})$) if

$$A_\sigma = \bigcup_{s \in A} \begin{cases} A_{gt_i} & \text{if } s = x_i \text{ for some } i \\ \{s\sigma\} & \text{otherwise} \end{cases}$$

Lemma 2 (Argument Substitution). *Let $A_\sigma = urep(A, \{x_i \mapsto A_{gt_i}\})$ where A, f, σ as in the definition above of uniform replacement. Then $(A)\sigma \geq A_\sigma$ where $(A)\sigma = \bigcup_{s \in A} s\sigma$.*

Proof. Follows from Property 14 that $\{gt_i\} \geq A_{gt_i}$.

Lemma 3 (Uniform Replacement Candidate). *Let s be a term, $f \in F_{AC}$, and $\sigma = \{x_i \mapsto gt_i\}$ be a ground substitution. Let $c_s = \langle A_s, C_s \rangle \in cands(s, f)$ and $c_{gt_i} = \langle A_{gt_i}, C_{gt_i} \rangle \in cands(gt_i, f)$. Let $A_{s\sigma} = urep(A_s, \{x_i \mapsto A_{gt_i}\})$ and*

$$C_{s\sigma} = \bigcup_{\langle B, ss \rangle \in C_s} \{\langle urep(B, \{x_i \mapsto A_{gt_i}\}), ss\sigma \rangle\}$$

Then $c_{s\sigma} = \langle A_{s\sigma}, C_{s\sigma} \rangle$ (denoted $c_{s\sigma} = urep(c_s, \{x_i \mapsto A_{gt_i}\})$) is a candidate of $s\sigma$.

Proof. Since every $ss \in A_s$ is at some elevatable position λ in s, in $s\sigma$ also, λ is an elevatable position. Because of the way candidates are defined, the above replacement of each variable by the candidate derived from its substitution in σ, the above construction gives a valid candidate for $s\sigma$.

In the example at the beginning of this section, candidates c_1, c_4 are obtained by uniform replacement.

Definition 27 (Maximum Replacement). Let $\sigma = \{x_i \mapsto gt_i\}$ and $c_{gt_i} = \langle A_{gt_i}, C_{gt_i} \rangle = max(cands(gt_i, f))$, the maximum candidate of gt_i. Then, $mrep(c_s, \sigma) = urep(c_s, \{x_i \mapsto A_{gt_i}\})$. Similarly, if A is any multiset of f-blocked terms, then $mrep(A, \sigma) = urep(A, \{x_i \mapsto A_{gt_i}\})$.

Lemma 4 (Biggest Candidate). *Let $s\sigma$ be any ground instance of s using some ground substitution $\sigma = \{x_i \mapsto gt_i\}$. Let $c_{s\sigma} = \langle A_{s\sigma}, C_{s\sigma} \rangle = max(cands(s\sigma, f))$. Let the parent candidate of $c_{s\sigma}$ be c_s. Let $c_m = \langle A_m, C_m \rangle = mrep(c_s, \sigma)$. Then $c_{s\sigma} = c_m$.*

Proof. By contradiction. Assume $c_{s\sigma} \neq c_m$. This implies that there is at least one elevatable position λ in s with $s/\lambda = x_j$ a variable and the contribution of $s\sigma/\lambda = gt_j$ to $c_{s\sigma}$ and c_m are different.

Let $\langle A^m_{gt_j}, C^m_{gt_j}\rangle$ be the maximum candidate of gt_j. By definition of *mrep* this is used to contribute to c_m. Let some other (i.e. smaller) candidate $\langle A_{gt_j}, C_{gt_j}\rangle$ of gt_j be used to contribute to $c_{s\sigma}$. We can now construct a candidate $c'_{s\sigma}$ of $s\sigma$ with $c'_{s\sigma} \succ_c c_{s\sigma}$ by keeping all other things the same, but only at position λ using $\langle A^m_{gt_j}, C^m_{gt_j}\rangle$ instead of $\langle A_{gt_j}, C_{gt_j}\rangle$.

This contradicts that $c_{s\sigma} = max(cands(s\sigma, f))$.

Property 28 (Abstraction Property 1). Let $f \in F_{AC}$, A, B be multisets of f-blocked terms, and σ any ground substitution. Then $fcount(A, f) > fcount(B, f)$ implies $fcount(mrep(A, \sigma), f) > fcount(mrep(B, \sigma), f)$.

Proof. $fcount(A, f) > fcount(B, f)$ implies that $Vars(B) \subseteq Vars(A)$, since all non-variable terms have an $fcount$ of 1. Also, in *mrep*, any non-variable term t is replaced by $t\sigma$ which is also a non-variable with $fcount$ of 1. (Note that this property is also preserved by the second abstraction $abs(A) = f(A)$ since $s \succ_{ac} t$ implies $Vars(s) \subseteq Vars(t)$.)

Property 29 (Abstraction Property 2). Let $f \in F_{AC}$, A, B be multisets of f-blocked terms, and σ any ground substitution. Then $(fcount(A, f) \geq fcount(B, f))$ implies $fcount(mrep(A, \sigma), f) \geq fcount(mrep(B, \sigma), f)$.

Proof. Similar to the previous property.

Lemma 5 (Ground Stability Property). *Let s, t be any terms with $s \succ_{ac} t$. Let $\sigma = \{x_i \mapsto gt_i\}$ be any ground substitution such that $s\sigma$ and $t\sigma$ are ground. Then $s\sigma \succ_{ac} t\sigma$.*

Proof. We use induction on $\langle |t|, |s|\rangle$. The base case when t is a variable or a constant is easy. So, let $s = f(s_1, \ldots, s_n)$ and $t = g(t_1, \ldots, t_m)$. Consider the cases used to show $s \succ_{ac} t$. In all cases except $f = g \in F_{AC}$, a straightforward use of the inductive hypothesis leads to a proof.

Consider the case of $f = g \in F_{AC}$. Let $c_{t\sigma}$ be the biggest candidate of $t\sigma$. Let $c_t = \langle A_t, C_t\rangle$ be the parent candidate of $c_{t\sigma}$. Then, $c_{t\sigma} = \langle A_{t\sigma}, C_{t\sigma}\rangle = mrep(c_t, \sigma)$. Since $s \succ_{ac} t$, we must have a candidate $c_s = \langle A_s, C_s\rangle$ of s with $c_s \succ c_t$. Let $c_{s\sigma} = \langle A_{s\sigma}, C_{s\sigma}\rangle = mrep(c_s, \sigma)$ be the biggest candidate of $s\sigma$. We prove $c_{s\sigma} \succ_c c_{t\sigma}$ by considering the cases used to show $c_s \succ_c c_t$.

1. $A_s \succ_{ac} A_t$: Without loss of generality, we assume $A_s \cap A_t = \phi$ for common terms make the same contributions to $A_{s\sigma}$ and $A_{t\sigma}$ which are obtained by maximum replacement in A_s and A_t respectively.
   Consider $tt \in A_t - A_s$. Since $A_s \succ A_t$, we must have $ss \in A_s - A_t$ with $ss \succ_{ac} tt$. Also, ss is not a variable since $x \not\succ t$ for any t. Hence $ss\sigma \in A_{s\sigma}$. By induction, $ss\sigma \succ_{ac} tt\sigma$. If tt is not a variable then $tt\sigma$ is itself the contribution of tt to $A_{t\sigma} = mrep(A_t, \sigma)$. If tt is a variable x_i, then also $\{tt\sigma\} = \{gt_i\} \geq A_{gt_i}$. Hence ss makes a bigger contribution to $A_{s\sigma}$ than tt does to $A_{t\sigma}$. Thus $A_{s\sigma} \succ A_{t\sigma}$.

2. $(A_s \succeq_{ac} A_t)$ and $C_s \succ C_t$: As in the previous case, $A_{s\sigma} = mrep(A_s, \sigma) \geq mrep(A_t, \sigma) = A_{t\sigma}$ from $A_s \geq A_t$, since all terms in A_s and A_t are strictly smaller in size than s and t respectively. If $A_{s\sigma} \succ A_{t\sigma}$ we are done. So, let $A_{s\sigma} = A_{t\sigma}$ (since these are multisets of ground terms).
We now show $C_{s\sigma} \succ C_{t\sigma}$. Note that $C_{s\sigma}$ $(C_{t\sigma})$ is constructed using maximum replacement in C_s (C_t). Let $\langle A, tt \rangle \in C_t - C_s$ and $\langle A, ss \rangle \in C_s - C_t$ be the pair such that $\langle abs(A_s - B), ss \rangle \succ \langle abs(A_t - A), tt \rangle$.
By the definition of uniform replacement, $C_{s\sigma}$ includes $\langle mrep(B, \sigma), ss\sigma \rangle$ whereas $C_{t\sigma}$ includes $\langle mrep(A, \sigma), tt\sigma \rangle$. By Property 29,
$fcount(mrep((A_s - B), \sigma), f) \geq fcount(mrep((A_t - A), \sigma), f)$ since
$fcount((A_s - B), f) \geq fcount((A_t - A), f)$. If $fcount(mrep((A_s - B), \sigma), f) > fcount(mrep((A_t - A), \sigma), f)$, then we are done.
If $fcount(mrep((A_s - B), \sigma), f) = fcount(mrep((A_t - A), \sigma), f)$, then $ss\sigma \succ_{ac} tt\sigma$ by induction since $ss \succ_{ac} tt$.
So, we have $C_{s\sigma} \succ C_{t\sigma}$.

Since $c_{t\sigma} = mrep(t, \sigma)$ is the biggest candidate of $t\sigma$, and $c_{s\sigma} \succ_c c_{t\sigma}$ we have $s\sigma \succ_{ac} t\sigma$.

Theorem 30 (Stability Property). *Let s, t be any terms with $s \succ_{ac} t$, and $\sigma = \{x_i \mapsto t_i\}$ be any substitution. Then $s\sigma \succ_{ac} t\sigma$.*

Proof. (Sketch)
It is easy to see that any substitution σ can be written as a sequence (composition) of simple substitutions of the form $\sigma = \{x \mapsto y\}$ and $\sigma = \{x \mapsto h(z_1, \cdots, z_k)\}$, where h is a function symbol of arity $k \geq 0$. It thus suffices to prove that $\succ_{ac}$ is preserved under these two kinds of substitutions.

The stability proof for $\sigma = \{x \mapsto y\}$ follows easily by case analysis guided by the definition of $\succ_{ac}$. The proof for $\sigma = \{x \mapsto h(z_1, \cdots, z_k)\}$ is interesting especially for the case when $f \succ h$, where $f \in F_{ac}$, as different occurrences of x in s, t can lead to many different candidates in $s\sigma$ and $t\sigma$; other cases can be easily considered by case analysis.

We consider the case of $f \succ h$. For every candidate of s (and t) in which x appears uniquely in the Arguments component, k candidates are generated in $s\sigma$ (and $t\sigma$), one for each argument z_i. Given $s \succ_{ac} t$, for every (uncommon) candidate of t, there is a bigger candidate of s; then for every corresponding candidate $t\sigma$, it is possible to find a bigger candidate of $s\sigma$. Unlike in the proof of ground stability, the concept of biggest candidate cannot be used since terms with variables are being considered, and we cannot compare a candidate due to the argument z_1, for instance, with a candidate due to the argument z_2 of h. If x occurs many times in the Arguments component of candidates of s and t, even then for every corresponding candidate of $t\sigma$ in which different arguments of $h(z_1, \cdots, z_k)$ may be used for different occurrences of x, a bigger candidate of $s\sigma$ can be suitably constructed.

7 Conclusion

We have discussed an RPO-like scheme for defining a well-founded ordering on AC-equivalent terms. The scheme works for general terms (including non-ground as well as ground terms). If the precedence relation on function symbols is total, then the scheme defines a total well-founded ordering on AC-equivalent ground terms. Distributivity axioms can be oriented in the proper direction by making $x * (y + z) > (x * y) + (x * z)$ when both $*$ and $+$ are AC operators and $* > +$. Orderings defined using this scheme can be easily implemented.

The proposed scheme is general and it simplifies the definitions in our earlier paper [7], even though the basic concepts of candidates and constructions for generating candidates in the two papers are related. In fact, it was our attempt to simplify the definition in [7] and related insight leading to the proposed definition. Three different orderings for the same precedence relation on function symbols are discussed. They all first compare terms by first ignoring symbols smaller than AC operators. In case that is not sufficient to compare terms, subterms with smaller symbols which get elevated and their contexts are compared (in the reverse order). The orderings differ in how these contexts are compared.

To define candidates and for elevation, it is required that every AC function symbol should be comparable with other symbols in the precedence relation. In this sense, the precedence relation on function symbols need not be total, insofar as the requirement to have a total ordering on ground terms is relaxed.

A weakness of the proposed ordering scheme is that unlike in the case of RPO for non-AC ground terms, it is not possible to define a family of orderings by incrementally adding precedence on function symbols. It is unclear how to generalize the concept of a candidate if precedence relation between an AC symbol and other symbols is unknown.

References

1. Bachmair, L., and Plaisted, D.A. (1985): Termination orderings for associative-commutative rewriting systems. *J. Symbolic Computation,* 1, 329-349
2. Ben Cherifa, A., and Lescanne, P. (1987): Termination of rewriting systems by polynomial interpretations and its implementation. *Science of Computer Programming,* 9, 2, 137-160.
3. Delor, C., Puel, L. (1993): Extension of the associative path ordering to a chain of associative commutative symbols. Proc. of *5th Intl. Conf. on Rewrite Techniques and Applications (RTA-93)*, LNCS, Springer-Verlag, 389-404.
4. Dershowitz, N. (1987): Termination of rewriting. *J. Symbolic Computation,* 3, 69-116.
5. Gnaeding, I., and Lescanne, P. (1986): Proving termination of associative-commutative rewriting systems by rewriting. Proc. of *8th Intl. Conf. on Automated Deduction (CADE-8)*, Oxford, LNCS 230 (ed. Siekmann), Springer Verlag, 52-60.
6. Kapur, D., and Sivakumar, G. (1995): Maximal extensions of simplification orderings. Proc. of *15th Conf. on Foundations of Software Technology and Theoretical Computer Science* (ed. Thiagarajan), Bangalore, India, Springer Verlag LNCS 1026, 225-239, Dec. 1995.

7. Kapur, D., and Sivakumar, G. (1997): A total ground path ordering for proving termination of AC-Rewrite systems. Proc. *Rewriting Techniques and Applications, 8th Intl. Conf., RTA-97*, Sitges, Spain, June 1997, Springer LNCS 1231 (ed. H. Comon), 142-156.
8. Kapur, D., and Sivakumar, G.: *A recurive path ordering for proving associative-commutative termination* Technical Report, Department of Computer Science, State University of New York, Albany, NY, May 1998.
9. Kapur, D., Sivakumar, G. and Zhang, H. (1995): A new ordering for proving termination of AC-rewrite systems. *J. Automated Reasoning,* 1995.
10. Kapur, D., and Zhang, H. (1995): An overview of Rewrite Rule Laboratory (RRL). *J. Computer and Mathematics with Applications,* 29, 2, 91-114.
11. Lankford, D.S. (1979): On proving term rewriting systems are Noetherian. Memo MTP-3, Lousiana State University.
12. Narendran, P., and Rusinowitch, M. (1991): Any ground associative commutative theory has a finite canonical system. In Book, R. (ed.) Proc. of *4th Intl. Conf. on Rewrite Techniques and Applications (RTA-91),* LNCS 488, 423-434.
13. Rubio, A. (1997): A total AC-compatible ordering with RPO scheme. Technical Report, Technical Univ. of Catalonia, Barcelona, Spain.
14. Rubio, A., Nieuwenhuis, R. (1993): A precedence-based total AC-compatible ordering. In Kirchner, C. (ed.) Proc. of *5th Intl. Conf. on Rewrite Techniques and Applications (RTA-93),* LNCS Springer-Verlag, 374-388.
15. Steinbach, J. (1989): Path and decomposition orderings for proving AC-termination. Seki-Report, SR-89-18, University of Kaiserslautern. See also "Improving associative path orderings," in: Proc. of *10th Intl. Conf. on Automated Deduction (CADE-10)*, Kaiserslautern, LNCS 449 (ed. Stickel), 411-425.

Decision Procedures and Model Building or How to Improve Logical Information in Automated Deduction

Alexander Leitsch

Institut für Computersprachen
Technische Universität Wien
Karlsplatz 13, 1040 Vienna, Austria
leitsch@logic.at

1 Introduction

The field of automated theorem proving is about 40 years old. During this time many new logic calculi were developed which thoroughly reshaped the discipline of deduction. The key feature of these calculi, in contrast to the "traditional" logic calculi, is efficient mechanizability. Instead of proof transformation (as in classical proof theory) *proof search* became the main issue. Programs searching for proofs of theorems formalized in some logical syntax are commonly called *theorem provers*. Thus most of the existing theorem provers can be considered as (deterministic) implementations of (nondeterministic) calculi: in fact their activity essentially consists in production of deductions till a proof (or a refutation) of the theorem under consideration is eventually found. In order to be useful theorem provers must (at least) be *efficient*, *sound* and *complete*. While soundness is absolutely mandatory, completeness may (in specific circumstances) sacrificed for higher efficiency. The first calculus which fulfilled all three requirements defined above was Robinson's resolution [21]. For a long time, particularly in the seventies and eighties, increasing efficiency under preservation of soundness and completeness was virtually the only goal in the field of automated deduction. This was the time where most of the refinements of resolution, tableaux- and connection type calculi and equational calculi were developed. Only few papers, in particular those of S.Y. Maslov and W.J. Joyner, addressed the logical quality of theorem provers, i.e. the amount of *logical information* they are capable to produce. The inverse calculus invented by S.Y. Maslov [16] was not just a new computational calculus; besides being complete the calculus could be put to use as decision procedure for the so-called K-class, a decidable first-order class properly containing the Skolem class. In fact the inverse calculus serves several purposes: 1. it is a general first-order theorem prover, 2. it terminates on K thus deciding the satisfiability problem for this class and 3. it is a metatheoretic tool to prove decidability of a first-order class. In particular the work of Maslov shows that, instead of proving provable theorems only, a calculus can be used to show that sentences are not derivable! A related approach of W.J. Joyner [11] is based

R. Caferra and G. Salzer (Eds.): Automated Deduction, LNAI 1761, pp. 62–79, 2000.

on resolution; in fact he demonstrated that "ordinary" resolution provers based on ordering refinements of resolution can be used as decision procedures for some important well-known (decidable) first-order classes. In his approach – like in this of Maslov – a theorem prover, instead of producing proofs of provable theorems only, is used as consistency checker in a systematic manner. The merit of Maslov and Joyner consists in the observation that *termination* of a calculus is as important as completeness. Note that, if a calculus is used as decision procedure, completeness is necessary – otherwise it is not sound! Due to the undecidability of first-order logic no sound and complete theorem prover can terminate on all input problems. But the systematic investigation *where* it terminates may help to improve the quality of inference systems: instead of using one fixed refinement of a calculus on all problems, a syntax check may yield membership of the problem to a decidable class; the corresponding decision procedure can then be used as a theorem prover. The requirement of termination is of particular importance in an interactive inference environment: frequently a problem is incompletely specified resulting in a nonprovable sentence; "blind" inference most probably yields nontermination and, consequently, no information.

Suppose that a complete resolution refinement terminates on a set of clauses $\mathcal{C}$ without producing the empty clause. All we know is that $\mathcal{C}$ is satisfiable, but we also want to know *why*! The answer must, of course, be a *model* of $\mathcal{C}$. In the first moment it seems to be absurd to ask for a model, after we have selected a method which just avoids production of models; in fact, resolution decision procedures merely produce sets of clauses, which – in case of satisfiability – only show the nonderivability of a contradiction. Nevertheless the produced sets (fixed points under the deduction operators) can sometimes be used to produce representations of Herbrand models in a purely deductive way. Therefore the construction of models can be considered as an end point of a deductive procedure. Note that model building as a postprocessing on termination sets differs from the method of search through finite domains. The former method is *symbolic*, while the latter one is *semantic* and, in some sense, "numeric". Although finite domain search is fruitful to many purposes, it clearly fails in cases where finite models do not exist. We will even demonstrate that, for some decision classes, the resolution decision method can be easily extended to a model building method on the corresponding termination sets. Thus some inference systems can be considered as provers, decision procedures and model building methods; in particular this holds for hyperresolution and (in case of equational clause logic) for positive resolution + ordered paramodulation.

The purpose of this paper is not to present new results on decision procedures and model building, but rather to discuss the corresponding potential of current inference systems in general and point to open problems, possible improvements and extensions of the methods. First of all we illustrate that *ordinary theorem provers can do much more* than just the task they were designed for. Besides of only deriving $\Box$ out of unsatisfiable sets of clauses, many traditional methods can act as decision procedures and even model generators; it is a matter of mathematical analysis to characterize the syntax classes where this *additional logical information* can be produced. Then we point out the limitations of the traditional deductive methods concerning termination and model building. The extension of the clause syntax via equational constraints and the introduction of disinference rules, as applied in the model builder RAMC [5], is one of the successful methods to increase the *semantic potential* of theorem provers. But still there are many types of models which cannot be constructed via equational constraints. We point out that metaterms might be an adequate tool for a further improvement of decision procedures and model building.

Generally we emphasize the need for *more intelligent* and not only for faster theorem provers. Indeed a theorem prover can be more than just a deterministic implementation of a logic calculus. It is a firm belief of the author that the systematic analysis of logical information (e.g. satisfiability and (counter-)models) will not only lead to more intelligent inference systems, but – in the long run – also to faster ones.

2 Notation and Definitions

A set of literals $\mathcal{A}$ *subsumes* a set of literals $\mathcal{B}$ if there exists a substitution θ s.t. $\mathcal{A}\theta \subseteq \mathcal{B}$ (we write $\mathcal{A} \leq_{ss} \mathcal{B}$). We define a *clause* as a condensed set of literals; a set of literals $\mathcal{D}$ is called *condensed* if there exists no proper subset $\mathcal{D}'$ of $\mathcal{D}$ s.t. $\mathcal{D}$ subsumes $\mathcal{D}'$. For example $\{P(x,a), P(a,x)\}$ is condensed and thus is a clause; $\mathcal{D} = \{P(x,a), P(a,a)\}$ is not condensed because it subsumes $\{P(a,a)\}$; $\{P(a,a)\}$ is called the condensation of $\mathcal{D}$. Clauses are written in form of disjunctions, thus $P(x,a) \vee P(a,x)$ stands for $\{P(a,x), P(x,a)\}$. We choose the condensed clause form in this paper because it is frequently needed for termination of resolution decision procedures. For details concerning condensing and termination we refer to [13] and [7]. The positive part of a clause C is denoted by C_+, the negative by C_-. If $\mathcal{C}$ is a set of clauses we write $P(\mathcal{C})$ for the subset of positive clauses in $\mathcal{C}$. By $sub(\mathcal{C})$ we denote a subsumption-reduced subset $\mathcal{D}$ of $\mathcal{C}$, where $\mathcal{D}$ is called *subsumption reduced* if for all $D_1, D_2 \in \mathcal{D}$ with $D_1 \leq_{ss} D_2$ it follows that $D_1 = D_2$.

We write $\mathrm{var}(E)$ for the set of variables occurring in an expression or a set of expressions E. $\tau(E)$ denotes the *term-depth* of E and $\tau_{\max}(x, E)$ the maximal depth of an occurrence of the variable x in E.

Substitutions are usually applied in postfix form and *mgu* stands for the most general unifier.

Resolution is defined as in [21]. For a formal definition of a resolution *refinement* see [13]. For every resolution refinement x we define an operator R_x s.t. for every clause set $\mathcal{C}$

$$R_x(\mathcal{C}) = \mathcal{C} \cup \rho_x(\mathcal{C})$$

where ρ_x is the set of all x-resolvents definable by clauses in $\mathcal{C}$. For hyperresolution the corresponding operator is denoted by R_H. If R_x is a resolution operator, the deductive closure is defined as

$$R_x^*(\mathcal{C}) = \bigcup_{i \in \mathbb{N}} R_x^i(\mathcal{C}).$$

Herbrand models Γ of a set of clauses $\mathcal{C}$ are usually denoted by the set of ground atoms over the signature of $\mathcal{C}$ which are true in Γ.

3 Theorem Provers as Decision Procedures

Due to the undecidability of first-order logic, all correct and complete theorem provers are nonterminating on some classes of formulas. In case of resolution theorem proving on clause logic, every complete refinement of resolution is nonterminating on some (infinite) class of satisfiable clause sets. Of course this does *not* mean that, typically, refinements are nonterminating on *all* satisfiable sets of clauses. In fact even unrestricted resolution terminates on satisfiable problems like

$$\mathcal{C}: \; \{\neg P(x, f(x)),\; P(f(y), y) \vee \neg Q(y),\; Q(a)\};$$

here the only new clause derivable by resolution is $P(f(a), a)$. Thus, by running a theorem prover, we may hope that, besides producing refutations of unsatisfiable clause sets, it will terminate (by chance) on satisfiable problems. At this point two questions arise:

(1) Should the typical inputs to resolution provers be unsatisfiable clause sets, i.e. is it realistic to assume satisfiability?

(2) Is it possible, without sacrificing efficiency, to improve the behavior of provers on satisfiable sets?

There is no trivial answer to question (1); satisfiable sets can be avoided altogether if we *know in advance* that the original problem A (where $\neg A$ has been transformed into clause form) is provable. But in this case we may ask, whether automated theorem proving should be focused on problems having well-known proofs. Suppose we admit that, in a realistic environment, there is no guarantee for the provability of A. Still we need not care about termination: We just apply different refinements and wait till some of them yields a solution; if all attempts to prove the theorem fail, we may try to find a finite model of $\mathcal{C}$ by exhaustive search through finite domains. We will try to show in this section that, in contrast to the approach defined above, there is a *systematic* way to improve termination of theorem provers – without inventing fancy refinements or expensive transformations. We will demonstrate that some part of theorem proving can be shifted from a purely experimental to a *mathematical* level and thus give a positive answer to question (2). Indeed many decidable subclasses of clause logic are (a) defined by simple syntactic criteria and (b) decidable by "ordinary" resolution refinements.

Example 1. Let $\mathcal{C}$ be the set of clauses

$$\{P(a),\; \neg P(x) \vee P(f(x)),\; \neg P(c)\}.$$

$\mathcal{C}$ is a clausal form of the negation of the sentence

$$A: \; [P(a) \wedge (\forall x)(P(x) \Rightarrow P(f(x)))] \Rightarrow (\forall y)P(y),$$

representing an "induction" axiom for P. Clearly A is not valid and thus $\mathcal{C}$ is satisfiable. Unrestricted resolution and positive resolution (coinciding with positive hyperresolution in this example) produce the infinite set of clauses $\{P(f^n(a)) \mid n \geq 1\}$ and thus do not terminate on $\mathcal{C}$. On the other hand, negative (hyper-)resolution and ordered resolution (based on a depth-ordering) do terminate. Indeed, negative resolution (one of the resolved clauses must be negative) does not produce any resolvent on $\mathcal{C}$. Moreover, in any "reasonable" atom ordering we have $P(x) < P(f(x))$, which – according to the ordering restriction – prevents the production of the resolvent $P(f(a))$.

The set of clauses $\mathcal{C}$ defined in example 1 belongs to different decidable classes discussed in [7]. In particular it belongs to the class $\mathcal{VARI}$: $\{\mathcal{C} \mid (\forall C \in \mathcal{C})|\text{var}(C)| \leq 1\}$, the set of all finite clause sets containing only clauses with at most one variable; $\mathcal{VARI}$ is decidable by ordered resolution. The required ordering is just

$$A <_d B \text{ iff } (1)\ \tau(A) < \tau(B) \text{ and}$$
$$(2)\ \tau_{\max}(x, A) < \tau_{\max}(x, B) \text{ for all } x \in \text{var}(A).$$

(see [6] and [13]). Note that the ordering refinement has to be applied *a posteriori*, i.e. the resolved atom under the most general unifier of the resolution may not be smaller than a literal in the resolvent. In the example above the resolvent of $P(a)$ and $P(x) \vee P(f(x))$ is blocked because the *mgu* is $\{x \leftarrow a\}$ and $P(a) <_d P(f(a))$.

Thus we know how $R_{<_d}$ behaves on $\mathcal{VARI}$ and recommend the following simple recipe: Test whether the input set $\mathcal{C}$ is in $\mathcal{VARI}$. If so then apply $R_{<_d}$ (we know it will terminate for sure); if not then we may try to locate $\mathcal{C}$ in another decision class; if also this fails we may apply an arbitrary refinement.

We have seen in Example 1 that negative hyperresolution terminates on $\mathcal{C}$, while the positive one does not. There is a syntactic property behind this phenomenon expressed in the decision classes $\mathcal{PVD}$ and $\mathcal{PVD}_+$.

Definition 1. *A (finite) set of clauses $\mathcal{C}$ is in $\mathcal{PVD}_+$ if for all clauses C in $\mathcal{C}$:*

(1) $\text{var}(C_+) \subseteq \text{var}(C_-)$,
(2) $\tau_{\max}(x, C_+) \leq \tau_{\max}(x, C_-)$ *for* $x \in \text{var}(C_+)$.

Roughly spoken, $\mathcal{C} \in \mathcal{PVD}_+$ if, in all clauses of $\mathcal{C}$, the positive part is "smaller" than the negative one (resulting in positive ground clauses and arbitrary negative clauses). It is shown in [14] and [7] that positive hyperresolution terminates on $\mathcal{PVD}_+$. The class $\mathcal{PVD}$ generalizes $\mathcal{PVD}_+$ under sign-renaming:

Definition 2. *$\mathcal{C} \in \mathcal{PVD}$ if there exists a sign-renaming η with $\eta(\mathcal{C}) \in \mathcal{PVD}_+$.*

Clearly the set $\mathcal{C}$: $\{P(a),\ \neg P(x) \vee P(f(x)),\ \neg P(c)\}$ is not in $\mathcal{PVD}_+$, but it is in $\mathcal{PVD}$; just apply the sign-renaming $\eta : \{P \leftarrow \neg P, \neg P \leftarrow P\}$. As a consequence, hyperresolution terminates on $\eta(\mathcal{C}) : \{\neg P(a),\ P(x) \vee \neg P(f(x)),\ P(c)\}$. This example shows that, in classifying a set of clauses, we might need some transformations on sets of clauses (like renaming). Although the test for an appropriate renaming w.r.t. $\mathcal{PVD}$ is NP-complete (see [4]) it is relatively cheap if few predicate symbols occur in the problem. The class $\mathcal{PVD}$ exemplifies the following principle:

> *Try to transform a set of clauses $\mathcal{C}$ into a set of clauses $\mathcal{D}$ s.t. $\mathcal{D}$ is member of a (well-known) decidable class and can be handled by an efficient refinement.*

In [14] a more general setting for sign-renaming and termination for hyperresolution is discussed: instead of term-depth any other *atom complexity measure* can be applied. In general we may think of a *prover generator* which, after some syntactic analysis, selects a refinement automatically. The syntactic criterion given by resolution decision theory addresses *termination*. If we succeed to locate $\mathcal{C}$ (or a corresponding transformed set $\mathcal{D}$) in a decidable class Γ, where Γ is decidable by the resolution operator R_Γ, then compute $R^*_\Gamma(\mathcal{C})$. Of course this choice will not always minimize the computing time. On the other hand it is a good choice in the sense of logical information; eventually we will find out whether $\mathcal{C}$ is satisfiable or not. Anyway, experiments in [7] indicate that resolution decision procedures behave well – also in practice; as a direct consequence of termination, decision procedures typically generate small and shallow clauses (at least on the decision class). Looking upon Example 1 we might suggest a much simpler procedure for attacking the problem. We observe that there exists a two-element model of $\mathcal{C}$ with domain $\{\bar{a}, \bar{c}\}$ and an interpretation function Φ defined by $\Phi(f)(\bar{a}) = \bar{a}$, $\Phi(f)(\bar{c}) = \bar{c}$, $\Phi(P)(\bar{a}) = \mathbf{t}$, $\Phi(P)(\bar{c}) = \mathbf{f}$. Then, why not adopt the following procedure:

(*) *Run a theorem prover in parallel with a finite model generator.*

The advantage of (*) is twofold: (a) it is easy to implement and (b) it yields more information (even a model) in case of satisfiability. On small domain size (roughly < 5) the method will be reasonably efficient, although – in contrast to resolution decision procedures – it strongly depends on the arity of predicate- and function symbols. So far the author does not know a systematic experimental comparison of these two approaches. The question remains whether, in principle, the methods differ in strength. In case that $\mathcal{C}$ is satisfiable but does not have finite models, (*) is clearly inappropriate (unless the prover itself acts as a logical decision procedure). This directly leads to the question:

> *Can resolution decision procedures terminate on sets of clauses not having finite models?*

The answer is *YES* (traditional symbolic methods can solve problems unsolvable by (*)). Just take the following example (M. Baaz 1996, see [9]):

Example 2.

$$\mathcal{C}: \{P(x,x),\ \neg P(f(x), f(y)) \vee P(x,y),\ \neg P(c, f(x))\}.$$

It is easy to see that $\mathcal{C}$ is satisfiable but does not have finite models. Moreover, hyperresolution and $<_d$-resolution both terminate on $\mathcal{C}$ (without producing any new clause) and thus detect satisfiability. If the principle (*) is realized by finite model generation with (a) negative (hyper-)resolution or with (b) linear resolution (with top-clause $\neg P(c, f(x))$), it is nonterminating on $\mathcal{C}$ and thus fails.

Sometimes termination can only be achieved by techniques which may reduce efficiency. One such method is the so-called "saturation" where instances of clauses are generated which cannot be obtained by most general unification. In particular saturation is used to obtain termination of resolution refinements on the Bernays Schönfinkel class and on the class $\mathcal{S}_+$ (see [7]). From some point on there is a clear trade-off between logical information and efficiency: extending the range of termination may lead to a deterioration of efficiency on unsatisfiable sets of clauses. It then depends on our priorities whether we use the faster or the stronger method.

As we should expect, the situation becomes more complex in presence of equality. First of all, many classes (like $\mathcal{VARI}$ and $\mathcal{PVD}$) become undecidable under admission of equality. Moreover equational inference methods like superposition and paramodulation are much more "fertile" than resolution and thus are hard to control. However there are some nontrivial classes where decision procedures based on resolution + ordered paramodulation or on the superposition calculus can be defined. We just mention the Ackermann class + equality [8], the monadic class + equality [1] and the class $\mathcal{PVD}_g^=$ (i.e. the class $\mathcal{PVD}$ with equality where all equational atoms are ground) [10]. Thus, also in equational clause logic, it is possible to systematically design calculi with a better behavior w.r.t. termination.

4 Extraction of Models

In section 3 we have shown how to improve the termination behavior of resolution theorem provers. It is fair to mention here that resolution is not the only computational method which is capable of deciding classes and building models. There exists corresponding research for semantic tableaux [12], constrained semantic tableaux [19] and hyper-tableaux [2]. It is just for the sake of clarity and simplicity that we focus on resolution and related methods, although many similar phenomena also occur in other computational calculi.

So let us assume that a resolution refinement R_x terminates on a set of clauses and yields the (finite) set $R_x^*(\mathcal{C})$ with $\Box \notin R_x^*(\mathcal{C})$. Although we know that $\mathcal{C}$ is satisfiable we are not yet in the position to specify a *single* model of $\mathcal{C}$. We also know that there must be a Herbrand model of $\mathcal{C}$, but there may be infinitely many ones and we do not know *how* they are *described* by $R_x^*(\mathcal{C})$. In fact it turns out that the problem of extracting a single model out of $R_x^*(\mathcal{C})$ strongly depends on the refinement R_x. While it is difficult for ordering refinements, it is relatively easy for hyperresolution, which – already by its design – is a model building procedure in principle. Thus, for illustrating model extraction, it is most convenient first to focus on hyperresolution.

If hyperresolution terminates on a set of Horn clauses $\mathcal{C}$ then $P(R_H^*(\mathcal{C}))$, the set of all positive unit clauses in the deductive closure, "directly" represents a

Herbrand model. Indeed the minimal Herbrand model is just defined by the set of all ground instances of $P(R^*_H(\mathcal{C}))$ over the Herbrand universe of $\mathcal{C}$. Computationally this makes sense only if the set $P(R^*_H(\mathcal{C}))$ is finite.

Definition 3. *Let $\mathcal{C}$ be a set of Horn clauses and $\mathcal{D} = P(R^*_H(\mathcal{C}))$; if $\mathcal{D}$ is finite we call it an* atomic representation *of the Herbrand model defined by the set of ground instances of $\mathcal{D}$ over the Herbrand universe of $\mathcal{C}$.*

Atomic representations enjoy several favorable properties:

(1) uniqueness,
(2) there are algorithms for evaluating (arbitrary) clauses over the representations and
(3) the equivalence of representations is decidable.

We believe that at least properties (1) and (2) should hold for any *computational* model representation. After the definition of basic algorithms in [9] solving 1. and 2. more efficient methods have been defined in [20].

Example 3. Let $\mathcal{C}$ be the set of clauses

$$\{P(a),\ \neg P(x) \vee P(f(x)),\ \neg P(c)\}.$$

R_H does not terminate on $\mathcal{C}$, although (of course) the infinite set $P(R^*_H(\mathcal{C}))$: $\{P(f^n(a)) \mid n \in \mathbb{N}\}$ represents a minimal Herbrand model of $\mathcal{C}$. But $\mathcal{C} \in \mathcal{PVD}$ via the sign renaming $\eta : \{P \leftarrow \neg P, \neg P \leftarrow P\}$ and we obtain

$$\mathcal{C}\eta = \{P(c), \neg P(f(x)) \vee P(x), \neg P(a)\}.$$

After this transformation we get $R^*_H(\mathcal{C}\eta) = \mathcal{C}\eta$ and thus $\{P(c)\}$ is the atomic representation of a (minimal) Herbrand model of $\mathcal{C}\eta$. But note, we are interested in a model of $\mathcal{C}$ and not of $\mathcal{C}\eta$! Clearly the interpretation Γ, defined by

$v_\Gamma(P(t)) = \mathbf{t}$ iff t is a ground term different from c,

is a Herbrand model of $\mathcal{C}$ (although not a minimal one!). However it is not trivial (and in general impossible) to obtain an atomic representation of Γ; here it works and we get $\mathcal{A}$: $\{P(a),\ P(f(x))\}$ as atomic representation of Γ. Note that $P(c)$ is the only ground P-atom which is not an instance of an atom in $\mathcal{A}$ (over $\Sigma = \{a, c, f\}$).

Already the simple example above indicates that constructing a model may be sophisticated, even if deciding satisfiability is trivial. In general a set of Horn clauses $\mathcal{C}$ in $\mathcal{PVD}$ might "need" some sign-renaming γ s.t. $\mathcal{C}\gamma \in \mathcal{PVD}$. But, in contrast to the example above, $\mathcal{C}\gamma$ need not be a set of Horn clauses; thus, although R_H terminates on $\mathcal{C}\gamma$ it need not produce an atomic representation of a model. However, for the well-known decision classes of hyperresolution like $\mathcal{PVD}$ and $\mathcal{OCCIN}$, models can be extracted by adding subsumption and a selection operation to hyperresolution [9].

Example 4. Let $\mathcal{C}$ be the set of clauses

$$\{P(f(a),a) \vee P(f(b),a),\ \neg P(f(x),a) \vee P(x,a),\ \neg P(f(x),x) \vee \neg P(x,x)\}.$$

$\mathcal{C}$ is in $\mathcal{PVD}$ but it is *essentially* non-Horn, i.e. $\mathcal{C}\eta$ is non-Horn for every sign-renaming η. But, in this case, $\mathcal{C}$ can be split into two sets of Horn clauses

$$\mathcal{C}_1 = \{P(f(a),a), \neg P(f(x),a) \vee P(x,a), \neg P(f(x),x) \vee \neg P(x,x)\} \text{ and}$$
$$\mathcal{C}_2 = \{P(f(b),a), \neg P(f(x),a) \vee P(x,a), \neg P(f(x),x) \vee \neg P(x,x)\}.$$

$\mathcal{C}_1$ and $\mathcal{C}_2$ are both in $\mathcal{PVD}_+$, but $\mathcal{C}_1$ is unsatisfiable and $\mathcal{C}_2$ is satisfiable (therefore, of course, $\mathcal{C}$ is satisfiable). Thus splitting makes backtracking necessary. If there are more positive non-unit ground clauses splitting itself may become quite expensive. Moreover there are sets in $\mathcal{PVD}$ which cannot be transformed to Horn via splitting at all.

Let us construct the closure $R_H^*(\mathcal{C})$ of $\mathcal{C}$ itself under hyperresolution. Then we obtain the set

$$R_H^*(\mathcal{C}) = \mathcal{C} \cup \{P(f(b),a) \vee P(a,a),\ P(f(a),a) \vee P(b,a),$$
$$P(a,a) \vee P(b,a),\ P(b,a),\ P(f(b),a)\}.$$

Even now splitting can be defective if we select $P(a,a)$ out of the first and $P(f(a),a)$ out of the second clause. But splitting is superfluous as all the non-unit clauses are subsumed by the unit clauses in $R_H^*(\mathcal{C})$. After subsumption the remaining set of clauses is

$$sub(R_H^*(\mathcal{C})) = \{P(b,a),\ P(f(b),a),\ \neg P(f(x),a) \vee P(x,a),$$
$$\neg P(f(x),x) \vee \neg P(x,x)\},$$

which is also deductively closed under R_H. Consequently the set of positive clauses $\mathcal{A}:\ \{P(b,a),\ P(f(b),a)\}$ is an atomic representation of a Herbrand model of $\mathcal{C}$.

Example 4 suggests that splitting can be replaced by deductive closure under R_H and subsumption. It also shows that by omitting subsumption wrong alternatives are still available. In general it may be the case that, even after application of R_H and subsumption, positive non-unit clauses remain in the set. Then, instead of splitting, we may *select* an atom out of a positive clause, delete the original clause and iterate the procedure.

Example 5. Let $\mathcal{C}$ be the set of clauses

$$\{P(a) \vee P(f(a)),\ \neg P(x) \vee \neg P(f(x))\}.$$

Here we have $sub(R_H^*(\mathcal{C})) = \mathcal{C}$ and we don't obtain positive unit clauses at once. But we may select both $P(a)$ or $P(f(a))$ out of the first clause of $\mathcal{C}$; the resulting clause sets are

$$\mathcal{C}_1 = \{P(a), \neg P(x) \vee \neg P(f(x))\} \text{ and } \mathcal{C}_2 = \{P(f(a)), \neg P(x) \vee \neg P(f(x))\}.$$

Both $\mathcal{C}_1$ and $\mathcal{C}_2$ are satisfiable and deductively closed under R_H; the corresponding atomic representations of Herbrand models are $\mathcal{A}_1 : \{P(a)\}$ and $A_2 : \{P(f(a))\}$.

We have seen that subsumption plays an important role in constructing atomic representations. Thus instead of the operator R_H we need hyperresolution + replacement [13] defined by

$$R_{Hr}(\mathcal{C}) = sub(R_H(\mathcal{C})).$$

In contrast to R_H, the operator R_{Hr} is not monotone, i.e. $\mathcal{C} \subseteq R_{Hr}(\mathcal{C})$ does not hold in general. By the completeness of R_{Hr} (see [13]), for every unsatisfiable set $\mathcal{C}$ there exist an i s.t. $\Box \in R^i_{Hr}(\mathcal{C})$ and thus (by definition of R_{Hr}) $R^i_{Hr}(\mathcal{C}) = \{\Box\}$ (note that every clause is subsumed by $\Box$). We may say that, on unsatisfiable sets of clauses $\mathcal{C}$, the replacement sequence $(R^i_{Hr}(\mathcal{C}))_{i \in \mathbb{N}}$ *converges* to $\Box$. On satisfiable sets of clauses the behavior of replacement sequences may be quite complicated. Fortunately on many decidable classes (like $\mathcal{PVD}$) we can guarantee that there exists always a number i with $R^i_{Hr}(\mathcal{C}) = R^{i+1}_{Hr}(\mathcal{C})$; we then say that $(R^i_{Hr}(\mathcal{C}))_{i \in \mathbb{N}}$ *converges* to $R^i_{Hr}(\mathcal{C})$ and denote that latter set by $R^*_{Hr}(\mathcal{C})$. There are ways to define the closure under replacement operators in general, but we do not need it here (we are only interested in working with finite termination sets).

We have seen in Example 5 that R_{Hr} has to be combined with a function selecting atoms out of positive clauses.

Definition 4. *An* atom selection function *is a function which maps sets of clauses into sets of clauses with the following properties*

(1) $\alpha(\mathcal{C}) = \mathcal{C}$ *if all positive clauses in* $\mathcal{C}$ *are unit and, otherwise,*
(2) $\alpha(\mathcal{C}) = (\mathcal{C} - \{C\}) \cup \{A\}$ *for a nonunit positive clause* $C \in \mathcal{C}$ *and an atom* A *in* C.

Now closure and selection can be combined in a single operator which may serve as key transformation for the model building procedure.

Definition 5. *Let* α *be an atom selection function; then the operator* T, *defined by*

$$T(\mathcal{C}) = \alpha(R^*_{Hr}(\mathcal{C}))$$

is called an mbh-operator *(corresponding to* α*).*

In general the application of α (even to deductively closed) sets of clauses is *incorrect* (it may produce unsatisfiable clause sets out of satisfiable ones)! The following class defines the range of applicability for the transformations T and α:

Definition 6. $\mathcal{PDC}$ *(positively disconnected) is the set of all sets of clauses* $\mathcal{C}$ *with the properties*

(1) $R^*_H(\mathcal{C})$ *is finite and*

(2) *If C is a positive clause in $R_H^*(\mathcal{C})$ and L, M are two different literals in C then* $\mathrm{var}(L) \cap \mathrm{var}(M) = \emptyset$.

Note that condition (2) alone would generalize Horn logic and thus yield an undecidable clausal class. The decision classes $\mathcal{PVD}$ and $\mathcal{OCCIN}$ for hyperresolution belong to $\mathcal{PDC}$. In [9] the following general result is proven:

Theorem 1. *Let T be an mbh-operator. Then $(T^i(\mathcal{C}))_{i \in \mathbb{N}}$ is convergent for all $\mathcal{C} \in \mathcal{PDC}$. The limes $T^k(\mathcal{C})$ is either the set $\{\square\}$ (then $k = 1$) or a nonempty finite satisfiable set of clauses $\mathcal{C}'$ s.t. all positive clauses in $\mathcal{C}'$ are unit; the set of these unit clauses then is an atomic representation of a Herbrand model of $\mathcal{C}$.*

The principle of computation via iteration of T is correct even under more general conditions: if α only selects atoms out of "disconnected" clauses (i.e. clauses fulfilling (2) above) then the computation $(T^i(\mathcal{C}))_{i \in \mathbb{N}}$ is correct; but we do not know whether it will terminate and, in case it terminates, whether all positive clauses in the resulting set will be unit (if not, we do not get an atomic model representation).

The situation becomes much more complex under resolution decision operators different from hyperresolution. The following example of a satisfiable set of clauses is quite famous in the area of automated model building:

Example 6.

$$\mathcal{C} = \{P(x) \vee P(f(x)),\ \neg P(x) \vee \neg P(f(x))\}.$$

$\mathcal{C}$ is a clausal form of the formula $(\forall x)(P(x) \leftrightarrow \neg P(f(x)))$. It is easy to see that $\mathcal{C}$ has two Herbrand models with the set of true atoms being $\mathcal{A}_1 = \{P(f^n(a)) \mid n \text{ even }\}$ and $\mathcal{A}_2 = \{P(f^n(a)) \mid n \text{ odd }\}$ for some constant symbol a. Moreover there exists a finite model with two elements.

It is easy to verify that hyperresolution, even under sign-renaming, does not terminate on $\mathcal{C}$. Moreover none of the two Herbrand models can be represented by a (finite) atomic representation. Using the $<_d$-ordering defined in Section 3 we simply obtain

$$R^*_{<_d}(\mathcal{C}) = \mathcal{C} \cup \{P(x) \vee \neg P(x)\}.$$

If we refine $R_{<_d}$ by deletion of tautologies (which preserves completeness) then nothing new at all is derived; anyway, the tautology does not provide any useful information. Thus $R_{<_d}$ essentially reproduces the set of clauses giving us the information of satisfiability but *nothing* about models.

In [25] and [7] a symbolic method of finite model building is defined which covers the Ackermann- and the monadic class (and thus also Example 6). Basically the method orients ground equations between elements of the Herbrand universe and uses the corresponding rewrite rules for narrowing on termination sets of an ordering refinement. The method is too sophisticated to be presented in detail here, but it can be demonstrated on the set of clauses from Example 6:

Suppose that we search for a model fulfilling the term equation $f(a) \doteq a$. Orienting this equation results in the rewrite rule $R:\ f(a) \to a$. Narrowing (see

[24]), based on R, terminates on $\mathcal{C}$ and yields the set

$$\mathcal{C}' : \mathcal{C} \cup \{P(a), \neg P(a)\}.$$

which is unsatisfiable, a fact which is trivial here but is detected by the ordering refinement in general. Thus clearly there is no model over the Herbrand universe fulfilling the equation $f(a) \doteq a$. The next attempt, however, is successful. We try the equation $f(f(a)) \doteq a$ which gives the rewrite rule $R' : f(f(a)) \to a$. Narrowing on $\mathcal{C}$ by R' gives the set

$$\mathcal{C}'' = \mathcal{C} \cup \{P(f(a)) \vee P(a), \neg P(f(a)) \vee \neg P(a)\}$$

which is satisfiable. Because, over the Herbrand universe, the elements a and $f(a)$ are the only normal forms under R' we know that there exists a two-element model of $\mathcal{C}$ with domain $\{\alpha, \beta\}$ and an interpretation φ of f with $\varphi(\alpha) = \beta$ and $\varphi(\beta) = \alpha$. Still the interpretation of the predicate symbol P has to be defined. Tammet's method only produces the domain and the interpretation of the function symbols (which, in general, is the harder part); it does not specify the model completely. Again this simple example illustrates the problems of symbolic model building.

In Section 3 we mentioned the problems arising in decision procedures if equality is added. So far there are computational decision methods for the Ackermann-class + equality and Monadic class + equality, but no model building procedures. To the best of the knowledge of the author, the class $\mathcal{PVD}_g^=$ is the only equational clause class where a model building procedure has been defined so far [10]. The method is based on positive resolution and ordered paramodulation and is similar to that for $\mathcal{PDC}$ defined above; its output on satisfiable sets of clauses are equational atomic ground-representations.

Definition 7. *A set*

$$\mathcal{A} : \{A_1, \ldots, A_n\} \cup \{s_1 \doteq t_1, \ldots, s_m \doteq t_m\}$$

where the A_i are ground atoms and the s_i, t_i are ground terms, is called an equational atomic ground-representation. *The represented Herbrand model is the set of all ground atoms M with $\mathcal{A} \models M$ (in equational clause logic).*

Note that me might also define the more general concept of equational model representations, where neither atoms nor equations need to be ground. In such a formalism, however, it is undecidable whether a ground atom is true in the represented model (by the possibility to encode the word problem of arbitrary equational theories). The expressive power of equational atomic ground-representations is much higher than this of ground atoms only and it is incomparable with atomic representations. Although the set of clauses $\mathcal{C} : \{P(x) \vee P(f(x)),\ \neg P(x) \vee \neg P(f(x))\}$ is not in $\mathcal{PVD}_g^=$ (because it is not in $\mathcal{PVD}$), the model $\{P(f^n(a)) \mid n \text{ even }\}$ is representable by $\{P(a), f(f(a)) \doteq a\}$, which is an equational atomic ground-representation. However, the decision procedure for $\mathcal{PVD}_g^=$ does not provide any means to extract this model from the set $\mathcal{C}$.

In symbolic model building, in contrast to finite domain search, the *syntactic representation* of models is a quite subtle matter. Trivially, infinite models like Herbrand models cannot be represented just by tables. But it is easy to show that clause sets which can be decided by proof theoretic procedures always have recursive models. Moreover, for most resolution decision procedures, models can be defined by algorithmically specifying a branch in an infinite semantic tree (which can be traversed without backtracking); this was already pointed out by W.J. Joyner [11]. However, such procedural specifications are not very helpful as they are not suited for *clause evaluation* (model checking). Thus, apart from model building itself, symbolic model representations and evaluation over representations are of interest per se and have been investigated in several papers, e.g. [17] and [20]. Efficient evaluation algorithms for clauses over symbolic representations, in turn, may be of importance to inference itself: they pave the way for implementing new forms of semantic resolution (over more complex models than just over settings [15]). The author firmly believes that in the future development of automated deduction such semantic methods will receive more attention than in the last decades. The investigation of the semantic potential of existing calculi is just a first and necessary step into this direction.

5 Extensions of Clause Logic

In Section 3 we have seen that there are clause sets having very simple models, where none of them can be described by an atomic representation. Thus in order to increase the power of model building procedures it is necessary to extend the syntax of clause logic. One way to do this is to introduce equality, another to introduce equational constraints. The first extensions of clause logic for the purpose of model building were investigated by R. Caferra and N. Zabel [5]. The method is called RAMC (Resolution and Model Construction) and has been improved in several papers [3], [18]. RAMC is a calculus on (equationally) constrained clause logic, which – besides inference rules – uses model building rules based on dis-inference principles. It is outside the scope of this paper to give a detailed description of RAMC (the reader is refered to the papers mentioned above). Instead we take an example out of the paper [3] and illustrate the use of the key techniques.

Example 7. Consider the set of clauses

$$\mathcal{C} = \{C_1 : P(x,x),\ C_2 : \neg P(x,y) \vee P(y,x),\ C_3 : P(x,y) \vee \neg P(f(x),f(y)),\\ C_4 : \neg P(x,y) \vee P(f(x),f(y)),\ C_5 : \neg P(c,f(x))\}.$$

Like the similar clause set in Example 2, $\mathcal{C}$ does not have finite models. But here neither positive nor negative hyperresolution terminate. Ordered resolution (e.g. based on $<_d$) does terminate, but (typically) does not produce an explicit model representation. RAMC is based on the fact that a clause in predicate logic can be considered as a representation of the set of all its ground instances. On the ground level some instances may be redundant either because they are tautologies or because they are subsumed by other (ground) clauses; moreover some instances can be used for resolutions and others cannot.

Let us consider $C_2 : \neg P(x,y) \vee P(y,x)$ first. If $C\theta$ is a ground instance with $x\theta = y\theta$ then $C_2\theta$ is a tautology and thus can be deleted. Therefore we restrict the set of ground instances by adding the constraint $x \neq y$, which results in the *constrained clause* $C_2' : \neg P(x,y) \vee P(y,x) : x \neq y$. The rule replacing C_2 by C_2' is called *distautology rule.* Similarly we can delete all ground instances $C_3\theta$ with $x\theta = y\theta$ because they are subsumed by $P(x,x)$ (or by the corresponding ground instances). Thus the so-called *dissubsumption rule* yields the clause

$$C_3' : \; P(x,y) \vee \neg P(f(x), f(y)) : x \neq y.$$

Similarly we can delete C_4 and replace it by

$$C_4' : \; \neg P(x,y) \vee P(f(x), f(y)) : x \neq y.$$

The new set of clauses obtained after this operations is

$$\begin{aligned} \mathcal{C}' = \{ & C_1 : P(x,x), \\ & C_2' : \neg P(x,y) \vee P(y,x) : x \neq y, \\ & C_3' : P(x,y) \vee \neg P(f(x), f(y)) : x \neq y, \\ & C_4' : \neg P(x,y) \vee P(f(x), f(y)) : x \neq y, \\ & C_5 : \neg P(c, f(x))\} \; . \end{aligned}$$

Still $\mathcal{C}'$ does not describe a model explicitly. To this aim a rule, called *GPL* (for Generating Pure Literal), is applied which generates constrained *unit* clauses. Consider the set of all ground instances of $\mathcal{C}'$: all occurrences of negative literals $\neg P(s,t)$ now fulfill $s \neq t$. Moreover all clauses containing complementary literals of the form $P(s,t)$ and $s \neq t$ either contain $\neg P(f(s), f(t))$ or $\neg P(s', t')$ for $f(s') = s$ and $f(t') = t$. In fact the constrained unit clause $C_6 : \neg P(x,y) : x \neq y$ does not infer with $P(x,x)$ and subsumes the ground instances of all the clauses C_2', C_3', C_4' and C_5. I.e. once we add C_6, all other clauses except C_1 can be deleted by the dissubsumption rule and satisfiability is preserved. What remains is the set of clauses

$$\mathcal{C}'' : \; \{C_1 : P(x,x), \; C_6 : \neg P(x,y) : x \neq y\}$$

which logically implies the original set $\mathcal{C}$ and represents the Herbrand model $\mathcal{M}$: $\{P(s,s) \mid s \in H(\mathcal{C})\}$. Therefore $\mathcal{C}''$ can be interpreted as a model representation for $\mathcal{C}$.

The generation of C_6 out of $\mathcal{C}'$ is by no means trivial and is only achieved by an extension of the original GPL-rule called *egpl*. The instances $P(s,t)$ for $s \neq t$ are *pure* (in the sense of the Davis–Putnam rules) only w.r.t. the instances of C_1, but not w.r.t. the instances of C_2', C_3' and C_4' which are in fact self-resolving constrained clauses. This is analyzed by the algorithm EGPL defined in [3] which, in this case, produces C_6.

Example 7 demonstrates that models can be constructed by using equational constraints for partitioning the set of ground instances defined by a set of clauses. It is not hard to show that the real power of the constraints lie in *inequalities* among variables. If the equational constraints contain only positive occurrences of $=$ then the constraints can be eliminated without changing the set of represented ground instances. In the set $\mathcal{A} : \{P(x,y) : x \neq y\}$ the inequality is "essential": There exists no (finite) set of atoms representing the same ground instances as $\mathcal{A}$ over the Herbrand universe $\{f^n(c) \mid n \in \mathbb{N}\}$; in particular this shows that atomic representations are not closed under complement. We see that, by the dis-rules, the calculus RAMC (essentially consisting of resolution, subsumption, the corresponding "dis-rules" and of GPL) extends the capacity of pure clause logic w.r.t. model construction. Clearly, the application of dissubsumption and of other dis-rules (which may lead to more complicated constraints) can become quite expensive. Thus, again, a classification prior to inference would make sense: If we find out by a syntax check that the set of clauses cannot be treated by hyperresolution (i.e. we have no guarantee that a model can be found) then we may try RAMC. In [18] it is shown that even RAMC is not successful in all cases where the sets of clauses possess models representable by constrained literals. But the inference systems RAMCET and EQMC defined in [18] are capable of producing all models having such representations.

Still the equational constraint formalism fails on examples like Example 6:

$$\mathcal{D} : \ \{P(x) \vee P(f(x)),\ \neg P(x) \vee \neg P(f(x))\}.$$

The only Herbrand models $\mathcal{M}_1 : \{P(f^{2n}(a)) \mid n \in \mathbb{N}\}$ and $\mathcal{M}_2 : \{P(f^{2n+1}(a)) \mid n \in \mathbb{N}\}$ are not representable via constrained literals. Therefore RAMC cannot handle this case (and is nonterminating). In Section 4 we have seen that the models $\mathcal{M}_1$ and $\mathcal{M}_2$ are representable by ground equational atomic representations: $\mathcal{M}_1$ by $\{P(a), f(f(a)) \doteq a\}$ and $\mathcal{M}_2$ by $\{P(f(a)), f(f(a)) \doteq a\}$. Note that here $\doteq$ is the equality predicate which plays a different role than $=$ in the equational constraints! But the problem remains that, so far, no reasonable general algorithms producing such representations are available.

An interesting and powerful mechanism to increase the expressive power of first-order calculi is provided by meta-terms (see [23] and [22]). Think about the expression $P(f^{2n}(a))$ as an element of the object language and extend the set $\mathcal{D}$ above to

$$\mathcal{D}' = \{P(x) \vee P(f(x)),\ \neg P(x) \vee \neg P(f(x)),\ P(f^{2n}(a))\}.$$

First of all, all ground instances $P(s) \vee P(f(s))$ are subsumed by the unit ground clauses represented by $P(f^{2n}(a))$ and thus the clause $P(x) \vee P(f(x))$ can be deleted. Secondly, there are no clash resolvents among $P(f^{2n}(a))$ and $\neg P(x) \vee \neg P(f(x))$. Indeed the only "meta"-resolvent which can be obtained within the clash is $\neg P(f^{2n+1}(a))$ which does not resolve with $P(f^{2n}(a))$. As a consequence, the set $\{\neg P(x) \vee \neg P(f(x)), P(f^{2n}(a))\}$ is stable under *meta-hyperresolution* and so $P(f^{2n}(a))$ represents a model of $\mathcal{C}$. Again, the problem of generating the appropriate meta-expressions remains. The following example shows that the meta-term formalism surpasses both equational constraints and equational atomic representations:

Example 8.

$$\mathcal{C} = \{\neg P(x,x),\ \neg P(x,y) \vee P(x,f(y)),\ P(x,f(x))\}.$$

It is not hard to realize that 1. $\mathcal{C}$ has no finite models and 2. $\mathcal{C}$ has only one Herbrand model, namely $\mathcal{M} : \{P(f^n(a)), f^m(a)) \mid n < m\}$. Although there exists a (very complicated) A-ordering refinement which terminates on $\mathcal{C}$ (the "usual" ones don't terminate) it does not yield a representation of a model. Moreover there are neither (equational) atomic nor constrained atomic representations of $\mathcal{M}$. In particular, as $\mathcal{C}$ is Horn (even under sign-renaming), hyperresolution does not terminate on $\mathcal{C}$. But, again, meta-terms can do the job.

In [22] an algorithm is defined which automatically generates meta-expressions by analyzing cycles within clauses (i.e. the possibilities of self-resolution). Applied to this example the algorithm first computes the meta-hyperresolvent $P(x, f^{n+1}(x))$ out of $P(x, f(x))$ and $\neg P(x,y) \vee P(x, f(y))$ (note that the "powers" of the second clause are of the form $\neg P(x,y) \vee P(x, f^{n+1}(y))$). The new meta-clause $P(x, f^{n+1}(x))$ then subsumes $P(x, f(x))$, which can be deleted. The resulting set of clauses

$$\mathcal{C}' : \{\neg P(x,x),\ \neg P(x,y) \vee P(x,f(y)),\ P(x,f^{n+1}(x))\}$$

is a fixed point under meta-hyperresolution and yields the model representation

$$\mathcal{A} = \{P(x, f^{n+1}(x))\}.$$

$\mathcal{A}$ then represents exactly the ground instances

$$\{P(f^m(a), f^{m+n+1}(a)) \mid m, n \in \mathbb{N}\}$$

over $H(\mathcal{C})$.

The method in [22] (originally) is not designed for automated model building and, unlike RAMC, does not work over a fixed universe. In particular it cannot automatically produce the meta-clauses $P(f^{2n}(a))$ or $P(f^{2n+1}(a))$ out of the set $\{P(x) \vee P(f(x)), \neg P(x) \vee \neg P(f(x))\}$. It would be interesting to modify the method according to the needs of model building.

Example 8 indicates that, in contrast to purely refutational theorem proving, termination and model building require *stronger formalisms* than those provided by first-order logic. With respect to model building meta-terms (and schematizations in general) cannot only lead to a speed-up of existing first-order calculi but, much more, to an increase of expressive power. A mathematical analysis leading to powerful and fast algorithms for meta-term generation could indeed cause a major breakthrough in the field of automated model building and of computational decision procedures.

References

1. Leo Bachmair, Harald Ganzinger, and Uwe Waldmann. Superposition with simplification as a decision procedure for the monadic class with equality. In *Computational Logic and Proof Theory, KGC'93*, pages 83–96. Springer, LNCS 713, 1993.
2. P. Baumgartner, U. Furbach, and I. Niemela. Hyper-tableaux. In *Logics in AI, JELIA'96*. Springer, 1996.
3. Ch. Bourely, R. Caferra, and N. Peltier. A method for building models automatically. Experiments with an extension of Otter. In *Proceedings of CADE-12*, pages 72–86. Springer, 1994. LNAI 814.
4. A. Brandl, C. Fermüller, and G. Salzer. Testing for renamability to classes of clause sets. In M. P. Bonacina and U. Furbach, editors, *Int. Workshop on First-Order Theorem Proving (FTP'97)*, RISC-Linz Report Series No. 97-50, pages 34–39. Johannes Kepler Universität, Linz (Austria), 1997.
5. R. Caferra and N. Zabel. A method for simultaneous search for refutations and models by equational constraint solving. *Journal of Symbolic Computation*, 13:613–641, 1992.
6. C. Fermüller. *Deciding Classes of Clause Sets by Resolution.* PhD thesis, Technische Universität Wien, 1991.
7. C. Fermüller, A. Leitsch, T. Tammet, and N. Zamov. *Resolution Methods for the Decision Problem.* LNAI 679. Springer, 1993.
8. C. Fermüller and G. Salzer. Ordered paramudulation and resolution as decision procedure. In A. Voronkov, editor, *Logic Programming and Automated Reasoning, 4th International Conference, LPAR'93, St. Petersburg, Russia, July 1993, Proceedings*, volume 698 of *Lecture Notes in Artificial Intelligence*, pages 122–133. Springer Verlag, 1993.
9. C.G. Fermüller and A. Leitsch. Hyperresolution and automated model building. *Journal of Logic and Computation*, 6(2):173–203, 1996.
10. C.G. Fermüller and A. Leitsch. Decision procedures and model building in equational clause logic. *Journal of the IGPL*, 6(1):17–41, 1998.
11. W.H. Joyner. Resolution strategies as decision procedures. *Journal of the ACM*, 23:398–417, 1976.
12. Stefan Klingenbeck. *Counter Examples in Semantic Tableaux.* PhD thesis, University of Karlsruhe, 1996.
13. A. Leitsch. *The resolution calculus.* Springer. Texts in Theoretical Computer Science, 1997.
14. Alexander Leitsch. Deciding clause classes by semantic clash resolution. *Fundamenta Informaticae*, 18:163–182, 1993.
15. Donald W. Loveland. *Automated Theorem Proving: A Logical Basis*, volume 6 of *Fundamental Studies in Computer Science.* North Holland, 1978.
16. S.Y. Maslov. The inverse method for establishing deducibility for logical calculi—. *Proc. Steklov Inst. Math.*, 98:25–96, 1968.
17. Robert Matzinger. Computational representations of Herbrand models using grammars. In *Computer Science Logic, CSL'96*, 1997.
18. Nicolas Peltier. *Nouvelles Techniques pour la Construction de Modèles finis ou infinis en Déduction Automatique.* PhD thesis, Institut National Polytechnique de Grenoble, 1997.
19. Nicolas Peltier. Simplifying formulae in tableaux. Pruning the search space and building models. In *Proceeding of Tableaux'97*, pages 313–327. Springer, 1997. LNAI 1227.

20. R. Pichler. Algorithms on atomic representations of herbrand models. In *Proc. of JELIA'98*, pages 199–215. Springer, LNAI 1489, 1998.
21. J. A. Robinson. A machine-oriented logic based on the resolution principle. *J. Assoc. Comput. Mach.*, 12:23–41, 1965.
22. G. Salzer. Deductive generalization and meta-reasoning, or how to formalize Genesis. In H. Kaindl, editor, *Proc. 7th Austrian Conference on Artificial Intelligence*, Informatik-Berichte 287, pages 103–115. Springer Verlag, 1991.
23. G. Salzer. *Unification of Meta-Terms.* Dissertation, Technische Universität Wien, Austria, 1991.
24. J.R. Slagle. Automated theorem-proving for theories with simplifiers, commutativity and associativity. *J. Association of Computing Machinery*, 21(4):622–642, 1974.
25. Tanel Tammet. Using resolution for deciding solvable classes and building finite models. In *Baltic Computer Science*, pages 33–64. Springer, LNCS 502, 1991.

Replacement Rules with Definition Detection*

David A. Plaisted and Yunshan Zhu

Department of Computer Science
University of North Carolina at Chapel Hill
Chapel Hill, NC 27599-3175
{plaisted|zhu}@cs.unc.edu

Abstract. The way in which a theorem prover handles definitions can have a significant effect on its performance. Many first-order clause form theorem provers perform badly on theorems such as those from set theory that are proven largely by expanding definitions. The technique of using replacement rules permits automatic proofs of such theorems to be found quickly in many cases. We present a refinement of the replacement rule method which increases its effectiveness. This refinement consists in recognizing which clauses are obtained from first-order definitions.

1 Introduction

Many theorems involve concepts that are defined in terms of other concepts. For example, continuity can be defined in terms of limits, and the subset relationship is defined in terms of set membership. In an application, one might define the sibling relationship in terms of the parent relationship. How a theorem prover handles such definitions can have a significant effect on its performance. Sometimes it is better to expand these definitions to obtain a proof, and sometimes not. The problem is even more severe for clause form theorem provers in first-order logic. If the definition of a predicate involves the introduction of new quantifiers, then the replacement of the predicate by its definition becomes difficult for a clause form theorem prover, because all quantifiers are eliminated in the translation to clause form. As a result, clause form theorem provers are often very weak on problems involving defined predicates, such as theorems of set theory. This problem was highlighted by Bledsoe in [Ble77]. The inability to handle such definitions efficiently is a common problem in clause form theorem proving, even if it is not always recognized as such, and one that is not handled well by a basic resolution theorem prover. However, clause form is attractive for theorem proving because it permits many simple complete theorem proving methods based on unification, and so it would be helpful to be able to simulate the replacement of predicates by their definitions in a clause form context.

As an example of the problem, suppose that we desire to prove that $(\forall x)((x \cap x) = x)$ from the axioms of set theory. A human would typically prove this by

* This research was partially supported by the National Science Foundation under grant CCR-9108904

R. Caferra and G. Salzer (Eds.): Automated Deduction, LNAI 1761, pp. 80–94, 2000.

noting that $(x \cap x) = x$ is equivalent to $((x \cap x) \subseteq x) \wedge (x \subseteq (x \cap x))$, then observe that $u \subseteq v$ is equivalent to $(\forall z)((z \in u) \supset (z \in v))$, and finally observe that $z \in (x \cap x)$ is equivalent to $(z \in x) \wedge (z \in x)$. After applying all of these equivalences to the original theorem, a human would observe that the result is a tautology, thus proving the theorem.

But for a resolution theorem prover, the situation is not so simple. The axioms needed for this proof are

$$(x = y) \equiv [(x \subseteq y) \wedge (y \subseteq x)]$$
$$(x \subseteq y) \equiv (\forall z)((z \in x) \supset (z \in y))$$
$$(z \in (x \cap y)) \equiv [(z \in x) \wedge (z \in y)]$$

When these are all translated into clause form and Skolemized, the intuition of replacing a formula by its definition gets lost in a mass of Skolem functions, and a resolution prover has a much harder time. This particular example may be easy enough for a resolution prover to obtain, but other examples that are easy for a human quickly become very difficult for a resolution theorem prover using the standard approach.

The problem is more general than set theory, and has to do with how definitions are treated by resolution theorem provers. We cannot directly replace $(x \subseteq y)$ in a resolution theorem prover by $(\forall z)((z \in x) \supset (z \in y))$ because this would entail introducing a new quantifier, and such quantifiers have already been eliminated in the translation to clause form. Resolution theorem provers often have trouble with theorems like this. Even the set of support strategy[WRC65], which restricts inferences to those related to the particular theorem being proved, doesn't always do the right thing because it does unification, not matching, and because it loses the sense of directionality of the definitions, since any literal can be resolved. Of course, in a higher order theorem prover, one can perform the rewrite and introduce explicit quantifiers, which is an advantage for higher-order theorem proving. But we are interested in increasing the power of first-order theorem provers, as well.

2 Replacement Rules

The philosophy of replacement rules is to simulate the replacement of predicates by their definitions in a Skolemized setting.

Definition 1. A *replacement rule* is an expression of the form $R \rightarrow_r L_1, L_2, \ldots, L_n$. R is called a *replacement literal.* A replacement rule $R \rightarrow_r L_1, L_2, \ldots, L_n$ corresponds to the clause $\{\neg R, L_1, L_2, \ldots, L_n\}$. The literals R and L_i can be either positive or negative. We denote the set of replacement rules as RR. We define the set of *relevant literals* RL and *relevant instances* RI recursively as follows: Initially, RL contains ground literals occurring in the input clauses, and RI is empty. Then RL and RI are modified by performing the following operation as many times as possible, until there is no more change: If $L \in RL$ and there is a replacement rule $C \in RR$ of the form $C = R \rightarrow_r L_1, L_2, \ldots, L_n$

where R is the replacement literal in C and $R\theta = L$, then $RL \leftarrow RL \cup \{L_1\theta, L_2\theta, \ldots, L_n\theta\}$, and $RI \leftarrow RI \cup \{\{\neg R\theta, L_1\theta, \ldots, L_n\theta\}\}$. Note that RL is a set of ground literals and RI is a set of ground clauses.

Clauses	Replacement Rules
1. $\{\neg Z \in X \cap Y, Z \in X\}$	$Z \in X \cap Y \rightarrow_r Z \in X$
2. $\{\neg Z \in X \cap Y, Z \in Y\}$	$Z \in X \cap Y \rightarrow_r Z \in Y$
3. $\{Z \in X \cap Y, \neg Z \in X, \neg Z \in Y\}$	$\neg Z \in X \cap Y \rightarrow_r \neg Z \in X, \neg Z \in Y$
4. $\{\neg X \subseteq Y, \neg U \in X, U \in Y\}$	$X \subseteq Y \rightarrow_r \neg U \in X, U \in Y$
5. $\{X \subseteq Y, g(X,Y) \in X\}$	$\neg X \subseteq Y \rightarrow_r g(X,Y) \in X$
6. $\{X \subseteq Y, \neg g(X,Y) \in Y\}$	$\neg X \subseteq Y \rightarrow_r \neg g(X,Y) \in Y$
Theorem: $\{\neg a \cap a \subseteq a\}$	

Table 1. Replacement rules for a set theory example

There are many ways that a clause can be made into a replacement rule. Later we will give a general method for doing this. For now, we just give an example. Table 1 contains clauses for a set theory problem and the corresponding replacement rules[1]. Both $\subseteq$ and $\cap$ are defined in terms of the predicate $\in$. The first three clauses define $\cap$, and the last three define $\subseteq$. "g(X,Y)" is a Skolem function. Replacement literals contain the concepts (predicates or functions) being defined. Intuitively, since the theorem involves $\cap$ and $\subseteq$, the proof of the theorem will involve instances of the input clauses that "define" $\subseteq$ and $\cap$. These instances can be generated using the replacement rules.

We illustrate the replacement strategy using the example from Table 1. Initially, $RL_0 = \{\neg a \cap a \subseteq a\}$ and $RI_0 = \emptyset$. The relevant literal $\neg a \cap a \subseteq a$ unifies with the replacement literal $\neg X \subseteq Y$ in 5) and 6). After one round of replacement, RI_1 contains instances $\{a \cap a \subseteq a, g(a \cap a, a) \in a \cap a\}$ and $\{a \cap a \subseteq a, \neg g(a \cap a, a) \in a\}$. RL_1 contains relevant literals $\{a \cap a \subseteq a, g(a \cap a, a) \in a \cap a, \neg g(a \cap a, a) \in a\}$. The new relevant literal $g(a \cap a, a) \in a \cap a$ unifies with the replacement literal $Z \in X \cap Y$ in 1), thus $RI_2 = RI_1 \cup \{\{\neg g(a \cap a, a) \in a \cap a, g(a \cap a, a) \in a\}\}$. $RL_2 = RL_1 \cup \{g(a \cap a, a) \in a\}$. No more new replacement rules can be applied to the relevant literals in RL_2. The union of RI_2 with the input clause set contains a propositionally unsatisfiable set of instances. We do not need to be concerned about directionality here, since unsatisfiability can be detected by a Davis and Putnam type propositional decision procedure[DP60,DLL62].

Replacement rules solve the problem of handling definitions in a first order setting very effectively, in many cases. Simple theorems can sometimes be proved by applying replacement in this way: generating a set of replacement instances, and demonstrating propositional unsatisfiability of the replacement instances

[1] The first-order clauses can also be represented as $\{not\ in(Z, intersection(X,Y)), in(Z,X)\}$. For clarity, we use $\in$ for predicate *in*, $\cap$ for function *intersection* and $\subseteq$ for predicate *subset*. We use infix instead of prefix operators.

using a decision procedure such as that of Davis and Putnam. This approach is not the same as meta-level replacement as presented in [Pau92], since the original clauses are not removed or even rewritten. Rather, a set of new replacement instances is added to the set of clauses. These replacement instances encode the relationship between the original clauses and their rewritten versions. However, the original clauses are still available for inference. This technique permits proofs to be found regardless of whether the original or rewritten clauses are the ones that are needed for the proof. The problem is how to choose the rules and their orientation automatically.

3 Methods for Choosing Replacement Rules

Before presenting our current approach, we survey some of the approaches we have tried in the past. The idea of [PG86] was to do the replacement of predicates by their definitions before translation to clause form, and then use a structure-preserving clause form translation and a particular variant of locking resolution. This approach was highly effective with a number of set theory problems. In [PP91], we performed replacement in a term-rewriting context and applied replacements much in the spirit of term rewriting rules. However, the rules and their orientations were chosen by the user. This approach was also effective on a number of theorems from set theory, including the composition of homomorphisms theorem. In [LP94], the replacement rules were used in a first-order clause form context, as illustrated above, but they were chosen by the user, and there were extra features added as well to enable some difficult proofs to be obtained. These rules were integrated into CLIN, an instance-based first-order prover that already had a propositional satisfiability tester built in. The prover CLIN-S of [CP94] had an automatic method for choosing the replacement rules, and was able to obtain a number of set theory problems fully automatically. It had two kinds of replacement rules, one kind that always replaced literals by others that were smaller, and the other that replaced literals by possibly larger literals. The former rules were applied more often than the latter ones. The RRTP theorem prover of [PP97] has automatic methods of choosing replacement rules, but the goal is not to detect definitions, but instead to perform a number of different kinds of replacement at the same time. This prover turned out to be very efficient for problems involving concept description languages [PP98]. Replacement rules have been extensively studied in [Par97]. We present a variant of the definitional replacement rule in [Par97]. We also emphasize the automatic generation of definitional replacement rules. The work of [GOP93] also seems relevant, because it proposes a criterion for eliminating defined concepts. It is also of note that [DHK98] considers this problem of how to replace predicates by their definitions in a systematic way in a first-order combinatory logic setting, and obtains a complete approach to higher-order logic in this manner.

The idea which we now propose is to detect which clauses were obtained from first-order formulas of the form $L \equiv A$, where L is a literal and A is a formula. Such clauses are then converted into replacement rules which have the same logical power as replacing L by A, without actually doing it.

Suppose a definition of the form $L \equiv (A_1 \vee A_2)$ is translated into clause form, where A_1 and A_2 are literals. Then we obtain the clauses

$$\neg L^1, A_1^0, A_2^0$$

$$L^0, \neg A_1^1$$

$$L^0, \neg A_2^1$$

where $\neg L^1$ is the Skolemized form of $\neg L$, and L^0 is the Skolemized form of L, and similarly for A_1 and A_2. For a definition of the form $L \equiv (A_1 \wedge A_2)$, we obtain the clauses

$$L^0, \neg A_1^1, \neg A_2^1$$

$$\neg L^1, A_1^0$$

$$\neg L^1, A_2^0$$

with notation as above. The pattern also can be extended to definitions of the form $L \equiv [A_1 \vee A_2 \vee \ldots A_n]$ and $L \equiv [A_1 \wedge A_2 \wedge \ldots A_n]$, as shown below. Such patterns can be detected, and replacement rules can be constructed that will have the effect of replacing L by its definition. We have integrated this approach into the OSHL theorem prover [PZ97], which is an instance-based prover that generates ground instances of the input clauses and tests them for propositional satisfiability.

We now make precise the criterion for detecting definitions and generating replacement rules.

Theorem 1. *Suppose the formula $L \equiv (Q_1 x_1) \ldots (Q_m x_m)(L_1 \vee L_2 \vee \ldots \vee L_n)$ is converted to clause form, where L is a quantifier-free literal, the Q_i are either $\forall$ or $\exists$, and the L_i are literals, possibly containing additional quantifiers. Then the resulting set of clauses will be of the form*

$\neg L \vee L_1^0 \vee L_2^0 \vee \ldots \vee L_n^0$
$L \vee \neg L_1^1$
$L \vee \neg L_2^1$
$\ldots$
$L \vee \neg L_n^1$

where the L_i^0 and L_i^1 are literals and the empty clause may be derived by unit resolution from the clauses

$(L_1^0 \vee L_2^0 \vee \ldots \vee L_n^0)\Theta$
$\neg L_1^1 \Theta$
$\neg L_2^1 \Theta$
$\ldots$
$\neg L_n^1 \Theta$

where Θ is a substitution replacing the variables of L by distinct new constant symbols.

Proof. We know that the formula $[(Q_1x_1)\ldots(Q_mx_m)(L_1 \vee L_2 \vee \ldots \vee L_n)] \wedge \neg[(Q_1x_1)\ldots(Q_mx_m)(L_1 \vee L_2 \vee \ldots \vee L_n)]$ is unsatisfiable, as are all instances of this formula obtained by replacing the variables of L by arbitrary terms. Since this formula is unsatisfiable, its Skolemized form is also unsatisfiable. The Skolemized form of this formula is the set of clauses

$(L_1^0 \vee L_2^0 \vee \ldots \vee L_n^0)$
$\neg L_1^1$
$\neg L_2^1$
$\ldots$
$\neg L_n^1.$

Since this set of clauses is unsatisfiable, there is a resolution proof of the empty clause. However, since only one of the clauses is a non-unit clause, there must be a unit resolution proof of the empty clause, as stated in the theorem. Moreover, if Θ is a substitution replacing the variables of L by distinct new constant symbols, we know that $[(Q_1x_1)\ldots(Q_mx_m)(L_1 \vee L_2 \vee \ldots \vee L_n)]\Theta \wedge \neg[(Q_1x_1)\ldots(Q_mx_m)(L_1 \vee L_2 \vee \ldots \vee L_n)]\Theta$ is unsatisfiable, so by similar reasoning there is a unit resolution refutation from its Skolemized form. By syntactic reasoning about the process of Skolemization, we can conclude that there is also a unit resolution refutation from the clauses

$(L_1^0 \vee L_2^0 \vee \ldots \vee L_n^0)\Theta$
$\neg L_1^1\Theta$
$\neg L_2^1\Theta$
$\ldots$
$\neg L_n^1\Theta.$

Furthermore, the Skolemized form of the formula $L \equiv (Q_1x_1)\ldots(Q_mx_m)(L_1 \vee L_2 \vee \ldots \vee L_n)$ is obtained from the Skolemized form of $[(Q_1x_1)\ldots(Q_mx_m)(L_1 \vee L_2 \vee \ldots \vee L_n)] \wedge \neg[(Q_1x_1)\ldots(Q_mx_m)(L_1 \vee L_2 \vee \ldots \vee L_n)]$ by adding the literal L or $\neg L$ to the resulting clauses. □

We note by duality that the same result applies to definitions of the form $L \equiv (Q_1x_1)\ldots(Q_mx_m)(L_1 \wedge L_2 \wedge \ldots \wedge L_n)$. This theorem gives an effective way to detect such definitions, as well.

As an example, consider the clauses

$\{\neg Z \in X \cap Y, Z \in X\}$
$\{\neg Z \in X \cap Y, Z \in Y\}$
$\{Z \in X \cap Y, \neg Z \in X, \neg Z \in Y\}$

We can choose L to be the literal $Z \in X \cap Y$ and choose Θ to replace X by a, Y by b, and Z by c. Then, according to theorem 1, the set of clauses

$\{Z \in X\}\Theta$
$\{Z \in Y\}\Theta$
$\{\neg Z \in X, \neg Z \in Y\}\Theta$

should be unsatisfiable, and the empty clause should be derivable from them using unit resolution. And it is easy to verify that the empty clause is derivable by unit resolution from

$\{c \in a\}$
$\{c \in b\}$
$\{\neg c \in a, \neg c \in b\}$

For clauses in which quantifiers Q_i appear, the clauses

$(L_1^0 \vee L_2^0 \vee \ldots \vee L_n^0)\Theta$
$\neg L_1^1\Theta$
$\neg L_2^1\Theta$
$\ldots$
$\neg L_n^1\Theta.$

might not be ground clauses. This is the case, for example, with the definition of $\subseteq$:

{not(subset(X,Y)), not(in(Z,X)), in(Z,Y)}.
{in(g(X,Y),X), subset(X,Y)}.
{not(in(g(X,Y),Y)), subset(X,Y)}.

The substitution Θ will not replace the variable Z by a constant in this case. The empty clause is still derivable by unit resolution even if there are quantifiers in the definition, which means that the literals L_i^0 or L_i^1 will contain variables that are not removed by Θ.

What this means is that in computing the set RI of relevant instances, some of these relevant instances may contain variables. In order to obtain ground instances, which we need for the propositional unsatisfiability test, these variables are instantiated to ground terms by unification of literals of RI with other relevant literals. This mechanism is essential to obtain the proof of the theorem p($X \cap Y$) =p(X)$\cap$p(Y), which is discussed below. The reason for this is that the definition of $X \subseteq Y$ is $\forall Z(Z \in X \supset Z \in Y)$, and this definition does not specify how Z is to be instantiated. Therefore, we need to unify with other literals to know how to instantiate Z.

It is not only single definitions that are of interest, but their interaction as well. In a mathematical theory, there is often a hierarchical definition of concepts. For example, in set theory, *subset* or *union* can be defined in terms of *membership*, and *equalset* can be defined in terms of *subset*. To prove a theorem involving *subset* and *intersection*, it is often necessary to expand the definitions of these concepts. In the replacement strategy, there are a number of replacement rules generated based on the input clauses. Instances of the input clauses are generated using these replacement rules. The generation of these instances in essence corresponds to the expansion of definitions.

A replacement rule can be manually generated by examining each clause and using human insight to select the replacement literal that represents the defined concept. However, there are patterns in input clauses noted in theorem 1 that often correspond to definitions, and these patterns can be used to generate replacement rules automatically.

Case 1.

First-Order Formula: $\forall \bar{X} p(\bar{X}) \leftrightarrow \exists \bar{Y} (q_1(\bar{X}, \bar{Y}) \wedge q_2(\bar{X}, \bar{Y}) \ldots \wedge q_n(\bar{X}, \bar{Y}))$

Clause Form:

$$[p(\bar{X}), \neg q_1(\bar{X}, \bar{Y}), \ldots, \neg q_n(\bar{X}, \bar{Y})].$$
$$[\neg p(\bar{X}), q_1(\bar{X}, \bar{f}(\bar{X}))].$$
$$\ldots$$
$$[\neg p(\bar{X}), q_n(\bar{X}, \bar{f}(\bar{X}))].$$

Case 2.

$$\forall \bar{X} p(\bar{X}) \leftrightarrow \exists \bar{Y} (q_1(\bar{X}, \bar{Y}) \vee \ldots \vee q_n(\bar{X}, \bar{Y}))$$
$$[\neg p(\bar{X}), q_1(\bar{X}, \bar{f}(\bar{X})), \ldots, q_n(\bar{X}, \bar{f}(\bar{X}))].$$
$$[p(\bar{X}), \neg q_1(\bar{X}, \bar{Y})].$$
$$\ldots$$
$$[p(\bar{X}), \neg q_n(\bar{X}, \bar{Y})].$$

Case 3.

$$\forall \bar{X} p(\bar{X}) \leftrightarrow \forall \bar{Y} (q_1(\bar{X}, \bar{Y}) \wedge \ldots \wedge q_n(\bar{X}, \bar{Y}))$$
$$[p(\bar{X}), \neg q_1(\bar{X}, \bar{f}(\bar{X})), \ldots, \neg q_n(\bar{X}, \bar{f}(\bar{X}))].$$
$$[\neg p(\bar{X}), q_1(\bar{X}, \bar{Y})].$$
$$\ldots$$
$$[\neg p(\bar{X}), q_n(\bar{X}, \bar{Y})].$$

Case 4.

$$\forall \bar{X} p(\bar{X}) \leftrightarrow \forall \bar{Y} (q_1(\bar{X}, \bar{Y}) \vee q_2(\bar{X}, \bar{Y}) \ldots \vee q_n(\bar{X}, \bar{Y}))$$
$$[\neg p(\bar{X}), q_1(\bar{X}, \bar{Y}), \ldots, q_n(\bar{X}, \bar{Y})].$$
$$[p(\bar{X}), \neg q_1(\bar{X}, \bar{f}(\bar{X}))].$$
$$\ldots$$
$$[p(\bar{X}), \neg q_n(\bar{X} \bar{f}(\bar{X}))].$$

Fig. 1. First-order formulas and clauses that often represent definitions

Definition 2. If S is a set of first-order clause such that $N \in S$ and $N\alpha = \{P, Q_1, \ldots, Q_n\}$ and if $\forall i (E_i \in S)$ where $E_i \alpha_i = \{\neg P, \neg Q_i\}$, where α and α_i are substitutions, then we call clause N a nucleus clause and we call the E_i electron clauses. The first-order literals P and Q_i can be either positive or negative.

Remark 1. Given a nucleus clause N such that $N\alpha = \{P, Q_1, \ldots, Q_n\}$ and its electron clauses E_i such that $E_i \alpha_i = \{\neg P, \neg Q_i\}$ where P contains at least one predicate, function or constant symbol that does not appear in any Q_i, replacement rules $\neg P \rightarrow_r Q_1, \ldots, Q_n$ and $P \rightarrow_r \neg Q_i$ are generated.

Figure 1 lists some common axiomatization of definitions. Their clause forms have patterns that are captured in nucleus and electron clauses. For example, in the set theory example in Table 1, the definition of $\cap$ corresponds to case 1 or 3, where $\bar{Y} = \emptyset$, and the definition of $\subseteq$ corresponds to case 4. Based on Definition 2, it is quite easy to test whether a clause $C \in S$ is a nucleus clause. One can nondeterministically select a literal R in C, assume R to be the replacement literal P, and check if $\forall i(E_i \in S)$, where $E_i\alpha_i = \{\neg P, \neg Q_i\}$. A set of clauses might generate multiple sets of replacement rules due to different ways of assigning replacement literals. For example, in a clause set with $\{\{p(X), \neg q(X)\}, \{\neg p(X), q(X)\}\}$, both $p(X)$ and $q(X)$ can be replacement literals. In this case, we generate two sets of replacement rules $p(X) \rightarrow_r q(X)$, $\neg p(X) \rightarrow_r \neg q(X)$ and $q(X) \rightarrow_r p(X)$, $\neg q(X) \rightarrow_r \neg p(X)$. This is not a problem for our approach, since no rewriting actually occurs. Both sets of replacement rules are used at the same time. In general, multiple replacement rules may be used at the same time, which may have the effect of replacing some literals by multiple definitions at the same time. The idea of nucleus and electron clauses can be extended to detect other patterns of definitions, such as a definition of the form $P \leftrightarrow (Q_1 \wedge Q_2) \vee Q_3$.

In OSHL, when the set theory flag is turned on, the replacement strategy is invoked before the instantiation procedures that generate semantically false instances. The replacement strategy terminates when a time limit is reached, or no more relevant literals can be generated. OSHL collects all relevant instances generated by the replacement strategy and combines them with the instances generated by instantiation to detect propositional unsatisfiability using a method much like that of Davis and Putnam [DP60,DLL62].

Nontermination of the process of replacement is not inherently a problem for this approach, since a propositional satisfiability test can be applied after each round of replacement. Thus we do not need to be concerned with whether the definitions are well-founded, in some sense. In fact, definition of a predicate $p(X, Y)$ as $p(Y, X)$ would not even cause nontermination for us. Other definitions could cause nontermination. However, if the replacement process is nonterminating, then after a certain time limit, the general theorem prover will be called, which might not be as efficient at finding a proof as the replacement rules would be.

We applied the replacement strategy to solve set theory problems. The technique is very effective and can generate the "right" instances very efficiently. Combining replacement rules with an efficient propositional decision procedure, OSHL can solve many set theory problems that are very difficult for other theorem provers. The automatic generation of replacement rules is also effective. Many definitions in set theory can be detected. Examples include intersection, union, subset, powerset, etc. Some definitions are not captured by nucleus or electron clauses. For these, we can either construct the replacement rules manually, or else break the definitions into smaller pieces, each of which will be of the form $L \equiv (A_1 \vee A_2)$ or $L \equiv (A_1 \wedge A_2)$, both of which our approach can detect. For example, a definition of the form $P \equiv [(Q_1 \wedge Q_2) \vee Q_3]$ can be broken down into the definitions $P \equiv (P_1 \vee Q_3)$ and $P_1 \equiv (Q_1 \wedge Q_2)$. This technique is somewhat like a structure-preserving translation to clause form [PG86].

4 Test Results

We now present results on application of replacement rules in set theory. All runs were done on a SUN Sparc-20. OSHL is programmed in Prolog and Otter [McC90] is implemented in C. Six problems were run, which we will call p1 through p6. These involved definitions of the set theory predicates "equal" and "subset" and the functions $\cup$, $\cap$, comp (complement), diff (difference), and p (powerset). We indicate which axioms were included in each problem by Ax[$=, \subseteq, \cup$], for example, indicating that the definitions of $=$, $\subseteq$, and $\cup$ were included in the set of axioms. The definitions were input as in table 2.

Definition of =:	{not(equal(X,Y)), subset(X,Y)}.
	{not(equal(X,Y)), subset(Y,X)}.
	{not(subset(X,Y)), not(subset(Y,X)), equal(X,Y)}.
Definition of $\subseteq$:	{not(subset(X,Y)), not(in(Z,X)), in(Z,Y)}.
	{in(g(X,Y),X), subset(X,Y)}.
	{not(in(g(X,Y),Y)), subset(X,Y)}.
Definition of $\cup$:	{in(X,Y), in(X,Z), not(in(X,union(Y,Z)))}.
	{in(X,union(Y,Z)), not(in(X,Y))}.
	{in(X,union(Y,Z)), not(in(X,Z))}.
Definition of $\cap$:	{not(in(X,Y)), not(in(X,Z)), in(X,intersect(Y,Z))}.
	{not(in(X,intersect(Y,Z))), in(X,Y)}.
	{not(in(X,intersect(Y,Z))), in(X,Z)}.
Definition of comp:	{not(in(X,Y)), not(in(X,comp(Y)))}.
	{in(X,Y), in(X,comp(Y))}.
Definition of diff:	{in(X,diff(Y,Z)), not(in(X,intersect(Y,comp(Z))))}.
	{not(in(X,diff(Y,Z))), in(X,intersect(Y,comp(Z)))}.
Definition of p :	{not(subset(X,Y)), in(X,p(Y))}.
	{not(in(X,p(Y))), subset(X,Y)}.

Table 2. Clauses defining set theory predicates and operators

The clauses and theorems for the various problems were as shown in table 3.

We note from the input clauses of problems p1 to p6 that axioms were often included that were not needed for the proof. The results on OSHL and Otter were as shown in table 4.

Problem p1: Ax[=,⊆,∩]
Negation of theorem:
{not(equal(a, intersect(a,a)))}.

Problem p2: Ax[=,⊆,∩]
Negation of theorem:
{not(equal(intersect(a,intersect(b,intersect(a,c))),
intersect(c,intersect(a,intersect(c,b)))))}.

Problem p3: Ax[=,⊆,∩,∪,p]
Negation of theorem:
{not(equal(p(intersect(a,b)),intersect(p(a),p(b))))}.

Problem p4: Ax[=,⊆,∩,∪,comp]
Negation of theorem:
{not(equal(comp(union(a,b)),intersect(comp(a),comp(b))))}.

Problem p5: Ax[=,⊆,∩,∪,p,comp]
Negation of theorem:
{not(equal(comp(union(a,b)),intersect(comp(a),comp(b))))}.

Problem p6: Ax[=,⊆,∩,∪,p,comp,diff]
Negation of theorem:
{neg(equal(diff(a,diff(a,b)),intersect(a,b)))}.

Table 3. Input clauses of problems p1 to p6

These runs were made with Otter using binary resolution and only the negation of the theorem in the set of support. We also ran all problems on Otter with all clauses in the set of support and used hyper-resolution, with essentially the same result: all problems except the first one timed out after 1000 seconds and generated many clauses, without finding a proof. Something that is not obvious from the figures of table 4 is that the proofs printed out by OSHL are often several pages long.

5 Comparison with Other Approaches

There have been a number of other approaches to set theory; meta-level replacement has already been mentioned. One difference of our approach is that it is a general technique for handling definitions and is not limited to set theory. Our approach also differs from some others that involve higher-order logic and thus can explicitly represent quantifiers in definitions.

Quaife[Qua92] has also obtained many proofs in set theory. He used Otter [McC90], a general first-order theorem prover, with some special settings for the switches. For example, he often preferred UR-resolution with set of support and preferred clauses not containing variables. Though this can be effective, the

Problem	OSHL Time	OTTER Time	OTTER clauses generated
p1	0.3	0.03	51
p2	2.3	1000+	41867
p3	11.25	1000+	27656
p4	1.35	1000+	105244
p5	2.0	1000+	54660
p6	2.17	1000+	23553

Table 4. Timing of OSHL and OTTER. Time is measured in seconds on a SPARC-20. 1000+ means that no proof is found in 1000 seconds.

combination of UR resolution and set of support is not complete in general. Quaife also chose particular clause weightings to guide the proof. For simple theorems, our approach seems to require less guidance. However, Quaife was able to prove harder theorems than we can obtain automatically at present.

The approach of Andrews [BA98] is interesting in that he also retains both the original clauses and their expanded forms. His approach is incorporated into a higher-order theorem prover, which is more expressive but has a higher overhead for simple theorems.

The Set-Var approach of [BF91] handles theorems in which set variables are universally and existentially quantified. For us, all set variables are universally quantified (in effect), which makes the theorems simpler. We do not know how the Set-Var approach would perform on theorems such as we have tried.

The approach of [COP90] is noteworthy in that they give a decision procedure for a fragment of set theory. It may be that our approach also provides a decision procedure for this same $(\forall)_0^{\prime}$ fragment of set theory. If so, then the use of efficient propositional decision procedures could actually give our approach an efficiency advantage. It may also be that not all of our examples fit within this fragment of set theory.

6 Discussion

Although we only ran six problems, the results are striking enough that some general conclusions can be drawn. Since many set theory problems are of the same general nature, it is clear even from these results that replacement rules are far superior to resolution on set theory problems which can be proved entirely by the replacement of predicates and operators by their definitions. In addition, we note that the replacement rule facility implemented here is fully automatic and does not recognize these problems as set theory problems. If all of the operators and predicates were renamed, the OSHL running times would be essentially the same. Since definitions are common in many theorems, a replacement rule facility such as this one would be a good addition to any theorem prover.

These problems were fairly simple, and so we would not expect the same efficiency on more complex problems, such as the composition of homomorphism problem [Qua92]. It is an interesting project to attempt to extend the results of this paper to harder theorems.

It would also be interesting to study the complexity of replacement using this mechanism. Of course, nothing in general can be said, because the process of replacement can generate long chains of replacement instances, or even be nonterminating on some examples. Some efficiency might be gained by generating the replacement rules during a preprocessing step. It appears that the replacement rules can be generated in time polynomial in the length of the input clause set, if all clauses have a bounded number of literals. In the general case, generating these rules might take exponential time.

We comment on the completeness of our approach. In general, we believe that the following is true: If a set S of clauses, with all definitions expanded, is propositionally unsatisfiable, then our method will be able to show that S is unsatisfiable. This is at least a limited completeness result. After replacement rule generation, the replacement instances together with the input clause set are given to a general theorem prover in our approach. We note that the clauses that have been identified as definitions are not dropped from the input clause set, which would lead to incompleteness.

Examples of possible applications in which replacement rules could prove valuable include hardware verification, in which the high-level behavior of a device can often be defined in terms of its detailed low-level gate-level behavior. Another application is concept description languages, which often involve definitions, and for which a replacement mechanism was recently shown to be efficient [PP97]. We also believe that state space planning problems can be solved quickly in this way, but we have not investigated this very far.

One limitation of this technique is that replacement is only performed on ground literals present in the input clauses. It is often useful to apply definition expansion to terms and literals generated during the course of a proof, as well. This could be done in a similar way, but of course there is less likelihood that such definition expansion will lead to a proof. We need to devote more attention to this area. It does not seem right to apply replacement to all ground literals that appear during the course of a proof, but it may be advantageous to apply it to some of them.

An interesting comparison can be made with these problems and the TPTP problem set [SS97], which has hundreds of set theory problems, each containing many, many axioms of set theory. The advantage of replacement over resolution and other strategies does not seem as striking on the TPTP problems as it does here, for some reason, and we do not fully understand why.

7 Conclusions

The replacement rule mechanism with automatic definition detection is efficient for proving many set theory problems, and is often far superior to resolution in this respect. It also holds promise for substantially increasing the power of first-order clause-form theorem provers on any problem in which the expansion of definitions is needed in the proof. Moreover, this mechanism requires no user interaction. Many theorem provers would benefit by incorporating some form of replacement rules.

Acknowledgments

Support from Ricardo Caferra during the first author's stay in Grenoble, France in the summer of 1998 contributed to the preparation of this paper.

References

[BA98] Matthew Bishop and Peter B. Andrews. Selectively instantiating definitions. In *Proceedings of the 15th International Conference on Automated Deduction*, pages 365–380, 1998.

[BF91] W. W. Bledsoe and G. Feng. Set-var. *Journal of Automated Reasoning*, 11(3):293–314, 1991.

[Ble77] W. W. Bledsoe. Non-resolution theorem proving. *Artificial Intelligence*, 9:1–35, 1977.

[COP90] D. Cantone, E.G. Omodeo, and A. Policriti. The automation of syllogistic II: optimization and complexity issues. *Journal of Automated Reasoning*, 6(2):173–187, 1990.

[CP94] Heng Chu and D. Plaisted. Semantically guided first-order theorem proving using hyper-linking. In *Proceedings of the Twelfth International Conference on Automated Deduction*, pages 192–206, 1994. Lecture Notes in Artificial Intelligence 814.

[DHK98] G. Dowek, T. Hardin, and C. Kirchner. Theorem proving modulo. Technical Report 3400, Institut National de Recherche en Informatique et en Automatique (INRIA), Le Chesnay, France, April 1998.

[DLL62] M. Davis, G. Logemann, and D. Loveland. A machine program for theorem-proving. *Communications of the ACM*, 5:394–397, 1962.

[DP60] M. Davis and H. Putnam. A computing procedure for quantification theory. *Journal of the Association for Computing Machinery*, 7:201–215, 1960.

[GOP93] D. Gabbay, J. Ohlbach, and D. Plaisted. Killer transformations. In *Proc. 1993 Workshop on Proof Theory in Modal Logic*, pages 1–45, Hamburg, Germany, 1993.

[LP94] S.-J. Lee and D. Plaisted. Use of replace rules in theorem proving. *Methods of Logic in Computer Science*, 1:217–240, 1994.

[McC90] W. McCune. Otter 2.0 (theorem prover). In M.E. Stickel, editor, *Proceedings of the 10th International Conference on Automated Deduction*, pages 663–4, July 1990.

[Par97] M. Paramasivam. *Instance-Based First-Order Methods Using Propositional Calculus Provers.* PhD thesis, University of North Carolina at Chapel Hill, 1997.

[Pau92] L.C. Paulson. Set theory for verification I: from foundations to functions. *Journal of Automated Reasoning*, 11(3):352–390, 1992.

[PG86] D. Plaisted and S. Greenbaum. A structure-preserving clause form translation. *Journal of Symbolic Computation*, 2:293–304, 1986.

[PP91] D. Plaisted and R Potter. Term rewriting: Some experimental results. *Journal of Symbolic Computation*, 11:149 – 180, 1991.

[PP97] M. Paramasivam and D. Plaisted. A replacement rule theorem prover. *Journal of Automated Reasoning*, 18(2):221–226, 1997.

[PP98] M. Paramasivam and D. Plaisted. Automated deduction techniques for classification in description logics. *Journal of Automated Reasoning*, 20(3):337–364, 1998.

[PZ97] D. Plaisted and Y. Zhu. Ordered semantic hyper linking. In *Proceedings of Fourteenth National Conference on Artificial Intelligence (AAAI97)*, Providence, Rhode Island, 1997.

[Qua92] A. Quaife. Automated deduction in NBG set theory. *Journal of Automated Reasoning*, 8(1):91–147, 1992.

[SS97] C.B. Suttner and G. Sutcliffe. The TPTP problem library (TPTP v2.0.0). Technical Report AR-97-01, Institut für Informatik, Technische Universität München, Germany, 1997.

[WRC65] L. Wos, G. Robinson, and D. Carson. Efficiency and completeness of the set of support strategy in theorem proving. *Journal of the Association for Computing Machinery*, 12:536–541, 1965.

On the Complexity of Finite Sorted Algebras

Thierry Boy de la Tour

LEIBNIZ Laboratory - IMAG (CNRS)
46, Av. Félix Viallet, 38031 Grenoble Cedex, France
Thierry.Boy-de-la-Tour@imag.fr,
WWW home page:
http://www-leibniz.imag.fr/ATINF/Thierry.Boy-de-la-Tour/welcome.html

Abstract. The general problem of testing the isomorphism of two given finite algebras is known to be isomorphism complete, i.e. polynomially equivalent to the graph isomorphism problem (**GI**). It is easy to see that this fact still holds when sorts are introduced. However, this isomorphism problem is relevant only for algebras (or interpretations) of a fixed signature, and in some cases, according to the signature, is much simpler than the general problem. We therefore establish exactly for which signatures is the associated isomorphism problem simpler than **GI**, and for which is it isomorphism complete. It turns out that for non-monadic signatures, this problem is isomorphism complete just as is the case without sorts, while the classification of monadic signatures is more complex and interesting in the presence of sorts.

1 Introduction

In the context of model building, it is very common to consider sorts in order to reduce the search space. It is also a trivial thought that things get more complex if we consider a formula with more non-logical symbols than another one. But then why not consider only one sort, and one function symbol encoding all others? Because the corresponding algebras would poorly represent the objects we are looking for, and the search would browse many meaningless structures. A search can only be efficient if the search space consists of reasonable candidates, not weird mixtures of unsuitable representations. We may question whether the art of finding a suitable, or "searchable" representation can rest on firm ground.

When we search for finite models of a first order sorted formula, the search space is determined by the set of non-logical symbols used in the formula, i.e. the signature. It is clear that some signatures are much simpler than others, for example the interpretations of a signature Σ with only one constant symbol cannot match the rich structure of graphs, while this is possible with a binary predicate symbol. Of course, there may be many ways to represent any kind of objects as finite algebras, and it may be difficult to establish what can possibly be represented in a given structure. We may however obtain negative results by considering the relative complexity of source and target structures of representations: the represented object is necessarily simpler than the structure into which it is encoded.

R. Caferra and G. Salzer (Eds.): Automated Deduction, LNAI 1761, pp. 95–108, 2000.

We will only consider transformations that preserve isomorphisms in order to ensure fair representations. We will also focus on a very elementary measure for the complexity of a structure: the computational complexity of the associated isomorphism problem. The reason is that the general isomorphism problem between finite algebras is known to be isomorphism complete, while it is believed that this class is disjoint from the class **P**. Hence finite interpretations of simple signatures, i.e. inducing a polynomial isomorphism test, are strictly simpler than those rich enough to embed graphs.

2 Preliminaries

Definition 1. *Given a finite set $\mathcal{S}$, whose elements are called* sorts, *the set of* first-order $\mathcal{S}$-types *is* $\mathfrak{T}_1(\mathcal{S}) = \bigcup_{k\in\mathbb{N}} \mathcal{S}^k \times (\mathcal{S} \uplus \{\mathrm{o}\})$.

For $t = \langle d_1, \ldots, d_k, r\rangle \in \mathfrak{T}_1(\mathcal{S})$, *if* $k \neq 0$ *then* t *is said to be* functional *of arity* k, *and is noted* $d_1 \times \ldots \times d_k \to r$; $\mathrm{dom}\, t$ *is* $d_1 \times \ldots \times d_k$ *and* $\mathrm{rng}\, t$ *is* r. *If* $k = 1$, t *is said to be* monadic, *and* atomic *if* $k = 0$.

A signature $\Sigma = \langle \mathcal{S}, \mathcal{F}, \tau\rangle$ *is given by a finite set* $\mathcal{S}$ *of* sorts, *a finite set* $\mathcal{F}$ *of* symbols *and a function* τ *from* $\mathcal{F}$ *to* $\mathfrak{T}_1(\mathcal{S})$. $f \in \Sigma$ *stands for* $f \in \mathcal{F}$, *and* Σ_f *for* $\tau(f)$. *If* Σ_f *is functional and* $\mathrm{rng}\,\Sigma_f = \mathrm{o}$, *then* f *is a* predicate *symbol. A signature* Σ *is* monadic *if* $\forall f \in \Sigma$, Σ_f *is either monadic or atomic.*

A sort interpretation $\mathcal{I}$ *of* $\mathcal{S}$ *is a function which associates a non empty set to each element of* $\mathcal{S}$, *such that* $\forall s, s' \in \mathcal{S}$, *if* $s \neq s'$ *then* $\mathcal{I}(s) \cap \mathcal{I}(s') = \emptyset$ *and* $\mathcal{I}(s) \cap \{\top, \bot\} = \emptyset$. $\mathcal{I}$ *is said to be* finite *iff* $\forall s \in \mathcal{S}, \mathcal{I}(s)$ *is finite.*

We naturally extend $\mathcal{I}$ *to the set of first order* $\mathcal{S}$*-types by:* $\mathcal{I}(\mathrm{o}) = \{\top, \bot\}$, $\forall s_1, \ldots, s_n \in \mathcal{S}, \mathcal{I}(s_1 \times \ldots \times s_n) = \prod_{i=1}^n \mathcal{I}(s_i)$ *and for any functional first-order* $\mathcal{S}$*-type* t, $\mathcal{I}(t)$ *is the set of functions from* $\mathcal{I}(\mathrm{dom}\, t)$ *to* $\mathcal{I}(\mathrm{rng}\, t)$.

A Σ-algebra $\mathcal{A} = \langle \mathcal{I}, v\rangle$, *or* interpretation of Σ, *is given by a sort interpretation* $\mathcal{I}$ *of* $\mathcal{S}$ *and a function* v *from* $\mathcal{F}$ *to* $\bigcup_{t\in\mathfrak{T}_1(\mathcal{S})} \mathcal{I}(t)$ *such that* $\forall f \in \Sigma, v(f) \in \mathcal{I}(\Sigma_f)$. *In the sequel,* $\mathcal{A}_f$ *stands for* $v(f)$, *and* $\mathcal{A}(t)$ *for* $\mathcal{I}(t)$. *From now on, we only consider* finite *algebras, i.e. such that the sort interpretation* $\mathcal{I}$ *is finite.*

Given two problems $\mathcal{P}$ and $\mathcal{Q}$, we note $\mathcal{P} \propto_P \mathcal{Q}$ when $\mathcal{P}$ polynomially reduces to $\mathcal{Q}$ (see [1]). We note **GI** the problem of graph isomorphism: given two graphs $G = \langle V, E\rangle$ and $G' = \langle V', E'\rangle$, **GI** is true of G, G' iff $\exists\alpha : G \cong G'$, i.e. α is a 1-1 function from V onto V' such that $\forall x, y \in V$, $\langle x, y\rangle \in E \Leftrightarrow \langle x^\alpha, y^\alpha\rangle \in E'$ (x^α denotes the image of x under the isomorphism α). We will also consider the usual brands of graphs, directed, labeled, multigraphs. Their isomorphism problem are known to be all polynomially equivalent to **GI**, i.e. *isomorphism complete* (see e.g. [2]). Other standard notions as paths, connexity, etc. will also be assumed.

We will obviously make extensive use of isomorphisms between (finite) algebras: given a signature Σ and two Σ-algebras $\mathcal{A}, \mathcal{B}$, an isomorphism between $\mathcal{A}$ and $\mathcal{B}$ is a function σ such that

- $\forall s \in \mathcal{S}$, σ is 1-1 from $\mathcal{A}(s)$ onto $\mathcal{B}(s)$,
- σ is the identity on $\mathcal{A}(\mathrm{o}) = \mathcal{B}(\mathrm{o})$,

- $\forall f \in \Sigma$, let n be the arity of Σ_f, $\forall \langle x_1, \ldots, x_n \rangle \in \mathcal{A}(\text{rng}\, \Sigma_f), \mathcal{B}_f(x_1^\sigma, \ldots, x_n^\sigma) = \mathcal{A}_f(x_1, \ldots, x_n)^\sigma$.

This is noted $\sigma : \mathcal{A} \cong \mathcal{B}$. Finally, we note $\mathbf{I}(\Sigma)$ the problem which, given two finite Σ-algebras $\mathcal{A}, \mathcal{B}$, is true iff $\exists \sigma$ such that $\sigma : \mathcal{A} \cong \mathcal{B}$.

Since we only consider isomorphism problems, we will provide polynomial time transformations from source structures (graphs, finite algebras) to target structures, while preserving isomorphisms *in both directions*. When isomorphic source objects are transformed into isomorphic target objects, we say that the transformation is *invariant* (intuitively, *only* their structure is transformed). If source objects are isomorphic whenever their transformed objects are isomorphic, the transformation is *accurate* (*all* the structure is transformed). A transformation both invariant and accurate is said to be *fair*.

As an example, we first prove that complexity increases by adding sorts.

Lemma 1. *Let* $\Sigma = \langle \mathcal{S}, \mathcal{F}, \tau \rangle$ *and* $\Sigma' = \langle \mathcal{S} \uplus \{s\}, \mathcal{F}, \tau \rangle$, *then* $\mathbf{I}(\Sigma) \propto_P \mathbf{I}(\Sigma')$.

Proof. Any Σ-algebra $\mathcal{A}$ can be transformed into a Σ'-algebra $\widetilde{\mathcal{A}}$ by extending it with a new element a: let $\widetilde{\mathcal{A}}(t) = \mathcal{A}(t)$ and $\widetilde{\mathcal{A}}_f = \mathcal{A}_f$ for all $t \in \mathcal{S}$ and $f \in \mathcal{F}$, and $\widetilde{\mathcal{A}}(s) = \{a\}$, where $a \notin \biguplus_{t \in \mathcal{S}} \mathcal{A}(t)$. This transformation is obviously polynomial.

The transformation is invariant since any isomorphism σ between two Σ-algebras $\mathcal{A}, \mathcal{B}$ can be extended to an isomorphism between $\widetilde{\mathcal{A}}$ and $\widetilde{\mathcal{B}}$ ($\mathcal{B}$ extended with b) by $a^\sigma = b$. It is accurate since any isomorphism $\sigma : \widetilde{\mathcal{A}} \cong \widetilde{\mathcal{B}}$ is 1-1 from $\widetilde{\mathcal{A}}(s)$ onto $\widetilde{\mathcal{B}}(s)$, hence $a^\sigma = b$, and the restriction of σ to $\biguplus_{t \in \mathcal{S}} \widetilde{\mathcal{A}}(t)$ is an isomorphism between $\mathcal{A}$ and $\mathcal{B}$. Hence the problem $\mathbf{I}(\Sigma)$ can be solved by using $\mathbf{I}(\Sigma')$ (whether the answer is yes or no) through this polynomial and fair transformation.

In the sequel, we will establish properties of specific signatures, the statement of which will be eased by the following notation: for a given $\mathcal{S}$ and any first-order $\mathcal{S}$-types $t_1, \ldots, t_n$, we note $\lceil t_1, \ldots, t_n \rceil$ for any signature $\Sigma = \langle \mathcal{S}, \mathcal{F}, \tau \rangle$ where $\mathcal{F}$ contains exactly n symbols $f_1, \ldots, f_n$ and $\forall i \in \{1 \ldots n\}, \tau(f_i) = t_i$. If $\mathcal{S}$ is not specified, we take the smallest possible one: the set of symbols appearing in the t_i's.

It is easy to see that complexity increases by *adding* arguments to functions.

Lemma 2. $\mathbf{I}(\lceil d_1 \times \ldots \times d_n \to r \rceil) \propto_P \mathbf{I}(\lceil d_0 \times \ldots \times d_n \to r \rceil)$.

Proof. Let $\Sigma = \langle \mathcal{S}, \{f\}, \tau \rangle$, and $\Sigma' = \langle \mathcal{S}', \{f\}, \tau' \rangle$ with $\mathcal{S} = \{d_1, \ldots, d_n, r\}$, $\tau(f) = d_1 \times \ldots \times d_n \to r$, $\mathcal{S}' = \mathcal{S} \cup \{d_0\}$ and and $\tau'(f) = d_0 \times \ldots \times d_n \to r$. We first consider the case where $d_0 \in \{d_1, \ldots, d_n, r\}$, that is $\mathcal{S} = \mathcal{S}'$.

We transform any Σ-algebras $\mathcal{A}$ into a Σ'-algebra $\widetilde{\mathcal{A}}$ by: $\forall s \in \mathcal{S}, \widetilde{\mathcal{A}}(s) = \mathcal{A}(s)$ and $\forall \langle x_0, \ldots, x_n \rangle \in \widetilde{\mathcal{A}}(d_0 \times \ldots \times d_n), \widetilde{\mathcal{A}}_f(x_0, \ldots, x_n) = \mathcal{A}_f(x_1, \ldots, x_n)$. This transformation is clearly polynomial: the graph of $\mathcal{A}_f$ is duplicated $|\mathcal{A}(d_0)|$ times. Since $\widetilde{\mathcal{A}}_f(x_0^\sigma, \ldots, x_n^\sigma) = \mathcal{A}_f(x_1^\sigma, \ldots, x_n^\sigma)$ and $\widetilde{\mathcal{A}}_f(x_0, \ldots, x_n)^\sigma = \mathcal{A}_f(x_1, \ldots, x_n)^\sigma$, it is obviously fair:

$$\begin{aligned}\sigma : \mathcal{A} \cong \mathcal{B} &\text{ iff } \forall \langle x_1, \dots, x_n \rangle \in \mathcal{A}(d_1 \times \dots \times d_n), \mathcal{B}_f(x_1^\sigma, \dots, x_n^\sigma) = \mathcal{A}_f(x_1, \dots, x_n)^\sigma \\ &\text{ iff } \forall \langle x_0, \dots, x_n \rangle \in \widetilde{\mathcal{A}}(d_0 \times \dots \times d_n), \widetilde{\mathcal{B}}_f(x_0^\sigma, \dots, x_n^\sigma) = \widetilde{\mathcal{A}}_f(x_0, \dots, x_n)^\sigma \\ &\text{ iff } \sigma : \widetilde{\mathcal{A}} \cong \widetilde{\mathcal{B}}.\end{aligned}$$

If d_0 is a new sort, we first add d_0 to Σ', which yields Σ'' and $\mathbf{I}(\Sigma) \propto_P \mathbf{I}(\Sigma'')$ by lemma 1. The previous case yields $\mathbf{I}(\Sigma'') \propto_P \mathbf{I}(\Sigma')$.

It is not as easy to prove that complexity increases by adding *objects* to a signature. More precisely, given two signatures $\Sigma = \langle \mathcal{S}, \mathcal{F}, \tau \rangle$ and $\Sigma' = \langle \mathcal{S}', \mathcal{F}', \tau' \rangle$, we say that $\Sigma \subseteq \Sigma'$ iff $\mathcal{S} \subseteq \mathcal{S}'$, $\mathcal{F} \subseteq \mathcal{F}'$ and $\forall f \in \mathcal{F}, \tau(f) = \tau'(f)$.

Definition 2. *To any signature Σ we associate a directed multigraph $G_\Sigma = \langle \mathcal{S}, \mathcal{E}_\Sigma, \mathrm{fst}_\Sigma, \mathrm{snd}_\Sigma \rangle$, where $\mathcal{E}_\Sigma$ is the set of $\langle f, i \rangle$ for $f \in \Sigma$ such that Σ_f is functional, with $\mathrm{rng}\, \Sigma_f \neq \mathbf{o}$ and i is an integer between 1 and the arity n of f; then for $\Sigma_f = d_1 \times \dots \times d_n \to r$, we take $\mathrm{fst}_\Sigma(\langle f, i \rangle) = d_i$ and $\mathrm{snd}_\Sigma(\langle f, i \rangle) = r$ (see figure 1).*

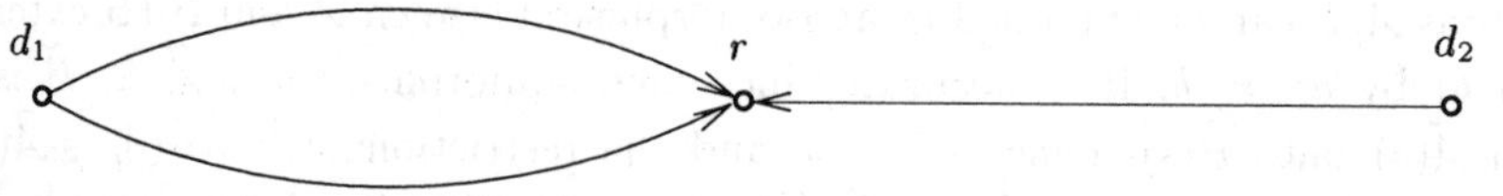

Fig. 1. G_Σ for $\Sigma = \lceil d_1 \times d_2 \to r, d_1 \to r, r \to \mathbf{o} \rceil$

We now come to the more difficult task of adding a new function symbol $g : d_1 \times \dots \times d_n \to t$ to a signature Σ while preserving isomorphisms. The trivial thing to do is to take some constant function for $\mathcal{A}_g$, but this necessarily involves an element of $\mathcal{A}(t)$, therefore disturbing the whole structure of the Σ-algebra $\mathcal{A}$. The solution is to add a new element a_t to $\mathcal{A}(t)$ in order to hold the "blind" value of $\mathcal{A}_g$. But then for any $f \in \Sigma$ with t among its domain sort, we have to provide a value for $\mathcal{A}_f(a_t)$, and hence to add other elements to other range sets in order to hold the images of these new elements, in an inductive way.

Lemma 3. *Let $\Sigma = \langle \mathcal{S}, \mathcal{F}, \tau_{\mathcal{F}} \rangle$ and $\Sigma' = \langle \mathcal{S}, \mathcal{F} \uplus \{g\}, \tau \rangle$, then $\mathbf{I}(\Sigma) \propto_P \mathbf{I}(\Sigma')$.*

Proof. Let $t = \mathrm{rng}\, \tau(g)$ if $\tau(g)$ is functional, and $t = \tau(g)$ otherwise.

If $t = \mathbf{o}$, to every Σ-algebra $\mathcal{A}$ we associate a Σ'-algebra $\widetilde{\mathcal{A}}$ defined by:

- $\forall s \in \mathcal{S}, \widetilde{\mathcal{A}}(s) = \mathcal{A}(s)$,
- $\forall f \in \Sigma, \widetilde{\mathcal{A}}_f = \mathcal{A}_f$,

– if $\tau(g)$ is functional, then $\forall \chi \in \mathcal{A}(\mathrm{dom}\,\tau(g)), \widetilde{\mathcal{A}}_g(\chi) = \top$; if $\tau(g)$ is atomic then $\widetilde{\mathcal{A}}_g = \top$.

This transformation is obviously polynomial and fair.

If $t \in \mathcal{S}$, let $\mathcal{S}_t$ be the set of $s \in \mathcal{S}$ such that there exists a path in G_Σ from t to s, and including t. Given a Σ-algebra $\mathcal{A}$, to every $s \in \mathcal{S}_t$ we associate a different a_s such that $a_s \notin \biguplus_{u \in \mathcal{S}} \mathcal{A}(u)$, and we build the Σ'-algebra $\widetilde{\mathcal{A}}$ defined by (see figure 2):

– $\forall s \in \mathcal{S} - \mathcal{S}_t, \widetilde{\mathcal{A}}(s) = \mathcal{A}(s)$, and $\forall s \in \mathcal{S}_t, \widetilde{\mathcal{A}}(s) = \mathcal{A}(s) \uplus \{a_s\}$,
– $\forall f \in \Sigma$, if $\tau(f)$ is atomic then $\widetilde{\mathcal{A}}_f = \mathcal{A}_f$,
– if $\tau(g)$ is atomic then $\widetilde{\mathcal{A}}_g = a_t$,
– if $\tau(g)$ is functional then $\forall \chi \in \widetilde{\mathcal{A}}(\mathrm{dom}\,\tau(g)), \widetilde{\mathcal{A}}_g(\chi) = a_t$,
– if $\tau(f) = d_1 \times \ldots \times d_n \to r$, then $\forall \langle x_1, \ldots, x_n \rangle \in \widetilde{\mathcal{A}}(d_1 \times \ldots \times d_n)$,

$$\widetilde{\mathcal{A}}_f(x_1, \ldots, x_n) = \text{ if } x_1 = a_{d_1} \text{ or}\ldots\text{or } x_n = a_{d_n} \text{ then } a_r \text{ else } \mathcal{A}_f(x_1, \ldots, x_n).$$

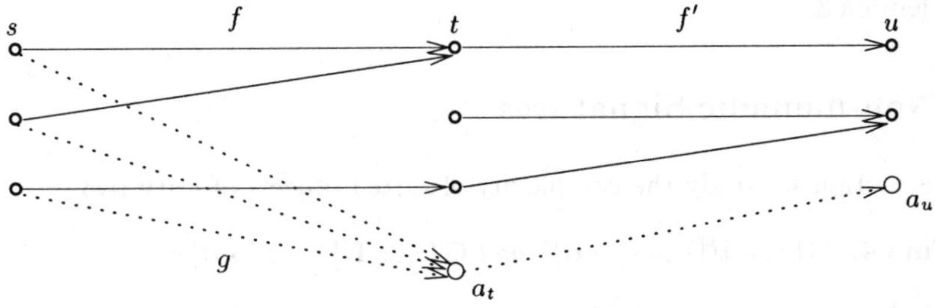

Fig. 2. Adding a $g : s \to t$ to $f : s \to t, f' : t \to u$

The transformation from $\mathcal{A}$ to $\widetilde{\mathcal{A}}$ is polynomial, and we have to prove that it is fair. Let $\mathcal{B}$ a Σ-algebra, and $\widetilde{\mathcal{B}}$ its extension as above with elements b_s.

If $\sigma : \mathcal{A} \cong \mathcal{B}$, then we extend σ to $\widetilde{\mathcal{A}}(s)$ by: $a_s^\sigma = b_s$. If $\tau(g)$ is atomic, we have $\widetilde{\mathcal{A}}_g^\sigma = a_t^\sigma = b_t = \widetilde{\mathcal{B}}_g$; if $\tau(g)$ is functional, then $\forall x \in \widetilde{\mathcal{A}}(\mathrm{dom}\,\tau(g)), \widetilde{\mathcal{B}}_g(x^\sigma) = b_t = a_t^\sigma = \widetilde{\mathcal{A}}_g(x)^\sigma$. Moreover, $\forall f \in \Sigma$, if $\tau(f)$ is atomic, then $\widetilde{\mathcal{A}}_f^\sigma = \mathcal{A}_f^\sigma = \mathcal{B}_f = \widetilde{\mathcal{B}}_f$. We now consider the case where $\tau(f)$ is functional, say $\tau(f) = d_1 \times \ldots \times d_n \to r$; $\forall \langle x_1, \ldots, x_n \rangle \in \mathcal{A}(d_1 \times \ldots \times d_n)$, we have

$$\begin{aligned}\widetilde{\mathcal{B}}_f(x_1^\sigma, \ldots, x_n^\sigma) &= \text{if } x_1^\sigma = b_{d_1} \text{ or}\ldots\text{or } x_n^\sigma = b_{d_n} \text{ then } b_r \text{ else } \mathcal{B}_f(x_1^\sigma, \ldots, x_n^\sigma)\\ &= \text{if } x_1 = a_{d_1} \text{ or}\ldots\text{or } x_n = a_{d_n} \text{ then } a_r^\sigma \text{ else } \mathcal{A}_f(x_1, \ldots, x_n)^\sigma\\ &= \widetilde{\mathcal{A}}_f(x_1, \ldots, x_n)^\sigma.\end{aligned}$$

The transformation is therefore invariant.

Conversely, let $\sigma : \widetilde{\mathcal{A}} \cong \widetilde{\mathcal{B}}$, we first prove that $\forall s \in \mathcal{S}_t, a_s^\sigma = b_s$ by induction on the length of the path form t to s in G_Σ. If this is 0, i.e. $s = t$, we have $\forall \chi \in \widetilde{\mathcal{A}}(\mathrm{dom}\, \tau(g)), a_t^\sigma = \widetilde{\mathcal{A}}_g(\chi)^\sigma = \widetilde{\mathcal{B}}_g(\chi^\sigma) = b_t$ (and similarly if $\tau(g)$ is atomic). If this is true of d_i (induction hypothesis) and there is an arrow in G_Σ form d_i to r, i.e. there is a $f \in \Sigma$ with $\tau(f) = d_1 \times \ldots \times d_n \to r$, then $a_r^\sigma = \widetilde{\mathcal{A}}_f(a_{d_1}, \ldots, a_{d_n})^\sigma = \widetilde{\mathcal{B}}_f(a_{d_1}^\sigma, \ldots, a_{d_n}^\sigma) = b_r$, since $a_{d_i}^\sigma = b_{d_i}$. This completes the induction.

Hence it is clear that $\forall s \in \mathcal{S}$, σ is 1-1 from $\mathcal{A}(s)$ onto $\mathcal{B}(s)$. $\forall f \in \Sigma$ such that $\tau(f)$ is functional, say $d_1 \times \ldots \times d_n \to r$, we have $\forall \langle x_1, \ldots, x_n \rangle \in \mathcal{A}(d_1 \times \ldots \times d_n)$,

$$\begin{aligned} \mathcal{A}_f(x_1, \ldots, x_n)^\sigma &= \widetilde{\mathcal{A}}_f(x_1, \ldots, x_n)^\sigma \text{ (since } x_i \neq a_{d_i}) \\ &= \widetilde{\mathcal{B}}_f(x_1^\sigma, \ldots, x_n^\sigma) \\ &= \mathcal{B}_f(x_1^\sigma, \ldots, x_n^\sigma) \text{ (since } x_i^\sigma \neq b_{d_i} = a_{d_i}^\sigma). \end{aligned}$$

Hence the transformation is fair.

Theorem 1. *if* $\Sigma \subseteq \Sigma'$ *then* $\mathbf{I}(\Sigma) \propto_P \mathbf{I}(\Sigma')$.

Proof. If $\Sigma = \langle \mathcal{S}, \mathcal{F}, \tau \rangle$ and $\Sigma' = \langle \mathcal{S}', \mathcal{F}', \tau' \rangle$, let $\Sigma'' = \langle \mathcal{S}', \mathcal{F}, \tau \rangle$, we obtain $\mathbf{I}(\Sigma) \propto_P \mathbf{I}(\Sigma'')$ by induction with lemma 1, and $\mathbf{I}(\Sigma'') \propto_P \mathbf{I}(\Sigma')$ by induction with lemma 3.

3 Non-monadic Signatures

In this section we study the complexity of sorted objects of arity two.

Lemma 4. $\mathbf{GI} \propto_P \mathbf{I}(\lceil s \times s \to \mathbf{o} \rceil)$ *and* $\mathbf{GI} \propto_P \mathbf{I}(\lceil s \times t \to \mathbf{o} \rceil)$.

Proof. An interpretation $\mathcal{A}$ of $s \times s \to \mathbf{o}$ is a binary relation on $\mathcal{A}(s)$, which is essentially a directed graph with $\mathcal{A}(s)$ as set of vertices. Also, any graph $G = \langle V, E \rangle$ can be considered as an adjacency relation, i.e. the interpretation $\mathcal{A}$ of Σ with $\Sigma_R = s \times t \to \mathbf{o}$ such that $\mathcal{A}(s) = V, \mathcal{A}(t) = E$, and $\forall v \in V, \forall e \in E, \mathcal{A}_R(v, e) = \top$ iff $v \in e$. These trivial transformations are fair.

These two cases will be the base for the five remaining cases of objects of arity two. We begin with the essentially unsorted case.

Lemma 5. $\mathbf{I}(\lceil s \times s \to \mathbf{o} \rceil) \propto_P \mathbf{I}(\lceil s \times s \to s \rceil)$.

Proof. If $R \in \Sigma, f \in \Sigma'$ with $\Sigma_R = s \times s \to \mathbf{o}$ and $\Sigma'_f = s \times s \to s$, and given a Σ-algebra $\mathcal{A}$, we consider two elements which are not in $\mathcal{A}(s)$, say $\mathfrak{t}$ and $\mathfrak{f}$, and we build the Σ'-algebra $\widetilde{\mathcal{A}}$ by $\widetilde{\mathcal{A}}(s) = \mathcal{A}(s) \uplus \{\mathfrak{t}, \mathfrak{f}\}$ and (see figure 3) $\forall x, y \in \mathcal{A}(s)$:

- $\widetilde{\mathcal{A}}_f(x, y) = \mathfrak{t}$ if $\mathcal{A}_R(x, y) = \top$, and $\mathfrak{f}$ otherwise,
- $\widetilde{\mathcal{A}}_f(x, \mathfrak{t}) = \widetilde{\mathcal{A}}_f(x, \mathfrak{f}) = \widetilde{\mathcal{A}}_f(\mathfrak{t}, y) = \widetilde{\mathcal{A}}_f(\mathfrak{f}, y) = \widetilde{\mathcal{A}}_f(\mathfrak{t}, \mathfrak{t}) = \widetilde{\mathcal{A}}_f(\mathfrak{f}, \mathfrak{f}) = \mathfrak{t}$,
- $\widetilde{\mathcal{A}}_f(\mathfrak{t}, \mathfrak{f}) = \widetilde{\mathcal{A}}_f(\mathfrak{f}, \mathfrak{t}) = \mathfrak{f}$.

R	a	b
a	$\perp$	$\top$
b	$\perp$	$\perp$

f	a	b	$\mathfrak{t}$	$\mathfrak{f}$
a	$\mathfrak{f}$	$\mathfrak{t}$	$\mathfrak{t}$	$\mathfrak{t}$
b	$\mathfrak{f}$	$\mathfrak{f}$	$\mathfrak{t}$	$\mathfrak{t}$
$\mathfrak{t}$	$\mathfrak{t}$	$\mathfrak{t}$	$\mathfrak{t}$	$\mathfrak{f}$
$\mathfrak{f}$	$\mathfrak{t}$	$\mathfrak{t}$	$\mathfrak{f}$	$\mathfrak{t}$

Fig. 3. From a $R : s \times s \to \mathbf{o}$ to a $f : s \times s \to s$

This transformation is polynomial, and invariant: given two Σ-algebras $\mathcal{A}$ and $\mathcal{B}$ (and $\widetilde{\mathcal{B}}$ is constructed with elements $\mathfrak{t}', \mathfrak{f}'$), it is easy to extend any $\sigma : \mathcal{A} \cong \mathcal{B}$ to a Σ'-isomorphism between $\widetilde{\mathcal{A}}$ and $\widetilde{\mathcal{B}}$, by taking $\mathfrak{t}^\sigma = \mathfrak{t}'$ and $\mathfrak{f}^\sigma = \mathfrak{f}'$.

Conversely, suppose that $\sigma : \widetilde{\mathcal{A}} \cong \widetilde{\mathcal{B}}$. We have $\forall x, y \in \widetilde{\mathcal{A}}(s), \widetilde{\mathcal{A}}_f(x,y)^\sigma = \widetilde{\mathcal{B}}_f(x^\sigma, y^\sigma) \in \{\mathfrak{t}', \mathfrak{f}'\}$, hence $\{\mathfrak{t}^\sigma, \mathfrak{f}^\sigma\} = \{\mathfrak{t}', \mathfrak{f}'\}$. $\forall z \in \{\mathfrak{t}, \mathfrak{f}\}$, by definition we have $\mathfrak{t}' = \widetilde{\mathcal{B}}_f(z^\sigma, z^\sigma) = \widetilde{\mathcal{A}}_f(z,z)^\sigma = \mathfrak{t}^\sigma$, and $\mathfrak{f}^\sigma = \mathfrak{f}'$, from which it is easy to conclude that $\sigma : \mathcal{A} \cong \mathcal{B}$, hence the transformation is fair.

In the next case, compared with the previous one, we release the constraints by taking one argument of a different sort. The main difference with the previous case is that we are no longer able to avoid $\mathfrak{f}^\sigma \neq \mathfrak{f}'$, but this only occurs in a particular, harmless case.

Lemma 6. $\mathbf{I}(\lceil s \times t \to \mathbf{o} \rceil) \propto_P \mathbf{I}(\lceil s \times t \to t \rceil) \propto_P \mathbf{I}(\lceil t \times s \to t \rceil)$.

Proof. As in the proof of lemma 5, if $\Sigma_R = s \times t \to \mathbf{o}$ and $\Sigma'_f = s \times t \to t$, and given a Σ-algebra $\mathcal{A}$ we build the Σ'-algebra $\widetilde{\mathcal{A}}$ by $\widetilde{\mathcal{A}}(s) = \mathcal{A}(s)$, $\widetilde{\mathcal{A}}(t) = \mathcal{A}(t) \uplus \{\mathfrak{t}, \mathfrak{f}\}$, and (see figure 4) $\forall \langle x, y \rangle \in \mathcal{A}(s \times t)$:

- $\widetilde{\mathcal{A}}_f(x,y) = \mathfrak{t}$ if $\mathcal{A}_R(x,y) = \top$, and $\mathfrak{f}$ otherwise,
- $\widetilde{\mathcal{A}}_f(x,\mathfrak{t}) = \widetilde{\mathcal{A}}_f(x,\mathfrak{f}) = \mathfrak{t}$.

This transformation is trivially polynomial and invariant.

R	a'	b'
a	$\perp$	$\top$
b	$\perp$	$\perp$

f	a'	b'	$\mathfrak{t}$	$\mathfrak{f}$
a	$\mathfrak{f}$	$\mathfrak{t}$	$\mathfrak{t}$	$\mathfrak{t}$
b	$\mathfrak{f}$	$\mathfrak{f}$	$\mathfrak{t}$	$\mathfrak{t}$

Fig. 4. From a $R : s \times t \to \mathbf{o}$ to a $f : s \times t \to t$

If $\sigma : \widetilde{\mathcal{A}} \cong \widetilde{\mathcal{B}}$, with $\mathcal{A}, \mathcal{B}$ two Σ-algebras, we have $\forall x \in \mathcal{A}(s), \mathfrak{t}^\sigma = \widetilde{\mathcal{A}}_f(x,\mathfrak{t})^\sigma = \widetilde{\mathcal{B}}_f(x^\sigma, \mathfrak{t}^\sigma) \in \{\mathfrak{t}', \mathfrak{f}'\}$, hence $\mathfrak{t}^\sigma = \widetilde{\mathcal{B}}_f(x^\sigma, \mathfrak{t}^\sigma) = \mathfrak{t}'$. If $\exists \langle x, y \rangle \in \mathcal{A}(s \times t)$ such that $\mathcal{A}_R(x,y) = \perp$, then $\mathfrak{f}^\sigma = \widetilde{\mathcal{B}}_f(x^\sigma, y^\sigma) \in \{\mathfrak{t}', \mathfrak{f}'\}$, hence $\mathfrak{f}^\sigma = \mathfrak{f}'$, from which it is easy to prove that $\sigma : \mathcal{A} \cong \mathcal{B}$. If $\forall \langle x, y \rangle \in \mathcal{A}(s \times t), \mathcal{A}_R(x,y) = \top$, then $\widetilde{\mathcal{B}}_f(x^\sigma, y^\sigma) = \mathfrak{t}^\sigma = \mathfrak{t}'$, and hence $\forall \langle x, y \rangle \in \mathcal{B}(s \times t), \mathcal{B}_R(x,y) = \top$, and $\mathcal{A}$ and $\mathcal{B}$ are also isomorphic. This proves that the transformation is fair. $\mathbf{I}(\lceil s \times t \to t \rceil) \propto_P \mathbf{I}(\lceil t \times s \to t \rceil)$ is obvious.

The next case is a further release of constraints by taking a third sort for the range. This time things get more complex, because the target structure has one more sort than the source, and we have to preclude any unwanted isomorphism on this new sort.

Lemma 7.

$$\mathbf{I}(\lceil s \times t \to \mathbf{o} \rceil) \propto_P \mathbf{I}(\lceil s \times t \to u \rceil)$$
$$\mathbf{I}(\lceil s \times s \to \mathbf{o} \rceil) \propto_P \mathbf{I}(\lceil s \times s \to u \rceil)$$

Proof. If $R \in \Sigma, f \in \Sigma'$ with $\Sigma_R = s \times t \to \mathbf{o}$ and $\Sigma'_f = s \times t \to u$, given a Σ-algebra $\mathcal{A}$ we build a Σ'-algebra $\widetilde{\mathcal{A}}$ in the following way. We first consider two sets S, T such that $S, T, \mathcal{A}(s), \mathcal{A}(t)$ are disjoint two by two, and $|S| = |\mathcal{A}(s)|+1, |T| = |\mathcal{A}(t)|+1$, and we also consider $\mathfrak{t}, \mathfrak{f}$ as above. $\widetilde{\mathcal{A}}$ is build as follows (see figure 5):

- $\widetilde{\mathcal{A}}(s) = \mathcal{A}(s) \uplus S, \widetilde{\mathcal{A}}(t) = \mathcal{A}(t) \uplus T, \widetilde{\mathcal{A}}(u) = \{\mathfrak{t}, \mathfrak{f}\}$,
- $\forall \langle x, y \rangle \in \widetilde{\mathcal{A}}(s \times t), \widetilde{\mathcal{A}}_f(x, y) = \mathfrak{t}$ if either $x \in S$ and $y \in T$, or $x \notin S, y \notin T$ and $\mathcal{A}_R(x, y) = \top$; otherwise $\widetilde{\mathcal{A}}_f(x, y) = \mathfrak{f}$.

The transformation from $\mathcal{A}$ to $\widetilde{\mathcal{A}}$ is obviously polynomial, and invariant: given Σ-algebras $\mathcal{A}, \mathcal{B}$ (and $\widetilde{\mathcal{B}}$ is constructed with sets S', T' and elements $\mathfrak{t}', \mathfrak{f}'$), any Σ-isomorphism $\sigma : \mathcal{A} \cong \mathcal{B}$ can be extended by $\mathfrak{t}^\sigma = \mathfrak{t}', \mathfrak{f}^\sigma = \mathfrak{f}'$, by any bijection from S to S' and from T to T').

R	a'	b'
a	$\bot$	$\top$
b	$\bot$	$\bot$

f	a'	b'	c'	d'	e'
a	$\mathfrak{f}$	$\mathfrak{t}$	$\mathfrak{f}$	$\mathfrak{f}$	$\mathfrak{f}$
b	$\mathfrak{f}$	$\mathfrak{f}$	$\mathfrak{f}$	$\mathfrak{f}$	$\mathfrak{f}$
c	$\mathfrak{f}$	$\mathfrak{f}$	$\mathfrak{t}$	$\mathfrak{t}$	$\mathfrak{t}$
d	$\mathfrak{f}$	$\mathfrak{f}$	$\mathfrak{t}$	$\mathfrak{t}$	$\mathfrak{t}$
e	$\mathfrak{f}$	$\mathfrak{f}$	$\mathfrak{t}$	$\mathfrak{t}$	$\mathfrak{t}$

Fig. 5. From a $R : s \times t \to \mathbf{o}$ to a $f : s \times t \to u$, with $S = \{c, d, e\}, T = \{c', d', e'\}$

If $\sigma : \widetilde{\mathcal{A}} \cong \widetilde{\mathcal{B}}$, we have $\{\mathfrak{t}^\sigma, \mathfrak{f}^\sigma\} = \{\mathfrak{t}', \mathfrak{f}'\}$ as above. Let $n = |\widetilde{\mathcal{A}}(s)|, m = |\widetilde{\mathcal{A}}(t)|$, we can view $\widetilde{\mathcal{A}}_f$ as a (n, m)-matrix; it clearly contains a sub-matrix uniformly equal to $\mathfrak{t}$ (this is $(\widetilde{\mathcal{A}}_f)_{|S \times T}$), hence the (n, m)-matrix $\widetilde{\mathcal{B}}_f$ contains a $(|S|, |T|)$-matrix uniformly equal to $\mathfrak{t}^\sigma$, and also a $(|S'|, |T'|)$-matrix uniformly equal to $\mathfrak{t}'$. Since $|S'| = |S| > n/2$ and $|T'| = |T| > m/2$, these sub-matrices have to intersect, hence $\mathfrak{t}^\sigma = \mathfrak{t}'$, and $\mathfrak{f}^\sigma = \mathfrak{f}'$ hold.

Suppose there is an $x \in S$ such that $x^\sigma \notin S'$, then $\forall y \in T, \widetilde{\mathcal{B}}_f(x^\sigma, y^\sigma) = \widetilde{\mathcal{A}}_f(x, y)^\sigma = \mathfrak{t}'$, hence $y^\sigma \notin T'$. Therefore $B^\sigma \cap T' = \emptyset$, hence $B^\sigma \subseteq \mathcal{B}(s)$, which is impossible since $|T^\sigma| = |T| = |T'| > |\mathcal{B}(s)|$. We conclude that $\forall x \in S, x^\sigma \in S'$, hence $\mathcal{A}(s)^\sigma = \mathcal{B}(s)$, and similarly $\mathcal{A}(t)^\sigma = \mathcal{B}(t)$, and we easily obtain $\sigma : \mathcal{A} \cong \mathcal{B}$, which proves that the transformation is fair. This proof holds if $s = t$ by taking $S = T$.

Theorem 2. *If Σ is a non-monadic signature, then* $\mathbf{I}(\Sigma)$ *is isomorphism complete.*

Proof. Σ contains a f such that Σ_f is not monadic. Let $r = \operatorname{rng} \Sigma_f$, s, t the last two sorts in $\operatorname{dom} \Sigma_f$ (we may have $s = t$), and $\tau = s \times t \to r$, by successive applications of lemma 2 we obtain $\mathbf{I}(\lceil\tau\rceil) \propto_P \mathbf{I}(\lceil\Sigma_f\rceil)$. By theorem 1, we also have $\mathbf{I}(\lceil\Sigma_f\rceil) \propto_P \mathbf{I}(\Sigma)$.

If $r = \mathbf{o}$, lemma 4 yields $\mathbf{GI} \propto_P \mathbf{I}(\lceil\tau\rceil)$. If r is a sort, we have three different cases. If $r \notin \{s,t\}$, we also use lemma 7 to get $\mathbf{GI} \propto_P \mathbf{I}(\lceil\tau\rceil)$, if $r = s = t$, we use lemma 5, and if $r \in \{s,t\}$ with $s \neq t$, we use lemma 6 to get the same result. We therefore have $\mathbf{GI} \propto_P \mathbf{I}(\lceil\tau\rceil) \propto_P \mathbf{I}(\lceil\Sigma_f\rceil) \propto_P \mathbf{I}(\Sigma) \propto_P \mathbf{GI}$ (this last fact is well-known, see e.g. [3] [4]).

4 Hard Monadic Signatures

In this section and the next we only consider monadic signatures. From now on, the term "monadic functions" refers to function symbols which are not predicate symbols. We will prove that the complexity of binary relations can be simulated by pairs of well chosen monadic functions. The criterion for a pair of functions to have this property is purely syntactic: they should have the same domain sort. In graph theoretic language, this means that this domain sort s, as a vertex of G_Σ, has an output degree (number of edges out of s, noted $\mathrm{d}^+(s)$) at least 2. We start with the case where these monadic functions have different domain and range sorts.

Lemma 8.

$$\mathbf{I}(\lceil t \times u \to \mathbf{o}\rceil) \propto_P \mathbf{I}(\lceil s \to t, s \to u\rceil)$$
$$\mathbf{I}(\lceil t \times t \to \mathbf{o}\rceil) \propto_P \mathbf{I}(\lceil s \to t, s \to t\rceil)$$

Proof. Let Σ be the signature with the unique symbol R and $\Sigma_R = t \times u \to \mathbf{o}$, and Σ' with only the symbols f, g and $\Sigma'_f = s \to t$ and $\Sigma'_g = s \to u$. To any Σ-algebra $\mathcal{A}$ we associate the Σ'-algebra $\widetilde{\mathcal{A}}$ defined by (see figure 6):

- $\widetilde{\mathcal{A}}(t) = \mathcal{A}(t), \widetilde{\mathcal{A}}(u) = \mathcal{A}(u)$,
- $\widetilde{\mathcal{A}}(s) = \{\langle x,y\rangle \in \mathcal{A}(t \times u) / \mathcal{A}_R(x,y) = \top\}$,
- $\forall \langle x,y\rangle \in \widetilde{\mathcal{A}}(s), \widetilde{\mathcal{A}}_f(\langle x,y\rangle) = x$ and $\widetilde{\mathcal{A}}_g(\langle x,y\rangle) = y$.

If $\sigma : \mathcal{A} \cong \mathcal{B}$, we extend σ to all $\langle x,y\rangle \in \widetilde{\mathcal{A}}(s)$ by $\langle x,y\rangle^\sigma = \langle x^\sigma, y^\sigma\rangle$. Since $\forall \langle x,y\rangle \in \mathcal{A}(t \times u)$, we have $\langle x,y\rangle \in \widetilde{\mathcal{A}}(s)$ iff $\mathcal{A}_R(x,y) = \top$ iff $\mathcal{B}_R(x^\sigma, y^\sigma) = \top$ iff $\langle x^\sigma, y^\sigma\rangle = \langle x,y\rangle^\sigma \in \widetilde{\mathcal{B}}(s)$, then σ is clearly 1-1 from $\widetilde{\mathcal{A}}(s)$ onto $\widetilde{\mathcal{B}}(s)$. We also have $\forall \langle x,y\rangle \in \widetilde{\mathcal{A}}(s), \widetilde{\mathcal{A}}_f(\langle x,y\rangle)^\sigma = x^\sigma = \widetilde{\mathcal{B}}_f(\langle x,y\rangle^\sigma)$, and similarly for g, hence $\sigma : \widetilde{\mathcal{A}} \cong \widetilde{\mathcal{B}}$.

If $\sigma : \widetilde{\mathcal{A}} \cong \widetilde{\mathcal{B}}$, then $\forall \langle x,y\rangle \in \widetilde{\mathcal{A}}(s)$, we have $\widetilde{\mathcal{B}}_f(\langle x,y\rangle^\sigma) = \widetilde{\mathcal{A}}_f(\langle x,y\rangle)^\sigma = x^\sigma$, and $\widetilde{\mathcal{B}}_g(\langle x,y\rangle^\sigma) = y^\sigma$, hence $\langle x,y\rangle^\sigma = \langle x^\sigma, y^\sigma\rangle$. Then $\forall \langle x,y\rangle \in \mathcal{A}(t \times u)$, we have $\mathcal{A}_R(x,y) = \top$ iff $\langle x,y\rangle \in \widetilde{\mathcal{A}}(s)$ iff $\langle x,y\rangle^\sigma \in \widetilde{\mathcal{B}}(s)$ iff $\mathcal{B}_R(x^\sigma, y^\sigma) = \top$, hence $\sigma : \mathcal{A} \cong \mathcal{B}$. The transformation is therefore fair, and it is trivially polynomial. This proof holds if $t = u$.

R	a'	b'
a	$\bot$	$\top$
b	$\top$	$\top$

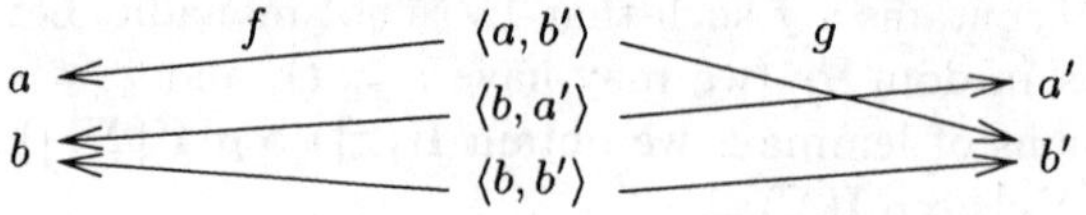

Fig. 6. From a $R : t \times u \to \mathbf{o}$ to a $f : s \to t, g : s \to u$

We now turn to the case where monadic functions have the same domain and range sort, which is more difficult than the previous one since we somehow have to "mix" in one set both the domain and the range of a function.

Lemma 9.

$$\mathbf{I}(\lceil s \times s \to \mathbf{o} \rceil) \propto_P \mathbf{I}(\lceil t \to t, t \to u \rceil)$$
$$\mathbf{I}(\lceil s \times s \to \mathbf{o} \rceil) \propto_P \mathbf{I}(\lceil t \to t, t \to t \rceil)$$

Proof. Let Σ be the signature with the unique symbol R and $\Sigma_R = s \times s \to \mathbf{o}$, and Σ' with only the symbols f, g and $\Sigma'_f = t \to t$ and $\Sigma'_g = t \to u$. To any Σ-algebra $\mathcal{A}$ we associate the Σ'-algebra $\widetilde{\mathcal{A}}$ defined by (see figure 7):

- $\widetilde{\mathcal{A}}(t) = \{\langle x, t \rangle / x \in \mathcal{A}(s)\} \uplus \{\langle y, z, t \rangle / y, z \in \mathcal{A}(s), \mathcal{A}_R(y, z) = \top\}$,
- $\widetilde{\mathcal{A}}(u) = \{\langle x, u \rangle / x \in \mathcal{A}(s)\} \uplus \{\langle y, z, u \rangle / y, z \in \mathcal{A}(s), \mathcal{A}_R(y, z) = \top\}$,
- $\forall \langle x, t \rangle \in \widetilde{\mathcal{A}}(t), \widetilde{\mathcal{A}}_f(\langle x, t \rangle) = \langle x, t \rangle$ and $\widetilde{\mathcal{A}}_g(\langle x, t \rangle) = \langle x, u \rangle$,
- $\forall \langle y, z, t \rangle \in \widetilde{\mathcal{A}}(t), \widetilde{\mathcal{A}}_f(\langle y, z, t \rangle) = \langle y, t \rangle$ and $\widetilde{\mathcal{A}}_g(\langle y, z, t \rangle) = \langle z, u \rangle$.

Remark that $\widetilde{\mathcal{A}}(t) \cap \widetilde{\mathcal{A}}(u) = \emptyset$ and $t = u \Rightarrow \widetilde{\mathcal{A}}(t) = \widetilde{\mathcal{A}}(u)$.

R	a	b
a	$\bot$	$\top$
b	$\top$	$\top$

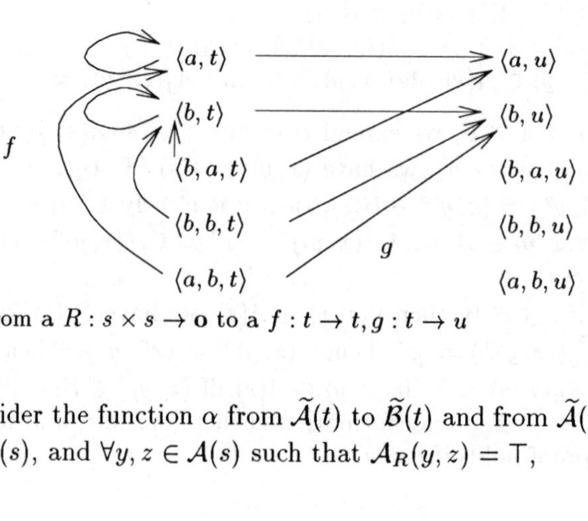

Fig. 7. From a $R : s \times s \to \mathbf{o}$ to a $f : t \to t, g : t \to u$

If $\sigma : \mathcal{A} \cong \mathcal{B}$, we consider the function α from $\widetilde{\mathcal{A}}(t)$ to $\widetilde{\mathcal{B}}(t)$ and from $\widetilde{\mathcal{A}}(u)$ to $\widetilde{\mathcal{B}}(u)$ defined by: $\forall x \in \mathcal{A}(s)$, and $\forall y, z \in \mathcal{A}(s)$ such that $\mathcal{A}_R(y, z) = \top$,

- $\langle x, t\rangle^\alpha = \langle x^\sigma, t\rangle$,
- $\langle y, z, t\rangle^\alpha = \langle y^\sigma, z^\sigma, t\rangle$,
- $\langle x, u\rangle^\alpha = \langle x^\sigma, u\rangle$,
- $\langle y, z, u\rangle^\alpha = \langle y^\sigma, z^\sigma, u\rangle$.

Since $\forall x \in \mathcal{A}(s)$, we have $\langle x, t\rangle \in \widetilde{\mathcal{A}}(t)$ iff $x \in \mathcal{A}(s)$ iff $x^\sigma \in \mathcal{B}(s)$ iff $\langle x^\sigma, t\rangle = \langle x, t\rangle^\alpha \in \widetilde{\mathcal{B}}(t)$; and $\forall y, z \in \mathcal{A}(s)$, we have $\langle y, z, t\rangle \in \widetilde{\mathcal{A}}(t)$ iff $\mathcal{A}_R(y, z) = \top$ iff $\mathcal{B}_R(y^\sigma, z^\sigma) = \top$ iff $\langle y^\sigma, z^\sigma, t\rangle = \langle y, z, t\rangle^\alpha \in \widetilde{\mathcal{B}}(t)$, then α is 1-1 from $\widetilde{\mathcal{A}}(t)$ onto $\widetilde{\mathcal{B}}(t)$, and similarly 1-1 from $\widetilde{\mathcal{A}}(u)$ onto $\widetilde{\mathcal{B}}(u)$.

By definition of $\alpha, \widetilde{\mathcal{A}}_f$ and $\widetilde{\mathcal{B}}_f$ we have $\forall x \in \mathcal{A}(s), \widetilde{\mathcal{A}}_f(\langle x, t\rangle)^\alpha = \langle x, t\rangle^\alpha = \langle x^\sigma, t\rangle = \widetilde{\mathcal{B}}_f(\langle x^\sigma, t\rangle) = \widetilde{\mathcal{B}}_f(\langle x, t\rangle^\alpha)$ and $\forall \langle y, z, t\rangle \in \widetilde{\mathcal{A}}(t), \widetilde{\mathcal{A}}_f(\langle y, z, t\rangle)^\alpha = \langle y, t\rangle^\alpha = \langle y^\sigma, t\rangle = \widetilde{\mathcal{B}}_f(\langle y^\sigma, z^\sigma, t\rangle) = \widetilde{\mathcal{B}}_f(\langle y, z, t\rangle^\alpha)$. Similarly, by definition of $\alpha, \widetilde{\mathcal{A}}_g$ and $\widetilde{\mathcal{B}}_g$ we have $\forall x \in \mathcal{A}(s), \widetilde{\mathcal{A}}_g(\langle x, t\rangle)^\alpha = \langle x, u\rangle^\alpha = \langle x^\sigma, u\rangle = \widetilde{\mathcal{B}}_g(\langle x^\sigma, t\rangle) = \widetilde{\mathcal{B}}_g(\langle x, t\rangle^\alpha)$, and $\forall \langle y, z, t\rangle \in \widetilde{\mathcal{A}}(t), \widetilde{\mathcal{A}}_g(\langle y, z, t\rangle)^\alpha = \langle z, u\rangle^\alpha = \langle z^\sigma, u\rangle = \widetilde{\mathcal{B}}_g(\langle y^\sigma, z^\sigma, t\rangle) = \widetilde{\mathcal{B}}_g(\langle y, z, t\rangle^\alpha)$. We conclude that $\alpha : \widetilde{\mathcal{A}} \cong \widetilde{\mathcal{B}}$, and that the transformation is invariant.

Conversely, if $\alpha : \widetilde{\mathcal{A}} \cong \widetilde{\mathcal{B}}$, then $\forall x \in \mathcal{A}(s), \widetilde{\mathcal{B}}_f(\langle x, t\rangle^\alpha) = \widetilde{\mathcal{A}}_f(\langle x, t\rangle)^\alpha = \langle x, t\rangle^\alpha$, i.e. $\langle x, t\rangle^\alpha$ is a fix point of $\widetilde{\mathcal{B}}_f$, hence is of the form $\langle y, t\rangle$, with $y \in \mathcal{B}(s)$, and this y is unique (for α is 1-1); this defines a function σ from $\mathcal{A}(s)$ to $\mathcal{B}(s)$. We also have $\forall \langle y, z, t\rangle \in \mathcal{A}(s), \widetilde{\mathcal{B}}_f(\langle y, z, t\rangle^\alpha) = \widetilde{\mathcal{A}}_f(\langle y, z, t\rangle)^\alpha = \langle y, t\rangle^\alpha$, hence $\langle y, z, t\rangle^\alpha$ is not a fixpoint of $\widetilde{\mathcal{B}}_f$, and should therefore be of the form $\langle y', z', t\rangle$. Since α is 1-1 from $\widetilde{\mathcal{A}}(t)$ onto $\widetilde{\mathcal{B}}(t)$, it is therefore also 1-1 form $\{\langle x, t\rangle / x \in \mathcal{A}(s)\}$ onto $\{\langle y, t\rangle / y \in \mathcal{B}(s)\}$, hence σ is also 1-1 from $\mathcal{A}(s)$ onto $\mathcal{B}(s)$.

$\forall x \in \mathcal{A}(s)$, since $x^\sigma \in \mathcal{B}(s)$, we have $\widetilde{\mathcal{B}}_g(\langle x^\sigma, t\rangle) = \langle x^\sigma, u\rangle$, and by definition of σ we have $\langle x^\sigma, t\rangle = \langle x, t\rangle^\alpha$, hence by isomorphism $\langle x^\sigma, u\rangle = \widetilde{\mathcal{A}}_g(\langle x, t\rangle)^\alpha = \langle x, u\rangle^\alpha$. We therefore have $\forall \langle y, z, t\rangle \in \widetilde{\mathcal{A}}(t), \widetilde{\mathcal{B}}_g(\langle y, z, t\rangle^\alpha) = \widetilde{\mathcal{A}}_g(\langle y, z, t\rangle)^\alpha = \langle z, u\rangle^\alpha = \langle z^\sigma, u\rangle$, while $\widetilde{\mathcal{B}}_f(\langle y, z, t\rangle^\alpha) = \langle y, t\rangle^\alpha = \langle y^\sigma, t\rangle$ has been established above. We know that $\langle y, z, t\rangle^\alpha$ is of the form $\langle y', z', t\rangle$, hence by definition of $\widetilde{\mathcal{B}}_f$ and $\widetilde{\mathcal{B}}_g$ we get $y' = y^\sigma$ and $z' = z^\sigma$.

We conclude that $\forall y, z \in \mathcal{A}(s), \mathcal{A}(y, z) = \top$ iff $\langle y, z, t\rangle \in \widetilde{\mathcal{A}}(t)$ iff $\langle y, z, t\rangle^\alpha = \langle y^\sigma, z^\sigma, t\rangle \in \widetilde{\mathcal{B}}(t)$ iff $\mathcal{B}(y^\sigma, z^\sigma) = \top$, hence that $\sigma : \mathcal{A} \cong \mathcal{B}$. Hence the transformation is fair, and trivially polynomial. This proof holds if $t = u$.

Theorem 3. *If Σ is a monadic signature such that* $\mathrm{d}^+(G_\Sigma) > 1$ *then* $\mathbf{I}(\Sigma)$ *is isomorphism complete.*

Proof. If $\mathrm{d}^+(G_\Sigma) > 1$, then $\exists s \in \mathcal{S}, \exists f, g \in \Sigma$ such that $\mathrm{dom}\, f = \mathrm{dom}\, g = s$. If $\mathrm{rng}\, f = s$ or $\mathrm{rng}\, g = s$, we use lemma 9, otherwise lemma 8, and we get $\mathbf{GI} \propto_P \mathbf{I}(\lceil \Sigma_f, \Sigma_g \rceil)$ (together with lemma 4). We then proceed as in theorem 2.

5 Easy Monadic Signatures

We now prove that the isomorphism problem for all other signatures, i.e. monadic such that G_Σ has output degree at most one, is polynomial. We first provide the simplest possible representation of the corresponding algebras.

Definition 3. *A graph $G = \langle V, E\rangle$ is a* partial function graph *(or PFG), if E is the graph of a partial function from V to V. A* labeled PFG *(or LPFG), is a vertex-labeled graph whose underlying graph is a PFG. The isomorphism problem between LPFG's is noted* **LPFGI**.

Lemma 10. *If Σ is monadic and $\mathrm{d}^+(G_\Sigma) \le 1$ then $\mathbf{I}(\Sigma) \propto_P$* **LPFGI**.

Proof. We transform Σ-algebras $\mathcal{A}$ into graphs. $\forall s \in \mathcal{S}$, let $\mathcal{P}_s$ be the set of predicate symbols of type $s \to \mathbf{o}$ in Σ, and $\forall x \in \mathcal{A}(s)$, let

$$\mathcal{P}_\mathcal{A}(x) = \{P \in \mathcal{P}_s / \mathcal{A}_P(x) = \top\} \text{ and } \mathcal{C}_\mathcal{A}(x) = \{c \in \Sigma / \Sigma_c = s \text{ and } \mathcal{A}_c = x\}.$$

To any $s \in \mathcal{S}$ and $x \in \mathcal{A}(s)$ we associate a different vertex $v(s,x)$ labeled by $\langle s, \mathcal{P}_\mathcal{A}(x), \mathcal{C}_\mathcal{A}(x)\rangle$. To any function symbol $f \in \Sigma$, say $\Sigma_f = s \to t$ (with possibly $s = t$), and any $x \in \mathcal{A}(s)$ we associate the directed edge $\langle v(s,x), v(t, \mathcal{A}_f(x))\rangle$ (see figure 8), thus constructing a labeled directed graph $U_\mathcal{A}$, called the *underlying graph* of $\mathcal{A}$. Remark that $\forall s \in \mathcal{S}, \forall x \in \mathcal{A}(s)$, there is at most one $f \in \Sigma$ such that $\operatorname{dom} f = s$, hence there is at most one edge out of $v(s,x)$. Hence the graph $U_\mathcal{A}$ is a LPFG. The transformation from $\mathcal{A}$ to $U_\mathcal{A}$ is polynomial.

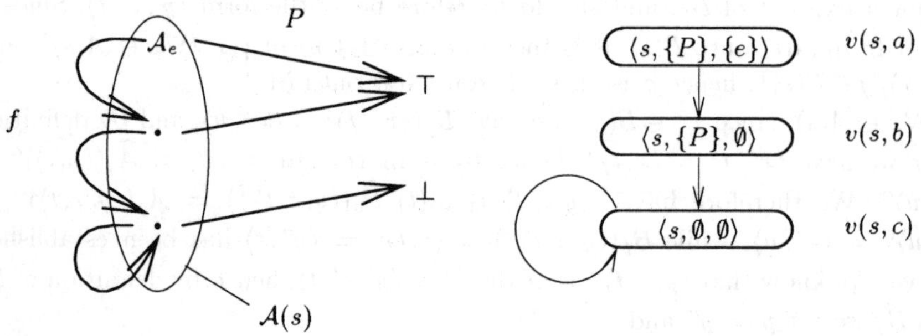

Fig. 8. An algebra $\mathcal{A}$ and the corresponding $U_\mathcal{A}$, with $f : s \to s, P : s \to \mathbf{o}, e : s$

We now consider two Σ-algebras $\mathcal{A}, \mathcal{B}$ and their underlying graphs $U_\mathcal{A}$ and $U_\mathcal{B}$ (where $U_\mathcal{B}$ is constructed as above with vertices $v'(s,x)$), and we first prove that the transformation is invariant.

If $\sigma : \mathcal{A} \cong \mathcal{B}$, let α be defined by $\forall s \in \mathcal{S}, \forall x \in \mathcal{A}(s), v(s,x)^\alpha = v'(s, x^\sigma)$, it preserves labels iff $\mathcal{P}_\mathcal{A}(x) = \mathcal{P}_\mathcal{B}(x^\sigma)$ and $\mathcal{C}_\mathcal{A}(x) = \mathcal{C}_\mathcal{B}(x^\sigma)$, which is obvious since $\forall P \in \mathcal{P}_s, \mathcal{B}_P(x) = \mathcal{A}_P(x^\sigma)$ and $\forall c \in \Sigma, c \in \mathcal{C}_\mathcal{A}(x)$ iff $\mathcal{A}_c = x$ iff $\mathcal{B}_c = \mathcal{A}_c^\sigma = x^\sigma$ iff $c \in \mathcal{C}_\mathcal{B}(x^\sigma)$. Edges are also preserved by α, since $\langle v(s,x), v(t, \mathcal{A}_f(x))\rangle^\alpha = \langle v(s, x^\sigma), v(t, \mathcal{B}_f(x^\sigma))\rangle$ is an edge of $U_\mathcal{B}$, hence $\alpha : U_\mathcal{A} \cong U_\mathcal{B}$.

Conversely, if $\alpha : U_\mathcal{A} \cong U_\mathcal{B}$, then $\forall s \in \mathcal{S}, \forall x \in \mathcal{A}(s)$, by the preservation of labels there is a unique $y \in \mathcal{B}(s)$ such that $v(s,x)^\alpha = v'(s,y)$, and we note it x^σ.

For any $f \in \sigma$, say $\Sigma_f = s \to t$, then $\forall x \in \mathcal{A}(s)$, the unique edge out of $v(s,x)^\alpha$ should be the image of the unique edge out of $v(s,x)$, i.e. $\langle v(s,x), v(t, \mathcal{A}_f(x))\rangle^\alpha = \langle v'(s,x^\sigma), v'(t, \mathcal{B}_f(x^\sigma))\rangle$, hence $\mathcal{A}_f(x)^\sigma = \mathcal{B}_f(x^\sigma)$. Moreover, for any $P \in \Sigma$, say $\Sigma_P = s \to \mathbf{o}$, then $\forall x \in \mathcal{A}(s)$, we have $\mathcal{A}_P(x) = \top$ iff $P \in \mathcal{P}_\mathcal{A}(x)$, part of the label of $v(s,x)$, iff (by the preservation of labels) $P \in \mathcal{P}_\mathcal{B}(x^\sigma)$, part of the label of $v'(s,x^\sigma)$, iff $\mathcal{B}_P(x^\sigma) = \top$. Similarly, for any $c \in \Sigma$, let $x = \mathcal{A}_c$ and $s = \Sigma_c$, we have $c \in \mathcal{C}_\mathcal{A}(x)$, part of the label of $v(s,x)$, hence $c \in \mathcal{C}_\mathcal{B}(x^\sigma)$, part of the label of $v'(s,x^\sigma)$, hence $\mathcal{B}_c = x^\sigma = \mathcal{A}_c^\sigma$. Hence $\sigma : \mathcal{A} \cong \mathcal{B}$.

Remark that not all LPFG's correspond to Σ-algebras, since the structure of labels is a special one. The following proof analyses the structure of PFG's, hence gives good insight into the structure of "simple" algebras.

Lemma 11. *The problem* **LPFGI** *is polynomial.*

Proof. Since testing the isomorphism of two graphs with n connex components each requires $O(n^2)$ tests of isomorphisms between connex components, we may only consider connex LPFG's. In such a graph $G = \langle V, E\rangle$, there is at least one undirected path between two vertices v_1, v_2. If $d^+(v_1) = d^+(v_2) = 0$, then such a path must contain a third vertex v with $d^+(v) \geq 2$, which is impossible. Hence there is at most one vertex r with $d^+(r) = 0$. If there is such a r, then the number of vertices exceeds the number of edges by one, hence G is a tree, with edges directed to the root r.

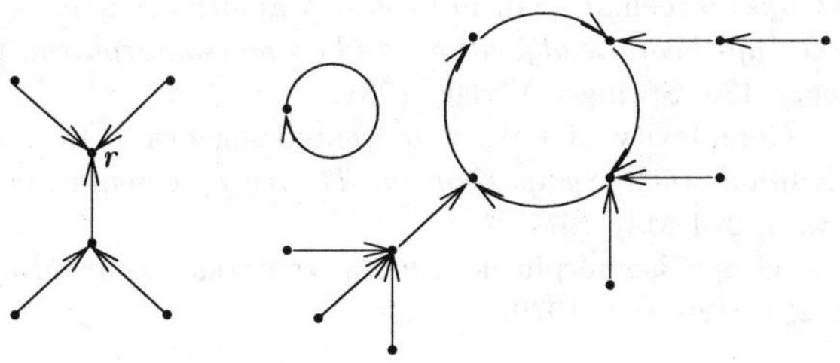

Fig. 9. Example of a PFG

If there is no root in G, i.e. $\forall v \in V, d^+(v) = 1$. Let $v_0 \in V$, and $\forall i \in \mathbb{N}, v_{i+1}$ is the unique vertex such that $\langle v_i, v_{i+1}\rangle \in E$. Since V is finite, $\exists i, j, i < j$ and $v_i = v_j$, hence G contains a cycle, of length $c = j - i$. By removing one edge from the cycle we obtain a connex LPFG with a root, hence a tree, which proves that G is a cycle of trees (figure 9).

It is clear that testing the isomorphism of two cycles of c labeled trees requires at most $O(c^2)$ tests of isomorphism between labeled trees, well-known to be polynomial.

Theorem 4. *If Σ is monadic and* $d^+(G_\Sigma) \leq 1$ *then* $\mathbf{I}(\Sigma)$ *is polynomial.*

Proof. This is a direct consequence of lemmas 10 and 11.

Therefore, if we agree that **GI** is not polynomial, we get the result that $\mathbf{I}(\Sigma)$ is not isomorphism complete only in the case that Σ is monadic and no two functions have the same domain sort. To state it differently, a finite Σ-algebra can fairly represent a graph if and only if either Σ is not monadic or contains at least two function symbols with the same domain. Remark that monadic predicates have no influence on $\mathbf{I}(\Sigma)$.

If we translate this result to standard first order signatures (without sorts), which is equivalent to the sorted case with $|S| = 1$, we get that $\mathbf{I}(\Sigma)$ is not isomorphism complete exactly when Σ is monadic *and* has at most one function symbol. In comparison, the sorted case has a much richer structure, since polynomial cases are obtained with any monadic Σ such that G_Σ is a PFG, and any PFG can be obtained as a G_Σ (more than once since atomic objects and monadic predicates are not represented in G_Σ). However, the PFG underlying a Σ-algebra $\mathcal{A}$ may not be any PFG, and is closely dependent on G_Σ. For instance, $U_\mathcal{A}$ may contain trees as connex components iff this is also the case of G_Σ. Hence our embedding of simple algebras into LPFG, though fair, is not an exact one.

References

1. M. Garey and D. S. Johnson. *Computers and intractability: a guide to the theory of* **NP**-*completeness.* Freeman, San Francisco, California, 1979.
2. C. Hoffmann. *Group-theoretic algorithms and graph isomorphism.* Lecture Notes in Computer Science 136. Springer Verlag, 1981.
3. Dexter Kozen. Complexity of finitely presented algebras. In *Conference Record of the Ninth Annual ACM Symposium on Theory of Computing*, pages 164–177, Boulder, Colorado, 2–4 May 1977.
4. Gary L. Miller. Graph isomorphism, general remarks. *Journal of Computer and System Sciences*, 18:128–142, 1979.

A Further and Effective Liberalization of the δ-Rule in Free Variable Semantic Tableaux

Domenico Cantone and Marianna Nicolosi Asmundo

Università di Catania, Dipartimento di Matematica
Viale A. Doria 6, I-95125 Catania, Italy
{cantone,nicolosi}@cs.unict.it

Abstract. In this paper, we present a further liberalization of the δ-rule in free variable semantic tableaux. It is effective in that (1) it is both a natural and intuitive liberalization, and (2) can reduce the proof size non elementarily as compared to previous versions of the δ-rule.

1 Introduction

Proof procedures for first-order predicate logic such as semantic tableaux need means to deal with existential quantifiers. In general there are two different ways to do this. One way is to Skolemize the formula to be proven in a pre-processing step, obtaining a purely universal formula at the expense of a richer signature. The other approach is not to use a preliminary Skolemization but to add a tableau expansion rule for treating the essentially existential formulae, so that Skolemization is performed during the proof construction when existential formulae are encountered on tableau branches. In substance, there is no difference in applying either of the two methods, but we believe that adding a rule for the existential formulae to the tableau expansion rules and eliminating the preliminary Skolemization phase makes the proof procedure more natural and is generally preferable.

In this paper we follow the second approach, presenting an expansion rule for existential formulae based on the global Skolemization technique described in [4] and [3]. The central idea of our method is to perform – during the proof – a "delayed" global Skolemization of the formula to be proven. This approach differs from the widespread "local" Skolemization technique in that the (infinitely many) Skolem function symbols for eliminating all existential quantifiers are introduced in a single shot.[1]

We will define a δ-rule going beyond existing δ-rules in the literature in that sense, which is able to reflect structural similarities in a natural way. This reduces the number of Skolem functors and of variables dependencies in the proofs.

[1] In [4] and [3] the possibility is contemplated to get rid of the universal quantifiers as well, returning a formula devoid of quantifiers.

R. Caferra and G. Salzer (Eds.): Automated Deduction, LNAI 1761, pp. 109–125, 2000.

2 Preliminaries

Before going into details, we introduce some notations and terminology.

2.1 Signatures and Languages

Let $\Sigma = (\mathcal{P}, \mathcal{F})$ be a *signature*, where $\mathcal{P}$ and $\mathcal{F}$ are countable collections of predicate and function symbols, respectively, and let *Var* be a fixed countable collection of individual variables. Then the *language* $\mathcal{L}_\Sigma$ is the collection of all first-order formulae involving besides the standard logical symbols, individual variables in *Var*, and predicate and function symbols of the signature Σ.

For any formula φ in the language $\mathcal{L}_\Sigma$, the collection of free variables occurring in φ is denoted by $\mathit{Free}(\varphi)$.

It is convenient to assume that the individual variables *Var* are arranged in a sequence $\ldots, x_{-2}, x_{-1}, x_0, x_1, x_2, \ldots$, and that two subsequences

- $\mathit{Var}^- = \{x_{-1}, x_{-2}, \ldots\}$ (to be used later for bound variables), and
- $\mathit{Var}^+ = \{x_0, x_1, x_2, \ldots\}$ (to be used later for free variables)

are singled out. Then by $\mathcal{L}_\Sigma^+$ we denote the collection $\{\varphi \in \mathcal{L}_\Sigma : \mathit{Free}(\varphi) \subseteq \mathit{Var}^+\}$.

Without loss of generality, we will assume in the following that no formula contains free occurrences of variables in Var^-.

Given a finite set $S \subseteq \mathit{Var}^+$, we denote by $\overrightarrow{S}$ the sequence of variables in S ordered by increasing index.

2.2 Structures and Assignments

A *structure* $\mathcal{M} = \langle \mathcal{D}, \mathcal{I} \rangle$ for a signature $\Sigma = (\mathcal{P}, \mathcal{F})$ consists of a domain $\mathcal{D}$ and of an interpretation $\mathcal{I}$ for the function and predicate symbols in Σ such that $P^\mathcal{I} : \mathcal{D}^{\mathrm{arity}(P)} \rightarrow \{\mathbf{true}, \mathbf{false}\}$, for every predicate symbol $P \in \mathcal{P}$, and $f^\mathcal{I} : \mathcal{D}^{\mathrm{arity}(f)} \rightarrow \mathcal{D}$, for every function symbol $f \in \mathcal{F}$.

An *assignment* A relative to a structure $\mathcal{M} = \langle \mathcal{D}, \mathcal{I} \rangle$ and to a language $\mathcal{L}_\Sigma$ is a mapping $A : \mathit{Var} \rightarrow \mathcal{D}$. An *$x$-variant* of an assignment A is an assignment A' such that $y^{A'} = y^A$, for every variable y different from x. We use the notation $A[x \leftarrow d]$ to denote the x-variant of A such that $x^A = d$, where $d \in \mathcal{D}$.

The notions of satisfiability and validity of a (set of) formula(e) are the standard ones. So, for instance, we write $(\mathcal{M}, A) \models \varphi$ to express that the formula φ is true when its predicate and function symbols are interpreted by $\mathcal{I}$, its free variables by A, and its logical symbols are interpreted in the classical way. In such a case we write also $\varphi^{\mathcal{I},A} = \mathbf{t}$. The notation $\mathcal{M} \models \varphi$ is used to indicate that $(\mathcal{M}, A) \models \varphi$, for every assignment A, whereas $\models \varphi$ denotes that $\mathcal{M} \models \varphi$, for every structure $\mathcal{M}$ over the signature of the language.

2.3 Unifying Notation

For the sake of simplicity we use Smullyan's unifying notation, which has the advantage of being compact, cutting down on the number of cases that must be considered. Smullyan divides the formulae of the language into four categories: conjunctive, disjunctive, universal, and existential formulae (called α-, β-, γ-, and δ-formulae, respectively). According to this notation, our interest is clearly devoted to δ-formulae.

Given a δ-formula δ, the notation $\delta_0(x)$ will be used to denote the formula φ, if δ is of the form $(\exists x)\varphi$, or $\neg\varphi$, if δ is of the form $\neg(\forall x)\varphi$. In any case, we will refer to $\delta_0(x)$ as *the instance of* δ and to x as *the quantified variable of* δ.

Likewise, for any γ-formula γ, $\gamma_0(x)$ denotes the formula φ of $\neg\varphi$, according to whether γ has the form $(\forall x)\varphi$ or $\neg(\exists x)\varphi$, respectively.

Let us define the complement operator $\mathtt{C}$ over a language $\mathcal{L}_\Sigma$:

$$\mathtt{C}(X) = \begin{cases} Z & \text{if } X = \neg Z \\ \neg X & \text{otherwise.} \end{cases}$$

Then to each α- and β-formula, one can associate two components, denoted respectively by α_1, α_2 and by β_1, β_2, in the following way.

α	α_1	α_2
$X \wedge Y$	X	Y
$\neg(X \vee Y)$	$\mathtt{C}(X)$	$\mathtt{C}(Y)$
$\neg(X \supset Y)$	X	$\mathtt{C}(Y)$

β	β_1	β_2
$X \vee Y$	X	Y
$\neg(X \wedge Y)$	$\mathtt{C}(X)$	$\mathtt{C}(Y)$
$(X \supset Y)$	$\mathtt{C}(X)$	Y

The following equivalences hold:

$$\models \alpha \equiv \alpha_1 \wedge \alpha_2 \qquad \models \beta \equiv \beta_1 \wedge \beta_2 \qquad \models \gamma \equiv (\forall x)\gamma_0(x) \qquad \models \delta \equiv (\exists x)\delta_0(x)\,.$$

2.4 Different Variants of the δ-Rule

As semantic tableaux have recently been subject of a renewed interest, many attempts have been made to optimize them. One of the main goals has been to obtain shorter proofs by means of strategies which restrict the search space.

An important rôle has been played by the δ-rule, which has gone through various liberalization phases since its introduction in [7].

We start with the original proviso of the δ-rule in the context of ground tableaux, where the signature has been enriched with a countable collection $\mathcal{C}$ of *new* parameters of arity 0, so that the introduction of an "uncommitted" (new) parameter is always guaranteed (thus preserving the soundness of the system). That leads to the following formulation:

$$\frac{\delta}{\delta_0(p)}\,, \tag{1}$$

where p is a new parameter not occurring in the branch to which the δ-rule is applied.

A first liberalization of (1), due to Smullyan, allows the same parameter p to be used more than once, provided that either it does not occur on the current branch, or the following conditions hold simultaneously (cf. [7]):

- p does not occur in δ;
- p has not been previously introduced by any application of the δ-rule;
- δ contains no parameter that has been introduced by a δ-rule.

Notice that such restrictions allow to use, when expanding δ-formulae, parameters already introduced by expansions of γ-formulae.

On the other hand, the γ-rule for ground tableaux causes problems in closing branches. In fact it is too liberal, as it allows to substitute the quantified variable with an *arbitrary* and *fixed* ground term. Since the choice of a term could be the wrong one, the γ-rule may need to be applied several times to the same formula.

A solution to this problem has been the introduction of *free variables* in semantic tableaux, in order to postpone the instantiation of terms until when more information is available. In this case, the signature needs to be extended with a collection $\mathcal{F}'$ of *new* function symbols containing countably many function symbols of any given arity.

Accordingly, in *free variable tableaux* the δ-rule has been modified as follows:

$$\frac{\delta}{\delta_0(f(x_1,\ldots,x_n))}\,, \tag{2}$$

where $x_1,\ldots,x_n$ are the free variables occurring on the branch to which the δ-rule is applied, and f is a new function symbol (cf. [5]).

Subsequently, Hähnle and Schmitt realized that the proviso in (2) is too strong and can be weakened by requiring that $x_1,\ldots,x_n$ *are the free variables occurring in* δ *and* f *is a new function symbol*, thus introducing the δ^+-rule (cf. [6]). Clearly, reducing the number of free variables in Skolem terms make the tableau system more efficient, as it allows a faster closure of the branches.

Beckert, Hähnle and Schmitt observed later that even the requirement that the Skolem function symbol must be new to the branch can be weakened, leading them to the introduction of the following δ^{+^+}-rule (cf. [2]):

$$\frac{\delta}{\delta_0(f_{[\delta]}(x_1,\ldots,x_n))}\,, \tag{3}$$

where $x_1,\ldots,x_n$ are the free variables occurring in δ and $f_{[\delta]}$ is a new function symbol assigned to the collection of formulae which are identical to δ up to variable renaming (including renaming of bound variables).

Finally, another variant of the δ-rule, which has been called δ^*-rule, has been introduced by Baaz and Fermüller in [1], leading to a non-elementary speedup with respect to previous variants of the δ-rule. It can be formulated as (3) but with the proviso that $x_1\ldots,x_n$ are the *relevant variables* occurring in δ. More specifically, one first defines for any formula φ, the set $Rel(\varphi,x)$ of free variables that *occur relevantly* w.r.t. a free variable x as follows:

- If $x \notin Free(\varphi)$, then $Rel(\varphi, x) = \emptyset$.

Otherwise:

- If φ is an atomic formula, then $Rel(\varphi, x) = Free(\varphi) \setminus \{x\}$.
- If $\varphi = \neg\psi$, then $Rel(\varphi, x) = Rel(\psi, x)$.
- If $\varphi = \psi_1 \vee \psi_2$ and $x \notin Free(\psi_i)$, with $i \in \{1, 2\}$, then $Rel(\varphi, x) = Rel(\psi_{2-i}, x)$. If $x \in Free(\psi_1) \cap Free(\psi_2)$, then $Rel(\varphi, x) = Free(\varphi) \setminus \{x\}$. (Similarly for $\varphi = \psi_1 \wedge \psi_2$ and $\varphi = \psi_1 \supset \psi_2$.)
- If $\varphi = (Qy)\psi$, then $Rel(\varphi, x) = Rel(\psi, x) \setminus \{y\}$, where the occurrence of Q is *strong* in the original formula;[2] otherwise $Rel(\varphi, x) = Free(\varphi) \setminus \{x\}$.

If δ is a δ-formula with quantified variable x, then the set of *relevant variables* of δ is defined as $Rel(\delta_0(x), x)$. Notice that in general, the relevant variables of a formula δ can be a proper subset of $Free(\delta)$.

3 A New Liberalization of the δ-Rule

The new liberalization of the δ-rule presented in this paper, called δ^{*^*}-rule, is based on the combination of (a recursive generalization of) the concept of relevant variables together with the notion of *key formulae* (adapted from [4]).

As we will show, the overall effect will be not only a general reduction on the number of variable dependencies in Skolem functions, but also a wider reusability of the same Skolem symbols, thus leading to shorter tableau proofs.

3.1 Canonical and Key Formulae

The notion of *key formulae* is of great importance to the technique of global Skolemization, as it characterizes the formulae in the language that need to be assigned their own Skolem function symbol. We will see that to each formula there corresponds a unique key formula.

Before going into details, we intuitively clarify the concept with some examples.

Example 1. Suppose that during the construction of a tableau, we need to expand the δ-formula $(\exists x)r(x, y)$. Application of either the δ^{++}- or the δ^*-rule would result in the formula $r(g(y), y)$, with g a new function symbol.

If later in the proof, we have to expand the formula $(\exists w)r(w, z)$, again both δ-rules would recognize that the same Skolem function symbol g introduced for $(\exists x)r(x, y)$ can be reused, since the two δ-formulae are identical up to variable renaming. Thus, the expansion results in the formula $r(g(z), z)$.

However, if we need to expand the δ-formula $(\exists x)r(x, k(z))$, then both δ-rules would introduce a new Skolem function symbol, say f, resulting in the formula $r(f(z), k(z))$, whereas the δ^{*^*}-rule would recognize that the same previously introduced Skolem symbol g can be reused again, as all three δ-formulae share the same key formula $r(x_0, x_1)$, thus yielding $r(g(k(z)), k(z))$. □

---

[2] We recall that in our context an existential quantifier occurrence is strong if it is positive and that a universal quantifier one is strong if it is negative.

Example 2. Let us suppose that the following formulae occur in a tableau proof:

$$(\exists x)p(x,y) \qquad (\exists w)p(w,f(f(z))) \qquad (\exists x)p(x,h(h(h(z))))\,.$$

If we apply any of the previous versions of the δ-rule (see [5], [6], [2] and [1]), then we have to assign a different Skolem function symbol to each of them. On the other hand, applying the δ^{*^*}-rule, the same Skolem function symbol can be reused, since all the above formulae share the same key formula $p(x_0, x_1)$. □

We now proceed to formally define the notion of key formulae. This definition is slightly different from the one given in [4] and [3], since now a key formula is allowed to contain quantifiers.

We first define the notion of *canonical formulae.*

Definition 1. *A formula φ is said to be* canonical *(with respect to the variable x_0) if:*

- *there is a $k \geq 0$ such that the bound variables of φ are $\{x_{-1}, \ldots, x_{-k}\}$, these appear in φ in the order $x_{-1}, \ldots, x_{-k}$ from left to right, and each of them is quantified only once (though may occur multiply);*
- *there is an $n \geq 0$ such that $Free(\varphi) \setminus \{x_0\} = \{x_1, \ldots, x_n\}$, these variables appear in φ in the order $x_1, \ldots, x_n$ from left to right, and each of them appears only once in φ.* □

Every formula φ can be canonized with respect to a designated variable x, in the sense that there exists a unique corresponding canonical formula $\hat{\varphi}$, such that φ and $\hat{\varphi}\sigma$ are equal up to renaming of bound variables, where σ is a substitution free for φ which maps variables into variables and such that $x\sigma = x_0$.

Example 3. The canonical formula φ_1 with respect to x corresponding to the formula

$$\varphi = (\exists y)(\exists z)(R(x, f(y), z, h(w,w)) \wedge Q(u,v))$$

is

$$\varphi_1 = (\exists x_{-1})(\exists x_{-2})(R(x_0, f(x_{-1}), x_{-2}, h(x_1, x_2)) \wedge Q(x_3, x_4))\ .$$

□

We define key formulae to be canonical formulae that are most general with respect to substitutions.

Definition 2. *A formula φ is said to be a* key formula *if*

- *it is canonical with respect to x_0, and*
- *for each canonical formula ψ, if there is a substitution σ which is free for $(\exists x_0)\psi$ and such that $\varphi = \psi\sigma_{x_0}$, then $\psi = \varphi$.*[3] □

[3] We recall that σ_{x_0} denotes the substitution which leaves x_0 unchanged and otherwise is equal to σ.

To any formula of the language there uniquely corresponds a key formula, as the following lemma states.

Lemma 1. *Let ψ be a formula in the language $\mathcal{L}_\Sigma^+$ and let $x_i \in Var^+$ be any variable. Then there exists a unique key formula φ, denoted by $Key(\psi, x_i)$, and a non-empty collection of substitutions free for φ, denoted by $SubstKey(\psi, x_i)$, such that for each $\sigma \in SubstKey(\psi, x_i)$ we have*

- *ψ and $\varphi\sigma$ are identical up to renaming of bound variables,*
- *$x_0\sigma = x_i$, and*
- *x_i does not occur in $x\sigma$ for $x \neq x_0$.*

Sketch of the proof. The following algorithm construct a key formula φ and a substitution σ which satisfy the conditions of the lemma.

1. Rename all bound variables in ψ by $x_{-1}, x_{-2}, \ldots$, going from left to right. Let ψ_1 be the resulting formula.
2. Locate in ψ_1 the leftmost term t_1 not containing x_i or any bound variable and continue the process until a term t_n is found such that there is no further term not containing x_i or any of the bound variables. Let $t_1, \ldots, t_n$ be the sequence of terms so obtained.
3. Let φ be the formula resulting from simultaneously substituting in ψ_1 the terms $x, t_1, \ldots, t_n$ by the variables $x_0, x_1, \ldots, x_n$, respectively, and let $\sigma = \{x_0/x, x_1/t_1, \ldots, x_n/t_n\}$.
4. Return φ and σ.

Uniqueness of φ can easily be shown. ■

Example 4. We continue from Example 3. The key formula with respect to x corresponding to

$$\varphi = (\exists y)(\exists z)(R(x, f(y), z, h(w, w)) \wedge Q(u, v))$$

is

$$\varphi_2 = (\exists x_{-1})(\exists x_{-2})(R(x_0, f(x_{-1}), x_{-2}, x_1) \wedge Q(x_2, x_3)) \ .$$

A substitution σ satisfying the conditions of the above lemma is

$$\sigma = \{x_0/x,\ x_1/h(w, w),\ x_2/u,\ x_3/v\} \ .$$

Notice that we have

$$\varphi_2\sigma = (\exists x_{-1})(\exists x_{-2})(R(x, f(x_{-1}), x_{-2}, h(w, w)) \wedge Q(u, v)) \ .$$

□

3.2 Relevant Extracted Formulae

In [1] the notion of *relevant variables* of a formula φ with respect to a free variable x is introduced, in order to reduce the number of arguments in Skolem function symbols (cf. the end of Section 2.4). One can go further by using a recursive definition of relevant variables. Instead, we define the notion of *relevant extracted formulae*, that not only allows to reduce the number of arguments in Skolem terms (and thus the number of variable dependencies) but also, in combination with the notion of key formulae, allows to generate the same Skolem symbols for existentially quantified formulae that differ only in *irrelevant* subformulae such as, for instance, the formulae $(\exists x)(p(x) \wedge q)$ and $(\exists x)(r \vee p(x))$.

For the purpose of simplifying the statement of the following definition, we introduce the concept of "empty formula", to be denoted by Λ. We do not bother to interpret Λ in any particular way. We only require that both $\neg\Lambda$ and $(Qy)\Lambda$, where Q stands for any quantifier, are to be considered as syntactic variations of Λ, and that $\Lambda \oplus \psi$, $\psi \oplus \Lambda$, where $\oplus$ stands for any binary connective, are to be considered as syntactic variations of ψ, for any formula ψ.

Definition 3. *Let φ be a formula, and let S be a set of variables. We define the* relevant extracted formula *for φ w.r.t. S, denoted by $RelF(\varphi, S)$, as follows*

- *if $Free(\varphi) \cap S = \emptyset$, then $RelF(\varphi, S) = \Lambda$,*
- *otherwise:*

$$RelF(\varphi, S) = \begin{cases} \varphi & \text{if } \varphi \text{ is a literal} \\ RelF(\psi, S) & \text{if } \varphi = \neg\neg\psi \\ RelF(\alpha_1, S) \wedge RelF(\alpha_2, S) & \text{if } \varphi = \alpha \\ RelF(\beta_1, S) \vee RelF(\beta_2, S) & \text{if } \varphi = \beta \\ (\exists y) RelF(\delta_0(y), S \cup \{y\}) & \text{if } \varphi = \delta \equiv (\exists y)\delta_0(y) \\ (\forall y) RelF(\gamma_0(y), S \cup \{y\}) & \text{if } \varphi = \gamma \equiv (\forall y)\gamma_0(y) \end{cases}$$

□

The following lemma, which can be proven by structural induction and some elementary metalogic manipulations, gives two properties of relevant extracted formulae which will be used in the soundness proof of the δ^{*^*}-rule.

Lemma 2. *Let φ be a formula of the language $\mathcal{L}^+_\Sigma$, let $S = \{y_1, \ldots, y_r\}$ be a set of variables, and let $\psi = RelF(\varphi, S)$. If $RelF(\varphi, S) \neq \Lambda$, then*

(a) $\models \varphi \supset \psi$
(b) $\models (\exists y_1) \ldots (\exists y_r)\varphi \supset (\forall y_1) \ldots (\forall y_r)(\psi \supset \varphi)$.

□

3.3 The δ^{*^*}-Rule

Let again $\Sigma = (\mathcal{P}, \mathcal{F})$ be a fixed countable signature and let $\bar{\mathcal{F}}$ be a collection of function symbols, disjoint from $\mathcal{F}$ and such that $\bar{\mathcal{F}}$ contains countably many function symbols for any arity (constants are considered as function symbols of arity 0).

Then, we can define by recursion an *injective* map

$$h : \mathcal{L}_{\bar{\Sigma}} \times Var \to \bar{\mathcal{F}} \ ,$$

where $\bar{\Sigma} = (\mathcal{P}, \mathcal{F} \cup \mathrm{Range}(h))$, such that $\mathrm{arity}(h_{\varphi,x}) = |Free(\varphi) \setminus \{x\}|$, for all φ in $\mathcal{L}_{\bar{\Sigma}}$ and x in Var.[4]

Now we have everything at hand to give the formal definition of our δ^{*^*}-rule.

[4] We will use the notation $h_{\varphi,x}$ to denote the function symbol $h(\varphi, x)$. Also, for convenience, we will write just h_φ in place of h_{φ,x_0}.

Definition 4. *Let δ be a δ-formula in the signature $\bar{\Sigma}$ not involving any free variable in Var^-, let $\varphi_1 = Key(\delta_0(x), x)$, and let $\sigma \in SubstKey(\delta_0(x), x)$, where x is the quantified variable of δ. Also, let $\varphi_2 = RelF(\varphi_1, \{x_0\})$, and let $S_{\varphi_2} = Free(\varphi_2) \setminus \{x_0\}$. Then the δ^{*^*}-rule can be schematically described as follows:*

$$\frac{\delta}{\delta_0(h_{\varphi_2}(\overrightarrow{S_{\varphi_2}})\sigma)} \quad \text{if } \varphi_2 \neq \Lambda. \qquad \frac{\delta}{\delta_0(x)} \quad \text{if } \varphi_2 = \Lambda. \tag{4}$$

□

Example 5. Application of the δ^{*^*}-rule to the formula $(\exists x)(p(x,y) \wedge r(z))$ yields $p(f_1(y), y) \wedge r(z)$. According to the notation in the above definition, we have

$$\begin{aligned}
\delta &= (\exists x)(p(x,y) \wedge r(z)) \\
\delta_0(x) &= p(x,y) \wedge r(z) \\
\varphi_1 &= Key(\delta_0(x), x) = p(x_0, x_1) \wedge r(x_2) \\
\sigma &= \{x_1/y, x_2/z\} \\
\varphi_2 &= RelF(\varphi_1, \{x_0\}) = p(x_0, x_1) \\
S_{\varphi_2} &= Free(\varphi_2) \setminus \{x_0\} = \{x_1\} \quad \text{(hence } S_{\varphi_2}\sigma = \{y\}\text{)} \\
h_{\varphi_2} &= f_1 \,.
\end{aligned}$$

□

By using the above δ^{*^*}-rule in tableau proofs of formulae of the language $\mathcal{L}^+_{\Sigma}$, only a sub-signature of $\bar{\Sigma}$ is actually needed. This can recursively be defined as follows. Let $\Sigma_0 = \Sigma$ and $\bar{\mathcal{F}}_0 = \mathcal{F}$, and put for each $i \geq 1$

$$\begin{aligned}
\bar{\mathcal{F}}_i = \{h_\varphi : \varphi = RelF(Key(\delta_0(x), x), \{x_0\}), &\text{for some } \delta\text{-formula } \delta \text{ in the} \\
&\text{language } \mathcal{L}^+_{\Sigma_{i-1}}, \text{ with quantified variable } x\} \setminus \textstyle\bigcup_{j=0}^{i-1} \bar{\mathcal{F}}_j \\
\Sigma_i = (\mathcal{P}, \textstyle\bigcup_{j=0}^{i} \bar{\mathcal{F}}_j) \,.
\end{aligned}$$

Then the sub-signature of $\bar{\Sigma}$ we are interested in is

$$\Sigma_\infty = (\mathcal{P}, \textstyle\bigcup_{j=0}^{\infty} \bar{\mathcal{F}}_j) \,. \tag{5}$$

If for any sentence φ in the language $\mathcal{L}^+$, we denote by k_φ the maximal nesting depth of positive occurrences of existential quantifiers and of negative occurrences of universal quantifiers in φ, then it can be seen that any δ^{*^*}-tableau proof of φ can be carried out in the signature Σ_{k_φ}.

It is useful to introduce the following notion of *rank* of a formula ψ in the language $\mathcal{L}^+_{\Sigma_\infty}$ by putting:

$$rank(\psi) =_{Def} \min\{k \in \mathbb{N} : \psi \text{ is in the language } \mathcal{L}^+_{\Sigma_k}\} \,.$$

3.4 Naturalness of the δ^{*^*}-Rule

All δ-formulae sharing the same basic structure are assigned the same Skolem function symbol by the δ^{*^*}-rule. This leads to a more natural way of reasoning (compared to previous versions of δ-rules), as one is able, in a very simple syntactic manner, to abstract from irrelevant parts and terms of formulae.

What we obtain is a natural way to perform Skolemization by keeping oneself closer to the general concept of function. The following example makes our point clearer.

Example 6. Let us assume that we have the following formula:

$$(\forall x)(\exists y)(x \cdot y = e),$$

which asserts the existence of an inverse for any element w.r.t. the operation "$\cdot$" and relative to the (identity) element e. If we have to expand this formula in a tableau system with the δ^{*^*}-rule, first we have to instantiate the universal formula obtaining:

$$(\exists y)(x_1 \cdot y = e).$$

Then, an application of the δ^{*^*}-rule yields:

$$x_1 \cdot i(x_1, e) = e.$$

Now let us assume that we encounter also the formula

$$(\forall x)(\exists y)((a \cdot x) \cdot y = e),$$

where a is a parameter. Then, after applying to it the γ-rule and the δ^{*^*}-rule, we obtain

$$(a \cdot x_1) \cdot i((a \cdot x_1), e) = e.$$

Notice that by reusing the same Skolem symbol i, we were able to abstract from the terms in the formula. □

4 Completeness and Soundness of the δ^{*^*}-Rule

Since the δ^{*^*}-rule is a liberalization of the δ-rule, it follows that completeness is trivially preserved and does not have to be proven.

The soundness proof can be conducted in the standard way, by showing that the satisfiability of a tableau is preserved during the application of tableaux expansion rules.

Tableau proofs are for statements of a first-order language over a signature Σ, but they are carried out in the extended signature Σ_∞ (cf. (5)).

Given a tableau $\mathcal{T}$ for a sentence in a first-order language $\mathcal{L}_\Sigma^+$, a branch θ of $\mathcal{T}$ is said to be satisfied by a structure $\mathcal{M}$ over $\mathcal{L}_{\Sigma_\infty}^+$, and we write $\mathcal{M} \models \theta$, if $\mathcal{M} \models X$, for each formula X occurring in θ. A tableau $\mathcal{T}$ is said to be satisfied by $\mathcal{M}$ if at least one of its branches is satisfied by $\mathcal{M}$, in which case we write $\mathcal{M} \models \mathcal{T}$. A tableau (resp. a branch) is said to be *satisfiable* if it is satisfied by some structure.

Next we show how to extend a structure $\mathcal{M} = \langle \mathcal{D}, \mathcal{I} \rangle$, over an initial signature $\Sigma = (\mathcal{P}, \mathcal{F})$, into a structure $\mathcal{M}_\infty$, over the limit signature $\Sigma_\infty = (\mathcal{P}, \bigcup_{j=0}^{\infty} \bar{\mathcal{F}}_j)$. We define recursively a sequence $\{\mathcal{M}_i\}_{i \in \mathbb{N}}$ of structures $\mathcal{M}_i = \langle \mathcal{D}, \mathcal{I}_i \rangle$, for each signature Σ_i, where $\Sigma_0 = \Sigma$, $\mathcal{M}_0 = \mathcal{M}$, and $\mathcal{I}_0 = \mathcal{I}$, as follows. Let $h_\varphi \in \bar{\mathcal{F}}_{n+1}$, where $\varphi = \mathit{RelF}(\mathit{Key}(\delta_0(x), x), \{x_0\})$, for some δ-formula δ in the language $\mathcal{L}^+_{\Sigma_n}$, with quantified variable x, and let $k = \text{arity}(h_\varphi)$. For any k-tuple $\mathbf{b} \in \mathcal{D}^k$ we define $h_\varphi(\mathbf{b})$ in the following way:

(a) if $(\mathcal{M}_n, A) \models (\exists x_0)\varphi$, for some assignment A s.t. $\overrightarrow{S}^A_\varphi = \mathbf{b}$, then we put

$$h_\varphi^{\mathcal{I}_{n+1}}(\mathbf{b}) =_{Def} c \ , \qquad (6)$$

for some $c \in \mathcal{D}$ such that $(\mathcal{M}_n, A[x_0 \leftarrow c]) \models \varphi$,

(b) otherwise we put

$$h_\varphi^{\mathcal{I}_{n+1}}(\mathbf{b}) =_{Def} d \ ,$$

for an arbitrary $d \in \mathcal{D}$.

Finally, we define $\mathcal{M}_\infty = \langle \mathcal{D}, \mathcal{I}_\infty \rangle$, where $\mathcal{I}_\infty|_{\mathcal{P}\cup\mathcal{F}} = \mathcal{I}_0|_{\mathcal{P}\cup\mathcal{F}}$, and $\mathcal{I}_\infty|_{\bar{\mathcal{F}}_n} = \mathcal{I}_n|_{\bar{\mathcal{F}}_n}$, for any $n \geq 1$.

By reasoning as in the cases of other variants of free-variable tableau systems, it can be proven that satisfiability of tableaux for sentences in the initial signature Σ is preserved by applications of propositional tableau rules and of the γ-rule (see for instance [5]). Thus we focus our attention only on the δ^{*^*}-rule.

Lemma 3. *Satisfiability of tableaux for sentences in the initial signature $\Sigma = (\mathcal{P}, \mathcal{F})$ is preserved by applications of the δ^{*^*}-rule.*

Proof. Let $\mathcal{T}$ be a satisfiable tableau for a sentence of $\mathcal{L}^+$. We show that satisfiability is preserved by applications of the δ^{*^*}-rule.

Let $\mathcal{M}' = \langle \mathcal{D}, \mathcal{I}' \rangle$ be a structure satisfying a branch θ of $\mathcal{T}$, and let δ be a δ-formula occurring in θ. Let $\varphi_1 = \mathit{Key}(\delta_0(x), x)$ and $\sigma \in \mathit{SubstKey}(\delta_0(x), x)$, where x is the quantified variable of δ. Also, let $\varphi_2 = \mathit{RelF}(\varphi_1, \{x_0\})$ and $S_{\varphi_2} = \mathit{Free}(\varphi_2) \setminus \{x_0\}$. Let us put

$$\psi = \begin{cases} \delta_0(h_{\varphi_2}(S_{\varphi_2})\sigma) & \text{if } \varphi_2 \neq \Lambda \\ \delta_0(x) & \text{if } \varphi_2 = \Lambda. \end{cases}$$

By applying the δ^{*^*}-rule to the formula δ, the new branch $\theta' = \theta; \psi$ is produced.

It is enough to prove that the branch θ' is satisfiable. In fact we will show that it is satisfied by the structure $\mathcal{M}_\infty = \langle \mathcal{D}, \mathcal{I}_\infty \rangle$ constructed over $\mathcal{M} = \langle \mathcal{D}, \mathcal{I} \rangle$, where $\mathcal{I} = \mathcal{I}'|_{\mathcal{P}\cup\mathcal{F}}$.

We proceed by induction on the length of θ'. Thus, as inductive hypothesis, we may assume that $\mathcal{M}_\infty \models \theta$. We show that $\mathcal{M}_\infty \models \psi$ and to this purpose we distinguish the following two cases:

Case $\varphi_2 \neq \Lambda$. Let $r = \mathit{rank}(\delta)$. By inductive hypothesis $\mathcal{M}_\infty \models \delta$, and since $\mathcal{I}_r$ and $\mathcal{I}_\infty$ coincide over the predicate and function symbols of δ we have $\mathcal{M}_r \models \delta$. Let A be an arbitrary assignment over the variables of $\mathcal{L}_{\Sigma_\infty}$. Then $(\mathcal{M}_r, A) \models \delta$ and therefore $(\mathcal{M}_r, A) \models (\exists x)\delta_0(x)$. Since $\varphi_1\sigma$ and $\delta_0(x)$ coincide up to renaming of bound variables, we have $(\mathcal{M}_r, A) \models (\exists x)(\varphi_1\sigma)$, so that $(\mathcal{M}_r, A') \models (\exists x_0)\varphi_1(x_0)$, where $A' = A[x \leftarrow (x\sigma)^A]_{x\in \mathit{Free}(\varphi_1)}$. But then, $(\mathcal{M}_r, A'') \models \varphi_1(x_0)$, for some x_0-variant A'' of A'. By Lemma 2(a), $(\mathcal{M}_r, A'') \models \varphi_2(x_0)$, so that $(\mathcal{M}_r, A') \models (\exists x_0)\varphi_2(x_0)$. From the definition of $h_{\varphi_2}^{\mathcal{I}_{r+1}}$ (cf. (6)), it then follows that $(\mathcal{M}_{r+1}, A') \models \varphi_2(h_{\varphi_2}(\overrightarrow{S}_{\varphi_2}))$. Since $(\mathcal{M}_r, A') \models (\exists x_0)\varphi_1(x_0)$, we have immediately $(\mathcal{M}_{r+1}, A') \models (\exists x_0)\varphi_1(x_0)$, which, by Lemma 2(b), implies $(\mathcal{M}_{r+1}, A') \models (\forall x_0)(\varphi_2(x_0) \supset \varphi_1(x_0))$. Hence $(\mathcal{M}_{r+1}, A'') \models \varphi_2(x_0) \supset \varphi_1(x_0)$, for every x_0-variant A'' of A'. In particular, by putting $\bar{A}'' = A'[x_0 \leftarrow h_{\varphi_2}^{\mathcal{I}_{r+1}}(\overrightarrow{S}_{\varphi_2}^{A'})]$, we have $(\mathcal{M}_{r+1}, \bar{A}'') \models \varphi_2(x_0) \supset \varphi_1(x_0)$, so that $(\mathcal{M}_{r+1}, A') \models \varphi_2(h_{\varphi_2}(\overrightarrow{S}_{\varphi_2})) \supset \varphi_1(h_{\varphi_2}(\overrightarrow{S}_{\varphi_2}))$. Hence $(\mathcal{M}_{r+1}, A') \models \varphi_1(h_{\varphi_2}(\overrightarrow{S}_{\varphi_2}))$. But then $(\mathcal{M}_{r+1}, A) \models (\varphi_1(h_{\varphi_2}(\overrightarrow{S}_{\varphi_2})))\sigma$, which in turn implies $(\mathcal{M}_{r+1}, A) \models \delta_0(h_{\varphi_2}(\overrightarrow{S}_{\varphi_2})\sigma)$. Since $\mathcal{I}_{r+1}$ and $\mathcal{I}_\infty$ coincide over the symbols of $\delta_0(h_{\varphi_2}(\overrightarrow{S}_{\varphi_2})\sigma)$ and A is an arbitrarily chosen assignment, we obtain $\mathcal{M}_{r+1} \models \psi$ and therefore $\mathcal{M}_\infty \models \psi$.

Case $\varphi_2 = \Lambda$. Let $r = \mathit{rank}(\delta)$. As above, given an arbitrary assignment A over the variables of $\mathcal{L}_{\Sigma_\infty}$, we have $(\mathcal{M}_r, A) \models (\exists x)\delta_0(x)$. Since $\varphi_2 = \Lambda$, the variable x_0 does not occur in φ_1, and therefore the variable x does not occur in $\delta_0(x)$. Hence, we have immediately that $\mathcal{M}_\infty \models \delta_0(x)$, namely $\mathcal{M}_\infty \models \psi$, since $\mathcal{I}_r$ and $\mathcal{I}_\infty$ coincide over the symbols of $\delta_0(x)$ and A is an arbitrarily chosen assignment. ■

The above discussion can be summarized in the following theorem.

Theorem 1 (Soundness and Completeness). *The free-variable tableau system with the δ^{*^*}-rule is sound and complete.* □

5 Complexity Issues

In the present section we discuss the δ^{*^*}-rule from a proof complexity point of view. We observe first that the computation of key formulae and relevant extracted formulae is not expensive, as it can be done in linear time. Moreover:

1. for every unsatisfiable formula φ, a shortest closed δ^{*^*}-tableau for φ is never longer than a shortest closed δ^*-tableau for φ;
2. adopting the δ^{*^*}-rule in place of previous variants of the δ-rule can lead to reductions in proof length.

The first point follows by noticing that a linear simulation of a δ^*-tableau by a δ^{*^*}-tableau is always possible. The second point will be addressed in the following subsection.

5.1 Comparing the δ^{*^*}-Rule to Other Versions

The δ^{*^*}-rule is able to reduce the number of different Skolem functors in the proof and the arities of the introduced Skolem terms and, as we stressed before, this fact has a favorable impact on proof length.

Let us consider first the following example which shows that by reducing the arities of the introduced Skolem terms (reduction of variable dependencies), it is possible to obtain shorter proofs:

Example 7. Let us suppose we have to prove the unsatisfiability of:

$$\varphi = (\forall y)((\exists x)(p(x) \wedge (\neg p(y) \wedge r(x)))) \ .$$

Using a tableau system based on any of the previous versions of δ-rule, we would obtain the following tableau:

$$\begin{array}{c} (\forall y)((\exists x)(p(x) \wedge (\neg p(y) \wedge r(x)))) \\ (\exists x)(p(x) \wedge (\neg p(x_1) \wedge r(x))) \\ p(f(x_1)) \wedge (\neg p(x_1) \wedge r(f(x_1))) \\ p(f(x_1)) \\ \neg p(x_1) \\ r(f(x_1)) \\ \vdots \end{array}$$

and another instantiation of the universal formula is needed to close the tableau.

On the other hand, in a tableau system with the δ^{*^*}-rule, we get the following shorter proof, where closure is obtained by means of the substitution $\sigma = \{x_1/c\}$:

$$\begin{array}{c} (\forall y)((\exists x)(p(x) \wedge (\neg p(y) \wedge r(x)))) \\ (\exists x)(p(x) \wedge (\neg p(x_1) \wedge r(x))) \\ p(c) \wedge (\neg p(x_1) \wedge r(c)) \\ p(c) \\ \neg p(x_1) \\ r(c) \\ \bot \end{array}$$

Notice that while expanding the δ-formula $(\exists x)(p(x) \wedge (\neg p(x_1) \wedge r(x)))$, we did not have to consider the free variable x_1 in the construction of the relative Skolem term, since $p(x_0) \wedge r(x_0)$ is its relevant extracted key formula (in other words, the part $\neg p(x_1)$ has been recognized as irrelevant). □

5.2 Exponential Speedup

In fact, using the δ^{*^*}-rule instead of the δ^*-rule can lead to exponentially shorter proofs.

Theorem 2. *There is a class of formulae $\{\varphi_n\}_{(n\geq 1)}$ such that, if $b^*(n)$ (resp. $b^{*^*}(n)$) is the number of branches of the shortest closed tableau for φ_n using the δ^*-rule (resp. δ^{*^*}-rule), then the shortest closed tableau for φ_n using the δ^*-rule has*

$$b^*(n) = \Theta(2^{b^{*^*}(n)})$$

branches.

Proof. We recursively define the following class of formulae:

$$\varphi_1 = \mathbf{false}$$
$$\varphi_n = (\forall x)(\forall y)(\varphi_{n-1} \lor [p_n(x,y) \land ((\forall v)(\exists z)(\neg p_n(z, f(v))) \lor (\forall w)(\exists z)(\neg p_n(z, f(f(w)))))])$$

for $n \geq 2$.

The theorem is then proven by showing that

1. $b^{*^*}(n) = \Theta(n)$ (i.e. $b^{*^*}(n)$ is linear in n),
2. $b^*(n) = \Theta(2^n)$ (i.e. $b^*(n)$ is exponential in n).

Intuitively, the reason for the different behavior of the δ^*- and the δ^{*^*}-rule on the above formula class is that the δ^{*^*}-rule uses *the same* Skolem function symbol h to Skolemize the two existential formulae in the second part of φ_n; therefore, a single copy of the literal $p_n(x_1, y_1)$ is sufficient to close the two branches that contain these existential formulae, and the closed tableau $\mathcal{T}_n^{*^*}$ for φ_n contains only *one* copy of $\mathcal{T}_{n-1}^{*^*}$. The δ^*-rule, on the other hand, introduces two *different* Skolem function symbols h and g. As a result, two instances $p_n(x_1, y_1)$ and $p_n(x_2, y_2)$ have to be generated; this, however, means that the closed tableau $\mathcal{T}_n^*$ for φ_n must contain *two* copies of $\mathcal{T}_{n-1}^*$.

$b^{*^*}(n)$ is linear in n. It is easy to see that the tableau $\mathcal{T}_n^{*^*}$ shown in Figure 1 is a smallest closed δ^{*^*}-tableau for φ_n. The number $b^{*^*}(n)$ of branches of $\mathcal{T}^{*^*}(n)$ satisfies the recurrence relation

$$b^{*^*}(n) = b^{*^*}(n-1) + 2\,, \text{ for } n \geq 1,$$

which implies that $b^{*^*}(n) = \Theta(n)$.

$b^*(n)$ is exponential in n. Similar to the previous case, it is easy to see that the tableau $\mathcal{T}_n^*$ shown in Figure 2 is a smallest closed δ^*-tableau for φ_n. The number $b^*(n)$ of branches of $\mathcal{T}^*(n)$ satisfies the following recurrence relation

$$b^*(n) = 2b^*(n-1) + 2\,, \text{ for } n \geq 1,$$

which implies that $b^*(n) = \Theta(2^n)$. ∎

Notice that the above proof is based only on one of the two main features of the δ^{*^*}-rule, namely the fact that it uses the concept of key formulae for assigning Skolem function symbols to δ-formulae. The same result can be proven solely on the basis of the second main feature of the δ^{*^*}-rule, which is to ignore non-relevant sub-formulae.

5.3 Non-elementary Speedup

By applying the δ^{*^*}-rule, it is also possible to gain a non-elementary speedup in proof length over previous versions of the δ-rule, specifically over Baaz and Fermüller's δ^*-rule.

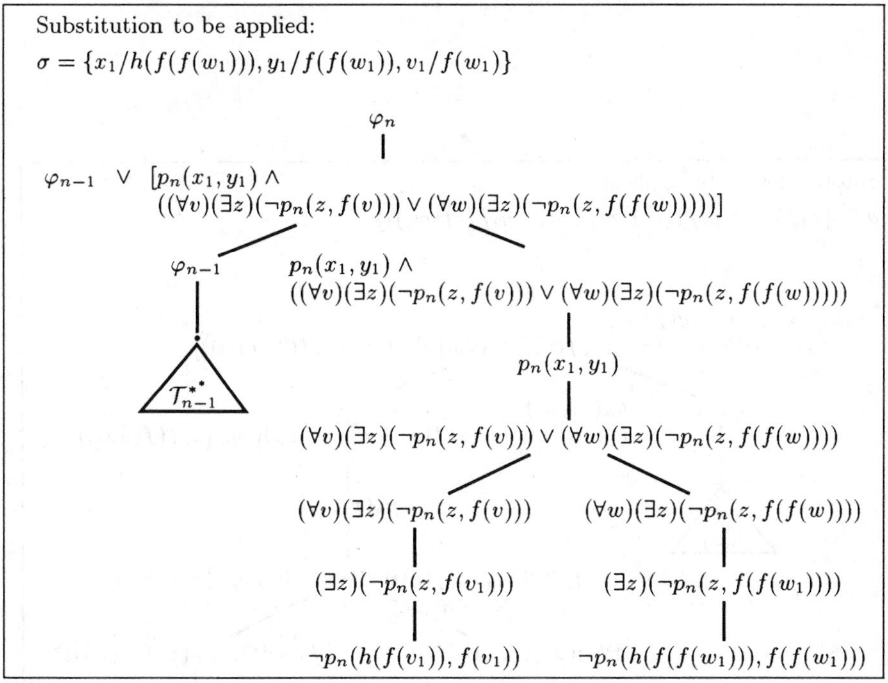

Fig. 1. A minimal δ^{**}-tableau for φ_n that is closed after application of the substitution σ shown at the top.

The proof follows exactly the same lines of [1], to which we refer the reader for details. Here we only indicate the variant of the "justifying formula" presented in [1], which must be used in our case:

$$(\forall x_1)\cdots(\forall x_n)(\forall y)[(C_1 \vee C_2) \supset (C_1 \vee (\exists z)[C_2\{y/z\} \vee (P(y) \wedge (R(z) \wedge \neg P(y)))])].$$

6 Conclusions and Directions of Future Research

We have introduced a new version of the δ-rule in free variable semantic tableau. The new rule carries mainly two features:

1. it assigns the same Skolem function symbol to existential formulae which are identical up to irrelevant subformulae;
2. it abstracts from the terms present in an existential formula.

As we already pointed out, both features, independently, enable a non-elementary reduction in proof complexity. Moreover key formulae and extracted key formulae are not expensive to calculate.

Global Skolemization has already been implemented in the language *SETL*. As a next step, we plan to implement a semantic tableau system employing

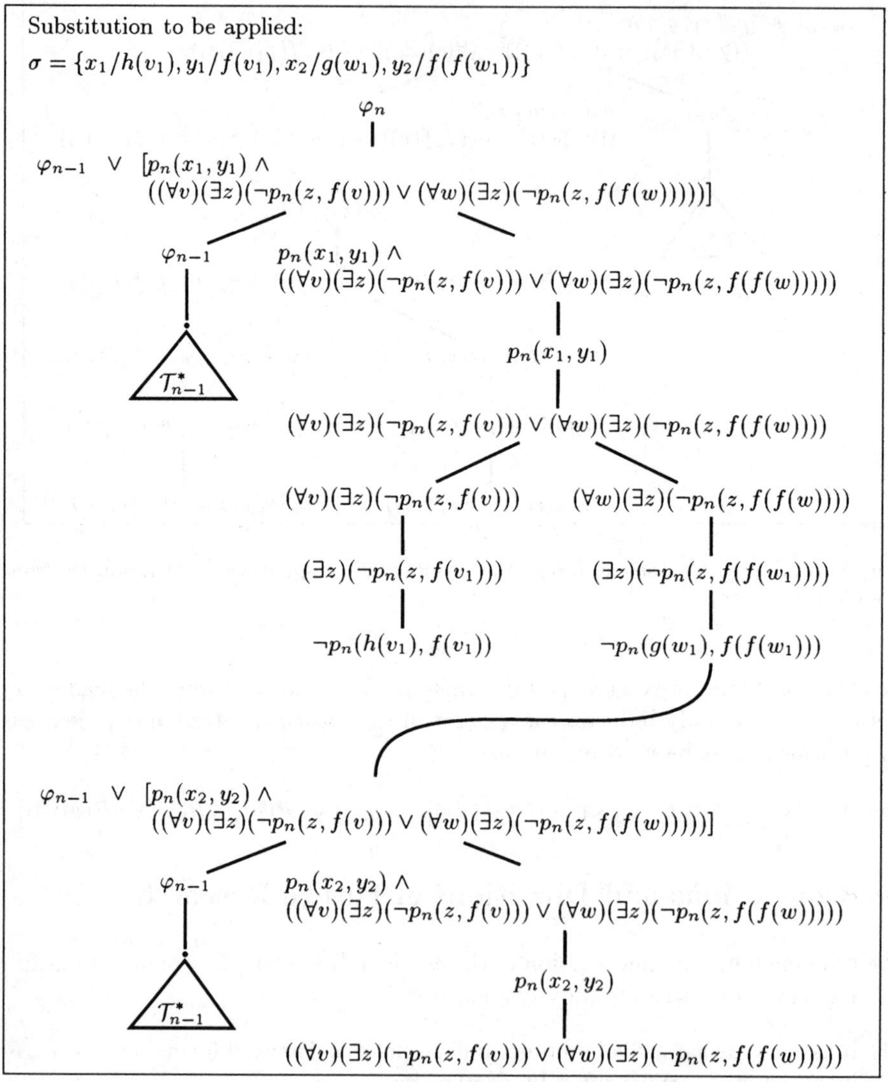

Fig. 2. A minimal δ^*-tableau for φ_n that is closed after application of the substitution σ shown at the top.

the δ^{*^*}-rule and additional optimizations. We believe that our version of the δ-rule offers many advantages over previous versions and a good ratio between reduction in proof length and costs of execution.

What we want to emphasize as the main point of our work is not the fact that it is possible at all to gain a non-elementary speedup, but that our rule (in particular due to the second feature mentioned above) triggers Skolemization in a quite natural way. If a proof introduces functions in a generalizing manner, we keep closer to the usual *intuition* of what the meaning of a function is, i.e., an abstraction that is applicable to *different* elements.

Acknowledgments

The authors thank heartily Wolfgang Ahrendt and Bernhard Beckert for many enlightening discussions and suggestions and for their generous support in the preparation of a first draft of the paper.

This work has been partially supported by the C.N.R. of Italy, coordinated project SETA, by M.U.R.S.T. Project "Tecniche speciali per la specifica, l'analisi, la verifica, la sintesi e la trasformazione di programmi", and by project "Deduction in Set Theory: A Tool for Software Verification" under the 1998 and 1999 Vigoni Programs.

References

1. M. Baaz, C.G. Fermüller. Non-elementary speedups between different versions of tableaux. In 4th *International Workshop, TABLEAUX'95* LNCS n. 918, 1995.
2. B. Beckert, R. Hähnle and P. Schmitt. The even more liberalized δ-rule in free variable semantic tableaux. In *Computational Logic and Proof Theory*, Proceedings of the 3rd Kurt Gödel Colloquium, Brno, August 1993. Springer, LNCS 713, pp. 108-119.
3. D. Cantone, M. Nicolosi Asmundo and E. Omodeo. Global Skolemization with grouped quantifiers. In *Proceedings of APPIA-GULP PRODE'97: Joint Conference on Declarative Programming*, pp. 405-413, 1997.
4. M.D. Davis and R. Fechter. A free variable version of the first-order predicate calculus. *Journal of Logic and Computation*, 1(14):431-451, 1991.
5. M. Fitting. *First-Order Logic and Automated Theorem Proving*. Springer, New York, 1990.
6. R. Hähnle and P. Schmitt. The liberalized δ-rule in free variable semantic tableaux. *Journal of Automated Reasoning*, 13(2):211-221, 1994.
7. R. Smullyan. *First-Order Logic*. Springer, New York, 1968.

A New Fast Tableau-Based Decision Procedure for an Unquantified Fragment of Set Theory*

Domenico Cantone[1] and Calogero G. Zarba[2]

[1] Università di Catania, Dipartimento di Matematica
Viale A. Doria 6, I-95125 Catania, Italy
cantone@cs.unict.it

[2] Stanford University, Computer Science Department,
Gates Building, Stanford CA 94305, USA
zarba@theory.stanford.edu

Abstract. In this paper we present a new fast tableau-based decision procedure for the ground set-theoretic fragment Multi-Level Syllogistic with Singleton (in short **MLSS**) which avoids the interleaving of model checking steps.

The underlying tableau calculus is based upon the system **KE**.

1 Introduction

In the last few years many fragments of set theory have been proved decidable [6, 5]. However, the problem of finding *efficient* decision procedures for these fragments still remains largely unexplored.

In this paper we present a new fast tableau-based decision procedure for the ground set-theoretic fragment Multi-Level Syllogistic with Singleton (in short **MLSS**).

Tableaux have the appealing feature that it is easy to extract a counter-example from an open and saturated branch, but on the other hand they can be highly inefficient if the splitting rules are not designed properly, at least for certain classes of formulae. We address this anomaly by presenting a tableau calculus based on the system **KE** introduced in [7] which forces tableau branches to be mutually exclusive. This results in an exponential speed-up with respect to Smullyan tableau-based calculi.[1]

In addition, in the procedure we are going to describe useful cuts are recognized in constant time, without the interleaving model-checking steps approach used in [1, 4, 9]. Moreover, useless cuts that might be executed by an exhaustive search strategy are totally avoided. This will have the overall effect to considerably speed up the saturation process with respect to the previous approaches.

* Work partially supported by the C.N.R. of Italy, coordinated project SETA, by M.U.R.S.T. Project "Tecniche speciali per la specifica, l'analisi, la verifica, la sintesi e la trasformazione di programmi", and by project "Deduction in Set Theory: A Tool for Software Verification" under the 1998 Vigoni Program.

[1] See [7] for further details about the cited speed-up.

R. Caferra and G. Salzer (Eds.): Automated Deduction, LNAI 1761, pp. 126–136, 2000.

Our decision procedure has been implemented as part of the Stanford Temporal Prover, STeP [2], a system which supports the computer-aided verification of reactive, real time and hybrid systems based on temporal specification. The integration of our decision procedure with STeP First-Order Reasoning and STeP's other decision procedures is done using the method described in [3].

The paper is organized as follows. In Section 2 we introduce some preliminary concepts which will be useful in what follows. In Section 3 we present a decidable tableau calculus for **MLSS**, whose proof of correctness is given in Section 4. Finally, after giving in Section 5 some experimental results, in Section 6 we hint at some directions of future research.

2 Preliminaries

In this section we introduce the syntax and semantics of **MLSS**, as well as the concept of realization.

2.1 Syntax

The unquantified set-theoretic fragment **MLSS** contains

- a denumerable infinity of variables,
- the constant $\emptyset$ (empty set),
- the operator symbols $\sqcup$ (union), $\sqcap$ (intersection), $-$ (set difference) and $[\bullet]$ (singleton),
- the predicate symbols $\sqsubseteq$ (membership) and $\approx$ (equality), and
- the logical connectives $\neg$, $\wedge$ and $\vee$.[2]

Plainly, the predicate $\sqsubseteq$ and the finite enumeration operator $[\bullet, \bullet, \ldots, \bullet]$ can be expressed in **MLSS** by noticing that $s \sqsubseteq t$ is equivalent to $s \sqcup t \approx t$ and that $[t_1, t_2, \ldots, t_k]$ can be expressed by $[t_1] \sqcup \ldots \sqcup [t_k]$.

We denote by T_φ the collection of all terms occurring in the formula φ, and we use the abbreviations $s \not\sqsubseteq t$ and $s \not\approx t$ to denote $\neg(s \sqsubseteq t)$ and $\neg(s \approx t)$, respectively .

2.2 Semantics

The semantics of **MLSS** is based upon the von Neumann standard cumulative hierarchy $\mathcal{V}$ of sets defined by:

$$\begin{aligned} \mathcal{V}_0 &= \emptyset \\ \mathcal{V}_{\alpha+1} &= \mathcal{P}(\mathcal{V}_\alpha)\,, && \text{for each ordinal } \alpha \\ \mathcal{V}_\lambda &= \textstyle\bigcup_{\mu<\lambda} \mathcal{V}_\mu\,, && \text{for each limit ordinal } \lambda \\ \mathcal{V} &= \textstyle\bigcup_{\alpha \in On} \mathcal{V}_\alpha\,, \end{aligned}$$

[2] In our treatment, $\neg\neg p$ is considered to be a syntactic variation of p.

where $\mathcal{P}(S)$ is the power set of S and On denotes the class of all ordinals. It can easily be seen that there can be no membership cycle in $\mathcal{V}$, namely sets in $\mathcal{V}$ are well-founded with respect to membership.

An ASSIGNMENT M over a collection V of variables is any function $M : V \to \mathcal{V}$. Given an assignment M over the variables of a formula φ, we denote with $M\varphi$ the truth-value obtained by interpreting each variable v in φ with the set Mv and the set symbols and logical connectives according to their standard meaning (thus, for instance, $\sqcup$, $\sqcap$, $-$, $[\bullet]$, $\sqsubset$, and $\approx$ are interpreted as the set operators $\cup$, $\cap$, $\setminus$, $\{\bullet\}$, and as the set predicates $\in$ and $=$, respectively).

A SET MODEL for a formula φ is an assignment M over the collection of variables occurring in φ such that $M\varphi$ evaluates to true.

A formula φ is SATISFIABLE if it has a set model.

2.3 Realizations

Let $G = (N, \widehat{\sqsubset})$ be a directed acyclic graph, and let (P, T) be a bipartition of N. Also, let $\{u_x : x \in P\}$ be a family of sets.

Definition 1. *The* REALIZATION *of $G = (N, \widehat{\sqsubset})$ relative to $\{u_x : x \in P\}$ and to (P, T) is the assignment R over N recursively defined by:*

$$\begin{aligned} Rx &= \{u_x\}\,, && \text{for } x \text{ in } P \\ Rt &= \{Rs : s \mathrel{\widehat{\sqsubset}} t\}\,, && \text{for } t \text{ in } T. \end{aligned}$$

Observe that R is well-defined since G is acyclic.

Next we define the function $h : N \to \mathbb{N}$ (called the HEIGHT), by putting:

$$h(t) = \begin{cases} 0 & \text{if } t \in P \text{ or } s \mathrel{\widehat{\not\sqsubset}} t, \text{ for all } s \in N \\ \max\{h(s) : s \mathrel{\widehat{\sqsubset}} t\} + 1 & \text{otherwise.} \end{cases}$$

The following lemma states the main properties of realizations.

Lemma 1. *Let $G = (P \cup T, \widehat{\sqsubset})$ be a directed acyclic graph, with $P \cap T = \emptyset$. Also, let $\{u_x : x \in P\}$ and R be respectively a family of sets and the realization of G relative to $\{u_x : x \in P\}$ and (P, T). Assume that:*

(a) *$u_x \neq u_y$ for all distinct x, y in P;*
(b) *$u_x \neq Rt$, for all x in P and t in $P \cup T$.*[3]

Then the following properties hold:

(i) *if $s \mathrel{\widehat{\sqsubset}} t$ then $h(s) < h(t)$, for all s in $P \cup T$ and t in T;*
(ii) *if $Rt_1 = Rt_2$ then $h(t_1) = h(t_2)$, for all t_1, t_2 in $P \cup T$;*
(iii) *if $Rs \in Rt$ then $h(s) < h(t)$, for all s, t in $P \cup T$.*

[3] Notice that conditions (a) and (b) can always be satisfied by letting the u_x's be pairwise distinct sets of cardinality no less than $|P \cup T|$, since $|Rt| < |P \cup T|$.

Proof. **(i)** is immediate.

(ii) If either t_1 or t_2 is in P, the claim is ensured by conditions (a) and (b). On the other hand, if $t_1, t_2 \in T$, we proceed by induction on $\max\{h(t_1), h(t_2)\}$. The base case ($\max\{h(t_1), h(t_2)\} = 0$) is trivial. For the inductive step, suppose $Rt_1 = Rt_2$ and, without lost of generality, that $h(t_1) > 0$. Then there exists s such that $s \mathrel{\widehat{\sqsubseteq}} t_1$ and $h(t_1) = h(s) + 1$. Since $s \mathrel{\widehat{\sqsubseteq}} t_1$, it follows that $Rs \in Rt_1$ and therefore $Rs \in Rt_2$. Moreover, there exists s' such that $Rs' = Rs$ and $s' \mathrel{\widehat{\sqsubseteq}} t_2$. By inductive hypothesis $h(s) = h(s')$. Finally, $h(t_2) \geq h(s') + 1 = h(s) + 1 = h(t_1)$. Exchanging the rôles of t_1 and t_2 it is also possible to deduce $h(t_2) \leq h(t_1)$. Thus $h(t_1) = h(t_2)$.

(iii) If $Rs \in Rt$ then there exists some s' such that $Rs' = Rs$ and $s' \mathrel{\widehat{\sqsubseteq}} t$. For (i) $h(s') < h(t)$ and for (ii) $h(s) = h(s')$. Thus $h(s) < h(t)$. □

3 The Tableau Calculus

In this section we describe a tableau calculus for **MLSS**. See [8] for a complete introduction to semantic tableaux.

We extend the notion of closed tableau as follows:

Definition 2. *A branch θ of a tableau $\mathcal{T}$ is closed if it contains:*

- *two complementary formulae ψ, $\neg\psi$, or*
- *a membership cycle of the form $t_0 \sqsubseteq t_1 \sqsubseteq \ldots \sqsubseteq t_0$, or*
- *a literal of the form $t \not\approx t$, or*
- *a literal of the form $s \sqsubseteq \mathbf{\emptyset}$.*

A tableau is CLOSED *if all its branches are closed.*

3.1 Saturation Rules

Our calculus has two kinds of rules: *saturation* and *fulfilling* rules. Moreover, we impose the restriction that *no new term will be created by any application of a saturation rule.* Thus, for instance, the rule

$$s \sqsubseteq t_1 \Longrightarrow s \sqsubseteq t_1 \sqcup t_2$$

can be applied to a branch θ of a tableau for φ *only* if the term $t_1 \sqcup t_2$ is already in T_φ. Under this fundamental restriction, the full collection of saturation rules is shown in Table 1. Notice also that in the first two rules for equality, ℓ stands for a literal, and the substituted term is restricted to be a top-level term occurring in ℓ. This will prevent the search space from exploding.

A branch is said to be LINEARLY SATURATED if no saturation rule produces new formulae.

propositional rules		rules for $\sqcup$	
$p \wedge q$	$\Longrightarrow p, q$	$s \not\sqsubseteq t_1 \sqcup t_2$	$\Longrightarrow s \not\sqsubseteq t_1, s \not\sqsubseteq t_2$
$\neg(p \vee q)$	$\Longrightarrow \neg p, \neg q$	$s \sqsubseteq t_1$	$\Longrightarrow s \sqsubseteq t_1 \sqcup t_2$
$p \vee q, \neg p$	$\Longrightarrow q$	$s \sqsubseteq t_2$	$\Longrightarrow s \sqsubseteq t_1 \sqcup t_2$
$p \vee q, \neg q$	$\Longrightarrow p$	$s \sqsubseteq t_1 \sqcup t_2, s \not\sqsubseteq t_1$	$\Longrightarrow s \sqsubseteq t_2$
$\neg(p \wedge q), p$	$\Longrightarrow \neg q$	$s \sqsubseteq t_1 \sqcup t_2, s \not\sqsubseteq t_2$	$\Longrightarrow s \sqsubseteq t_1$
$\neg(p \wedge q), q$	$\Longrightarrow \neg p$	$s \not\sqsubseteq t_1, s \not\sqsubseteq t_2$	$\Longrightarrow s \not\sqsubseteq t_1 \sqcup t_2$
rules for $\sqcap$		rules for $-$	
$s \sqsubseteq t_1 \sqcap t_2$	$\Longrightarrow s \sqsubseteq t_1, s \sqsubseteq t_2$	$s \sqsubseteq t_1 - t_2$	$\Longrightarrow s \sqsubseteq t_1, s \not\sqsubseteq t_2$
$s \not\sqsubseteq t_1$	$\Longrightarrow s \not\sqsubseteq t_1 \sqcap t_2$	$s \not\sqsubseteq t_1$	$\Longrightarrow s \not\sqsubseteq t_1 - t_2$
$s \not\sqsubseteq t_2$	$\Longrightarrow s \not\sqsubseteq t_1 \sqcap t_2$	$s \sqsubseteq t_2$	$\Longrightarrow s \not\sqsubseteq t_1 - t_2$
$s \not\sqsubseteq t_1 \sqcap t_2, s \sqsubseteq t_1$	$\Longrightarrow s \not\sqsubseteq t_2$	$s \not\sqsubseteq t_1 - t_2, s \sqsubseteq t_1$	$\Longrightarrow s \sqsubseteq t_2$
$s \not\sqsubseteq t_1 \sqcap t_2, s \sqsubseteq t_2$	$\Longrightarrow s \not\sqsubseteq t_1$	$s \not\sqsubseteq t_1 - t_2, s \not\sqsubseteq t_2$	$\Longrightarrow s \not\sqsubseteq t_1$
$s \sqsubseteq t_1, s \sqsubseteq t_2$	$\Longrightarrow s \sqsubseteq t_1 \sqcap t_2$	$s \sqsubseteq t_1, s \not\sqsubseteq t_2$	$\Longrightarrow s \sqsubseteq t_1 - t_2$
rules for $[\bullet]$		rules for equality	
	$\Longrightarrow t_1 \sqsubseteq [t_1]$	$t_1 \approx t_2, \ell$	$\Longrightarrow \ell\{t_2/t_1\}$
$s \sqsubseteq [t_1]$	$\Longrightarrow s \approx t_1$	$t_1 \approx t_2, \ell$	$\Longrightarrow \ell\{t_1/t_2\}$
$s \not\sqsubseteq [t_1]$	$\Longrightarrow s \not\approx t_1$	$s \sqsubseteq t, s' \not\sqsubseteq t$	$\Longrightarrow s \not\approx s'$

Table 1. Saturation rules.

3.2 Fulfilling Rules

A fulfilling rule can be applied to an open linearly saturated branch, provided that its associated *precondition* and *subsumption requirement* are, respectively, true and false. Table 2 summarizes the fulfilling rules and their associated preconditions and subsumption requirements. Notice that even fulfilling rules (that, incidentally, in our calculus are exactly the splitting rules) are not allowed to introduce new terms, with the exception of the last one, which introduces fresh parameters x not occurring in the branch to which it is applied.

Remark 1. Notice that literals of type $s \not\sqsubseteq t_1 \sqcap t_2$ and $s \not\sqsubseteq t_1 - t_2$ do not trigger any split rule, as would happen in an exhaustive search strategy.

Notice also the asymmetry in the precondition for $\sqcap$: no split needs to occur if for some term $t_1 \sqcap t_2$ in T_φ a literal $s \sqsubseteq t_2$ occurs in a branch.

In early versions of this work all sorts of cut rules were allowed, whereas a careful analysis of the correctness proof has pointed out that most of them can be avoided.

Remark 2. Observe that if the literals $s_1 \approx s_2$, $t_1 \approx t_2$, $s_1 \not\approx t_1$, $s_1 \not\approx t_2$, $s_2 \not\approx t_1$, $s_2 \not\approx t_2$ occur in a branch, an exhaustive search strategy would apply a splitting rule to each inequality, thereby generating 2^4 branches, whereas in our calculus at most 2 branches will eventually be created.

Remark 3. It is possible to further strengthen the subsumption requirement associated to the last fulfilling rule by noticing that if a literal $t \not\approx \emptyset$ occurs in a

fulfilling rule	precondition	subsumption requirement
$p \mid \neg p$	$p \vee q$ is in θ	p is in θ or $\neg p$ is in θ
$\neg p \mid p$	$\neg(p \wedge q)$ is in θ	$\neg p$ is in θ or p is in θ
$s \sqsubset t_1 \mid s \not\sqsubset t_1$	$t_1 \sqcup t_2 \in T_\varphi$ $s \sqsubset t_1 \sqcup t_2$ is in θ	$s \sqsubset t_1$ is in θ or $s \not\sqsubset t_1$ is in θ
$s \sqsubset t_2 \mid s \not\sqsubset t_2$	$t_1 \sqcap t_2 \in T_\varphi$ $s \sqsubset t_1$ is in θ	$s \sqsubset t_2$ is in θ or $s \not\sqsubset t_2$ is in θ
$s \sqsubset t_2 \mid s \not\sqsubset t_2$	$t_1 - t_2 \in T_\varphi$ $s \sqsubset t_1$ is in θ	$s \sqsubset t_2$ is in θ or $s \not\sqsubset t_2$ is in θ
$x \sqsubset t_1, x \not\sqsubset t_2 \mid x \not\sqsubset t_1, x \sqsubset t_2$	$t_1, t_2 \in T_\varphi$ $t_1 \not\approx t_2$ is in θ	$\exists x : (x \sqsubset t_1$ is in θ and $x \not\sqsubset t_2$ is in $\theta)$ or $\exists x : (x \not\sqsubset t_1$ is in θ and $x \sqsubset t_2$ is in $\theta)$

Table 2. Fulfilling rules.

branch θ, then it is enough to require that $x \sqsubset t$ occurs in θ for some x, thus obtaining the *linear* fulfilling rule

$$t \not\approx \emptyset \Longrightarrow x \sqsubset t \ (x \text{ new parameter})$$

This improvement will be used in Example 1.

More generally, one can maintain a *transitivity graph* [3] whose nodes are labeled with terms in $P_\theta \cup T_\varphi$ and edges are labeled with $\sqsubseteq$, $\not\approx$ or $\not\sqsubseteq$. Then, if a literal $t_1 \not\approx t_2$ occurs in a branch θ, we may check whether there exists a path from t_1 to t_2 (or from t_2 to t_1) with edges labeled with $\sqsubseteq$, and the fulfilling rule would then be:

$$t_1 \not\approx t_2, t_1 \sqsubseteq t_2 \Longrightarrow x \sqsubset t_2, x \not\sqsubset t_1 \ (x \text{ new parameter}) .$$

We should also notice that if the literals $t_1 \not\approx t_2$, $t_1 \sqsubseteq \ldots \sqsubseteq t_2$ occur in a branch θ, we do not need to apply any fulfilling rule at all. Soundness of such optimizations is an easy matter.

Example 1. Table 1 contains a closed tableau with 3 branches for proving the validity of the formula $\neg(x \approx [y] \wedge x \approx y \sqcup z) \vee (y \approx \emptyset \wedge x \approx z)$.

We denote with φ_i the formula labeling node i, and provide justifications for the construction of the tableau.

- $\varphi_2, \varphi_3, \varphi_4, \varphi_5$ and φ_7 are obtained by means of propositional rules;
- φ_6 and φ_{17} are obtained by means of the second fulfilling rule;
- $\varphi_8, \varphi_9, \varphi_{13}$ and φ_{14} are obtained by means of the last fulfilling rule;
- $\varphi_{10}, \varphi_{12}, \varphi_{16}, \varphi_{20}, \varphi_{21}$ and φ_{23} are obtained by means of equality rules;
- $\varphi_{11}, \varphi_{15}$ and φ_{19} are obtained by means of rules for $\sqcup$;
- the optimization promised in Remark 3 is used to deduce φ_{18};

$$
\begin{array}{ll}
1. & \neg(\neg(x \approx [y] \wedge x \approx y \sqcup z) \vee (y \approx \emptyset \wedge x \approx z)) \\
2. & x \approx [y] \wedge x \approx y \sqcup z \\
3. & \neg(y \approx \emptyset \wedge x \approx z) \\
4. & x \approx [y] \\
5. & x \approx y \sqcup z
\end{array}
$$

6. $y \approx \emptyset$			17.	$y \not\approx \emptyset$
7. $x \not\approx z$			18.	$w \in y$
			19.	$w \in y \sqcup z$
8.	$w \in x$	13. $w \notin x$	20.	$w \in x$
9.	$w \notin z$	14. $w \in z$	21.	$w \in [y]$
10.	$w \in y \sqcup z$	15. $w \in y \sqcup z$	22.	$w \approx y$
11.	$w \in y$	16. $w \in x$	23.	$y \in y$
12.	$w \in \emptyset$	$\perp$		$\perp$
	$\perp$			

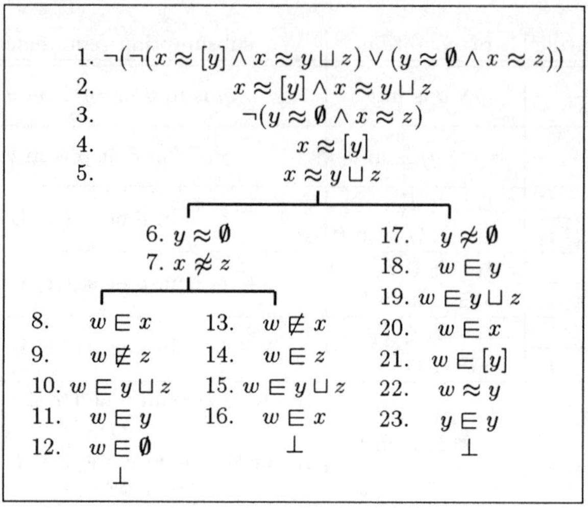

Fig. 1. A closed tableau for $\neg(\neg(x \approx [y] \wedge x \approx y \sqcup z) \vee (y \approx \emptyset \wedge x \approx z))$

– φ_{22} is obtained by means of a rule for $[\bullet]$.

The tableau is closed since the leftmost branch contains the contradiction φ_{12}, the central branch contains two complementary literals $\varphi_{13}, \varphi_{16}$, and the rightmost branch contains a membership cycle (φ_{23}).

Finally, notice that to prove the same formula, the approach described in [4] produced a tableau with 8 branches

4   The Decision Procedure

In this section, after introducing some definition and terminology, we state our decision procedure and prove its correctness.

Definition 3. *To any branch θ of a tableau $\mathcal{T}$ for a formula φ we associate the following objects:*

P_θ: *the collection of parameters added to θ;*

V_θ: *the collection of variables and parameters occurring in θ;*

P_θ': *the collection of parameters $\{x \in P_\theta$: there is no t in T_φ such that $x \approx t$ occurs in $\theta\}$;*

T_θ': *the set $T_\varphi \cup (P_\theta \setminus P_\theta')$;*

G_θ: *the oriented graph $(P_\theta' \cup T_\theta', \widehat{\in})$, where $s \widehat{\in} t$ if and only if the literal $s \in t$ occurs in θ;*

R_θ: *a realization of G_θ relative to the partition (P_θ', T_θ') and to pairwise distinct sets u_x, for $x \in P_\theta'$, each having cardinality no less than $|P_\theta' \cup T_\theta'|$;*

M_θ: *the assignment over V_θ defined by $M_\theta v = R_\theta v$, for each v in V_θ.*

Definition 4. *An open branch θ is* SATURATED *if it is linearly saturated and all its subsumption requirements are fulfilled.*

Definition 5. *A branch θ is said to be* COHERENT *if $R_\theta t = M_\theta t$, for all t in $P_\theta \cup T_\varphi$.*

Procedure 1 (MLSS-Satisfiability Test).

Input: an **MLSS**-formula φ.

1. Let $\mathcal{T}$ be the tableau consisting of a single node labeled with φ;
2. linearly saturate $\mathcal{T}$ by strictly applying to it all possible saturation rules until either $\mathcal{T}$ is closed or no new formula can be produced;
3. if $\mathcal{T}$ is closed, announce that φ is unsatisfiable;
4. otherwise, if there exists an open and saturated branch θ in $\mathcal{T}$, announce that φ is satisfied by the model M_θ;
5. otherwise, let θ be a non-saturated open branch; apply to θ any fulfilling rule whose subsumption requirement is false and go to step 2.

4.1 Termination

We begin to prove total correctness of Procedure 1 by first showing termination, and leave the proof of partial correctness for the next subsection.

Theorem 1. *Procedure 1 always terminate.*

Proof. Let φ be the root formula of the tableau limit $\mathcal{T}$ constructed by Procedure 1. Since steps 3 and 4 cause the procedure to terminate, and step 5 always add new formulae, to show termination it is enough to prove that $\mathcal{T}$ must be finite. Now, let θ be any branch in $\mathcal{T}$. Because of the restriction imposed to the application of the rules, $|T_\theta|$ is bounded by $|T_\varphi|^2$, and therefore $T_\varphi \cup T_\theta$ is finite. It follows that the number of literals occurring in θ is finite, as well as the number of formulae involving propositional connectives. Having shown that any branch in $\mathcal{T}$ is finite, in view of the König Lemma even $\mathcal{T}$ is finite. □

4.2 Partial Correctness

Let again φ be the root formula of the tableau $\mathcal{T}$ constructed by Procedure 1. Since all rules are plainly sound, if $\mathcal{T}$ is closed then φ is unsatisfiable. Otherwise the tableau $\mathcal{T}$ must contain an open and saturated branch θ. Thus, in order to establish the correctness of Procedure 1, it is enough to prove that the assignment M_θ (cf. Definition 3) satisfies the branch θ and, therefore, the formula φ.

The following lemma is easily proved by induction on the number of applications of the inferences rules.

Lemma 2. *In any branch θ if $x \in P'_\theta$ then:*

(a) there can be no term t in $T_\varphi \cup P_\theta$ different from x such that $x \approx t$ occurs in θ;

(b) there can be no term s in $T_\varphi \cup P_\theta$ such that $s \sqsubseteq x$ occurs in θ.

In order to show that the assignment M_θ models correctly all formulae occurring in an open and saturated branch θ, we first show in the following lemma that the realization R_θ models correctly all literals in an open and saturated branch θ, provided that terms are just considered as "complex names" for variables (namely operators are not interpreted).

Lemma 3. *Let θ be an open and saturated branch. Then:*

(i) *if $s \sqsubseteq t$ occurs in θ, then $R_\theta s \in R_\theta t$;*
(ii) *if $t_1 \approx t_2$ occurs in θ, then $R_\theta t_1 = R_\theta t_2$;*
(iii) *if $t_1 \not\approx t_2$ occurs in θ, then $R_\theta t_1 \neq R_\theta t_2$;*
(iv) *if $s \not\sqsubseteq t$ occurs in θ, then $R_\theta s \notin R_\theta t$.*

Proof. **(i)** Let $s \sqsubseteq t$ be in θ. By Lemma 2, $t \notin P'_\theta$, and by construction of R_θ it trivially follows that $R_\theta s \in R_\theta t$.
(ii) Let $t_1 \approx t_2$ be in θ. If either $t_1 \in P'_\theta$ or $t_2 \in P'_\theta$ then by Lemma 2 it must be $t_1 = t_2$ and therefore $R_\theta t_1 = R_\theta t_2$. If $t_1, t_2 \in T'_\theta$ but $R_\theta t_1 \neq R_\theta t_2$, suppose w.l.o.g. that there is some a such that $a \in R_\theta t_1$ and $a \notin R_\theta t_2$. Then there exists s such that $R_\theta s = a$ and $s \sqsubseteq t_1$ occurs in θ. Since θ is saturated, $s \sqsubseteq t_2$ must also occur in θ, and by (i) $a = R_\theta s \in R_\theta t_2$, a contradiction.
(iii) Let $t_1 \not\approx t_2$ be in θ but $R_\theta t_1 = R_\theta t_2$. W.l.o.g. we can assume that $t_1, t_2 \in T_\varphi$ (otherwise either at least one among t_1, t_2 is in P'_θ, and the claim easily follows from Lemma 2, or θ would contain a literal $t'_1 \not\approx t'_2$ with $t'_1, t'_2 \in T_\varphi$ and such that $t_1 \approx t'_1$ and $t_2 \approx t'_2$ are in θ; then $t'_1 \not\approx t'_2$ could play the rôle of $t_1 \not\approx t_2$ in the following discussion). By Lemma 1 we have $h(t_1) = h(t_2)$. We proceed by induction on $h(t_1)$. In the base case ($h(t_1) = 0$) we reach a contradiction, since by saturation there is some x such that either $x \sqsubseteq t_1$ and $x \not\sqsubseteq t_2$ occur in θ, or $x \not\sqsubseteq t_1$ and $x \sqsubseteq t_2$ occur in θ, and we would have $h(t_1) > 0$ in either cases. For the inductive step, w.l.o.g. let $x \sqsubseteq t_1$ and $x \not\sqsubseteq t_2$ be in θ (their occurrence is due to saturation), for some x. Then $R_\theta x \in R_\theta t_1$ that implies $R_\theta x \in R_\theta t_2$, so that there exists x' such that $R_\theta x = R_\theta x'$ and $x' \sqsubseteq t_2$ occurs in θ. Notice that $x' \neq x$ (otherwise θ would be closed). Since by Lemma 1 we have $h(x) = h(x') < h(t_1)$, we can apply the inductive hypothesis and obtain the contradiction $R_\theta x \neq R_\theta x'$.
(iv) Let $s \not\sqsubseteq t$ be in θ but $R_\theta s \in R_\theta t$. Then there exists s' different from s such that $R_\theta s = R_\theta s'$ and $s' \sqsubseteq t$ occurs in θ. By saturation $s \not\approx s'$ is in θ, and by (iii) $R_\theta s \neq R_\theta s'$, a contradiction. □

Next we show that even operators are correctly modeled by R_θ (and therefore by M_θ), for an open and saturated branch θ.

Lemma 4. *If a branch θ is open and saturated, then it is coherent.*

Proof. Let θ be an open and saturated branch. We prove that $R_\theta t = M_\theta t$, for each t in $P_\theta \cup T_\varphi$, by structural induction on t. The base case is trivial for variables. Concerning $\boldsymbol{\emptyset}$, notice that trivially $M_\theta \boldsymbol{\emptyset} = \emptyset$ and that $R_\theta \boldsymbol{\emptyset} = \emptyset$ since

θ is open. For the inductive step we prove only that $R_\theta(t_1 \sqcap t_2) = M_\theta(t_1 \sqcap t_2)$ (other cases are similar). Suppose that $a \in R_\theta(t_1 \sqcap t_2)$. Then there exists s such that $R_\theta s = a$ and $s \sqsubseteq t_1 \sqcap t_2$ occurs in θ, and since θ is saturated both $s \sqsubseteq t_1$ and $s \sqsubseteq t_2$ occur in θ. By Lemma 3 $R_\theta s \in R_\theta t_1$ and $R_\theta s \in R_\theta t_2$, and by inductive hypothesis $a \in M_\theta t_1 \cap M_\theta t_2 = M_\theta(t_1 \sqcap t_2)$. Conversely, if $a \in M_\theta(t_1 \sqcap t_2)$ then $a \in M_\theta t_1 \cap M_\theta t_2$, and by inductive hypothesis $a \in R_\theta t_1 \cap R_\theta t_2$. After noticing that, because of the restrictions imposed to the application of the rules, it must be the case that $t_1, t_2 \in T_\varphi$, it follows that there exist s', s'' such that $Rs' = Rs'' = a$ and both $s' \sqsubseteq t_1$ and $s'' \sqsubseteq t_2$ occur in θ. By saturation, either $s' \sqsubseteq t_2$ or $s' \not\sqsubseteq t_2$ occurs in θ. In the former case $s' \sqsubseteq t_1 \sqcap t_2$ occurs in θ, and therefore $a \in R_\theta(t_1 \sqcap t_2)$. In the latter case $s' \not\approx s''$ occurs in θ, and therefore $R_\theta s' \neq R_\theta s''$, a contradiction. □

The following theorem concludes the proof of partial correctness.

Theorem 2. *If θ is an open and saturated branch, then it is satisfiable, and indeed it is satisfied by M_θ.*

Proof. Let θ be an open and saturated branch. By combining together Lemma 3 and 4, it follows that M_θ satisfies all literals occurring in θ. Finally, proceeding by structural induction, it easy to see that even formulae involving propositional connectives are satisfied by M_θ. □

5 Some Experimental Results

On a 200 Mhz ULTRA-Spark Sun workstation, the formulae $\neg(x \approx [y] \wedge x \approx y \sqcup z) \vee (y \approx \emptyset \wedge x \approx z)$ (cf. Example 1) and $a \sqcup (b \sqcup c) \approx (a \sqcup b) \sqcup c$ were proved valid in 0.03 seconds and 0.02 seconds, respectively, whereas the formula $\neg(x \sqsubseteq y \wedge x \not\sqsubseteq z_1 \wedge z_1 \sqcup z_2 \sqsubseteq [y])$ was recognized not to be valid in 0.04 seconds.

Moreover, using the basic notion of pair $(a, b) =_{\text{Def}} \{\{a\}, \{a, b\}\}$ due to Kuratowski, it has been possible to prove the validity of $(a, b) \neq (u, b) \vee (a = u \wedge b = v)$ in 0.08 seconds. Similar theorems have also been proved for 3-tuples, 4-tuples and 5-tuples in 0.24, 0.58 and 1.79, respectively.

6 Future Plans

We plan to further investigate heuristics which allow to strengthen subsumption requirements, as hinted in Remark 3.

Also, we intend to study thoroughly the cases in which cuts are really needed, in order to further optimize our calculus.

Finally, we plan to generalize our tableau calculus and relative saturation strategy to extensions of **MLSS** (cf. [6, 5]).

Acknowledgments

The authors wish to thank Bernhard Beckert, Nikolaj S. Bjørner, and Tomás E. Uribe for helpful comments. The second author wishes to thank Prof. Zohar Manna for having given him the opportunity to visit his REACT group.

References

1. Bernhard Beckert and Ulrike Hartmer. A tableau calculus for quantifier-free set theoretic formulae. In *Proceedings, International Conference on Theorem Proving with Analytic Tableaux and Related Methods, Oisterwijk, The Netherlands*, LNCS 1397, pages 93–107. Springer, 1998.
2. Nikolaj S. Bjørner, Anca Browne, Eddie S. Chang, Michael Colón, Arjun Kapur, Zohar Manna, Henny B. Sipma, and Tomás E. Uribe. STeP: Deductive-algorithmic verification of reactive and real-time systems. In *Proc. 8th Intl. Conference on Computer Aided Verification*, volume 1102 of *LNCS*, pages 415–418. Springer-Verlag, July 1996.
3. Nikolaj S. Bjørner, Mark E. Stickel, and Tomás E. Uribe. A practical integration of first-order reasoning and decision procedures. In *Proc. of the* 14th *Intl. Conference on Automated Deduction*, volume 1249 of *LNCS*, pages 101–115. Springer-Verlag, July 1997.
4. Domenico Cantone. A fast saturation strategy for set-theoretic Tableaux. In Didier Galmiche, editor, *Proceedings of the International Conference on Automated Reasoning with Analytic Tableaux and Related Methods*, volume 1227 of *LNAI*, pages 122–137, Berlin, May13–16 1997. Springer.
5. Domenico Cantone and Alfredo Ferro. Techniques of computable set theory with applications to proof verification. *Comm. Pure Appl. Math.*, XLVIII:1–45, 1995.
6. Domenico Cantone, Alfredo Ferro, and Eugenio Omodeo. *Computable set theory*, volume no.6 Oxford Science Publications of *International Series of Monographs on Computer Science*. Clarendon Press, 1989.
7. Marcello D'Agostino and Marco Mondadori. The taming of the cut. Classical refutations with analytic cut. *Journal of Logic and Computation*, 4(3):285–319, June 1994.
8. Melvin C. Fitting. *First-Order Logic and Automated Theorem Proving*. Graduate Texts in Computer Science. Springer-Verlag, Berlin, 2nd edition, 1996. 1st ed., 1990.
9. Calogero G. Zarba. Dimostrazione automatica di formule inisiemistiche con tagli analitici. Tesi di Laurea, Università di Catania (in Italian), July 1998.

Interpretation of a Mizar-Like Logic in First Order Logic

Ingo Dahn*

University of Koblenz-Landau
Department of Computer Science
Rheinau 1, D-56075 Koblenz
dahn@uni-koblenz.de

1 Introduction

Automated theorem provers for first order logic have reached a state where they can give useful support for interactive theorem proving. However, most real world problems handled in interactive theorem proving are formulated in a typed language. First order provers have currently rather limited capabilities to handle types. Therefore type information has to be encoded in an efficient way. What is most efficient, depends on the type system as well as on the first order prover at hand.

In this paper we describe a general purpose interpretation of a large fragment of the typed logic used in the MIZAR MATHEMATICAL LIBRARY [Rud92,Try93] into untyped first order logic. This poses also new challenging problems for first order automated provers (see [DahWer97]). A general definition of an interpretation based on concepts from abstract model theory sets the theoretical framework.

2 Semantic Foundations

Libraries of theorems are basically collections of sentences that are assumed to be true in a given class of models. In this abstract setting, automated theorem provers provide a potential library - the library of all formulas they can prove. The correctness proof for the calculus underlying a specific prover provides evidence that all formulas in this potential library are true in the class of all their models.

The semantics of the formulas is fixed. Hence it can serve as a basis for the consistent combination of knowledge from various sources. Abstract model theory has provided a theoretical framework to study semantic interrelations between several deductive systems. Therefore, we give slight generalizations of its most basic definitions from [Ba74].

Abstract model theory has abstracted from the syntax of a particular language. The only essential property of a logic in this setting is to determine

* Supported by the Deutsche Forschungsgemeinschaft

R. Caferra and G. Salzer (Eds.): Automated Deduction, LNAI 1761, pp. 137–151, 2000.

whether a particular formula is valid in a particular model. At this stage we do not care about how the logic determines validity in detail. We only want to be a little more specific on formulas and models. These are connected by the concept of a signature. Again, there is currently no need to define what a signature is. We simply note that each *logic* $\mathcal{L}$ accepts a specific set $\Sigma_{\mathcal{L}}$ of signatures. For example, some logics may require all signatures to include special symbols like $=$ or $\in$. For each signature $\sigma \in \Sigma_{\mathcal{L}}$, the logic fixes a class of models $Mod_{\sigma}^{\mathcal{L}}$, a set of formulas $\Phi_{\sigma}^{\mathcal{L}}$ and a relation $\models_{\sigma}^{\mathcal{L}}$which determines whether a formula $H \in \Phi_{\sigma}^{\mathcal{L}}$ holds in a model $M \in Mod_{\sigma}^{\mathcal{L}}$ $(M \models_{\sigma}^{\mathcal{L}} H)$.

Then, an $\mathcal{L}$-*theory* of signature σ is simply a subset of $\Phi_{\sigma}^{\mathcal{L}}$. This is sufficient to define the concepts of models and semantic consequence for each such abstract logic $\mathcal{L}$.

Definition 1. *For each $\mathcal{L}$-theory T of signature σ the class of all $\mathcal{L}$-*models *of T is the class $Mod_{\sigma}^{\mathcal{L}}(T)$ of all M in $Mod_{\sigma}^{\mathcal{L}}$, such that $M \models_{\sigma}^{\mathcal{L}} H$ for all $H \in T$.*

This induces the consequence relation, denoted also by $\models_{\sigma}^{\mathcal{L}}$:

Definition 2. *A formula $A \in \Phi_{\sigma}^{\mathcal{L}}$ is a* consequence *of a theory $T \subseteq \Phi_{\sigma}^{\mathcal{L}}$ $(T \models_{\sigma}^{\mathcal{L}} A)$ if and only if $M \models_{\sigma}^{\mathcal{L}} A$ for each model M from $Mod_{\sigma}^{\mathcal{L}}(T)$.*

3 Interpretations

In order to use theorems proved by one system (the source system) to enhance the knowledge of another system (the target system), the logic of the second system must be interpreted in the logic of the first system. From the point of view of system architecture this is a mediation service [WiGe97].

For our intended application we think of the source system as an automated prover with logic $\mathcal{S}$, while the target system is a library of formulas from a logic $\mathcal{T}$. However, the same considerations can be applied in order to combine the libraries of two interactive theorem provers as well.

We have to interpret proof problems from $\mathcal{T}$ as proof problems in $\mathcal{S}$ that can be solved by the source system. Our interpretation has to ensure that the consequences proved by the source system are valid consequences in the target logic. In order to be useful, it is not necessary that the source is able to handle *all* knowledge that the target system can handle - some interesting subset suffices and there can be required some translation procedure ν between the formulas of the source logic and that of the target logic. Also, the models of the two logics can be quite different (for example, think of an interpretation of a geometric model like a plane as an arithmetic model consisting of pairs of Cartesian coordinates). This interpretation μ of the models requires some translation ι of between their signatures.

The following definition provides the concept of interpretation with an exact meaning.

Definition 3. *An* interpretation *I of a logic $\mathcal{T}$ in a logic $\mathcal{S}$ consists of a set $\Sigma^I \subseteq \Sigma_{\mathcal{T}}$ of signatures, for each $\sigma \in \Sigma^I$ an $\mathcal{S}$-theory $\Theta_{I,\sigma}$ and three mappings:*

- ι maps a set of signatures Σ^I into $\Sigma_{\mathcal{S}}$,
- μ maps $Mod_\sigma^{\mathcal{T}}$ into $Mod_{\iota(\sigma)}^{\mathcal{S}}(\Theta_{I,\sigma})$ for each $\sigma \in \Sigma^I$,
- ν maps for each $\sigma \in \Sigma^I$ a subset of $\Phi_\sigma^{\mathcal{T}}$ into $\Phi_{\iota(\sigma)}^{\mathcal{S}}$

such that for all $\sigma \in \Sigma^I$, for each sentence H in the domain of ν and for each model M from $Mod_\sigma^{\mathcal{T}}$

$$M \models_\sigma^{\mathcal{T}} H \text{ if and only if } \mu(M) \models_{\iota(\sigma)}^{\mathcal{S}} \nu(H).$$

The second of these conditions requires that the models in the range of μ satisfy some set of conditions $\Theta_{I,\sigma}$ which can be stated in the source logic.

Example 1. Let the source logic $\mathcal{S}$ be equational logic and let the target logic $\mathcal{T}$ be full first order logic. We obtain an interpretation I by taking Σ_I as the set of signatures containing equality, ι as the operation, that deletes all predicates except equality, μ as the giving the reduct of a model to its equational part, $\Theta_{I,\sigma}$ as the empty theory and ν as the identity on equational first order sentences.

Example 2. Take 2-sorted first order logic as source logic $\mathcal{S}$, full monadic second order logic as target logic $\mathcal{T}$ and $\Sigma^I = \Sigma_{\mathcal{T}}$ as the set of all signatures. ι extends each first order signature by a second sort *set*, μ extends each first order model by adding the powerset of its universe as a second sort and the set theoretic $\in$ as a new relation between elements of the universe and elements of sort *set*, i. e. subsets of the universe. These 2-sorted models will satisfy a number of 2-sorted first order conditions that can be put into the theory $\Theta_{I,\sigma}$, for example the axiom of extensionality or the collection schema

$$\exists X : set\ \forall y\,(y \in X \leftrightarrow H(y)).$$

In this example, not all $\mathcal{S}$-models of $\Theta_{I,\sigma}$ will be in the range of μ, for example by the Löwenheim-Skolem theorem there are models of this theory where there are countably many objects of sort *set*, hence the sort of sets cannot be a full powerset in these models. Models of $\Theta_{I,\sigma}$ are called *weak models* in the theoretical foundations of higher order theorem provers.

Example 3. Let $\mathcal{S}$ be a first order logic with a designated binary symbol $\prec$. $\mathcal{T}$ is now ordinary first order logic, not using $\prec$ in any of its signatures. For M a $\mathcal{T}$-model of signature σ, let $\mu(M)$ be an expansion of M to $\sigma \cup \{\prec\}$ by interpreting $\prec$ as a well-ordering of the universe. It is a well-known consequence of the axiom of choice that this is always possible. Then, the schema of transfinite induction

$$\forall x\,(\forall y\,(y \prec x \rightarrow H(y)) \rightarrow H(x)) \rightarrow \forall z\,(H(z))$$

can be included in the theory $\Theta_{I,\sigma}$ for each formula H of signature $\sigma \cup \{\prec\}$ and can be used by theorem provers for the source logic $\mathcal{S}$. Again, there will be weak models, i. e. models of $\Theta_{I,\sigma}$, where the ordering $\prec$ is not a well-founded.

The following theorem states that the existence of an interpretation of a target logic $\mathcal{T}$ in source logic $\mathcal{S}$ justifies the use of translations of theorems from $\mathcal{S}$ in $\mathcal{T}$.

Theorem 1. *Let I be an interpretation of the logic $\mathcal{T}$ in the logic $\mathcal{S}$. Let $\sigma \in \Sigma^I$, $\Gamma \subseteq \Phi_\sigma^\mathcal{T}$, $A \in \Phi_\sigma^\mathcal{T}$. Then $\nu(\Gamma) \cup \Theta_{I,\sigma} \models_{\iota(\sigma)}^\mathcal{S} \nu(A)$ implies that $\Gamma \models_\sigma^\mathcal{T} A$, where $\nu(\Gamma)$ denotes the image of Γ under ν.*

Proof. If M is a $\mathcal{T}$-model of Γ, then $\mu(M)$ must be an $\mathcal{S}$-model of $\nu(\Gamma) \cup \Theta_{I,\sigma}$. Hence, $\mu(M)$ is also a model of $\nu(A)$ and therefore M must be a model of $\nu(A')$.**qed**

We mention that the converse of the theorem holds under the additional assumption that there are no weak models, i.e. $Mod_{\iota(\sigma)}^\mathcal{S}(\Theta_{I,\sigma})$ is the image of $Mod_\sigma^\mathcal{T}$ under μ.

Having an interpretation of a logic $\mathcal{T}$ in a logic $\mathcal{S}$ does not mean that there is a procedure to translate proofs from a calculus for $\mathcal{S}$ into proofs in a calculus for $\mathcal{T}$. Thus, in the third example above, proofs in a calculus for $\mathcal{S}$ can make use of transfinite induction, which cannot be translated directly in ordinary first order logic. If a calculus for $\mathcal{T}$ is complete, then it can merely be said that there must be a proof of the sentence A from Γ in this calculus.

4 Basic Properties of the Mizar Mathematical Library

The MIZAR MATHEMATICAL LIBRARY is a collection of mathematical papers (*articles*), written in the MIZAR language. This library has evolved over more than 10 years and consists of more than 20.000 theorems.

All theorems in the MIZAR MATHEMATICAL LIBRARY are proved from the axioms of TARSKI-GROTHENDIECK set theory (see [Ta38]). This is a set theoretic system, stronger than the more familiar system of ZERMELO and FRAENKEL with the axiom of choice. Especially, there is an unbounded class of strongly inaccessible cardinals.

4.1 On the Mizar Type System

TARSKI-GROTHENDIECK set theory is formulated in first order logic using variables for objects of a single type - *set*. Basic symbols are only the equality symbol $=$ and the membership symbol $\in$. MIZAR treats also the real numbers, the natural numbers and the arithmetic operations as primitive. However, from a theoretical point of view, these could be introduced as derived concepts.

There are some tools to introduce new types - called modes - in MIZAR. All these types are subtypes of *set*, i.e. ultimately, every object occurring in formulas in the MIZAR MATHEMATICAL LIBRARY is a set. Since $=$ and $\in$ take arbitrary arguments of type *set*, there can occur also arguments of all other types on both sides of these symbols. [MLC99] is the official description of the MIZAR syntax.

Given types can be restricted by additional properties, called attributes. Attributes are predicates with a designated argument. We call the other arguments parameters of the attribute. When a type S_1 is introduced by restricting a type S (the mother mode of S_1 in MIZAR terminology) by attributes $A_1,\ldots,A_n$, this means that S_1 is exactly the type of all objects of type S that satisfy the additional conditions $A_1,...,A_n$. Parameters of S_1 are the parameters of S and the parameters of the attributes. This restriction of a type can also be paraphrased by saying that $A_1,...,A_n$ are the conditions that permit an object of type S also to have the subtype S_1. The meaning of the attributes must have been defined before. The characteristic property

$$\forall (X : S) (A_1 (X) \wedge \ldots \wedge A_n (X) \leftrightarrow \exists (Y : S) (Y = X)) \tag{1}$$

can be used only when it has been proved that there is an object of type S that satisfies $A_1,...,A_n$.

Whenever a denotes a set, it is possible to introduce the type *element_of* (a). For example the type of real numbers is constructed in this way from the set of real numbers. Whenever *element_of* (a) is introduced by the user, MIZAR generates the obligation to prove that a is nonempty. The characteristic property

$$\forall (X : set) (X \in a \leftrightarrow \exists (Y : element\_of (a)) (Y = X)) \tag{2}$$

can be used only when this proof obligation has been satisfied.

a used in the example above, can be a term with parameters. E.g. a can be $\wp (X)$ where $\wp$ denotes the power set functor and X is a variable for sets. Then it is possible to prove a sentence like

$$\forall X \; (\forall (Y : element\_of (\wp (X))) \; Y \subset X) .$$

In this way, type constructors can have object parameters. All variables must be bound by quantifiers. This applies especially to variables which occur as parameters in terms that denote types (modes).

When a new mode is introduced in MIZAR, all parameters that are used must have modes which have been defined before. Therefore, no variable can occur as a parameter in its own type.

A MIZAR signature is a (possibly infinite) sequence of mode, functor[1] and predicate declarations, such that each declaration uses only concepts that have been defined before.

For each type there is an infinite number of variables of this type. Variables of types with different declarations are different. When a predicate or functor symbol expects as nth argument according to its declaration an object of type S, then all terms occuring at this position must have a declared value of a subtype of S.

In the formation of MIZAR formulas, the definition of a quantified formula is restricted by the following condition.

If F is a well formed formula and X is a free variable of F, then $\exists X \; F$ and $\forall X \; F$ are well formed formulas if and only if none of the variables occuring as parameters in the type of X is bound by a quantifier inside F.

[1] We follow the MIZAR usage to speak of *functions* when certain objects are meant and of *functors* when we mean the function symbols of a signature of the MIZAR logic.

For example,

$$\forall X : set\ \forall Y : element\_of(\wp(X))\ Y \subseteq X$$

is well formed, while

$$\forall Y : element\_of(\wp(X))\ \forall X : set\ Y \subseteq X$$

is not.

Theories, theorems and proofs in MIZAR contain only sentences, i.e. formulas without free variables[2]. Hence, the outermost quantifiers of such sentences quantify variables with ground types. Such variables can be instantiated with ground terms only and such an instantiation will make the type terms of the next-inner variables of the sentence ground etc.

Type checking can be done algorithmically in the MIZAR type system. More precisely, each functor symbol t must be declared in Mizar with a unique minimal type S. Of course, values of t will also have all types of which S is a restriction. The MIZAR parser may introduce tacitly hidden arguments of t in order to make sure that all parameters of S are determined by the arguments of t. Especially, the value type of a ground term will be ground. It is also possible that t can be proved to be equal to an object of a different type. For example, it can be proved that empty lists of elements of different types are equal. This way of reconsidering an object as an object of a different type must be justified by a proof also in MIZAR.

As we stated above, MIZAR adds internally type parameters to terms in order to ensure the uniqueness of the value type. For the following we strengthen this by requiring that all type parameters of the value type of a functor declaration occur as parameters of the functor.

4.2 Semantics of Mizar Types

Models of the logic of the MIZAR MATHEMATICAL LIBRARY are models of TARSKI-GROTHENDIECK set theory. Subsequently we assume that such models exist, i.e. that the MIZAR logic is consistent.

set is the top type of the MIZAR type system. Consequently, the universe of models of the MIZAR logic consists of all objects of type *set*.

These models are augmented by predicates for MIZAR modes (types). These predicates have a designated argument (say, the first) for the objects of the given type and potentially other arguments for the parameters.

n-ary predicate symbols are interpreted as n-ary relations over the universe. A predicate may require arguments of particular types in sentences. In these cases we do not care about the behaviour of the relation outside these types, since the

[2] This may not be apparent from MIZAR articles since quantifiers may be ommitted for better readability or hidden in declarations which are valid for larger sections of such an article.

truth value of well formed sentences will only depend on the interpretation of the predicate for legal values of the arguments.

Let f be an n-ary functor symbol of σ with arguments of type $S_1, \ldots, S_n$ and values declared to be of (minimal) type S. Then, in a MIZAR interpretation of σ, f must be interpreted as an n-ary mapping from the universe of the model into itself such that for all instantiations ρ of the arguments of f and of the type parameters of $S_1, \ldots, S_n$ for which the instance a_i of the i-th argument of f satisfies the type predicate of $S_i\rho$, the value of the mapping at $(a_1, \ldots, a_n)$ satisfies the type predicate of S.

It may happen – given a MIZAR theory which has a model – that such a mapping does not exist on that model for some freely chosen new declaration of f. In this case, these declarations are inconsistent with the given theory and there is no MIZAR model to interpret.

In order to define the truth value of a sentence in a MIZAR model, for each ground type and each member of the model's universe, a constant of that type is added to the signature. This constant is canonically interpreted as the corresponding element. This process is repeated a countable number of times. Note that this repetition does not create new types but only adds more notations for types that have been generated in the first step. Then, for this extended language, the truth value of a sentence is defined as usual by induction on the complexity of the sentence.

For example, $\exists X : S\ F(X)$ is true in the model if and only if $F(a)$ is true for some constant of type S.

4.3 A Remark on the Power of the Mizar Type System

It is important to note that terms denoting types can have only object variables - there are no type variables in MIZAR. Nevertheless, type constructors known from type systems of other logics, can be modelled even in a restricted subsystem of MIZAR.

From a set theoretic point of view, types in MIZAR denote classes. Some of these classes are so small that they can be represented as *sets*. We may call a type S *small* if

$$\exists\,(X : set)\,\forall\,(Y : S)\,(Y \in X)$$

can be proved. Then, by the collection schema, it can be proved that there is some a such that objects of type S are exactly the objects of type $element\_of\,(a)$.

Functions are special sets. Hence the semantics of the type of all functions is given by a predicate which selects all objects of type *set* that satisfy a certain property (being $function-like$). If a and b are objects of type *set*, it is possible to define the type of all functions from a into b by a predicate that selects those functions with domain a and range being a subset of b.

But when S_1, S_2 are small types represented as

$$element\_of\,(a_1)\,, element\_of\,(a_2)\,,$$

it can be even proved that the class of all functions taking arguments of type S_1 and having values of type S_2 is small, i.e. there is an object $function\,(a_1, a_2)$ of type *set* which describes exactly the type of all functions from a_1 into a_2. Hence this type can be introduced as

$$element\_of\,(function\,(a_1, a_2))\,.$$

Using the MIZAR *function* type constructor it should be possible to interpret classical logics based on the type system used by λ-calculus (e.g. the logic of the HOL system) in the MIZAR logic. However, this is outside the scope of the present paper.

5 Interpretations of Mizar Formulas in First Order Logic

Currently, the most advanced automated theorem provers take formulas in untyped first order logic as input. In order to apply them to extend a library of formulas – like the MIZAR MATHEMATICAL LIBRARY – the logic of the library must be interpreted in untyped first order logic. We propose some way to do this for the MIZAR logic.

There is a naive interpretation of the MIZAR logic in first order logic by expanding all definitions. For example, $\forall X : element\_of\,(a)\ H\,(X)$ translates into

$$\forall X : set\ (X \in a \rightarrow H\,(X))\,.$$

Given a type S_1 as the restriction of the type S by the attributes $A_1, \ldots, A_n$ as described in section 4.1, then a Mizar formula $\forall X : S_1\ H\,(X)$ could be translated into

$$\forall Y : S\ (A_1\,(Y) \wedge \ldots \wedge A_n\,(Y) \rightarrow H\,(Y))\,.$$

This process could be continued until there remain only variables of type *set*. When the resulting formulas are handed over to a first order theorem prover, the prover has to solve many proof obligations to ensure the type correctness conditions. For example, to prove $H\,(a)$ for an object a of type S_1 from the assumption $\forall X : S_1\ H\,(X)$, the assumptions $A_1\,(a)\,, \ldots, A_n\,(a)$ have to be confirmed. This creates heavy deductive overload, especially for provers working with depth bound strategies.

The following interpretation intends to carry over algorithmic typechecking from MIZAR to automated theorem provers by encoding type information into terms in order to prevent the generation of additional proof problems due to type checking obligations. The interpretation will work on a large class of formulas from the MIZAR logic (not only on clauses). Running a resolution prover on an interpreted MIZAR theory will yield a unification failure when the prover tries to bind a term to a variable which does not have an appropriate type. Restrictions of this method are discussed in the last section. In the following, the MIZAR logic takes the role of the target logic $\mathcal{T}$ and first order logic is the source logic $\mathcal{S}$. Recall that an interpretation does not necessary entail a possibility to translate proofs in the target logic into proofs in the source logic. Thus we shall not be concerned with the problem of translating proofs from automated theorem provers into proofs in the MIZAR logic.

Let M be a model of TARKI-GROTHENDIECK set theory and let

$$S\,(x, u_1, \ldots, u_n)$$

be a MIZAR mode, seen as a predicate with argument x and parameters $u_1, \ldots, u_n$. For all $a_1, \ldots, a_n \in |M|$, where $|M|$ denotes the universe of M

$$\{x \in |M| : M \models^{\mathcal{T}}_{\sigma} S\,(x, a_1, \ldots, a_n)\} \neq \emptyset.$$

Hence, there is an $n+1$-ary function f_S on $|M|$ such that

$$M \models^{\mathcal{T}}_{\sigma} S\,(f_S\,(a, a_1, \ldots a_n)\,, a_1, \ldots, a_n)$$

for all $a, a_1, \ldots, a_n \in |M|$ and $f_S\,(a, a_1, \ldots, a_n) = a$ if $M \models S\,(a, a_1, \ldots, a_n)$. This means that $f_S\,(x, a_1, \ldots, a_n)$ maps $|M|$ into the interpretation of

$$S\,(x, a_1, \ldots, a_n)$$

in M and is the identity on the set of elements that satisfy this relation.

Note that f_S can be introduced as the Skolem function needed to eliminate the existentioal quantifier in the formula

$$\forall X, U_1, \ldots, U_n \exists Y\,(S\,(Y, U_1, \ldots, U_n) \wedge (S(X, U_1, \ldots, U_n) \rightarrow Y = X))\,.$$

The following Lemma is an immediate consequence of this definition of f_S.

Lemma 1. *Let* $U = \{x \in |M| : M \models^{\mathcal{T}}_{\sigma} S\,(x, a_1, \ldots, a_n)\}$ *and let* f_S *also denote the unary function defined by* $f_S\,(x, a_1, \ldots, a_n)$. *Then*

- U is the range of f_S,
- f_S is idempotent on U,
- the following conditions are equivalent for all $x \in |M|$:
  1. $x \in U$,
  2. $f_S\,(x) = x$.
  3. x is an object of type S with parameters $a_1, \ldots, a_n$.

A MIZAR signature σ consists - beside the type of all sets and the predicate symbols $=$ and $\in$ - of a set of user defined MIZAR modes, relations and functors. Our interpretation does not need a restriction on the admissible signatures, i. e. $\Sigma^I = \Sigma_{\mathcal{T}}$. For each MIZAR signature σ let $\iota\,(\sigma)$ be the first order signature which contains beside $=$ and $\in$ these symbols and new $n+1$-ary functors f_S for each MIZAR mode S from σ with n parameters.

If M is a MIZAR model of such a sorted signature σ, then let $\mu\,(M)$ be the first order model of signature $\iota\,(\sigma)$ with the same universe as M, $\in$ as in M, and the remaining relations and functors defined as follows.

Relations are defined as in M for arguments in their specific domains. If one of the arguments in $\mu(M)$ is outside this domain, we fix a truth value for this relation in an arbitrary way.

Similarly, functors are interpreted in $\mu(M)$ on their domains in M as in M and in an arbitrary but fixed way for the remaining arguments.

The new functors f_S are interpreted as described above. This completes the description of the mappings ι and μ. We complete our definition of an interpretation of the MIZAR logic into first order logic by giving the description of the mapping ν which translates MIZAR formulas into first order formulas and the description of $\Theta_{I,\sigma}$.

In fact, we shall extend ν to work on well formed terms in the MIZAR logic. $\nu(H)$ will be defined by recursion on the structure of H. However, the induction schema has to be chosen carefully, since the type declarations of variables and functors may contain complex terms.

Let H be a well formed sentence in the MIZAR logic. Without loss of generality we can assume that each variable is bound in H by exactly one quantifier. If necessary, this can be achieved by renaming of variables. The ordering $\prec$ on the variables of H is defined as follows.

Definition 4. *$X \prec Y$ if and only if the quantifier that binds Y in H is in the range of a quantifier that binds X.*

Note that variables that are bound by the outermost quantifiers of H are minimal with respect to this ordering. Moreover, all variables in terms occuring as instances of parameters of the type of a variable X are below X.

ω denotes the first infinite ordinal. If G is a subformula or subterm of H, the *rank* of G is an ordinal number defined as follows.

Definition 5. *Let*

$$n = \max(\{card\{X \mid X \prec Y\} + 1 \mid Y \text{ occurs in } G\} \cup \{0\}).$$

Let d be the term depth of G[3] *Then let*

$$rank(G) = \omega \cdot n + d.$$

Note that a proper subterm of a term has a strictly smaller rank than the term itself. Moreover, if the variable X occurs in a term t and the parameters of the type of X are instantiated with the terms $t_1, \ldots, t_n$, than the ranks of $t_1, \ldots, t_n$ must be strictly smaller than the rank of X, since their variables are strictly below X. Moreover the rank of X is not bigger than the rank of t. The rank of ground terms is the ordinary term depth. When t is a term with outermost functor symbol f, by our provision on (hidden) functor arguments of f, the parameters of the value type of t have a rank which is strictly less than the rank of t.

[3] Formulas are considered as terms in an extended signature where logical connectives and quantifiers are considered as ordinary operators.

Now we define $\nu(H)$ by transfinite induction on the rank of subterms and subformulas of H[4]. Hence we can assume that ν has been already defined for all proper subformulas, subterms and type parameters.

When X is a variable of a type S with parameters $u_1, \ldots, u_n$ let

$$\nu(X) = f_S(X, \nu(u_1), \ldots, \nu(u_n)).$$

Whenever f is a functor of σ taking arguments of type $S_1, \ldots, S_n$ and declared as giving values of type S, $t_1, \ldots, t_n$ are terms of type $S_1, \ldots, S_n$ respectively, we define

$$\nu(f(t_1, \ldots, t_n)) = f_S(f(\nu(t_1), \ldots, v(t_n))).$$

Especially, if f is a constant, then $\nu(f) = f_S(f)$. Note that by the definition of f_S above

$$\mu(M) \models^S_\sigma f_S(f) = f.$$

If r is a predicate, then let

$$\nu(r(t_1, \ldots, t_n)) = r(\nu(t_1), \ldots, \nu(t_n)).$$

i.e. relation symbols are not changed. This is of special importance for the equality predicate, since it gives provers a chance to utilize their special treatments of equality. ν distributes over quantifiers and propositional operators. Especially, variables following a quantifier remain unchanged. The theory $\Theta_{I,\sigma}$ contains beside the axioms of TARSKI-GROTHENDIECK set theory additional informations on the declarations in use. When f is a functor as above, we add to $\Theta_{I,\sigma}$ the universal closure of

$$f_S(f(v(X_1), \ldots, \nu(X_n))) = f(\nu(X_1), \ldots, \nu(X_n)) \tag{3}$$

where $X_1, \ldots, X_n$ are variables of type $S_1, \ldots, S_n$ respectively. Moreover we add

$$\forall X\, f_{set}(X) = X$$

and

$$\forall X\, f_S(f_S(X)) = f_S(X)$$

When the type S_1 is defined by restricting the type S by the attributes $A_1,\ldots,A_n$, we add

$$\forall X\ (A_1(f_S(X)) \wedge \ldots \wedge A_n(f_S(X)) \leftrightarrow f_{S_1}(f_S(X)) = f_S(X)) \tag{4}$$
$$\forall X\ (f_S(f_{S_1}(X)) = f_{S_1}(X))$$

When S is defined as *element_of* (a),

$$\forall X\,(X \in \nu(a) \leftrightarrow f_S(X) = X)$$

is added to $T'_{I,\sigma}$.

[4] Readers not acquainted with transfinite induction might prefer to map the finite number of ordinals which occur as ranks of subterms and subformulas of H in an order-preserving way onto an initial segment of natural numbers and to use ordinary induction on these modified ranks.

Theorem 2. *I as defined above by the mappings ι, μ, ν and the first order theories $\Theta_{I,\sigma}$ is an interpretation of the* MIZAR *logic into untyped first order logic.*

Proof. The first thing to show is, that first order models in the range of μ satisfy $\Theta_{I,\sigma}$. Since $\in$ and $=$ are not changed by μ, a model $\mu(M)$ must be a model of TARSKI-GROTHENDIECK set theory, since the MIZAR model M is.

If f is a functor symbol that is declared to take arguments of type $S_1, \ldots, S_n$ and to yield a value of type S, 3 expands into

$$f_S(f(f_{S_1}(X_1), \ldots, f_{S_n}(X_n))) = f(f_{S_1}(X_1), \ldots, f_{S_n}(X_n))$$

(we discard parameters of the argument types to simplify the notation). Now let $a_1, \ldots, a_n$ be arbitrary elements of $|\mu(M)| = |M|$. Then for $i = 1 \ldots n$ we have $S_i(f_{S_i}(a_i))$ by the definition of f_{S_i}. Hence $f_{S_1}(a_1), \ldots, f_{S_n}(a_n)$ are in the domain of f and hence $S(f(f_{S_1}(a_1), \ldots, f_{S_n}(a_n)))$. Therefore, since f_S is defined to be the identity on S,

$$f_S(f(f_{S_1}(a_1), \ldots, f_{S_n}(a_n))) = f(f_{S_1}(a_1), \ldots, f_{S_n}(a_n)).$$

Since the hole universe of M consists of elements of type *set* and this must be the range of f_{set}. The functions f_S are the identity on their respective ranges, hence f_{set} is the identity.

Now suppose S_1 is defined by restricting the type S by the attributes A_1,...,A_n. Let $a \in |M|$ be arbitrary and let $b = f_S(a)$. Hence

$$M \models_\sigma^{\mathcal{T}} (A_1(b) \wedge \ldots \wedge A_n(b) \leftrightarrow \exists X : S_1\, b = x)$$

by (1). The right hand side of this equivalence means that $S_1(b)$ holds and is by Lemma 1 also equivalent with $f_{S_1}(b) = b$. Now, replacing b by $f_S(A)$, we confirm (4). b is also a member of the set of all objects of type S, on which f_S is idempotent. Hence, also $f_S(f_{S_1}(a)) = f_{S_1}(a)$. The last sentence of $\Theta_{I,\sigma}$ reflects similarly (2).

The remaining third condition of the definition of an interpretation states, that the translation ν does not change the truth value of MIZAR sentences. First we show by induction on the form of t that for each legal MIZAR term t and for each instantiation of its variables the value of t in M equals the value of $\nu(t)$ in $\mu(M)$. More precisely, a nested induction is required, where the outer induction goes over the number of parameters occurring in the involved types.

If t is a variable of sort S, then the value of t satisfies the predicate characterizing S, hence $t = f_S(t) = \nu(t)$. If t is a compound term $f(t_1, \ldots, t_n)$ where f is declared as above, then by induction hypothesis

$$\nu(t) = f_S(f(\nu(t_1), \ldots, v(t_n))) = f_S(f(t_1, \ldots, t_n)) = f(t_1, \ldots, t_n) = t$$

by Lemma 1.

The truth value of atomic formulas has not been changed for arguments of the sorts admitted according to the MIZAR declarations. Only such arguments occur in translations of legal MIZAR formulas by ν. The induction over propositional connectives is trivial.

Now, consider a MIZAR formula $\exists X : S\, H(X)$.

$$\nu(\exists X : S\, H(X)) = \exists X\, \nu(H(X)).$$

If $M \models^{\mathcal{T}}_{\sigma} \exists X : S\, H(X)$, say $M \models^{\mathcal{T}}_{\sigma} H[a/X]$ for some a such that $S(a)$, then $\mu(M) \models^{\mathcal{S}}_{\iota(\sigma)} \nu(H)[a/X]$, Hence $\mu(M) \models^{\mathcal{S}}_{\iota(\sigma)} \exists X\, \nu(H(X))$. Conversely, assume that $\mu(M) \models^{\mathcal{S}}_{\iota(\sigma)} \exists X\, \nu(H(X))$, say $\mu(M) \models^{\mathcal{S}}_{\iota(\sigma)} \nu(H(a))$. a need not be of sort S, but we can observe, that X occurs inside H always inside f_S. Moreover by Lemma 1 $f_S(f_S(a)) = f_S(a)$ Therefore, the element $b = f_S(a) = f_S(b)$ is of sort S and we have that also $\mu(M) \models^{\mathcal{S}}_{\iota(\sigma)} \nu(H(b))$, hence $M \models^{\mathcal{T}}_{\sigma} H(b)$. This yields $M \models^{\mathcal{T}}_{\sigma} \exists X : S\, H(X)$. The universal quantifier can be treated similarly.**qed**

6 Modifications

Consider the following sentence which states that each relation can be extended.

$$\forall A\colon set \forall B\colon set \forall C\colon set(A \subseteq B \to \forall F\colon relation(A,C) \exists G\colon relation(B,C) F \subseteq G).$$

Let $f_s.f_r$ denote the function symbols introduced for the type constructors *set* and *relation*. Then this sentence is translated by the method described in the last section into

$$\forall A \forall B \forall C(f_s(A) \subseteq f_s(B) \to \forall F \exists G f_r(F, f_s(A), f_s(C)) \subseteq f_r(G, f_s(B), f_s(C))).$$

Note that this translation is performed prior to generating clauses for a prover. Since f_s is the identity function, it can be omitted. The resulting formula yields the clause

$$A \subseteq B \to f_r(F, A, C) \subseteq f_r(s(A, B, C, F), B, C),$$

where s is a new Skolem function.

Suppose we want to infer that each functions can be extended in a similar way to a relation, where functions are defined as special relations. f_f denotes the function symbol introduced for the function type constructor. The negated goal gives the clauses

$$a \subseteq b$$

$$\neg f_f(h(a,b,c), a, b) \subseteq f_r(G, b, c)$$

for new Skolem symbols a, b, c, h. Since relations are functions, the theory describing the interpretation yields

$$f_r(f_f(X, A, B), A, B) = f_f(X, A, B).$$

Hence, f_f can be replaced already in the non-clause form by a term starting with f_r. Then a simple resolution step completes the proof.

On the other hand, as expected, it cannot be proved from the above formula that each function can be extended similarly to a function with an extended domain.

7 Discussion

The interpretation we have given encodes type information into first order terms. It is a general purpose interpretation working for any target first order prover. It has been especially useful in experiments with provers that communicate at runtime within the ILF system [DGHW97]. In order to save time during the communication it was necessary to use the same type encoding for all provers. When working with a single prover, better results may be achieved by taking specific properties of the prover or the actual proof problem into account. The ideal solution might be an automated prover having unification implemented in an exchangeable module, so that various type checking algorithms can be used.

For example the SPASS prover treats unary predicates as types [GaMeWe97] and tries to detect type clashes early. Hence, for this particular prover, the naive interpretation which translates quantification of typed variables into quantification relativized by type predicates, is most efficient – at least for the monomorphic case. For SPASS, the theory $\Theta_{I,\sigma}$ contains axioms describing the declaration of functor symbols and for each type an axiom saying that it is not empty.

[Mel88] proposes a method for encoding monomorphic types that translates also checking the subtype relation into unification problems. This method introduces new variables into the terms. These auxiliary variables in the first order clauses can lead to a larger search space, unless they are treated in a special way by the automated provers.

The input language of some provers (e. g. 3TaP and ProTeIn) supports the encoding of monomorphic tree-like type systems in clauses. When our method is applied in this situation and the modifications described in the last section are applied, our encoding will differ from them only by using nested functor symbols instead of additional list arguments. Since both encodings lead to unifiability checks of the same complexity, they can be considered as being of equal power. But our interpretation has the advantage that it works also on non-clauses and can deal with object type parameters.

In the interpretation given above we have made some simplifications compared with the full MIZAR language. We have not considered the set constructor, which, given a set object a and a formula H, constructs an object representing the set of all $x \in a$ such that $H(x)$. This leads to the phenomenon that terms can contain formulas. Handling this situation requires an additional induction over a countable hierarchy of formulas such that terms of level $n+1$ can contain formulas of level n.

We also did not consider types that are defined as classes of structures. This is not a severe restriction since the MIZAR constructors and selectors of structure classes can be translated into ordinary functors. Overloading of functors poses a serious limitation to the interpretation given here. In MIZAR it occurs in the form of redefinitions of value types. They redeclare the value type of a term depending on the types of the arguments. These redeclarations cannot be encoded into the term structure such that type checking is performed during unification in first order theorem provers. The reason is that unification works without backtracking from terms to their arguments. It cannot correct a unification clash when it discovers that arguments carry encodings of a more specific type. Nevertheless, it is possible to express overloading by first order formulas so that it can be handled by deductive means.

Recently, Christoph Wernhard has extracted 47 new proof problems for first order provers from an article in the MIZAR library with the ILF system. Unlike earlier test suites, these problems make use of a polymorphic type constructor. The proof problems can be downloaded from the following URL:

`www-irm.mathematik.hu-berlin.de/~ilf/miz2atp/download.html`

These problems use the naive translation mentioned above. They are formulated such that the involved type information can be easily recovered. Authors of theorem provers are encouraged to modify their provers in order to make efficient use of the type information contained in the problems. The interpretation given above intends to be just one step into this direction.

References

[Ba74] K. J. Barwise: Axioms for abstract model theory; Ann. Math. Logic vol. 7 (1974), 221–265

[DahWer97] I. Dahn, C. Wernhard: First Order Proof Problems Extracted from an Article in the MIZAR Mathematical Library. RISC-Linz Report Series, No. 97-50, pp. 58–62, Johannes Kepler Universität Linz, 1997.

[DGHW97] B. I. Dahn, J. Gehne, Th. Honigmann, A. Wolf: Integration of Automated and Interactive Theorem Proving in ILF. In Proc. CADE-14, pp. 57-60, Springer, 1997.

[GaMeWe97] H. Ganzinger, C. Meyer, C. Weidenbach: Soft Typing for Ordered Resolution. In Proc. CADE-14, pp. 321-335, Springer, 1997.

[Mel88] Mellish, C. S.: Implementing Systemic Classification by Unification. Comp. Ling. 14, 1988, pp 40 – 51

[MLC99] The Mizar Library Committee: Syntax of the Mizar Language. http://www.mizar.org/language/syntax.txt

[Rud92] P. Rudnicki: An Overview of the Mizar Project. Proceedings of the 1992 Workshop on Types for Proofs and Programs, Chalmers University of Technology, Bastad 1992.

[Ta38] A. Tarski "Uber unerreichbare Kardinalzahlen, Fund. Math., vol.30 (1938), pp.68-69

[Try93] A. Trybulec: Some Features of the Mizar Language, ESPRIT Workshop, Torino 1993.

[WiGe97] G. Wiederhold, M. Genesereth: The Basis for Mediation. To appear IEEE Expert

An $\mathcal{O}((n \cdot \log n)^3)$-Time Transformation from Grz into Decidable Fragments of Classical First-Order Logic

Stéphane Demri[1] and Rajeev Goré[2*]

[1] Laboratoire LEIBNIZ - C.N.R.S.
46 av. Félix Viallet, 38000 Grenoble, France
demri@imag.fr

[2] Automated Reasoning Project and Dept. of Computer Science
Australian National University, ACT 0200 Canberra, Australia
rpg@arp.anu.edu.au

Abstract. The provability logic Grz is characterized by a class of modal frames that is not first-order definable. We present a simple embedding of Grz into decidable fragments of classical first-order logic such as FO^2 and the guarded fragment. The embedding is an $\mathcal{O}((n.log\ n)^3)$-time transformation that neither involves first principles about Turing machines (and therefore is easy to implement), nor the semantical characterization of Grz (and therefore does not use any second-order machinery). Instead, we use the syntactic relationships between cut-free sequent-style calculi for Grz, S4 and T. We first translate Grz into T, and then we use the relational translation from T into FO^2.

1 Introduction

Propositional modal logics have proved useful in many areas of computer science because they capture interesting properties of binary relations (Kripke frames) whilst retaining decidability (see e.g. [Var97,Ben99]). By far the most popular method for automating deduction in these logics has been the method of analytic tableaux (see e.g. [Fit83,Rau83,Gor99]), particularly because of the close connection between tableaux calculi and known cut-free Gentzen systems for these logics.

An alternative approach is to translate propositional modal logics into classical first-order logic since this allows us to use the wealth of knowledge in first-order theorem proving to mechanize modal deduction (see e.g. [Mor76], [Ohl88], [Her89], [dMP95], [Non96], [Ohl98]). Let FO^n be the fragment of classical first-order logic using at most n individual variables and no function symbols. Any modal logic characterized by a first-order definable class of modal frames can be translated into FO^n for some fixed $n \geq 2$. The *decidable* modal logic K4, for example, is characterised by transitive frames, definable using the first-order

* Supported by an Australian Research Council Queen Elizabeth II Fellowship.

R. Caferra and G. Salzer (Eds.): Automated Deduction, LNAI 1761, pp. 152–166, 2000.

formula $(\forall x, y, z)(R(x, y) \wedge R(y, z) \Rightarrow R(x, z))$ containing 3 variables. Since FO^3 is undecidable and FO^2 is decidable, translating K4 into first-order logic does not automatically retain decidability. Of course, the exact fragment delineated by the translation is decidable. The only known first-order decision procedure for that particular fragment except the one that mimicks the rules for K4 is the one recently published in [GHMS98]. Therefore, blind translation is not useful if this means giving up decidability.

Moreover, it is well-known that many *decidable* propositional modal logics are characterised by classes of Kripke frames which are not first-order definable, and that the "standard" relational translation (see e.g. [Mor76,Ben83]) is unable to deal with such logics. The class of such "second order" modal logics includes logics like G and Grz which have been shown to have "arithmetical" interpretations as well as logics like S4.3.1 which have interpretations as logics of linear time (without a next-time operator) [Gor94].

Somewhat surprisingly, faithful translations into classical logic (usually augmented with theories) have been found for some propositional modal logics even when these logics are characterized by classes of frames that are not first-order definable. For instance, the modal logic K augmented with the McKinsey axiom is captured by the framework presented in [Ohl93]. Similarly, the provability logic G[1] that admits arithmetical interpretations [Sol76] is treated within the set-theoretical framework defined in [dMP95]. Both techniques in [Ohl93,dMP95] use a version of classical logic augmented with a theory. Alternatively, G can also be translated into classical logic by first using the translation into K4 defined in [BH94] and then a translation from K4 into classical logic (see e.g. [Ben83]).

The fact that G can be translated into a *decidable* fragment of classical logic follows from a purely complexity theory viewpoint, as shown next. Take a modal logic $\mathcal{L}$ that is in the complexity class $\mathbf{C}$ and let $\mathbf{C}'$ be another complexity class. Here a *logic* is to be understood as a set of formulae and therefore a logic is exactly a *(decision) problem* in the usual sense in complexity theory. That is, as a language viewed as a set of strings built upon a given alphabet. By definition (see e.g. [Pap94]), for any fragment of classical logic that is $\mathbf{C}$-hard with respect to $\mathbf{C}'$ many-one reductions[2], there is a mapping f in $\mathbf{C}'$ such that any modal formula $\phi \in \mathcal{L}$ iff $f(\phi)$ is valid in such a first-order fragment. From the facts that G is in **PSPACE** (see e.g. [BH94,Lad77]), validity in FO^2 is **NEXPTIME**-hard [Für81] (see also [Lew80]) and $\mathbf{PSPACE} \subseteq \mathbf{NEXPTIME}$, it is easy to conclude that there exists a polynomial-time transformation from G into validity in FO^2.

As is well-known, this illustrates the difference between the fact that a propositional modal logic K + ϕ is characterised by a class of frames which is not first-order definable, and the existence of a translation from K + ϕ into first-order logic. The weak point with this theoretical result is that the definition of f might require the use of first principles about Turing machines. If this is so, then realising the map f requires cumbersome machinery since we must first

[1] Also called GL (for Gödel and Löb), KW, K4W, PrL.

[2] Also called "transformation", see e.g. [Pap94].

completely define a Turing machine that solves the problem. This is why the translations in [Ohl93,BH94,dMP95] are much more refined and practical (apart from the fact that they allow to mechanise the modal logics under study).

Another well-known modal logic that is characterized by a class of modal frames that is not first-order definable is the provability logic Grz (for Grzegorczyk). The main contribution of this paper is the definition of an $\mathcal{O}(n.log\ n)$-time transformation from Grz into S4, using cut-free sequent-style calculi for these respective logics. Renaming techniques from [Min88] are used in order to get the $\mathcal{O}(n.log\ n)$-time bound. Then, we present a cubic-time transformation from S4 into T, again using the cut-free sequent-style calculi for these respective logics. Both reductions proceed via an analysis of the proofs in cut-free sequent calculi from the literature. The second reduction is a slight variant of the one presented in [CCM97] (see also [Fit88]). The reduction announced in the title can be obtained by translating T into FO^2, which is known to be decidable (see e.g. [Mor75]). Furthermore, the formula obtained by reduction belongs to the decidable guarded fragment of classical logic (see e.g. [ANB98]) for which a resolution decision procedure has been defined in [Niv98].

In [Boo93, Chapter 12], a (non polynomial-time) transformation from Grz into G is defined. By using renamings of subformulae, it is easy to extract from that transformation, an $\mathcal{O}(n.log\ n)$-time transformation from Grz into G [Boo93, Chapter 12]. There exists an $\mathcal{O}(n)$-time transformation from G into K4 [BH94]. There exists an $\mathcal{O}(n^4.log\ n)$-time transformation from K4 into K using [CCM97] and renamings of subformulae. Finally, there exists an $\mathcal{O}(n)$-time transformation from K into FO^2 [Ben83]. Combining these results gives an $\mathcal{O}(n^4.(log\ n)^5)$-time transformation from Grz into FO^2, a decidable fragment of first-order logic.

The translation proposed in this paper is therefore a more refined alternative since it requires only time in $\mathcal{O}((n.log\ n)^3)$. As a side-effect, we obtain an $\mathcal{O}(n.log\ n)$-time transformation from Grz into S4 and an $\mathcal{O}((n.log\ n)^3)$-time transformation from Grz into T. Using the space upper bound for S4-validity from [Hud96], we obtain that Grz requires only space in $\mathcal{O}(n^2.(log\ n)^3)$. We are not aware of any tighter bound for Grz in the literature. Furthermore, our purely proof-theoretical analyses of the cut-free sequent-style calculi, and sometimes of the Hilbert-style proof systems, gives a simple framework to unify the transformations involved in [Boo93,BH94,CCM97]. As we intend to report in a longer paper, it is also possible to generalise our method to handle other "second order" propositional modal logics like S4.3.1 using the calculi from [Gor94] (see also [DG99] for a generalisation and extension in the Display Logic framework [Bel82]). This paper is a completed version of [DG98].

2 Basic Notions

In the present paper, we assume that the modal formulae are built from a countably infinite set $\texttt{For}_0 \stackrel{\text{def}}{=} \{\mathrm{p}_{i,j} : i,j \in \omega\}$ of atomic propositions using the usual connectives $\Box, \neg, \Rightarrow, \wedge$. Other standard abbreviations include $\vee, \Leftrightarrow, \Diamond$. The set of modal formulae is denoted $\texttt{For}$. An occurrence of the subformula ψ in ϕ is *positive* [resp. *negative*] iff it is in the scope of an even [resp. odd] number of negations, where as usual, every occurrence of $\phi_1 \Rightarrow \phi_2$ is treated as an occurence of $\neg(\phi_1 \wedge \neg\phi_2)$. For instance $\Box p_{0,0}$ [resp. $\Box p_{0,1}$] has a positive [resp. negative] occurrence in $(\Box\Box p_{0,1}) \Rightarrow (p_{0,1} \wedge \Box p_{0,0})$. We write $mwp(\phi)$ [resp. $mwn(\phi)$] to denote the number of positive [resp. negative] occurrences of $\Box$ in ϕ. We write $|\phi|$ to denote the *size* of the formula ϕ, that is the number of symbols occurring in ϕ. ϕ is also represented as a string of characters.

We recall that the standard Hilbert system K is composed of the following axiom schemes: the tautologies of the Propositional Calculus (PC) and $\Box p \Rightarrow (\Box(p \Rightarrow q) \Rightarrow \Box q)$. The inference rules of K are *modus ponens* (from p and $p \Rightarrow q$ infer q) and *necessitation* (from p infer $\Box p$). By abusing our notation, we may identify the system K with its set of theorems, allowing us to write $\phi \in K$ to denote that ϕ is a *theorem* of K. Analogous notation is used for the following well-known extensions of K: T $\stackrel{\text{def}}{=}$ K + $\Box p \Rightarrow p$, K4 $\stackrel{\text{def}}{=}$ K + $\Box p \Rightarrow \Box\Box p$, S4 $\stackrel{\text{def}}{=}$ K4 + $\Box p \Rightarrow p$ and Grz $\stackrel{\text{def}}{=}$ S4 + $\Box(\Box(p \Rightarrow \Box p) \Rightarrow p) \Rightarrow \Box p$. Numerous variants of the system Grz (having the same set of theorems) can be found in the literature (see for instance [GHH97]).

We call GT, G$S4$ and GGrz the cut-free versions of the Gentzen-style calculi defined in [OM57,Avr84] where the sequents are built from finite sets of formulae. Moreover, the weakening rule is absorbed in the initial sequents. For instance, the initial sequents of all the Gentzen-style calculi used in the paper are of the form $\Gamma, \phi \vdash \Delta, \phi$ where "," denotes set union. The common core of rules for the systems GT, G$S4$ and GGrz are presented in Figure 1.

The introduction rules for $\Box$ on the right-hand side are the following:

$$\frac{\Gamma \vdash \phi}{\Sigma, \Box\Gamma \vdash \Box\phi, \Delta}\ (\vdash \Box)_T \qquad \frac{\Box\Gamma \vdash \phi}{\Sigma, \Box\Gamma \vdash \Box\phi, \Delta}\ (\vdash \Box)_{S4}$$

$$\frac{\Box\Gamma, \Box(\phi \Rightarrow \Box\phi) \vdash \phi}{\Sigma, \Box\Gamma \vdash \Box\phi, \Delta}\ (\vdash \Box)_{Grz}$$

where $\Box\Gamma \stackrel{\text{def}}{=} \{\Box\psi : \psi \in \Gamma\}$. Moreover, we assume that in Σ, there is no formula of the form $\Box\psi$. This restriction is not essential for completeness (and for soundness) but it is used in the proof of Lemma 5. Each rule $(\vdash \Box)_T$, $(\vdash \Box)_{S4}$ and

$$\Gamma, \phi \vdash \Delta, \phi \text{ (initial sequents)} \qquad \frac{\Gamma \vdash \Delta, \phi}{\Gamma, \neg\phi \vdash \Delta}\ (\neg \vdash) \qquad \frac{\Gamma, \phi \vdash \Delta}{\Gamma \vdash \Delta, \neg\phi}\ (\vdash \neg)$$

$$\frac{\Gamma, \phi_1, \phi_2 \vdash \Delta}{\Gamma, \phi_1 \wedge \phi_2 \vdash \Delta}\ (\wedge \vdash) \qquad \frac{\Gamma \vdash \Delta, \phi_1 \quad \Gamma \vdash \Delta, \phi_2}{\Gamma \vdash \Delta, \phi_1 \wedge \phi_2}\ (\vdash \wedge)$$

$$\frac{\Gamma \vdash \Delta, \phi_1 \quad \Gamma, \phi_2 \vdash \Delta}{\Gamma, \phi_1 \Rightarrow \phi_2 \vdash \Delta}\ (\Rightarrow \vdash) \qquad \frac{\Gamma, \phi_1 \vdash \Delta, \phi_2}{\Gamma \vdash \Delta, \phi_1 \Rightarrow \phi_2}\ (\vdash \Rightarrow) \qquad \frac{\Gamma, \Box\phi, \phi \vdash \Delta}{\Gamma, \Box\phi \vdash \Delta}\ (\Box \vdash)$$

Fig. 1. Common core of rules

$(\vdash \Box)_{Grz}$ belongs respectively to $\mathtt{G}T$, $\mathtt{G}S4$ and $\mathtt{G}Grz$. For each $\mathcal{L} \in \{T, S4, Grz\}$, we know that for any sequent $\Gamma \vdash \Delta$, the formula $(\bigwedge_{\phi \in \Gamma} \phi) \Rightarrow (\bigvee_{\phi \in \Delta} \phi) \in \mathcal{L}$ iff[3] the sequent $\Gamma \vdash \Delta$ is derivable in $\mathtt{G}\mathcal{L}$ (see e.g. [OM57,Avr84,Gor99]). Consequently, if $\Gamma \vdash \Delta$ is derivable in $\mathtt{G}\mathcal{L}$, then so is $\Gamma, \Gamma' \vdash \Delta, \Delta'$.

3 A Transformation from Grz into S4

Let $f : \mathtt{For} \times \{0,1\} \to \mathtt{For}$ be the following map:

- for any $\mathrm{p} \in \mathtt{For}_0$, $f(\mathrm{p}, 0) \stackrel{\text{def}}{=} f(\mathrm{p}, 1) \stackrel{\text{def}}{=} \mathrm{p}$
- $f(\neg\phi, i) \stackrel{\text{def}}{=} \neg f(\phi, 1-i)$ for $i \in \{0,1\}$
- $f(\phi_1 \wedge \phi_2, i) \stackrel{\text{def}}{=} f(\phi_1, i) \wedge f(\phi_2, i)$ for $i \in \{0,1\}$
- $f(\phi_1 \Rightarrow \phi_2, i) \stackrel{\text{def}}{=} f(\phi_1, 1-i) \Rightarrow f(\phi_2, i)$ for $i \in \{0,1\}$
- $f(\Box\phi, 1) \stackrel{\text{def}}{=} \Box(\Box(f(\phi,1) \Rightarrow \Box f(\phi,0)) \Rightarrow f(\phi,1))$ $\quad f(\Box\phi, 0) \stackrel{\text{def}}{=} \Box f(\phi, 0)$.

In $f(\phi, i)$, the index i should be seen as information about the *polarity* of ϕ in the translation process as is done in [BH94] for the translation from G into K4. Observe that if we replace the definition of $f(\Box\phi, 1)$ above by $f(\Box\phi, 1) \stackrel{\text{def}}{=} \Box(f(\Box(\phi \Rightarrow \Box\phi) \Rightarrow \phi, 1))$, we get the same map.

Since the rule of *replacement of equivalents* is admissible in Grz, one can show by induction on the length of ϕ that for any $\phi \in \mathtt{For}$ and for any $i \in \{0,1\}$, $\phi \Leftrightarrow f(\phi, i) \in Grz$. Moreover,

Lemma 1. *For any $\phi \in \mathtt{For}$, $\phi \Rightarrow f(\phi,1) \in K \subseteq S4$ and $f(\phi,0) \Rightarrow \phi \in K \subseteq S4$.*

Proof. The proof is by simultaneous induction on the structure of ϕ. The base case when ϕ is an atomic proposition is immediate. By way of example, let us treat the cases below in the induction step:

(1) $\phi_1 \wedge \phi_2 \Rightarrow f(\phi_1 \wedge \phi_2, 1) \in K$ $\quad$ (2) $\Box\phi_1 \Rightarrow f(\Box\phi_1, 1) \in K$

(3) $f(\neg\phi_1, 0) \Rightarrow \neg\phi_1 \in K$ $\quad$ (4) $f(\Box\phi_1, 0) \Rightarrow \Box\phi_1 \in K$.

(1) By the induction hypothesis, $\phi_1 \Rightarrow f(\phi_1, 1) \in K$ and $\phi_2 \Rightarrow f(\phi_2, 1) \in K$. By easy manipulation at the propositional level, $\phi_1 \wedge \phi_2 \Rightarrow f(\phi_1, 1) \wedge f(\phi_2, 1) \in K$. By definition of f, $\phi_1 \wedge \phi_2 \Rightarrow f(\phi_1 \wedge \phi_2, 1) \in K$.
(2) By the induction hypothesis, $\phi_1 \Rightarrow f(\phi_1, 1) \in K$. By easy manipulation at the propositional level, $\phi_1 \Rightarrow (\Box(f(\phi,1) \Rightarrow \Box f(\phi,0)) \Rightarrow f(\phi_1,1)) \in K$. It is known that the regular rule (from $\psi_1 \Rightarrow \psi_2$ infer $\Box\psi_1 \Rightarrow \Box\psi_2$) is admissible in K. So, $\Box\phi_1 \Rightarrow \Box(\Box(f(\phi,1) \Rightarrow \Box f(\phi,0)) \Rightarrow f(\phi_1,1)) \in K$. By the definition of f, $\Box\phi_1 \Rightarrow f(\Box\phi_1, 1) \in K$.

[3] As is usual, the empty conjunction is understood as the *verum* logical constant $\top$ (or simply $\mathrm{p}_{0,0} \vee \neg\mathrm{p}_{0,0}$) and the empty disjunction is understood as the *falsum* logical constant $\bot$ (or simply $\mathrm{p}_{0,0} \wedge \neg\mathrm{p}_{0,0}$).

(3) By the induction hypothesis, $\phi_1 \Rightarrow f(\phi_1, 1) \in K$. By easy manipulation at the propositional level, $\neg f(\phi_1, 1) \Rightarrow \neg\phi_1 \in K$. By definition of f, $f(\neg\phi_1, 0) \Rightarrow \neg\phi_1 \in K$.
(4) By the induction hypothesis, $f(\phi_1, 0) \Rightarrow \phi_1 \in K$. Since the regular rule is admissible in K, $\Box f(\phi_1, 0) \Rightarrow \Box\phi_1 \in K$. By the definition of f, $f(\Box\phi_1, 0) \Rightarrow \Box\phi_1 \in K$.

Theorem 1. *A formula $\phi \in Grz$ iff $f(\phi, 1) \in S4$.*

Proof. If $f(\phi, 1) \in S4$, then *a fortiori* $f(\phi, 1) \in Grz$, and since $\phi \Leftrightarrow f(\phi, 1) \in Grz$, we then obtain $\phi \in Grz$.

Now assume $\phi \in Grz$, hence the sequent $\vdash \phi$ has a cut-free proof in GGrz. We can show that in the given cut-free proof of $\vdash \phi$, for every sequent $\Gamma \vdash \Delta$ with cut-free proof Π', the sequent $f(\Gamma, 0) \vdash f(\Delta, 1)$ admits a cut-free proof in G$S4$. Here, f is extended to sets of formulae in the natural way. So, we shall conclude that $\vdash f(\phi, 1)$ is derivable in GS4 and therefore $f(\phi, 1) \in S4$. The proof is by induction on the structure of the derivations.
Base case: When $\Gamma \vdash \Delta$ is an initial sequent $\Gamma', \psi \vdash \psi, \Delta'$, we can show that $f(\Gamma', 0), f(\psi, 0) \vdash f(\psi, 1), f(\Delta', 1)$ has a cut-free proof in G$S4$ since $f(\psi, 0) \Rightarrow f(\psi, 1) \in S4$. By completeness of G$S4$, $f(\psi, 0) \vdash f(\psi, 1)$ has a proof in G$S4$.
Induction step: The structural rules pose no difficulties because by definition f is homomorphic with respect to the comma. By way of example, the proof step (in GGrz)

$$\dfrac{\begin{array}{c}\vdots\\ \Box\Gamma', \Box(\psi \Rightarrow \Box\psi) \vdash \psi\end{array}}{\Gamma, \Box\Gamma' \vdash \Box\psi, \Delta}\ (\vdash \Box)_{Grz}$$

is transformed into the proof steps (in G$S4$)

$$\dfrac{\dfrac{\begin{array}{c}\vdots\\ \Box f(\Gamma', 0), \Box(f(\psi, 1) \Rightarrow \Box f(\psi, 0)) \vdash f(\psi, 1)\end{array}}{\Box f(\Gamma', 0) \vdash \Box(f(\psi, 1) \Rightarrow \Box f(\psi, 0)) \Rightarrow f(\psi, 1)}\ (\vdash\Rightarrow)}{f(\Gamma, 0), \Box f(\Gamma', 0) \vdash \Box(\Box(f(\psi, 1) \Rightarrow \Box f(\psi, 0)) \Rightarrow f(\psi, 1)), f(\Delta, 1)}\ (\vdash \Box)_{S4}$$

The induction hypothesis is used here since $\Box f(\Gamma', 0), \Box(f(\psi, 1) \Rightarrow \Box f(\psi, 0)) \vdash f(\psi, 1)$ has a (cut-free) proof in G$S4$. Furthermore, by definition,

- $f(\Box\Gamma', 0) = \Box f(\Gamma', 0)$; $f(\Box\psi, 1) = \Box(\Box(f(\psi, 1) \Rightarrow \Box f(\psi, 0)) \Rightarrow f(\psi, 1))$;
- $f(\Box(\psi \Rightarrow \Box\psi), 0) = \Box(\Box(f(\psi, 1) \Rightarrow \Box f(\psi, 0)))$.

Observe that $f(\Gamma, 0)$ does not contain any formula of the form $\Box\psi'$. The proof (in GGrz) below left is transformed into the proof (in G$S4$) below right

$$\dfrac{\begin{array}{c}\vdots\\ \Gamma, \Box\psi, \psi \vdash \Delta\end{array}}{\Gamma, \Box\psi \vdash \Delta}\ (\Box \vdash) \qquad \dfrac{\begin{array}{c}\vdots\\ f(\Gamma, 0), \Box f(\psi, 0), f(\psi, 0) \vdash f(\Delta, 1)\end{array}}{f(\Gamma, 0), \Box f(\psi, 0) \vdash f(\Delta, 1)}\ (\Box \vdash)$$

Indeed, $f(\Box\psi, 0) = \Box f(\psi, 0)$. The other cases are not difficult to obtain and they are omitted here.

A close examination of f shows that f is not computable in $\mathcal{O}(n.log\ n)$-time. Indeed, the right-hand side in the definition of $f(\Box\phi, 1)$ requires several recursive calls to f and the computation of f is therefore exponential-time. However, we can use a slight variant of f that uses renamings as done in [Min88]. Specifically, we have, (Renaming) $\phi \in S4$ iff $\Box(\mathrm{p}_{new} \Leftrightarrow \psi) \Rightarrow \phi' \in S4$ where ϕ' is obtained from ϕ by replacing every occurrence of ψ in ϕ by the atomic proposition p_{new} not occurring in ϕ.

Let ϕ be a modal formula we wish to translate from Grz into S4. Let $\phi_1, \ldots, \phi_m$ be an enumeration (without repetition) of all the subformulae of ϕ in increasing order with respect to the size such that the n first formulae are all the atomic propositions occurring in ϕ. We shall build a formula $g(\phi)$ using $\{\mathrm{p}_{i,j} : 1 \leq i \leq m,\ j \in \{0,1\}\}$ such that $g(\phi) \in S4$ iff $f(\phi, 1) \in S4$. Moreover, $g(\phi)$ can be computed in time $\mathcal{O}(|\phi|.log\ |\phi|)$. For $i \in \{1, \ldots, m\}$, we associate a formula ψ_i as shown in Figure 2 and let $g(\phi) \stackrel{\text{def}}{=} (\bigwedge_{i=1}^{m} \psi_i) \Rightarrow \mathrm{p}_{m,1}$.

Lemma 2.
(1) $f(\phi, 1) \in S4$ iff $g(\phi) \in S4$ (2) computing $g(\phi)$ requires time in $\mathcal{O}(|\phi|.log\ |\phi|)$ (3) $|g(\phi)|$ is in $\mathcal{O}(|\phi|.log\ |\phi|)$ (4) $mwp(g(\phi)) + mwn(g(\phi))$ is in $\mathcal{O}(|\phi|)$.

Proof. (2)-(4) is by simple inspection of the definition of $g(\phi)$. The idea of the proof of (1) is to effectively build $g(\phi)$ from $f(\phi, 1)$ by successively applying transformations based on (Renaming). Such a process requires exponential-time in ϕ (since $|f(\phi, 1)|$ can be exponential in $|\phi|$). However, we can build $g(\phi)$ in a tractable way (see (2)-(4)) since g translates and renames simultaneously.
(1) Let us build $g(\phi)$ from $f(\phi, 1)$ by successively applying transformations based on (Renaming). For any atomic proposition $\mathrm{q} = \phi_i$ occurring in $f(\phi, 1)$, replace the positive [resp. negative] occurrences of q by $\mathrm{p}_{i,1}$ [resp. $\mathrm{p}_{i,0}$]. Let us say that we obtain the formula ψ (this shall be our current working formula). The *constraint* formula, say C, is defined as $C \stackrel{\text{def}}{=} \bigwedge_{i=1}^{n} \Box(\mathrm{p}_{i,1} \Leftrightarrow \mathrm{p}_{i,0})$. Along the steps, we shall have that $f(\phi, 1) \in S4$ iff $C \Rightarrow \psi \in S4$. The next steps consist of replacing subformulae ψ' in ψ by their renaming equivalent and then to update C appropriately until $\psi = \mathrm{p}_{m,1}$. For instance, take a subformula $\psi' = \mathrm{p}_{i,1} \wedge \mathrm{p}_{j,1}$ in ψ. Replace every occurrence of $\mathrm{p}_{i,1} \wedge \mathrm{p}_{j,1}$ in ψ by $\mathrm{p}_{k,1}$ with $\phi_k = \phi_i \wedge \phi_j$. The

Form of ϕ_i	ψ_i
p	$\Box(\mathrm{p}_{i,0} \Leftrightarrow \mathrm{p}_{i,1})$
$\neg\phi_j$	$\Box(\mathrm{p}_{i,1} \Leftrightarrow \neg\mathrm{p}_{j,0}) \wedge \Box(\mathrm{p}_{i,0} \Leftrightarrow \neg\mathrm{p}_{j,1})$
$\phi_{i_1} \wedge \phi_{i_2}$	$\Box(\mathrm{p}_{i,1} \Leftrightarrow (\mathrm{p}_{i_1,1} \wedge \mathrm{p}_{i_2,1})) \wedge \Box(\mathrm{p}_{i,0} \Leftrightarrow (\mathrm{p}_{i_1,0} \wedge \mathrm{p}_{i_2,0}))$
$\phi_{i_1} \Rightarrow \phi_{i_2}$	$\Box(\mathrm{p}_{i,1} \Leftrightarrow (\mathrm{p}_{i_1,0} \Rightarrow \mathrm{p}_{i_2,1})) \wedge \Box(\mathrm{p}_{i,0} \Leftrightarrow (\mathrm{p}_{i_1,1} \Rightarrow \mathrm{p}_{i_2,0}))$
$\Box\phi_j$	$\Box(\mathrm{p}_{i,1} \Leftrightarrow \Box(\Box(\mathrm{p}_{j,1} \Rightarrow \Box\mathrm{p}_{j,0}) \Rightarrow \mathrm{p}_{j,1})) \wedge \Box(\mathrm{p}_{i,0} \Leftrightarrow \Box\mathrm{p}_{j,0})$

Fig. 2. Definition of ψ_i

constraint formula C is updated as follows: $C := C \wedge \Box(\mathtt{p}_{k,1} \Leftrightarrow (\mathtt{p}_{i,1} \wedge \mathtt{p}_{j,1}))$. The other cases are omitted and they use the decomposition from Figure 2. So, when ψ is equal to $\mathtt{p}_{m,1}$, $f(\phi, 1) \in S4$ iff $C \Rightarrow \mathtt{p}_{m,1} \in S4$. It is easy to see that $(\bigwedge_{i=1}^{m} \psi_i) \Rightarrow \mathtt{p}_{m,1} \in S4$ iff $C \Rightarrow \mathtt{p}_{m,1}$. Indeed, the set of conjuncts of C is a subset of the set of conjuncts of $\bigwedge_{i=1}^{m} \psi_i$. So, if $C \Rightarrow \mathtt{p}_{m,1} \in S4$, then $g(\phi) \in S4$. In order to show that the converse also holds, let us define the binary relation DEP between atomic propositions. Let $\mathtt{p}_{i_1,j_1}$ and $\mathtt{p}_{i_2,j_2}$ be atomic propositions occurring in $\bigwedge_{i=1}^{m} \psi_i$. We write $\mathtt{p}_{i_1,j_1}$ DEP $\mathtt{p}_{i_2,j_2}$ to denote that there is a conjunct of $\bigwedge_{i=1}^{m} \psi_i$ of the form $\Box(\psi_1' \Leftrightarrow \psi_2')$ such that either $\mathtt{p}_{i_1,j_1}$ occurs in ψ_1' and $\mathtt{p}_{i_2,j_2}$ occurs in ψ_2' or $\mathtt{p}_{i_1,j_1}$ occurs in ψ_2' and $\mathtt{p}_{i_2,j_2}$ occurs in ψ_1'. Let DEP^* be the smallest equivalence relation including DEP. It is easy to see that if $g(\phi) \in S4$, then $C \Rightarrow \mathtt{p}_{m,1} \in S4$ since for all the atomic propositions $\mathtt{q}$ occurring in $\bigwedge_{i=1}^{m} \psi_i$ but not in C, not $\mathtt{q} DEP^* \mathtt{p}_{m,1}$.

Theorem 2. *Grz requires space in* $\mathcal{O}(n^2.(log\ n)^3)$.

An equivalent statement is that there exists a deterministic Turing machine in **SPACE**($\mathcal{O}(n^2.(log\ n)^3)$) that solves the Grz-provability problem. This follows from the facts that S4 requires space in $\mathcal{O}(n^2.log\ n)$ [Hud96], computing $g(\phi)$ requires space in $\mathcal{O}(|\phi|.log\ |\phi|)$, and $|g(\phi)|$ is in $\mathcal{O}(|\phi|.log\ |\phi|)$. Putting these together gives that checking whether $g(\phi)$ is an S4-theorem requires space in $\mathcal{O}((|\phi|.log\ |\phi|)^2.log(|\phi|.log\ |\phi|))$, that is space in $\mathcal{O}(|\phi|^2.(log\ |\phi|)^3)$. By the way, one can show that Grz is **PSPACE**-hard by using mappings from propositional intuitionistic logic into Grz (see e.g. [CZ97]).

4 A Transformation from S4 into T

Let $h : \mathtt{For} \times \omega \times \{0,1\} \rightarrow \mathtt{For}$ be the following map ($n \in \omega$, $i \in \{0,1\}$):

- for any $\mathtt{p} \in \mathtt{For}_0$, $h(\mathtt{p}, n, 0) \stackrel{\text{def}}{=} h(\mathtt{p}, n, 1) \stackrel{\text{def}}{=} \mathtt{p}$
- $h(\neg\phi, n, i) \stackrel{\text{def}}{=} \neg h(\phi, n, 1-i)$
- $h(\phi_1 \wedge \phi_2, n, i) \stackrel{\text{def}}{=} h(\phi_1, n, i) \wedge h(\phi_2, n, i)$
- $h(\phi_1 \Rightarrow \phi_2, n, i) \stackrel{\text{def}}{=} h(\phi_1, n, 1-i) \Rightarrow h(\phi_2, n, i)$
- $h(\Box\phi, n, 1) \stackrel{\text{def}}{=} \Box h(\phi, n, 1)$
- $h(\Box\phi, n, 0) \stackrel{\text{def}}{=} \begin{cases} \Box^n h(\phi, n, 0) \text{ if } n \geq 1 \\ \Box h(\phi, n, 0) \text{ otherwise} \end{cases}$

The map h is a slight variant of the map $\mathcal{M}_{S4,T}$ defined in [CCM97] which itself is a variant of a map defined in [Fit88]. The main difference is that we do not assume that the formulae are in negative normal form (which is why a third argument dealing with polarity is introduced here). In that sense, we follow [Fit88, Section 3]. Furthermore, since we are dealing here with validity instead of inconsistency, the treatment of the modal operators is dual.

Lemma 3. *For any formula $\phi \in \mathtt{For}$ and for any $0 \leq m \leq n$,*

(1) $\phi \Leftrightarrow h(\phi, n, 0) \in S4$ *and* $\phi \Leftrightarrow h(\phi, n, 1) \in S4$.
(2) $h(\phi, n, 0) \Rightarrow h(\phi, m, 0) \in T$ *and* $h(\phi, m, 1) \Rightarrow h(\phi, n, 1) \in T$.
(3) $h(\phi, n, 0) \Rightarrow h(\phi, n, 1) \in T$.

Proof. The proof of (1) uses the facts that the rule of *replacement of equivalents* is admissible in S4 and $\Box^n \psi \Leftrightarrow \Box\psi \in S4$ for any $n \geq 1$ and for any $\psi \in \mathtt{For}$. The proof of (2) is by simultaneous induction on the size of the formula. By way of example, let us show in the induction step that $h(\Box\phi, n, 0) \Rightarrow h(\Box\phi, m, 0) \in T$. By induction hypothesis, $h(\phi, n, 0) \Rightarrow h(\phi, m, 0) \in T$. It is known that the regular rule is admissible for T. So, by applying this rule n times on $h(\phi, n, 0) \Rightarrow h(\phi, m, 0)$, we get that $\Box^n h(\phi, n, 0) \Rightarrow \Box^n h(\phi, m, 0) \in T$. Since $\Box^n h(\phi, m, 0) \Rightarrow \Box^m h(\phi, m, 0) \in T$ (remember $m \leq n$ and $\Box\psi \Rightarrow \psi \in T$), then $\Box^n h(\phi, n, 0) \Rightarrow \Box^m h(\phi, m, 0) \in T$.
(3) If $n = 0$, then $h(\phi, n, 0) = h(\phi, n, 1) = \phi$. Now assume $n \geq 1$. The proof is by induction on the structure of ϕ. The base case when ϕ is an atomic proposition is immediate. Let us treat the cases $\phi = \neg\phi'$ and $\phi = \Box\phi'$ in the induction step. By Induction Hypothesis, $h(\phi', n, 0) \Rightarrow h(\phi', n, 1) \in T$. By manipulation at the propositional level, $\neg h(\phi', n, 1) \Rightarrow \neg h(\phi', n, 0) \in T$. By definition of h, $h(\neg\phi', n, 0) \Rightarrow h(\neg\phi', n, 1) \in T$. Moreover, by applying n times the regular rule (admissible in T) on $h(\phi', n, 0) \Rightarrow h(\phi', n, 1)$, we get $\Box^n h(\phi', n, 0) \Rightarrow \Box^n h(\phi', n, 1) \in T$. Moreover,

- $\Box^n h(\phi', n, 1) \Rightarrow \Box h(\phi', n, 1) \in T$;
- $\Box^n h(\phi', n, 0) = h(\Box\phi', n, 0)$;
- $\Box h(\phi', n, 1) = h(\Box\phi', n, 1)$.

So, $h(\Box\phi', n, 0) \Rightarrow h(\Box\phi', n, 1) \in T$.

The map h is extended to sets of formulae in the most natural way.

Lemma 4. *Let $\Gamma \vdash \Delta$ be a sequent that has a (cut-free) proof Π in* $\mathtt{G}S4$ *such that the maximum number of* $(\vdash \Box)_{S4}$*-rule inferences in any branch is at most n. Then, $h(\Gamma, n, 0) \vdash h(\Delta, n, 1)$ has a (cut-free) proof in* $\mathtt{G}T$.

Lemma 4 is an extension of Lemma 2.2 in [CCM97].

Proof. The proof is by double induction on n and then on the length of the proof Π of $\Gamma \vdash \Delta$. The length of Π is just the number of nodes of the proof tree.
Base case (i): $n = 0$. By definition, $h(\Gamma, 0, 0) = \Gamma$ and $h(\Delta, 0, 1) = \Delta$. Any proof of $\Gamma \vdash \Delta$ in $\mathtt{G}S4$ with no applications of $(\vdash \Box)_{S4}$ is also a proof of $\Gamma \vdash \Delta$ in $\mathtt{G}T$.
Induction step (i): assume that for any sequent $\Gamma \vdash \Delta$ having a (cut-free) proof in GS4 such that the maximum number of $(\vdash \Box)_{S4}$-rule inferences in any branch is at most $n - 1 \geq 0$, $h(\Gamma, n-1, 0) \vdash h(\Delta, n-1, 1)$ has a (cut-free) proof in GT. Now, let $\Gamma \vdash \Delta$ be a sequent that has a (cut-free) proof Π in GS4 such that the maximum number of $(\vdash \Box)_{S4}$-rule inferences in any branch is at most n. We use an induction on the length of Π.

Base case (ii): $\Gamma \vdash \Delta$ is an initial sequent $\Gamma', \phi \vdash \Delta', \phi$. By Lemma 3(3), $h(\phi, n, 0) \Rightarrow h(\phi, n, 1) \in T$. So, $h(\phi, n, 0) \vdash h(\phi, n, 1)$ has a cut-free proof in $\mathtt{G}T$ by completeness of $\mathtt{G}T$ with respect to T. Hence, $h(\Gamma', n, 0), h(\phi, n, 0) \vdash h(\Delta', n, 1), h(\phi, n, 1)$ has a cut-free proof in $\mathtt{G}T$.
Induction step (ii): assume that for any sequent $\Gamma \vdash \Delta$ having a (cut-free) proof Π of length at most $n' - 1 \geq 1$ in GS4 such that the maximum number of $(\vdash \Box)_{S4}$-rule inferences in any branch is at most n, $h(\Gamma, n, 0) \vdash h(\Delta, n, 1)$ has a (cut-free) proof in GT. Now, let $\Gamma \vdash \Delta$ be a sequent that has a (cut-free) proof Π in GS4 of length n' such that the maximum number of $(\vdash \Box)_{S4}$-rule inferences in any branch is at most n. Among the Boolean connectives, we only treat here the case for the conjunction since the cases for $\neg$ and $\Rightarrow$ are similar. The proof Π below (in $\mathtt{G}S4$)

$$\frac{\begin{array}{c}\vdots\\ \Gamma', \phi_1, \phi_2 \vdash \Delta'\end{array}}{\Gamma', \phi_1 \wedge \phi_2 \vdash \Delta'}\ (\wedge \vdash)$$

is transformed into the proof below (in $\mathtt{G}T$) using the induction hypothesis (ii)

$$\frac{\begin{array}{c}\vdots\\ h(\Gamma', n, 0), h(\phi_1, n, 0), h(\phi_2, n, 0) \vdash h(\Delta', n, 1)\end{array}}{h(\Gamma', n, 0), h(\phi_1 \wedge \phi_2, n, 0) \vdash h(\Delta', n, 1)}\ (\wedge \vdash)$$

The proof Π below (in $\mathtt{G}S4$)

$$\frac{\begin{array}{c}\vdots\\ \Gamma' \vdash \Delta', \phi_1 \quad \Gamma' \vdash \Delta', \phi_2\end{array}}{\Gamma' \vdash \Delta', \phi_1 \wedge \phi_2}\ (\vdash \wedge)$$

is transformed into the proof below (in $\mathtt{G}T$) using the induction hypothesis (ii)

$$\frac{\begin{array}{c}\vdots\\ h(\Gamma', n, 0) \vdash h(\Delta', n, 1), h(\phi_1, n, 1) \quad h(\Gamma', n, 0) \vdash h(\Delta', n, 1), h(\phi_2, n, 1)\end{array}}{h(\Gamma', n, 0) \vdash h(\Delta', n, 1), h(\phi_1 \wedge \phi_2, n, 1)}\ (\vdash \wedge)$$

Consider the proof Π below:

$$\frac{\begin{array}{c}\Pi'\\ \vdots\\ \Box\Gamma'' \vdash \phi\end{array}}{\Gamma', \Box\Gamma'' \vdash \Box\phi, \Delta'}\ (\vdash \Box)_{S4}$$

In the proof Π' of $\Box\Gamma'' \vdash \phi$ in $\mathtt{G}S4$, the maximum number of $(\vdash \Box)_{S4}$-rule inferences in any branch is less than $n-1$. By induction hypothesis (i), $h(\Box\Gamma'', n-1, 0) \vdash h(\phi, n-1, 1)$ has a cut-free proof, say Π'', in $\mathtt{G}T$. So, the proof below is obtained in $\mathtt{G}T$:

$$\dfrac{\begin{array}{c}\Pi'' \\ \vdots \\ \Box^{n-1}h(\Gamma'',n-1,0) \vdash h(\phi,n-1,1)\end{array}}{h(\Gamma',n,0),\Box^{n}h(\Gamma'',n-1,0) \vdash \Box h(\phi,n-1,1),h(\Delta',n,1)}\ (\vdash\Box)_T$$

For $\psi \in \Gamma''$, $h(\psi,n,0) \Rightarrow h(\psi,n-1,0) \in T$ by Lemma 3(2). By using n applications of the regular rule, for $\psi \in \Gamma''$, $\Box^n h(\psi,n,0) \Rightarrow \Box^n h(\psi,n-1,0) \in T$. Similarly, by Lemma 3(2) $h(\Box\phi,n-1,1) \Rightarrow h(\Box\phi,n,1) \in T$. By soundness of $\mathtt{G}T$, the formula $\varphi \in T$ where:

$$\varphi \stackrel{\text{def}}{=} ((\bigwedge_{\psi\in\Gamma'} h(\psi,n,0)) \wedge (\bigwedge_{\psi\in\Gamma''} \Box^n h(\psi,n-1,0))) \Rightarrow (h(\Box\phi,n-1,1) \vee \bigvee_{\psi\in\Delta'} h(\psi,n,1)).$$

For $\psi \in \Gamma''$, $\Box^n h(\psi,n-1,0)$ occurs negatively in φ and $h(\Box\phi,n-1,1)$ occurs positively in φ. By the Monotonicity of Entailment Lemma [AM86],

$$((\bigwedge_{\psi\in\Gamma'} h(\psi,n,0)) \wedge (\bigwedge_{\psi\in\Gamma''} \Box^n h(\psi,n,0))) \Rightarrow (h(\Box\phi,n,1) \vee \bigvee_{\psi\in\Delta'} h(\psi,n,1)) \in T$$

By completeness of $\mathtt{G}T$, we get that $h(\Gamma',n,0),h(\Box\Gamma'',n,0) \vdash h(\Box\phi,n,1)$, $h(\Delta',n,1)$ has a cut-free proof in $\mathtt{G}T$. In order to conclude the proof, let us treat the last case. Consider the proof Π below in $\mathtt{G}S4$:

$$\dfrac{\begin{array}{c}\vdots \\ \Gamma',\Box\phi,\phi \vdash \Delta'\end{array}}{\Gamma',\Box\phi \vdash \Delta'}\ (\Box\vdash)$$

By induction hypothesis (ii), $h(\Gamma',n,0),\Box^n h(\phi,n,0),h(\phi,n,0) \vdash h(\Delta',n,1)$ has a cut-free proof in $\mathtt{G}T$. So,

$$s_1 \stackrel{\text{def}}{=} h(\Gamma',n,0),\Box^n h(\phi,n,0),\Box^{n-1}h(\phi,n,0),\ldots$$
$$\ldots,\Box h(\phi,n,0),h(\phi,n,0) \vdash h(\Delta',n,1)$$

has also a cut-free proof in $\mathtt{G}T$. The above proof is transformed into (in $\mathtt{G}T$)

$$\dfrac{\dfrac{\begin{array}{c}\vdots \\ s_1\end{array}}{h(\Gamma',n,0),\Box^n h(\phi,n,0),\Box^{n-1}h(\phi,n,0),\ldots,\Box h(\phi,n,0) \vdash h(\Delta',n,1)}\ (\Box\vdash)}{h(\Gamma',n,0),\Box^n h(\phi,n,0),\Box^{n-1}h(\phi,n,0),\ldots,\Box^2 h(\phi,n,0) \vdash h(\Delta',n,1)}\ (\Box\vdash)$$

$$\vdots$$

$$\dfrac{h(\Gamma',n,0),\Box^n h(\phi,n,0),\Box^{n-1}h(\phi,n,0) \vdash h(\Delta',n,1)}{h(\Gamma',n,0),h(\Box\phi,n,0) \vdash h(\Delta',n,1)}\ (\Box\vdash)$$

Lemma 5. *Let $\Gamma \vdash \Delta$ be a sequent such that the number of negative occurrences of $\Box$ in $\bigwedge_{\phi \in \Gamma} \phi \Rightarrow \bigvee_{\psi \in \Delta} \psi$ is n. If $\Gamma \vdash \Delta$ has a (cut-free) proof in* GS4*, then $\Gamma \vdash \Delta$ has a (cut-free) proof in* GS4 *such that the $(\vdash \Box)_{S4}$-rule is applied at most $n+1$ times to the same formula in every branch.*

Lemma 5 is also an extension of Lemma 2.4 in [CCM97]. However, its proof mainly relies on the analysis of the proof of [CCM97, Lemma 2.4]. So it is included here in order to make the paper self-contained.

Proof. First, observe that if $\Gamma \vdash \Delta$ is derivable in GS4 and if ψ has a negative [resp. positive] occurrence in $(\bigwedge_{\phi \in \Gamma} \phi) \Rightarrow (\bigvee_{\phi \in \Delta} \phi)$, then for any cut-free proof Π of $\Gamma \vdash \Delta$, every occurrence of ψ in Π can only occur in the left-hand side [resp. in the right-hand side] of sequents. So if the inference below

$$\frac{\Box \Gamma'' \vdash \phi}{\Gamma', \Box \Gamma'' \vdash \Box \phi, \Delta'} (\vdash \Box)_{S4}$$

occurs in a proof Π of $\Gamma \vdash \Delta$, then any $\Box \psi \in \Box \Gamma''$ occurs with negative polarity in $(\bigwedge_{\phi \in \Gamma} \phi) \Rightarrow (\bigvee_{\phi \in \Delta} \phi)$. Moreover, consider the following $(\vdash \Box)_{S4}$ inferences in a proof Π of $\Gamma \vdash \Delta$:

$$\frac{\Box \Gamma'_2 \vdash \phi_2}{\Gamma_2, \Box \Gamma'_2 \vdash \Box \phi_2, \Delta_2} (\vdash \Box)_{S4}$$
$$\vdots$$
$$\frac{\Box \Gamma'_1 \vdash \phi_1}{\Gamma_1, \Box \Gamma'_1 \vdash \Box \phi_1, \Delta_1} (\vdash \Box)_{S4}$$
$$\vdots$$

Then $\Gamma'_1 \subseteq \Gamma'_2$. Let Π be a (cut-free) proof of $\Gamma \vdash \Delta$ in GS4. Assume there is a branch in Π containing $n+1+k$ $(k \geq 1)$ $(\vdash \Box)_{S4}$ inferences introducing the same formula $\Box \psi$. Let us eliminate at least one $(\vdash \Box)_{S4}$ inference on that branch as done in [CCM97]. Consider the sequence $inf_1, \ldots, inf_{n+1+k}$ of inferences of the form $(1 \leq i \leq n+1+k)$,

$$\frac{\Box \Gamma'_i \vdash \psi}{\Gamma_i, \Box \Gamma'_i \vdash \Box \psi, \Delta_i} (\vdash \Box)_{S4}$$

We assume that if $i < j$, then inf_j occurs above inf_i. Let Γ' be the set of the formulae of the form $\Box \psi'$ where $\Box \psi'$ has a negative occurrence in $(\bigwedge_{\phi \in \Gamma} \phi) \Rightarrow (\bigvee_{\phi \in \Delta} \phi)$. Since $\Gamma'_1 \subseteq \ldots \subseteq \Gamma'_{n+1+k}$ and $card(\Gamma') = n$, there exist $i_0 \in \{1, \ldots, n+1\}$ and $j_0 \in \{i_0, \ldots, n+2\}$ such that $\Gamma'_{i_0} = \Gamma'_{j_0}$. So, in that branch of Π, we can replace the sequence shown below left by the sequence shown below right:

$$\dfrac{\dfrac{\begin{array}{c}\Pi' \\ \vdots \\ \Box\Gamma'_{j_0} \vdash \psi\end{array}}{\Gamma_{j_0}, \Box\Gamma'_{j_0} \vdash \Box\psi, \Delta_{j_0}}(\vdash\Box)_{S4}}{\begin{array}{c}\vdots \\ \Box\Gamma'_{i_0} \vdash \psi\end{array}} \quad \dfrac{\Box\Gamma'_{i_0} \vdash \psi}{\Gamma_{i_0}, \Box\Gamma'_{i_0} \vdash \Box\psi, \Delta_{i_0}}(\vdash\Box)_{S4} \qquad \qquad \dfrac{\begin{array}{c}\Pi' \\ \vdots \\ \Box\Gamma'_{j_0} \vdash \psi\end{array}}{\Gamma_{j_0}, \Box\Gamma'_{j_0} \vdash \Box\psi, \Delta_{j_0}}(\vdash\Box)_{S4}$$

Theorem 3. *A formula* $\phi \in S4$ *iff* $h(\phi, (mwn(\phi) + 1).mwp(\phi), 1) \in T$.

Theorem 3 is a mere consequence of Lemma 4 and Lemma 5. Its proof uses the sequent calculi G$S4$ and GT whereas in [CCM97] the proofs manipulate Fitting's non prefixed calculi for S4 and T [Fit83]. Observe the map h is a variant of a map defined in [Fit88]. Let us write $h'(\phi)$ to denote the formula $h(\phi, (mwn(\phi)+1).mwp(\phi), 1)$.

By close examination of the definition of $h'(\phi)$,

1. computing $h'(\phi)$ requires time in $\mathcal{O}(|\phi|^3)$;
2. $|h'(\phi)|$ is in $\mathcal{O}(|\phi|^3)$.

So a formula $\phi \in Grz$ iff $h'(g(\phi)) \in T$.

1. Computing $h'(g(\phi))$ requires time in $\mathcal{O}((|\phi|.log\ |\phi|)^3)$ (remember $mwp(g(\phi))$ $+mwn(g(\phi))$ is in $\mathcal{O}(|\phi|)$;
2. $|h'(g(\phi))|$ is in $\mathcal{O}((|\phi|.log\ |\phi|)^3)$.

The relational translation from T into FO^2 (see e.g. [Ben83]) with a smart recycling of the variables requires only linear-time and the size of the translated formula is also linear in the size of the initial formula. We warn the reader that in various places in the literature it is stated that the relational translation exponentially increases the size of formulae; this is erroneous. Using this "smart" relational transformation, the composition of various transformations in the paper provides an $\mathcal{O}((n.log\ n)^3)$-time transformation from Grz into the decidable fragment FO^2 of classical logic. It is easy to see that the resulting formula is in the guarded fragment of classical logic (see e.g. [ANB98]), for which a proof procedure based on resolution is proposed in [Niv98]. Alternatively, after translating Grz into T, the techniques from [Sch97] could also be used to translate T into classical logic. These are possibilities to obtain a decision procedure for Grz using theorem provers for classical logic.

We are currently investigating whether this translation can be extended to first-order Grz (FOGrz). But the set of valid formulae for first-order Gödel-Löb logic, a close cousin of FOGrz, is not recursively enumerable [Boo93, Chapt. 17], and we suspect that this result also holds for FOGrz.

References

[AM86] M. Abadi and Z. Manna. Modal theorem proving. In J. H. Siekmann, editor, *CADE-8*, pages 172–189. Springer Verlag, LNCS 230, 1986.

[ANB98] H. Andreka, I. Nemeti, and J. van Benthem. Modal languages and bounded fragments of predicate logic. *Journal of Philosophical Logic*, 27(3):217–274, 1998.

[Avr84] A. Avron. On modal systems having arithmetical interpretations. *The Journal of Symbolic Logic*, 49(3):935–942, 1984.

[Bel82] N. Belnap. Display logic. *Journal of Philosophical Logic*, 11:375–417, 1982.

[Ben83] J. van Benthem. *Modal logic and classical logic.* Bibliopolis, 1983.

[Ben99] J. van Benthem. The Range of Modal Logic - An Essay in Memory of George Gargov. *Journal of Applied Non-Classical Logics*, 1999. To appear.

[BH94] Ph. Balbiani and A. Herzig. A translation from the modal logic of provability into K4. *Journal of Applied Non-Classical Logics*, 4:73–77, 1994.

[Boo93] G. Boolos. *The Logic of Provability.* Cambridge University Press, 1993.

[CCM97] S. Cerrito and M. Cialdea Mayer. A polynomial translation of S4 into T and contraction-free tableaux for S4. *Logic Journal of the IGPL*, 5(2):287–300, 1997.

[CZ97] A. Chagrov and M. Zakharyaschev. *Modal Logic.* Clarendon Press, Oxford, 1997.

[DG98] S. Demri and R. Goré. An $\mathcal{O}((n.log\ n)^3)$-time transformation from Grz into decidable fragments of classical first-order logic. In *2nd International Workshop on First-Order Theorem Proving, Vienna*, pages 127–134. TU-Wien Technical Report E1852-GS-981, 1998.

[DG99] S. Demri and R. Goré. Theoremhood preserving maps as a characterisation of cut elimination for provability logics. Technical Report, A.R.P., A.N.U., 1999. Forthcoming.

[dMP95] G. d'Agostino, A. Montanari, and A. Policriti. A set-theoretical translation method for polymodal logics. *Journal of Automated Reasoning*, 15:317–337, 1995.

[Fit83] M. Fitting. *Proof methods for modal and intuitionistic logics.* D. Reidel Publishing Co., 1983.

[Fit88] M. Fitting. First-order modal tableaux. *Journal of Automated Reasoning*, 4:191–213, 1988.

[Für81] M. Fürer. The computational complexity of the unconstrained limited domino problem (with implications for logical decision problems). In *Logical machines: Decision problems and complexity*, pages 312–319. LNCS 171, Springer-Verlag, 1981.

[GHH97] R. Goré, W. Heinle, and A. Heuerding. Relations between propositional normal modal logics: an overview. *Journal of Logic and Computation*, 7(5):649–658, 1997.

[GHMS98] H. Ganzinger, U. Hustadt, C. Meyer, and R. Schmidt. A resolution-based decision procedure for extensions of K4. In *2nd Workshop on Advances in Modal Logic (AiML'98), Uppsala, Sweden*, 1998. to appear.

[Gor94] R. Goré. Cut-free sequent and tableau systems for propositional Diodorian modal logics. *Studia Logica*, 53:433–457, 1994.

[Gor99] R Goré. Tableaux methods for modal and temporal logics. In M. d'Agostino, D. Gabbay, R. Hähnle, and J. Posegga, editors, *Handbook of Tableaux Methods.* Kluwer, Dordrecht, 1999. To appear.

[Her89] A. Herzig. *Raisonnement automatique en logique modale et algorithmes d'unification*. PhD thesis, Université P. Sabatier, Toulouse, 1989.

[Hud96] J. Hudelmaier. Improved decision procedures for the modal logics K, T and S4. In H. Buning, editor, *Computer Science Logic (CSL'95)*, pages 320–334. LNCS 1092, Springer-Verlag, 1996.

[Lad77] R. Ladner. The computational complexity of provability in systems of modal propositional logic. *SIAM Journal of Computing*, 6(3):467–480, 1977.

[Lew80] H. Lewis. Complexity results for classes of quantificational formulas. *Journal of Computer and System Sciences*, 21:317–353, 1980.

[Min88] G. Mints. Gentzen-type and resolution rules part I: propositional logic. In P. Martin-Löf and G. Mints, editors, *International Conference on Computer Logic, Tallinn*, pages 198–231. Springer Verlag, LNCS 417, 1988.

[Mor75] M. Mortimer. On language with two variables. *Zeitschrift für Mathematik Logik und Grundlagen der Mathematik*, 21:135–140, 1975.

[Mor76] Ch. Morgan. Methods for automated theorem proving in non classical logics. *IEEE Transactions on Computers*, 25(8):852–862, 1976.

[Niv98] H. de Nivelle. A resolution decision procedure for the guarded fragment. In C. Kirchner and H. Kirchner, editors, *CADE-15, Lindau, Germany*, pages 191–204. LNAI 1421, Springer-Verlag, 1998.

[Non96] A. Nonnengart. Resolution-based calculi for modal and temporal logics. In M. McRobbie and J. Slaney, editors, *CADE-13*, pages 599–612. LNAI 1104, Springer-Verlag, 1996.

[Ohl88] H.J. Ohlbach. *A resolution calculus for modal logics*. PhD thesis, FB Informatik Univ. of Kaiserslautern, 1988.

[Ohl93] H.J. Ohlbach. Optimized translation of multi modal logic into predicate logic. In A. Voronkov, editor, *LPAR'93*, pages 253–264. Springer-Verlag, LNAI 698, 1993.

[Ohl98] H. J. Ohlbach. Combining Hilbert style and semantic reasoning in a resolution framework. In C. Kirchner and H. Kirchner, editors, *CADE-15, Lindau, Germany*, pages 205–219. LNAI 1421, Springer-Verlag, 1998.

[OM57] M. Ohnishi and K. Matsumoto. Gentzen method in modal calculi. *Osaka Mathematical Journal*, 9:113–130, 1957.

[Pap94] Ch. Papadimitriou. *Computational Complexity*. Addison-Wesley Publishing Company, 1994.

[Rau83] W. Rautenberg. Modal tableau calculi and interpolation. *The Journal of Philosophical Logic*, 12:403–423, 1983.

[Sch97] R. Schmidt. *Optimised Modal Translation and Resolution*. PhD thesis, Fakultät der Universität des Saarlandes, 1997.

[Sol76] R. Solovay. Provability interpretations of modal logics. *Israel Journal of Mathematics*, 25:287–304, 1976.

[Var97] M. Vardi. Why is modal logic so robustly decidable? In *Descriptive complexity and finite models, A.M.S.*, 1997.

Implicational Completeness of Signed Resolution

Christian G. Fermüller

Institut für Computersprachen
Technische Universität
Resselgasse 3/3/E185.2
A-1040 Wien, Austria
ChrisF@logic.at

1 Implicational Completeness - A Neglected Topic

Every serious computer scientist and logician knows that resolution is complete for first-order clause logic. By this, of course, one means that the empty clause (representing contradiction) is derivable by resolution from every unsatisfiable set of clauses $\mathcal{S}$. However, there is another – less well known – concept of completeness for clause logic, that is often referred to as "Lee's Theorem" (see, e.g., [8]): Char-tung Lee's dissertation [7] focused on an interesting observation that (in a corrected version and more adequate terminology) can be stated as follows:

Theorem 1 (Lee). *Let $\mathcal{S}$ be a set of clauses. For every non-tautological clause C that is logically implied by $\mathcal{S}$ there is clause D, derivable by resolution from $\mathcal{S}$, such that D subsumes C.*

Observe that this theorem amounts to a *strengthening* of refutational completeness of resolution: If $\mathcal{S}$ is unsatisfiable then it implies every clause; but the only clause that subsumes every clause (including the empty clause) is the empty clause, which therefore must be derivable by resolution from $\mathcal{S}$ according to the theorem.

At least from a logical point of view, Lee's "positive" completeness result is as interesting as refutational completeness. Nevertheless this classic result – which we prefer to call *implicational completeness* of resolution – is not even mentioned in most textbooks and survey articles on automated deduction. The main reason for this is probably the conception that implicational completeness, in contrast to refutational completeness, is of no practical significance. Moreover, it fails for all important *refinements* of Robinson's original resolution calculus. In addition, Lee's proof [7] is presented in an unsatisfactory manner (to say the least). A fourth reason for the widespread neglect of implicational completeness might be the fact that Lee (and others at that time) did not distinguish between *implication* and *subsumption* of clauses. However, nowadays, it is well known that the first relation between clauses is undecidable [10], whereas sophisticated and efficient algorithms for testing the latter one are at the core of virtually all successful resolution theorem provers (see, e.g., [4]). With hindsight, this is decisive for the significance of Lee's Theorem.

R. Caferra and G. Salzer (Eds.): Automated Deduction, LNAI 1761, pp. 167–174, 2000.

We will provide a new and independent proof of implicational completeness in a much more general setting, namely *signed resolution*. An additional motivation is that this result is needed for an interesting application: computing optimal rules for the handling of quantifiers in many-valued logics (see [9]). In fact, we provide a self-contained presentation of signed resolution (compare [5, 2]).

Readers mainly interested in classical logic are reminded that classical clause logic is just the simplest case of signed resolution. Even for this special case our proof is new and independent from the (rather intricate) ones presented in [7] and [8].

2 Signed Clause Logic

Atomic formulae – or: *atoms* – are build up from predicate, function and variable symbols as usual. (Constants are considered as function symbols of arity 0.) By the *Herbrand base* (corresponding to some signature) we mean the set of all *ground* atoms; i.e., atoms that do not contain variable symbols. We consider the reader to be familiar with other standard notions, like *substitution*, *most general unifier (mgu)* etc.

Let W be a fixed finite set; here always considered as the set of truth values. A *literal* (over W) is an expression $S{:}\, P$, where P is an atom and $S \subseteq W$. A *(signed) clause* is a finite set of literals.[1]

An *assignment* associates truth values (i.e., elements of W) with atoms. A *complete assignment to a set of atoms* K is defined as a set of literals $\{\{\psi(P)\}{:}\, P \mid P \in K\}$, where ψ is a total function from K to W. An *(Herbrand-)interpretation* is a complete assignment of the Herbrand base.

For any set of atoms K the corresponding *literal set* $\Lambda(K)$ is the set $\{V{:}\, A \mid A \in K, V \subseteq W, V \neq \emptyset\}$.

To assist concise statements about the relation between arbitrary sets of literals we use the following notation:

For a set of literals C let $\widehat{C}$ be the equivalent set that consists of singleton-as-sign literals only. More exactly, $\widehat{C} = \{\{v\}{:}\, A \mid S{:}\, A \in C, v \in S\}$. We say that C is *contained* in another set of literals D if $\widehat{C} \subseteq \widehat{D}$.

An interpretation I *satisfies* a clause set $\mathcal{S}$ iff for all ground instances C' of each $C \in \mathcal{S}$: $\widehat{C'} \cap I \neq \emptyset$. I is called an *H-model* of $\mathcal{S}$. $\mathcal{S}$ is *(H-)unsatisfiable* if it has no H-model. Since an analogue of Herbrand's theorem holds for signed clause logic (see, e.g., [1, 2]) we can restrict our attention to H-models.

The significance of this notions lies in the fact that formulae of any first-order finite-valued logic can effectively be translated to finite sets of signed clauses in such a way that the clause set is unsatisfiable iff the original formula is valid in the source logic. (See, e.g., [6, 2] for a detailed presentation of this fact.)

---

[1] In classical clause logic we have $W = \{\mathbf{true}, \mathbf{false}\}$. Literals $\mathbf{true}{:}\, P$ and $\mathbf{false}{:}\, P$ are traditionally denoted as simply as P and $\neg P$, respectively.

3 Signed Resolution

The conclusion of the following inference rule:

$$\frac{\{S\colon P\} \cup C_1 \qquad \{R\colon Q\} \cup C_2}{(\{S \cap R\colon P\} \cup C_1 \cup C_2)\sigma} \text{ binary resolution}$$

is called a *binary resolvent* of the variable disjoint *parent clauses* $\{S\colon P\} \cup C_1$ and $\{R\colon Q\} \cup C_2$, if $S \neq R$ and σ is an mgu of the atoms P and Q.

Like in the classical case we need a *factorization rule* to obtain a refutationally complete calculus:

$$\frac{C}{C\sigma} \text{ factorization}$$

where σ is an mgu of a subset of C. $C\sigma$ is called a *factor* of C.

The combination of factorization and binary resolution does not yet guarantee that the empty clause can be derived from all unsatisfiable sets of clauses. We also have to remove literals with empty signs by the following *simplification rule:*[2]

$$\frac{C \cup \{\emptyset\colon P\}}{C} \text{ simplification}$$

C is called a *simplification* of C' if it results from C' by removing all literals with empty sign. (I.e., by applying the simplification rule to C' as often as possible.)

The *merging rule* unites literals that share the same atom. It is not needed for completeness but helps to reduce the search space and to simplify the completeness proof.[3]

$$\frac{\{S_1\colon P\} \cup \ldots \cup \{S_n\colon P\} \cup C}{\{S_1 \cup \ldots \cup S_n\colon P\} \cup C} \text{ merging}$$

C is called a *normal form* or *normalized* version of C' if it results from C' by applying the simplification rules and the merging rule to C' as often as possible. I.e., all literals with empty signs are removed and all different literals in C have different atoms.

One can combine factoring, simplification, merging, and binary resolution into a single resolution rule. This corresponds to a particular strategy for the application of these rules.

The following alternative version of signed resolution can be considered as a combination of a series of binary resolution and simplification steps into one "macro inference step", called *hyperresolution* in [5].

$$\frac{\{S_1\colon P_1\} \cup C_1 \qquad \ldots \qquad \{S_n\colon P_n\} \cup C_n}{(C_1 \cup \ldots \cup C_n)\sigma} \text{ hyperresolution}$$

2 Alternatively, one can dispose with the simplification rule by defining a clause to be empty if all literals have empty sets as signs.

3 The merging rule is needed for completeness if clauses are not treated modulo idempotency of disjunction (e.g., as multisets as opposed to sets).

where $S_1 \cap \ldots \cap S_n = \emptyset$ and σ is the mgu of the atoms P_i $(1 \leq i \leq n)$. The conclusion is called a *hyperresolvent.*

It is useful to consider resolution as a set operator (mapping sets of clauses into sets of clauses).

Definition 1. *For a set of clauses S let $\mathcal{R}_b(S)$ be the set of all binary resolvents of (variable renamed) normalized factors of clauses in S. The transitive and reflexive closure of the set operator $\mathcal{R}_b$ is denoted by $\mathcal{R}_b^*$.*

Similarly, we define $\mathcal{R}_m(S)$ as the set of all hyperresolvents of (variable renamed) normalized factors of clauses in S. $\mathcal{R}_m^*$ denotes the transitive and reflexive closure of $\mathcal{R}_m$.

Definition 2. *A resolution operator $\mathcal{R}$ is* refutationally complete *if, for all clause sets S, S unsatisfiable implies $\{\} \in \mathcal{R}^*(S)$.*

A resolution operator $\mathcal{R}$ is called implicationally complete *if, for all clause sets S and clauses C, either C is a tautology or C is subsumed by some $C' \in \mathcal{R}^*(S)$ whenever S implies C.*

Observe that hyperresolution does *not* enjoy implicational completeness: Consider, e.g., the propositional clauses

$$\{\{u, v\}\colon A\} \quad \text{and} \quad \{\{u, w\}\colon A\},$$

where u, v, w are pairwise different truth values. The hyperresolution rule is not applicable. The (non-tautological) clause $\{\{u\}\colon A\}$ is implied by $\{\{\{u, v\}\colon A\}, \{\{u, w\}\colon A\}\}$, without being subsumed by one of its members.

4 Implication and Subsumption

Definition 3. *For a clause $C = \{S_1\colon P_1, \ldots S_n\colon P_n\}$ let*

$$[\neg C] = \{\{W - S_1\colon P_1\gamma\}, \ldots \{W - S_n\colon P_n\gamma\}\},$$

where γ is a substitution that replaces each variable in C by a new constant. (W is the set of all truth values.)

Proposition 1. *For every clause C and interpretation I*[4]*: I is a model of $[\neg C]$ iff I does not satisfy C.*

Proof. Follows from the definition of $[\neg C]$.

Definition 4. *A clause C* subsumes *a clause D if some instance of C is contained in D; more formally: if $\widehat{C\theta} \subseteq \widehat{D}$, for some substitution θ. A set of clauses $\mathcal{S}$* implies *a clause C if all models of $\mathcal{S}$ satisfy C.*

We state some simple facts about implication of clauses and subsumption.

[4] Of course, the Herbrand universe has to include also the new constants occurring in $[\neg C]$.

Proposition 2. *Let C and D be clauses. If C subsumes D then $\{C\}$ implies D.*

Proof. Follows from the definitions of subsumption and implication, respectively.

Observe that the converse of Proposition 2 does not hold. E.g., $\{\{u\}: P(x), \{v\}: P(f(x))\}$ implies but does not subsume $\{\{u\}: P(x), \{v\}: P(f(f(x)))\}$ if $u \neq v$. Whereas the problem to decide whether a clause C subsumes a clause D is NP-complete (see [3], it is undecidable whether $\{C\}$ implies D, in general as proved in [10].

Proposition 3. *Let S be a clause set and C be a non-tautological clause. S implies C iff $S \cup [\neg C]$ is unsatisfiable.*

Proof. Follows from Proposition 1 and the definition of implication.

Lemma 1. *Let C and D be non-tautological clauses. C subsumes D iff there exists a ground substitution θ s.t. $\{C\theta\} \cup [\neg D]$ is unsatisfiable.*

Proof. $\Rightarrow$: Suppose $\widehat{C\sigma} \subseteq \widehat{D}$. Then also $\widehat{C\sigma\gamma} \subseteq \widehat{D\gamma}$, where γ is the substitution replacing every variable by a new constant in $[\neg D]$. This implies that for each literal $V: A \in \widehat{C\sigma\gamma}$, there is a clause of form $\{V': A\} \in [\neg D]$ such that $V \cap V' = \emptyset$. This means that $\{C\sigma\gamma\} \cup [\neg D]$ is unsatisfiable.

$\Leftarrow$: Suppose $\{C\theta\} \cup [\neg D]$ is unsatisfiable, where $C\theta$ is ground. Since D is non-tautological, $[\neg D]$ is satisfiable. Therefore, for each literal $\{v\}: A \in \widehat{C\theta}$ there has to exist a clause $\{S: A\} \in [\neg D]$ s.t. $v \notin S$. This implies $\widehat{C\theta} \subseteq \widehat{D}$. In other words: C subsumes D.

5 Semantic Trees for Signed Clause Logic

Our completeness proof is based on the concept of semantic trees. It differs from the proofs in [1] and [6]; but generalizes the completeness proof in [2] for singletons-as-signs resolution to (unrestricted) signed resolution.

As usual in automated deduction, we consider a tree as growing downwards; i.e. the *root* is the top node of a tree. A node or edge α *is above* a node or edge β if α is part of the path (considered as alternating sequence of nodes and edges) connecting β with the root. A *branch* of T is a path that starts with the root and either is infinite or else ends in a leaf node of T.

Definition 5. *Let W be a finite set of truth values and K be a set of ground atoms. For any subset Δ of the literal set $\Lambda(K)$ of K we say that Δ* omits *the assignment A_K to K if $\Delta \cap A_K = \emptyset$. A finitely branching tree T is a* semantic tree *for K if finite, non-empty subsets of $\Lambda(K)$ label the edges of T in the following way:*

(1) The set of the sets of literals labeling all edges leaving one node is an H-unsatisfiable set of clauses.

(2) *For each branch of T the union of the sets of literals labeling the edges of the branch omits exactly one complete assignment A_K to K. For short, we say that* the branch omits A_K *as well as any interpretation containing A_K.*
(3) *For each complete assignment A_K to K there is a branch of T s.t. this branch omits A_K.*

The union of all sets of literals labeling the edges of the path from the root down to some node α of T forms the refutation set *of α.*

For a set of clauses S any semantic tree T for $A(S)$ represents an exhaustive survey of all possible H-interpretations. Each branch omits exactly one H-interpretation and each H-interpretation is omitted by at least one branch.

Definition 6. *A clause C* fails *at a node α of a semantic tree T if some ground instance of C is contained in the refutation set of that node. A node α is a* failure node *for a clause set S if some clause of S fails at α but no clause in S fails at a node above α. A node is called an* inference node *if all of its successor nodes are failure nodes. T is* closed *for S if there is a failure node for S on every branch of T.*

Theorem 2. *A set of clauses S is unsatisfiable iff there is a finite subset $K \subseteq A(S)$ s.t. every semantic tree for K is closed for S.*

Proof. $\Rightarrow$: Let T be a semantic tree for $A(S)$, the Herbrand base of S. By definition of a semantic tree, any branch B of T omits exactly one complete assignment to $A(S)$, which extends to an H-interpretation $\mathcal{M}$ of S. If S is unsatisfiable then $\mathcal{M}$ does not satisfy all clauses in S. This means that there is some ground instance C' of a clause C in S s.t. $\widehat{C'} \cap \mathcal{M} = \emptyset$. But since B omits only the literals of $\Lambda(A(S))$ that are true in $\mathcal{M}$ this implies that the union of labels of the edges of B contains C'; i.e., C' is contained in the refutation set of some node of B. We have thus proved that every branch of T contains a failure node for some clause of S. In other words, T is closed for S. Moreover, by König's Lemma, the number of nodes in T that are situated above a failure node is finite. But this implies that for each unsatisfiable set of clauses S there is a finite unsatisfiable set S' of ground instances of clauses of S. Since any semantic tree that is closed for S' is also closed for S it is sufficient to base the tree on a finite subset of $A(S)$: the set K of ground atoms occurring in S'. Observe that we have not imposed any restriction on the form of the tree. Thus every semantic tree for K is closed for S.

$\Leftarrow$: Let T be a closed semantic tree for a finite $K \subseteq A(S)$. Suppose $\mathcal{M}$ is an H-model of S; i.e. for all ground instances C' of $C \in S$ we have $\mathcal{M} \cap \widehat{C'} \neq \emptyset$. By definition of a semantic tree, $\mathcal{M}$ is omitted by some branch B of T. Since T is closed, some clause $C \in S$ fails at a node α of B. That means that some ground instance C' of C is contained in the refutation set of α. Therefore $\mathcal{M} \cap \widehat{C'} \neq \emptyset$ implies that $\mathcal{M}$ contains some literal that also occurs in some refuation set of a node on B. But this contradicts the assumption that B omits $\mathcal{M}$. Therefore S is unsatisfiable.

Theorem 2 is the basis for refutional completeness proofs for many different versions and refinements of signed resolution (see [2]). Our task here is to show that it can be used to prove implicational completeness as well.

6 Implicational Completeness

Theorem 3. *$\mathcal{R}_b$ is implicationally complete. More precisely, if C is a non-tautological clause that is implied by a set of clause S then there exists a $D \in \mathcal{R}_b^*(S)$ s.t. D subsumes C.*

Proof. By Propositon 3 $S \cup [\neg C]$ is unsatisfiable. Hence, by Theorem 2 there is a finite subset K of $A(S \cup [\neg C])$ s.t. every semantic tree for K is closed for $S \cup [\neg C]$.

Let $[\neg C] = \{\{V_1\colon A_1\}, \ldots, \{V_n\colon A_n\}\}$ and W be the set of all truth values. Since C is non-tautological $W - V_i$ is not empty. Without loss of generality we may assume C to be normalized; i.e., $A_i \neq A_j$ if $i \neq j$. We choose a semantic tree T for K that starts with the following subtree:

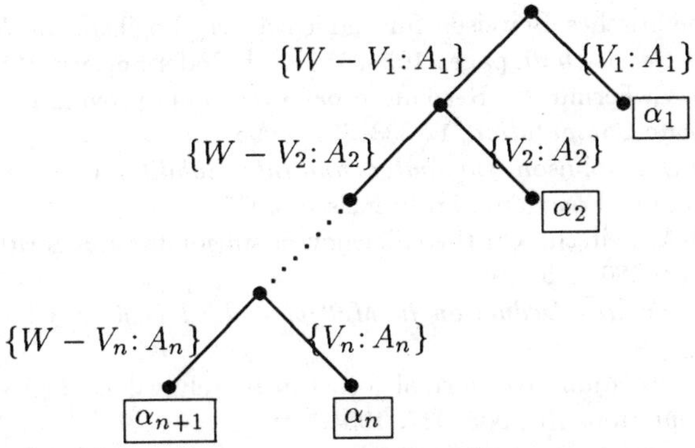

The subtrees of T rooted in the nodes $\alpha_1, \ldots, \alpha_n$, respectively, are arbitrary (since these nodes obviously are failure nodes).

For the construction of the subtree T_{n+1} of T rooted in α_{n+1} we have to take care that it does not contain a failure node for any clause in $[\neg C]$. This can be achieved as follows. Let $V_1^1, \ldots, V_1^k$ be the subsets of V_1 that contain all but one element of V_1. (If V_1 is a singleton simply skip this part of the construction of T.) Attach k successor nodes $\beta_1, \ldots, \beta_k$ to α_{n+1}. Label the edges to these new nodes by $\{V_1^1\colon A_1\}$, …, $\{V_1^k\colon A_1\}$, respectively. Clearly, the refutation set of β_i $(1 \leq i \leq k)$ omits exactly one assignment to the atom A_1. By proceeding in the same way for $A_2, \ldots A_n$ we arrive at a partial semantic tree T_C, each branch of which omits exactly one assignment to the atoms occurring in $[\neg C]$. Thus no literals signing atoms of $[\neg C]$ will have to occur below T_C. Therefore we can assume that the only failure nodes in T of clauses in $[\neg C]$ are $\alpha_1, \ldots, \alpha_n$. In other words: all failure nodes in T_{n+1} are failure nodes for clauses in S.

The only restriction (in addition to the requirement that T is a semantic tree for K) that we pose on the structure of T below T_C is that the literals labeling edges directly connected to a common node all contain the same atom. This way the following statement is easily seen to follow from condition (1) of the definition of a semantic tree.

(R) Let α be an inference node in T. Let $C_1, \ldots C_n$ be the clauses failing at its successor nodes $\beta_1, \ldots \beta_n$, respectively. Then some resolvent $D \in \mathcal{R}_b^*(\{C_1, \ldots C_n\})$ fails at α.

Since T is closed for $S \cup [\neg C]$ it must contain at least one inference node. Therefore, by iteratively adding resolvents to $S \cup [\neg C]$ and applying **(R)**, we must eventually derive a clause D that fails at the node α_{n+1}. Since T_{n+1} contains no failure nodes for clauses in $[\neg C]$ we conclude that $D \in \mathcal{R}_b^*(S)$. By Theorem 2 it follows that $\{D\theta\} \cup [\neg C]$ is unsatisfiable, where θ is a ground substitution such that $D\theta$ is contained in the refutation set of node α_{n+1}. By Lemma 1 it follows that D subsumes C.

References

1. M. Baaz. Automatisches Beweisen für endlichwertige Logiken. In *Jahrbuch 1989 der Kurt Gödel-Gesellschaft*, pages 105–107. Kurt Gödel Society, 1989.
2. M. Baaz and C. G. Fermüller. Resolution-based theorem proving for many-valued logics. *J. Symbolic Computation*, 19:353–391, 1995.
3. M.S. Garey and D.S. Johnson. *Computers and Intractability: A Guide to the Theory of NP-Completeness.* Freeman, San Francisco, 1979.
4. G. Gottlob and A. Leitsch. On the efficiency of subsumbtion algorithms. *Journal of the ACM*, 32(2):280–295, 1985.
5. R. Hähnle. *Automated Deduction in Multiple-valued Logics.* Clarendon Press, Oxford, 1993.
6. R. Hähnle. Short conjunctive normal forms in finitely-valued logics. *Journal of Logic and Computation*, 4(6):905–927, 1994.
7. R.C.T. Lee. *A completeness theorem and a computer program for finding theorems derivable from given axioms.* Ph.D. Thesis, University of California, Berkely, 1967.
8. A. Leitsch. *The Resolution Calculus.* Springer, Berlin, Heidelberg, New York, 1997.
9. G. Salzer. Optimal axiomatizations for multiple-valued operators and quantifiers based on semi-lattices. In *13th Int. Conf. on Automated Deduction (CADE'96)*, LNCS (LNAI). Springer, 1996.
10. M. Schmidt-Schauss. Implication of clauses is undecidable. *Theoretical Computer Science*, 59:287–296, 1988.

An Equational Re-engineering of Set Theories*

Andrea Formisano[1] and Eugenio Omodeo[2]

[1] University "La Sapienza" of Rome, Department of Computer Science
formisan@dsi.uniroma1.it
[2] University of L'Aquila, Department of Pure and Applied Mathematics
omodeo@univaq.it

This is hence the advantage of our method: that immediately ⋯ and with the only guidance of characters and through a safe and really analytic method, we bring to light truths that others had barely achieved by an immense mind effort and by chance. And therefore we are able to present within our century results which, otherwise, the course of many thousands of years would hardly deliver.
(G. W. Leibniz, 1679)

Abstract. New successes in dealing with set theories by means of state-of-the-art theorem-provers may ensue from terse and concise axiomatizations, such as can be moulded in the framework of the (fully equational) Tarski-Givant map calculus. In this paper we carry out this task in detail, setting the ground for a number of experiments.
Keywords: Set Theory, relation algebras, first-order theorem-proving, algebraic logic.

1 Introduction

Like other mature fields of mathematics, Set Theory deserves sustained efforts that bring to light richer and richer decidable fragments of it [6], general inference rules for reasoning in it [35, 2], effective proof strategies based on its domain-knowledge [3], and so forth.

Advances in this specialized area of automated reasoning tend to be steady but slow compared to the overall progress in the field. Many experiments with set theories have hence been carried out with standard theorem-proving systems. Still today such experiments pose considerable stress on state-of-the-art theorem provers, or demand the user to give much guidance to proof assistants; they therefore constitute ideal benchmarks. Moreover, in view of the pervasiveness of Set Theory, they are likely —when successful in something tough— to have a strong echo amidst computer scientists and mathematicians. Even for those who are striving to develop something entirely *ad hoc* in the challenging arena of set theories, it is important to assess what can today be achieved by unspecialized proof methods and where the context-specific bottlenecks of Set Theory precisely reside.

* Work partially supported by the CNR of Italy, coordinated project SETA, and by MURST 40%, "Tecniche speciali per la specifica, l'analisi, la verifica, la sintesi e la trasformazione di programmi".

R. Caferra and G. Salzer (Eds.): Automated Deduction, LNAI 1761, pp. 175–190, 2000.

In its most popular first-order version, namely the Zermelo-Skolem-Fraenkel axiomatic system ZF, set theory (very much like Peano arithmetic) presents an immediate obstacle: it does not admit a finite axiomatization. This is why the von Neumann-Bernays-Gödel theory GB of sets and classes is sometimes preferred to it as a basis for experimentation [4, 34, 27]. Various authors (e.g., [19, 23, 24]) have been able to retain the traits of ZF, by resorting to higher-order features of specific theorem-provers such as Isabelle.

In this paper we will pursue a minimalist approach, proposing a purely equational formulation of both ZF and finite set theory. Our approach heavily relies on [33], but we go into much finer detail with the axioms, resulting in such a concise formulation as to offer a good starting point for experimentation (with Otter [18], say, or with a more markedly equational theorem-prover). Our formulation of the axioms is based on the formalism $\mathcal{L}^{\times}$ of [33] (originating from [32]), which is equational and devoid of variables, but somewhat out of standards. Luckily, a theory stated in $\mathcal{L}^{\times}$ can easily be emulated through a first-order system, simply by treating the meta-variables that occur in the schematic formulation of its axioms (both the logical axioms and the ones endowed with a genuinely set-theoretic content) as if they were first-order variables. In practice, this means treating ZF as if it were an extension of the theory of relation algebras [17, 29, 21, 8, 10]; an intuitive explanation —a rough one, in view of well-known limitative results—[1] of why we can achieve a finite axiomatization is that variables are not supposed to range over sets but over the dyadic (i.e. binary) relations on the universe of sets.

Taken in its entirety, Set Theory offers a *panorama of alternatives* (cf. [28], p.x); that is, it consists of axiomatic systems not equivalent (and sometimes antithetic, cf. [20]) to one another. This is why we will not produce the axioms of just one theory and will also touch the theme of 'individuals' (ultimate entities entering in the formation of sets). Future work will expand the material of this paper into a toolkit for assembling set theories of all kinds—after we have singled out, through experiments, formulations of the axioms that work decidedly better than others.

2 Syntax and Semantics of $\mathcal{L}^{\times}$

$\mathcal{L}^{\times}$ is a ground equational language where one can state properties of dyadic relations —MAPS, as we will call them— over an unspecified, yet fixed, *domain $\mathcal{U}$ of discourse*. In this paper, the map whose properties we intend to specify is the membership relation $\in$ over the class $\mathcal{U}$ of all sets. The language $\mathcal{L}^{\times}$ consists of *map equalities* $Q{=}R$, where Q and R are *map expressions*:

[1] Two crucial limitative results are: that no consistent extension of the Zermelo theory is finitely axiomatizable (Montague, 1961), and that the variety of representable relation algebras is not finitely based (Monk, 1964).

Definition 1. MAP EXPRESSIONS are all terms of the following signature:

symbol :	$\emptyset$	$1\!\!1$	ι	$\in$	$\cap$	Δ	$\circ$	$^{-1}$	$^{-}$	$\setminus$	$\cup$	$\dagger$
degree :	0	0	0	0	2	2	2	1	1	2	2	2
priority :					5	3	6	7		2	2	4

(Of these, $\cap, \Delta, \circ, \setminus, \cup, \dagger$ will be used as left-associative infix operators, $^{-1}$ as a postfix operator, and $^{-}$ as a line topping its argument.) □

For an *interpretation* of $\mathcal{L}^{\times}$, one must fix, along with a nonempty $\mathcal{U}$, a subset $\in^{\Im}$ of $\mathcal{U}^2 =_{\text{Def}} \mathcal{U} \times \mathcal{U}$. Then each map expression P comes to designate a specific map $P^{\Im}$ (and, accordingly, any equality $Q{=}R$ between map expressions turns out to be either true or false), on the basis of the following evaluation rules:

$$\emptyset^{\Im} =_{\text{Def}} \emptyset, \qquad 1\!\!1^{\Im} =_{\text{Def}} \mathcal{U}^2, \qquad \iota^{\Im} =_{\text{Def}} \{[a,a] : a \text{ in } \mathcal{U}\};$$
$$(Q \cap R)^{\Im} =_{\text{Def}} \{ [a,b] \in Q^{\Im} : [a,b] \in R^{\Im} \};$$
$$(Q \Delta R)^{\Im} =_{\text{Def}} \{ [a,b] \in \mathcal{U}^2 : [a,b] \in Q^{\Im} \text{ if and only if } [a,b] \notin R^{\Im} \};$$
$$(Q \circ R)^{\Im} =_{\text{Def}} \{ [a,b] \in \mathcal{U}^2 : \text{there are } cs \text{ in } \mathcal{U} \text{ for which } [a,c] \in Q^{\Im} \text{ and } [c,b] \in R^{\Im} \};$$
$$(Q^{-1})^{\Im} =_{\text{Def}} \{ [b,a] : [a,b] \in Q^{\Im} \}.$$

Of the operators and constants in the signature of $\mathcal{L}^{\times}$, only a few deserve being regarded as *primitive* constructs; indeed, we choose to regard as *derived* constructs the ones for which we gave no evaluation rule, as well as others that we will tacitly add to the signature:

$\overline{P} \equiv_{\text{Def}} P \Delta 1\!\!1$	$P \dagger Q \equiv_{\text{Def}} \overline{\overline{P} \circ \overline{Q}}$
$P \setminus Q \equiv_{\text{Def}} P \cap \overline{Q}$	$\mathsf{funPart}(P) \equiv_{\text{Def}} P \setminus P \circ \overline{\iota}$
$P \cup Q \equiv_{\text{Def}} \overline{\overline{P} \setminus Q}$	etc.

The interpretation of $\mathcal{L}^{\times}$ obviously extends to the new constructs; e.g.,

$$(P \dagger Q)^{\Im} =_{\text{Def}} \{ [a,b] \in \mathcal{U}^2 : \text{for all } c \text{ in } \mathcal{U}, \text{ either } [a,c] \in P^{\Im} \text{ or } [c,b] \in Q^{\Im} \},$$
$$\mathsf{funPart}(P)^{\Im} =_{\text{Def}} \{[a,b] \in P^{\Im} : [a,c] \notin P^{\Im} \text{ for any } c \neq b\},$$

so that $\mathsf{funPart}(P){=}P$ will mean "P is a partial function", very much like $\mathsf{Fun}(P)$ to be seen below.

Through abbreviating definitions, we can also define shortening notation for map equalities that follow certain patterns, e.g.,

$$\mathsf{Fun}(P) \equiv_{\text{Def}} P^{-1} \circ P \setminus \iota = \emptyset$$
$$\mathsf{Total}(P) \equiv_{\text{Def}} P \circ 1\!\!1 = 1\!\!1$$

so that $\mathsf{Total}(P)$ states that for all a in $\mathcal{U}$ there is at least one pair $[a,b]$ in $P^{\Im}$.

Remark 1. It is at times useful (cf. [5]) to represent a map expression P by a labeled oriented graph G with two designated nodes s_0, s_1 named *source* and *sink*, whose edges are labeled by sub-expressions of P.

A non-deterministic algorithm to construct G, s_0, s_1 runs as follows: either

– G consists of a single edge, labeled P, leading from s_0 to s_1; or

- P is of the form Q^{-1}, and G, s_1, s_0 (with source and sink interchanged) represents Q; or
- P is of the form $Q \circ R$, the disjoint graphs G', s_0, s'_2 and G'', s''_2, s_1 represent Q and R respectively, and one obtains G by combination of G' with G'' by 'gluing' s''_2 onto s'_2 to form a single node; or
- P is of the form $Q \cap R$, the disjoint graphs G', s'_0, s'_1 and G'', s''_0, s''_1 represent Q and R respectively, and one obtains G from G' and G'' by gluing s''_0 onto s'_0 to form s_0 and by gluing s''_1 onto s'_1 to form s_1.

As an additional related convention, one can either

- label both s_0 and s_1 by $\forall$, to convert a representation G, s_0, s_1 of P into a representation of the equality $P = \mathbb{1}$; or
- label both s_0 and s_1 by $\exists$, to represent the inequality $P \neq \emptyset$ (which is a short for the equality $\mathbb{1} \circ P \circ \mathbb{1} = \mathbb{1}$); or
- label the source by $\forall$ and the sink by $\exists$, to represent the statement $\mathsf{Total}(P)$.

□

3 Specifying Set Theories in $\mathcal{L}^\times$

One often strives to specify the class $\mathcal{C}$ of interpretations that are of interest in some application through a collection of equalities that must be true in every $\Im$ of $\mathcal{C}$. The task we are undertaking here is of this nature; our aim is to capture through simple map equalities the interpretations of $\in$ that comply with

- standard Zermelo-Fraenkel theory, on the one hand;
- a theory of finite sets ultimately based on individuals, on the other hand.

In part, the game consists in expressing in $\mathcal{L}^\times$ common set-theoretic notions. To start with something obvious,

$$\notin \ \equiv_{\mathsf{Def}} \overline{\in}, \qquad \ni \ \equiv_{\mathsf{Def}} \in^{-1}, \qquad \not\ni \ \equiv_{\mathsf{Def}} \overline{\ni};$$

$\varepsilon_0 \varepsilon_1 \cdots \varepsilon_n \equiv_{\mathsf{Def}} \varepsilon_0 \circ \varepsilon_1 \circ \cdots \circ \varepsilon_n$, where each ε_i stands for one of $\in, \notin, \ni, \not\ni, \mathbb{1}$. To see something slightly more sophisticated:

Example 1. With respect to an interpretation $\Im$, one says that a *intersects* b if a and b have some element in common, i.e., there is a c for which $c \in^{\Im} a$ and $c \in^{\Im} b$. A map expression P such that $P^{\Im} = \{[a,b] \in \mathcal{U}^2 : a \text{ intersects } b\}$ is $\ni\in$.

Likewise, one can define in $\mathcal{L}^\times$ the relation a *includes* b (i.e., 'no element of b fails to belong to a'), by the map expression $\overline{\not\ni\in}$. The expression $\overline{\ni\notin \cup \iota}$ translates the relation a *is strictly included in* b, and so on.

Let a *splits* b mean that every element of a intersects b and that no two elements of a intersect each other. These conditions translate into the map expression defined as follows:

$$\mathsf{splits} \equiv_{\mathsf{Def}} (\not\ni \dagger \ni\in) \cap \overline{(\ni \cap \ni \circ (\ni\in \cap \bar{\iota}))} \circ \mathbb{1}.$$

□

Secondly, the reconstruction of set theory within $\mathcal{L}^\times$ consists in restating ordinary axioms (and, subsequently, theorems), through map equalities.

Example 2. One of the many ways of stating the much-debated AXIOM OF CHOICE (under adequately strong remaining axioms) is by claiming that *when a splits some b, there is a c which is also split by a and which does not strictly include any other set split by a.* Formally:

(Ch) $$\mathsf{Total}(\overline{\mathsf{splits}\circ\mathbb{1}}\cup\mathsf{splits}\setminus\mathsf{splits}\circ\overline{\ni\notin\cup\iota}),$$

where the second and third occurrence of splits could be replaced by $\not\ni\dagger\ni\in$.

The original version of this axiom in [36] stated that if a is a set whose elements all are sets endowed with elements and mutually disjoint, then $\bigcup a$ includes at least one subset having one and only one element in common with each element of a. To relate this version of **(Ch)** with ours,[2] notice that a set a splits some b if and only if a consists of pairwise disjoint non-void sets (and, accordingly, a splits $\bigcup a$). Moreover, an inclusion-minimal c split by a must have a singleton intersection with each d in a (otherwise, of two elements in $c \cap d$, either one could be removed from c); conversely, if c is included in $\bigcup a$ and has a singleton intersection with each d in a, then none of its elements e can be removed (otherwise $c \setminus \{e\}$ would no longer intersect the d in a to which e belongs). □

In the third place, we are to prove theorems about sets by equational reasoning, moving from the equational specification of the set axioms. To discuss this point we must refer to an inferential apparatus for $\mathcal{L}^{\times}$; we hence delay this discussion to much later (cf. Sec.8).

4 Extensionality, Subset, Sum-Set, and Power-Set Axioms

Two derived constructs, ∂ and $\mathfrak{F}$, will be of great help in stating the properties of membership simply:

$$\partial(P) \equiv_{\mathrm{Def}} \overline{P\circ\notin}, \qquad \mathfrak{F}(P) \equiv_{\mathrm{Def}} \partial(P)\setminus\overline{P}\circ\in.$$

Plainly, $a\partial(Q)^{\Im}b$ and $a\mathfrak{F}(R)^{\Im}b$ will hold in an interpretation $\Im$ if and only if, respectively,

- all cs in $\mathcal{U}$ for which $aQ^{\Im}c$ holds are 'elements' of b (in the sense that $c\in^{\Im}b$);
- the elements of b are precisely those c in $\mathcal{U}$ for which $aR^{\Im}c$ holds.

Our first axiom, EXTENSIONALITY, states that *sets are the same whose elements are the same*:

(E) $$\mathfrak{F}(\ni)=\iota.$$

A useful variant of this axiom is the scheme $\mathsf{Fun}(\mathfrak{F}(P))$, where P ranges over all map expressions.

Two rather elementary postulates, the POWER-SET axiom and the SUM-SET axiom, state that *for any set a, there is a set comprising as elements all sets included in a, and there is one which comprises all elements of elements of a*:

($\mathcal{P}ow$) $$\mathsf{Total}(\partial(\overline{\not\ni}\in)),$$

[2] For 19 alternative versions of this axiom, cf. [25], p.309.

$(\mathcal{U}n)$ $\mathsf{Total}(\,\partial(\ni\ni)\,)$.

A customary strenghtening of the sum-set axiom is the TRANSITIVE EMBEDDING axiom, stating that *every b belongs to a set a which is transitively closed w.r.t. membership*, in the sense specified by trans here below:

(T) $\mathsf{Total}(\,\in\circ\mathsf{trans}\,)$, where $\mathsf{trans} \equiv_{\mathsf{Def}} \iota\cap\partial(\,\ni\ni\,)$.

Here, by requiring $\mathsf{trans}^{\Im}$ to be contained in $\iota^{\Im}$, we have made it represent a collection of sets; then, the further requirement that $\mathsf{trans}^{\Im}$ be contained in $\partial(\,\ni\ni\,)^{\Im}$ amounts to the condition that *$c\in^{\Im}a$ holds when a, d, and c are such that a $\mathsf{trans}^{\Im}$ a, $a\ni^{\Im}d$, and $d\ni^{\Im}c$ hold.*

The SUBSET axioms enable one to extract from any given a the set b consisting of those elements of a that meet a condition specified by means of a predicate expression P. In this form, still overly naïve, this 'separation' principle could be stated as simply as: $\mathsf{Total}(\,\mathcal{F}(\ni\cap P)\,)$. This would suffice (taking $\emptyset$ as P) to ensure the existence of a *null* set, devoid of elements. We need the following more general form of separation (whence the previous one is obtained by taking ι as Q):

(S) $\mathsf{Total}\big(\,\mathcal{F}(\,\mathsf{funPart}(\,Q\,)\circ\ni\cap P\,)\,\big)$.

The latter states that *to every set a, there corresponds a set b which is null unless there is exactly one d fulfilling $aQ^{\Im}d$, and which in the latter case consists of all elements c of d for which $aP^{\Im}c$ holds.*

Example 3. Plainly, $\mathsf{funPart}(\,\ni\,)^{\Im}$ is the map holding between c and d in $\mathcal{U}$ iff $c = \{d\}$, i.e. d is the sole element of c; moreover $\mathsf{funPart}(\,\ni\circ\mathsf{funPart}(\,\ni\,)\,)^{\Im}$ is the map holding between a and d iff there is exactly one singleton c in a and d is the element of that particular c. Thus, the instance

$$\mathsf{Total}\big(\,\mathcal{F}(\,\mathsf{funPart}(\,\ni\circ\mathsf{funPart}(\,\ni\,)\,)\circ\ni\cap\not\ni\,)\,\big)$$

of **(S)** states that to every set a there corresponds a set b which is null unless there is exactly one singleton $c = \{d\}$ in a, and which in the latter case consists of all elements of d that do not belong to a. □

5 Pairing and Finiteness Axioms

A list $\pi_0, \pi_1, \ldots, \pi_n$ of maps are said to be CONJUGATED QUASI-PROJECTIONS if they are (partial) functions and they are, collectively, *surjective*, in the sense that for any list $a_0, \ldots, a_n$ of entities in $\mathcal{U}$ there is a b in $\mathcal{U}$ such that $\pi_i(b) = a_i$ for $i = 0, 1, \ldots, n$. We assume in what follows that π_0, π_1 are map expressions designating two conjugated quasi-projections. It is immaterial whether they are added as primitive constants to $\mathcal{L}^{\times}$, or they are map expressions suitably chosen so as to reflect one of the various notions of ordered pair available around, and subject to axioms that are adequate to ensure that the desired conditions, namely

(Pair) $\pi_0^{-1}\circ\pi_1 = \mathbb{1}$, $\mathsf{Fun}(\,\pi_0\,)$, $\mathsf{Fun}(\,\pi_1\,)$, $\in\ni = \mathbb{1}$,

hold (cf. [33], pp.127–135). Notice that the clause $\mathbf{(Pair)}_4$ of this PAIRING AXIOM will become superfluous when the replacement axiom scheme will enter into play (cf. [16], pp.9–10).

Example 4. A use of the $\boldsymbol{\pi}_b$s is that they enable one to represent set-theoretic functions by means of entities f of $\mathcal{U}$ such that no two elements b, c of f for which $\boldsymbol{\pi}_0^{\Im}$ yields a value have $\boldsymbol{\pi}_0^{\Im}(b) = \boldsymbol{\pi}_0^{\Im}(c)$. Symbolically, we can define the class of these *single-valued sets* as

$$\mathsf{sval} \equiv_{\mathsf{Def}} \boldsymbol{\iota} \cap \overline{\boldsymbol{\sigma} \circ \in}, \qquad \text{where } \boldsymbol{\sigma} \equiv_{\mathsf{Def}} \ni \circ (\boldsymbol{\pi}_0 \circ \boldsymbol{\pi}_0^{-1} \cap \overline{\boldsymbol{\iota}}).$$

Cantor's classical theorem that the power-set of a set has more elements than the set itself can be phrased (cf. [2], p.410) as follows: *for every set a and for every function f, there is a subset b of a which is not 'hit' by the function f* (restricted to the set a in question).[3] A rendering of this theorem in $\mathcal{L}^{\times}$ could be $\mathsf{Total}(\overline{\not\ni \in} \cap \overline{\ni \circ \mathsf{funPart}(P)})$, but this would not faithfully reflect the idea that the theorem concerns set-theoretic functions rather than functions, $\mathsf{funPart}(P)$, of $\mathcal{L}^{\times}$. The distinction is subtle but important, because the subsets F of $\mathcal{U}^2$ that candidate as values for map expressions are not necessarily entities of the same kind as the 'sets' f belonging to $\mathcal{U}$; on the one hand, F qualifies as a function when no two pairs $[a, b]$, $[a, d]$ in F share the same first component and differ in their second components; on the other hand, f qualifies as a 'function' when $f \, \mathsf{sval}^{\Im} f$ holds—the convenience to require also that $\boldsymbol{\pi}_0^{\Im}(d)$ and $\boldsymbol{\pi}_1^{\Im}(d)$ both exist for each $d \in^{\Im} f$ seems to be a debatable matter of taste.

The typical use of $\boldsymbol{\pi}_0$ and $\boldsymbol{\pi}_1$ is illustrated by a translation of Cantor's theorem more faithful than the above, which exploits the possibility to encode the pair a, f by an entity c with $\boldsymbol{\pi}_0^{\Im}(c) = a$ and $\boldsymbol{\pi}_1^{\Im}(c) = f$:

$$\mathsf{Total}(\overline{\boldsymbol{\pi}_0 \circ \not\ni \in} \cap \overline{(\boldsymbol{\pi}_0 \circ \ni \circ \boldsymbol{\pi}_0^{-1} \cap \boldsymbol{\pi}_1 \circ (\overline{\boldsymbol{\sigma}} \cap \ni)) \circ \boldsymbol{\pi}_1}) \qquad (\boldsymbol{\sigma} \text{ as before}).$$

The latter states that to every c there corresponds a b such that

- if it exists, $\boldsymbol{\pi}_0^{\Im}(c)$ includes b;
- if $\boldsymbol{\pi}_0^{\Im}(c) = a$ and $\boldsymbol{\pi}_1^{\Im}(c) = f$ both exist, then $b \neq \boldsymbol{\pi}_1^{\Im}(d)$ for any d in f such that $\boldsymbol{\pi}_0^{\Im}(d) = e$ exists and belongs to a and no d' in f other than d fulfills $\boldsymbol{\pi}_0^{\Im}(d') = e$. □

A standard technique used to derive statements of the form $\mathsf{Total}(\mathcal{F}(R))$, which are often very useful, is by breaking $\mathcal{F}(R)$ into an equivalent expression of the form $(P \circ \boldsymbol{\pi}_0^{-1} \cap \boldsymbol{\pi}_1^{-1}) \circ \mathcal{F}(\boldsymbol{\pi}_0 \circ \ni \cap \boldsymbol{\pi}_1 \circ Q)$, where $\mathsf{Total}(P)$ is easier to prove. Exploiting the graph representation of map expressions introduced in Remark 1, this situation can be depicted as follows:

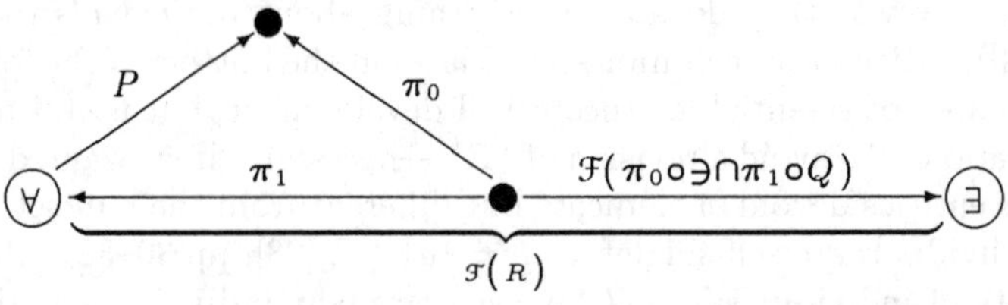

The desired totality of $\mathcal{F}(R)$ will then follow, in view of **(Pair)**$_1$ and of **(S)**, **(Pair)**$_2$. For example, by means of the instantiation $P \equiv \in \circ \mathsf{trans}$, $Q \equiv \boldsymbol{\iota}$ of

[3] This was one of the first major theorems whose proof was automatically found by a theorem prover, cf. [1]. This achievement originally took place in the framework of typed lambda-calculus.

this proof scheme, we obtain $\mathsf{Total}\big(\mathcal{F}(\boldsymbol{\iota})\big)$, where $\mathcal{F}(\boldsymbol{\iota})$ designates the *singleton-formation* operation $a \mapsto \{a\}$ on $\mathcal{U}$; then, by taking

$$P \equiv \big((\boldsymbol{\pi}_0 \cup \overline{\boldsymbol{\pi}_0 \circ \mathbb{1}}) \circ \in \cap (\boldsymbol{\pi}_1 \cup \overline{\boldsymbol{\pi}_1 \circ \mathbb{1}}) \circ \mathcal{F}(\boldsymbol{\iota}) \circ \in\big) \circ \partial(\ni\ni)$$

and

$$Q \equiv \boldsymbol{\pi}_0 \circ \ni \cup \boldsymbol{\pi}_1,$$

we obtain the totality of $\mathcal{F}(\boldsymbol{\pi}_0 \circ \ni \cup \boldsymbol{\pi}_1)$, which designates the *adjunction* operation $[a, b] \mapsto a \cup \{b\}$. Similarly, one gets the totality of $\mathcal{F}(\overline{\not\ni \in})$, $\mathcal{F}(\ni\ni)$, $\mathcal{F}(\boldsymbol{\pi}_0 \cup \boldsymbol{\pi}_1)$, of any $\mathcal{F}(R)$ such that both $R \backslash Q = \emptyset$ and $\mathsf{Total}\big(\partial(Q)\big)$ are known for some Q, etc. Even the full **(S)** could be derived with this approach from its restrained version $\mathsf{Total}\big(\mathcal{F}(\boldsymbol{\pi}_0 \circ \ni \cap \boldsymbol{\pi}_1 \circ P)\big)$.

Under the set axioms **(E)**, ($\mathcal{P}ow$), **(S)**, **(Pair)** introduced so far, it is reasonable to characterize a set a as being *finite* if and only if every set b of which a is an element has an element which is minimal w.r.t. inclusion (cf. [31], p.49). Intuitively speaking, in fact, the set formed by all infinite cs in the power-set $\wp(a)$ of a has no minimal elements when a is infinite, because every such c remains infinite after a single-element removal. Conversely, if a belongs to some b which has no minimal elements, then the intersection of b with $\wp(a)$ has no minimal elements either, and hence a is infinite. In conclusion, to instruct a theory concerned exclusively with finite sets, one can adopt the following FINITENESS AXIOM:

(F) $\mathsf{finite} = \boldsymbol{\iota}$, where $\mathsf{finite} \equiv_{\mathrm{Def}} \boldsymbol{\iota} \cap \big(\mathbb{1} \circ (\in \cap ((\boldsymbol{\iota} \cup \not\ni \in) \dagger \not\in)) \dagger \not\ni\big)$.

Here, by requiring $\mathsf{finite}^{\mathfrak{I}}$ to be contained in $\boldsymbol{\iota}^{\mathfrak{I}}$, we have made it represent a collection of sets (the collection of *all* sets, if **(F)** is postulated); then, the further requirement that $\mathsf{finite}^{\mathfrak{I}}$ be contained in $\big(\mathbb{1} \circ (\in \cap ((\boldsymbol{\iota} \cup \not\ni \in) \dagger \not\in)) \dagger \not\ni\big)^{\mathfrak{I}}$ amounts to the condition that *when both a* $\mathsf{finite}^{\mathfrak{I}}$ *a and* $b \ni^{\mathfrak{I}} a$ *hold, there is a* $c \in^{\mathfrak{I}} b$ *such that no* $d \in^{\mathfrak{I}} b$ *other than c itself is included in c.*

6 Bringing Individuals into Set Theory: Foundation and Plenitude Axioms

Taken together with the *foundation* axiom to be seen below, the axioms **(E)**, ($\mathcal{P}ow$), **(T)**, **(S)**, **(Pair)**, and **(F)** discussed above constitute a full-blown theory of finite sets. However, they do not say anything about *individuals* (or 'urelements', cf. [14]), entities that common sense places at the bottom of the formation of sets. These are not essential for theoretical development, but useful to model practical situations. To avoid a revision of **(E)** —necessary, if we wanted to treat individuals as entities devoid of elements but different from the null set— let us agree that individuals are self-singletons $a = \{a\}$ (cf. [28], pp.30–32). Moreover, to bring plenty of individuals into $\mathcal{U}$ (at least as many individuals as there are sets, hence infinitely many individuals), we require that *there are individuals outside the sum-set of any set*. Here comes the PLENITUDE AXIOM:

(Ur) $\mathsf{Total}(\overline{\ni\ni} \circ \mathsf{ur})$, where $\mathsf{ur} \equiv_{\mathrm{Def}} \boldsymbol{\iota} \cap \mathcal{F}(\boldsymbol{\iota})$.

To develop a theory of *pure* sets, one will postulate 'lack' of individuals, by adopting the axiom $\mathsf{ur} = \emptyset$ instead of plenitude.

When individuals are lacking, the FOUNDATION (or 'regularity') axiom ensures that the membership relation $\in^{\Im}$ is cycle-free—more generally, under infinity and replacement axioms (see Sec.7 below), it can be used to prove that $\in^{\Im}$ is well-founded on $\mathcal{U}$ (cf. [7], Ch.2 Sec.5). Regularity is usually stated as follows: *when some b belongs to a, there is a c also belonging to a that does not intersect a.* On the surface, this statement has the same structure as the version of the axiom of choice seen at the end of Sec.2; in $\mathcal{L}^{\times}$ it can hence be rendered by

$$\mathsf{Total}(\,\overline{\ni\mathbb{1}}\cup\ni\setminus\ni\in\,).$$

Example 5. To ascertain that the existence of a membership cycle would conflict with regularity stated in the form just seen, one can use singleton-formation together with the adjunction operation and with the quasi-projections π_0, π_1, to form the set $a = \{b_0, \ldots, b_n\}$ out of any given list $b_0, \ldots, b_n$ of sets. If, by absurd hypothesis, $b_0 \in^{\Im} b_1 \in^{\Im} \cdots \in^{\Im} b_n \in^{\Im} b_0$ could hold, then every element b_j of a would intersect a, since $b_n \in^{\Im} a \cap b_0$ and $b_{i-1} \in^{\Im} a \cap b_i$ would hold for $i = 1, \ldots, n$. □

To reconcile the above statement of regularity with individuals, we can recast it as

(R) $$\mathsf{Total}\big(\,(\,\not\ni\cup\mathbb{1}\circ\mathsf{ur}\,)\dagger\emptyset\cup\ni\setminus\ni\circ(\,\iota\setminus\mathsf{ur}\,)\circ\in\setminus\mathbb{1}\circ\mathsf{ur}\,\big),$$

which means: *unless every b in a is an individual, there is a c in a such that every element of $a \cap c$ is an individual and c itself is not an individual.*

As is well-known (cf. [16], p.35), foundation helps one in making the definitions of basic mathematical notions very simple. In our framework, we propose to adopt the following definition of the class of *natural numbers*:[4]

$$\mathsf{nat} \equiv_{\mathsf{Def}} \iota \cap \Big(\ni\circ\big(\mathcal{F}(\,\ni\cup\iota\,)\setminus\iota\,\big)\dagger\overline{(\,\iota\cup\in\,)\cap\ni\mathbb{1}}\,\Big),$$

which means: *a is a natural number if for every b in $a \cup \{a\}$ other than the null set, there is a c in a such that $b = c \cup \{c\}$ and $b \neq c$.*

7 An Infinity Axiom and the Replacement Axioms

Similarly, under the foundation axiom, the definition of *ordinal numbers* becomes

$$\mathsf{ord} \equiv_{\mathsf{Def}} (\,\mathsf{trans}\setminus\ni\circ\mathsf{ur}\circ\mathbb{1}\,)\cap(\,\not\ni\dagger(\,\in\cup\iota\cup\ni\,)\dagger\not\in\,),$$

where trans is the same as in **(T)**, hence $\mathsf{trans}\setminus\iota=\emptyset$ holds, and hence (thanks to **(R)**) $\not\ni\dagger(\,\in\cup\iota\cup\ni\,)\dagger\not\in$ requires that an ordinal be totally ordered by membership.

The existence of infinite sets is often postulated by claiming that $\mathsf{ord}\setminus\mathsf{nat}$ is not empty: $\mathbb{1}\circ(\,\mathsf{ord}\setminus\mathsf{nat}\,)\circ\mathbb{1}=\mathbb{1}$, or equivalently $\mathsf{Total}\big(\,\mathbb{1}\circ(\,\mathsf{ord}\setminus\mathsf{nat}\,)\,\big)$. The following more essential formulation of the INFINITY axiom, based on [22] and presupposing **(R)**, seems preferable to us:[5]

(I) $$\mathsf{Total}\Big(\,\mathbb{1}\circ\big(\,\partial(\,\ni\ni\,)\cap\partial(\,\ni\ni\,)^{-1}\setminus\in\setminus\ni\setminus\iota\setminus\ni\circ\overline{\in\triangle\ni}\circ\in\,\big)\Big).$$

[4] From this simple start one can rapidly reach the definition of important data structures, e.g., ordered and oriented finite trees.

[5] Here, like in the case of **(Ur)** (which could have been stated more simply as $\mathsf{Total}(\,\not\ni\circ\mathsf{ur}\,)$), our preference goes to a formulation whose import is as little dependent as possible from the remaining axioms.

What **(I)** means is: *There are distinct sets* a_0, a_1 *such that the sum-set of either one is included in the other, neither one belongs to the other, and for any pair* c_0, c_1 *with* c_0 *in* a_0 *and* c_1 *in* a_1*, either* c_0 *belongs to* c_1 *or* c_1 *belongs to* c_0*.*[6] [7] Of course this axiom is antithetic to the axiom **(F)** seen earlier: one can adopt either one, but only one of the two.

In a theory with infinite sets, the REPLACEMENT AXIOM SCHEME plays a fundamental rôle. Two simple-minded versions of it are:

$$\mathsf{Total}\big(\,\partial(\,\ni\circ\mathsf{funPart}(\,Q\,)\,)\,\big), \qquad \mathsf{Total}\big(\,\partial(\,\ni\circ\mathcal{F}(\,Q\,)\circ\ni\,)\,\big).$$

Both of these state —under different conditions on a certain map P— that to every c there corresponds a (superset of a) set of the form $P[c] =_{\mathrm{Def}} \{u : vP^{\mathfrak{I}}u$ for some $v{\in}^{\mathfrak{I}}c\}$. The former applies when P ($\equiv \mathsf{funPart}(\,Q\,)$) designates a function, the latter when $\mathcal{F}(\,P\,)$ (with $P \equiv \mathcal{F}(\,Q\,)\circ\ni$) designates a total map. A formulation of replacement closer in spirit to the latter is adopted in [30], but it is the former that we generalize in what follows.

Parameter-less replacement, like a parameter-less subset axiom scheme, would be of little use. Given an entity d of $\mathcal{U}$, we can think that $\pi_0^{\mathfrak{I}}(d)$ represents the domain c to which one wants to restrict a function, and $\pi_1^{\mathfrak{I}}(d)$ represents a list of parameters. To state replacement simply, it is convenient to add to the conditions on the π_is a new one. Specifically, we impose that distinct entities never encode the same pair:[8]

(Pair)$_5$ $$\pi_0\circ\pi_0^{-1}\cap\pi_1\circ\pi_1^{-1}\setminus\iota=\emptyset.$$

The simplest formulation of replacement we could find in $\mathcal{L}^{\times}$, so far, is:

(Repl) $$\mathsf{Total}\big(\,\partial(\,(\,\pi_0\circ\ni\circ\pi_0^{-1}\cap\pi_1\circ\pi_1^{-1}\,)\circ\mathsf{funPart}(\,Q\,)\,)\,\big)\,.$$

This means: *To every pair d there corresponds a set comprising the images, under the functional part of Q, of all pairs e that fulfill the conditions* $\pi_0^{\mathfrak{I}}(e){\in}^{\mathfrak{I}}\pi_0^{\mathfrak{I}}(d)$, $\pi_1^{\mathfrak{I}}(e) = \pi_1^{\mathfrak{I}}(d)$.

Example 6. To see that **(Pair)**$_4$ can be derived from **(Pair)**$_{1,2,3}$, **(T)**, **(S)**, and **(Repl)**, one can argue as follows. Thanks to **(S)**, a null set $\{\}$ exists: $\overline{\mathbb{1}{\in}}\circ\mathbb{1}=\mathbb{1}$. Then, by virtue of **(T)**, a set to which this null set belongs exists too: $\overline{\mathbb{1}{\in}}\circ{\in}\circ\mathbb{1}=\mathbb{1}$. Again through **(T)**, we obtain a set c to which both of the preceding sets belong: $\overline{\mathbb{1}{\in}}\circ(\,{\in}\cap{\in}{\in}\,)\circ\mathbb{1}=\mathbb{1}$. The latter c can be combined with any given a to form a pair d fulfilling both $\pi_0^{\mathfrak{I}}(d) = c$ and $\pi_1^{\mathfrak{I}}(d) = a$, by **(Pair)**$_1$. Two uses of **(Repl)**, referring to the single-valued maps

$$Q_\ell \equiv_{\mathrm{Def}} \pi_0\circ\overline{\ni\mathbb{1}} \cap \pi_\ell \,\triangle\, \pi_0\circ\ni\mathbb{1} \cap \pi_{1-\ell}$$

with $\ell = 0$ and $\ell = 1$ respectively, will complete the job. Indeed, the first use of **(Repl)** will form from d a set c_a comprising a and $\{\}$ as elements; the second

---

[6] Notice that when c belongs to a_ℓ ($\ell = 0, 1$), then $c \subsetneq a_{1-\ell}$; hence there is a c' in $a_{1-\ell} \setminus c$, so that c belongs to c'. Then $c' \subsetneq a_\ell$, and so on. Starting w.l.o.g. with c_0 in a_0, one finds distinct sets $c_0, c_1, c_2, \ldots$ with $c_{\ell+2\cdot i}$ in a_ℓ for $\ell = 0, 1$ and $i = 0, 1, 2, \ldots$.

[7] For the sake of completeness, let us mention here that for a statement not relying on **(R)**, the following cumbersome expression should be subtracted from the argument of Total in **(I)**: $(\,\ni\circ\pi_0^{-1}\cap\ni\circ\pi_1^{-1}\,)\circ(\,\pi_0\circ{\in}\circ\pi_0^{-1}\cap\pi_1\circ{\in}\circ\pi_1^{-1}\cap\pi_1\circ\ni\circ\pi_0^{-1}\cap$ $\overline{\pi_0\circ{\in}\circ\pi_1^{-1}}\,)\circ(\,\pi_0\circ{\in}\cap\pi_1\circ{\in}\,)$.

[8] Notice that **(Pair)**$_{2,3,4,5}$ can be superseded (retaining **(Pair)**$_1$) by the definitions

$$\pi_0 \equiv_{\mathrm{Def}} \mathsf{funPart}(\,\ni\circ\mathsf{funPart}(\,\ni\,)\,), \qquad \pi_1 \equiv_{\mathrm{Def}} \ni\ni\cap\big(\,(\,\overline{\ni\ni}\cup\pi_0\,)\dagger\iota\,\big)\cap(\,\not\ni\dagger\ni\mathbb{1}\,).$$

use of **(Repl)** will form from a pair d_a, with components c_a and b, a set c_{ab} comprising a and b as elements, for any given b.

Notice that either use of **(Repl)** in the above argument has exploited a single parameter, which was a and b respectively. □

8 Setting Up Experiments on a Theorem-Prover

A MAP CALCULUS, i.e, an inferential apparatus for $\mathcal{L}^\times$ is defined in [33], pp.45–47, along the following lines:

- A certain number of equality schemes are chosen as *logical axioms*. Each scheme comprises infinitely many map equalities $P{=}Q$ such that $P^{\Im} = Q^{\Im}$ holds in every interpretation $\Im$; syntactically it differs from an ordinary map equality in that *meta-variables*, which stand for arbitrary map expressions, may occur in it.
- *Inference rules* are singled out for deriving new map equalities $V{=}W$ from two equalities $P{=}Q$, $R{=}S$ (either assumed or derived earlier). Of course $V^{\Im} = W^{\Im}$ must hold in any interpretation $\Im$ fulfilling both $P^{\Im} = Q^{\Im}$ and $R^{\Im} = S^{\Im}$. The smallest collection $\Theta^\times(\mathtt{E})$ of map equalities that comprises a given collection E (of *proper* axioms) together with all instances of the logical axioms, and which is closed w.r.t. application of the inference rules, is regarded as the *theory* generated by E.

A variant of this formalism, which differs in the choice of the logical axioms (because $\cap$ and $\triangle$ seem preferable to $\cup$ and $^-$ as primitive constructs), is shown in Figure 1 (see also [9]).

We omit the details here, although we think that the choice of the logical axioms can critically affect the performance of automatic deduction within our theories. Ideally, only minor changes in the formulation E of the set axioms should be necessary if the logical axioms are properly chosen and then they are bootstrapped with inventories of useful lemmas concerning primitive as well as secondary map constructs. Similarly, in the automation of GB, one has to bestow some care to the treatment of Boolean constructs (cf. [26], pp.107–109).

To follow [33] orthodoxly, we should treat $\mathcal{L}^\times$ as an autonomous formalism, on a par with first-order predicate calculus. This, however, would pose us two problems: we should develop from scratch a theorem-prover for $\mathcal{L}^\times$, and we should cope with the infinitely many instances of **(S)** and of **(Repl)**. Luckily, this is unnecessary if we treat as first-order variables the meta-variables that occur in the logical axioms or in **(S)**, **(Repl)** (as well as in induction schemes, should any enter into play either as additional axioms or as theses to be proved). Within the framework of first-order logic, the logical axioms lose their status and become just axioms on *relation algebras*, conceptually forming a chapter of axiomatic set theory interesting *per se*, richer than Boolean algebra and more fundamental and stable than the rest of the axiomatic system.

Attempts (some of which very challenging) that one might carry out with any first-order theorem prover have the following flavor:

$P \cup Q \equiv_{\mathrm{Def}} P \triangle Q \triangle P \cap Q$	$P \subseteq Q \equiv_{\mathrm{Def}} P \cap Q = P$

$$
\begin{aligned}
P \triangle P &= \emptyset \\
P \triangle (Q \triangle P) &= Q \\
R \cap Q \triangle R \cap P &= (P \triangle Q) \cap R \\
P \cap P &= P \\
\mathbb{1} \cap P &= P \\
(P \star_1 Q) \star_1 R &= P \star_1 (Q \star_1 R) \\
\iota \circ P &= P \\
P^{-1^{-1}} &= P \\
(P \star_2 Q)^{-1} &= Q^{-1} \star_2 P^{-1} \\
(P \triangle Q) \circ R &\subseteq Q \circ R \cup P \circ R
\end{aligned}
$$

From $P \circ Q \cap R = \emptyset$ derive $P^{-1} \circ R \cap Q = \emptyset$

From $P \subseteq Q$ derive $P \circ R \subseteq Q \circ R$

Substitution laws for equals (cf. [12])

Either $P = \emptyset$ or $\mathbb{1} \circ P \circ \mathbb{1} = \mathbb{1}$ holds

$\star_1 \in \{\triangle, \cap, \circ\}$ and $\star_2 \in \{\cap, \circ\}$

Fig. 1. Logical axioms and inference rules for $\mathcal{L}^{\times}$, plus a splitting rule.

- Under the axioms **(E)**, $(\mathcal{P}ow)$, **(T)**, **(S)**, $\mathbf{(Pair)}_{1,2,3,4}$, **(R)**, $\mathsf{ur} = \emptyset$, and **(F)**, prove $(\mathcal{U}n)$, **(Repl)**, **(Ch)**, $\mathsf{Fun}(\mathcal{F}(P))$, and $\mathsf{trans} \circ \overline{\iota} \setminus \mathbb{1} \in \setminus \ni = \emptyset$,[9] as theorems.
- Under the axioms **(E)**, $(\mathcal{U}n)$, **(S)**, **(Pair)**, **(R)**, and **(Ur)**, prove that the following map equations hold $\in \circ (\in \cdots \in) \cap \iota = \mathsf{ur}$, $\mathsf{nat} \cap \mathsf{ur} = \emptyset$, $\mathsf{ord} \cap \mathsf{ur} = \emptyset$, $\in \circ \mathsf{ord} \setminus \mathsf{ord} \circ \mathbb{1} = \emptyset$, $\emptyset \dagger \notin \triangle \mathbb{1} \circ \overline{\mathsf{ord}} \circ \in \cup \mathbb{1} \circ \big(\in \cap ((\ni \triangle \iota) \dagger \notin) \big) = \mathbb{1}$,[10] etc.
- Under the axioms **(E)**, $(\mathcal{P}ow)$, $(\mathcal{U}n)$, **(S)**, $\mathbf{(Pair)}_{1,2,3,5}$, and **(Repl)**, prove $\mathbf{(Pair)}_4$ as a theorem; moreover, prove Cantor's theorem, prove the totality of $\mathcal{F}(\emptyset)$, $\mathcal{F}(\iota)$, $\mathcal{F}(\overline{\not\ni \in})$, $\mathcal{F}(\ni\ni)$, $\mathcal{F}(\ni \cup \iota)$, $\mathcal{F}(\pi_0 \cup \pi_1)$, $\mathcal{F}(\pi_0 \circ \ni \cup \pi_1)$, and of $\mathcal{F}\big(\mathsf{funPart}(Q) \circ \ni \cup \mathsf{setPart}(P)\big)$, where $\mathsf{setPart}(P) \equiv_{\mathrm{Def}} P \cap \partial(P) \circ \mathbb{1}$.

We count on the opportunity to soon start a systematic series of experiments of this nature, for which we are inclined to using Otter. We plan to perform extensive experimentation with theories of numbers and sets specified in $\mathcal{L}^{\times}$, and we are eager to compare the results of our experiments with the work of others. Otter is attractive in this respect, because it has been the system underlying experiments of the kind we have in mind, as reported in [26, 27]. Moreover, the fact that Otter encompasses full first-order logic —and not just an equational

9 The last of these states that the null set belongs to every transitively closed non-null set.

10 The last two of these state that elements of ordinals are ordinals and that every non-null set of ordinals has a minimum w.r.t. $\in$.

fragment of it— paves the way to combined reasoning tactics which intermix term rewriting steps with steps that, e.g., perform resolution of $\mathbb{1} \circ P \circ \mathbb{1} = \mathbb{1}$ against $P = \emptyset$, or (cf. [32, 15]) of $P \circ \mathbb{1} = \mathbb{1}$ against $\mathbb{1} \circ \overline{P} = \mathbb{1}$.

9 A Case-Study Experiment Run on Otter

By way of example, let us consider the problem of showing the equivalence between two formulations of extensionality, which are $\mathfrak{F}(\ni) = \iota$ and the scheme $\mathsf{Fun}(\mathfrak{F}(P))$. Our proof assistant is Otter 3.05, run under Linux. Our deductive apparatus for $\mathcal{L}^{\times}$ is the one shown in Figure 1, but occasionally we have better results with an explicit distributive law for $\circ$ w.r.t. $\cup$, and with a suitable substitute for the *cycle law* (cf. [11], pp.2–3), as shown in Figure 2.

$(P \triangle Q) \circ R \subseteq Q \circ R \cup P \circ R$
From $P \subseteq Q$ derive $P \circ R \subseteq Q \circ R$
From $P \circ Q \cap R = \emptyset$ derive $P^{-1} \circ R \cap Q = \emptyset$

$\Rrightarrow$

$(P \cup Q) \circ R = Q \circ R \cup P \circ R$
$P^{-1} \circ \big(R \cap (P \circ Q \triangle R)\big) \cap Q = \emptyset$

Fig. 2. Modifications to the laws of $\mathcal{L}^{\times}$, useful in some experiments.

Deriving the equivalence between these two statements from the axioms and inference rules of Figure 1, appears to be out of reach of the current system; hence we start with a separate derivation of $\mathfrak{F}(\ni) = \iota$ from $\mathsf{Fun}(\mathfrak{F}(P))$.

As a useful preliminary, Otter is exploited to get $\iota \subseteq \mathfrak{F}(\ni)$, a fact which does not depend on the hypothesis $\mathsf{Fun}(\mathfrak{F}(P))$. The main step of the proof is $\iota \subseteq \overline{\overline{Q^{-1}} \circ \overline{Q}}$, whence $\iota \subseteq \overline{\overline{\overline{Q^{-1}}} \circ Q}$ and $\iota \subseteq \overline{\overline{Q^{-1}} \circ \overline{\overline{Q}}} \cap \overline{\overline{\overline{Q^{-1}}} \circ Q}$ follow. Now it suffices to recall that $\mathfrak{F}(\ni) \equiv_{\mathrm{Def}} \overline{\ni \circ \notin} \cap \overline{\not\ni \circ \in}$. Proving $\iota \subseteq \mathfrak{F}(\ni)$ in a single shot, though feasible, requires one to bootstrap the logical axioms by adding suitable hypotheses and lemmas concerning algebraic properties of $\triangle$, $\cap$, $^{-1}$, and the defined map construct $^{-}$. (An excerpt of these can be found in Figure 3, together with the definition of $^{-}$ in term of $\triangle$ we adopted.) However, each of the four major steps in the above outline of the proof can be obtained in fully automatic mode from the axioms of Figure 1.

To complete the derivation of $\mathfrak{F}(\ni) = \iota$, it suffices to instantiate P as $\ni$ in the hypothesis $\mathsf{Fun}(\mathfrak{F}(P))$, and to observe that, taken together, $\mathsf{Fun}(Q)$, $R \subseteq Q$, and $\mathsf{Total}(R)$ yield $R = Q$—in particular, with the instantiation $Q \equiv$

$$\overline{P} = P \triangle \mathbb{1}$$

$$\overline{\overline{P}} = P \qquad \overline{P^{-1}} = \overline{P}^{-1}$$

$$(P \triangle Q)^{-1} = Q^{-1} \triangle P^{-1} \qquad \overline{P} \cap Q = Q \triangle P \cap Q$$

$$\iota = \iota^{-1} \qquad P \circ \iota = \iota \circ P$$

Fig. 3. Some tiny lemmas useful to speed-up proof discovery in Otter.

$\mathcal{F}(\ni)$ and $R \equiv \iota$, one gets the desired conclusion. The implication $\mathsf{Fun}(Q) \wedge R \subseteq Q \wedge \mathsf{Total}(R) \rightarrow R = Q$ is rather difficult for Otter to prove, unless with the replacements shown in Figure 2.

We are left with the task of deriving $\mathsf{Fun}(\mathcal{F}(P))$ from $\mathcal{F}(\ni) = \iota$. The main step here is the law $\overline{R \circ Q} \circ Q^{-1} \subseteq \overline{R}$ (which Otter is able to prove in automatic mode), whence $\overline{R \circ Q} \circ Q^{-1} \circ \overline{Q} \subseteq \overline{R} \circ \overline{Q}$ (i.e., $\overline{R \circ Q} \circ Q^{-1} \circ \overline{Q} \cap \overline{\overline{R} \circ \overline{Q}} = \emptyset$) and $\overline{Q^{-1} \circ R^{-1}} \circ \overline{\overline{R} \circ \overline{Q}} \cap \subseteq \overline{Q^{-1} \circ \overline{Q}}$ (i.e., $\overline{Q^{-1} \circ R^{-1}} \circ \overline{\overline{R} \circ \overline{Q}} \cap Q^{-1} \circ \overline{Q} = \emptyset$, by cycle law) follow. The latter specializes both into $\overline{\not\ni \circ P^{-1}} \circ \overline{\overline{P} \circ \in} \subseteq \overline{\not\ni \circ \in}$ and into $\overline{\ni \circ \overline{P^{-1}}} \circ \overline{P \circ \notin} \subseteq \overline{\ni \circ \notin}$. On another side, $\mathcal{F}(P)^{-1} \circ \mathcal{F}(P) \subseteq \overline{\not\ni \circ P^{-1}} \circ \overline{\overline{P} \circ \in}$ and $\mathcal{F}(P)^{-1} \circ \mathcal{F}(P) \subseteq \overline{\ni \circ \overline{P^{-1}}} \circ \overline{P \circ \notin}$ both hold (the derived law $P \subseteq Q \rightarrow R \circ P \subseteq R \circ Q$ intervenes crucially here), and hence we obtain $\mathcal{F}(P)^{-1} \circ \mathcal{F}(P) \subseteq \mathcal{F}(\ni) = \iota$, which leads to the desired conclusion.

The time-consumption in similar experiments can be significantly reduced by exploiting collections of useful tiny lemmas (regarding $^{-}$, $\cup$, etc.).

10 Conclusions

The language $\mathcal{L}^{\times}$ may look distasteful to reading, but it ought to be clear that techniques for moving back and forth between first-order logic and map logic exist and are partly implemented (cf. [33, 13, 5, 9]); moreover they can be ameliorated, and can easily be extended to meet the specific needs of set theories. Thanks to these, the automatic crunching of set axioms of the kind discussed in this paper can be hidden inside the back-end of an automated reasoner.

Anyhow, we think that it is worthwhile to riddle through experiments our expectation that a basic machine reasoning layer designed for $\mathcal{L}^{\times}$ may significantly raise the degree of automatizability of set-theoretic proofs. This expectation relies on the merely equational character of $\mathcal{L}^{\times}$ and on the good properties of the map constructs; moreover, when the calculus of $\mathcal{L}^{\times}$ gets emulated by means of first-order predicate calculus, we see an advantage in the finiteness of the axiomatization of ZF.

Acknowledgements

We are grateful to Marco Temperini, with whom we have enjoyed a number of discussions on subjects related to this paper, and have begun the experiments reported in Sec.9.

The example at the end of Sec.7 was suggested by Alberto Policriti.

We should also like to thank an anonymous referee for very useful comments, which are valuable also for our future experimentation plan.

References

[1] P. B. Andrews, D. Miller, E. Longini Cohen, and F. Pfenning. Automating higher-order logic. In W. W. Bledsoe and D. W. Loveland eds., *Automated theorem proving: After 25 years*, 169–192. American Mathematical Society, Contemporary Mathematics vol.29, 1984.

[2] S. C. Bailin and D. Barker-Plummer. $\mathcal{Z}$-match: An inference rule for incrementally elaborating set instantiations. *J. Automated Reasoning*, 11(3):391–428, 1993. (Errata in *J. Automated Reasoning*, 12(3):411–412, 1994).

[3] J. G. F. Belinfante. On a modification of Gödel's algorithm for class formation. *AAR Newsletter* No.34, 10–15, 1996.

[4] R. Boyer, E. Lusk, W. McCune, R. Overbeek, M. Stickel, and L. Wos. Set theory in first-order logic: Clauses for Gödel's axioms. *J. Automated Reasoning*, 2(3):287–327, 1986.

[5] D. Cantone, A. Cavarra, and E. G. Omodeo. On existentially quantified conjunctions of atomic formulae of $\mathcal{L}^+$. In M. P. Bonacina and U. Furbach, eds., *Proc. of the FTP97 International workshop on first-order theorem proving*, RISC-Linz Report Series No.97-50, pp. 45–52, 1997.

[6] D. Cantone, A. Ferro, and E. G. Omodeo. *Computable set theory. Vol. 1. Int. Series of Monographs on Computer Science.* Oxford University Press, 1989.

[7] P. J. Cohen. Set Theory and the continuum hypothesis. Benjamin, New York, 1966.

[8] I. Düntsch. Rough relation algebras. *Fundamenta Informaticae*, 21:321–331, 1994.

[9] A. Formisano, E. G. Omodeo, and M. Temperini. Plan of activities on the map calculus. In J. L. Freire-Nistal, M. Falaschi, and M. Vilares Ferro, eds., *Proc. of the AGP98 Joint Conference on Declarative Programming*, pp. 343–356, A Coruña, Spain, 1998.

[10] M. F. Frias, A. M. Haeberer, and P. A. S. Veloso. A finite axiomatization for fork algebras. *J. of the IGPL*, 5(3):311–319, 1997.

[11] S. R. Givant. *The Structure of Relation Algebras Generated by Relativization*, volume 156 of *Contemporary Mathematics.* American Mathematical Society, 1994.

[12] D. Gries and F. B. Schneider. *A logical approach to discrete math. Texts and Monographs in Computer Science.* Springer-Verlag, 1994.

[13] A. M. Haeberer, G. A. Baum, and G. Schmidt. On the smooth calculation of relational recursive expressions out of first-order non-constructive specifications involving quantifiers. In *Proc. of the International Conference on Formal Methods in Programming and their Applications.* LNCS 735:281–298. Springer-Verlag, 1993.

[14] T. J. Jech *Set theory*, Academic Press, New York, 1978.

[15] B. Jónsson and A. Tarski. Representation problems for relation algebras. *Bull. Amer. Math. Soc.*, 54, 1948;

[16] J.-L. Krivine *Introduction to axiomatic set theory*, Reidel, Dordrecht. Holland, 1971.

[17] R. C. Lyndon The representation of relational algebras. *Annals of Mathematics*, 51(3):707–729, 1950.
[18] W. W. McCune. Otter 3.0 reference manual and guide. Technical Report ANL-94/6, Argonne National Laboratory, 1994. (Revision A, august 1995).
[19] Ph. A. J. Noël. Experimenting with Isabelle in ZF set theory. *J. Automated Reasoning*, 10(1):15–58, 1993.
[20] E. G. Omodeo and A. Policriti. Solvable set/hyperset contexts: I. Some decision procedures for the pure, finite case. *Comm. Pure App. Math.*, 48(9-10):1123–1155, 1995. Special Issue in honor of J.T. Schwartz.
[21] E. Orlowska. Relational semantics for nonclassical logics: Formulas are relations. In Wolenski, J. ed. *Philosophical Logic in Poland*, pages 167–186, 1994.
[22] F. Parlamento and A. Policriti. Expressing infinity without foundation. *J. Symbolic Logic*, 56(4):1230–1235, 1991.
[23] L. C. Paulson. Set Theory for verification: I. From foundations to functions. *J. Automated Reasoning*, 11(3):353–389, 1993.
[24] L. C. Paulson. Set Theory for verification. II: Induction and recursion. *J. Automated Reasoning*, 15(2):167–215, 1995.
[25] L. C. Paulson and K. Grąbczewski. Mechanizing set theory. *J. Automated Reasoning*, 17(3):291–323, 1996.
[26] A. Quaife. Automated deduction in von Neumann-Bernays-Gödel Set Theory. *J. Automated Reasoning*, 8(1):91–147, 1992.
[27] A. Quaife. *Automated development of fundamental mathematical theories.* Kluwer Academic Publishers, 1992.
[28] W. V. Quine. *Set theory and its logic.* The Belknap Press of Harvard University Press, Cambridge, Massachussetts, revised edition, 3rd printing, 1971.
[29] G. Schmidt and T. Ströhlein. Relation algebras: concepts of points and representability. *Discrete Mathematics*, 54:83–92, 1985.
[30] J. R. Shoenfield. *Mathematical logic.* Addison Wesley, 1967.
[31] A. Tarski. Sur les ensembles fini. *Fundamenta Mathematicae*, 6:45–95, 1924.
[32] A. Tarski. On the calculus of relations. *Journal of Symbolic Logic*, 6(3):73–89, 1941.
[33] A. Tarski and S. Givant. *A formalization of set theory without variables*, volume 41 of *Colloquium Publications.* American Mathematical Society, 1987.
[34] L. Wos. *Automated reasoning. 33 basic research problems.* Prentice Hall, 1988.
[35] L. Wos. The problem of finding an inference rule for set theory. *J. Automated Reasoning*, 5(1):93–95, 1989.
[36] E. Zermelo. Untersuchungen über die Grundlagen der Mengenlehre I. In *From Frege to Gödel - A source book in Mathematical Logic, 1879-1931*, pages 199–215. Harvard University Press, 1977.

Issues of Decidability for Description Logics in the Framework of Resolution

Ullrich Hustadt and Renate A. Schmidt

Department of Computing, Manchester Metropolitan University,
Chester Street, Manchester M1 5GD, United Kingdom
{U.Hustadt,R.A.Schmidt}@doc.mmu.ac.uk

Abstract. We describe two methods on the basis of which efficient resolution decision procedures can be developed for a range of description logics. The first method uses an ordering restriction and applies to the description logic $\mathcal{ALB}$, which extends $\mathcal{ALC}$ with the top role, full role negation, role intersection, role disjunction, role converse, domain restriction, range restriction, and role hierarchies. The second method is based solely on a selection restriction and applies to reducts of $\mathcal{ALB}$ without the top role and role negation. The latter method can be viewed as a polynomial simulation of familiar tableaux-based decision procedures. It can also be employed for automated model generation.

1 Introduction

Since the work of Kallick [13] resolution-based decision procedures for subclasses of first-order logic have drawn continuous attention [5, 7, 12]. There are two research areas where decidability issues also play a prominent role: extended modal logics and description logics [6, 9, 14]. Although is is not difficult to see that most of the logics under consideration can be translated into first-order logic, the exact relation to decidable subclasses of first-order logic and in particular to subclasses decidable by resolution is still under investigation. A recent important result describes a resolution decision procedure for the guarded fragment using a non-liftable ordering refinement [5]. But, the restrictions on the polarity of guards in guarded formulae are too strong to capture description logics with role negation (correspondingly, extended modal logics with relational negation).

Description logics with role negation can be embedded into the class One-Free, for which a resolution decision procedure using a non-liftable ordering refinement exists [7, 19]. However, this method cannot be extended easily to description logics with transitive roles. The method of this paper is based on the resolution framework of Bachmair and Ganzinger [4] which is also suitable for overcoming the problems associated with transitivity axioms, in particular, non-termination of resolution on the relational translation of certain transitive modal logics [3, 8].

The most prominent description logic is $\mathcal{ALC}$ [18]. It can be embedded into a subclass of the Bernays-Schönfinkel class, called basic path logic, which can

R. Caferra and G. Salzer (Eds.): Automated Deduction, LNAI 1761, pp. 191–205, 2000.

be decided by resolution and condensing using any compatible ordering or selection strategy [17]. This embedding was used in recent experimental work which provides evidence that resolution theorem provers can serve as reasonable and efficient inference tools for description logics [11, 15].

In this paper we consider an expressive description logic, which we believe has not been considered before in the literature on description logics or modal logics. We call the logic $\mathcal{ALB}$ which is short for 'attribute language with boolean algebras on concepts and roles'. $\mathcal{ALB}$ extends $\mathcal{ALC}$ with the top role, full role negation, role intersection, role disjunction, role converse, domain restriction, range restriction, and role hierarchies.

We describe two methods on the basis of which efficient resolution decision procedures can be developed for a number of description logics. The first method uses an ordering restriction and applies to $\mathcal{ALB}$ and its reducts. The second method is based solely on a selection restriction and applies to reducts of $\mathcal{ALB}$ without the top role and role negation. On $\mathcal{ALC}$, the latter method can be viewed as a polynomial simulation of tableaux-based theorem proving. This result is a first contribution towards a better understanding of the relationship of tableaux-based and resolution-based reasoning for description logics, similar to our understanding of the relationship of various calculi for propositional logic [20].

This paper is organised as follows. In Section 2 we introduce the description logic $\mathcal{ALB}$ and give an embedding into first-order logic. The two resolution decision procedures described in this paper are instances of a general resolution calculus outlined in Section 3. Section 4 describes a decision procedure for the satisfiability of general $\mathcal{ALB}$ knowledge bases which is based on an ordering refinement of resolution. Section 5 describes a decision procedure for the satisfiability of descriptive knowledge bases over a reduct of $\mathcal{ALB}$ based on a selection refinement. We show in Section 6 that with this decision procedure we can polynomially simulate standard tableaux decision procedures for $\mathcal{ALC}$. In Section 7 we turn our attention to automated model generation. The Conclusion mentions related work.

2 Syntax and Semantics of $\mathcal{ALB}$

We start with the definition of the description logic $\mathcal{ALB}$. The signature is given by a tuple $\Sigma = (\mathsf{O}, \mathsf{C}, \mathsf{R})$ of three disjoint alphabets, the set C of *concept symbols*, the set R of *role symbols*, and the set O of *object symbols*. *Concept terms* (or just *concepts*) and *role terms* (or just *roles*) are defined as follows. Every concept symbol is a concept and every role symbol is a role. If C and D are concepts, and R and S are roles, then $\top$, $\bot$, $C \sqcap D$, $C \sqcup D$, $\neg C$, $\forall R.C$, and $\exists R.C$ are *concept terms*, and ∇, $\triangle$, $R \sqcap S$, $R \sqcup S$, $\neg R$, R^{-1} (*converse*), $R{\restriction}C$ (*domain restriction*), and $R{\downharpoonright}C$ (*range restriction*) are roles. Concept and role symbols are also called *atomic* terms.

A *knowledge base* has two parts: A *TBox* comprising of terminological sentences and an *ABox* comprising of assertional sentences. *Terminological sen-*

Embedding of sentences:

$$\Pi(C \mathrel{\dot\sqsubseteq} D) = \forall x{:}\, \pi(C,x) \rightarrow \pi(D,x) \qquad \Pi(R \mathrel{\dot\sqsubseteq} S) = \forall x,y{:}\, \pi(R,x,y) \rightarrow \pi(S,x,y)$$
$$\Pi(C \doteq D) = \forall x{:}\, \pi(C,x) \leftrightarrow \pi(D,x) \qquad \Pi(R \doteq S) = \forall x,y{:}\, \pi(R,x,y) \leftrightarrow \pi(S,x,y)$$
$$\Pi(a \in C) = \pi(C,\underline{a}) \qquad \Pi((a,b) \in R) = \pi(R,\underline{a},\underline{b})$$

where $\underline{a}$ and $\underline{b}$ are constants uniquely associated with a and b.
Embedding of terms:

$$\pi(A,X) = p_A(X) \qquad \pi(P,X,Y) = p_P(X,Y)$$
$$\pi(\neg C,X) = \neg\pi(C,X) \qquad \pi(\neg R,X,Y) = \neg\pi(R,X,Y)$$
$$\pi(\top,X) = \top \qquad \pi(\nabla,X,Y) = \top$$
$$\pi(\bot,X) = \bot \qquad \pi(\Delta,X,Y) = \bot$$
$$\pi(C \sqcap D,X) = \pi(C,X) \wedge \pi(D,X) \qquad \pi(R \sqcap S,X,Y) = \pi(R,X,Y) \wedge \pi(S,X,Y)$$
$$\pi(C \sqcup D,X) = \pi(C,X) \vee \pi(D,X) \qquad \pi(R \sqcup S,X,Y) = \pi(R,X,Y) \vee \pi(S,X,Y)$$
$$\pi(\forall R.C,X) = \forall y{:}\, \pi(R,X,y) \rightarrow \pi(C,y) \qquad \pi(R{\restriction}C,X,Y) = \pi(R,X,Y) \wedge \pi(C,Y)$$
$$\pi(\exists R.C,X) = \exists y{:}\, \pi(R,X,y) \wedge \pi(C,y) \qquad \pi(R{\upharpoonleft}C,X,Y) = \pi(R,X,Y) \wedge \pi(C,X)$$
$$\pi(R^{-1},X,Y) = \pi(R,Y,X)$$

where X and Y are meta-variables for variables and constants, and p_A (respectively p_P) denotes a unary (binary) predicate symbol uniquely associated with the concept symbol A (role symbol P). The variable y is distinct from X.

Fig. 1. The standard embedding of $\mathcal{ALB}$ into first-order logic

tences are of the form $C \mathrel{\dot\sqsubseteq} D$, $C \doteq D$, $R \mathrel{\dot\sqsubseteq} S$, and $R \doteq S$, and *assertional sentences* are of the form $a \in C$ and $(a,b) \in R$, where C and D are concepts, R and S are roles, and a and b are object symbols.

A symbol S_0 *uses* a symbol S_1 *directly* in a TBox T if and only if T contains a sentence of the form $S_0 \doteq E$ or $S_0 \mathrel{\dot\sqsubseteq} E$ such that S_1 occurs in E. A symbol S_0 *uses* S_n if and only if there is a chain of symbols $S_0, \ldots, S_n$ such that S_i uses S_{i+1} directly, for every i, $1 \leq i \leq n-1$. A knowledge base Γ is said to contain a *terminological cycle* if and only if some symbol uses itself in the TBox of Γ.

The standard definition of knowledge bases imposes the following restrictions on the set of admissible terminological sentences: (i) The left-hand sides of terminological sentences have to be concept symbols or role symbols, (ii) any concept or role symbol occurs at most once on the left-hand side of any terminological sentence, and (iii) there are no terminological cycles. Knowledge bases obeying these restrictions are known as *descriptive knowledge bases*. In this context terminological sentences are called *definitions*. When no restrictions are imposed, we speak of *general knowledge bases*.

The semantics of $\mathcal{ALB}$ is specified by the embedding into first-order logic defined in Figure 1.

All common inferential services for knowledge bases, like subsumption tests for concepts, TBox classification, realization, retrieval, can be reduced to tests of the satisfiability of a knowledge base.

3 The Resolution Framework

We adopt the resolution framework of Bachmair and Ganzinger [4], from which we recall some basic definitions.

As usual clauses are assumed to be multisets of literals. The components in the variable partition of a clause are called split components, that is, split components do not share variables. A clause which is identical to its split component is indecomposable. The condensation $\text{Cond}(C)$ of a clause C is a minimal subclause of C which is a factor of C.

In the framework inference rules are parameterised by an ordering $\succ$ and a selection function S. A well-founded and total ordering on ground literals is called *admissible* if it is compatible with a certain *complexity measure* c_L on ground literals L. If $c_L \succ c_{L'}$ implies $L \succ L'$ for any two ground literals L and L', then the ordering is said to be *compatible*. For the exact requirements orderings have to satisfy refer to [4]. A *selection* function assigns to each clause a possibly empty set of occurrences of negative literals. If C is a clause, then the literal occurrences in $S(C)$ are *selected*. No restrictions are imposed on the selection function.

The calculus consists of general *expansion rules* of the form

$$\frac{N}{N_1 \mid \cdots \mid N_n},$$

each representing a finite derivation of the leaves $N_1, \ldots, N_k$ from the root N. The following rules describe how derivations can be expanded at leaves.

Deduce:
$$\frac{N}{N \cup \{\text{Cond}(C)\}}$$
if C is either a resolvent or a factor of clauses in N.

Delete:
$$\frac{N \cup \{C\}}{N}$$
if C is a tautology or N contains a clause which is a variant of C.

Split:
$$\frac{N \cup \{C \cup D\}}{N \cup \{C\} \mid N \cup \{D\}}$$
if C and D are variable-disjoint.

Resolvents and factors are derived by the following rules.

Ordered Resolution:
$$\frac{C \cup \{A_1\} \quad D \cup \{\neg A_2\}}{(C \cup D)\sigma}$$
where (i) σ is the most general unifier of A_1 and A_2, (ii) no literal is selected in C and $A_1\sigma$ is strictly $\succ$-maximal with respect to $C\sigma$, and (iii) $\neg A_2$ is either selected, or $\neg A_2\sigma$ is maximal with respect to $D\sigma$ and no literal is selected in D. $C \vee A$ is called the *positive premise* and $D \vee \neg B$ the *negative premise*.[1]

Ordered Factoring:
$$\frac{C \cup \{A_1, A_2\}}{(C \cup \{A_1\})\sigma}$$
where (i) σ is the most general unifier of A_1 and A_2; and (ii) no literal is selected in C and $A_1\sigma$ is $\succ$-maximal with respect to $C\sigma$.

We will restrict our attention to derivations which are generated by strategies in which "Delete", "Split", and "Deduce" are applied in this order. In addition, no application of the "Deduce" expansion rule with identical premises and identical consequence may occur twice on the same path in the derivation.

4 Decidability by Ordered Resolution

The conversion to clausal form of first-order formulae resulting from the translation of $\mathcal{ALB}$ knowledge bases, makes use of a particular form of structural transformation (or renaming) [2, 16]. For ease of presentation we assume any first-order formula ϕ is in negation normal form.

Let $\mathrm{Pos}(\phi)$ be the set of positions of a formula ϕ. If λ is a position in ϕ, then $\phi|_\lambda$ denotes the subformula of ϕ at position λ and $\phi[\lambda \leftarrow \psi]$ is the result of replacing ϕ at position λ by ψ. We associate with each element λ of $\Lambda \subseteq \mathrm{Pos}(\phi)$ a predicate symbol Q_λ and a literal $Q_\lambda(x_1, \ldots, x_n)$, where $x_1, \ldots, x_n$ are the free variables of $\phi|_\lambda$, Q_λ does not occur in ϕ and two symbols Q_λ and $Q_{\lambda'}$ are equal only if ϕ_λ and $\phi_{\lambda'}$ are variant formulae. The *definition* of Q_λ is the formula

$$\mathrm{Def}_\lambda(\phi) = \forall\, x_1, \ldots, x_n {:} (Q_\lambda(x_1, \ldots, x_n) \leftrightarrow \phi|_\lambda).^2$$

Define $\mathrm{Def}_\Lambda(\phi)$ inductively by: $\mathrm{Def}_\emptyset(\phi) = \phi$ and

$$\mathrm{Def}_{\Lambda\cup\{\lambda\}}(\phi) = \mathrm{Def}_\Lambda(\phi[\lambda \leftarrow Q_\lambda(x_1, \ldots, x_n)]) \wedge \mathrm{Def}_\lambda(\phi)$$

where λ is maximal in $\Lambda\cup\{\lambda\}$ with respect to the prefix ordering on positions. Let $\mathrm{Pos}_r(\phi)$ be the set of positions of non-atomic subformulae of ϕ with at least one free variable. By Ξ we denote the transformation taking $\Pi(\Gamma)$ to its *definitional form* $\mathrm{Def}_{\mathrm{Pos}_r(\Pi(\Gamma))}(\Pi(\Gamma))$.

Theorem 1. *Let Γ be any knowledge base. $\Xi\Pi(\Gamma)$ can be computed in polynomial time, and Γ is satisfiable iff $\Xi\Pi(\Gamma)$ is satisfiable.*

Next we characterise a class of clauses which we call *DL-clauses*. Let C be a clause and L a literal in C. We refer to a literal L as *embracing* in C if for every L' in C, $\mathcal{V}(L') \cap \mathcal{V}(L) \neq \emptyset$[3] implies $\mathcal{V}(L') \subseteq \mathcal{V}(L)$ (that is, it contains all variables occurring in the split component in which it occurs). A term t in C is called *embracing* if for every L' in C, $\mathcal{V}(L') \cap \mathcal{V}(t) \neq \emptyset$ implies $\mathcal{V}(L) \subseteq \mathcal{V}(t)$. A term is called *compound* if it is neither a variable nor a constant. A literal L is *singular* if it contains no compound term and $\mathcal{V}(L)$ is a singleton. A literal is *flat* if it is non-ground and contains no compound term.

In the context of this paper a *regular* literal has either no compound term arguments or if it does then there is a compound term argument which contains

[1] As usual we implicitly assume that the premises have no common variables.

[2] As any formula ϕ is assumed to be in negation normal form, we could of course also use $\mathrm{Def}^+_\lambda(\phi) = \forall\, x_1, \ldots, x_n {:} (Q_\lambda(x_1, \ldots, x_n) \rightarrow \phi|_\lambda)$ without altering the validity of our results.

[3] $\mathcal{V}(L)$ denotes the set of variables of L.

all the variables of the literal and does not itself have a compound term argument. By definition, L is a *DL-literal* if the following is true.

1. L is regular,
2. L is either monadic or dyadic, and contains at most 2 variables,
3. L is ground whenever it contains a constant symbol, and
4. the maximal arity of any function symbol in L is 1.

A clause C is a *DL-clause*, if

1. when C contains a compound term t, then t is embracing,
2. C is ground whenever C contains a constant symbol,
3. all literals in C are DL-literals, and
4. the argument multisets of all flat, dyadic literals coincide.

Property (4) is important to enable us to employ an ordering which is stable under substitutions. It excludes clauses like $\{p(x,x), q(x,y)\}$. In order to avoid possibly unbounded chains of variables across literals we would need to restrict resolution inferences to the literal $q(x,y)$. But, when such clauses are present it is in general not possible to devise an ordering stable under substitution such that only the second literal is maximal. By contrast, clauses like $\{p(x,x), q(x,x)\}$ and $\{p(x,y), q(x,y)\}$ are DL-clauses, and may occur in a derivation from $\Xi\Pi(\Gamma)$.

Lemma 2. *Let Γ be a knowledge base. Every clause in the clausal form of $\Xi\Pi(\Gamma)$ belongs to the class of DL-clauses.*

For every ground literal L, let the complexity measure c_L be the multiset of arguments of L. We compare complexity measures by the multiset extension of the strict subterm ordering $\succ^s_{mul}$. The ordering is lifted from ground to non-ground expressions as follows: $E \succ E'$ if and only if $E\sigma \succ E'\sigma$, for all ground instances $E\sigma$ and $E'\sigma$. We show that ordered resolution and ordered factoring on DL-clauses with respect to any ordering $\succ_{cov}$ which is compatible with this complexity measure will result in DL-clauses.

Lemma 3. *Let $C = \{L_1, L_2\} \cup D$ be an indecomposable, DL-clause with σ a most general unifier of L_1 and L_2 such that $L_1\sigma$ is $\succ_{cov}$-maximal with respect to $D\sigma$. The split components of $(\{L_1\} \cup D)\sigma$ are DL-clauses.*

Proof. Since C is indecomposable and contains at least two literals, it is not a ground clause. By property (2) it contains no constants. So, the most general unifier σ will not introduce any constant symbols. Also, there are no compound terms in the codomain of σ, since all compound terms in C are embracing. Therefore, σ is a variable renaming. It is straightforward to see that variable renamings preserve the properties (1)–(4). □

Lemma 4. *Let $C_1 = \{A_1\} \cup D_1$ and $C_2 = \{\neg A_2\} \cup D_2$ be two variable-disjoint, indecomposable, DL-clauses such that A_1 and A_2 are unifiable with most general unifier σ, and $A_1\sigma$ and $A_2\sigma$ are $\succ_{cov}$-maximal with respect to $D_1\sigma$ and $D_2\sigma$, respectively. The split components of $(D_1 \cup D_2)\sigma$ are DL-clauses.*

Proof. It is not difficult to show that the following holds:

1. A_1 is embracing in C_1.
2. If A_1 is a flat, singular literal, then C_1 contains only flat, singular literals.
3. If A_1 is flat, then C_1 contains no compound term.
4. If $A_1\sigma$ contains a compound term t, then for no variable x in C_2 is $x\sigma$ a compound term, and t is embracing in $(D_1 \cup D_2)\sigma$.
5. If A_1 contains a compound term t, then for no variable x in C_1, is $x\sigma$ a compound term and t is embracing in $(D_1 \cup D_2)\sigma$.

Analogously, for $\neg A_2$ and C_2. Let E be a split component of $(D_1 \cup D_2)\sigma$.

1. It follows that no compound term in E has a compound term argument and that compound terms in E are embracing.
2. Suppose $A_1\sigma$ contains a constant. Then either A_1 or A_2 is ground. Since A_1 and $\neg A_2$ are embracing, E is a unit ground clause.
3. It follows from (1) and (2) that all literals in E are DL-literals.
4. Only if $A_1\sigma = A_2\sigma$ is a flat, dyadic literal does E possibly contain a flat, dyadic literal $L\sigma$. The argument multiset of L coincide with that of either A_1 or A_2. Therefore, the argument multiset of $L\sigma$ coincides with $A_1\sigma$. So, does the argument multiset of any flat, dyadic literal in E. □

Theorem 5. *Let Γ be a knowledge base of $\mathcal{ALB}$ and let N be the clausal form of $\Xi\Pi(\Gamma)$. Then any derivation from N by ordered resolution and ordered factoring based on $\succ_{cov}$ terminates.*

Proof. By Theorem 1 and Lemmas 2, 3 and 4, because any class of non-variant, condensed, indecomposable DL-clauses built from finitely many predicate and function symbols is finitely bounded; and the fact that any application of "Deduce" will be followed immediately by applications of the "Split" rule, as well as the fact that "Delete" is applied eagerly. □

The techniques used by Tammet and Zamov to decide the classes One-Free [19] and KS [7] can also be utilised to provide a decision procedure for the class of DL-clauses. However, these techniques are based on non-liftable orderings which have limitations regarding the application of some standard simplification rules.

5 Decidability by Selection

Most decision procedures presented in the literature for the satisfiability problem of concepts and knowledge bases in description logics are specialised tableaux-based transformation systems. Since derivations in these system are quite different from those of a resolution decision procedure based on an ordering refinement, very little can be said about the relative proof or search complexity of these systems. In this section we define a resolution decision procedure based solely on the use of a particular selection function for a reduct of $\mathcal{ALB}$ including $\mathcal{ALC}$.

In the next section we will establish that this procedure is able to polynomially simulate standard tableaux-based transformation systems for $\mathcal{ALC}$, thereby establishing a result relating resolution and tableaux decision procedures.

We focus on descriptive knowledge bases Γ over reducts of $\mathcal{ALB}$ without role negation and the top role. Determining the satisfiability of Γ using a tableaux decision procedure is a two-step process. For a non-empty TBox, concept and role symbols in the ABox are *unfolded* in the first step, that is, replaced by the right-hand side of their definitions, before the tableaux-based transformation system is applied to the ABox, in the next step.

To simulate the unfolding steps in our resolution decision procedure, we have to restrict resolution inferences with clauses stemming from the translation of terminological sentences of the form $S \doteq E$ and $S \dot{\sqsubseteq} E$ to the literals associated with S. As only negative literals can be selected, it is necessary to transform the given knowledge base. Essentially, for concepts, occurrences of $\neg A$ will be replaced by a new symbol $\overline{A}$, and for roles, positive occurrences[4] of P will be replaced by a new symbol P^d while negative occurrences will be replaced by P^u.

Without loss of generality, all expressions occurring in Γ are assumed to be in negation normal form. Formally, let $\mathrm{D}_{\doteq}(\Gamma)$ denote the set of symbols $S_0 \in \mathsf{C} \cup \mathsf{R}$ such that Γ contains a terminological sentence $S_0 \doteq E$. We obtain the transformed knowledge base $\overline{\Gamma}$, defined over $(\mathsf{O}, \overline{\mathsf{C}}, \overline{\mathsf{R}})$, in the following way. Extend C to $\overline{\mathsf{C}}$, by adding a concept symbol $\overline{A}$ for every concept symbol A in $\mathrm{D}_{\doteq}(\Gamma)$. Replace R by $\overline{\mathsf{R}}$, which is obtained by replacing every role symbol $P \in \mathrm{D}_{\doteq}(\Gamma)$ by new symbols P^u and P^d. The following steps transform Γ to $\overline{\Gamma}$.

1. Replace concept definitions $A \doteq C$, by $A \dot{\sqsubseteq} C$ and $\neg A \dot{\sqsubseteq} \mathrm{nnf}(\neg C)$, and replace role definitions $P \doteq R$, by $P^d \dot{\sqsubseteq} R$ and $R \dot{\sqsubseteq} P^u$, where $\mathrm{nnf}(\neg C)$ is the negation normal form of $\neg C$.
2. Replace every occurrence of a concept $\neg A$, for A in $\mathrm{D}_{\doteq}(\Gamma)$, by $\overline{A}$.
3. Replace every positive occurrence of a role symbol $P \in \mathrm{D}_{\doteq}(\Gamma)$ by P^d, and every negative occurrence of P by P^u.
4. For every concept symbol A in $\mathrm{D}_{\doteq}(\Gamma)$, add the sentence $A \dot{\sqsubseteq} \neg\overline{A}$ and add for every role symbol P in $\mathrm{D}_{\doteq}(\Gamma)$, the sentence $P^d \dot{\sqsubseteq} P^u$.

For example, if Γ contains the terminological axioms $A \doteq B \sqcup C$, $B \dot{\sqsubseteq} \forall P.C$, and $P \doteq R \sqcap S$ where A, B, and C are concept symbols and P, R, and S are role symbols, then the transformed knowledge base contains:

$$
\begin{array}{ll}
A \dot{\sqsubseteq} B \sqcup C & P^d \dot{\sqsubseteq} R \sqcap S \\
\overline{A} \dot{\sqsubseteq} \neg B \sqcap \neg C & R \sqcap S \dot{\sqsubseteq} P^u \\
A \dot{\sqsubseteq} \neg\overline{A} & P^d \dot{\sqsubseteq} P^u \\
B \dot{\sqsubseteq} \forall P^u.C &
\end{array}
$$

[4] An occurrence of a subformula (subexpression) is a *positive occurrence* if it is one inside the scope of an even number of (explicit or implicit) negations, and an occurrence is a *negative occurrence* if it is one inside the scope of an odd number of negations.

The reason for transforming concept definitions differently from role definitions is that no negative information about roles in the form of ground unit clauses can be derived.

In this section, the definitional form is produced by a variant $\overline{\Xi}$ of the transformation Ξ described in the previous section. First, $\overline{\Xi}$ uses *definitions*, $\mathrm{Def}_\lambda(\phi)$, of the form

$$\forall x_1, \ldots, x_n \colon (Q_\lambda(x_1, \ldots, x_n) \rightarrow \phi|_\lambda) \text{ or } \forall x_1, \ldots, x_n \colon (\phi|_\lambda \rightarrow Q_\lambda(x_1, \ldots, x_n)),$$

depending on whether $\phi|_\lambda$ occurs positively or negatively in ϕ. Second, only subformulae χ associated with non-atomic terms in $\overline{\Gamma}$, with the exception of non-atomic terms in terminological sentences introduced by step 4 of the transformation, are renamed. In particular, this means for subformulae χ of the form $\forall y \colon (\phi(x,y) \rightarrow \psi(y))$ or $\exists y \colon (\phi(x,y) \wedge \psi(y))$, $\overline{\Xi}$ will only introduce definitions for χ itself and $\phi(x,y)$ and $\psi(y)$ if necessary, but not for $\neg\phi(x,y) \vee \psi(y)$ and $\phi(x,y) \wedge \psi(y)$. Third, two symbols Q_λ and $Q_{\lambda'}$ are equal iff ϕ_λ and $\phi_{\lambda'}$ are variant formulae. Thus, every newly introduced symbol Q_λ is associated with an expression E of the original language, and hence, we will denote Q_λ by p_E.

For the sample knowledge base above we obtain the following set of clauses.

$$\begin{array}{ll}
\{\neg p_A(x), p_B(x), p_C(x)\} & \{\neg p^d_P(x,y), p_R(x,y)\} \\
\{\neg p_{\overline{A}}(x), \neg p_B(x)\} & \{\neg p^d_P(x,y), p_S(x,y)\} \\
\{\neg p_{\overline{A}}(x), \neg p_C(x)\} & \{\neg p_R(x,y), \neg p_S(x,y), p^u_P(x,y)\} \\
\{\neg p_A(x), \neg p_{\overline{A}}(x)\} & \{\neg p^d_P(x,y), p^u_P(x,y)\} \\
\{\neg p_B(x), \neg p^u_P(x,y), p_C(x)\} &
\end{array}$$

To keep the clause set small, no renaming was performed on the non-atomic terms $\neg B$, $\neg C$, $\neg B \sqcup \neg C$, etc.

Define a dependency relation $\succ^1_c$ on the predicate symbols by $p_A \succ^1_c p_B$, if there is a definition $\phi \rightarrow \psi$ in $\overline{\Xi}\Pi(\overline{\Gamma})$ such that p_A occurs in ϕ and p_B occurs in ψ. Let $\succ_S$ be an ordering on the predicate symbols in $\overline{\Xi}\Pi(\overline{\Gamma})$ which is compatible with the transitive closure of $\succ^1_c$. Due to the acyclicity of the terminology and due to fact that we split role definitions, it is possible to find such an ordering.

While an ordering restriction of resolution and factoring is optional, our selection function $S_{\mathcal{TAB}}$ selects the literal $\neg p_{\overline{A}}(x)$ in a clause $\{\neg p_{\overline{A}}(x), \neg p_A(x)\}$ originating from $A \dot{\sqsubseteq} \neg\overline{A}$. For all other clauses C, let L be an occurrence of a negative literal in C with predicate symbol p_A. Then L is selected in C if and only if either the predicate symbol of L is $\succ_S$-maximal in C, or L is a literal of the form $\neg p_A(s,y)$, where s is a ground term and y is a variable. In our sample clause set above all negative literal occurrences are selected except for the last two clauses in the left column, where in each case only $\neg p_{\overline{A}}(x)$ is selected. All clauses originating from a terminological sentence or from a definition introduced by $\overline{\Xi}$ contain negative literals, one of which is selected. Consequently, no factoring steps are possible and the clauses may only be used as negative premises of resolution steps. Observe that all clauses originating from the translation of assertional sentences are ground unit clauses.

In all clauses except those of the form

$$\{\neg p_A(x)_+, \neg p_R(x,y), p_B(y)\} \tag{1}$$

the selected literal (marked by $_+$) contains all variables of the clause, and with the exception of

$$\{\neg p_A(x)_+, p_R(x, f(x))\} \quad \text{and} \quad \{\neg p_A(x)_+, p_B(f(x))\} \tag{2}$$

no variables occur as arguments of compound terms.

Inferences with premises like (1) are problematic, since the resolvent may contain more free variables than the positive premise of the inference step. Suppose we have derived a clause of the form $\{p_{A_1}(\underline{a}), p_{A_2}(\underline{a}), p_{A_3}(\underline{a})\}$ (momentarily ignoring the "Split" rule) and $\overline{\Xi\Pi}(\overline{\Gamma})$ contains $\{\neg p_{A_i}(x)_+, \neg p_{R_i}(x,y), p_{B_i}(y)\}$, for $1 \leq i \leq 3$. Without taking further restrictions into account, we can derive the clause

$$\{\neg p_{R_1}(\underline{a},x), p_{B_1}(x), \neg p_{R_2}(\underline{a},y), p_{B_2}(y), \neg p_{R_3}(\underline{a},z), p_{B_3}(z)\}.$$

It contains more variables than any clause in $\overline{\Xi\Pi}(\overline{\Gamma})$.

In general, the positive premise of a resolution inference step with a clause like (1) is a ground clause $\{p_0(s)\} \cup D_1$ such that no literals in D_1 are selected. The conclusion of the inference step is a clause $C_1 = \{\neg p_1(s,y)_+, p_2(y)\} \cup D_1$, with one free variable. However, the literal $\neg p_1(s,y)$ is selected by $S_{\mathcal{TAB}}$ and no inference steps are possible on $\{p_2(y)\} \cup D_1$ (which again contains no selected literals). The only clauses we can derive containing a positive literal with predicate symbol p_1 will be ground clauses, that is, clauses of the form $C_2 = \{p_1(s,t)\} \cup D_2$. The conclusion of an inference step between C_1 and C_2 is the ground clause $\{p_2(t)\} \cup D_1 \cup D_2$. Consequently, all clauses occurring in a derivation from the clausal form of $\overline{\Xi\Pi}(\overline{\Gamma})$ contain at most two variables.

Note that C_1 is not a DL-clause. Also note for the argument it is important that a negative binary literal occurs in (1). This is the reason for excluding role negation as well as the top role from the language.

The problem with inferences involving negative premises of the forms (2) is that resolvents may contain terms of greater depth than the positive premise of the inference. Nevertheless, we can still show that there is an upper bound on the depth of terms.

With every literal $L = (\neg)p(t_1, \ldots, t_n)$ we associate a complexity measure $c_L = (p, \{t_1, \ldots, t_n\})$. Complexity measures on ground literals are compared by the ordering $\succ_c^{\text{lit}}$ given by the lexicographic combination of the ordering $\succ_S$ and the multiset extension of the strict subterm ordering $\succ_{mul}^{s}$. The ordering is lifted from ground to non-ground expressions in the usual way. The ordering on clauses is the multiset extension of $\succ_c^{\text{lit}}$. It is straightforward to check that any inference step from a positive premise C by (ordered) resolution or (ordered) factoring will result in a clause D such that c_C is greater than c_D with respect to $\succ_c^{\text{mul}}$.

Theorem 6. *Let Γ be a descriptive knowledge base and let N be the clausal form of $\overline{\Xi\Pi}(\overline{\Gamma})$. Then any derivation from N by (ordered) resolution with selection as determined by $S_{\mathcal{TAB}}$ and (ordered) factoring terminates.*

6 Simulation of Tableaux for $\mathcal{ALC}$

We now consider the relation between the selection-based decision procedure and a standard tableaux decision procedure for $\mathcal{ALC}$.

Recall, for example, from [18], the definition of unfolding and the inferences rules. Unfolding iteratively replaces the concept, respectively role, symbols in ABox sentences by the right-hand sides of their definitions. For example, given $A \doteq B \sqcup C$ and $B \sqsubseteq \forall P.C$ two consecutive unfolding steps replace $a \in A$ first by $a \in B \sqcup C$ and then by $a \in (\forall P.C) \sqcup C$. Note that fully unfolding all definitions may lead to an exponential increase in the size of the ABox. For this reason it is advisable to interleave unfolding steps with applications of the transformation rules described next. This is known as *lazy unfolding* [1, 10].

The set of transformation rules for testing the satisfiability of an $\mathcal{ALC}$-ABox are:

1. $\Delta \Rightarrow_{\sqcap} \Delta \cup \{a \in C, a \in D\}$, if $a \in (C \sqcap D)$ is in Δ, $a \in C$ and $a \in D$ are not both in Δ.
2. $\Delta \Rightarrow_{\sqcup} \Delta \cup \{a \in E\}$, if $a \in (C \sqcup D)$ is in Δ, neither $a \in C$ nor $a \in D$ is in Δ, and $E = C$ or $E = D$.
3. $\Delta \Rightarrow_{\exists} \Delta \cup \{(a, b) \in R, b \in C\}$, if $a \in \exists R.C$ is in Δ, there is no c such that both $(a, c) \in R$ and $c \in C$ are in Δ, and b is a new object symbol with respect to Δ.
4. $\Delta \Rightarrow_{\forall} \Delta \cup \{b \in C\}$, if $a \in \forall R.C$ and $(a, b) \in R$ are in Δ, and $b \in C$ is not in Δ.
5. $\Delta \Rightarrow_{\perp} \Delta \cup \{a \in \perp\}$, if $a \in A$ and $a \in \neg A$ are in Δ, where A is a concept symbol.

Let $\Rightarrow_{\mathcal{TAB}}$ be the transitive closure of the union of the transformation rules given above. An ABox Δ contains a *clash* if $a \in \perp$ is in Δ. An ABox Δ is satisfiable iff there exists an ABox Δ' such that (i) $\Delta \Rightarrow_{\mathcal{TAB}} \Delta'$, (ii) no further applications of $\Rightarrow_{\mathcal{TAB}}$ to Δ' are possible, and (iii) Δ' is clash-free.

The correspondence between the tableaux-based decision procedure and the selection-based decision procedure is not difficult to see. Remember that for every concept C and every role R, which may possibly occur in an ABox during a satisfiability test, there exist corresponding predicate symbols p_C and p_R in the clausal form of $\overline{\Xi}\Pi(\overline{\Gamma})$. Likewise for every object symbol a we will have a corresponding term t_a.

Lazy unfolding steps can be simulated by resolution inference steps with the clauses we obtain from the translation of the TBox. Suppose the knowledge base Γ contains either the terminological sentence $A \sqsubseteq C$ or $A \doteq C$. Then unfolding will replace an assertional sentence $a \in A$ by $a \in C$. Correspondingly, our clause set contains the clauses $\{\neg p_A(x)_+, p_C(x)\}$ and $\{p_A(t_a)\}$ and one resolution step produces $\{p_C(t_a)\}$. Suppose Γ contains $A \doteq C$ and $a \in \neg A$. In this case, unfolding replaces the assertional sentence by $a \in D$, where D is the negation normal form of $\neg C$. Since $A \in \mathrm{D}_{\doteq}(\Gamma)$, occurrences of $\neg A$ have been replaced by $\overline{A}$ in $\overline{\Gamma}$, and the clause set contains $\{\neg p_{\overline{A}}(x)_+, p_D(x)\}$ and $\{p_{\overline{A}}(t_a)\}$. We derive $\{p_D(t_a)\}$. These inference steps obey the restrictions enforced by the selection function S_{TAB}. p_C and p_D are the predicate symbols associated with the concepts C and D. Thus, in case C and D are non-atomic concept terms, the clause set contains additional clauses originating from the translation of the definition $\forall x{:}p_C(x) \rightarrow \pi(C,x)$. The inference steps described above will be followed by resolution steps with these clauses which completes the unfolding step.

Transformation by the inference rules is simulated according to the following.

1. An application of the $\Rightarrow_\sqcap$ rule corresponds to a resolution inference step between a ground clause $\{p_{C\sqcap D}(t_a)\}$ and clauses $\{\neg p_{C\sqcap D}(x), p_C(x)\}$ and $\{\neg p_{C\sqcap D}(x), p_D(x)\}$, generating the resolvents $\{p_C(t_a)\}$ and $\{p_D(t_a)\}$.
2. An application of the $\Rightarrow_\sqcup$ rule corresponds to a resolution inference step between a ground unit clause $\{p_{C\sqcup D}(t_a)\}$ and $\{\neg p_{C\sqcup D}(x), p_C(x), p_D(x)\}$. We then apply the splitting rule to the conclusion $\{p_C(t_a), p_D(t_a)\}$ which will generate two branches, one on which our set of clauses contains $\{p_C(t_a)\}$ and one on which it contains $\{p_D(t_a)\}$.
3. An application of the $\Rightarrow_\exists$ rule corresponds to resolution inference steps between $\{p_{\exists R.C}(t_a)\}$, $\{\neg p_{\exists R.C}(x), p_R(x, f(x))\}$, and $\{\neg p_{\exists R.C}(x), p_C(f(x))\}$. This will add $\{p_R(t_a, f(t_a))\}$ and $\{p_C(f(t_a))\}$ to the clause set. The term $f(t_a)$ corresponds to the new object symbol b introduced by the $\Rightarrow_\exists$ rule, that is, $t_b = f(t_a)$.
4. An application of the $\Rightarrow_\forall$ rule corresponds to two consecutive inference steps. Here, the set of clauses contains $\{p_{\forall R.C}(t_a)\}$ and $\{p^u_R(t_a, t_b)\}$ (to obtain $\{p^u_R(t_a, t_b)\}$ an inference step with a clause $\{\neg p^d_R(x,y), p^u_R(x,y)\}$ may be necessary). First, $\{p_{\forall R.C}(t_a)\}$ is resolved with $\{\neg p_{\forall R.C}(x), \neg p^u_R(x,y), p_C(y)\}$ to obtain $\{\neg p^u_R(t_a, y), p_C(y)\}$. Then this clause is resolved with $\{p^u_R(t_a, t_b)\}$ to obtain $\{p_C(t_b)\}$.
5. For applications of the $\Rightarrow_\perp$ rule we distinguish two cases. If A is not in $\mathrm{D}_{\doteq}(\Gamma)$, then the set of clauses contains $\{p_A(t_a)\}$ and $\{p_{\neg A}(t_a)\}$. Two consecutive inference steps using these two clauses and $\{\neg p_{\neg A}(x)_+, \neg p_A(x)\}$, the definition of $\neg A$, produce the empty clause. Otherwise, A is in $\mathrm{D}_{\doteq}(\Gamma)$ and the set of clauses contains $\{p_A(t_a)\}$ and $\{p_{\overline{A}}(t_a)\}$. In this case the empty clause can be derived with $\{\neg p_{\overline{A}}(x)_+, \neg p_A(x)\}$.

All these resolution inference steps strictly obey the restrictions enforced by the selection function S_{TAB}. Consequently:

Theorem 7. *The selection-based resolution decision procedure with selection function S_{TAB} p-simulates tableaux-based decision procedures for $\mathcal{ALC}$.*

Moreover, the described procedure provides a basis for defining tableaux-based decision procedures for extensions of $\mathcal{ALC}$ with role hierarchies, role conjunction and/or role disjunction.

For example, Theorem 7 also holds in the presence of role conjunction. Descriptions of tableaux-based procedures often hide some of the inferential effort in side conditions of inference rules. Commonly the following modified version of the $\Rightarrow_\forall$ rule is used.

4′. $\Delta \Rightarrow_\forall \Delta \cup \{b \in C\}$ if $a \in \forall R.C$ is in Δ and $(a,b) \in R$ holds in Δ, and $b \in C$ is not in Δ.

By definition, $(a,b) \in R_1 \sqcap \ldots \sqcap R_n$ *holds in* Δ if and only if, for all i, $1 \leq i \leq n$, $(a,b) \in R_i$ is in Δ.

Obviously, the implicit inferential steps needed to determine whether $(a,b) \in R$ holds in Δ, for complex roles R, have to be taken into account when establishing a relationship to the selection-based decision procedure. Then it becomes evident that any tableaux inference step can be simulated by at most two inference steps in the selection-based decision procedure.

For example, reconsider the knowledge base containing $B \dot{\sqsubseteq} \forall P.C$ and $P \doteq R \sqcap S$. Assume that, in addition, the knowledge base contains the assertional sentences $a \in B$ and $(a,b) \in P$. Unfolding will replace P by $R \sqcap S$. By an application of the analogue of $\Rightarrow_\sqcap$ for roles, $(a,b) \in R$ and $(a,b) \in S$ will be derived. Then, $b \in C$ will be derived by using the modified version of $\Rightarrow_\forall$.

The clauses corresponding to the two assertional sentences are $\{p_B(\underline{a})\}$ and $\{p^d_P(\underline{a},\underline{b})\}$. Simulating the unfolding step and applying $\Rightarrow_\sqcap$ we derive $\{p_R(\underline{a},\underline{b})\}$ and $\{p_S(\underline{a},\underline{b})\}$ from $\{\neg p^d_P(x,y), p_R(x,y)\}$ and $\{\neg p^d_P(x,y), p_S(x,y)\}$. Then resolution steps with $\{\neg p_R(x,y), \neg p_S(x,y), p^u_P(x,y)\}$ give $\{p^u_P(\underline{a},\underline{b})\}$. Finally, $\{p_C(\underline{b})\}$ can be obtained by the simulation of inference with the $\Rightarrow_\forall$ rule.

7 Model Generation

As with tableaux-based procedures our selection-based procedure lends itself for the construction of a model when the empty clause was not derived. We briefly describe how this can be done. The results of this section concern the reduct of $\mathcal{ALB}$ without the top role and role negation.

First, define a translation mapping which maps the first-order syntax back to the original syntax. This exploits the one to one correspondence between ground terms and objects, and predicate symbols and concept and role subexpressions. For any ground term t_a, let $\widehat{t_a}$ denote the object symbol a uniquely associated with t_a. Let $\widehat{C}$ and $\widehat{R}$ denote the concept and role obtained by replacing any occurrences of $\overline{A}$ by $\neg A$, and P^u and P^d by P, respectively. Now, define the mapping Π^{-1} by $\Pi^{-1}(\{p_C(t_a)\}) = \widehat{t_a} \in \widehat{C}$, $\Pi^{-1}(\{p_R(t_a,t_b)\}) = (\widehat{t_a},\widehat{t_b}) \in \widehat{R}$ and the straightforward extension to clauses and sets of clauses.

By a model we mean a set I of ground atoms. The presence of an atom A in I means A is true in I, and the absence of A means $\neg A$ is true in I. In general, a clause C is true in I iff for all ground substitutions σ there is a literal L in $C\sigma$ which is true in I. Falsehood is defined dually.

Theorem 8. *Let Γ be a descriptive knowledge base, N the clausal form of $\Xi\Pi(\overline{\Gamma})$, and N_∞ a satisfiable, saturated clause set derivable from N by using the selection-based decision procedure. Let I be the set of ground positive unit clauses in N_∞. Then, I is a model of N_∞ and N, and $\Pi^{-1}(I)$ is a model of Γ.*

Proof. As noted before, during the derivation only ground unit clauses and clauses of the form $\{\neg p_1(s,y), p_2(y)\}$ (with s ground) are generated. To prove that I is a model of N_∞ we have to show that any ground instance of a clause C in N_∞ is true in I. This obviously holds for any of the positive ground unit clauses in N_∞. Also, any negative ground unit clause $\{\neg A\}$ is true in I. Let $C = \{\neg A\sigma\} \cup D\sigma$ be the ground instance of clause in N_∞ with selected literal $\neg A$. If $A\sigma$ is not in I, then C is true. Otherwise, $\{A\sigma\}$ is an element of N_∞ and we have derived $D\sigma$ at one stage of the derivation. Consequently, one of the split components of $D\sigma$ is in N_∞. The split components of a ground clause are unit ground clauses, for which we have already shown that they are true in I. It follows that C is true in I. Hence I is a model of N_∞ and also N.

By Theorem 7 and the correspondence between predicate symbols and ground terms in the clause set and the symbols in the knowledge base, it follows that $\Pi^{-1}(I)$ is identical to a clash-free knowledge base Γ_∞ derivable from Γ such that no further applications of $\Rightarrow_{\mathit{TAB}}$ are possible. It follows from the results of [18] that $\Pi^{-1}(I) = \Gamma_\infty$ is (a syntactic representation of) a model of Γ. □

The finite model property is an immediate consequence of Theorems 5 and 8.

Corollary 9. *Let Γ be a descriptive knowledge base. If Γ is satisfiable, then it has a model of finite size.*

8 Conclusion

The class of DL-clauses is not comparable with the guarded fragment or the loosely guarded fragment. In the guarded fragments the conditional quantifiers may not include negations or disjunctions. On the other hand, the guarded fragments allow predicates of arbitrary arity. Recently it has been shown that the extension of the guarded fragment with two interacting transitive relations and equality is undecidable. However, basic modal logic plus transitivity is known to be decidable. Therefore, looking at more restricted classes than the guarded fragment may lead to better characterisations of the connection between modal logics and decidable subclasses of first-order logic (e.g. [8]).

The class of DL-clauses is more restrictive than the class One-Free, which stipulates that quantified subformulae have at most one free variable. But it is possible to extend $\mathcal{ALB}$ by certain restricted forms of role composition (e.g., positive occurrences), for which the procedure described in Section 4 remains a decision procedure. The corresponding clausal class is distinct from the One-Free class. It is known from the literature on algebraic logic that arbitrary occurrences of composition in the presence of role negation leads to undecidability, though.

The resolution decision procedures of [7, 19] have the disadvantage that they are based on a non-liftable ordering refinement. As a consequence certain standard simplification rules, e.g. tautology deletion, have to be restricted for completeness. Real world knowledge bases typically contain hundreds of concept definitions. The corresponding clauses can be used to derive an extensive number of tautologies. Our approach does not have this drawback. In addition to using liftable orderings, the resolution framework here is equipped with a general notion of redundancy which accommodates most standard simplification rules including tautology deletion, condensing, subsumption deletion, as well as non-standard theory-specific simplification rules. For a discussion of redundancy and fairness consult [4].

Acknowledgements. The authors wish to thank the anonymous referees for their comments. The work of the first author was supported by EPSRC Grant GR/K57282.

References

1. F. Baader, B. Hollunder, B. Nebel, H.-J. Profitlich, and E. Franconi. An empirical analysis of optimization techniques for terminological representation systems or "making KRIS get a move on". *Applied Intelligence*, 4(2):109–132, 1994.
2. M. Baaz, C. Fermüller, and A. Leitsch. A non-elementary speed-up in proof length by structural clause form transformation. In *Proc. LICS'94*, pages 213–219. IEEE Computer Society Press, 1994.
3. L. Bachmair and H. Ganzinger. Ordered chaining calculi for first-order theories of binary relations. Research report MPI-I-95-2-009, Max-Planck-Institut für Informatik, Saarbrücken, Germany, 1995. To appear in *J. ACM*.
4. L. Bachmair and H. Ganzinger. A theory of resolution. Research report MPI-I-97-2-005, Max-Planck-Institut für Informatik, Saarbrücken, Germany, 1997. To appear in J. A. Robinson and A. Voronkov (eds.), *Handbook of Automated Reasoning*.
5. H. de Nivelle. A resolution decision procedure for the guarded fragment. In *Proc. CADE-15*, LNAI 1421, pages 191–204. Springer, 1998.
6. F. M. Donini, M. Lenzerini, D. Nardi, and A. Schaerf. Deduction in concept languages: From subsumption to instance checking. *J. Logic and Computation*, 4:423–452, 1994.
7. C. Fermüller, A. Leitsch, T. Tammet, and N. Zamov. *Resolution Method for the Decicion Problem*. LNCS 679. Springer, 1993.
8. H. Ganzinger, U. Hustadt, C. Meyer, and R. A. Schmidt. A resolution-based decision procedure for extensions of K4. To appear in *Advances in Modal Logic, Volume 2*. CSLI Publications, 1999.
9. E. Hemaspaandra. The price of universality. *Notre Dame J. Formal Logic*, 37(2):174–203, 1996.
10. I. Horrocks. *Optimising Tableaux Decision Procedures for Description Logics*. PhD thesis, University of Manchester, Manchester, UK, 1997.
11. U. Hustadt and R. A. Schmidt. On evaluating decision procedures for modal logic. In *Proc. IJCAI'97*, pages 202–207. Morgan Kaufmann, 1997.
12. W. H. Joyner Jr. Resolution strategies as decision procedures. *J. ACM*, 23(3):398–417, 1976.
13. B. Kallick. A decision procedure based on the resolution method. In *Information Processing 68, Volume 1*, pages 269–275. North-Holland, 1968.
14. M. Marx. Mosaics and cylindric modal logic of dimension 2. In *Advances in Modal Logic, Volume 1*, Lecture Notes 87, pages 141–156. CSLI Publications, 1996.
15. M. Paramasivam and D. A. Plaisted. Automated deduction techniques for classification in description logic systems. *J. Automated Reasoning*, 20:337–364, 1998.
16. D. A. Plaisted and S. Greenbaum. A structure-preserving clause form translation. *J. Symbolic Computation*, 2:293–304, 1986.
17. R. A. Schmidt. Decidability by resolution for propositional modal logics. To appear in *J. Automated Reasoning*.
18. M. Schmidt-Schauß and G. Smolka. Attributive concept description with complements. *Artifical Intelligence*, 48:1–26, 1991.
19. T. Tammet. Using resolution for extending KL-ONE-type languages. In *Proc. CIKM'95*, 1995.
20. A. Urquhart. The complexity of propositional proofs. *Bull. Symbolic Logic*, 1(4):425–467, 1995.

Extending Decidable Clause Classes via Constraints

Reinhard Pichler

Technische Universität Wien
reini@logic.at

Abstract. There are several well known possibilities which constrained clauses (= c-clauses, for short) provide in addition to standard clauses. In particular, many (even infinitely many) standard clauses can be represented by a single c-clause. Hence, many parallel inference steps on standard clauses can be encoded in a single inference step on c-clauses. The aim of this work is to investigate another possibility offered by constrained clauses: We shall try to combine resolution based decision procedures with constrained clause logic in order to increase the expressive power of the resulting decision classes. Therefore, there are two questions on which this paper focuses:

1. In what sense do constrained clauses actually provide additional expressive power in comparison with standard clauses? The answer given here is that only constraints made up from conjunctions of disequations constitute a genuine extension w.r.t. standard clauses.
2. Is it possible to extend decision classes of standard clauses by the use of constrained clauses? The main result of this work is a positive answer to this question, namely a theorem which shows that standard clause classes decidable by certain resolution refinements remain decidable even if they are extended by constraints consisting of conjunctions of disequations.

In order to prove the termination of our decision procedures on constrained clauses, some kind of compactness theorem for unification problems will be derived, thus extending a related result from [9].

1 Introduction

The usefulness of constrained clauses (*c-clauses*, for short) in automated deduction is generally acknowledged: Constraints allow the representation of (possibly infinitely) many standard clauses in a single c-clause. Hence, a single inference step on c-clauses may in fact represent many analogous inference steps on standard clauses carried out in parallel. Furthermore, c-clauses play an important role in automated model building, since they allow a finite representation of (Herbrand) models which would require an infinite representation in standard clause logic (cf. [3]).

In [3], a refutational calculus on c-clauses was introduced, combining refutational rules with rules for model construction. This calculus was later modified

R. Caferra and G. Salzer (Eds.): Automated Deduction, LNAI 1761, pp. 206–220, 2000.

and applied to decidable classes of c-clauses (cf. [2]). However, the focus of the latter work was still on model building, i.e.: the authors present an algorithm for automated model building, which is applicable to known decision classes. The decision classes themselves are literal translations from standard clause logic.

The aim of this work is to combine decision procedures based on resolution refinements with c-clause logic in order to extend the decision classes themselves. Therefore, the first question to be answered here is in what sense do constrained clauses actually provide additional expressive power in comparison with standard clauses. The answer given in Section 3 is that only constraints made up from conjunctions of disequations constitute a genuine extension w.r.t. standard clauses. A *disequation normal form* of constrained clauses will be defined in order to formalize this result. We then investigate the extension of decidable classes of standard clauses to c-clauses in disequation normal form. To this end, in Section 4, we shall modify the c-clause calculus of Caferra et al. so as to make it suitable as a decision procedure. In Section 5, the strong compactness of sets of equations proven in [9] will be slightly extended. The main result of this work will be proven in Section 6 where we show that a standard clause class decidable by certain resolution refinements remains decidable even if the clauses are extended by constraints consisting of arbitrary conjunctions of disequations. Finally, in Section 7, the main results of this paper are summarized and some directions for future research will be mentioned.

2 Preliminaries

As far as constrained clause logic is concerned, we shall follow the approach of Caferra et al. (cf. [3] and [2]), who in turn make use of equational problems in the sense of [1]). Hence, in this section, we shall revise very briefly some basic definitions and results on equational problems and constrained clauses, which are needed in the subsequent sections. For any details, the original papers (in particular, [1] and [3]) have to be referred to.

Recall from [1], that an *equational problem* is defined as a formula of the form $\exists \boldsymbol{w} \forall \boldsymbol{y} \mathcal{P}(\boldsymbol{w}, \boldsymbol{x}, \boldsymbol{y})$, where $\mathcal{P}(\boldsymbol{w}, \boldsymbol{x}, \boldsymbol{y})$ is a quantifier-free formula with equality "=" as the only predicate symbol. Without loss of generality, we can assume that $\mathcal{P}(\boldsymbol{w}, \boldsymbol{x}, \boldsymbol{y})$ is in negation normal form, i.e.: every occurrence of the negation symbol $\neg$ has been shifted directly in front of an equation. By writing a negated equation $\neg(s = t)$ as a disequation $s \neq t$, all occurrences of the negation symbol can be eliminated. The trivially true problem is denoted by $\top$ and the trivially false one by $\bot$. An important special case of equational problems are *unification problems*, which contain neither universal quantifiers nor disequalities.

In the context of constrained clauses in the sense of [3], equational problems are only interpreted over the free term algebra. Furthermore, variables of a single sort are considered, i.e.: they may only take values from the same Herbrand universe H. A Herbrand interpretation over H is given through an H-ground substitution σ, whose domain coincides with the free variables of the equational problem. The trivial problem $\top$ evaluates to $\mathbf{T}$ in every interpretation. Likewise,

$\perp$ always evaluates to **F**. A single equation $s = t$ is validated by a ground substitution σ, if $s\sigma$ and $t\sigma$ are syntactically identical. Analogously, a single disequation $s \neq t$ is validated by σ, if $s\sigma$ and $t\sigma$ are syntactically different. The interpretation of the connectives $\wedge$, $\vee$, $\exists$ and $\forall$ is as usual. A ground substitution σ which validates an equational problem $\mathcal{P}$ is called a *solution*.

In analogy with [1] and [9], we use the following notation for comparing the syntactical form and the solution sets of equational problems, respectively: By $\mathcal{P} \equiv \mathcal{Q}$, we denote syntactical identity. $\mathcal{P} \approx \mathcal{Q}$ means that both problems have the same solution set and $\mathcal{P} \leq \mathcal{Q}$ means that all solutions of $\mathcal{P}$ are also solutions of $\mathcal{Q}$.

In [3], *constrained clauses* (c-clauses, for short) are defined as pairs $[c : \mathcal{P}]$, where c is a clause and $\mathcal{P}$ is an equational problem. Intuitively, $[c : \mathcal{P}]$ denotes the set $c\sigma$ of ground clauses, where σ is a ground solution of $\mathcal{P}$. Two c-clauses $[c : \mathcal{P}]$ and $[d : \mathcal{Q}]$ are equivalent, iff they represent the same set of ground instances. In [3], the equivalence of two c-clauses is denoted by $[c : \mathcal{P}] \equiv [d : \mathcal{Q}]$.

A *Herbrand interpretation* $\mathcal{I}$ w.r.t. some Herbrand universe H is given by a subset $\mathcal{I}(P) \subseteq H^n$ for every n-ary predicate symbol P. A ground atom $P(\mathbf{s})$ evaluates to **T** in $\mathcal{I}$, iff $\mathbf{s} \in \mathcal{I}(P)$. The generalization to negative ground literals $\neg P(\mathbf{s})$ and to ground clauses $L_1(\mathbf{s}_1) \vee \ldots \vee L_n(\mathbf{s}_n)$ follows from the usual interpretation of $\neg$ and $\vee$. A c-clause $[c : \mathcal{P}]$ evaluates to **T** in $\mathcal{I}$, iff $c\sigma$ evaluates to **T** for every ground solution σ of $\mathcal{P}$. The evaluation of a c-clause $[c : \mathcal{P}]$ to **T** in an interpretation $\mathcal{I}$ is denoted by $\mathcal{I} \models [c : \mathcal{P}]$.

Caferra et al. defined a calculus on c-clauses consisting of refutational rules (c-factorization, c-resolution), model construction rules (e.g.: c-dissubsumption) and structural rules (e.g.: transformations of the constraint part without changing the overall meaning of the c-clause). The original calculus was later extended to include resolution refinements (e.g. A-ordering resolution and semantic clash resolution, cf. [3], [2]). The definition of the cRes rule (= c-resolution) and the cDsub rule (= c-dissubsumption) is given below, since they form the basis of our calculus to be defined in Section 4. For the remaining rules and any details, the original papers (in particular [3]) have to be referred to.

Definition 2.1. (cRes Rule and cDsub Rule) *The following rules are part of the calculus of Caferra et al.:*

1. *c-resolution: Let L denote some literal symbol (i.e.: a predicate symbol or a negated predicate symbol) and let L^d denote its dual. Then the following clause may be derived via the cRes rule from the c-clauses $[L(\mathbf{s}) \vee c : X]$ and $[L^d(\mathbf{t}) \vee d : Y]$:*

$$\frac{[L(\mathbf{s}) \vee c : X] \qquad [L^d(\mathbf{t}) \vee d : Y]}{[c \vee d : X \wedge Y \wedge \mathbf{s} = \mathbf{t}]}$$

2. *c-dissubsumption: For c-clauses $[L_1(\mathbf{s}_1) \vee \ldots \vee L_n(\mathbf{s}_n) : X]$ and $[L_1(\mathbf{t}_1) \vee \ldots \vee L_n(\mathbf{t}_n) \vee c : Y]$, the cDsub rule allows the derivation of the following c-clause:*

$$\frac{[L_1(\mathbf{s}_1) \vee \ldots \vee L_n(\mathbf{s}_n) : X] \qquad [L_1(\mathbf{t}_1) \vee \ldots\ L_n(\mathbf{t}_n) \vee c : Y]}{[L_1(\mathbf{t}_1) \vee \ldots\ L_n(\mathbf{t}_n) \vee c : Y \wedge Z]}$$

where $Z \equiv \neg(\exists \boldsymbol{x})(X \wedge \boldsymbol{s}_1 = \boldsymbol{t}_1 \wedge \ldots \wedge \boldsymbol{s}_n = \boldsymbol{t}_n)$. *Furthermore, the original c-clause* $[L_1(\boldsymbol{t}_1) \vee \ldots \vee L_n(\boldsymbol{t}_n) \vee c : Y]$ *may be replaced by the new c-clause* $[L_1(\boldsymbol{t}_1) \vee \ldots \vee L_n(\boldsymbol{t}_n) \vee c : Y \wedge Z]$.

3 Disequation Normal Form

The constraint part of a c-clause may play two essentially different roles: On the one hand, it may be simply a short-hand notation for a more complex standard clause or for a finite set of standard clauses, respectively. On the other hand, constraints may give us a means for a finite representation of clause sets, which only have an infinite representation in standard clause logic, e.g.: Over the Herbrand universe with signature $\Sigma = \{f, a\}$, the c-clause $C_1 = [P(x, y) : x = f(y) \vee (\exists z) y = f(z)]$ is equivalent to the set $\mathcal{C}_1 = \{P(f(y), y), P(x, f(z))\}$ of standard clauses. On the other hand, the c-clause $C_2 = [P(x, y) : x \neq y]$ has no finite representation in standard clause logic.

In [9], it is shown that (apart from some trivial cases) disequations cannot be represented by a finite disjunction of equations (cf. [9], Theorem 6.3). Moreover, in [8], an algorithm is presented for the following problem: Given terms $t, t_1, \ldots, t_n$ over an infinite Herbrand universe H. Is there a finite set of terms $\{s_1, \ldots, s_m\}$, s.t. the set of H-ground instances of t which are not instances of any term t_i, is identical to the union of the sets of H-ground instances of the terms s_j. In our terminology of c-clauses, this problem can be reformulated in the following way: Let $t, t_1, \ldots, t_n$ be terms over an infinite Herbrand universe s.t. t has no variables in common with the t_i's. Moreover, let $\boldsymbol{y}$ denote the set of all variables occurring in the t_i's and let P be a unary predicate symbol. Then the algorithm from [8] decides the the following question: Can the c-clause $[P(t) : \forall \boldsymbol{y} \, (t \neq t_1 \wedge \ldots \wedge t \neq t_n)]$ be represented by a finite set of standard clauses?

In this section, we shall prove a related result, namely: only disequations or conjunctions of disequations are more than just short-hand notations of clause sets that could be represented in standard clause logic as well. These considerations will be formalized by defining the so-called *disequation normal form* (= DeqNF) of c-clauses and by showing that every finite set of c-clauses with arbitrary constraints can be effectively transformed into an equivalent finite set of c-clauses in DeqNF.

Definition 3.1. (Disequation Normal Form) *Let* $C = [c : \mathcal{P}]$ *be a c-clause over an infinite Herbrand universe* H. *We say that* C *is in* disequation normal form *(= DeqNF), iff the following conditions hold:*

1. $\mathcal{P}$ *is a quantifier-free conjunction of disequations or the empty conjunction* $\top$.
2. *All variables of the constraint part* $\mathcal{P}$ *also occur in the clause part* c.

Theorem 3.1. Transformation into DeqNF) *Let* H *be an infinite Herbrand universe and let* $\mathcal{C}$ *be a finite set of arbitrary c-clauses over* H. *Then* $\mathcal{C}$ *can be* *effectively transformed into an equivalent finite set of c-clauses $\mathcal{C}'$ in disequation normal form.*

Proof: We have to apply several transformation steps to every clause $[c : \mathcal{P}] \in \mathcal{C}$, until all resulting c-clauses have the desired form:

- Step 1 (definition with constraints):
  By [1], the equational problem $\mathcal{P}$ can be transformed into an equivalent equational problem $\mathcal{P}'$ in "definition with constraints solved form", i.e.: $\mathcal{P}' \equiv \bot$ or $\mathcal{P}' \equiv \top$ or $\mathcal{P}'$ is a disjunction of problems $\mathcal{P}_i$ of the form

  $$(\exists w_1) \dots (\exists w_m) x_1 = t_1 \wedge \dots \wedge x_k = t_k \wedge z_1 \neq u_1 \wedge \dots \wedge z_l \neq u_l,$$

  where all variables $x_1, \dots, x_k$ occur only once in $\mathcal{P}_i$. Moreover, replacing the the constraint part by some equivalent equational problem does not change the semantics of a c-clause. Hence, $[c : \mathcal{P}]$ is equivalent to $[c : \mathcal{P}']$, where the following three cases have to be distinguished for $\mathcal{P}'$:
  If $\mathcal{P}' \equiv \top$, then $[c : \mathcal{P}']$ already is in DeqNF. If $\mathcal{P}' \equiv \bot$, then $\mathcal{P}$ has no solutions and, therefore, $[c : \mathcal{P}]$ is trivially true in every interpretation. Hence, $[c : \mathcal{P}]$ may be deleted from $\mathcal{C}$. Otherwise, $\mathcal{P}' \equiv \mathcal{P}_1 \vee \dots \vee \mathcal{P}_n$, where the disjuncts $\mathcal{P}_i$ are of the above form. The following steps deal with the latter case.
- Step 2 (elimination of disjunctions):
  Let $\mathcal{P} \equiv \mathcal{P}_1 \vee \dots \vee \mathcal{P}_n$. Then $[c : \mathcal{P}]$ is equivalent to the c-clause set $\{[c : \mathcal{P}_1], \dots, [c : \mathcal{P}_n]\}$. This equivalence follows immediately from the definition of the semantics of c-clauses: If $c\sigma$ is a ground instance of $[c : \mathcal{P}]$, then σ is a solution of $\mathcal{P}$ and, therefore, of some disjunct $\mathcal{P}_i$. Hence, $c\sigma$ is also a ground instance of $[c : \mathcal{P}_i]$. Likewise, every ground instance $c\sigma$ of some c-clause $[c : \mathcal{P}_i]$ is a ground instance of $[c : \mathcal{P}]$.
- Step 3 (elimination of existential quantifiers):
  Let $\mathcal{P}_i$ be an equational problem of the form $(\exists w_1) \dots (\exists w_m) \mathcal{Q}$, where $\mathcal{Q} \equiv x_1 = t_1 \wedge \dots \wedge x_k = t_k \wedge z_1 \neq u_1 \wedge \dots \wedge z_l \neq u_l$ and all variables $x_1, \dots, x_k$ occur only once in $\mathcal{P}_i$. The bound variables $w_1, \dots, w_m$ can be renamed without changing the meaning of the equational problem. Hence, we may assume w.l.o.g. that they do not occur in the clause part. But then we are allowed to apply the following "structural rule" from [3]:

  $$[c : \mathcal{Q}] \equiv [c : (\exists w) \mathcal{Q}], \text{ if } w \text{ does not occur in } c.$$

  Hence, applying this rule m-times yields the following equivalence:

  $$[c : \mathcal{P}_i] \equiv [c : x_1 = t_1 \wedge \dots \wedge x_k = t_k \wedge z_1 \neq u_1 \wedge \dots \wedge z_l \neq u_l]$$

- Step 4 (elimination of equations):
  Let $[c : \mathcal{Q}]$ be a c-clause with $\mathcal{Q} \equiv x_1 = t_1 \wedge \dots \wedge x_k = t_k \wedge z_1 \neq u_1 \wedge \dots \wedge z_l \neq u_l$, s.t. the variables $x_1, \dots, x_k$ occur only once in $\mathcal{Q}$. Then there exists another "structural rule" from [3], which is applicable in this situation, namely:

  $$[c : x_i = t_i \wedge \mathcal{Q}'] \equiv [c\{x_i \leftarrow t_i\} : \mathcal{Q}'\{x_i \leftarrow t_i\}], \text{ if } x_i \notin var(t_i).$$

Hence, we can apply this rule k-times to get the following equivalence:

$[c : \mathcal{Q}] \equiv [c\sigma : (z_1 \neq u_1 \wedge \ldots \wedge z_l \neq u_l)\sigma]$, where $\sigma = \{x_1 \leftarrow t_1, \ldots, x_k \leftarrow t_k\}$.

– Step 5 (elimination of "additional" free variables):
Let $[d : \mathcal{R}]$ be a c-clause resulting from step 4 above. Furthermore, let $var(\mathcal{R}) - var(d) = \{v_1, \ldots, v_\alpha\}$. Then the transformation from step 3 can also be applied in the opposite direction, i.e.: all variables in $var(\mathcal{R}) - var(d)$ may be existentially quantified. Hence, the following equivalence holds:

$$[d : \mathcal{R}] \equiv [d : (\exists v_1) \ldots (\exists v_\alpha)\mathcal{R}]$$

– Step 6 (alternative way of eliminating the existential quantifiers):
Let $[d : (\exists v_1) \ldots (\exists v_\alpha)\mathcal{R}]$ be a c-clause whose constraint part is a quantified conjunction of disequations. Since the Herbrand universe H is assumed to be infinite, we may apply the so-called "cleaning rule" CR_3 from [1], Section 3.2:

$$(\exists \boldsymbol{v})(d_1 \vee y_1 \neq t_1) \wedge \ldots \wedge (d_l \vee y_l \neq t_l) \wedge \mathcal{P}' \equiv (\exists \boldsymbol{v})\mathcal{P}',$$

provided that the d_i's are arbitrary disjunctions of equations and disequations, each y_i is a variable and each $y_i \neq t_i$ is a non-trivial disequation which contains an existentially quantified variable v_j not occurring in $\mathcal{P}'$.
Then we can apply the *cleaning rule* CR_3 to $(\exists v_1) \ldots (\exists v_\alpha)\mathcal{R}$ by taking the d_i's to be empty and $\mathcal{P}'$ to be the conjunction of all disequations containing no existentially quantified variable. Hence, all disequations which contain a bound variable may be deleted. But then the prefix of existential quantifiers may also be deleted, since the resulting conjunction of disequations contains no bound variables anymore. Therefore, the following c-clauses are equivalent:

$$[d : (\exists v_1) \ldots (\exists v_\alpha)\mathcal{R}] \equiv [d : z_{j_1} \neq u_{j_1} \wedge \ldots \wedge z_{j_{l'}} \neq u_{j_{l'}}],$$

where $\{j_1, \ldots, j_{l'}\} = \{j | z_j \neq u_j$ contains no bound variable $v_i\}$. ◇

The steps 5 and 6 in the above proof were carried out separately for the sake of better readability. Note, however, that these two steps together result in the deletion of all disequations that contain an "additional" free variable v_i after step 4. Hence, in practice, they will naturally be contracted to a single transformation step. In fact, this is exactly what the normalization rule of our c-clause calculus in Definition 4.1 will do.

4 A Resolution-Based Calculus in c-Clause Logic

The original calculus of Caferra et al. (and, in particular, the cRes rule and cDsub rule recalled in Definition 2.1) provides the basis for the construction of a decision procedure for certain classes of c-clauses. However, some modifications are required to make sure that the resulting calculus fulfills several conditions, e.g.: Decision classes of standard clauses will be extended to decidable classes of c-clauses in DeqNF. Hence, the c-clause calculus should preserve the DeqNF. Note that neither the cRes rule nor the cDsub rule from [3] have this property. Furthermore, for every clause part, only finitely many constraint parts should be generated by our c-clause calculus. Again, the cRes rule and the cDsub rule from [3] are problematical since it is not clear how the number of constraint parts can be controlled. Starting from an arbitrary resolution refinement R_x on standard clauses, we define the following calculus $\mathcal{I}_x$ on c-clauses:

Definition 4.1. (Calculus $\mathcal{I}_x$ on c-clauses) *Let R_x be some resolution refinement on standard clauses. Then the calculus $\mathcal{I}_x$ on c-clauses in DeqNF is defined through the following rules and rule application strategy:*

Rules of $\mathcal{I}_x$:

1. *Refined c-resolution: Let L denote some literal symbol (i.e.: a predicate symbol or a negated predicate symbol) and let L^d denote its dual. Furthermore, let $[L(\boldsymbol{s}_1) \vee \ldots \vee L(\boldsymbol{s}_n) \vee c : X]$ and $[L^d(\boldsymbol{t}_1) \vee \ldots \vee L^d(\boldsymbol{t}_m) \vee d : Y]$ be variable disjoint c-clauses in DeqNF. Then we define the $cRes_x$ rule in the following way:*

$$\frac{[L(\boldsymbol{s}_1) \vee \ldots \vee L(\boldsymbol{s}_n) \vee c : X] \qquad [L^d(\boldsymbol{t}_1) \vee \ldots \vee L^d(\boldsymbol{t}_m) \vee d : Y]}{[(c \vee d)\sigma : (X \wedge Y)\sigma]} \; cRes_x,$$

   where $\sigma = mgu(\{\boldsymbol{s}_1, \ldots, \boldsymbol{s}_n, \boldsymbol{t}_1, \ldots, \boldsymbol{t}_m\})$ and $(c \vee d)\sigma$ is an R_x-resolvent of $L(\boldsymbol{s}_1) \vee \ldots \vee L(\boldsymbol{s}_n) \vee c$ and $L^d(\boldsymbol{t}_1) \vee \ldots \vee L^d(\boldsymbol{t}_m) \vee d$.
2. *Normalization: Let $[c : \mathcal{P}]$ be a c-clause derived by the $cRes_x$ rule above and let $u_{i_1} \neq v_{i_1}, \ldots, u_{i_k} \neq v_{i_k}$ denote the disequations in $\mathcal{P}$ containing a variable which does not occur in c. Then every disequation $u_{i_\alpha} \neq v_{i_\alpha}$ may be either replaced by $\perp$ (if $u_{i_\alpha} \equiv v_{i_\alpha}$ holds) or deleted (otherwise).*
3. *c-subsumption: Let $[c : X_1]$, …, $[c : X_k]$ be c-clauses in the data base and let $[c : X_{k+1}]$ be a new $cRes_x$-resolvent. Then $[c : X_{k+1}]$ may be deleted, if $X_{k+1} \leq X_1 \vee \ldots \vee X_k$.*

Rule Application Strategy $\mathcal{I}_x$:

We require that the c-subsumption rule be applied immediately to every newly derived c-clause. Furthermore, normalization has to be applied to every $cRes_x$ resolvent before it is added to the data base. As far as fairness is concerned, we choose the simple strategy of level saturation, i.e.: The whole generation of c-clauses derivable by n applications of the $cRes_x$ rule has to be derived before a resolvent is derived via $n+1$ $cRes_x$ rule applications.

The above calculus $\mathcal{I}_x$ differs from the original definition of Caferra et al. in various ways (cf. [3]), e.g.: Analogously to Robinson's original definition of resolution, we consider factoring and resolution as a single inference step (cf. [11]). More importantly, we apply the unifying substitution σ explicitly both to the clause part and to the constraint part whereas, in [3], the unification is carried out implicitly by adding the corresponding equations $\boldsymbol{s}_i = \boldsymbol{t}_i$ to the constraints.

Furthermore, the definition of c-subsumption given above can be considered as the original cDsub rule from [3] and [2] together with a very restricted rule application strategy, namely: The cDsub rule may only be applied if all c-clauses involved have the same clause part and if, moreover, a finite number of applications of this rule ultimately leads to the actual deletion of $[c : X_{k+1}]$.

The Correctness of the calculus $\mathcal{I}_x$ is easy to prove: The correctness of the resolution refinement cRes_x follows immediately from the corresponding correctness in standard clause logic. Furthermore the deletion of c-clauses via c-subsumption may only affect the completeness (but not the correctness) of a calculus. As far as the normalization rule is concerned, we have to distinguish two cases: A disequation $u_{i_\alpha} \neq v_{i_\alpha}$ where $u_{i_\alpha} \equiv v_{i_\alpha}$ holds, is trivially unsolvable. Hence, it is correct to replace it by $\perp$. If $u_{i_\alpha} \neq v_{i_\alpha}$ contains a variable not occurring in the clause part and $u_{i_\alpha} \not\equiv v_{i_\alpha}$ holds, then we may apply the transformation steps 5 and 6 from Theorem 3.1 and delete this disequation.

On the other hand, the completeness of $\mathcal{I}_x$ is not so trivial. In particular, the compatibility of the c-subsumption rule with any resolution refinement need not necessarily hold. In [10], the completeness of the calculus of Caferra et al. is shown by extending the well-known concept of semantic trees from standard clauses to c-clauses. In [6], the completeness of unrefined resolution R_0, A-ordering resolution $\text{R}_{<_A}$ and semantic clash resolution $\text{R}_{\mathcal{M}}$ are proven via semantic trees in standard clause logic. Analogously, the refutational completeness of the calculi $\mathcal{I}_0$, $\mathcal{I}_{<_A}$ and $\mathcal{I}_{\mathcal{M}}$ based on these resolution refinements can be shown via semantic trees in c-clause logic.

5 Compactness of Unification Problems

We ultimately want to show how the termination of a resolution refinement R_x on standard clauses can be carried over to the corresponding calculus $\mathcal{I}_x$ on c-clauses. To this end, the strong compactness of sets of equations proven in [9] will be slightly extended in Theorem 5.3. For the proof of this theorem, some more basic terminology and results are required, which are revised in the following subsections:

5.1 Unification Revisited

Throughout this section we assume that the Herbrand universe H is non-trivial and the set of variables V is finite. The following definitions form the basis of the considerations in [9]:

Definition 5.1. (Solved Form of an Equation Set) *An equation set $\mathcal{E}$ is called* solved, *iff it has the form $\{v_1 = t_1, \ldots, v_n = t_n\}$ s.t. the v_i's are pairwise distinct variables which do not occur on the right-hand side of any equation. The variables $v_1, \ldots, v_n$ are said to be* eliminable *and the remaining variables from V are called* parameters.

Definition 5.2. (Dimension of an Equation Set) *Let $\mathcal{E}$ be a solvable set of equations and let $\mathcal{E}'$ be some solved form equivalent to $\mathcal{E}$. Then $dim(\mathcal{E})$ (=* dimension *of $\mathcal{E}$) denotes the number of parameters in $\mathcal{E}'$.*

The following results on the dimension $dim(\mathcal{E})$ of an equation set $\mathcal{E}$ are proven in [9], Propositions 3.3 and 3.5, respectively:

Proposition 5.1. (Well-Defined Dimension of an Equation Set) *The dimension $dim(\mathcal{E})$ of a (solvable) set of equations is well-defined, i.e.: all solved forms $\mathcal{E}'$ equivalent to $\mathcal{E}$ have the same number of parameters.*

Proposition 5.2. (Dimension and Solution Sets) *Let $\mathcal{E}_1$ and $\mathcal{E}_2$ be two solvable sets of equations. Then the following implication holds: If the solutions of $\mathcal{E}_1$ are a proper subset of the solutions of $\mathcal{E}_2$, then $dim(\mathcal{E}_1) < dim(\mathcal{E}_2)$.*

A result similar to our Theorem 5.3 is proven in [9], Theorem 3.11:

Theorem 5.1. (Strong Compactness of Equation Sets) *Let $\mathcal{E}$ and $\mathcal{E}_1, \ldots, \mathcal{E}_n$ be equation sets over an infinite Herbrand universe. Then the following implication holds: If $\mathcal{E} \approx \mathcal{E}_1 \vee \ldots \vee \mathcal{E}_n$, then there exists some j s.t. $\mathcal{E} \approx \mathcal{E}_j$*

5.2 Multiset Orderings

Multisets are a common technique in termination proofs with a broad field of applications. The termination proof in Theorem 5.3 and, hence, also in Theorem 6.1 is based on a multiset ordering. The following definitions and results are taken from [4], Section 2:

Let $(S, <)$ be a partially-ordered set, where $<$ denotes a transitive and irreflexive binary relation on elements of S. Multisets over S are unordered collections of elements from S, that may have multiple occurrences of identical elements. By $\mathcal{M}(S)$ we denote the set of all finite multisets over S.

Let N denote the natural numbers. Then a multiset $M \in \mathcal{M}(S)$ can be either written in set notation or as a function $M : S \to N$, where $M(x)$ denotes the number of occurrences of the element $x \in S$ in the multiset M, e.g.: Let $S = \{a, b, \ldots\}$. Then the multiset $M = \{a, b, a, b, b, b\}$ corresponds to the function $M : S \to N$ with $M(a) = 2$, $M(b) = 4$ and $M(x) = 0$ otherwise.

The partial ordering $<$ on S can be extended to a partial ordering $\prec$ on the multisets in $\mathcal{M}(S)$ in the following way: Let $M, M' \in \mathcal{M}(S)$. Then $M' \prec M$, iff there exists a non-empty multiset $X \subseteq M$ and a multiset $Y \in \mathcal{M}(S)$, s.t. $M' = (M - X) \cup Y$ and for every $y \in Y$, there exists an $x \in X$ with $y < x$. Intuitively, $M' \prec M$ holds, iff M' is obtained from M by replacing at least one element in M (i.e.: those in X) by an arbitrary, finite number of elements from S (i.e.: those in Y), that are all strictly smaller than one of the removed elements.

The main reason why multisets are such a useful tool in termination proofs is the property of "well-foundedness", which the multiset ordering $\prec$ inherits from the original partial ordering $<$, i.e.: A partially-ordered set $(S, <)$ is said to be well-founded, if there is no infinite, strictly decreasing sequence of elements $s_1 > s_2 > \ldots$ from S. Then the following theorem holds:

Theorem 5.2. *Let $(S,<)$ be a partially-ordered set and $\prec$ the multiset extension. Then the following equivalence holds: $(S,<)$ is well-founded, iff $(\mathcal{M}(S),\prec)$ is well-founded.*

Proof: see [4], p. 467.

5.3 Compactness Theorem

We are now ready to prove the following compactness theorem of unification problems:

Theorem 5.3. (Compactness of Unification Problems) *Let H be an infinite Herbrand universe and let V be a finite set of variables. Moreover, let $\mathcal{N} = \{Y_1, Y_2, Y_3 \ldots\}$ be an infinite set of unification problems over H with variables in V.*

Then there is a finite subset $\mathcal{N}' \subseteq \mathcal{N}$, s.t. $\mathcal{N}'$ is equivalent to the whole set $\mathcal{N}$. In particular, there exists a K s.t. for all $n > K$, the condition $Y_1 \wedge \ldots \wedge Y_K \leq Y_n$ holds.

Proof:
Restriction to disjunctions of equations: W.l.o.g. we can assume that every unification problem Y_i is in CNF, i.e.: $Y_i \equiv (Z_{i1} \wedge \ldots \wedge Z_{in_i})$, where every Z_{ij} is a disjunction of equations. Furthermore, let $\mathcal{M} = \{Z_{11}, \ldots, Z_{1n_1}, Z_{21}, \ldots, Z_{2n_2}, \ldots\}$. It is then sufficient to show that there exists a finite subset $\mathcal{M}' \subseteq \mathcal{M}$, s.t. $\mathcal{M}'$ is equivalent to the whole set $\mathcal{M}$. Hence, w.l.o.g. we can restrict our considerations to the case where every unification problem $Y_i \in \mathcal{N}$ is a disjunction of equations, i.e.: $Y_i \equiv e_{i1} \vee \ldots \vee e_{ik_i}$

Multiset of dimensions: Suppose that some unification problem S is in DNF, i.e.: $S \equiv Z_1 \vee \ldots \vee Z_N$, where every Z_i is a conjunction of equations. Furthermore, assume that all conjunctions Z_i are solvable. Then, by Proposition 5.1, the dimension $dim(Z_i)$ is well-defined (Recall that the dimension of a unification problem $\mathcal{P}$ denotes the number of unbound variables in a most general unifier of $\mathcal{P}$). Hence, for a unification problem S in DNF, we can define the multiset of dimensions as $DIM(S) := \{dim(Z_1), \ldots, dim(Z_N)\}$. If S is unsolvable, we set $DIM(S) := \emptyset$. The proof of Theorem 5.3 will then be based on the following idea: Let $S_n \equiv Y_1 \wedge \ldots \wedge Y_n$ denote the conjunction of the first n unification problems from $\mathcal{N}$ and let S'_n be an equivalent problem in DNF. We have to provide an appropriate algorithm for computing the DNF S'_n s.t. the following implication holds:

$$S_n \not\approx S_{n-1} \Rightarrow DIM(S'_n) \prec DIM(S'_{n-1}),$$

i.e.: If the solutions of S_n are a proper subset of the solutions of S_{n-1}, then the multiset $DIM(S'_n)$ is strictly smaller than $DIM(S'_{n-1})$. (The details of such an algorithm are given below.) Note that the natural numbers with $<$ are well-founded. Hence, also multisets over the natural numbers with $\prec$ are well-founded, i.e.: There exists no infinite, strictly decreasing sequence of multisets

$DIM(S'_{n_1}), DIM(S'_{n_2}), \ldots$. But then $S_n \approx S_{n-1}$ holds for all but finitely many n's. Thus there exists a K s.t. for all $n > K$, the condition $Y_1 \wedge \ldots \wedge Y_{n-1} \approx Y_1 \wedge \ldots \wedge Y_{n-1} \wedge Y_n$ (or, equivalently, $Y_1 \wedge \ldots \wedge Y_{n-1} \leq Y_n$) holds. We can, therefore, conclude by a simple induction argument that $Y_1 \wedge \ldots \wedge Y_K \leq Y_n$ holds for all $n > K$.

Incremental computation of the DNF: It only remains to provide an algorithm for computing a sequence of DNFs S'_n equivalent to $S_n \equiv Y_1 \wedge \ldots \wedge Y_n$, s.t. the implication

$$S_n \not\approx S_{n-1} \Rightarrow DIM(S'_n) \prec DIM(S'_{n-1})$$

holds. We construct the DNFs S'_n inductively as follows:
By assumption, $S_1 \equiv Y_1 \equiv e_{11} \vee \ldots \vee e_{1k_1}$ already is in DNF, i.e.: $S'_1 := S_1$. Now suppose that $S'_{n-1} \equiv Z_1 \vee \ldots \vee Z_N$ is the DNF corresponding to S_{n-1}. Then $S_n \equiv Y_1 \wedge \ldots \wedge Y_{n-1} \wedge Y_n \equiv S_{n-1} \wedge Y_n$ is equivalent to the following problem:

$$\begin{aligned} S_n &\approx (Z_1 \vee \ldots \vee Z_N) \wedge (e_{n1} \vee \ldots \vee e_{nk_n}) \\ &\approx (Z_1 \wedge (e_{n1} \vee \ldots \vee e_{nk_n})) \vee \ldots \vee (Z_N \wedge (e_{n1} \vee \ldots \vee e_{nk_n})) \end{aligned}$$

In order to transform this problem into a disjunctive normal form S'_n, we transform every disjunct $Z_i \wedge (e_{n1} \vee \ldots \vee e_{nk_n})$ into an equivalent problem D_i in DNF in the following way:

$$D_i := \begin{cases} Z_i \quad \text{if there exists a } j \text{ s.t. } (Z_i \wedge e_{nj}) \approx Z_i \\ \bot \quad \text{if for all } j\text{: } (Z_i \wedge e_{nj}) \approx \bot \\ (Z_i \wedge e_{nj_1}) \vee \ldots \vee (Z_i \wedge e_{nj_l}) \quad \text{otherwise,} \\ \quad \text{where } \{j_1, \ldots, j_l\} = \{j \mid Z_i \wedge e_{nj} \text{ is solvable}\} \end{cases}$$

Finally, all unsolvable problems D_i have to be deleted from S'_n. Then every D_i and, therefore, also the disjunction S'_n clearly is in DNF. Moreover, the equivalence $D_i \approx Z_i \wedge (e_{n1} \vee \ldots \vee e_{nk_n})$ and, hence, also the equivalence $S'_n \approx S_n$ are easy to prove. Furthermore, the multiset $DIM(S'_n)$ can be computed from $DIM(S'_{n-1})$ in the following way:

1. If $D_i \equiv Z_i$, then $dim(Z_i) \in DIM(S'_{n-1})$ is left unchanged in $DIM(S'_n)$.
2. If $D_i \equiv \bot$, then $dim(Z_i) \in DIM(S'_{n-1})$ is deleted from $DIM(S'_n)$.
3. If $D_i \equiv (Z_i \wedge e_{nj_1}) \vee \ldots \vee (Z_i \wedge e_{nj_l})$ (according to case 3 of the above definition of D_i), then $dim(Z_i)$ is replaced by $dim(Z_i \wedge e_{nj_1}), \ldots, dim(Z_i \wedge e_{nj_l})$.

Remember that case 3 of the definition of D_i only applies if $Z_i \wedge e_{nj_\alpha} < Z_i$ for all α, i.e.: the solutions of every problem $(Z_i \wedge e_{nj_\alpha})$ are a proper subset of the solutions of Z_i. But then, by Proposition 5.2, $dim(Z_i \wedge e_{nj_\alpha}) < dim(Z_i)$ also holds. Hence, by the definition of multiset orderings, $DIM(S'_n) = DIM(S'_{n-1})$, iff case 1 applies to all disjuncts D_i of S'_n, and $DIM(S'_n) \prec DIM(S'_{n-1})$ otherwise. In other words, $DIM(S'_n) = DIM(S'_{n-1})$, iff $S_n \approx S'_{n-1}$, and $DIM(S'_n) \prec DIM(S'_{n-1})$ otherwise. ◇

6 Extension of Decision Classes to c-Clause Logic

The target of this section is to show how decision classes from standard clause logic can be extended by adding appropriate constraints. To this end, we first have to show that the termination of a resolution refinement R_x on standard clauses can be easily carried over to the corresponding calculus $\mathcal{I}_x$ on c-clauses:

Theorem 6.1. (Termination of $\mathcal{I}_x$) *Let R_x be a resolution refinement on standard clauses and let $\mathcal{I}_x$ be the corresponding calculus on c-clauses according to Definition 4.1. Furthermore, let $\mathcal{C} = \{[c_1 : \mathcal{P}_1], \ldots, [c_n : \mathcal{P}_n]\}$ be a set of c-clauses over some infinite Herbrand universe H, s.t. $\mathcal{C}$ is in disequation normal form and $\mathcal{C}' = \{c_1, \ldots, c_n\}$ is the corresponding set of standard clauses consisting of the clause parts of $\mathcal{C}$. By $R_x(\mathcal{C}')$, we denote the clauses derivable from $\mathcal{C}'$ via finitely many applications of the resolution refinement R_x. Likewise, the set of c-clauses derivable from $\mathcal{C}$ via $\mathcal{I}_x$ will be denoted as $\mathcal{I}_x(\mathcal{C})$. Then the following implication holds:*

If $R_x(\mathcal{C}')$ is finite, then $\mathcal{I}_x(\mathcal{C})$ is also finite.

Proof: Suppose that $R_x(\mathcal{C}')$ is finite. We have to prove, that $\mathcal{I}_x(\mathcal{C})$ is also finite, i.e.: there are only finitely many distinct clause parts and constraint parts in $\mathcal{I}_x(\mathcal{C})$:

- (Clause parts):
  By the definition of $\mathcal{I}_x$, the set $\mathcal{D} := \{c \mid [c : \mathcal{P}] \in \mathcal{I}_x(\mathcal{C})\}$ of clause parts produced by $\mathcal{I}_x$ is contained in the set $\mathrm{R}_x(\mathcal{C}')$ of standard clauses generated by R_x. Hence, the set $\mathcal{D}$ of clause parts in $\mathcal{I}_x(\mathcal{C})$ is finite.
- (Constraint parts):
  We have to show that for every clause part c in $\mathcal{I}_x(\mathcal{C})$, there are only finitely many distinct constraint parts X_i s.t. $[c : X_i] \in \mathcal{I}_x(\mathcal{C})$. Suppose, on the contrary, that there is an infinite sequence $[c : X_1]$, $[c : X_2]$, $[c : X_3], \ldots$ of c-clauses in $\mathcal{I}_x(\mathcal{C})$ such that for all $n > 1$, $[c : X_n]$ is not c-subsumed by the previously derived c-clauses $\{[c : X_1], \ldots, [c : X_{n-1}]\}$. The X_i's are conjunctions of disequations over the infinite Herbrand universe H with variables in the finite set $V = var(c)$. Therefore, the equational problems $\neg X_1$, $\neg X_2$, $\neg X_3, \ldots$ are disjunctions of equations over the infinite Herbrand universe H with variables in the finite set V. By Theorem 5.3, we know that there is a K s.t. for all $n > K$: $\neg X_1 \wedge \ldots \wedge \neg X_K \leq \neg X_n$ or, equivalently, $X_n \leq X_1 \vee \ldots \vee X_K$ holds. But then, by Definition 4.1, $\{[c : X_1], \ldots, [c : X_K]\}$ c-subsumes $[c : X_n]$ for all $n > K$, which contradicts the assumption. ◇

The following theorem constitutes the main result of this work:

Theorem 6.2. (Decision Procedure $\mathcal{I}_x$) *Let R_x denote either unrefined resolution R_0, A-ordering resolution $R_{<_A}$ or semantic clash resolution $R_{\mathcal{M}}$. Furthermore, let $\mathcal{K}$ denote a class of standard clauses over an infinite Herbrand universe H, s.t. $\mathcal{K}$ is decidable by R_x. Then $\mathcal{K}$ can be extended to the decidable class $\mathcal{K}'$ of c-clauses in the following way:*

$\mathcal{C}' = \{[c_1 : \mathcal{P}_1], \ldots, [c_n : \mathcal{P}_n]\}$ is in $\mathcal{K}'$, iff $\mathcal{C} := \{c_1, \ldots, c_n\}$ is a set of standard clauses in $\mathcal{K}$ and for all $i \in \{1, \ldots, n\}$, $\mathcal{P}_i$ is a quantifier-free conjunction of disequations with $var(\mathcal{P}_i) \subseteq var(c_i)$.

Then $\mathcal{I}_x$ is a decision procedure for the class $\mathcal{K}'$.

Proof: First of all, we have to make sure that the class $\mathcal{K}'$ is closed w.r.t. the calculus $\mathcal{I}_x$: But the clause parts of the derivable c-clauses result from applications of R_x to $\mathcal{K}$. Furthermore, all input c-clauses are in disequation normal form, which is preserved by the rules from $\mathcal{I}_x$. Hence, the resulting c-clauses are in $\mathcal{K}'$. (Note that the DeqNF may be destroyed by cRes_x since the constraint part of the resolvent may contain variables not occurring in the clause part, e.g.: In case of unrefined resolution R_0, the c-clause $[P(x) : y \neq a \wedge y \neq b]$ may be derived by the cRes_0 rule from $[P(x) \vee Q(y) : y \neq a]$ and $[\neg Q(y') : y' \neq b]$. However, by the rule application strategy, the normalization rule must be applied to the resolvent, which allows for the elimination of these variables, i.e.: in the above example, only the c-clause $[P(x) : \top]$ is actually stored.)

The refutational completeness of the calculus $\mathcal{I}_x$ based on the above mentioned resolution refinements R_x is proven in [10] (cf. the remark in Section 4). The termination of the calculus $\mathcal{I}_x$ on the class $\mathcal{K}'$ follows from the Theorem 6.1. ◇

The following examples illustrate how this theorem can lead to a genuine extension of standard clause classes decidable by A-ordering resolution $\mathrm{R}_{<_A}$ or semantic clash resolution $\mathrm{R}_{\mathcal{M}}$, respectively.

Example 6.1. (extension of the decision class MON)* Let the following clauses and c-clauses be defined over the Herbrand universe H with signature $\Sigma = \{a^0, b^0, f^2\}$, where the exponent denotes the arity of each symbol. Recall from [7] that the class MON* is decidable by an A-ordering resolution refinement. MON* essentially denotes those sets of clauses, where all predicate symbols have arity 1 and variables may only occur in variable arguments or in functional arguments of the form $g(y_1, \ldots, y_\alpha)$, e.g.: $\mathcal{C}' := \{P(x), P(f(x,y)) \vee Q(x), \neg Q(a)\}$. Then the following sets $\mathcal{C}_1$ and $\mathcal{C}_2$ of c-clauses in disequation normal form are obtained from $\mathcal{C}'$ by adding appropriate constraints:

By Theorem 6.2, the c-clause set $\mathcal{C}_1 := \{[P(x) : \top], [P(f(x,y)) \vee Q(x) : x \neq y], [\neg Q(a) : \top]\}$ belongs to a decidable class of c-clauses even though it does not have a finite representation in standard clause logic.

The c-clause set $\mathcal{C}_2 := \{[P(x) : \top], [P(f(x,y)) \vee Q(x) : y \neq a \wedge y \neq b], [\neg Q(a) : \top]\}$ is based on the same set of standard clauses and, therefore, belongs to a decidable class of c-clauses by Theorem 6.2. However, for this Herbrand universe, the equational problem $y = a \vee y = b \vee (\exists u)(\exists v) y = f(u,v)$ is valid. Hence, $\mathcal{C}_2$ is equivalent to the c-clause set $\{[P(x) : \top], [P(f(x,y)) \vee Q(x) : (\exists u)(\exists v) y = f(u,v)], [\neg Q(a) : \top]\}$ which, in turn, is equivalent to the standard clause set $\mathcal{C}_2' = \{P(x), P(f(x, f(u,v))), \neg Q(a)\}$. Note that the set $\mathcal{C}_2'$ is outside the class MON*, due to the nested functional term in $P(f(x, f(u,v)))$. Hence, in this case, the transformation into c-clauses allows for an extension of the decidable standard clause class itself.

Example 6.2. (extension of the decision class PVD) Let the following clauses and c-clauses be defined over the Herbrand universe H with signature $\Sigma = \{a^0, f^2, g^1\}$. In [7], the class PVD is shown to be decidable by hyperresolution. Recall that PVD (= positive variable dominated) consists of the sets of clauses, where all variables from unnegated literals also occur in negated ones and where furthermore the maximum depth of occurrence of each variable in the unnegated literals is not greater than the maximum depth of occurrence of this variable in the negated literals, e.g.: $\mathcal{C}' := \{\neg P(x), P(g(x)) \vee Q(f(y,x)), \neg Q(x)\}$. Then the set $\mathcal{C} = \{[\neg P(x) : \top], [P(g(x)) \vee Q(f(y,x)) : x \neq y], [\neg Q(x) : x \neq a]\}$ does not have a finite representation in standard clause logic. Nevertheless, by Theorem 6.2, it belongs to a decidable class of c-clauses.

7 Concluding Remarks and Future Work

After briefly revising some basic concepts concerning equational problems and constrained clauses, we have provided an answer to the question in what sense constraints actually do increase the expressive power of clauses. The result was formalized by defining the so-called disequation normal form (= DeqNF) of c-clauses, i.e.: the constraint part consists of conjunctions of disequations and contains only variables which also occur in the clause part. Furthermore we proved that every finite set of c-clauses can be effectively transformed into an equivalent finite set of c-clauses in DeqNF. The main result of this paper is the extension of standard clause classes decidable by certain resolution refinements to decidable classes of c-clauses in DeqNF.

So far, we have only considered clause classes which are decidable by some resolution refinement. However, many more ingredients for resolution-based decision procedures can be found in the literature (cf. [5]), e.g.: subsumption, the splitting rule, condensing, partial saturation, etc. Furthermore, there are several paramodulation-based decision procedures for decision classes containing equality. It still remains to investigate, how a standard clause calculus based on these methods can be extended to c-clause logic without destroying the refutational completeness and the termination property.

In [5], resolution based decision methods for many classes of standard clauses are presented. The expressive power gained through the extension of these classes to c-clause logic and potential applications of the resulting languages deserve further study. In particular, what kind of problems can be expressed by the resulting classes of c-clauses in DeqNF?

References

[1] H. Comon, P. Lescanne: Equational Problems and Disunification, Journal of Symbolic Computation, Vol 7, pp. 371–425, (1989).

[2] R.Caferra, N.Peltier: Decision Procedures using Model Building Techniques, Proceedings of CSL'95, LNCS 1092, pp.130–144, Springer (1996).

[3] R.Caferra, N.Zabel: Extending Resolution for Model Construction, Proceedings of Logics in AI - JELIA'90, LNAI 478, pp. 153–169, Springer (1991).
[4] N.Dershowitz, Z.Manna: Proving Termination with Multiset Orderings, in Communications of the ACM, Vol 22, No 8, pp. 465–475 (1979).
[5] C.Fermüller, A.Leitsch, T.Tammet, N. Zamov: Resolution Methods for the Decision Problem. LNAI 679, Springer (1993).
[6] R.Kowalski, P.J.Hayes: Semantic Trees in Automated Theorem Proving, in Machine Intelligence 4, pp. 87–101 (1969).
[7] A.Leitsch: The Resolution Calculus, Texts in Theoretical Computer Science, Springer (1997).
[8] J.-L.Lassez, K.Marriott: Explicit Representation of Terms defined by Counter Examples, Journal of Automated Reasoning, Vol 3, pp. 301–317 (1987).
[9] J.-L.Lassez, M.J.Maher, K.Marriott: Unification Revisited, Foundations of Logic and Functional Programming, LNCS 306, pp. 67–113, Springer (1986).
[10] R.Pichler: Completeness and Redundancy in Constrained Clause Logic, in Proceedings of FTP'98 (Int. Workshop on First-Order Theorem Proving), Technical Report E1852-GS-981 of Technische Universität Wien, pp. 193–203, available from `http://www.logic.at/ftp98`, Vienna (1998).
[11] J.A.Robinson: A machine oriented logic based on the resolution principle, Journal of the ACM, Vol 12, No 1, pp. 23–41 (1965).

Completeness and Redundancy in Constrained Clause Logic

Reinhard Pichler

Technische Universität Wien
reini@logic.at

Abstract. In [6], a resolution-based inference system on c-clauses (i.e. constrained clauses) was introduced, incorporating powerful deletion rules for redundancy elimination. This inference system was extended to resolution refinements in subsequent papers of Caferra et al. (e.g. [4] and [5]). The completeness proofs given for the purely refutational calculi (i.e.: the inference systems without deletion rules) are basically "translations" of the corresponding results from standard clause logic to constrained clause logic (= c-clause logic, for short).
This work focuses on the deletion rules of the calculi of Caferra et al. and, in particular, on the c-dissubsumption rule, which is considerably more powerful than the usual subsumption concept in standard clause logic. We will show that the "conventional" method for proving the completeness of (standard clause) resolution refinements with subsumption fails when the powerful deletion rules of Caferra et al. are considered. Therefore, in order to prove the completeness of the c-clause calculi, a different strategy is required. To this end, we shall extend the well-known concept of semantic trees from standard clause logic to c-clause logic.
In general, purely non-deterministic application of the inference rules is not sufficient to ensure refutational completeness. It is intuitively clear, that some sort of "fairness" must be required. The completeness proof via semantic trees gives us a hint for defining precisely what it means for a rule application strategy to be "fair".
Finally other methods for proving completeness and defining redundancy criteria are contrasted with completeness via semantic trees and c-dissubsumption. In particular, it is shown that the redundancy criteria within the ordering-based approaches of Bachmair/Ganzinger (cf. [2]) and Nieuwenhuis/Rubio (cf. [11]) are incomparable with c-dissubsumption.

1 Introduction

In [6], a refutational calculus based on factoring and resolution is carried over in a natural way from standard clause logic to constrained clause logic (= c-clause logic, for short). This inference system was extended to resolution refinements in subsequent papers of Caferra et al. (e.g. [4] and [5]). The completeness of the resulting calculi is proven in 2 steps: First the *ground completeness* is proven, exploiting the fact that ground resolution on c-clauses coincides with ground

R. Caferra and G. Salzer (Eds.): Automated Deduction, LNAI 1761, pp. 221–235, 2000.

resolution on standard clauses. Then the completeness for (general) c-clauses is shown by proving the *lifting property* of c-factoring and (possibly refined) c-resolution.

However, one is not contented with the purely refutational calculus. In order to increase the efficiency, rules for deleting "redundant" clauses (e.g.: tautologies and subsumed clauses) have to be added to the inference system. But this deletion of (c-)clauses may, in principle, destroy the completeness of the original refutational calculus. Hence, the compatibility of the deletion rules incorporated into the inference system with the original refutational rules is not trivial and must be proven separately for every refutational calculus, e.g.: in [10] the completeness of hyperresolution and of A-ordering resolution, respectively, when combined with tautology deletion and subsumption is proven for standard clauses.

The classical deletion rules in standard clause logic aim at the deletion of the "whole" clause, if it is detected to be redundant. Of course, these concepts of redundancy elimination can be easily translated to c-clause logic. However, the additional expressive power provided by c-clause logic not only allows the deletion of redundant c-clauses as a whole but also the deletion of redundant "parts" of a c-clause by introducing additional constraints. This is what the so-called model construction rules defined by Caferra et al. actually do (cf. [6]).

Obviously, on the one hand, the additional power of the deletion rules will, in general, make the resulting inference system on c-clauses more efficient (if we take into account only the number of derived clauses and if we do not care about the actual cost for checking the redundancy), since the deletion of only parts of the ground instances of a c-clause may already suffice to prevent the deduction of certain resolvents. On the other hand, the refutational completeness of the resulting inference system is by no means trivial. An example in Section 4 illustrates that the completeness proof in [10] for A-ordering resolution together with subsumption is no longer valid if c-dissubsumption is applied. Hence, the original proof idea for the purely refutational calculus (i.e.: first proving the ground completeness and then the lifting property) will no longer suffice and, therefore, a different strategy for the completeness proof is called for. To this end, we shall extend the well-known concept of semantic trees to c-clause logic.

In general, purely non-deterministic application of the inference rules is not sufficient to ensure refutational completeness. It is intuitively clear, that some sort of "fairness" must be required. The completeness proof via semantic trees gives us a hint for defining an appropriate rule application strategy, thus making the concept of "fairness" precise. The principal result of this work is summarized in Definition 3.2 and Theorem 3.2, i.e.: a precise definition of an inference system based on a c-resolution refinement and a sufficient criterion for its refutational completeness. Theorem 3.2 can then be applied to prove the completeness of inference systems based on two common c-resolution refinements, namely semantic clash c-resolution and A-ordering c-resolution (cf. Theorem 3.3).

In [7], the concept of H-subsumption was introduced, which is a much stronger redundancy criterion than the familiar subsumption rule. Example 4.2 shows that in general the usual completeness proof for resolution refinements with subsumption no longer works, if H-subsumption is applied. However, by showing that H-subsumption is a special case of the c-dissubsumption rule of Caferra et al., the completeness of semantic clash resolution or A-ordering resolution in combination with H-subsumption is an immediate consequence of Theorem 3.3.

Finally the completeness criterion via semantic trees and the rules for redundancy elimination of Caferra et al. are compared with other approaches in the literature. In particular, it is shown that the redundancy criteria within the ordering-based approaches of Bachmair/Ganzinger (cf. [2]) and Nieuwenhuis/Rubio (cf. [11]) are incomparable with c-dissubsumption, i.e.: There exist clauses which may be deleted by the redundancy criteria from [2] and [11] but which cannot be deleted by c-dissubsumption, and vice versa.

This work is structured as follows: In Section 2, some principal aspects of the rule system of Caferra et al. and the concept of semantic trees are revised very briefly. In Section 3, the completeness of inference sytsems based on some c-resolution refinement and the non-refutational rules of Caferra et al. is investigated. In Section 4, subsumption on standard clauses is revisited. Finally, in Section 5, the completeness criterion via semantic trees and the rules for redundancy elimination of Caferra et al. are compared with other approaches in the literature. In Section 6, the main results of this work are summarized and directions for future research are indicated.

2 Basic Concepts

2.1 Equational Problems and Constrained Clauses

As far as constrained clause logic is concerned, we shall follow the approach of Caferra et al. (cf. [6] and [5]), who in turn make use of equational problems in the sense of [3]). Hence, in this section, we shall revise very briefly some basic definitions and results on equational problems and constrained clauses, which are needed in the subsequent sections. For any details, the original papers (in particular, [3] and [6]) have to be referred to.

Recall from [3], that an *equational problem* is defined as a formula of the form $\exists \boldsymbol{w} \forall \boldsymbol{y} \mathcal{P}(\boldsymbol{w}, \boldsymbol{x}, \boldsymbol{y})$, where $\mathcal{P}(\boldsymbol{w}, \boldsymbol{x}, \boldsymbol{y})$ is a quantifier-free formula with equality "=" as the only predicate symbol. Without loss of generality, we can assume that $\mathcal{P}(\boldsymbol{w}, \boldsymbol{x}, \boldsymbol{y})$ is in negation normal form, i.e.: every occurrence of the negation symbol $\neg$ has been shifted directly in front of an equation. By writing a negated equation $\neg(s = t)$ as a disequation $s \neq t$, all occurrences of the negation symbol can be eliminated. The trivially true problem is denoted by $\top$ and the trivially false one by $\bot$.

In the context of constrained clauses in the sense of [6], equational problems are only interpreted over the free term algebra. Furthermore, variables of a single sort are considered, i.e.: they may only take values from the same Herbrand universe H. A Herbrand interpretation over H is given through an H-ground substitution σ, whose domain coincides with the free variables of the equational problem. The trivial problem $\top$ evaluates to **T** in every interpretation. Likewise, $\bot$ always evaluates to **F**. A single equation $s = t$ is validated by a ground substitution σ, if $s\sigma$ and $t\sigma$ are syntactically identical. Analogously, a single disequation $s \neq t$ is validated by σ, if $s\sigma$ and $t\sigma$ are syntactically different. The interpretation of the connectives $\wedge$, $\vee$, $\exists$ and $\forall$ is as usual. A ground substitution σ which validates an equational problem $\mathcal{P}$ is called a *solution*. In contrast to the papers of Caferra et al., we distinguish between the notation "$\equiv$" (to denote syntactical identity of equational problems) and "$\approx$" (for the equivalence of equational problems).

In [6], *constrained clauses* (c-clauses, for short) are defined as pairs $[c : \mathcal{P}]$, where c is a clause and $\mathcal{P}$ is an equational problem. Intuitively, $[c : \mathcal{P}]$ denotes the set $c\sigma$ of ground clauses, where σ is a ground solution of $\mathcal{P}$. Two c-clauses $[c : \mathcal{P}]$ and $[d : \mathcal{Q}]$ are equivalent, iff they represent the same set of ground instances. In [6], the equivalence of two c-clauses is denoted by $[c : \mathcal{P}] \equiv [d : \mathcal{Q}]$.

A *Herbrand interpretation* $\mathcal{I}$ w.r.t. some Herbrand universe H is given by a subset $\mathcal{I}(P) \subseteq H^n$ for every n-ary predicate symbol P. A ground atom $P(\boldsymbol{s})$ evaluates to **T** in $\mathcal{I}$, iff $\boldsymbol{s} \in \mathcal{I}(P)$. The generalization to negative ground literals $\neg P(\boldsymbol{s})$ and to ground clauses $L_1(\boldsymbol{s}_1) \vee \ldots \vee L_n(\boldsymbol{s}_n)$ follows from the usual interpretation of $\neg$ and $\vee$. A c-clause $[c : \mathcal{P}]$ evaluates to **T** in $\mathcal{I}$, iff $c\sigma$ evaluates to **T** for every ground solution σ of $\mathcal{P}$. The evaluation of a c-clause $[c : \mathcal{P}]$ to **T** in an interpretation $\mathcal{I}$ is denoted by $\mathcal{I} \models [c : \mathcal{P}]$.

2.2 A Rule System on Constrained Clauses

Caferra et al. defined a calculus based on unrefined c-resolution for constrained clauses (cf. [6]) which was then further developed to c-resolution refinements like semantic c-resolution and semantic clash c-resolution (cf. [4] and [5]). Furthermore, ordering refinements were already discussed in the original paper [6]. Analogously to standard clause logic, many more c-resolution refinements are conceivable. Throughout this paper, we shall therefore use the notation cRes_x to denote an arbitrary c-resolution refinement.

The calculus of Caferra et al. comprises 3 kinds of rules, namely refutational rules, model construction rules and structural rules. The rule definitions of the refutational rules and of those model construction rules which aim at the deletion of parts of c-clauses, play the most important role as far as completeness is concerned. Their definition is recalled below. In contrast to the cDtaut- and cDsub-rule, the other model construction rules (i.e.: the cDfact-, cDres-, GPL-, EGPL-, GMPL-rule) and the structural rules do not delete any ground instances of c-clauses, i.e.: The cDfact-rule and the cDres-rule replace a c-clause by two new c-clauses which contain together exactly the same set of ground instances as the original c-clause. Moreover, the GPL-, EGPL- and GMPL-rule add new c-clauses and the structural rules allow the transformation of a c-clause into an equivalent c-clause. For details on these rules, the original papers have to be referred to (e.g.: [6], [4], [5]).

Definition 2.1.(Refutational Rules and Redundancy Elimination Rules) *Let $H(\mathcal{C})$ be a fixed Herbrand universe. Then the rules cFact, cRes, cDtaut and cDsub are defined as follows:*

1. *(Binary) c-factorization: ¿From the c-clause $C = [L(\overline{s}) \vee L(\overline{t}) \vee c : X]$ over the Herbrand universe $H(\mathcal{C})$, the following c-clause may be derived:*

$$\frac{[L(\overline{s}) \vee L(\overline{t}) \vee c : X]}{[L(\overline{s}) \vee c : X \wedge \overline{s} = \overline{t}]} \quad cFact(C)$$

2. *c-resolution: Let $C_1 = [L(\overline{s}) \vee c : X]$ and $C_2 = [L^d(\overline{t}) \vee d : Y]$ be c-clauses over $H(\mathcal{C})$. Then the following c-clause may be derived:*

$$\frac{[L(\overline{s}) \vee c : X] \qquad [L^d(\overline{t}) \vee d : Y]}{[c \vee d : X \wedge Y \wedge \overline{s} = \overline{t}]} \quad cRes(C_1, C_2)$$

3. *c-distautology: Let $C = [L_{i_1}(\overline{s}_{i_1}) \vee L_{i_2}(\overline{s}_{i_2}) \vee c : X]$ be a c-clause over $H(\mathcal{C})$, where the order of the literals is chosen s.t. the first 2 literal symbols are complementary, i.e.: $L_{i_1} = L^d_{i_2}$. By the c-distautology rule, the original c-clause C may be replaced by the following c-clause "cDtaut(C)":*

$$\frac{[L_{i_1}(\overline{s}_{i_1}) \vee L_{i_2}(\overline{s}_{i_2}) \vee c : X]}{[L_{i_1}(\overline{s}_{i_1}) \vee L_{i_2}(\overline{s}_{i_2}) \vee c : X \wedge \overline{s}_{i_1} \neq \overline{s}_{i_2}]}$$

4. *c-dissubsumption: Let $C_1 = [L_1(\overline{s}_1) \vee \ldots \vee L_n(\overline{s}_n) : X]$ be a c-clause over $H(\mathcal{C})$ with a fixed order of the literals and let $\overline{x}$ denote the free variables of the constraint X. Furthermore let $C_2 = [M_{i_1}(\overline{t}_{i_1}) \vee \ldots \vee M_{i_n}(\overline{t}_{i_n}) \vee c : Y]$ be c-clause over $H(\mathcal{C})$ with some appropriately chosen order of the literals, s.t. the literal symbols L_j and M_{i_j} are identical. Then, by the c-dissubsumption rule, the original c-clause C_2 may be replaced by the following c-clause "cDsub(C_1, C_2)":*

$$\frac{[L_1(\overline{s}_1) \vee \ldots \vee L_n(\overline{s}_n) : X] \qquad [M_{i_1}(\overline{t}_{i_1}) \vee \ldots \vee M_{i_n}(\overline{t}_{i_n}) \vee c : Y]}{[M_{i_1}(\overline{t}_{i_1}) \vee \ldots \vee M_{i_n}(\overline{t}_{i_n}) \vee c : Y \wedge Z]}$$

   where $Z \equiv \neg(\exists \overline{x})(X \wedge \overline{s}_1 = \overline{t}_{i_1} \wedge \ldots \wedge \overline{s}_n = \overline{t}_{i_n})$.

The 2 redundancy elimination rules defined above have the following meaning: The cDtaut-rule eliminates all tautological ground instances $C\tau$ from the original c-clause C. Likewise, the cDsub-rule allows the deletion of those ground instances $C_2\tau$ from C_2, which are subsumed by the c-clause C_1.

2.3 Semantic Trees in c-clause Logic

In [9], the concept of *semantic trees* is introduced and several definitions like *failure node, inference node* and *closed semantic tree* are given for standard clause logic. Since these definitions can be taken over almost literally from standard clauses to c-clauses, they are not repeated here. Definition 2.2 of completeness via semantic trees is slightly modified w.r.t. the original definition in [9].

Definition 2.2. (Completeness via Semantic Trees) *Let $cRes_x$ be a c-resolution refinement. Then $cRes_x$ is called* complete via semantic trees, *iff for every unsatisfiable set of c-clauses $\mathcal{C}$ the following conditions hold:*

1. *There is a finite semantic tree T with some particular property $\mathcal{P}$, s.t. T is closed for $\mathcal{C}$.*
2. *Let T be a closed, finite semantic tree T with property $\mathcal{P}$. Then there is an inference node N in T and there are c-clauses $C_1, \ldots, C_k$ in $\mathcal{C}$ which fail at nodes $N_1, \ldots, N_k$ immediately below N but not at N itself, s.t. there is a c-clause D which is derived by $cRes_x$ from c-factors of $C_1, \ldots, C_k$ and which fails at N.*
3. *The semantic tree which results from deleting the nodes immediately below N from T (N, T according to condition 2 above) can be reduced to a semantic tree T' which is closed for $\mathcal{C} \cup \{D\}$ and which again has property $\mathcal{P}$.*

Although our Definition 2.2 differs slightly from the one given in [9], the following theorem on the relationship between refutational completeness and completeness via semantic trees can be proven by exactly the same ideas as Theorem 2 in [9].

Theorem 2.1. (Refutational Completeness) *Let $cRes_x$ be a c-resolution refinement which is complete via semantic trees. Then $cRes_x$ is refutationally complete, i.e.: for every unsatisfiable set $\mathcal{C}$ of c-clauses the empty c-clause $\underline{\square}$ can be derived in the refutational calculus consisting of the cFact-rule and the $cRes_x$-rule (and, possibly, structural rules).*

3 Complete Inference Systems

By Theorem 2.1, completeness via semantic trees is a sufficient criterion for the completeness of the purely refutational calculus. In order to investigate the effect of the non-refutational rules of Caferra et al. on a closed semantic tree, we introduce a binary relation "$\Rightarrow$" on c-clauses in a derivation. Roughly speaking, "$C \Rightarrow D$" means that C is either replaced by D or c-dissubsumed by D. In Theorem 3.1 we shall show that, whenever a c-clause C, that fails at some node N, is deleted through a non-refutational rule, then there is a c-clause D, s.t. $C \Rightarrow D$ and D fails at N.

Definition 3.1. (Relations "$\Rightarrow$" and "$\Rightarrow^*$") *Let $\mathcal{C}_0, \mathcal{C}_1, \ldots$ be the sets of c-clauses in a derivation. We define a binary relation "$\Rightarrow$" on c-clauses as follows: Suppose that for some c-clause C there exists an $i \geq 0$ s.t. $C \in \mathcal{C}_i$ but $C \notin \mathcal{C}_{i+1}$. Then we distinguish 2 cases:*

1. *c-dissubsumption is applied to C: Suppose that there is a c-clause $D \in \mathcal{C}_i$ s.t. the cDsub-rule w.r.t. D is applied to C and $C' = cDsub(D, C)$. Then $C \Rightarrow D$ and $C \Rightarrow C'$.*
2. *Any other non-refutational rule is applied to C: If there is a single c-clause $C' \in \mathcal{C}_{i+1}$ s.t. C is replaced by C', then $C \Rightarrow C'$. Likewise, if C is replaced by 2 c-clauses $C_1, C_2 \in \mathcal{C}_{i+1}$, then $C \Rightarrow C_1$ and $C \Rightarrow C_2$.*

By "$\Rightarrow^*$" we denote the reflexive and transitive closure of the relation "$\Rightarrow$".

Theorem 3.1. (Effect of Non-refutational Rules) *Let $\mathcal{C}$ be an unsatisfiable set of c-clauses and T be a finite semantic tree which is closed for $\mathcal{C}$. Let $C \in \mathcal{C}$ be a c-clause which fails at a leaf node N of T. Furthermore suppose that $\mathcal{C}'$ is obtained from $\mathcal{C}$ by applying some model construction rule (i.e.: cDtaut, cDsub, cDfact, cDres) or structural rule to C s.t. $C \notin \mathcal{C}'$. Then there is a c-clause $D \in \mathcal{C}'$, s.t. $C \Rightarrow D$ and D fails at N.*

Proof (Sketch): Note that failure of a c-clause C at some node N only depends on the set of ground instances contained in C and not on a specific representation of C. The structural rules leave the set of ground instances of a c-clause unchanged. The model construction rules of c-disfactorization and c-disresolution replace the original c-clause C by 2 new c-clauses C_1 and C_2 s.t. the ground instances of C are partitioned into the 2 sets of ground instances of C_1 and C_2. Therefore, we only consider c-distautolgy and c-dissubsumption here, since these are the only rules which lead to the actual deletion of ground instances. Let $C = [c : X]$ and let $c\sigma$ be an instance of C which fails at N.

1. cDtaut: Suppose that C is replaced by the c-clause $C' = \text{cDtaut}(C) = [c : X \wedge Y]$. But a tautology cannot fail at any node and, hence, the ground instance $c\sigma$ is still contained in C'. Furthermore, by Definition 3.1, $C \Rightarrow C'$.
2. cDsub: Suppose that some of the instances of C are deleted by applying the cDsub-rule to C w.r.t. some c-clause $D \in \mathcal{C}$. Then, by Definition 3.1, $C \Rightarrow D$ and $C \Rightarrow C'$, where $C' = cDsub(D, C)$. We have to distinguish 2 cases:
   (a) If $c\sigma$ is not among the deleted ground instances, then the resulting c-clause C' still fails at N.
   (b) If $D = [d : Y]$ subsumes $c\sigma$, then there exists a ground instance $d\tau$ of D, s.t. all literals of $d\tau$ are contained in the literals of $c\sigma$. But then $d\tau$ fails at any node at which $c\sigma$ fails. Hence, also D fails at N. ◇

We are now ready to formulate the main result of this work, namely a precise definition of an inference system in constrained clause logic (including, in particular, a concrete definition of the notion of "fairness") and a sufficient condition for its refutational completeness (cf. Definition 3.2 and Theorem 3.2):

Definition 3.2. (Inference System Based on a c-resolution Refinement) *Let $cRes_x$ be a c-resolution refinement. Then we define the inference system $\mathcal{I}_x$ through the following rule system and rule application strategy.*

- **Rule system:**
  1. *Refutational rules: cFact, $cRes_x$*
  2. *Model construction rules: cDsub, cDtaut, cDfact, cDres*
  3. *Structural rules: normalization rules, variable elimination rules*
- **Rule application strategy:**
  The rules may be applied non-deterministically. However, the following 3 restrictions must be complied with:

1. *Fairness w.r.t. $cRes_x$: Suppose that the current c-clause set $\mathcal{C}_t$ at some stage in the deduction process contains the c-clauses $C_1, \ldots, C_k$ to which $cRes_x$ can be applied. Then, after a finite number of steps, the $cRes_x$-resolvent D of appropriate c-factors $C'_1, \ldots, C'_k$ must be actually derived. If a c-resolution step is due and some c-clause C_i is no longer contained in the new c-clause set $\mathcal{C}_{t'}$, then all $cRes_x$-resolvents which exist for (c-factors of) $D_1, \ldots, D_k$ have to be derived instead, where $D_i \in \mathcal{C}_{t'}$ and $C_i \Rightarrow^* D_i$.*
2. *Availability of appropriate c-factors: If a resolution step is to be carried out on the c-clauses $C_1, \ldots, C_k$, then appropriate c-factors must be available, i.e.: If L_i is the literal to be resolved upon in c-clause C_i, then all c-factors of C_i which result from unifying L_i with any subset of literals in C_i have to be derived before.*
3. *Normalization of the empty clause: If a c-clause $[\Box, X]$ is derived, s.t. $X \not\approx \bot$, then the normalization rule yielding the empty clause $\underline{\Box}$ has to be applied.*

Remark: The above condition of "fairness w.r.t. cRes_x" of a rule application strategy is a generalization of the usual level saturation strategy, i.e.: A c-clause set $\mathcal{C}_i$ is transformed to the set $\mathcal{C}_{i+1}$ by first deriving all possible (refined) c-resolvents from $\mathcal{C}_i$ and then simplifying the resulting set by finitely many applications of structural and model construction rules.

Theorem 3.2. (Completeness of an Inference System Based on a c-resolution Refinement) *Let $cRes_x$ be a c-resolution refinement and $\mathcal{I}_x$ be the inference system based on $cRes_x$ according to Definition 3.2. If $cRes_x$ is* complete via semantic trees, *then the inference system $\mathcal{I}_x$ is* refutationally complete, *i.e.: If $\mathcal{C}$ is an unsatisfiable set of c-clauses and the rules of $\mathcal{I}_x$ are applied to $\mathcal{C}$ according to the rule application strategy of $\mathcal{I}_x$, then eventually the empty c-clause $\underline{\Box}$ is derived.*

Proof (Sketch): Let $\mathcal{C}$ be an unsatisfiable set of c-clauses. By assumption, the c-resolution refinement cRes_x is complete via semantic trees. Hence, by condition 1 of Definition 2.2, there is a finite semantic tree T with some particular property $\mathcal{P}$, s.t. T is closed for $\mathcal{C}$. We prove the refutational completeness of $\mathcal{I}_x$ by induction on the number of nodes n of T:

If T has 1 node (i.e.: T consists of the root node only), then some c-clause in $\mathcal{C}$ must fail at the root of T. But only a c-clause of the form $[\Box, X] \in \mathcal{C}$ with $X \not\approx \bot$ can fail at the root node. By condition 3 of the rule application strategy, we have to apply the normalization rule, thus deriving the empty c-clause $\underline{\Box}$.

If T has $n > 1$ nodes then by condition 2 of Definition 2.2, there is an inference node N in T and there are c-clauses $C_1, \ldots, C_k$ in $\mathcal{C}$ which fail immediately below N s.t. there is a c-clause D derivable by cRes_x from c-factors of $C_1, \ldots, C_k$, s.t. D fails at N. According to condition 1 of the rule application strategy, this resolution step eventually has to be carried out. Now suppose that some c-clause C_i is deleted prior to this resolution step. Then Theorem 3.1 together with a simple induction argument guarantees the existence of a c-clause D_i in the current c-clause set, s.t. $C_i \Rightarrow^* D_i$ and either D_i fails at N or D_i can take the place of C_i in the resolution step at the inference node N. In the latter case, the rule application strategy requires that this resolution step be actually carried out. But this leads to a closed semantic tree with less than n nodes, to which the induction hypothesis can be applied. ◇

We now put Theorem 3.2 to work by applying it to inference systems based on two common c-resolution refinements, namely semantic clash resolution and A-ordering resolution. For a precise definition of these resolution refinements on c-clauses, cf. [5] and [11], respectively.

Theorem 3.3. (Complete Inference Systems) *Let H be a Herbrand universe. Furthermore let $\mathcal{M}$ be an interpretation over H and let $<_A$ be an A-ordering over H. Then the inference systems $\mathcal{I}_{\mathcal{M}}$ and $\mathcal{I}_{<_A}$ based on the c-resolution refinements $cRes_{\mathcal{M}}$ and $cRes_{<_A}$, respectively, are refutationally complete.*

Proof (Sketch): By Theorem 3.2 it suffices to prove that $cRes_{\mathcal{M}}$ and $cRes_{<_A}$ are complete via semantic trees. But the completeness proof for semantic clash resolution and A-ordering resolution on standard clauses given in [9] can be easily extended to c-clauses. ◇

4 Subsumption on Standard Clauses

The c-dissubsumption rule defined for c-clauses in Definition 2.1 restricts the admissible set of ground instances of a c-clause by strengthening the constraints. To this aim, usually, new disequations are added. In some cases this introduction of disequations can be simulated in standard clause logic by replacing the original clause through an appropriate instance thereof. However, in general, this kind of simulation is not possible. Example 4.1 shows both cases.

Example 4.1. Let $\mathcal{C} = \{C_1, C_2, C_3, C_4, C_5\}$ be a clause set over the Herbrand universe $H(\Sigma)$ with $\Sigma = \{a, f, P, Q\}$, and let the C_i's be defined as follows:

$$C_1 = P(x,y) \vee Q(x,y) \qquad C_3 = P(x,x) \qquad C_5 = \neg P(a, f(a))$$
$$C_2 = P(x,a) \qquad C_4 = \neg Q(a, f(a))$$

The clause C_1 corresponds to the c-clause $[P(x,y) \vee Q(x,y) : \top]$ and C_2 to $[P(x,a) : \top]$. An application of the cDsub-rule yields the c-clause $cDsub(C_2, C_1)$ $= [P(x,y) \vee Q(x,y) : y \neq a] = [P(x,y) \vee Q(x,y) : (\exists z) y = f(z)]$, which corresponds to the standard clause $P(x, f(z)) \vee Q(x, f(z))$.

On the other hand, c-dissubsumption w.r.t. $[P(x,x) : \top]$ allows us to restrict the original c-clause $[P(x,y) \vee Q(x,y) : \top]$ to $[P(x,y) \vee Q(x,y) : x \neq y]$. But neither may the original clause $P(x,y) \vee Q(x,y)$ be deleted completely (without destroying the completeness) nor can the resulting c-clause be represented by a finite set of standard clauses.

Hence, the c-dissubsumption rule given in Definition 2.1 is naturally more powerful than an analogous subsumption rule defined on standard clauses. But even if the application of c-dissubsumption is restricted to cases where it leads to the actual deletion of the subsumed clause, the resulting rule is still more powerful than the usual subsumption rule in standard clause logic. The subsumption concept obtained from restricting c-dissubsumption to actual clause deletion in standard clause logic is the so-called *H-subsumption* (a term coined in [7] in order to emphasize, that this subsumption concept is parameterized by a specific Herbrand universe H), i.e.: Let $\mathcal{C}$ be a set of clauses over the Herbrand universe H and D be a clause over H. Then H-subsumption is defined as follows: $\mathcal{C} \leq^H_{ss} D$ $\Leftrightarrow$ "$\mathcal{C}$ H-subsumes D" $\Leftrightarrow$ there exists a finite subset $\mathcal{C}'$ of $\mathcal{C}$ s.t. for all ground substitutions τ based on H, there is a clause $C \in \mathcal{C}'$ s.t. $C \leq_{ss} D\tau$.

Analogously to the combination of resolution refinements with the usual subsumption rule, resolution refinements can be combined with H-subsumption. However, the usual proof found in the literature for the completeness of A-ordering resolution and semantic clash resolution together with ordinary subsumption cannot be simply extended to H-subsumption. This is due to the fact that the following lemma, which plays a crucial role in the usual completeness proof, no longer works, if H-subsumption is used.

Lemma 4.1. *Let Res_x denote the set of clauses derivable either by A-ordering resolution or by semantic clash resolution. Furthermore let $\mathcal{C}' \leq_{ss} \mathcal{C}$ and $D \in Res_x(\mathcal{C})$. Then $\mathcal{C}' \cup Res_x(\mathcal{C}') \leq_{ss} D$, i.e.: either $\mathcal{C}' \leq_{ss} D$ or there is an R_x-resolvent $D' \in Res_x(\mathcal{C}')$ s.t. $D' \leq_{ss} D$.*

Proof: cf. [10], Theorem 4.2.1 and Lemma 4.2.3

The following counter-example shows, that the above lemma does not hold for H-subsumption, i.e.: Even though $\mathcal{C}' \leq^H_{ss} \mathcal{C}$ and $D \in Res_x(\mathcal{C})$, then D is not necessarily H-subsumed by $\mathcal{C}' \cup Res_x(\mathcal{C}')$.

Example 4.2. Let $\mathcal{C}' = \{C_1, C_2, C_3, C_4, C_5\}$ and $\mathcal{C} = \{C_6, C_7\}$ be clause sets over the Herbrand universe $H(\Sigma)$ with $\Sigma = \{a, f, P, Q, R\}$, and let the C_i's be defined as follows:

$$C_1 = P(f(x)) \qquad C_4 = R(a) \qquad C_6 = P(x) \vee Q(x)$$
$$C_2 = Q(a) \qquad C_5 = R(f^2(x)) \qquad C_7 = \neg Q(x) \vee R(y)$$
$$C_3 = \neg Q(x) \vee R(f(a))$$

Let $<_d$ be the well-known A-ordering defined on the term depth and the maximal depth of variable occurrences (cf. [10], Example 3.3.1) and let the interpretation $\mathcal{M}$ be given through the atom representation $\mathcal{M} := \{P(x), Q(x), R(f(a))\}$.

Then $C_8 = P(x) \vee R(y)$ is an $R_{<_d}$-resolvent and an $R_{\mathcal{M}}$-resolvent of C_6 and C_7, but C_8 is neither H-subsumed by $\mathcal{C}' \cup Res_{<_d}(\mathcal{C}')$ nor by $\mathcal{C}' \cup Res_{\mathcal{M}}(\mathcal{C}')$. Note that this is due to the fact that the (unrefined) resolvent $R(f(a)) \in Res(C_2, C_3)$ is neither an $R_{<_d}$-resolvent nor an $R_{\mathcal{M}}$-resolvent.

However, with Theorem 3.3 at our disposal, the completeness of A-ordering resolution and semantic clash resolution with H-subsumption is a simple corollary.

5 Ordering-Based Redundancy Criteria

Bachmair and Ganzinger introduced a general framework for proving the completeness of an inference system (cf. [2]). Within this framework, they also provide an abstract redundancy criterion, which allows the deletion of clauses while preserving the refutational completeness of the calculus. Their ideas were further developed by Nieuwenhuis and Rubio (cf. [11]). In particular, they modified the redundancy criterion to allow for slightly more powerful deletion rules and to provide a general pattern for completeness proofs.

Both the criteria of Bachmair/Ganzinger and of Nieuwenhuis/Rubio aim at the deletion of the whole clause, rather than just the redundant parts. Hence, as Example 4.1 in Section 4 already illustrated, the power of deletion rules based on these criteria naturally cannot compare with the power of the deletion rules given in Definition 2.1. But then the question arises as to whether the deletion rules from Section 2.2 are still more powerful, if we restrict their application to those cases where they lead to the actual deletion of the whole clause. In particular, the cDsub-rule then collapses to the H-subsumption discussed in Section 4. We shall show in this section, that both redundancy criteria from [2] and from [11] are incomparable with H-subsumption.

In [2], the following concrete redundancy criterion (based on an abstract criterion not discussed here) is defined: A ground clause C is redundant w.r.t. a clause set $\mathcal{C}$, if there exist ground instances $C_1, \ldots, C_n$ of clauses in $\mathcal{C}$ s.t.: $C_1, \ldots, C_n \models C$ and $C_i < C$ for all i. A non-ground clause C is redundant w.r.t. a clause set $\mathcal{C}$, if all its ground instances are redundant.

In order to deal with subsumption, ground instances of clauses are considered as pairs consisting of the original clause and the instantiating substitution. An ordering on clauses covering subsumption can then be defined as follows:

$$(C, \sigma) < (D, \tau) :\Leftrightarrow \begin{array}{l} 1.\ C\sigma < D\tau \text{ or} \\ 2.\ C\sigma = D\tau \text{ and } C \text{ properly subsumes } D. \end{array}$$

The following two propositions show, that the redundancy criterion of Bachmair/Ganzinger is incomparable with H-subsumption:

Proposition 5.1. (H-subsumed Clause) *There is a clause set $\mathcal{C}$ and a clause $C \in \mathcal{C}$, s.t. C may be deleted by H-subsumption but C is not redundant by the criterion of Bachmair/Ganzinger.*

Proof (Sketch): Consider the clause set $\mathcal{C} = \{C_1, C_2, C_3, C_4\}$ over the Herbrand universe $H(\Sigma)$ with $\Sigma = \{a, f, P\}$, where the C_i's are defined as follows:

$$\begin{array}{ll} C_1 = P(x, f(y)) & C_3 = P(a, f(x)) \\ C_2 = P(f(x), y) & C_4 = P(f(x), a) \end{array}$$

Then both relations $\{C_1, C_4\} \leq_{ss}^{H} C_2$ and $\{C_2, C_3\} \leq_{ss}^{H} C_1$ hold.

Note that C_1 and C_2 have the common ground instance $P(f(a), f(a))$, i.e.: $C_1\sigma_1 = C_2\sigma_2$, where $\sigma_1 = \{x \leftarrow f(a), y \leftarrow a\}$ and $\sigma_2 = \{x \leftarrow a, y \leftarrow f(a)\}$.

By the transitivity and irreflexivity of $<$, it is impossible that both inequalities $(C_1, \sigma_1) < (C_2, \sigma_2)$ and $(C_2, \sigma_2) < (C_1, \sigma_1)$ are true. Hence, either C_1 or C_2 is not redundant in the sense of [2], although this clause may be deleted by H-subsumption. ◇

Proposition 5.2. (Redundant Clause) *There is a clause set $\mathcal{C}$ and a clause $C \in \mathcal{C}$, s.t. C is redundant by the criterion of Bachmair/Ganzinger but C may not be deleted by H-subsumption.*

Proof (Sketch): Consider the clause set $\mathcal{C} = \{C_1, C_2, C_3\}$ over the Herbrand universe $H(\Sigma)$ with $\Sigma = \{a, f, P, Q, R, S\}$, where the C_i's are defined as follows:

$$C_1 = P(a) \vee Q(f(a)) \qquad C_3 = Q(f(a)) \vee R(f(a)) \vee S(f(a))$$
$$C_2 = \neg P(a) \vee R(f(a))$$

Then C_3 is clearly implied by C_1 and C_2, since $Q(f(a)) \vee R(f(a)) \models C_3$ and $Q(f(a)) \vee R(f(a))$ is an unrefined resolvent of C_1 and C_2. Hence, C_3 is redundant by the criterion of Bachmair/Ganzinger. On the other hand, C_3 is not H-subsumed by $\{C_1, C_2\}$. ◇

The definition of an inference system (and, in particular, of redundancy criteria) in [11] is an abstraction from the Bachmair/Ganzinger approach sketched above. We shall briefly revise the prinicipal concepts of the Nieuwenhuis/Rubio approach and then compare the power of their redundancy criteria with H-subsumption.

Let $RC(\mathcal{C})$ denote the redundant clauses and let $RI(\mathcal{C})$ denote the redundant inferences w.r.t. the clause set $\mathcal{C}$. The pair (RC,RI) of redundancy criteria is called *correct*, if the following conditions hold:

1. $RC(\mathcal{C}) \subset RC(\mathcal{C} \cup \mathcal{D})$ and $RI(\mathcal{C}) \subset RI(\mathcal{C} \cup \mathcal{D})$ for any clause sets $\mathcal{C}$ and $\mathcal{D}$.
2. $RC(\mathcal{C}_j) \subset RC(\mathcal{C}_\infty)$ and $RI(\mathcal{C}_j) \subset RI(\mathcal{C}_\infty)$ for any theorem proving derivation $\mathcal{C}_0, \mathcal{C}_1, \ldots$ and any $j \geq 0$.

Let the sequence of clause sets $\mathcal{C}_0, \mathcal{C}_1, \ldots$ be a *theorem proving derivation*, i.e.: $\mathcal{C}_{i+1}$ is obtained from $\mathcal{C}_i$ by either adding a new clause via an inference rule or by deleting a clause via the redundancy criterion RC. The set $\mathcal{C}_\infty$ of *persisting clauses* is defined as $\mathcal{C}_\infty := \bigcup_j (\bigcap_{k \geq j} \mathcal{C}_k)$. The theorem proving derivation is called *fair*, if every inference π from $\mathcal{C}_\infty = \bigcup_j (\bigcap_{k \geq j} \mathcal{C}_k)$ is redundant w.r.t. some $\mathcal{C}_j$.

Analogously to the Bachmair/Ganzinger approach, concrete redundancy criteria RC and RI are defined in [11]:

- A ground clause C is in $RC(\mathcal{C})$, if there exist ground instances $C_1, \ldots, C_n$ of clauses in $\mathcal{C}$ s.t.: $C_1, \ldots, C_n \models C$ and $C_i \leq C$ for all i. A non-ground clause C is redundant w.r.t. a clause set $\mathcal{C}$, if all its ground instances are in $RC(\mathcal{C})$.
- Let π be a ground inference with conclusion C and maximal premise D. Then π is in $RI(\mathcal{C})$, if there exist ground instances $C_1, \ldots, C_n$ of clauses in $\mathcal{C}$ s.t.: $C_1, \ldots, C_n \models C$ and $C_i < D$ for all i. A non-ground inference π is redundant w.r.t. a clause set $\mathcal{C}$, if all its ground instances are in $RI(\mathcal{C})$.

The concrete redundancy criterion RC is slightly more powerful than the one of Bachmair/Ganzinger (since it allows ground clauses smaller than or equal to the redundant clause rather than strictly smaller clauses). Therefore, Proposition 5.2 also provides an example of a clause which is redundant in the sense of [11] but not H-subsumed. The opposite case is established by the following proposition:

Proposition 5.3. (H-subsumed Clause) *There is a derivation sequence* $\mathcal{C}_0$, $\mathcal{C}_1, \ldots$ *and a clause* $C \in \bigcup_{i \geq 0} \mathcal{C}_i$, *s.t.* C *may be deleted by H-subsumption but* C *is not redundant by a correct redundancy criterion in the sense of Nieuwenhuis/Rubio.*

Proof (Sketch): Suppose that there is a redundancy criterion RC that covers H-subsumption. Consider the clause set $\mathcal{C} = \{C_1, \ldots, C_5\}$ over the Herbrand universe $H(\Sigma)$ with $\Sigma = \{a, f, P\}$, where the C_i's are defined as follows:

$$\begin{array}{ll} C_1 = P(x, f(y)) & C_4 = \neg P(x, f(y)) \vee P(f(x), y) \\ C_2 = P(f(x), a) & C_5 = \neg P(f(x), y) \vee P(x, f(y)) \\ C_3 = P(a, f(x)) & \end{array}$$

Then the following resolvents can be derived:

$C_6 = Res(C_4, C_1) = P(f(x), y)$ and also $C_1 = Res(C_5, C_6) = P(x, f(y))$,
$C_4^{(n)} = \neg P(x, f^n(y)) \vee P(f^n(x), y)$ with $C_4^{(1)} = C_4$ and $C_4^{(n+1)} = Res(C_4^{(n)}, C_4)$,
$C_5^{(n)} = \neg P(f^n(x), y) \vee P(x, f^n(y))$ with $C_5^{(1)} = C_5$ and $C_5^{(n+1)} = Res(C_5^{(n)}, C_5)$.

Note that the relations $\{C_1, C_2\} \leq_{ss}^H C_6$ and $\{C_6, C_3\} \leq_{ss}^H C_1$ hold. Furthermore, all resolvents from either $C_4^{(n)}$ or $C_5^{(n)}$ with a clause from $\{C_1, C_2, C_3, C_6\}$ are H-subsumed by either C_1 or C_6, e.g.: $Res(C_4^{(n)}, C_1) = P(f^n(x), y)$ is an instance of C_6.

Then we can define the following theorem proving derivation:

$$\begin{array}{llll} & & \mathcal{C}_1 := \mathcal{C}_0 \cup \{C_6\}, & \mathcal{C}_2 := \mathcal{C}_1 - \{C_1\}, \\ \mathcal{C}_3 := \mathcal{C}_2 \cup \{C_4^{(2)}\}, & \mathcal{C}_4 := \mathcal{C}_3 \cup \{C_5^{(2)}\}, & \mathcal{C}_5 := \mathcal{C}_4 \cup \{C_1\}, & \mathcal{C}_6 := \mathcal{C}_5 - \{C_6\}, \\ \mathcal{C}_7 := \mathcal{C}_6 \cup \{C_4^{(3)}\}, & \mathcal{C}_8 := \mathcal{C}_7 \cup \{C_5^{(3)}\}, & \mathcal{C}_9 := \mathcal{C}_8 \cup \{C_6\}, & \mathcal{C}_{10} := \mathcal{C}_9 - \{C_1\}, \end{array}$$

etc.

Then $\mathcal{C}_\infty := \bigcup_j (\bigcap_{k \geq j} \mathcal{C}_k) = \{C_2, C_3\} \cup \{C_4^{(n)}, C_5^{(n)}; n \geq 1\}$. But the redundancy criterion RC is not correct, since $C_1 \in RC(\mathcal{C}_0) \not\subseteq RC(\mathcal{C}_\infty)$. However, the deletion of C_1 from $\mathcal{C}_1, \mathcal{C}_9, \ldots$ is clearly allowed by H-subsumption. ◇

Remarks:

- This kind of "oscillation" can be prevented by imposing the restriction, that no previously deleted clause may ever be derived again. By using a semantic tree argument similar to Section 3, it is trivial to prove that this restriction does not destroy the refutational completeness. However, it is not so clear how this restriction can be justified by an ordering argument, e.g.: In the sense of [2], neither the clause C_1 nor C_6 is redundant w.r.t. $\mathcal{C}$.

– Note that the concrete redundancy criterion RC from [11] actually does cover H-subsumption. However, the proof given for the correctness of the redundancy criteria in [11], Lemma 5.2. is slightly inaccurate, as was shown by Proposition 5.3 above.

6 Concluding Remarks and Future Work

First, the completeness of the calculus of Caferra et al. (including the redundancy elimination rules of c-dissubsumption and c-distautology) has been proven. This completeness result has then been carried over to H-subsumption in standard clause logic. The comparison with other redundancy concepts has basically shown that H-subsumption is a very strong redundancy criterion. In particular, the example from Proposition 5.2 of a clause that is not H-subsumed but redundant in the sense of Bachmair/Ganzinger and Nieuwenhuis/Rubio should not be overestimated: Actually, the "concrete" redundancy criterion of clause implication given in [2] and [11] is not really concrete, since it is not decidable on the non-ground level. Hence, even in cases where the criteria of [2] and [11] are stronger than H-subsumption, the latter criterion still seems to be about the strongest genuine concretisation of the abstract redundancy criteria that we can possibly expect. Future work should, therefore, concentrate on a thorough complexity analysis and on the design of an efficient algorithm for H-subsumption (and/or c-dissubsumption) rather than on the search for stronger concrete redundancy criteria.

The completeness proof in Section 3 was only carried out for c-clauses without equality. Likewise, the completeness of H-subsumption was only concluded for standard clauses without equality. In [8], the semantic tree method is extended to transfinite semantic trees so as to cover clauses with equality. Furthermore, some new definitions and a new proof strategy (namely, transfinite induction) are introduced to prove the completeness of several calculi using paramodulation and some refinements thereof via transfinite semantic trees. For details, [8] has to be referred to. However, analogously to Theorem 3.1, it can be shown that the "maximum consistent tree" does not grow when one of the non-refutational rules from Caferra et al. is applied. But then an extension of Theorem 3.2 to an inference system based on a c-resolution refinement and a c-paramodulation refinement should not be too difficult.

¿From a theoretical point of view, this extension to clauses with equality is necessary to arrive at a final judgement in the comparison between the power of H-subsumption and the redundancy concepts of [2] and [11]. A more practical motivation for this kind of extension is the search for an appropriate definition of a "fair" rule application strategy also in case of clauses with equality. In Section 3, a natural definition of fairness of a rule application strategy came as a by-product of the completeness proof. Note that the concept of "fair" theorem proving derivations from [2] and [11] is rather abstract. In particular, the set $\mathcal{C}_\infty$ of persisting clauses is not available during the deduction process itself.

Again, our definition of fairness from Definition 3.2 can be seen as some kind of concretisation of the corresponding concepts from [2] and [11].

References

[1] Ch. Bourely, R.Caferra, N.Peltier: A Method for Building Models automatically. Experiments with an Extension of Otter. Proceedings of CADE-12, LNAI 814, pp. 72–86 Springer (1994).

[2] L.Bachmair, H.Ganzinger: Rewrite-based Equational Theorem Proving with Selection and Simplification, Journal of Logic and Computation, Vol 4 No 3, pp. 217–247 (1994).

[3] H. Comon, P. Lescanne: Equational Problems and Disunification, Journal of Symbolic Computation, Vol 7, pp. 371–425 (1989).

[4] R.Caferra, N.Peltier: Extending semantic Resolution via automated Model Building: applications, Proceedings of IJCAI'95, Morgan Kaufmann (1995)

[5] R.Caferra, N.Peltier: Decision Procedures using Model Building Techniques, Proceedings of CSL'95, LNCS 1092, pp.130–144, Springer (1996).

[6] R.Caferra, N.Zabel: Extending Resolution for Model Construction, Proceedings of Logics in AI - JELIA'90, LNAI 478, pp. 153–169, Springer (1991).

[7] C.Fermüller, A.Leitsch: Hyperresolution and Automated Model Building, Journal of Logic and Computation, Vol 6 No 2, pp.173–230 (1996).

[8] J.Hsiang, M. Rusinowitch: Proving Refutational Completeness of Theorem-Proving Strategies: The Transfinite Semantic Tree Method, Journal of the ACM, Vol 38 No 3, pp. 559–587 (1991).

[9] R.Kowalski, P.J.Hayes: Semantic Trees in Automated Theorem Proving, Machine Intelligence 4, pp. 87–101, Edinburgh University Press (1969).

[10] A.Leitsch: The Resolution Calculus, Texts in Theoretical Computer Science, Springer (1997).

[11] R.Nieuwenhuis, A.Rubio: Theorem Proving with ordering and equality constrained clauses, Journal of Symbolic Computation, Vol 11, pp. 1–32 (1995).

Effective Properties of Some First Order Intuitionistic Modal Logics

Aida Pliuškevičienė

Institute of Mathematics and Informatics
Akademijos 4, Vilnius 2600, Lithuania
aida@ktl.mii.lt

Abstract. Indexed sequent calculi are constructed for first-order intuitionistic modal logics K, K4, T, S4 with the Barcan axiom as well as for KB, B, and S5, where the Barcan formula is derivable. Effective properties, namely, admissibility of the cut rule, Harrop properties, and the interpolation property for the calculi under consideration are proved using proof-theoretical methods. Based on the constructed sequent calculi, computer-aided tableaux-like and resolution calculi can be obtained.

1 Introduction

Modal logics based on logics weaker than the classical logic have been studied by various authors in different aspects. Most of these investigations deal with modal logics, based on an intuitionistic propositional logic and known as intuitionistic modal logics. Using model-theoretical methods, some results on the model theory for these logics as well as the relation between intuitionistic and classical modal logics have been obtained (see, e.g., [10], [15]). Some effective properties for intuitionistic modal logics have been obtained, too. Namely, the cut-free sequent calculi for $S4$-type intuitionistic propositional logic has been constructed by H. Ono in [10]. There are many studies concerning disjunction and existence properties for intermediate and super-intuitionistic predicate logics using semantic methods. More complex disjunction and existence properties (later named Harrop disjunction and existence properties) have been investigated for the intuitionistic predicate calculus and fragments of arithmetic in [1] and for some intermediate predicate logics in [9]. Some methods used to prove the Harrop-type properties are based on the proof that the set of provable formulas of the calculus is closed under modus ponens (see [1]), others (for example, [9]) are based on Kripke semantics. The interpolation theorem for $S4$-type and $S5$-type intuitionistic propositional modal logics (investigated in [10]) or some of their extensions have been proved by algebraic methods in [7]. Analogous positive results regarding admissibility of the cut rule, Harrop properties, and the interpolation property are not known for the first-order intuitionistic modal logics with the Barcan axiom. The proof-theoretical investigations of first-order classical modal logics can be found, for example, in [3]. To obtain a cut-free calculus for the classical modal logic $S5$ an indexing has been introduced by

R. Caferra and G. Salzer (Eds.): Automated Deduction, LNAI 1761, pp. 236–250, 2000.

S. Kanger in [5]. In [3] M. Fitting extended Kanger's ideas of indexing to construct analytic and semi-analytic tableaux (and called them prefixed tableau systems) for various classical modal logics. Cut-free indexed (prefixed) calculi for the first-order classical modal logics K, T, $K4$, $S4$ with the Barcan axiom as well as for KB and B (where the Barcan formula is derivable) have been constructed in [11]. In [12] it has been shown that traditional formulations of the Harrop disjunction and existence properties (by the same token, the conventional definition of the Harrop formula) are not suitable for the classical modal logics. Therefore, the notions of extended disjunction and existence properties for predicate modal logics K, $K4$, T, $S4$ as well as these logics with the Barcan axiom have been introduced. Using the proof-theoretical approach, it has been proved that these logics possess the properties introduced. It has been shown in [2] that the Craig Interpolation Theorem fails when the constant domain axiom scheme $\forall x \Box A(x) \equiv \Box \forall x A(x)$ is added to $S5$, or indeed, to any weaker extension of quantified K.

In this paper three effective properties, namely, (a) admissibility of the cut rule, (b) Harrop-type properties, (c) the interpolation-type property for some first-order intuitionistic modal logics with the Barcan axiom are investigated using proof-theoretical methods. These properties are very important in the development (and application) of theorem proving methods for classical and non-classical logics. The soundness and completeness of various resolution procedures (used as a basis for computer-aided proof systems) can be proved through explicit translations between resolution refutations and a cut–free Gentzen-type calculus (see, e.g., [8]). Based on the constructed sequent calculi, computer-aided tableaux-like and resolution calculi can be obtained. Harrop-type disjunction and existence properties allow us to get some invertibility of the rules $(\to \vee)$ and $(\to \exists)$. On the other hand, these properties serve as a useful tool to obtain non-derivability results in intuitionistic modal logics. The interpolation-type property can be interpreted as invertibility of the cut rule. In the logics where the cut rule is admissible, the invertibility of the cut rule serves as a measure of efficiency of the logic under consideration.

In the paper sequent cut–free calculi for intuitionistic modal logics K, $K4$, T, $S4$ with the Barcan axiom as well as for KB, B and $S5$, where the Barcan formula is derivable, are constructed using the index technique from [11]. Relying on the constructed sequent calculi, the Harrop disjunction and existence properties are proved constructively. It is shown that in contrast to classical predicate modal logics, a traditional formulation of the Harrop disjunction (existence) property for intuitionistic and intermediate logics is the same as the modal Harrop disjunction (existence) property for the intuitionistic modal logics considered. However, the usual constraints on the shape of the Harrop formulas can be weakened for non-reflexive intuitionistic modal logics K, K4, KB, i.e., an extension of the Harrop-type property is valid for the logics mentioned. An analogue of the interpolation theorem (Lemma 8) is proved for the intuitionistic modal logics under consideration. This lemma actually asserts some invertibility of the cut rule. Unlike non-constructive algebraic and model-theoretical methods, the constructive method, used to prove this invertibility, explicitly presents a way of constructing the cut formula. As it is known, the use of the cut rule in derivation can sharply reduce the length of derivation.

2 Gentzen-Type Calculi for Intuitionistic Modal Logics Considered

Let us consider first-order modal logics over K based on the intuitionistic logic, namely, K, T, $K4$, $S4$ with the Barcan axiom (i.e., the formula $\forall x \Box A(x) \supset \Box \forall x A(x)$) and the logics KB, B, $S5$, where the Barcan formula is derivable. The logics considered are in signature $\{\supset, \vee, \&, \forall, \exists, \Box\}$. Formulas are built up by means of logic connectives and modality $\Box$ starting from predicate variables, as usual. We don't use the modal operator $\Diamond$ (possibility), although, unlike classical modal logics, $\Diamond A$ cannot be considered as an abbreviation of $\neg \Box \neg A$. The symbol $\neg$ is used for the abbreviation of $A \supset \bot$, where $\bot$ stands for the constant "false". Let HJ be a Hilbert-type calculus for the first-order intuitionistic logic without equality (see, e.g., [6]). The intuitionistic modal logics considered are denoted by LJ, where $L \in \{K, T, K4, S4, KB, B, S5\}$, and defined by the postulates of HJ complemented by relevant axioms as follows:

A1. $\Box A \supset A$ (reflexivity);
A2. $A \supset \Box \neg \Box \neg A$ (Brouwerian Axiom or symmetry);
A3. $\Box(A \supset B) \supset (\Box A \supset \Box B)$;
A4. $\Box A \supset \Box \Box A$ (transitivity);
A5. $\forall x \Box A(x) \supset \Box \forall x A(x)$ (Barcan Axiom),

and the rule of inference **R**: $A/\Box A$ (rule of Necessitation).

Then, HLJ is a Hilbert-type calculus containing the Barcan formula and corresponding to the first-order intuitionistic modal logic LJ defined as follows:

KJ is $A3 + R$	KBJ is $KJ + A2$
TJ is $KJ + A1$	BJ is $KJ + A1 + A2$
$K4J$ is $KJ + A4$	$S5J$ is $KJ + A1 + A2 + A4$.
$S4J$ is $KJ + A1 + A4$	

The calculi HKJ, HTJ, $HK4J$, $HS4J$ under consideration have the Barcan Axiom explicitly. In the calculi $HKBJ$, HBJ, $HS5J$ the Barcan Axiom is derivable.

Let us examine the Gentzen-type calculi for the logic under consideration. A sequent is an expression of the form $\Gamma \to \Delta$, where Γ is an arbitrary finite (possibly empty) multiset of formulas (i.e., the order of formulas in Γ is disregarded) and Δ consists of one formula at most. Let us only consider such sequents in which no variable occurs free and bound at the same time. The formula $\mathfrak{A} = (A_1 \& \ldots \& A_n) \supset B$ is called an image formula of the sequent $A_1, \ldots, A_n \to B$. If $n = 0$, then $\mathfrak{A} = B$, and if Δ is empty, then $\mathfrak{A} = \mathop{\&}\limits_{i=1}^{n} A_i \supset \bot$, where $\bot$ is false.

Let LJ be the logic considered. Then Gentzen-type sequent calculus GLJ for any logic LJ has the following postulates (see, e.g., [8]).

Axioms: $\Gamma, A \to A$, where A is an elementary formula; $\bot, \Gamma \to \Delta$.

Recall that below in the paper, including the rules of inference, Δ consists of one formula at most.

The rules of inference for logical connectives are defined as follows.

$$\frac{A, \Gamma \to B}{\Gamma \to A \supset B}\ (\to\supset) \qquad \frac{A \supset B, \Gamma \to A; \quad B, \Gamma \to \Delta}{A \supset B, \Gamma \to \Delta}\ (\supset\to)$$

$$\frac{\Gamma \to A; \quad \Gamma \to B}{\Gamma \to A \& B}\ (\to \&) \qquad \frac{A, B, \Gamma \to \Delta}{A \& B, \Gamma \to \Delta}\ (\& \to)$$

$$\frac{\Gamma \to A}{\Gamma \to A \vee B}\ (\to \vee) \qquad \frac{A, \Gamma \to \Delta; \quad B, \Gamma \to \Delta}{A \vee B, \Gamma \to \Delta}\ (\vee \to)$$

$$\frac{\Gamma \to B}{\Gamma \to A \vee B}\ (\to \vee)$$

$$\frac{\Gamma \to A(t)}{\Gamma \to \exists x A(x)}\ (\to \exists) \qquad \frac{A(b), \Gamma \to \Delta}{\exists x\ A(x), \Gamma \to \Delta}\ (\exists \to)$$

$$\frac{\Gamma \to A(b)}{\Gamma \to \forall x A(x)}\ (\to \forall) \qquad \frac{A(t), \forall x\ A(x), \Gamma \to \Delta}{\forall x\ A(x), \Gamma \to \Delta}\ (\forall \to)$$

where the term t in $(\to \exists)$ and $(\forall \to)$ is an arbitrary term free for x in $A(x)$, and b, named eigenvariable, in the rules $(\exists \to)$ and $(\to \forall)$ does not occur in the conclusion of these rules.

The rules of inference for modality $\Box$ are different in the appropriate calculi. There are four different modal rules for the considered modal logics:

$$\frac{\Gamma \to A}{\Sigma, \Box\Gamma \to \Box A}\ (\Box_1) \qquad \frac{\Gamma, \Box\Gamma \to A}{\Sigma, \Box\Gamma \to \Box A}\ (\Box_2)$$

$$\frac{\Box\Gamma \to A}{\Sigma, \Box\Gamma \to \Box A}\ (\to \Box) \qquad \frac{A, \Box A, \Gamma \to \Delta}{\Box A, \Gamma \to \Delta}\ (\Box \to)$$

These modal rules correspond to the considered modal logics as the following table shows:

KJ	$K4J$	TJ	$S4J$	KB	B	$S5$
$(\Box_1)$	$(\Box_2)$	$(\Box_1)$ $(\Box \to)$	$(\to \Box)$ $(\Box \to)$	$(\Box_1)$	$(\Box_1)$ $(\Box \to)$	$(\to \Box)$ $(\Box \to)$

All the calculi considered have the rule $(cut^{\Box})$ as follows:

$$\frac{\Gamma \to \Box A; \quad \Box A, \Gamma \to \Delta}{\Gamma \to \Delta}\ (cut^{\Box}).$$

Besides, calculi GKJ, GTJ, $GK4J$, and $GS4J$ have the following rule of inference corresponding to the Barcan Axiom:

$$\frac{\Gamma \to \forall x \Box A(x)}{\Gamma \to \Box \forall x A(x)} (\to \Box\forall).$$

Instead of the rule $(\to \Box\forall)$ corresponding to the Barcan Axiom, calculi $GKBJ$, GBJ, and $GS5J$ have the rule (BA)

$$\frac{A, \Gamma \to}{\Gamma \to \Box\neg\Box A} (BA).$$

The rule (BA) corresponds to the Brouwerian Axiom.

A rule of inference is called admissible in a calculus if, by adding this rule, we do not extend the set of derivable sequents in the calculus.

Lemma 1. *In GLJ the following structural rules of weakening*

$$\frac{\Gamma \to}{\Gamma \to A} (\to W) \qquad \frac{\Gamma \to \Delta}{A, \Gamma \to \Delta} (W \to)$$

are admissible.

Proof. Let us rename the eigenvariables of applications of the rules of inference $(\to \forall)$, $(\exists \to)$ so that they do not enter formula A indicated in the conclusion of $(\to W), (W \to)$. Afterwards, the proof is carried out by induction on the height of the given derivation.

Lemma 2. *In GLJ the following structural rule of contraction*

$$\frac{A, A, \Gamma \to \Delta}{A, \Gamma \to \Delta} (C \to)$$

is admissible.

Proof. By induction on $|A|\omega + h(V)$, where $|A|$ is the complexity of the formula A, and $h(V)$ is the height of the given derivation.

Theorem 1. *The rule of inference*

$$\frac{\Gamma \to A; \quad A, \Sigma \to \Delta}{\Gamma, \Sigma \to \Delta} (cut),$$

where the cut formula of the (cut) has a different shape from $\Box A$, is admissible in GLJ.

Proof. By traditional transformations.

Remark 1. The necessity of the rule of inference $(cut^{\Box})$ in GLJ can be illustrated, for example, by derivation of the sequent $\forall x \Box A(x) \to \Box(\forall x A(x) \vee B)$ in any calculi GLJ under consideration or the sequent $A \to \Box(\Box\neg A \supset B)$ in GLJ, where $L \in \{\text{KB}, \text{B}\}$.

Theorem 2. *Let A be any formula, then $HLJ \vdash A \Leftrightarrow GLJ \vdash \rightarrow A$.*

Proof. Analogously as in [6, §77] using the admissibility of (cut) in GLJ.

Remark 2. Note that no cut-free Gentzen-type formulation for intuitionistic predicate modal logics with the Barcan axiom is known. To obtain cut-free calculi for the classical modal logics mentioned, indexed calculi have been introduced in [11].

3 Cut-Free Indexed Calculi

Let us introduce formulas with indices. Let $\alpha, \beta, \gamma, \dots$ be variables for the indices. Each predicate symbol P having its own index γ is denoted by P^γ. A predicate symbol without an index is regarded as a symbol with the index 1. Two identical predicate symbols with different indices are considered as different symbols.

A formula A with the index β is denoted by $(A)^\beta$ and defined in the following way:

1. $(E)^\beta = E^\beta$, where E is an elementary formula;
2. $(A \odot B)^\beta = (A)^\beta \odot (B)^\beta$, $\odot \in \{\supset, \&, \vee\}$;
3. $(\sigma A)^\beta = \sigma (A)^\beta$, $\sigma \in \{\Box, \exists x, \forall x\}$.

An index is introduced in different ways for analytic logics LJ, where $LJ \in \{KJ,\ TJ,\ K4J,\ S4J\}$ and for semi-analytic logics $KBJ,\ BJ$ (see, e.g., [3] for the term of analytic and semi-analytic logics). Note that in spite of the fact that $S5J$ is not an analytic logic, the indexing for this logic is introduced in a similar way as for the analytic logics. Let $\gamma_1, \dots, \gamma_m$ be all different indices entering the sequent $\Gamma \rightarrow \Delta$ as indices of the formulas from Γ, Δ. From now on, let us denote the analytic logics considered by LJ^B (the index B in this notation means that these logics contain the Barcan axiom explicitly) and semi-analytic ones by LJ^S.

An arbitrary positive integer i will be called an index (by analogy to [5]) in the logics LJ^B and $S5J$. The relation $\alpha \leq \beta$ for two arbitrary indices α and β is defined in the usual way for the integers. In the logics LJ^S the index σ is a finite sequence of positive integers (by analogy with [3]).

The indexed sequent calculus ILJ for any logic LJ has the same axioms and rules of inference for logic connectives and quantifiers as GLJ.

Instead of the special rules of inference concerning modality $\Box$ in the appropriate calculi for logics LJ, namely, $(\Box_1)$, $(\Box_2)$, $(\rightarrow \Box)$, $(\Box \rightarrow)$, and rules $(\rightarrow \Box\forall)$, (BA), $(cut^\Box)$ two modal rules are added.

The rule of inference for modality in succedent is of the shape:

$$\frac{\Gamma' \rightarrow (A)^\delta}{\Gamma \rightarrow \Box(A)^\sigma}\ (\rightarrow \Box^i).$$

Let $\gamma_1, \ldots, \gamma_m$ be all the indices entering the conclusion of this rule. Then δ and Γ' in the rule $(\to \Box^i)$ are defined as follows:

$$\delta = \begin{cases} j+1, & \text{for logics } LJ^B\text{, where } \sigma \text{ is a positive integer } j; \\ \delta, & \text{for } S5J\text{, where } \delta \notin \{\gamma_1, \ldots, \gamma_m\}\text{, and } \sigma \text{ and } \delta \\ & \text{are positive integers, i.e. } \delta \text{ is a new index;} \\ \sigma i, & \text{for logics } LJ^S\text{, where } \sigma \text{ is a sequence of integers,} \\ & i \text{ is any integer, and } \sigma i \text{ is not an initial segment} \\ & \text{of any index } \gamma \text{ from } \Gamma. \end{cases}$$

$$\Gamma' = \begin{cases} \Gamma, & \text{for logics } S5J\text{, and } LJ^S \text{ or, in case of } LJ^B, \\ & \text{if } \sigma = j = \max(\gamma_1, \ldots, \gamma_m)\ ; \\ \Gamma', & \text{otherwise, where } \Gamma' \text{ is obtained from } \Gamma \text{ by deleting} \\ & \text{all the formulas with the indices greater than } \sigma. \end{cases}$$

Remark 3. Note that in the case of indexed calculi for the first-order classical modal logics three succedent rules $(\to \Box^i_1)$, $(\to \Box^i_2)$, and $(\to \Box^\alpha)$ were formulated (see [11]). The rule $(\to \Box^i)$ formulated above is really a scheme that includes all three of the rules mentioned.

The rule of inference for modality in antecedent is of the common shape for all calculi ILJ, but the meaning of the index δ is different in the appropriate calculi:

$$\frac{(A)^\delta, \Box(A)^\sigma, \Gamma \to \Delta}{\Box(A)^\sigma, \Gamma \to \Delta}\ (\Box^i \to),$$

where $\delta \in \{\gamma_1 \ldots \gamma_m\}$, and $\gamma_1, \ldots, \gamma_m$ are all the indices entering the conclusion of this rule. This is the only restriction on the index δ for logic $S5J$.

The other logics considered need some additional restrictions on the index δ. Namely, for logics LJ^B $\delta = i + k$, if $\sigma = i$, and the meaning of k corresponds to the modal logics as the following table shows.

K^B	$K4^B$	T^B	$S4^B$
$k = 1$	$k \geq 1$	$k = 0$ or $k = 1$	$k \geq 0$

If such a k does not exist, the rule cannot be applied.

In the case of logic KBJ $\delta \neq \sigma$ and $\delta = \sigma_1 ji$ or $\delta = \sigma_1$, if $\sigma = \sigma_1 j$; for logic BJ $\delta = \sigma$ or δ is determined in the same way as for KBJ.

Remark 4. The choice of index in the rules $(\to \Box^i)$ and $(\Box^i \to)$ of ILJ^S corresponds to the restrictions on the prefix in the prefixed tableau introduced by Fitting [3] for logics KB and B.
For logics LJ^B, as well as for logic $S5J$, it suffices to take a positive integer as an index instead of a sequence of positive integers.

Lemma analogous to Lemmas 1, 2 can be proved in ILJ.

Lemma 3. *In ILJ the structural rules of weakening* $(\rightarrow W)$, $(W \rightarrow)$, *and contraction* $(C \rightarrow)$ *are admissible.*

Proof. In the case of rule $(W \rightarrow)$ we must rename not only the eigenvariables of applications of the rules of inference $(\rightarrow \forall)$, $(\exists \rightarrow)$ but

a) in the case of calculi ILJ^S $(IS5J)$, the index δ in applications of the rule of inference $(\rightarrow \Box^i)$ is also renamed in such a way that it would not be an initial segment of the index (the index, respectively) of formula A indicated in the conclusion of $(W \rightarrow)$;

b) in the case of the other calculi no renaming of indices in any applications of the rule of inference $(\rightarrow \Box^i)$ is necessary.

In the case of rule $(\rightarrow W)$ it is necessary to rename only the eigenvariables of applications of the rule of inference $(\exists \rightarrow)$.

4 Admissibility of the Cut Rule in Indexed Calculi

In order to prove the admissibility of cut in ILJ it is necessary to prove some lemmas allowing to preserve the derivability of sequents under the substitution of indices for some indices in the sequent. It should be noted that a regular substitution (formulated in the lemma below) is valid only for the calculus $IS5J$.

Lemma 4. *Let* $IS5J \vdash \Gamma, \Pi^i \rightarrow \Delta^i$, *where* $i \notin \Gamma$. *Then* $IS5J \vdash \Gamma, \Pi^j \rightarrow \Delta^j$ *for an arbitrary index j. Moreover, a given derivation and a reconstructed one has the same height.*

Proof. By induction on the height of the given derivation of the sequent $\Gamma, \Pi^i \rightarrow \Delta^i$. It is not difficult to get convinced (applying induction on the height) that all the axioms and rules of inference (r) for logical connectives are transformed to the axioms and the same rules of inference (r) substituting the index j for all the occurrences of i. Let us consider modal rules.

1. Let $(r) = (\rightarrow \Box^i)$ and the rule be of the form:

$$\frac{\Gamma, \Pi^i \rightarrow (A)^\delta}{\Gamma, \Pi^i \rightarrow (\Box A)^i} (\rightarrow \Box^i).$$

We get from the restrictions on the indices in the rule $(\rightarrow \Box^i)$ that $\delta \notin \{\gamma_1, \ldots, \gamma_m\}$, where $\gamma_1, \ldots, \gamma_m$ are all the indices entering the conclusion of this rule. If δ is the same as the index j then, using the induction hypothesis, we substitute some new index τ $(\tau \notin \{j, \gamma_1, \ldots, \gamma_m\})$ for δ. According to the statement of this lemma, derivations of the sequents $\Gamma, \Pi^i \rightarrow (A)^\tau$, and $\Gamma, \Pi^i \rightarrow (A)^\delta$ have the same height. Using the induction hypothesis and having substituted the index j for i in the premise (reconstructed premise) of $(\rightarrow \Box^i)$, we can apply this rule and get a desired derivation of the conclusion of the rule.

2. Let $(r) = (\Box^i \rightarrow)$. Then the rule is of the form:

$$\frac{\Gamma, B^\delta, \Box B^\sigma, \Pi^i \rightarrow \Delta^i}{\Gamma, \Box B^\sigma, \Pi^i \rightarrow \Delta^i} (\Box^i \rightarrow).$$

We get from the restrictions on the indices in the rule $(\Box^i \rightarrow)$ that $\delta \in \{\gamma_1 \dots \gamma_m\}$, and $\gamma_1, \dots, \gamma_m$ are all the indices entering the conclusion of this rule. This is the only restriction on the index δ for logic $IS5J$. Having substituted the index j for i in the premise of $(\Box^i \rightarrow)$ we can apply this rule and get a desired derivation of the conclusion of the rule in spite of the meaning of the index δ.

Remark 5. Lemma 4 is not valid for the other calculi considered. For example, let us consider the sequent $S = \Box(A^1 \supset B^1), \Box A^1 \rightarrow B^2$. This sequent is the premise of the application of the rule $(\rightarrow \Box^i)$ in the derivation of axiom $A3: \ \Box(A \supset B) \supset (\Box A \supset \Box B)$ in ILJ, where $L \in \{K,\ T,\ K4,\ S4\}$. Hence $ILJ \vdash S$. Let us apply Lemma 4 to this derivable sequent and substitute integer 3 for index 2 in S. It is easy to verify that the sequent $\Box(A^1 \supset B^1), \Box A^1 \rightarrow B^3$ is not derivable in IKJ and in ITJ. Counterexamples for the other considered calculi can be constructed.

The following lemmas, needed to prove Theorem 3, deal with the substitution of indices in the calculi considered, except the calculus $IS5J$.

Lemma 5. *Let* $ILJ^B \in \{ITJ,\ IS4J\}$. *Let* $ILJ^B \vdash \Gamma, \Pi_0^{i+1}, \dots, \Pi_k^{i+k+1} \rightarrow A^{i+k+1}$, *where* $i \geq \max(\gamma_1, \dots, \gamma_n)$, *and* $\gamma_1, \dots, \gamma_n$ *are all the indices entering* Γ *or* $i \geq 1$, *if* Γ *is empty (i.e.,* $(i+j) \notin \Gamma$ *if* $1 \leq j \leq k+1$*). Then* $ILJ^B \vdash \Gamma, \Pi_0^i, \dots, \Pi_k^{i+k} \rightarrow A^{i+k}$.

Proof. By induction on the height of the given derivation. Let us consider some characteristic cases.

1. Let $(r) = (\Box^i \rightarrow)$. Then the rule is of the form:

$$\frac{\Gamma, B^{l+h}, \Box B^l, \Pi_0^{i+1}, \dots, \Pi_k^{i+k+1} \rightarrow A^{i+k+1}}{\Gamma, \Box B^l, \Pi_0^{i+1}, \dots, \Pi_k^{i+k+1} \rightarrow A^{i+k+1}} (\Box^i \rightarrow).$$

We get from the conditions of the lemma and the restrictions on indices in the rule $(\Box^i \rightarrow)$ that $l \leq i$ or $i < l \leq i+k+1$. Only the case $l+h = i+j$, where $1 \leq j \leq k+1$, is interesting. In the first case (i.e., $l \leq i$), $h \geq j$ if $l+h = i+j$. The situation $l = i$ and $h = 1$ may occur only for $ILJ^B \in \{ITJ,\ IS4J\}$. Applying the induction hypothesis to the premise of $(\Box^i \rightarrow)$ considered we get a premise $S_1 = \Gamma, B^{i+j-1}, \Box B^l, \Pi_0^i, \dots, \Pi_k^{i+k} \rightarrow A^{i+k}$. In the second case (i.e., $i < l \leq i+k+1$), $l = i+m$, where $1 \leq m \leq k+1$. So, if $l+h = i+j$ then $0 \leq h \leq k$. According to the induction hypothesis we get a premise $S_1 = \Gamma, B^{i+j-1}, \Box B^{i+m-1}, \Pi_0^i, \dots, \Pi_k^{i+k} \rightarrow A^{i+k}$. In both cases, applying $(\Box^i \rightarrow)$ to S_1 we get the desired derivation. Note that this lemma is not valid for calculi $ILJ^B \in \{IKJ,\ IK4J\}$, because the application of $(\Box^i \rightarrow)$ will fail when $l = i$ and $h = 1$.

2. Let $(r) = (\rightarrow \Box^i)$ and the rule be of the form:

$$\frac{\Gamma, \Pi_0^{i+1}, \dots, \Pi_k^{i+k+1} \rightarrow B^{i+k+1+1}}{\Gamma, \Pi_0^{i+1}, \dots, \Pi_k^{i+k+1} \rightarrow \Box B^{i+k+1}} (\rightarrow \Box^i).$$

Applying the induction hypothesis to the premise of $(\rightarrow \Box^i)$ we get a proof of a sequent $S_1 = \Gamma, \Pi_0^i, \dots, \Pi_k^{i+k} \rightarrow B^{i+k+1}$. Applying $(\rightarrow \Box^i)$ to S_1 we get the desired derivation.

Lemma 6. *Let* $ILJ^B \in \{IK4J,\ IS4J\}$. *Let* $ILJ^B \vdash \Gamma, \Pi_0^{i+1}, \ldots, \Pi_k^{i+k+1} \to A^{i+k+1}$, *where* $i \geq \max(\gamma_1, \ldots, \gamma_n)$, *and* $\gamma_1, \ldots, \gamma_n$ *are all the indices entering* Γ *or* $i \geq 1$, *if* Γ *is empty (i.e.,* $(i+j) \notin \Gamma$ *if* $1 \leq j \leq k+1$*). Then* $ILJ^B \vdash \Gamma, \Pi_0^{i+m}, \ldots, \Pi_k^{i+k+m} \to A^{i+k+m}$, *where* $m > 1$.

Proof. Similar to the proof of Lemma 5. Let us note some differences when the following case is considered.

Let $(r) = (\Box^i \to)$. Then the rule is of the form:

$$\frac{\Gamma, B^{l+h}, \Box B^l, \Pi_0^{i+1}, \ldots, \Pi_k^{i+k+1} \to A^{i+k+1}}{\Gamma, \Box B^l, \Pi_0^{i+1}, \ldots, \Pi_k^{i+k+1} \to A^{i+k+1}} (\Box^i \to).$$

The case $l+h = i+j$ and $l = i+j$, i.e., $h = 0$, may occur only if $ILJ^B = IS4J$. This lemma cannot be proved for calculi $ILJ^B \in \{IKJ,\ ITJ\}$, because the application of $(\Box^i \to)$ will fail when $l = i$, $l+h = i+j$, where $j = 1$, and $m > 1$.

Lemma 7. *Let* $ILJ^S \vdash \Gamma, \Pi^{\sigma ij} \to A^{\sigma ij}$, *where* σ *is a finite (may be empty) sequence of positive integers,* i, j *are some positive integers and* σij *is not an initial segment of any index* γ *from* Γ. *Then* $ILJ^S \vdash \Gamma, \Pi^\delta \to A^\delta$, *where for* $IKBJ$ $\delta \in \{\sigma, \sigma ik\}$, *and for* IBJ $\delta \in \{\sigma, \sigma i, \sigma ik\}$.

Proof. Let us substitute δ for all the occurrences of the subsequence σij in any index in the given derivation. It is not difficult to get convinced that after such a substitution all the axioms and the application of any rule of inference (r) are transformed to the axioms and the applications of the same rule of inference (r). Let us consider only one specific case, where $(r) = (\Box^i \to)$.

Let the rule under consideration be of the form:

$$\frac{\Gamma, B^{\sigma i}, \Box B^{\sigma ij}, \Pi^{\sigma ij} \to A^{\sigma ij}}{\Gamma, \Box B^{\sigma ij}, \Pi^{\sigma ij} \to A^{\sigma ij}} (\Box^i \to).$$

Let δ be σ. Having replaced all the occurrences of the subsequence σij in any index of the application of this rule by σ we get the application of the same rule, namely:

$$\frac{\Gamma, B^{\sigma i}, \Box B^{\sigma}, \Pi^{\sigma} \to A^{\sigma}}{\Gamma, \Box B^{\sigma}, \Pi^{\sigma} \to A^{\sigma}} (\Box^i \to).$$

Theorem 3 (Admissibility of *(cut)* **in** ILJ**).** *The rule of inference*

$$\frac{\Gamma \to A; \quad A, \Sigma \to \Delta}{\Gamma, \Sigma \to \Delta} (cut)$$

is admissible in ILJ *provided no variable occurs both free and bound at the same time in the conclusion of this rule.*

Proof. By induction on $|A|\omega + h(V_1) + h(V_2)$, where $|A|$ is the complexity of the cut formula of (cut), $h(V_1)$, $h(V_2)$ are heights of the derivations of premises. The cases are considered in the usual way, when the cut formula of the (cut) is of the shape different from $\Box A^i$ or this cut formula (in the derivation at least one of premises of the (*cut*) rule considered) had not been introduced by the rule of inference applied last (in this case we have a parametric cut in terms of [14]).

Let us consider only some cases regarding the principal cut (for the term see [14]).

Derivations of premises of (*cut*) are of the following shape:

$$\dfrac{\mathcal{D}_1\left\{\dfrac{\mathcal{D}'_1\{\Gamma' \to A^\delta}{\Gamma \to \Box A^\sigma}(\to \Box^i)\right. \qquad \dfrac{\mathcal{D}'_2\{A^\gamma, \Box A^\sigma, \Sigma \to \Delta}{\Box A^\sigma, \Sigma \to \Delta}(\Box^i \to)}{\Gamma, \Sigma \to \Delta}(cut).$$

Applying (*cut*) to the conclusions of the derivations $\mathcal{D}_1$, $\mathcal{D}'_2$ and using the induction hypothesis, we get a derivation of the sequent $S = A^\gamma, \Gamma, \Sigma \to \Delta$ where $\gamma \in \{\gamma_1, \ldots, \gamma_m\}$, and $\gamma_1, \ldots, \gamma_m$ are all the indices entering the right premise of (*cut*), i.e., sequent $\Box A^\sigma, \Sigma \to \Delta$.

Let us consider the following cases:

1. The calculus under consideration is ILJ^B where $L \in \{K,\ K4,\ T,\ S4\}$. Let the index σ in the cut formula be i. Then, δ in the sequent $S_1 = \Gamma' \to A^\delta$ of the derivation $\mathcal{D}'_1$ is $i+1$, and $\delta \notin \Gamma'$. According to the restriction on the index in the rule of $(\Box^i \to)$, the index γ in the sequent S is $i+k$ and the meaning of k depends on the calculus considered.

(a) Let $k = 1$. Then, applying (*cut*) to S_1 and S and using the induction hypothesis and Lemma 3, we get $ILJ^B \vdash \Gamma, \Sigma \to \Delta$. Note that the analyzed case is only possible for calculus IKJ.

(b) Let $k \neq 1$. If $k = 0$ (this situation may only occur for calculus $ILJ^B \in \{ITJ,\ IS4J\}$) relying on Lemma 5, let us reconstruct the derivation $\mathcal{D}'_1$. We get $ILJ^B \vdash S'_1 = \Gamma' \to A^i$. If $k > 1$ (this situation may only occur for calculus $ILJ^B \in \{IK4J,\ IS4J\}$) let us reconstruct the derivation $\mathcal{D}'_1$ relying on Lemma 6. In this case we get $ILJ^B \vdash S'_1 = \Gamma' \to A^{i+k}$. Now, applying (*cut*) to S'_1 and S and using the induction hypothesis and Lemma 3, we get $ILJ^B \vdash \Gamma, \Sigma \to \Delta$.

2. The calculus under consideration is $IS5J$. The index of the cut formula is an integer δ and $\delta \notin \Gamma'$. Relying on Lemma 4, let us reconstruct the derivation $\mathcal{D}'_1$ into a derivation of the sequent $S'_1 = \Gamma \to A^\gamma$ where γ is the same as in the sequent S. Applying (*cut*) to S'_1 and S and using the induction hypothesis and Lemma 3, we get $IS5J \vdash \Gamma, \Sigma \to \Delta$.

3. The calculus under consideration is ILJ^S. The index of the cut formula is a sequence of integers, namely $\sigma = \sigma i$. Then, δ in the sequent S_1 is σij and σij is not an initial segment of any index from Γ. The index γ in the sequent S is defined for IKB as $\gamma \in \{\sigma, \sigma ik\}$, and for IB as $\gamma \in \{\sigma, \sigma i, \sigma ik.\}$ Relying on Lemma 7, let us reconstruct the derivation $\mathcal{D}'_1$. We get $ILJ^S \vdash S'_1 = \Gamma \to A^\gamma$. Then, applying (*cut*) to S'_1 and S and using the induction hypothesis and Lemma 3, we get the desired derivation.

Theorem 4. *Let S be an index-free sequent, then $GLJ \vdash S \Leftrightarrow ILJ \vdash S$.*

Proof. This theorem states the equivalence of indexed and indexed-free calculi with respect to indexed-free sequents. It is clear that a formula without any index can be considered as the formula with index 1. In order to prove the "if" part of the theorem, relying on Theorem 2 it suffices to prove the axioms from

A1–A5 of HLJ, associated with L, in the respective calculus ILJ. Theorem 3 is used in the induction step. The proof of "only–if" part requires some additional consideration analogously to [11].

5 Harrop Properties

We shall deal here with two properties which are analogues of the properties proved by R. Harrop [1] for the intuitionistic propositional logic and intuitionistic number theory. Later these properties called by T. Nakamura as the Harrop disjunction property (HDP) and the Harrop existence property (HEP) were investigated for some intermediate predicate logics in [9]. T. Nakamura showed by Kripke semantics that intermediate logic LD, i.e., an intuitionistic predicate logic complemented with $\forall x(P(x) \vee Q) \supset \forall x P(x) \vee Q$, had (HDP) and (HEP).

Let us recall and modify some notions.

Definition 1. *Let $A \in LJ$, where $L \in \{K, T, K4, S4, KB, B, S5\}$. Then A is a Harrop formula (H-formula) if every occurrence of the disjunction and the existence quantifier is only within the premise of some implication.*

Definition 2. *Let $A \in LJ$, where $L \in \{K, K4, KB\}$. Then A is a strong Harrop formula (sH-formula) if every occurrence of the disjunction and the existence quantifier is either within the premise of some implication or in the scope of necessity operator $\Box$.*

Definition 3. *The sequent S of the shape $\Gamma \to A \vee B$ or $\Gamma \to \exists x A(x)$ is said to be of Harrop-type (strong Harrop-type) if each formula of Γ is the H-formula (sH-formula).*

It is trivial that any Harrop-type sequent S is a strong Harrop-type sequent, but not vice versa.

Definition 4. *A logic LJ is said to have a modal Harrop disjunction property (MHDP) (a strong modal Harrop disjunction property (sMHDP)) provided that the Harrop-type (strong Harrop-type) sequent of the shape $\Gamma \to A \vee B$ is derivable in the appropriate sequent calculi ILJ iff $\Gamma \to A$ or $\Gamma \to B$ is derivable in the same ILJ.*

Definition 5. *A logic L is said to have a modal Harrop existence property (MHEP) (a strong modal Harrop existence property (sMHEP)) provided that the Harrop-type (strong Harrop-type) sequent of the shape $\Gamma \to \exists x A(x)$ is derivable in the appropriate sequent calculi ILJ iff there exists a term t such that the sequent $\Gamma \to A(t)$ is derivable in the same ILJ.*

Theorem 5 (Modal Harrop Disjunction and Existence Properties).

a) Intuitionistic modal logics with the Barcan axiom LJ where $L \in \{K, K4, T, S4, KB, B, S5\}$ have the modal Harrop disjunction property and the modal Harrop existence property.

b) Intuitionistic modal logics with the Barcan axiom LJ where $L \in \{K, K4, KB\}$ have the strong modal Harrop disjunction property and the strong modal Harrop existence property.

Proof. The "if" part of the theorem is trivial. In the "only–if" part it is essential that, according to Theorem 3, a cut–free derivation can be constructed in calculi ILJ. The proof of part a) is analogous to the syntactical proof of the Harrop theorem for the intuitionistic logic (see, e.g., [13]).

To prove part b), let us consider the non-indexed calculi GLJ where $L \in \{\mathrm{K}, \mathrm{K4}, \mathrm{KB}\}$. The proof is carried out by induction on the number of applications of the rules of inference that are below all the applications of rules for $\vee$ and $\exists$ in the given derivation. From the shape of the rules of calculi considered and the sequent examined, we have only two possibilities to start a derivation. If the last step in the given derivation is the application of a logical rule, the case is considered as in part a). Note that the last step cannot be the application of the rule $(\Box_1)$, $(\Box_2)$, $(\to \Box)$, $(\to \Box\forall)$ or (BA), although it can be the application of the rule $(cut^{\Box})$. In this case, the end of the given derivation is of the form:

$$\frac{S_1\Big\{\Gamma \to \Box A; \quad S_2\Big\{\Box A, \Gamma \to \Delta}{\Gamma \to \Delta}\,(cut^{\Box}),$$

where $\Delta \in \{A \vee B,\ \exists x A(x)\}$.

Based on Definition 2 and by the induction hypothesis applied to S_2 we can get the derivation of the sequent $S_3 = \Box A, \Gamma \to \Delta'$, where $\Delta' \in \{A,\ B,\ A(t)\}$. Applying $(cut^{\Box})$ to S_1, S_3 we get the desired derivation. To get sMHDP and sMHEP for the indexed calculi it suffices to apply Theorem 4.

Remark 6. A logic possessing the strong modal Harrop disjunction (existence) property has the modal Harrop disjunction (existence) property, too. Note that in contrast to classical predicate modal logics (see [12]), traditional formulation of the Harrop disjunction (existence) property for intuitionistic and intermediate logics (see, e.g., [1], [9]) is the same as the modal Harrop disjunction (existence) property for the intuitionistic modal logics considered.

Example 1. According to Definition 3 the sequent $\Box(\Box P \vee \Box Q) \to \Box P \vee \Box Q$ is of strong Harrop-type. It is easy to verify that it is not derivable in KJ, $K4J$, and KBJ. Therefore, based on (sMHDP) neither $\Box(\Box P \vee \Box Q) \to \Box P$ nor $\Box(\Box P \vee \Box Q) \to \Box Q$ are derivable in KJ, $K4J$, and KBJ. On the other hand, this sequent is derivable in TJ and $S4J$, but it is not of Harrop-type. So, (MHDP) cannot be applied to this sequent.

Example 2. According to Definition 3 the sequent $\Box(\Box P(a) \vee \Box P(b)) \to \exists x \Box P(x)$ is of strong Harrop-type. It is easy to verify that it is not derivable in KJ, $K4J$, and KBJ. Therefore, there does not exist any term t such that the sequent $\Box(\Box P(a) \vee \Box P(b)) \to \Box P(t)$ is derivable in ILJ, where $L \in \{K,\ K4,\ KB\}$. The sequent $\Box P(a) \vee \Box P(b) \to \exists x \Box P(x)$ is derivable in KJ, $K4J$, and KBJ, but it is not of strong Harrop-type. Both sequents considered in this example are derivable in T, but both of them are not of Harrop-type.

6 Analogue of the Interpolation Property

As shown in [2], the Interpolation Theorem does not hold for the first-order classical modal logics with the Barcan axiom. The same negative results can be obtained for the intuitionistic version of these modal logics. However, as follows from [7], the Interpolation Theorem is valid for the intuitionistic propositional $S4$-type and $S5$-type logics considered in [10]. The Craig Interpolation Theorem for the intuitionistic predicate logic with constant domains was first considered in [4] by the semantic approach. We examine here the possibility of constructing a cut formula in the cut rule so that it is invertible. This theorem can be treated as some analogue of the interpolation theorem.

Definition 6. *Let P^i be any predicate symbol with an index. Then P is called a basis of P^i. Let Γ be an arbitrary multiset of formulas. Then $V(\Gamma)$ is a set of all different variables, constants (apart from $\perp$), function symbols, and bases of predicates with an index entering Γ.*

Lemma 8 (Invertibility of (*cut*) **in** *ILJ*). *Let $ILJ \vdash \Gamma \rightarrow \Delta$. Then for any partition (Γ_1, Γ_2) of the multiset Γ there exists a formula C (called an interpolant) such that:*

1) $ILJ \vdash \Gamma_1 \rightarrow C$; $ILJ \vdash C, \Gamma_2 \rightarrow \Delta$ (invertibility condition);

2) $V(C) \subseteq V(\Gamma_1 \cup \Delta) \cap V(\Gamma_2 \cup \Delta)$ (intersection condition);

3) the index of C does not exceed the indices from Γ_1, Γ_2, Δ (index condition).

Proof. The lemma is proved by induction on the height h of the derivation, relying on the fact that ILJ does not contain the cut rule. If $h = 0$, then the proof is carried out in the same way as in [13]. Let $h > 0$ and (k) be the rule applied last in the given derivation. Let us consider only the case $(k) = (\rightarrow \Box^i)$. Then the end of the derivation is of the form:

$$\frac{\Gamma' \rightarrow (A)^\delta}{\Gamma \rightarrow \Box(A)^\sigma}\,(\rightarrow \Box^i),$$

where $\delta = i + 1$ if $\sigma = i$. Let $\gamma_1, \ldots, \gamma_m$ be all the indices entering the conclusion of the rule $(\rightarrow \Box^i)$. Then Γ' is obtained from Γ by deleting all the formulas with the indices greater than σ, if $\sigma < \max(\gamma_1, \ldots, \gamma_m)$. Otherwise, i.e., if $\sigma = \max(\gamma_1, \ldots, \gamma_m)$, then Γ' is the same as Γ. So, $\Gamma' \subseteq \Gamma$ and every partition (Γ_1, Γ_2) of the multiset Γ has a corresponding (induced, in terms of [13]) partition (Γ_1', Γ_2') of the multiset Γ'. By the induction assumption $ILJ \vdash S_1 = \Gamma_1' \rightarrow C$, and $ILJ \vdash S_2 = C, \Gamma_2' \rightarrow (A)^{i+1}$. An interpolant C also satisfies the intersection and index conditions. Let us consider two subcases.

1. Formula C has the index $i+1$. Since $i+1 \notin \Gamma_1'$, we can apply $(\rightarrow \Box^i)$ to the sequent S_1 and get $ILJ \vdash S_1' = \Gamma_1' \rightarrow \Box(C)^i$. Using the admissibility of $(W \rightarrow)$ and relying on the restriction of the indices in the rule $(\Box^i \rightarrow)$, having applied $(\Box^i \rightarrow)$ to S_2, we get $ILJ \vdash S_2' = \Box(C)^i, \Gamma_2' \rightarrow (A)^{i+1}$. Applying $(\rightarrow \Box^i)$ to the sequent S_2' we get $ILJ \vdash S_3' = \Box(C)^i, \Gamma_2' \rightarrow \Box(A)^i$. Derivations of the sequents S_1' and S_3' (or the sequents obtained from these sequents having applied $(W \rightarrow)$, if Γ' is not the same as Γ) are the desired ones and the formula $\Box(C)^i$ is the interpolant in this case.

2. Formula C has the index less than $i+1$. In this case, relying on the index condition we can apply $(\rightarrow \Box^i)$ to the sequent S_2 and get $ILJ \vdash S_2' = C, \Gamma_2' \rightarrow \Box(A)^i$. Derivations of the sequents S_1 and S_2' or the sequents obtained from these sequents having applied $(W \rightarrow)$ are the desired ones and the formula C is the interpolant in this case.

References

1. Harrop, R.: Concerning formulas of the types $A \rightarrow B \vee C$, $A \rightarrow (Ex)B(x)$ in intuitionistic formal systems. *Journal of Symbolic Logic* **25** (1960) 27–32.
2. Fine, K.: Failures of the interpolation lemma in quantified modal logic. *Journal of Symbolic Logic* **44** (1979) 201–206.
3. Fitting, M.C.: *Proof Methods for Modal and Intuitionistic Logics.* D. Reidel, Dordrecht (1983).
4. Gabbay, D.: Craig interpolation theorem for intuitionistic logic and extensions, Part III. *Journal of Symbolic Logic* **42** (1977) 269–271.
5. Kanger, S.G.: Provability in logic, Vol. 1. Acta Univ. Stock., Stockholm Studies in Philosophy (1957).
6. Kleene, S.C.: *Introduction to Metamathematics.* North-Holland, Amsterdam (1952).
7. Luppi, C.: On the interpolation property of some intuitionistic modal logics. *Arch. Math. Logic* **35** (1996) 173–189.
8. Mints, G.: *Resolution Strategies for the Intuitionistic Logic.* Constraint Programming, NATO ASI Series, Springer Verlag (1994) 289–311.
9. Nakamura, T.: Disjunction property for some intermediate predicate logics. *Reports on Mathematical Logic* **15** (1983) 33–39.
10. Ono, H.: On some intuitionistic modal logics. *Publ. R.I.M.S. Kyoto Univ.* **13** (1977) 687–722.
11. Pliuškevičienė A.: Cut–free indexed calculi for modal logics containing the Barcan axiom. In: M. Kracht et al. (eds.): *Advances in Modal Logic '96.* CSLJ Publications (1997) 155–170.
12. Pliuškevičienė A.: Extended disjunction and existence properties for some predicate modal logics. *Logic Journal of the IGPL* **6** (1998) 775–787.
13. Takeuti G.: *Proof Theory.* North-Holland, Amsterdam, American Elsevier, inc, New-York (1975).
14. Wansing H.: Strong cut-elimination for constant domain first-order S5. *Logic Journal of the IGPL* **3** (1995) 797–810.
15. Wolter, F., Zakharyaschev, M.: On the relation between intuitionistic and classical modal logics. *Algebra and Logic* **36** (1997) 121-155.

Hidden Congruent Deduction

Grigore Roşu* and Joseph Goguen

Department of Computer Science & Engineering
University of California at San Diego

1 Introduction

Cleverly designed software often fails to satisfy its requirements strictly, but instead satisfies them *behaviorally*, in the sense that they *appear* to be satisfied under every experiment that can be performed on the system. A good example is the traditional implementation of sets by lists, where union as implemented by append fails to strictly satisfy basic laws like commutativity and idempotency, but does satisfy them behaviorally. It is becoming increasingly clear that behavioral specification is more appropriate to software engineering than traditional approaches that rely on strict satisfaction of axioms, and it is therefore becoming increasingly important to develop powerful techniques for behavioral verification. This paper presents some techniques of this kind in the area called *hidden algebra*, clustered around the central notion of *coinduction*. We believe hidden algebra is the natural next step in the evolution of algebraic semantics and its first order proof technology. Hidden algebra originated in [7], and was developed further in [8, 10, 3, 12, 5] among other places; the most comprehensive survey currently available is [12].

Proofs by coinduction are *dual* to proofs by induction, in that the former are based on a largest congruence, and the latter on a smallest subalgebra (e.g., see [12]). Inductive proofs require choosing a set of constructors, often called a basis; the dual notion is *cobasis*, and as with bases for induction, the right choice can result in a dramatically simplified proof. An interesting complication is that the best choice may not be part of the given signature, but rather contain operations that can be defined over it.

An important recent development is the notion of *congruent* operations (these were called "coherent"[1] in [5, 4], where they were introduced), which considerably expands the applicability of hidden algebra and coinduction by allowing operations that have more than one hidden argument, thus going well beyond what is possible in coalgebra (e.g., see [14, 17]).

The most significant contributions of this paper are a slightly more general notion of congruence, the notion of cobasis, some rules of deduction for hidden algebra, and an easy to check criterion for operations to be congruent; the first

* On leave from Fundamentals of Computer Science, Faculty of Mathematics, University of Bucharest, Romania.

[1] We feel that the word "congruent" better describes the role that these operations actually play.

R. Caferra and G. Salzer (Eds.): Automated Deduction, LNAI 1761, pp. 251–266, 2000.

two items build on work in [4]. There is also a hidden version of the so called "theorem of constants," and Theorem 5, which says congruent operations can be added or subtracted to the set of behavioral operations as convenient, still yielding an equivalent specification. The main conceptual advance of this paper is to extend all the main concepts and results of hidden algebra to encompass operations with more than one hidden argument.

Because of space limitations, we must omit some proofs, and assume familiarity with many sorted first order equational logic, including the notions of many sorted signature, algebra, homomorphism, term, equation, and satisfaction; e.g., see [12, 11]. We let $f;g$ denote the composition of $f\colon A \to B$ with $g\colon B \to C$. Recall that $T_\Sigma(X)$ denotes the Σ-algebra of all Σ-terms with variables from X.

2 Hidden Algebra

Definition 1. *A* hidden signature *is* (Ψ, D, Σ), *often denoted just* Σ, *where*

- Ψ *is a* V*-sorted signature and* D *is a* Ψ*-algebra, called the* data algebra,
- Σ *is a* $(V \cup H)$*-sorted signature extending* Ψ *and such that each operation in* Σ *with both its arguments and its result visible lies in* Ψ, *and*
- V *and* H *are disjoint sets, called* visible sorts *and* hidden sorts, *respectively.*

For technical reasons, we assume that for every element d *in the data algebra* D *there exists exactly one constant in* Ψ, *also denoted* d.

The operations in Σ *with one hidden argument and visible result are called* attributes, *those with one hidden argument and hidden result are called* methods, *and those with visible arguments and hidden result are called* hidden constants. *A* hidden subsignature of Σ *is a hidden signature* (Ψ, D, Γ) *with* $\Gamma \subseteq \Sigma$. *A* behavioral *(or* hidden*)* Σ-specification *or* -theory *is a triple* (Σ, Γ, E), *where* Σ *is a hidden signature,* Γ *is a hidden subsignature of* Σ, *and* E *is a set of* Σ*-equations. The operations in* $\Gamma - \Psi$ *are called* behavioral.

A hidden Σ-algebra *is a many sorted* Σ*-algebra* A *such that* $A|_\Psi = D$.

Behavioral operations are the ones that can be used in experiments, i.e., they define behavioral equivalence. The results of experiments lie in the data algebra. Philosophically, an assertion that an operation is behavioral seems a kind of sentence; in this view, it is accidental that the set of such sentences forms a signature, as in the "extended signatures" of [4].

Example 1. Below is a behavioral specification for sets, written in the CafeOBJ language [5] (however, the CafeOBJ parser does not accept it, because behavioral operations with more than one hidden argument are currently prohibited):

```
mod* SET1 { *[ Set ]* pr(NAT)
bop _in_ : Nat Set -> Bool  ** attribute
op empty : -> Set           ** hidden const
bop add  : Nat Set -> Set   ** method
bop _U_  : Set Set -> Set   ** 2 hidden args!
```

```
bop _&_    : Set Set -> Set   ** 2 hidden args!
bop neg    : Set -> Set       ** method
vars N N' : Nat  vars X X' : Set
eq N in empty = false .
eq N in add(N',X) = (N == N') or (N in X) .
eq N in (X U X')  = (N in X)  or (N in X') .
eq N in (X & X')  = (N in X) and (N in X') .
eq N in neg(X)    = not (N in X) . }
```

Here "`*[Set]*`" declares `Set` to be a hidden sort, "`bop`" indicates a behavioral operation, and "`pr(NAT)`" indicates that the module `NAT` of natural numbers is imported in "protecting" mode, i.e., the naturals are not compromised by the new declarations and equations. The constant `empty` is the only non-behavioral operation, and `neg` is complement with respect to the set of all natural numbers. It seems undeniable that set union is a natural example motivating our generalization; there are also many other examples. We will see later that this spec is equivalent to another having `in` as its only behavioral operation.

Definition 2. *Given a hidden signature Γ, an (appropriate) Γ-*context *of sort s is a visible term in $T_\Gamma(\{z\} \cup Z)$ having exactly one occurrence of a special variable*[2] *z of sort s, where Z is an infinite set of special variables. We let $C_\Gamma[z : s]$ denote the set of all Γ-contexts of sort s, and $var(c)$ the finite set of variables of c, except z. Given a hidden signature Σ, a hidden subsignature Γ of Σ, and a Σ-algebra A, each Γ-context c generates a map $A_c \colon A_s \to (A^{var(c)} \to D)$ defined as $A_c(a)(\theta) = a_\theta^*(c)$, where a_θ^* is the unique extension of the map (denoted a_θ) that takes z to a and each $z' \in var(c)$ to $\theta(z')$. The equivalence given by $a \equiv_\Sigma^\Gamma a'$ iff $A_c(a) = A_c(a',)$ for all Γ-contexts c is called Γ-*behavioral equivalence on A. *Given any equivalence $\sim$ on A, an operation σ in $\Sigma_{s_1 \ldots s_n, s}$ is* congruent for $\sim$ *iff $A_\sigma(a_1, \ldots, a_n) \sim A_\sigma(a'_1, \ldots, a'_n)$ whenever $a_i \sim a'_i$ for $i = 1 \ldots n$. An operation σ is Γ-*behaviorally congruent for A *iff σ is congruent for $\equiv_\Sigma^\Gamma$; we will often say just "congruent" instead of "behaviorally congruent"*[3]. A hidden Γ-congruence on A *is an equivalence on A which is the identity on visible sorts and such that each operation in Γ is congruent for it.*

The following is the basis for several of our results, especially coinduction; it generalizes a similar result in [12] to operations that can have more than one hidden argument.

Theorem 1. *Given a hidden subsignature Γ of Σ and a hidden Σ-algebra A, then Γ-behavioral equivalence is the largest hidden Γ-congruence on A.*

Proof. We first show that $\equiv_\Sigma^\Gamma$ is a hidden Γ-congruence. It is straightforward that it is the identity on visible sorts because we can take the context $c = z$. Now let $\sigma : s_1 \ldots s_n \to s$ be any operation in Γ, let $a_1 \equiv_{\Sigma,s_1}^\Gamma a'_1, \ldots, a_n \equiv_{\Sigma,s_n}^\Gamma a'_n$, let c be any Γ-context of sort s, and let $\theta\colon var(c) \to A$ be any map. Let

[2] "Special variables" are assumed different from all other current variable.

[3] A similar notion has been given by Padawitz [16].

$z_1, \ldots, z_n$ be variables in Z distinct from z and from those in $var(c)$, and take the Γ-contexts $c_j = c[\sigma(z_1, \ldots, z_{j-1}, z, z_{j+1}, \ldots, z_n)]$ of sorts s_j and the maps $\theta_j \colon \{z_1, \ldots, z_{j-1}, z, z_{j+1}, \ldots, z_n\} \cup var(c) \to A$ to be defined by $\theta_j(z_i) = a'_i$ for $1 \leq i < j$, $\theta_j(z_i) = a_i$ for $j < i \leq n$, and $\theta_j(z') = \theta(z')$ for $z' \in var(c)$, for $1 \leq j \leq n$. Notice that $A_c(A_\sigma(a_1, \ldots, a_n)) = A_{c_1}(a_1)(\theta_1)$, that $A_{c_j}(a_j)(\theta_j) = A_{c_j}(a'_j)(\theta_j)$ for all $1 \leq j \leq n$ because $a_j \equiv^\Gamma_{\Sigma,s_j} a'_j$ and c_j and θ_j are appropriate Γ-contexts and maps, that $A_{c_j}(a'_j)(\theta_j) = A_{c_{j+1}}(a_{j+1})(\theta_{j+1})$ for all $1 \leq j < n$, and that $A_{c_n}(a'_n)(\theta_n) = A_c(A_\sigma(a'_1, \ldots, a'_n))(\theta)$. Then $A_c(A_\sigma(a_1, \ldots, a_n))(\theta) = A_c(A_\sigma(a'_1, \ldots, a'_n))(\theta)$, that is, $A_\sigma(a_1, \ldots, a_n) \equiv^\Gamma_{\Sigma,s} A_\sigma(a'_1, \ldots, a'_n)$. Therefore σ is Γ-behaviorally congruent for A, and so $\equiv^\Gamma_\Sigma$ is a hidden Γ-congruence.

Now let $\sim$ be another hidden Γ-congruence on A and let $a \sim_s a'$. Because each operation in Γ is congruent for $\sim$, $A_c(a)(\theta) \sim A_c(a')(\theta)$ for any Γ-context c of sort s and any map $\theta \colon var(c) \to A$, and because $\sim$ is the identity on visible sorts, $A_c(a)(\theta) = A_c(a')(\theta)$. Therefore $a \equiv^\Gamma_{\Sigma,s} a'$, that is, $\sim \subseteq \equiv^\Gamma_\Sigma$.

Definition 3. *A hidden Σ-algebra A Γ-*behaviorally satisfies *a conditional Σ-equation $e = (\forall X)\ t = t'$* **if** *$t_1 = t'_1, \ldots, t_n = t'_n$ iff for each $\theta \colon X \to A$, if $\theta(t_i) \equiv^\Gamma_\Sigma \theta(t'_i)$ for $i = 1, \ldots, n$, then $\theta(t) \equiv^\Gamma_\Sigma \theta(t')$; in this case we write $A \models^\Gamma_\Sigma e$. If E is a set of Σ-equations, we write $A \models^\Gamma_\Sigma E$ if A Γ-behaviorally satisfies each equation in E. When Σ and Γ are clear from context, we may write $\equiv$ and $\models$ instead of $\equiv^\Gamma_\Sigma$ and $\models^\Gamma_\Sigma$, respectively. We say that A* behaviorally satisfies *(or* is a model of*) a behavioral specification $\mathcal{B} = (\Sigma, \Gamma, E)$ iff $A \models^\Gamma_\Sigma E$, and in this case we write $A \models \mathcal{B}$; we write $\mathcal{B} \models e$ whenever $A \models \mathcal{B}$ implies $A \models^\Gamma_\Sigma e$. An operation $\sigma \in \Sigma$ is* behaviorally congruent for *$\mathcal{B}$ iff σ is behaviorally congruent for every $A \models \mathcal{B}$.*

Example 2. Let SET2 be SET1 without the operation neg and the last equation. Then one model of SET2 is finite lists of natural numbers, with in as membership, empty the empty list, add placing a number at the front of a list, _U_ appending two lists, and _&_ giving a list containing each element in the first list that also appears in the second. Notice that multiple occurrences of natural numbers are allowed in the "sets" of this model. Two lists are behaviorally equivalent iff they contain exactly the same natural numbers, without regard to order or number of occurrences. This implementation of sets goes back to the earliest days of LISP, and until now, its correctness has seemed a bit mysterious, at least to the authors of this paper.

Proposition 1. *If $\mathcal{B} = (\Sigma, \Gamma, E)$ is a behavioral specification, then all operations in Γ and all hidden constants are behaviorally congruent for $\mathcal{B}$.*

Example 3. All operations in SET1 in Example 1 are congruent. We will show that they are still be congruent when in is the only behavioral operation.

The following reduces behavioral congruence to behavioral satisfaction of a certain equation, thus underlining the assertional character of this property.

Proposition 2. *Given a behavioral specification $\mathcal{B} = (\Sigma, \Gamma, E)$ and an operation $\sigma \in \Sigma_{v_1 \ldots v_m h_1 \ldots h_k, s}$, let e_σ be the conditional Σ-equation $(\forall Y, x_1, x_1', ..., x_k, x_k')\ \sigma(Y, x_1, ..., x_k) = \sigma(Y, x_1', ..., x_k')$ **if** $x_1 = x_1', ..., x_k = x_k'$, where $Y = \{y_1 : v_1, ..., y_m : v_m\}$. Then*

1. *σ is Γ-behaviorally congruent for a hidden Σ-algebra A iff $A \models_\Sigma^\Gamma e_\sigma$, and*
2. *σ is behaviorally congruent for $\mathcal{B}$ iff $\mathcal{B} \models e_\sigma$.*

The next result supports the elimination of hidden universal quantifiers in proofs.

Theorem 2 (Theorem of Hidden Constants). *If $\mathcal{B} = (\Sigma, \Gamma, E)$ is a behavioral specification, e is the Σ-equation $(\forall Y, X)\ t = t'$ **if** $t_1 = t_1', ..., t_n = t_n'$, and e_X is the $(\Sigma \cup X)$-equation $(\forall Y)\ t = t'$ **if** $t_1 = t_1', ..., t_n = t_n'$, where $\Sigma \cup X$ is the hidden signature obtained from Σ adding the variables in X as hidden constants, then $\mathcal{B} \models e$ iff $\mathcal{B}_X \models e_X$, where $\mathcal{B}_X = (\Sigma \cup X, \Gamma, E)$.*

Proof. Suppose $\mathcal{B} \models e$, let A' be a $(\Sigma \cup X)$-algebra such that $A' \models \mathcal{B}_X$, and let A be the Σ-algebra $A|_\Sigma$. Notice that the Γ-behavioral equivalences on A and A' coincide, and that $A \models_\Sigma^\Gamma E$. Let $\theta : Y \to A'$ be such that $\theta(t_i) = \theta(t_i')$ for $i = 1...n$, and let $\tau : Y \cup X \to A'$ be defined by $\tau(y) = \theta(y)$ for all $y \in Y$, and $\tau(x) = A_x'$ for all $x \in X$. Notice that $\tau(t_i) = \theta(t_i) = \theta(t_i') = \tau(t_i')$ for $i = 1...n$, and $A \models_\Sigma^\Gamma e$ since $A \models_\Sigma^\Gamma E$. Therefore $\tau(t) = \tau(t')$, so that $\theta(t) = \theta(t')$. Consequently, $A' \models_{\Sigma \cup X}^\Gamma e_X$, so that $\mathcal{B}_X \models e_X$.

Conversely, suppose $\mathcal{B}_X \models e_X$, let A be a Σ-algebra with $A \models \mathcal{B}$, and let $\tau : Y \cup X \to A$ be such that $\tau(t_i) = \tau(t_i')$ for $i = 1...n$. Let A' be the $(\Sigma \cup X)$-algebra with the same carriers as A, and the same interpretations of operations in Σ, but with $A_x' = \tau(x)$ for each x in X. Notice that the Γ-behavioral equivalences on A and A' coincide. Also notice that $A' \models_{\Sigma \cup X}^\Gamma E$, so that $A' \models_{\Sigma \cup X}^\Gamma e_X$. Let $\theta : Y \to A'$ be the map defined by $\theta(y) = \tau(y)$ for each $y \in Y$. It is straightforward that $\theta(t_i) = \tau(t_i) = \tau(t_i') = \theta(t_i')$ for $i = 1...n$, so that $\theta(t) = \theta(t')$, that is, $\tau(t) = \tau(t')$. Therefore $A \models_\Sigma^\Gamma e$, so that $\mathcal{B} \models e$.

The following justifies implication elimination for conditional hidden equations:

Proposition 3. *Given behavioral specification $\mathcal{B} = (\Sigma, \Gamma, E)$ and $t_1, t_1', ..., t_n, t_n'$ ground hidden terms, let E' be $E \cup \{(\forall\emptyset)\ t_1 = t_1', ..., (\forall\emptyset)\ t_n = t_n'\}$, and let $\mathcal{B}'$ be the behavioral specification (Σ, Γ, E'). Then*

$$\mathcal{B}' \models (\forall X)\ t = t' \quad \textit{iff} \quad \mathcal{B} \models (\forall X)\ t = t' \ \textbf{if}\ t_1 = t_1', ..., t_n = t_n'.$$

3 Rules of Inference

This section introduces and justifies our rules for hidden congruent deduction. $\mathcal{B} = (\Sigma, \Gamma, E)$ is a fixed hidden specification throughout. The following shows soundness.

Proposition 4. *The following hold:*

1. $\mathcal{B} \models (\forall X)\, t = t$,
2. $\mathcal{B} \models (\forall X)\, t = t'$ *implies* $\mathcal{B} \models (\forall X)\, t' = t$,
3. $\mathcal{B} \models (\forall X)\, t = t'$ *and* $\mathcal{B} \models (\forall X)\, t' = t''$ *imply* $\mathcal{B} \models (\forall X)\, t = t''$,
4. *If* $\mathcal{B} \models (\forall Y)\, t = t'$ **if** $t_1 = t'_1, ..., t_n = t'_n$ *and* $\theta : Y \to T_\Sigma(X)$ *is a substitution such that* $\mathcal{B} \models (\forall X)\, \theta(t_i) = \theta(t'_i)$ *for* $i = 1...n$, *then* $\mathcal{B} \models (\forall X)\, \theta(t) = \theta(t')$,
5. *If* $\sigma \in \Sigma_{s_1...s_n,s}$ *and* $t, t' \in T_{\Sigma,s_j}(X)$ *for some* $1 \leq j \leq n$, *then*
   a) *if* $s_j \in V$ *then* $\mathcal{B} \models (\forall Z_j, X)\, \sigma(Z_j, t) = \sigma(Z_j, t')$, *where* Z_j *is the set of variables* $\{z_1 : s_1, ..., z_{j-1} : s_{j-1}, z_{j+1} : s_{j+1}, ..., z_n : s_n\}$ *and* $\sigma(Z_j, t)$ *is the term* $\sigma(z_1, ..., z_{j-1}, t, z_{j+1}, ..., z_n)$, *and*
   b) *if* $s_j \in H$ *and* σ *is congruent then* $\mathcal{B} \models (\forall Z_j, X)\, \sigma(Z_j, t) = \sigma(Z_j, t')$.

Notice that if $\sigma \in \Sigma_{s_1...s_n,s}$ is a congruent operation for $\mathcal{B}$ and t_i, t'_i are Σ-terms in $T_{\Sigma,s_i}(X)$ such that $\mathcal{B} \models (\forall X)\, t_i = t'_i$ for all $i = 1...n$, then it is easily seen that $\mathcal{B} \models (\forall X)\, \sigma(t_1, ..., t_n) = \sigma(t'_1, ..., t'_n)$. Substituting equal terms into a term is not always sound for behavioral satisfaction, because 5 above is not valid for non-congruent operations; the rules below take account of this fact. We define $\Vdash$ by $\mathcal{B} \Vdash (\forall X)\, t = t'$ iff $(\forall X)\, t = t'$ is derivable from $\mathcal{B}$ using (1)–(5) below.

(1) Reflexivity : $$\frac{}{(\forall X)\, t = t}$$

(2) Symmetry : $$\frac{(\forall X)\, t = t'}{(\forall X)\, t' = t}$$

(3) Transitivity : $$\frac{(\forall X)\, t = t',\ (\forall X)\, t' = t''}{(\forall X)\, t = t''}$$

(4) Substitution : $$\frac{(\forall Y)\, l = r \in E,\ \theta : Y \to T_\Sigma(X)}{(\forall X)\, \theta(l) = \theta(r)}$$

(5) Congruence :

a) $$\frac{(\forall X)\, t = t',\ sort(t, t') \in V}{(\forall Z_j, X)\, \sigma(Z_j, t) = \sigma(Z_j, t'),\ \text{for each } \sigma \in \Sigma}$$

b) $$\frac{(\forall X)\, t = t',\ sort(t, t') \in H}{(\forall Z_j, X)\, \sigma(Z_j, t) = \sigma(Z_j, t'),\ \text{for each congruent } \sigma \in \Sigma}$$

Rule (5b) is not fully syntactic, because the notion of congruent operation is semantic. But Proposition 1 tells us that all visible and all behavioral operations, as well as all hidden constants are congruent, so we already have many cases where (5) can be applied. Later we will see how other operations can be shown congruent; this is important because our inference system becomes more powerful with each new operation proved congruent. The following result expresses soundness of these rules for both equational and behavioral satisfaction.

Proposition 5. *Given a* Σ*-equation* $(\forall X)\, t = t'$, *if* $\mathcal{B} \Vdash (\forall X)\, t = t'$ *then* $E \models_\Sigma (\forall X)\, t = t'$ *and* $\mathcal{B} \models (\forall X)\, t = t'$. *If all operations are behaviorally congruent, then equational reasoning is sound for the behavioral satisfaction.*

The rules (1)–(5) above differ from those in [4] in allowing both congruent and non-congruent operations. CafeOBJ's behavioral rewriting [5] is a special case in the same way that standard rewriting is a special case of equational deduction. Unlike equational deduction, these rules are not complete for behavioral satisfaction, but they do seem to provide proofs for most cases of interest.

3.1 Coinduction and Cobases

In this subsection, we assume $\mathcal{B}' = (\Sigma', \Gamma', E')$ is a *conservative extension* of $\mathcal{B}$, i.e., Σ is a hidden subsignature of Σ' and for every model A of $\mathcal{B}$ there exists a model A' of $\mathcal{B}'$ such that $A'|_\Sigma = A$. Also let Δ be a hidden subsignature of Σ'.

Definition 4. *Given a variable z of hidden sort h, let $T_{\Sigma'}(\Gamma', \Delta; z, Z)$ be the set of all Σ'-terms γ with variables in $\{z\} \cup Z$, such that $\sigma_n \in \Delta$ and $\sigma_j, ..., \sigma_{n-1} \in \Gamma'$ for each occurrence of z, where $(\sigma_1, ..., \sigma_n)$ is the sequence of operations in Σ' from the root of γ to that z and $j = \max\{1, \sup\{k \mid k \leq n \text{ and } \sigma_k \text{ is visible}\}\}$*[4].

Then Δ is a cobasis *(is* context complete*) for $\mathcal{B}$ iff for every Γ-context c of hidden sort h, there is some Σ'-term γ in $T_{\Sigma'}(\Gamma', \Delta; z, Z)$ (in $T_\Delta(\{z\} \cup Z)$) such that $\mathcal{B}' \models (\forall z, Z)\ c = \gamma$, where $Z = var(c)$.*

Often $\mathcal{B} = \mathcal{B}'$ and $\Delta = \Gamma$, and in this case Δ is both context complete and a cobasis for $\mathcal{B}$. The following justifies coinduction in this and in the general situation:

Theorem 3. *If Δ is a cobasis for $\mathcal{B}$, if t, t' are Σ-terms of hidden sort h with variables in X, and if $\mathcal{B}' \models (\forall Z_j, X)\ \delta(Z_j, t) = \delta(Z_j, t')$ for all appropriate $\delta \colon s_1 ... s_n \to s$ in Δ and $1 \leq j \leq n$ (that is, $s_j = h$), where Z_j is the set of variables $\{z_1 : s_1, ..., z_{j-1} : s_{j-1}, z_{j+1} : s_{j+1}, ..., z_n : s_n\}$ and $\delta(Z_j, t)$ is the term $\delta(z_1, ..., z_{j-1}, t, z_{j+1}, ..., z_n)$, then $\mathcal{B} \models (\forall X)\ t = t'$.*

Proof. *We first show that $\mathcal{B}' \models (\forall Z, X)\ \gamma[t] = \gamma[t']$ for all γ in $T_{\Sigma'}(\Gamma', \Delta; z, Z)$. Let A' be a hidden Σ'-algebra such that $A' \models \mathcal{B}'$, let $\varphi' : X \to A'$ and $\theta' : Z \to A'$ be any two assignments, and let $a = \varphi'(t)$ and $a' = \varphi'(t')$. Let $Q \subseteq T_{\Sigma'}(\Gamma', \Delta; z, Z)$ be the set of all Σ'-terms γ with variables in $\{z\} \cup Z$, such that $\sigma_n \in \Delta$ and $\sigma_j, ..., \sigma_{n-1} \in \Gamma'$ for each occurrence of z in γ, where $(\sigma_1, ..., \sigma_n)$ is the sequence of operations in Σ' from the root of γ to that z and $j = \sup\{k \mid k \leq n \text{ and } \sigma_k \text{ is visible}\}\} \geq 1$.*

> *We prove by structural induction on $\gamma \in T_{\Sigma'}(\Gamma', \Delta; z, Z)$ the following assertion: if $\gamma \in Q$ then $A'_\gamma(a)(\theta') = A'_\gamma(a')(\theta')$ else $A'_\gamma(a)(\theta') \equiv^{\Gamma'}_{\Sigma'} A'_\gamma(a')(\theta')$. If $\gamma = z' \in Z$ then $A'_\gamma(a)(\theta') = \theta'(z') = A'_\gamma(a')(\theta')$. Now suppose that $\gamma = \sigma(\gamma_1, ..., \gamma_k, z, z, ..., z)$, where $\sigma : s_1 ... s_n \to s$, $k \leq n$, and $\gamma_1, ..., \gamma_k \in T_{\Sigma'}(\Gamma', \Delta; z, Z)$ (without restricting the generality, we suppose that the possible occurrences of z as arguments of σ are the last $n - k$*

[4] Notice that if there is no $k < n$ such that σ_k is visible then the supremum is 0 and $j = 1$, that is, the supremum is taken over natural numbers.

arguments). Let $a_i = A'_{\gamma_i}(a)(\theta')$ and $a'_i = A'_{\gamma_i}(a')(\theta')$ for all $i = 1, ..., k$, and notice that $A'_\gamma(a)(\theta') = A'_\sigma(a_1, ..., a_k, a, a, ..., a)$ and $A'_\gamma(a')(\theta') = A'_\sigma(a'_1, ..., a'_k, a', a', ..., a')$. By the induction hypothesis, $a_i \equiv^{\Gamma'}_{\Sigma'} a'_i$ for all $i = 1, ..., k$. One distinguishes the following cases:

Case 1: *$\sigma \in \Delta$. Since $A' \models^{\Gamma'}_{\Sigma'} (\forall Z_j, X)\, \delta(Z_j, t) = \delta(Z_j, t')$ for all appropriate $\delta \in \Delta$ (in particular for σ) and j, one can easily show:*

$$\begin{aligned} A'_\sigma(a_1, ..., a_k, a, a, ..., a) &\equiv^{\Gamma'}_{\Sigma'} A'_\sigma(a_1, ..., a_k, a', a, ..., a) \\ &\equiv^{\Gamma'}_{\Sigma'} A'_\sigma(a_1, ..., a_k, a', a', ..., a) \\ &\vdots \quad \vdots \\ &\equiv^{\Gamma'}_{\Sigma'} A'_\sigma(a_1, ..., a_k, a', a', ..., a'). \end{aligned}$$

Now one distinguishes two subcases:

Case 1.1: *$\sigma \in \Delta - \Gamma'$. Then $\gamma_1, ..., \gamma_k \in Q$, so by the induction hypothesis, $a_i = a'_i$ for all $i = 1, ..., k$. Therefore $A'_\gamma(a)(\theta') \equiv^{\Gamma'}_{\Sigma'} A'_\gamma(a')(\theta')$. If $\gamma \in Q$ then the sort of σ is visible, that is, $A'_\gamma(a)(\theta') = A'_\gamma(a')(\theta')$.*

Case 1.2: *$\sigma \in \Delta \cap \Gamma'$. Since σ is congruent, $A'_\sigma(a_1, ..., a_k, a', a', ..., a') \equiv^{\Gamma'}_{\Sigma'} A'_\sigma(a'_1, ..., a'_k, a', a', ..., a')$. Therefore $A'_\gamma(a)(\theta') \equiv^{\Gamma'}_{\Sigma'} A'_\gamma(a')(\theta')$. If the sort of σ is visible then $A'_\gamma(a)(\theta') = A'_\gamma(a')(\theta')$. If $\gamma \in Q$ and the sort of σ is hidden then $k = n$ and $\gamma_1, ..., \gamma_n \in Q$, in which case $a_i = a'_i$ for all $i = 1, ..., n$, and hence $A'_\gamma(a)(\theta') = A'_\gamma(a')(\theta')$.*

Case 2: *$\sigma \in \Gamma' - \Delta$. Then $k = n$ and since σ is behaviorally congruent, $A'_\sigma(a_1, ..., a_k, a', a', ..., a') \equiv^{\Gamma'}_{\Sigma'} A'_\sigma(a'_1, ..., a'_k, a', a', ..., a')$, that is, $A'_\gamma(a)(\theta') \equiv^{\Gamma'}_{\Sigma'} A'_\gamma(a')(\theta')$. If the sort of σ is visible then $A'_\gamma(a)(\theta') = A'_\gamma(a')(\theta')$. If $\gamma \in Q$ and the sort of σ is hidden then $\gamma_1, ..., \gamma_n \in Q$, in which case $a_i = a'_i$ for all $i = 1, ..., n$, and hence $A'_\gamma(a)(\theta') = A'_\gamma(a')(\theta')$.*

Case 3: *$\sigma \in \Sigma' - \Gamma' - \Delta$. Then $k = n$ and $\gamma_1, ..., \gamma_n \in Q$. So by the induction hypothesis, $a_i = a'_i$ for all $i = 1, ..., n$, so $A'_\gamma(a)(\theta') = A'_\gamma(a')(\theta')$.*

Thus $\mathcal{B}' \models (\forall Z, X)\, \gamma[t] = \gamma[t']$ for all γ in $T(\Gamma', \Delta; z, Z)$. Let c be a Γ-context for t and t' over z, and let γ be a term in $T_{\Sigma'}(\Gamma', \Delta; z, Z)$ with $\mathcal{B}' \models (\forall z, Z)\, c = \gamma$, where $Z = var(c)$. Let A be any hidden Σ-algebra such that $A \models \mathcal{B}$, let $\varphi: X \to A$ be any assignment, let $a = \varphi(t)$ and $a' = \varphi(t')$, and let A' be a hidden Σ'-algebra such that $A' \models \mathcal{B}'$ and $A'|_\Sigma = A$.

Then $A' \models^{\Gamma'}_{\Sigma'} (\forall z, Z)\; c = \gamma$ and $A' \models^{\Gamma'}_{\Sigma'} (\forall Z, X)\; \gamma[t] = \gamma[t']$. Let $\theta: Z \to A$ be any assignment and let $\psi: Z \cup X \to A'$ be defined as θ on Z and as φ on X. Notice that $\varphi(\gamma[t]) = A'_\gamma(a)(\theta)$ and $\varphi(\gamma[t']) = A'_\gamma(a')(\theta)$. Then $A'_c(a)(\theta) = A'_\gamma(a)(\theta)$, $A'_c(a')(\theta) = A'_\gamma(a')(\theta)$, and $A'_\gamma(a)(\theta) = A'_\gamma(a')(\theta)$. Since θ was chosen arbitrarily, $A'_c(a) = A'_c(a')$, that is, $A_c(a) = A_c(a')$. Hence $a \equiv^{\Gamma}_{\Sigma} a'$. Q.E.D.

We now introduce our inference rule for coinduction:

$$\text{(6) } \Delta\text{-Coinduction:} \quad \frac{(\forall Z_j, X)\, \delta(Z_j, t) = \delta(Z_j, t') \text{ for all } \delta \in \Delta \text{ and } 1 \leq j \leq n}{(\forall X)\; t = t'}$$

The Δ-Coinduction inference rule above should be read as follows: Given $t, t' \in T_\Sigma(X)$ such that $(\forall Z_j, X)\ \delta(Z_j, t) = \delta(Z_j, t')$ is derivable from $\mathcal{B}'$ for all appropriate $\delta : s_1 ... s_n \to s$ in Δ and $1 \le j \le n$, then $(\forall X)\ t = t'$ is derivable from $\mathcal{B}$. Notice that equations previously proved by coinduction can be used.

Proposition 6. *Define* $\Vdash_\Delta$ *by* $\mathcal{B} \Vdash_\Delta (\forall X)\ t = t'$ *iff* $(\forall X)\ t = t'$ *is derivable from* $\mathcal{B}$ *under rules (1)–(6). Then* $\Vdash_\Delta$ *is sound for behavioral satisfaction if* Δ *is a cobasis for* $\mathcal{B}$.

Notice that $\Vdash_\Delta$ is not necessarily sound with respect to equational satisfaction. The special case of Δ-coinduction where Δ consists of all the attributes is called *attribute coinduction.* Kumo [9] implements this special case, and will soon implement the coinduction rule (6) in its general form.

Definition 5. *Given a (not necessary hidden) signature* Σ, *a* derived operation $\gamma : s_1 ... s_n \to s$ *of* Σ *is a term in* $T_{\Sigma,s}(\{z_1, ..., z_n\})$, *where* $z_1, ..., z_n$ *are special variables of sorts* $s_1, ..., s_n$. *For any* Σ*-algebra* A, *the interpretation of* γ *in* A *is the map* $\gamma_A : A_{s_1} \times \cdots \times A_{s_n} \to A_s$ *defined as* $\gamma_A(a_1, ..., a_n) = \theta(\gamma)$, *where* $\theta : \{z_1, ..., z_n\} \to A$ *takes* z_i *to* a_i *for all* $i = 1...n$. *We let* $Der(\Sigma)$ *denote the signature of all derived operations of* Σ.

A common case is that $\mathcal{B}' = (Der(\Sigma), \Gamma, E)$ and Δ is a subsignature of derived operations over Γ. The following further extends the applicability of coinduction:

Proposition 7. *If* $\mathcal{B}' = (Der(\Sigma), \Gamma, E)$ *then* $\mathcal{B}'$ *is a conservative extension of* $\mathcal{B}$, *and if in addition* $\Delta \subseteq Der(\Gamma)$ *is context complete for* $\mathcal{B}$, *then* Δ *is a cobasis for* $\mathcal{B}$.

In many cases, the form of equations suggests which operations to put into Δ, as in the `STACK` specification (Example 5), where it is easily seen that any context over `top`, `push` and `pop` is equivalent to a context over only `top` and `pop`. Following [1,2], an algorithm for reducing the number of contexts based on context rewriting is given in [15] for certain behavioral specifications[5] to reduce the number of contexts; it can be applied to get a context complete Δ (when $\mathcal{B}' = (Der(\Sigma), \Gamma, E)$, see Proposition 7).

The first effective algebraic proof technique for behavioral properties was context induction, introduced by Rolf Hennicker [13] and further developed in joint work with Michel Bidoit; unfortunately, context induction can be awkward to apply in practice, as noticed in [6]. Hidden coinduction was originally proposed as a way to avoid these kinds of awkwardness.

4 Proving Congruence

This section discusses techniques for proving that operations are congruent with respect to Γ. We first give a general method that requires deduction, and then

[5] [15] allows just one hidden sort with all operations having at most one hidden sort, but we think the method will extend to the current framework.

a more specific but surprisingly applicable method that only requires checking the form of equations.

Example 4. The following behavioral theory of sets, again written in CafeOBJ, differs from that in Example 1 by having just one behavioral operation, in:

```
mod* SET { *[ Set ]* pr(NAT)
bop _in_ : Nat Set -> Bool       ** attribute
op empty : -> Set                ** hidden constant
op add   : Nat Set -> Set        ** method
op _U_   : Set Set -> Set        ** two hidden args
op _&_   : Set Set -> Set        ** two hidden args
op neg   : Set -> Set            ** method
vars N N' : Nat  vars X X' : Set
eq N in empty = false .
eq N in add(N',X) = (N == N') or (N in X) .
eq N in (X U X')  = (N in X)  or (N in X') .
eq N in (X & X')  = (N in X) and (N in X') .
eq N in neg(X)    = not (N in X) . }
```

We prove that all operations are congruent. By Proposition 1, both in and empty are congruent. Let Δ be the signature of NAT together with in and notice that Δ is a cobasis for SET (because Δ contains exactly the signature of NAT and the behavioral operations), so the six inference rules are sound for the behavioral satisfaction.

Congruence of add*:* By Proposition 2, we have to prove that

$\mathtt{SET} \models (\forall N : \mathtt{Nat}, X, X' : \mathtt{Set})\ \mathtt{add}(N, X) = \mathtt{add}(N, X')\ \mathbf{if}\ X = X'$.

By the theorem of hidden constants (Theorem 2), this is equivalent to proving

$\mathtt{SET}_X \models (\forall N : \mathtt{Nat})\ \mathtt{add}(N, x) = \mathtt{add}(N, x')\ \mathbf{if}\ x = x'$,

where $\mathtt{SET}_X$ adds to SET two hidden constants, x and x'. By Proposition 3, it is equivalent to

$\mathtt{SET}' \models (\forall N : \mathtt{Nat})\ \mathtt{add}(N, x) = \mathtt{add}(N, x')$,

where $\mathtt{SET}'$ adds to $\mathtt{SET}_X$ the equation $(\forall \emptyset)\ x = x'$. Now we use the six inference rules to prove that $\mathtt{SET}' \Vdash_{\{\mathtt{in}\}} (\forall N : \mathtt{Nat})\ \mathtt{add}(N, x) = \mathtt{add}(N, x')$. The following inferences give the proof:

1. $\mathtt{SET}' \Vdash_{\{\mathtt{in}\}} (\forall M, N : \mathtt{Nat})\ M = M$ (1)
2. $\mathtt{SET}' \Vdash_{\{\mathtt{in}\}} (\forall M, N : \mathtt{Nat})\ x = x'$ (4)
3. $\mathtt{SET}' \Vdash_{\{\mathtt{in}\}} (\forall M, N : \mathtt{Nat})\ M\ \mathtt{in}\ x = M\ \mathtt{in}\ x'$ (5)
4. $\mathtt{SET}' \Vdash_{\{\mathtt{in}\}} (\forall M, N : \mathtt{Nat})\ (M == N) = (M == N)$ (1)
5. $\mathtt{SET}' \Vdash_{\{\mathtt{in}\}} (\forall M, N : \mathtt{Nat})\ (M == N)\,\mathtt{or}\,(M\ \mathtt{in}\ x) = (M == N)\,\mathtt{or}\,(M\ \mathtt{in}\ x')$ (5)
6. $\mathtt{SET}' \Vdash_{\{\mathtt{in}\}} (\forall M, N : \mathtt{Nat})\ M\ \mathtt{in}\ \mathtt{add}(N, x) = (M == N)\ \mathtt{or}\ (M\ \mathtt{in}\ x)$ (4)
7. $\mathtt{SET}' \Vdash_{\{\mathtt{in}\}} (\forall M, N : \mathtt{Nat})\ M\ \mathtt{in}\ \mathtt{add}(N, x') = (M == N)\ \mathtt{or}\ (M\ \mathtt{in}\ x')$ (4)
8. $\mathtt{SET}' \Vdash_{\{\mathtt{in}\}} (\forall M, N : \mathtt{Nat})\ M\ \mathtt{in}\ \mathtt{add}(N, x) = M\ \mathtt{in}\ \mathtt{add}(N, x')$ (2,3)
9. $\mathtt{SET}' \Vdash_{\{\mathtt{in}\}} (\forall N : \mathtt{Nat})\ \mathtt{add}(N, x) = \mathtt{add}(N, x')$ (6)

The rest follows by the soundness of the six rule inference system.

Congruence of _U_*:* By Proposition 2, Theorem 2 and Proposition 3, this is equivalent to $\mathtt{SET}' \models (\forall \emptyset)\ x_1\ \mathtt{U}\ x_2 = x'_1\ \mathtt{U}\ x'_2$, where $\mathtt{SET}'$ adds to SET the hidden constants x_1, x'_1, x_2, x'_2 and the equations $(\forall\emptyset)\ x_1 = x'_1, (\forall\emptyset)\ x_2 = x'_2$. One can infer the following:

1. $\mathsf{SET}' \Vdash_{\{\mathtt{in}\}} (\forall N : \mathtt{Nat})\ N\ \mathtt{in}\ x_1 = N\ \mathtt{in}\ x'_1$ (1, 4, 5)
2. $\mathsf{SET}' \Vdash_{\{\mathtt{in}\}} (\forall N : \mathtt{Nat})\ N\ \mathtt{in}\ x_2 = N\ \mathtt{in}\ x'_2$ (1, 4, 5)
3. $\mathsf{SET}' \Vdash_{\{\mathtt{in}\}} (\forall N : \mathtt{Nat})\ (N\ \mathtt{in}\ x_1)\,\mathtt{or}\,(N\ \mathtt{in}\ x_2) = (N\ \mathtt{in}\ x'_1)\,\mathtt{or}\,(N\ \mathtt{in}\ x'_2)$ (5)
4. $\mathsf{SET}' \Vdash_{\{\mathtt{in}\}} (\forall N : \mathtt{Nat})\ N\ \mathtt{in}\ (x_1\ \mathtt{U}\ x_2) = (N\ \mathtt{in}\ x_1)\ \mathtt{or}\ (N\ \mathtt{in}\ x_2)$ (4)
5. $\mathsf{SET}' \Vdash_{\{\mathtt{in}\}} (\forall N : \mathtt{Nat})\ N\ \mathtt{in}\ (x'_1\ \mathtt{U}\ x'_2) = (N\ \mathtt{in}\ x'_1)\ \mathtt{or}\ (N\ \mathtt{in}\ x'_2)$ (4)
6. $\mathsf{SET}' \Vdash_{\{\mathtt{in}\}} (\forall N : \mathtt{Nat})\ N\ \mathtt{in}\ (x_1\ \mathtt{U}\ x_2) = N\ \mathtt{in}\ (x'_1\ \mathtt{U}\ x'_2)$ (2, 3)
7. $\mathsf{SET}' \Vdash_{\{\mathtt{in}\}} (\forall\emptyset)\ x_1\ \mathtt{U}\ x_2 = x'_1\ \mathtt{U}\ x'_2$ (6)

The rest follows by the soundness of the six rule inference system. The congruence property for _&_ and **neg** follow similarly.

A similar approach was used in proving the congruence of the operations in the previous example. We capture it in the following method for proving the congruence of an operation $\sigma : wh_1...h_k \to s$ for a hidden specification $\mathcal{B} = (\Sigma, \Gamma, E)$:

METHOD FOR PROVING CONGRUENCE:

- *Step 1:* Choose a suitable $\Delta \subseteq \Sigma$ and show that it is a cobasis. Usually Δ is just Γ, in which case it is automatically a cobasis.
- *Step 2:* Introduce appropriate new hidden constants $x_1, x'_1, ..., x_k, x'_k$, and new equations $(\forall\emptyset)\ x_1 = x'_1,...,(\forall\emptyset)\ x_k = x'_k$. Let $\mathcal{B}'$ denote the new hidden specification.
- *Step 3:* Show $\mathcal{B}' \Vdash_{\Delta} (\forall Y)\ \sigma(Y, x_1, ..., x_k) = \sigma(Y, x'_1, ..., x'_k)$, where Y is a set of appropriate visible variables.

The correctness of this method follows from Proposition 2, Theorem 2 and Proposition 3. Let's see how it works on another example:

Example 5. The following is a CafeOBJ behavioral theory of stacks of natural numbers:

```
mod* STACK { *[Stack]* pr(NAT)
bop top  : Stack -> Nat            ** attribute
bop pop  : Stack -> Stack          ** method
op  push : Nat Stack -> Stack      ** method
var N : Nat  var X : Stack
eq top(push(N,X)) = N .
beq pop(push(N,X)) = X . }
```

Let us prove the congruence of **push** using the method described above:

- *Step 1:* Let Δ be the signature of **NAT** together with **top** and **pop**. Then Δ is a cobasis for **STACK** because it contains exactly the data signature and the behavioral operations.

– *Step 2:* Introduce two hidden constants x and x' and the equation $(\forall\emptyset)\ x = x'$. Let STACK′ be the new hidden specification.
– *Step 3:* Prove $(\forall N : \texttt{Nat})\ \texttt{push}(N, x) = \texttt{push}(N, x')$. One natural proof is:

1. $\texttt{STACK}' \Vdash_{\{\texttt{top},\texttt{pop}\}} (\forall N : \texttt{Nat})\ \texttt{top}(\texttt{push}(N, x)) = N$ (4)
2. $\texttt{STACK}' \Vdash_{\{\texttt{top},\texttt{pop}\}} (\forall N : \texttt{Nat})\ \texttt{top}(\texttt{push}(N, x')) = N$ (4)
3. $\texttt{STACK}' \Vdash_{\{\texttt{top},\texttt{pop}\}} (\forall N : \texttt{Nat})\ \texttt{top}(\texttt{push}(N, x)) = \texttt{top}(\texttt{push}(N, x'))$ (2), (3)
4. $\texttt{STACK}' \Vdash_{\{\texttt{top},\texttt{pop}\}} (\forall N : \texttt{Nat})\ \texttt{pop}(\texttt{push}(N, x)) = x$ (4)
5. $\texttt{STACK}' \Vdash_{\{\texttt{top},\texttt{pop}\}} (\forall N : \texttt{Nat})\ \texttt{pop}(\texttt{push}(N, x')) = x'$ (4)
6. $\texttt{STACK}' \Vdash_{\{\texttt{top},\texttt{pop}\}} (\forall N : \texttt{Nat})\ x = x'$ (4)
7. $\texttt{STACK}' \Vdash_{\{\texttt{top},\texttt{pop}\}} (\forall N : \texttt{Nat})\ \texttt{pop}(\texttt{push}(N, x)) = \texttt{pop}(\texttt{push}(N, x'))$ (2, 3)
8. $\texttt{STACK}' \Vdash_{\{\texttt{top},\texttt{pop}\}} (\forall N : \texttt{Nat})\ \texttt{push}(N, x) = \texttt{push}(N, x')$ (6)

4.1 A Congruence Criterion

Let $\mathcal{B} = (\Sigma, \Gamma, E)$ be a hidden specification and let $\sigma : v_1...v_m h_1...h_k \to h$ be an operation in Σ, where $v_1, ..., v_m$ are visible sorts and $h_1, ..., h_k, h$ are hidden sorts. If $W = \{y_1 : v_1, ..., y_m : v_m, x_1 : h_1, ..., x_k : h_k\}$ is a set of variables then $\sigma(W)$ denotes the term $\sigma(y_1, ..., y_m, x_1, ..., x_k)$. Then

Theorem 4. *If Δ is a cobasis of $\mathcal{B}$ in a conservative extension $\mathcal{B}' = (\Sigma', \Gamma', E')$ of $\mathcal{B}$ and if for each appropriate $\delta\colon\ s_1...s_n \to s$ in Δ, there is some γ in $T_{\Gamma'}(Z_j \cup W)$ such that*[6] *$\mathcal{B}' \models (\forall Z_j, W)\ \delta(Z_j, \sigma(W)) = \gamma$ for $j = 1, ..., n$, then σ is behaviorally congruent for $\mathcal{B}$.*

Proof. *By Proposition 2, the Theorem of Hidden Constants (Theorem 2) and Proposition 3, it suffices to show $\mathcal{B}_{X,X'} \models (\forall Y)\ \sigma(Y, x_1, ..., x_k) = \sigma(Y, x'_1, ..., x'_k)$, where $\mathcal{B}_{X,X'} = (\Sigma \cup X \cup X', \Gamma, E \cup \{(\forall\emptyset)\ x_1 = x'_1, ..., (\forall\emptyset)\ x_k = x'_k\})$. Let $\mathcal{B}'_{X,X'}$ be the hidden specification $(\Sigma' \cup X \cup X', \Gamma', E' \cup \{(\forall\emptyset)\ x_1 = x'_1, ..., (\forall\emptyset)\ x_k = x'_k\})$. Note that $\mathcal{B}'_{X,X'}$ conservatively extends $\mathcal{B}_{X,X'}$ and that Δ is a cobasis for $\mathcal{B}_{X,X'}$. We claim that $\mathcal{B}'_{X,X'} \models (\forall Z_j, Y)\ \delta(Z_j, \sigma(Y, x_1, ..., x_k)) = \delta(Z_j, \sigma(Y, x'_1, ..., x'_k))$. Indeed, it is easy to see that $\mathcal{B}'_{X,X'}$ satisfies $(\forall Z_j, W)\ \delta(Z_j, \sigma(W)) = \gamma$, so by 4 of Proposition 4, $\mathcal{B}'_{X,X'}$ satisfies $(\forall Z_j, Y)\ \delta(Z_j, \sigma(Y, x_1, ..., x_k)) = \gamma_x$ and $\mathcal{B}'_{X,X'}$ satisfies $(\forall Z_j, Y)\ \delta(Z_j, \sigma(Y, x'_1, ..., x'_k)) = \gamma_{x'}$, where γ_x and $\gamma_{x'}$ are γ where each variable x_i in X is replaced by the corresponding constants x_i and x'_i, respectively, and since γ contains only operations in Γ' (which are behaviorally congruent for $\mathcal{B}'_{X,X'}$), by 4 of Proposition 4, we get $\mathcal{B}'_{X,X'} \models (\forall Z_j, Y)\ \gamma_x = \gamma_{x'}$. Then by Theorem 3, $\mathcal{B}_{X,X'} \models (\forall Y)\ \sigma(Y, x_1, ..., x_k) = \sigma(Y, x'_1, ..., x'_k)$, that is, σ is behaviorally congruent for $\mathcal{B}$.*

Corollary 1 (Congruence Criterion). *If for each appropriate $\delta\colon\ s_1...s_n \to s$ in Γ and each $j = 1, ..., n$ such that $s_j = h$, there is some γ in $T_\Gamma(Z_j \cup W)$ such that the Σ-equation $(\forall Z_j, W)\ \delta(Z_j, \sigma(W)) = \gamma$ is in*[7] *E, then σ is behaviorally congruent for $\mathcal{B}$.*

---

[6] We use the same notational conventions as in Theorem 3.
[7] Modulo renaming of variables.

Most examples fall under this easy to check syntactic criterion, including all those in this paper, and it would be easy to implement the criterion in a system like CafeOBJ.

5 Reducing the Behavioral Operations

The fewer operations Δ has, the easier it is to apply the Δ-coinduction rule. Most often, Δ contains the data signature and only behavioral operations, either all or some of them. Hence it is important to have as few behavioral operations as possible in a hidden specification.

Definition 6. *Hidden specifications $\mathcal{B}_1 = (\Sigma, \Gamma_1, E_1)$ and $\mathcal{B}_2 = (\Sigma, \Gamma_2, E_2)$ over the same hidden signature are* equivalent *iff for any hidden Σ-algebra A, $A \models \mathcal{B}_1$ iff $A \models \mathcal{B}_2$, and in this case $\equiv_\Sigma^{\Gamma_1} = \equiv_\Sigma^{\Gamma_2}$ on A.*

Assumption: $\mathcal{B}_1 = (\Sigma, \Gamma_1, E)$ and $\mathcal{B}_2 = (\Sigma, \Gamma_2, E)$ are two hidden specifications over the same signature with the same equations and with $\Gamma_1 \subseteq \Gamma_2$; also the Σ-equations in E have no conditions of hidden sort.

Proposition 8. *$\mathcal{B}_1$ is a conservative extension of $\mathcal{B}_2$. Moreover, $\mathcal{B}_1$ and $\mathcal{B}_2$ are equivalent iff $A \models \mathcal{B}_1$ implies $\equiv_\Sigma^{\Gamma_1} \subseteq \equiv_\Sigma^{\Gamma_2}$ for every hidden Σ-algebra A.*

Proof. Since every Γ_1-context is a Γ_2-context, $\equiv_\Sigma^{\Gamma_2} \subseteq \equiv_\Sigma^{\Gamma_1}$ in any hidden Σ-algebra A. Let A be a hidden Σ-algebra such that $A \models \mathcal{B}_2$, let e be any Σ-equation in E, say $(\forall X)\ t = t'$ **if** *$t_1 = t'_1, \ldots, t_n = t'_n$, and let $\theta : X \to A$ be any assignment such that $\theta(t_1) \equiv_\Sigma^{\Gamma_1} \theta(t'_1)$, ..., $\theta(t_n) \equiv_\Sigma^{\Gamma_1} \theta(t'_n)$. As $t_1, t'_1, \ldots, t_n, t'_n$ have visible sorts, one gets that $\theta(t_1) = \theta(t'_1)$, ..., $\theta(t_n) = \theta(t'_n)$. Since $A \models \mathcal{B}_2$, $\theta(t) \equiv_\Sigma^{\Gamma_2} \theta(t')$, so $\theta(t) \equiv_\Sigma^{\Gamma_1} \theta(t')$. Therefore $A \models_\Sigma^{\Gamma_1} e$. Consequently $A \models \mathcal{B}_1$, that is, $\mathcal{B}_1$ is a conservative extension of $\mathcal{B}_2$.*

If $\mathcal{B}_1$ and $\mathcal{B}_2$ are equivalent then $A \models \mathcal{B}_1$ implies $\equiv_\Sigma^{\Gamma_1} \subseteq \equiv_\Sigma^{\Gamma_2}$ since $\equiv_\Sigma^{\Gamma_2} = \equiv_\Sigma^{\Gamma_1}$. Conversely, suppose that $A \models \mathcal{B}_1$. Then $\equiv_\Sigma^{\Gamma_1} \subseteq \equiv_\Sigma^{\Gamma_2}$, and as $\equiv_\Sigma^{\Gamma_2} \subseteq \equiv_\Sigma^{\Gamma_1}$, one gets that $\equiv_\Sigma^{\Gamma_1} = \equiv_\Sigma^{\Gamma_2}$ and implicitly $A \models \mathcal{B}_2$. On the other hand, if $A \models \mathcal{B}_2$ then $A \models \mathcal{B}_1$ as proved above, and implicitly $\equiv_\Sigma^{\Gamma_1} = \equiv_\Sigma^{\Gamma_2}$.

Theorem 5. *$\mathcal{B}_1$ and $\mathcal{B}_2$ are equivalent iff all operations in Γ_2 are behaviorally congruent for $\mathcal{B}_1$.*

Proof. If $\mathcal{B}_1$ and $\mathcal{B}_2$ are equivalent then $\equiv_\Sigma^{\Gamma_1} = \equiv_\Sigma^{\Gamma_2}$ for any hidden Σ-algebra A with $A \models \mathcal{B}_1$. Since the operations in Γ_2 are congruent for $\equiv_\Sigma^{\Gamma_2}$ (see Theorem 1), they are also congruent for $\equiv_\Sigma^{\Gamma_1}$, so they are behaviorally congruent for $\mathcal{B}_1$.

Conversely, suppose that all operations in Γ_2 are behaviorally congruent for $\mathcal{B}_1$ and let A be a hidden Σ-algebra such that $A \models \mathcal{B}_1$. Then for every $a, a' \in A_h$ such that $a \equiv_{\Sigma,h}^{\Gamma_1} a'$, for every Γ_2-context c and for every $\theta : var(c) \to A$, we get $A_c(a)(\theta) = A_c(a')(\theta)$, that is, $a \equiv_{\Sigma,h}^{\Gamma_2} a'$. Therefore $\equiv_\Sigma^{\Gamma_1} \subseteq \equiv_\Sigma^{\Gamma_2}$, so by Proposition 8, $\mathcal{B}_1$ and $\mathcal{B}_2$ are equivalent.

Example 6. We show that the restriction on conditional equations cannot be removed with the following behavioral theory (in CafeOBJ syntax):

```
mod* B1 { *[ S ]*
bop f : S -> Bool        ** attribute
op  g : S -> Bool        ** attribute
vars X X' : S
bceq g(X) = g(X') if X == X' . }
```

Notice that g is congruent for `B1`. Now consider another CafeOBJ behavioral theory where g is also behavioral:

```
mod* B2 { *[ S ]*
bop f : S -> Bool        ** attribute
bop g : S -> Bool        ** attribute
vars X X' : S
bceq g(X) = g(X') if X == X' . }
```

Let Σ be the (common) signature of `B1` and `B2`, containing the operations on the booleans plus `f : S -> Bool` and `g : S -> Bool`. Then for any hidden Σ-algebra A, $A \models$ `B1` iff $A_f(a) = A_f(a')$ implies $A_g(a) = A_g(a')$ for any $a, a' \in A_s$, and $A \models$ `B2` under no restrictions. Therefore `B1` and `B2` are not equivalent because there exist hidden Σ-algebras satisfying `B2` which do not satisfy `B1`. Because `B1` and `B2` satisfy all the hypotheses in Theorem 5 except the one regarding the conditional equations, it follows that this restriction is needed.

Example 7. `SET1` of Example 1 and `SET` of Example 4 are equivalent, because all behavioral operations in `SET1` are congruent for `SET`. Similarly, `STACK` of Example 5 is equivalent to the behavioral specification where `push` is also behavioral.

Theorem 6. *If Γ_1 is context complete*[8] *for $\mathcal{B}_2$ then $\mathcal{B}_1$ and $\mathcal{B}_2$ are equivalent.*

Proof. Let A be any hidden Σ-algebra such that $A \models \mathcal{B}_1$, and let $a \equiv^{\Gamma_1}_{\Sigma,h} a'$. Since for every Γ_2-context c over z of sort h there is some γ in $T_{\Gamma_1}(\{z\} \cup var(c))$ such that $\mathcal{B}_1 \models (\forall z, var(c))\ c = \gamma$, we get that $A_c = A_\gamma$ as functions $A_h \to (A^{var(c)} \to D)$, where A_γ is defined similarly to A_c, that is, $A_\gamma(a)(\theta) = a^*_\theta(\gamma)$. As γ has visible sort and contains only operations in Γ_1 (which are congruent for $\equiv^{\Gamma_1}_{\Sigma}$), we get $A_\gamma(a)(\theta) = A_\gamma(a')(\theta)$ for any $\theta\colon var(c) \to A$. Therefore $A_c(a)(\theta) = A_c(a')(\theta)$ for any θ, that is, $a \equiv^{\Gamma_2}_{\Sigma,h} a'$. Therefore $\equiv^{\Gamma_1}_{\Sigma} \subseteq \equiv^{\Gamma_2}_{\Sigma}$, and so by Proposition 8, $\mathcal{B}_1$ and $\mathcal{B}_2$ are equivalent.

Example 8. Let `LIST` be the following behavioral specification:

```
mod* LIST { *[ List ]* pr(NAT)
bop car  : List -> Nat
bop cdr  : List -> List
bop cons : Nat List -> List
bop _in_ : Nat List -> Bool
```

[8] This makes sense because $\mathcal{B}_1$ is a conservative extension of $\mathcal{B}_2$.

```
vars N N' : Nat  var L : List
eq  car(cons(N,L)) = N .
beq cdr(cons(N,L)) = L .
eq N' in cons(N,L) = (N == N') or (N in L) . }
```

If Ψ is its data signature (natural numbers and booleans), and Σ and E are its hidden signature and equations, then the spec is $(\Sigma, \Psi \cup \{\texttt{car}, \texttt{cdr}, \texttt{cons}, \texttt{in}\}, E)$. By the congruence criterion (Corollary 1), `cons` is congruent for $\texttt{LIST1} = (\Sigma, \Psi \cup \{\texttt{car}, \texttt{cdr}, \texttt{in}\}, E)$, and so Theorem 5 implies that `LIST` and `LIST1` are equivalent. They have many models, including the standard finite lists and infinite lists. Note that `car` and `in` can behave unexpectedly on the unreachable states, , and all the states are unreachable here.

Another interesting behavioral specification is $\texttt{LIST2} = (\Sigma, \Psi \cup \{\texttt{car}, \texttt{cdr}\}, E)$, for which `cons` is also behaviorally congruent, but `in` is not necessarily congruent, because it can be defined in almost any way on states which are not a `cons` of other states.

Finally let `LIST3` be the behavioral specification $(\Sigma, \Psi \cup \{\texttt{in}\}, E)$. Again by the congruence criterion, `cons` is behaviorally congruent for `LIST3`. One model for `LIST3` is the Σ-algebra of finite lists (with any choice for `car(nil)` and `cdr(nil)`, such as 0 and `nil`), in which two lists are behaviorally equivalent iff they contain the same natural numbers (without regard to their order and number of occurrences). Therefore `car` and `cdr` are not behaviorally congruent for `LIST3`.

References

1. Narjes Berregeb, Adel Bouhoula, and Michaël Rusinowitch. Observational proofs with critical contexts. In *Fundamental Approaches to Software Engineering*, volume 1382 of *Lecture Notes in Computer Science*, pages 38–53. Springer-Verlag, 1998.
2. Michael Bidoit and Rolf Hennicker. Behavioral theories and the proof of behavioral properties. *Theoretical Computer Science*, 165:3–55, 1996.
3. Rod Burstall and Răzvan Diaconescu. Hiding and behaviour: an institutional approach. In A. William Roscoe, editor, *A Classical Mind: Essays in Honour of C.A.R. Hoare*, pages 75–92. Prentice-Hall, 1994.
4. Răzvan Diaconescu. Behavioral coherence in object-oriented algebraic specification. Technical Report IS–RR–98–0017F, Japan Advanced Institute for Science and Technology, June 1998. Submitted for publication.
5. Răzvan Diaconescu and Kokichi Futatsugi. *CafeOBJ Report: The Language, Proof Techniques, and Methodologies for Object-Oriented Algebraic Specification*. World Scientific, 1998. AMAST Series in Computing, volume 6.
6. Marie-Claude Gaudel and Igor Privara. Context induction: an exercise. Technical Report 687, LRI, Université de Paris-Sud, 1991.
7. Joseph Goguen. Types as theories. In George Michael Reed, Andrew William Roscoe, and Ralph F. Wachter, editors, *Topology and Category Theory in Computer Science*, pages 357–390. Oxford, 1991. Proceedings of a Conference held at Oxford, June 1989.
8. Joseph Goguen and Răzvan Diaconescu. Towards an algebraic semantics for the object paradigm. In Hartmut Ehrig and Fernando Orejas, editors, *Proceedings,*

Tenth Workshop on Abstract Data Types, pages 1–29. Springer, 1994. Lecture Notes in Computer Science, Volume 785.
9. Joseph Goguen, Kai Lin, Akira Mori, Grigore Roşu, and Akiyoshi Sato. Tools for distributed cooperative design and validation. In *Proceedings, CafeOBJ Symposium*. Japan Advanced Institute for Science and Technology, 1998. Numazu, Japan, April 1998.
10. Joseph Goguen and Grant Malcolm. Proof of correctness of object representation. In A. William Roscoe, editor, *A Classical Mind: Essays in Honour of C.A.R. Hoare*, pages 119–142. Prentice-Hall, 1994.
11. Joseph Goguen and Grant Malcolm. *Algebraic Semantics of Imperative Programs*. MIT, 1996.
12. Joseph Goguen and Grant Malcolm. A hidden agenda. *Theoretical Computer Science*, to appear 1999. Also UCSD Dept. Computer Science & Eng. Technical Report CS97–538, May 1997.
13. Rolf Hennicker. Context induction: a proof principle for behavioral abstractions. *Formal Aspects of Computing*, 3(4):326–345, 1991.
14. Bart Jacobs and Jan Rutten. A tutorial on (co)algebras and (co)induction. *Bulletin of the European Association for Theoretical Computer Science*, 62:222–259, 1997.
15. Michihiro Matsumoto and Kokichi Futatsugi. Test set coinduction — toward automated verification of behavioral properties —. In *Proceedings of the Second International Workshop on Rewriting Logic and its Applications*, Electronic Notes in Theoretical Computer Science. Elsevier Science, to appear 1998.
16. Peter Padawitz. Towards the one-tiered design of data types and transition systems. In *WADT'97*, volume 1376 of *Lecture Notes in Computer Science*, pages 365–380. Springer, 1998.
17. Horst Reichel. An approach to object semantics based on terminal co-algebras. *Mathematical Structures in Computer Science*, 5:129–152, 1995.

Resolution-Based Theorem Proving for SH_n-Logics

Viorica Sofronie-Stokkermans

Max-Planck-Institut für Informatik, D-66123 Saarbrücken, Germany
sofronie@mpi-sb.mpg.de

Abstract. In this paper we illustrate by means of an example, namely SH_n-logics, a method for translation to clause form and automated theorem proving for first-order many-valued logics based on distributive lattices with operators.

1 Introduction

In this paper we present a method for translation to clause form and automated theorem proving in finitely-valued logics having as algebras of truth values distributive lattices with certain types of operators. Many non-classical logics that occur in practical applications fall in this class. One of the advantages of distributive lattices (with well-behaved operators) is the existence, in such cases, of good representation theorems, such as the Priestley representation theorem. The method for translation to clause form we present here uses the Priestley dual of the algebra of truth values. The ideas behind this method are very natural, even if the algebraic notions used may at first sight seem involved. This is why in this paper we illustrate the ideas by one example, namely SH_n-logics. SH_n-logics are a series of propositional finitely-valued logics based on Symmetric Heyting algebras of order $\underline{n}$. The particular properties of SH_n-logics allow us to further improve the efficiency of the automated theorem proving procedure for certain types of formulae in SH_n-logics, by exploiting the structure of the Priestley dual of the algebra of truth values. This effect is difficult to explain in a general setting; the case of SH_n-logics can be considered a case-study, in which we take first steps in this direction.

The main sources of inspiration for our work are the many-valued resolution method of Baaz and Fermüller [BF95], and the results of Hähnle [Häh96]. Our method exploits the particular structure of the algebra of truth values, and leads to a reduction of the number of clauses compared to methods using the algebra of truth values, especially when the difference between the number of elements of the algebra of truth values and the number of elements of its Priestley dual is large. Resolution procedures are also discussed (in particular, a hyperresolution procedure that extends the results established for regular clauses in [Häh96]).

The paper is structured as follows. In Section 2 we briefly present the main notions needed in the paper. In Section 3 SH_n-logics are defined. In Section 4 our method for translation to clause form for SH_n-logics is presented. In Section 5

R. Caferra and G. Salzer (Eds.): Automated Deduction, LNAI 1761, pp. 267–281, 2000.

resolution-based methods for automated theorem proving are briefly presented. In Section 6 we compare our method with other approaches. Section 7 contains some conclusions.

2 Preliminaries

2.1 Partially-Ordered Sets and Lattices

In what follows we assume known standard notions, such as partially-ordered set and lattice, order-filter and order-ideal in partially-ordered sets, meet- and join-irreducible elements, and (prime) filter and (prime) ideal in lattices. For the definitions and further information we refer to [DP90]. Given a partially-ordered set $(P, \leq)$, by $\mathcal{O}(P)$ we will denote the set of order-filters of P; for every $i \in P$, we will use the following notations: $\uparrow i = \{j \in P \mid j \geq i\}$, and $\downarrow i = \{j \in P \mid i \geq j\}$. Note also that every ideal in a finite distributive lattice is of the form $\downarrow i$ and every filter is of the form $\uparrow i$ for some element i in the lattice; such an ideal (resp. filter) is prime iff i is meet-irreducible (resp. join-irreducible).

2.2 Priestley Pepresentation

The Priestley representation theorem [DP90] states that every distributive lattice A is isomorphic to the lattice of clopen (i.e. closed and open) order filters of the ordered topological space having as points the prime filters of A, ordered by inclusion, and the topology generated by the sets of the form $X_a = \{F \mid F$ prime filter, $a \in F\}$ and their complements as a subbasis. The partially ordered set of all prime filters of A, ordered by inclusion, and endowed with the topology mentioned above will be denoted $D(A)$ (we will refer to it as the dual of A). $E(X)$. In particular, if A is finite, the topology on $D(A)$ is discrete, and A is isomorphic to $\mathcal{O}(D(A))$.

2.3 Many-Valued Logics

We now give a (semantics-based) definition of many-valued logics, which closely follows the definition in [BF95].

Let A be a (finite) set of truth values. The semantics of a many-valued logic $\mathcal{L}$ with language $(X, O, P, \Sigma, \mathcal{Q})$ (where X is a (countably) infinite set of variables; O a set of function symbols; P a set of predicate symbols; Σ a finite set of logical operators; and $\mathcal{Q}$ a finite set of (one-place) quantifiers) is given as follows:

(i) to every $\sigma \in \Sigma$ with arity n we associate a truth function $\sigma_A : A^n \to A$;
(ii) to every quantifier Q we associate a truth function $\overline{Q} : \mathcal{P}(A)\backslash\{\emptyset\} \to A$.

Definition 1. *An interpretation for a language $(X, O, P, \Sigma, \mathcal{Q})$ and a set of truth values A is a tuple (D, I, d) where D is a non-empty set, the* domain, *I is a* signature interpretation, *i.e. a map assigning a function $I(f) : D^n \to D$ to every n-ary function symbol $f \in O$, and a function $I(R) : D^n \to A$ to every n-ary predicate symbol $R \in P$, and $d : X \to D$ a* variable assignment.

Every interpretation $\mathcal{I} = (D, I, d)$ induces a valuation $v_{\mathcal{I}} : \mathsf{Fma}(\mathcal{L}) \to A$ on the set $\mathsf{Fma}(\mathcal{L})$ of formulae of $\mathcal{L}$ as follows. (For further details we refer to [BF95].)

(1) $v_{\mathcal{I}}(x) = d(x)$ for all variables $x \in X$,
(2) $v_{\mathcal{I}}(f(t_1, \ldots, t_n)) = I(f)(v_{\mathcal{I}}(t_1), \ldots, v_{\mathcal{I}}(t_n))$ for all n-ary function symbols $f \in O$, $n \geq 0$,
(3) $v_{\mathcal{I}}(R(t_1, \ldots, t_n)) = I(R)(v_{\mathcal{I}}(t_1), \ldots, v_{\mathcal{I}}(t_n))$ for all n-ary predicate symbols $R \in P$, $n \geq 0$,
(4) $v_{\mathcal{I}}(\sigma(\phi_1, \ldots, \phi_n)) = \sigma_A(v_{\mathcal{I}}(\phi_1), \ldots, v_{\mathcal{I}}(\phi_n))$ for all logical operators $\sigma \in \Sigma$,
(5) $v_{\mathcal{I}}((Qx)\phi) = \overline{Q}(\{w \mid \exists d \in D \text{ s.t. } v_{\mathcal{I}_{x,d}}(\phi) = w\})$ for all quantifiers Q, where $\mathcal{I}_{x,d}$ is identical with $\mathcal{I}$ except for assigning d to the variable x.

A formula ϕ will be called *valid* iff for all interpretations $\mathcal{I}$, $v_{\mathcal{I}}(\phi) = 1$; ϕ will be called *satisfiable* iff there exists an interpretation $\mathcal{I}$ with $v_{\mathcal{I}}(\phi) = 1$.

3 SH_n-Logics

The propositional SH_n-logics were introduced by Iturrioz in [Itu82]. The language of SH_n-logics is a propositional language, whose formulae are built from propositional variables taken from a set Var, with operations $\vee$ (disjunction), $\wedge$ (conjunction), $\Rightarrow$ (intuitionistic implication), $\sim, \neg$ (a De Morgan resp. an intuitionistic negation), and a family $\{S_i \mid i = 1, \ldots, n-1\}$ of unary operations (expressing the degree of truth of a formula). The set of formulae in the variables Var will be denoted Fma(Var). Recently, Iturrioz noticed that SH_n-logics provide a source of examples for L_{t_f}-logics, which have been introduced by Rasiowa to formalize the reasoning of a poset of intelligent agents. A Hilbert style axiomatization of SH_n-logics is given in [Itu82] and [IO96]. We present it below:

Axioms: (A1) $a \Rightarrow (b \Rightarrow a)$
(A2) $(a \Rightarrow (b \Rightarrow c)) \Rightarrow ((a \Rightarrow b) \Rightarrow (a \Rightarrow c))$
(A3) $(a \wedge b) \Rightarrow a$
(A4) $(a \wedge b) \Rightarrow b$
(A5) $(a \Rightarrow b) \Rightarrow ((a \Rightarrow c) \Rightarrow (a \Rightarrow (b \wedge c)))$
(A6) $a \Rightarrow (a \vee b)$
(A7) $b \Rightarrow (a \vee b)$
(A8) $(a \Rightarrow c) \Rightarrow ((b \Rightarrow c) \Rightarrow ((a \vee b) \Rightarrow c))$
(A9) $\sim\sim a \leftrightarrow a$
(A10) $S_i(a \wedge b) \leftrightarrow S_i(a) \wedge S_i(b)$
(A11) $S_i(a \Rightarrow b) \leftrightarrow (\bigwedge_{k=i}^{n} S_k(a) \Rightarrow S_k(b))$
(A12) $S_i(S_j(a)) \leftrightarrow S_j(a)$, for every $i, j = 1, \ldots, n-1$
(A13) $S_1(a) \Rightarrow a$
(A14) $S_i(\sim a) \leftrightarrow \sim S_{n-i}a$, for $i = 1, \ldots, n-1$
(A15) $S_1(a) \vee \neg S_1(a)$

where $\neg a = (a \Rightarrow \sim (a \Rightarrow a))$ and $a \leftrightarrow b$ is an abbreviation for $(a \Rightarrow b) \wedge (b \Rightarrow a)$.

Inference rules:

$$\text{(R1)}\ \frac{a,\ a \Rightarrow b}{b} \qquad \text{(R2)}\ \frac{a \Rightarrow b}{\sim b \Rightarrow \sim a} \qquad \text{(R3)}\ \frac{a \Rightarrow b}{S_1(a) \Rightarrow S_1(b)}$$

3.1 Algebraic Semantics for Propositional SH_n-Logics

In [Itu82,Itu83], Iturrioz gave a lattice-based semantics for SH_n-logics, by means of symmetrical Heyting algebras of order n, or for short SH_n-algebras.

Definition 2. *An abstract algebra* $A = (A, 0, 1, \wedge, \vee, \Rightarrow, \neg, \sim, S_1, \ldots, S_{n-1})$ *is said to be a* symmetric Heyting algebra of order n *(SH_n-algebra for short) if:*

(1) $(A, 0, 1, \wedge, \vee, \Rightarrow, \neg)$ *is a Heyting algebra, i.e.* $(A, 0, 1, \wedge, \vee)$ *is a bounded distributive lattice; for every* $a, b \in A$, $a \Rightarrow b$ *is the pseudocomplement of* a *relative to* b*, i.e. the largest element* c *of* A *with* $a \wedge c \leq b$*; and* $\neg a = a \Rightarrow 0$*;*
(2) $\sim$ *is a De Morgan negation on* A*, i.e.* $\sim 0 = 1$, $\sim 1 = 0$*, and, for every* $a, b \in A$, $\sim(a \vee b) = \sim a \wedge \sim b$, $\sim(a \wedge b) = \sim a \vee \sim b$*, and* $\sim\sim a = a$*;*
(3) For every $a, b \in A$ *and for all* $i, j \in \{1, \ldots, n-1\}$*, the following hold:*
(S1) $S_i(a \wedge b) = S_i(a) \wedge S_i(b)$,
(S2) $S_i(a \Rightarrow b) = \bigwedge_{k=i}^{n} (S_k(a) \Rightarrow S_k(b))$,
(S3) $S_i(S_j(a)) = S_j(a)$*, for every* $i, j = 1, \ldots, n-1$,
(S4) $S_1(a) \vee a = a$,
(S5) $S_i(\sim a) = \sim S_{n-i}(a)$*, for* $i = 1, \ldots, n-1$,
(S6) $S_1(a) \vee \neg S_1(a) = 1$*, with* $\neg a = a \Rightarrow 0$.

The class of SH_n-algebras is a variety, which will be denoted $\mathsf{SH_n}$ in what follows. Iturrioz [Itu83] proved that this variety is generated by one finite SH_n-algebra, S_{n^2} (represented in the left-hand side of Figure 1), defined as follows.

Definition 3 (S_{n^2}). *Let* $n \geq 2$ *and let* S_{n^2} *be the cartesian product* $L_n \times L_n$ *where* $L_n = \{0, \frac{1}{n-1}, \ldots, \frac{n-2}{n-1}, 1\}$*. Consider the following operations on* S_{n^2}*:*

(1) $(x_1, y_1) \wedge (x_2, y_2) = (\mathsf{min}(x_1, x_2), \mathsf{min}(y_1, y_2))$,
(2) $(x_1, y_1) \vee (x_2, y_2) = (\mathsf{max}(x_1, x_2), \mathsf{max}(y_1, y_2))$,
(3) $\sim (x, y) = (1 - y, 1 - x)$ *for every* $(x, y) \in S_{n^2}$,
(4) $S_i(x, y) = (S_i(x), S_i(y))$*, where* $S_i(\frac{j}{n-1}) = \begin{cases} 1 & \text{if } i + j \geq n, \\ 0 & \text{if } i + j < n, \end{cases}$
(5) $(x_1, y_1) \Rightarrow (x_2, y_2) = (x_1 \to x_2, y_1 \to y_2)$,
(6) $\neg(x, y) = (x \to 0, y \to 0)$,

where $\to$ *is the Heyting relative pseudocomplementation on* L_n*, i.e.* $a \to b = \begin{cases} 1 & \text{if } a \leq b \\ b & \text{if } a > b \end{cases}$ *and for every* $a \in L_n$, $\neg a := a \to 0 = \begin{cases} 1 & \text{if } a = 0 \\ 0 & \text{if } a > 0 \end{cases}$.

In [Itu82] it is proved that SH_n-logics are sound and complete with respect to the variety of SH_n-algebras. Since the variety $\mathsf{SH_n}$ is generated by S_{n^2} it follows that the SH_n-logics can be regarded as many-valued logics having S_{n^2} as an algebra of truth values.

A Priestley representation theorem for SH_n-algebras is established in [Itu83], see also [SS97,SS99b]. In particular we give a description of the dual of the generator S_{n^2} of the variety of SH_n-algebras. The Priestley dual of S_{n^2}, $D(S_{n^2})$, is the set of prime filters of S_{n^2}, with the discrete topology, and ordered by inclusion. Every prime filter of S_{n^2} is of the form $\uparrow a$ where a is a join-irreducible

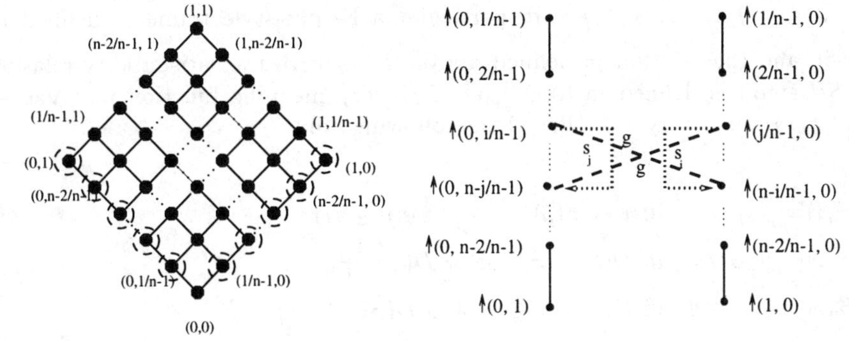

Fig. 1. S_{n^2} and its Priestley dual $D(S_{n^2})$

element of S_{n^2}. The set of join-irreducible elements of S_{n^2} (encircled in Figure 1) is $\{(0, \frac{i}{n-1}) \mid i = 1, \ldots, n-1\} \cup \{(\frac{i}{n-1}, 0) \mid i = 1, \ldots, n-1\}$.

Thus, $D(S_{n^2})$ (the right-hand side of Figure 1) is the set $\{\uparrow (0, \frac{i}{n-1}) \mid i = 1, \ldots, n-1\} \cup \{\uparrow (\frac{i}{n-1}, 0) \mid i = 1, \ldots, n-1\}$. Additional operations $g, s_1, \ldots, s_{n-1}$ are defined for every prime filter F of S_{n^2} by $g(F) = S_{n^2} \setminus \sim^{-1}(F)$, and $s_i(F) = S_i^{-1}(F)$. Therefore, $g(\uparrow (0, \frac{i}{n-1})) = \uparrow (\frac{n-i}{n-1}, 0)$; $g(\uparrow (\frac{i}{n-1}, 0)) = \uparrow (0, \frac{n-i}{n-1})$; and, for every $j = 1, \ldots, n-1$, $s_j(\uparrow (0, \frac{i}{n-1})) = \uparrow (0, \frac{n-j}{n-1})$; $s_j(\uparrow (\frac{i}{n-1}, 0)) = \uparrow (\frac{n-j}{n-1}, 0)$. By the Priestley representation theorem for SH_n-algebras, since the topology of $D(S_{n^2})$ is discrete, there exists an isomorphism of SH_n-algebras $\eta_{S_{n^2}} : S_{n^2} \simeq \mathcal{O}(D(S_{n^2}))$, defined for every $x \in S_{n^2}$ by $\eta_{S_{n^2}}(x) = \{\uparrow \alpha \in D(S_{n^2}) \mid x \in \uparrow \alpha\}$.

3.2 A Finite Kripke-Style Frame for SH_n-Logics

In [IO96], Iturrioz and Orłowska give a completeness theorem for SH_n-logics with respect to a Kripke-style semantics. We will show that one can regard $D(S_{n^2})$ as a particular Kripke-style frame for SH_n-logics, and that a formula is an SH_n-theorem iff it is valid in this frame. As in [IO96] where Kripke-style models for SH_n-logics are investigated, we will assume that all meaning functions for $D(S_{n^2})$ have as values order-filters.

Definition 4. *Let $m : \mathsf{Var} \to \mathcal{O}(D(S_{n^2}))$ be a meaning function, and let $\overline{m} : \mathsf{Fma}(\mathsf{Var}) \to \mathcal{O}(D(S_{n^2}))$ be the unique extension of m to formulae. We define:*

(i) $D(S_{n^2}) \overset{r}{\models}_{m,x} \phi$ *iff* $x \in \overline{m}(\phi)$;

(ii) $D(S_{n^2}) \overset{r}{\models}_{m} \phi$ *iff* $\overline{m}(\phi) = D(S_{n^2})$;

(iii) $D(S_{n^2}) \overset{r}{\models} \phi$ *iff* $D(S_{n^2}) \overset{r}{\models}_{m} \phi$ *for every* $m\colon \mathsf{Var} \to \mathcal{O}(D(S_{n^2}))$.

Theorem 1 ([SS97,SS99b]). *Every formula ϕ of SH_n-logic is an SH_n-theorem iff $D(S_{n^2}) \overset{r}{\models} \phi$.*

$(D(S_{n^2}), \leq, g, s_1, \ldots, s_{n-1})$ is in particular a Kripke-style frame as defined in [IO96], and the relation $\overset{r}{\models}$ defined above agrees with the satisfiability relation for SH_n-models defined in [IO96], i.e. for every meaning function $m : \mathsf{Var} \to \mathcal{O}(D(S_{n^2}))$ and every $x \in D(S_{n^2})$ the following hold:

$$
\begin{array}{lll}
D(S_{n^2}) \overset{r}{\models}_{m,x} p & \text{iff } x \in m(p), & \text{for } p \in \mathsf{Var}, \\
D(S_{n^2}) \overset{r}{\models}_{m,x} \phi \vee \psi & \text{iff } D(S_{n^2}) \overset{r}{\models}_{m,x} \phi \text{ or } D(S_{n^2}) \overset{r}{\models}_{m,x} \psi, & \\
D(S_{n^2}) \overset{r}{\models}_{m,x} \phi \wedge \psi & \text{iff } D(S_{n^2}) \overset{r}{\models}_{m,x} \phi \text{ and } D(S_{n^2}) \overset{r}{\models}_{m,x} \psi, & \\
D(S_{n^2}) \overset{r}{\models}_{m,x} \phi \Rightarrow \psi & \text{iff for all } y, \text{ if } x \leq y \text{ and } D(S_{n^2}) \overset{r}{\models}_{m,y} \phi \text{ then } D(S_{n^2}) \overset{r}{\models}_{m,y} \psi, & \\
D(S_{n^2}) \overset{r}{\models}_{m,x} \neg\phi & \text{iff for all } y, \text{ if } x \leq y \text{ then } D(S_{n^2}) \overset{r}{\not\models}_{m,y} \phi, & \\
D(S_{n^2}) \overset{r}{\models}_{m,x} S_i(\phi) & \text{iff } D(S_{n^2}) \overset{r}{\models}_{m,s_i(x)} \phi, & \\
D(S_{n^2}) \overset{r}{\models}_{m,x} \sim \phi & \text{iff } D(S_{n^2}) \overset{r}{\not\models}_{m,g(x)} \phi. &
\end{array}
$$

3.3 First-Order SH_n-Logics

Following [BF95] we define first-order SH_n-logics as many-valued logics having S_{n^2} as set of truth values.

A first-order SH_n-logic is defined by specifying a set X of variables, a set O of operation symbols and a set P of predicate symbols. The set of logical connectives is $\{\vee, \wedge, \Rightarrow, \neg, \sim\}$, and they are interpreted in S_{n^2} as explained in Definition 3. We allow only two quantifiers, namely $\exists$ and $\forall$, such that the truth functions $\overline{\forall}, \overline{\exists} : \mathcal{P}(S_{n^2}) \to (S_{n^2})$ are defined for every $\emptyset \neq W \subseteq S_{n^2}$ by:

$$\overline{\forall}(W) = \bigwedge_{w \in W} w; \ \overline{\exists}(W) = \bigvee_{w \in W} w.$$

Frames and interpretations are defined in the usual way (cf. Definition 1). Due to the fact that S_{n^2} is isomorphic to $\mathcal{O}(D(S_{n^2}))$, an alternative (equivalent) notion of frame (D, M) (and resp. interpretation $\mathcal{M} = (D, M, d)$) can be defined, where the signature interpretation M assigns with every n-ary predicate symbol $R \in P$ a function $M(R) : D^n \to \mathcal{O}(D(S_{n^2}))$. For every interpretation $\mathcal{M} = (D, M, d)$ in $\mathcal{O}(D(S_{n^2}))$, the induced valuation function $v_{\mathcal{M}} : \mathsf{Fma}(\mathcal{L}) \to \mathcal{O}(D(S_{n^2}))$ is defined in the usual way; so are the notions of validity and satisfiability.

Taking into account the fact that the largest element of the lattice $\mathcal{O}(D(S_{n^2}))$ is $D(S_{n^2})$, it follows that a formula ϕ is valid iff for all interpretations $\mathcal{M}$ in $\mathcal{O}(D(S_{n^2}))$, $v_{\mathcal{M}}(\phi) = D(S_{n^2})$; and satisfiable iff $v_{\mathcal{M}}(\phi) = D(S_{n^2})$ for some interpretation $\mathcal{M}$ in $\mathcal{O}(D(S_{n^2}))$.

4 Translation into Clause Form

The main idea of our approach is to use signed literals, where the signs are "possible worlds", i.e. elements of $D(S_{n^2})$ (corresponding to prime filters of truth values) instead of truth values (as done in [BF95]) or arbitrary sets of truth values (as done in [Häh94,Häh96]). The idea of using "valuations in $\{0,1\}$" instead of values appears already for instance in [Sco73] for the case of Łukasiewicz logics. In what follows, given an interpretation $\mathcal{M} = (D, M, d)$ in $\mathcal{O}(D(S_{n^2}))$ we use the following notations (where ϕ is a formula and α is an element of $D(S_{n^2})$):

$\boxed{\alpha}\ \phi^t$ in $\mathcal{M}$ means "ϕ is true at α" in the interpretation $\mathcal{M}$ (i.e. $\alpha \in v_{\mathcal{M}}(\phi)$)
$\boxed{\alpha}\ \phi^f$ in $\mathcal{M}$ means "ϕ is false at α" in the interpretation $\mathcal{M}$ (i.e. $\alpha \notin v_{\mathcal{M}}(\phi)$)

Note that if $\boxed{\beta}\ \phi^t$ in $\mathcal{M}$ and $\beta \leq \alpha$ then $\boxed{\alpha}\ \phi^t$ in $\mathcal{M}$.

Definition 5 (Literal, Clause). *Let L be an atomic formula and $\alpha \in D(S_{n^2})$. Then $\boxed{\alpha}\ L^t$ is a* positive literal *(with sign $\boxed{\alpha}$) and $\boxed{\alpha}\ L^f$ is a* negative literal *(with sign $\boxed{\alpha}$). A set of (positive or negative) signed literals is called a* (signed) clause. *A clause is called* negative (positive) *if it only contains negative (resp. positive) literals.*

Definition 6 (Signed CNF). *A* formula in signed conjunctive normal form (CNF) *is a finite set of signed clauses. We require that the clauses in a formula have disjoint variables.*

Definition 7 (Satisfiability). *A positive literal $\boxed{\alpha}\ L^t$ (resp. a negative literal $\boxed{\alpha}\ L^f$) is satisfied by an interpretation $\mathcal{M}$ in $\mathcal{O}(D(S_{n^2}))$ if L is true (resp. false) in $\mathcal{M}$ at α. A (positive or negative) literal is satisfiable if it is satisfied by some interpretation $\mathcal{M}$. A signed clause is satisfiable if at least one of its literals is satisfiable. A formula Φ in signed CNF is satisfiable if all clauses in Φ are simultaneously satisfiable by the same interpretation.*

We give a *structure-preserving* transformation method to clause form in first-order logic. The main idea of such methods is to introduce, for every non-atomic subformula ψ of ϕ, a new atomic formula of the form $P_\psi(\overline{x})$, where P_ψ is a new predicate symbol and $\overline{x}$ are the free variables in ψ.

Theorem 2. *The SH_n-formula ϕ is valid iff there exists no interpretation $\mathcal{M} = (D, M, d)$ in $\mathcal{O}(D(S_{n^2}))$ such that*

$$\left\{\begin{array}{c}
\boxed{\uparrow(0,1)}\ P_\phi^f \vee \boxed{\uparrow(1,0)}\ P_\phi^f \text{ in } \mathcal{M}, \\[1em]
(\boxed{\alpha}\ P_\psi(x_1,\dots,x_n)^t \vee \boxed{\alpha}\ \sigma(P_{\psi_1},\dots,P_{\psi_m})^f) \\
(\boxed{\alpha}\ P_\psi(x_1,\dots,x_n)^f \vee \boxed{\alpha}\ \sigma(P_{\psi_1},\dots,P_{\psi_m})^t) \\
\text{in } \mathcal{M}\text{; for every } \alpha \in D(S_{n^2}),\text{ for all subformulae } \psi = \sigma(\psi_1,\dots,\psi_m) \\
\text{of } \phi,\text{ and all instantiations in } D \text{ of the free variables } x_1,\dots,x_n \text{ of } \psi, \\[1em]
(\boxed{\alpha}\ P_\psi(x_1,\dots,x_n)^t \vee \boxed{\alpha}\ (Qx)P_{\psi_1}(x,x_1,\dots,x_n)^f) \\
(\boxed{\alpha}\ P_\psi(x_1,\dots,x_n)^f \vee \boxed{\alpha}\ (Qx)P_{\psi_1}(x,x_1,\dots,x_n)^t) \\
\text{in } \mathcal{M}\text{; for every } \alpha \in D(S_{n^2}),\text{ for all subformulae } \psi = (Qx)\psi_1(x,x_1,\dots,x_n) \\
\text{of } \phi,\text{ and all instantiations in } D \text{ of the free variables } x_1,\dots,x_n \text{ of } \psi.
\end{array}\right.$$

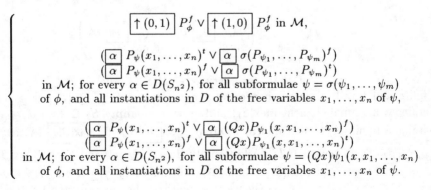

Proof: *(Sketch)* This is a consequence of the fact that a formula ϕ is valid iff there exists no interpretation $\mathcal{M}$ in $\mathcal{O}(D(S_{n^2}))$ such that ϕ is false in $\mathcal{M}$ at some world $\alpha \in D(S_{n^2})$ (and, thus, at some minimal world), taking into account the renamings mentioned before, and the fact that the minimal elements of $D(S_{n^2})$ are $\uparrow(0,1)$ and $\uparrow(1,0)$. □

The elimination rules for the operators and quantifiers use the correspondence between the operations on S_{n^2} and the associated operations on $D(S_{n^2})$ and $\mathcal{O}(D(S_{n^2}))$, as showed below.

Proposition 1. *The following hold for any atomic formulae $L, L_1, L_2, \dots, L_n$, in any given interpretation $\mathcal{M}$:*

$(\vee, t)$ $\boxed{\alpha}\ (L_1 \vee L_2)^t$ *iff* $\boxed{\alpha}\ L_1^t \vee \boxed{\alpha}\ L_2^t$;
$(\vee, f)$ $\boxed{\alpha}\ (L_1 \vee L_2)^f$ *iff* $\boxed{\alpha}\ L_1^f \wedge \boxed{\alpha}\ L_2^f$.
$(\wedge, t)$ $\boxed{\alpha}\ (L_1 \wedge L_2)^t$ *iff* $\boxed{\alpha}\ L_1^t \wedge \boxed{\alpha}\ L_2^t$;
$(\wedge, f)$ $\boxed{\alpha}\ (L_1 \wedge L_2)^f$ *iff* $\boxed{\alpha}\ L_1^f \vee \boxed{\alpha}\ L_2^f$.
(S_j, t) $\boxed{\alpha}\ (S_j(L_1))^t$ *iff* $\boxed{s_j(\alpha)}\ L_1^t$;
(S_j, f) $\boxed{\alpha}\ (S_j(L_1))^f$ *iff* $\boxed{s_j(\alpha)}\ L_1^f$.
$(\sim, t)$ $\boxed{\alpha}\ (\sim(L_1))^t$ *iff* $\boxed{g(\alpha)}\ L_1^f$;
$(\sim, f)$ $\boxed{\alpha}\ (\sim(L_1))^f$ *iff* $\boxed{g(\alpha)}\ L_1^t$.
$(\neg, t)$ $\boxed{\alpha}\ (\neg L)^t$ *iff for every* $\beta \geq \alpha$, $\boxed{\beta}\ L^f$;
$(\neg, f)$ $\boxed{\alpha}\ (\neg L)^f$ *iff there exists a* $\beta \geq \alpha$ *with* $\boxed{\beta}\ L^t$.
$(\Rightarrow, t)$ $\boxed{\alpha}\ (L_1 \Rightarrow L_2)^t$ *iff for every* $\beta \geq \alpha$, $\boxed{\beta}\ L_1^f \vee \boxed{\beta}\ L_2^t$.
$(\Rightarrow, f)$ $\boxed{\alpha}\ (L_1 \Rightarrow L_2)^f$ *iff* $\boxed{\max\{\beta \mid \beta \geq \alpha\}}\ L_1^t$, $\boxed{\alpha}\ L_2^f$, *and for every* α_1 *with* $\alpha \leq \alpha_1 < \max(\{\beta \mid \beta \geq \alpha\})$, $\boxed{\alpha_1}\ L_1^t \vee \boxed{s(\alpha_1)}\ L_2^f$.

Proof: *(Sketch)* The cases $(\vee, t)$, $(\vee, f)$, $(\wedge, t)$, $(\wedge, f)$, (S_j, t), (S_j, f), $(\sim, t)$, $(\sim, f)$, $(\neg, t)$, $(\neg, f)$, and $(\Rightarrow, t)$ follow immediately. We present the case $(\Rightarrow, f)$ in detail. We know that $\boxed{\alpha}\ (L_1 \Rightarrow L_2)^f$ iff for some $\beta \geq \alpha$, $\boxed{\beta}\ L_1^t$ and $\boxed{\beta}\ L_2^f$. By distributivity, the formula $\bigvee_{\beta \geq \alpha}(\boxed{\beta}\ L_1^t \wedge \boxed{\beta}\ L_2^f)$ can be written as

$$\bigwedge_{\substack{S_1, S_2, S_1 \cap S_2 = \emptyset \\ S_1 \cup S_2 = \{\beta \mid \beta \geq \alpha\}}} \left(\bigvee_{\beta_1 \in S_1} \boxed{\beta_1}\ L_1^t \vee \bigvee_{\beta_2 \in S_2} \boxed{\beta_2}\ L_2^f \right).$$

We then use the fact that, for every $\alpha \in D(S_{n^2})$, the set $\{\beta \mid \beta \geq \alpha\}$ is finite and totally ordered, hence every non-empty set $S_1 \subseteq \{\beta \mid \beta \geq \alpha\}$, contains a maximal element $\max(S_1)$ and every non-empty $S_2 \subseteq \{\beta \mid \beta \geq \alpha\}$ contains a minimal element $\min(S_2)$, and $\bigvee_{\beta_1 \in S_1} \boxed{\beta_1}\ L_1^t$ iff $\boxed{\max(S_1)}\ L_1^t$, resp. $\bigvee_{\beta_2 \in S_2} \boxed{\beta_2}\ L_2^f$ iff $\boxed{\min(S_2)}\ L_2^f$. Additionally, if $S_1 \cap S_2 = \emptyset$ and $S_1 \cup S_2 = \{\beta \mid \beta \geq \alpha\}$ it follows that $\max(S_1) \neq \min(S_2)$, and for every $\gamma \geq \alpha$ either $\gamma \in S_1$ (hence $\gamma \leq \max(S_1)$) or $\gamma \in S_2$ (hence $\gamma \geq \min(S_2)$). Let $m = \max\{\beta \mid \beta \geq \alpha\}$.

If $\mathsf{max}(S_1) \neq m$ then it has an immediate successor which will be denoted by $s(\mathsf{max}(S_1))$. Since $\gamma = s(\mathsf{max}(S_1)) \notin S_1$ it follows that it belongs to S_2. Hence, if $\mathsf{max}(S_1) \neq m$ then $\mathsf{min}(S_2) \leq s(\mathsf{max}(S_1))$. Therefore, the following hold:

$$\boxed{\alpha}\,(L_1 \Rightarrow L_2)^f \text{ iff } \bigwedge_{\substack{S_1,S_2,S_1\cap S_2=\emptyset\\ S_1\cup S_2=\{\beta\mid\beta\geq\alpha\}}} \left(\bigvee_{\beta_1\in S_1}\boxed{\beta_1}\,L_1^t \vee \bigvee_{\beta_2\in S_2}\boxed{\beta_2}\,L_2^f\right)$$

$$\text{iff } \boxed{m}\,L_1^t \wedge \boxed{\alpha}\,L_2^f \wedge \bigwedge_{\substack{S_1,S_2\neq\emptyset,S_1\cap S_2=\emptyset\\ S_1\cup S_2=\{\beta\mid\beta\geq\alpha\}}} \left(\boxed{\mathsf{max}(S_1)}\,L_1^t \vee \boxed{\mathsf{min}(S_2)}\,L_2^f\right)$$

$$\text{iff } \boxed{m}\,L_1^t \wedge \boxed{\alpha}\,L_2^f \wedge \bigwedge_{\beta\geq\alpha} \bigwedge_{\substack{S_1,\mathsf{max}(S_1)=\beta,\\ S_2=\uparrow\alpha\setminus S_1}} \left(\boxed{\beta}\,L_1^t \vee \boxed{\mathsf{min}(S_2)}\,L_2^f\right)$$

$$\text{iff } \boxed{m}\,L_1^t \wedge \boxed{\alpha}\,L_2^f \wedge \bigwedge_{\substack{S_1,\mathsf{max}(S_1)=m\\ S_2=\uparrow\alpha\setminus S_1}} \left(\boxed{m}\,L_1^t \vee \boxed{\mathsf{min}(S_2)}\,L_2^f\right) \wedge$$
$$\bigwedge_{\alpha\leq\beta<m} \bigwedge_{\substack{S_1,\mathsf{max}(S_1)=\beta,\\ S_2=\uparrow\alpha\setminus S_1}} \left(\boxed{\beta}\,L_1^t \vee \boxed{\mathsf{min}(S_2)}\,L_2^f\right)$$

$$\text{iff } \boxed{m}\,L_1^t \wedge \boxed{\alpha}\,L_2^f \wedge \bigwedge_{\alpha\leq\beta<m} \bigwedge_{\beta'\neq\beta,\beta'\leq s(\beta)} \left(\boxed{\beta}\,L_1^t \vee \boxed{\beta'}\,L_2^f\right)$$

$$\text{iff } \boxed{m}\,L_1^t \wedge \boxed{\alpha}\,L_2^f \wedge \bigwedge_{\alpha\leq\beta<m} \left(\boxed{\beta}\,L_1^t \vee \boxed{s(\beta)}\,L_2^f\right).$$

□

For quantifiers we have the following results (for related results cf. [Häh98]).

Lemma 1. *Let $\mathcal{I} = (D, I, d)$ be an interpretation of $\mathcal{L}$ in S_{n^2}, $v_{\mathcal{I}}$ the induced valuation, and let $a \in S_{n^2}$ be a join-irreducible element. The following hold:*

($\forall_1$) *$v_{\mathcal{I}}(\forall x\phi(x, x_1, \ldots, x_n)) \geq a$ iff $v_{\mathcal{I}_{x/d}}(\phi(x, x_1, \ldots, x_n)) \geq a$ for every instantiation $d \in D$ of x.*
($\forall_2$) *$v_{\mathcal{I}}(\forall x\phi(x, x_1, \ldots, x_n)) \not\geq a$ iff $v_{\mathcal{I}_{x/d}}(\phi(x, x_1, \ldots, x_n)) \not\geq a$ for some instantiation $d \in D$ of x, depending on $d(x_1), \ldots, d(x_n)$.*
($\exists_1$) *$v_{\mathcal{I}}(\exists x\phi(x, x_1, \ldots, x_n)) \geq a$ iff $v_{\mathcal{I}_{x/d}}(\phi(x, x_1, \ldots, x_n)) \geq a$ for some instantiation $d \in D$ of x, depending on $d(x_1), \ldots, d(x_n)$.*
($\exists_2$) *$v_{\mathcal{I}}(\exists x\phi(x, x_1, \ldots, x_n)) \not\geq a$ iff $v_{\mathcal{I}_{x/d}}(\phi(x, x_1, \ldots, x_n)) \not\geq a$ for every instantiation $d \in D$ of x.*

Proof: ($\forall_1$) and ($\forall_2$) follow immediately, taking into account that

$$v_{\mathcal{I}}(\forall x\phi(x, x_1, \ldots, x_n)) = \bigwedge\{w \mid \exists d \in D \ s.t.\ v_{\mathcal{I}_{x/d}}(\phi(x, x_1, \ldots, x_n)) = w\}.$$

($\exists_1$) For the direct implication, assume that $v_{\mathcal{I}}(\exists x\phi(x)) = \bigvee\{w \mid \exists d \in D \ s.t.\ v_{\mathcal{I}_{x/d}}(\phi(x, x_1, \ldots, x_n)) = w\} \geq a$. ¿From the fact that S_{n^2} is distributive and for every ϕ the set $\{w \mid \exists d \in D \ s.t.\ v_{\mathcal{I}_{x/d}}(\phi(x, x_1, \ldots, x_n)) = w\}$ is finite, it follows that $a = \bigvee\{w \mid \exists d \in D \ s.t.\ v_{\mathcal{I}_{x/d}}(\phi(x, x_1, \ldots, x_n)) = w\} \wedge a = \bigvee\{w \wedge a \mid \exists d \in D \ s.t.\ v_{\mathcal{I}_{x/d}}(\phi(x, x_1, \ldots, x_n)) = w\}$. By the fact that a is join-irreducible it then follows that $a = w \wedge a$ for some w such that there exists $d \in D$ with $v_{\mathcal{I}_{x/d}}(\phi(x, x_1, \ldots, x_n)) = w$, hence, $v_{\mathcal{I}_{x/d}}(\phi(x, x_1, \ldots, x_n)) \geq a$ for some $d \in D$ (depending on $d(x_1), \ldots, d(x_n)$). The converse follows immediately since if $v_{\mathcal{I}_{x/d}}(\phi(x, x_1, \ldots, x_n)) \geq a$ for some $d \in D$, then also $v_{\mathcal{I}}(\exists x \phi(x)) = \bigvee\{w \mid \exists d \in D \; s.t. \; v_{\mathcal{I}_{x/d}}(\phi(x, x_1, \ldots, x_n)) = w\} \geq a$.

($\exists_2$) follows immediately from ($\exists_1$). □

Proposition 2. *Let L be a literal and let $\mathcal{M} = (D, M, d)$ be an interpretation of $\mathcal{L}$ in $\mathcal{O}(D(S_{n^2}))$. The following hold:*

$(\forall, t)$ $\boxed{\alpha}$ $(\forall x L(x, x_1, \ldots, x_n))^t$ *in* $\mathcal{M}$ *iff* $\boxed{\alpha}$ $(L(x, x_1, \ldots, x_n))^t$ *in* $\mathcal{M}_{x/d}$ *for every instantiation* $d \in D$ *of* x.

$(\forall, f)$ $\boxed{\alpha}$ $(\forall x L(x, x_1, \ldots, x_n))^f$ *in* $\mathcal{M}$ *iff* $\boxed{\alpha}$ $(L(f(x_1, \ldots, x_n), x_1, \ldots, x_n))^f$ *in* $\mathcal{M}$ *(where f is a new function symbol).*

$(\exists, t)$ $\boxed{\alpha}$ $(\exists x L(x, x_1, \ldots, x_n))^t$ *in* $\mathcal{M}$ *iff* $\boxed{\alpha}$ $(L(f(x_1, \ldots, x_n), x_1, \ldots, x_n))^t$ *in* $\mathcal{M}$ *(where f is a new function symbol).*

$(\exists, f)$ $\boxed{\alpha}$ $(\exists x L(x, x_1, \ldots, x_n))^f$ *in* $\mathcal{M}$ *iff* $\boxed{\alpha}$ $(L(x, x_1, \ldots, x_n))^f$ *in* $\mathcal{M}_{x/d}$ *for every instantiation* $d \in D$ *of* x.

Proof: We know that all the elements $\alpha \in D(S_{n^2})$ are of the form $\uparrow a$, where a is a join-irreducible element in S_{n^2}. For every $\mathcal{M} = (D, M, d)$, let $v_{\mathcal{M}} : \mathsf{Fma}(\mathcal{L}) \to \mathcal{O}(D(S_{n^2}))$ be the valuation function induced by $\mathcal{M}$. Let $\mathcal{I} = (D, I, d)$ be the associated interpretation in S_{n^2} (obtained by composition with $\eta_{S_{n^2}}^{-1}$ when necessary). For every $\psi \in \mathsf{Fma}(\mathcal{L})$ we have $v_{\mathcal{M}}(\psi) = \eta_{S_{n^2}}(v_{\mathcal{I}}(\psi)) = \{\uparrow a \mid v_{\mathcal{I}}(\psi) \in \uparrow a\} = \{\uparrow a \mid v_{\mathcal{I}}(\psi) \geq a\}$. Thus, $\boxed{\alpha}$ ψ^t in $\mathcal{M}$ iff $\alpha = \uparrow a \in v_{\mathcal{M}}(\psi)$ iff $v_{\mathcal{I}}(\psi) \geq a$. Therefore, using Lemma 1 we have:

$(\forall, t)$ $\boxed{\alpha}$ $(\forall x L(x, x_1, \ldots, x_n))^t$ in $\mathcal{M}$ iff $v_{\mathcal{I}}(\forall x L(x, x_1, \ldots, x_n)) \geq a$, which, by Lemma 1 happens iff $v_{\mathcal{I}_{x/d}}(L(x, x_1, \ldots, x_n)) \geq a$ for every instantiation d of x. Thus, $\boxed{\alpha}$ $(\forall x L(x, x_1, \ldots, x_n))^t$ in $\mathcal{M}$ iff for every instantiation d of x, $\boxed{\alpha}$ $(L(x, x_1, \ldots, x_n))^t$ in $\mathcal{M}_{x/d}$.

$(\forall, f)$ $\boxed{\alpha}$ $(\forall x L(x, x_1, \ldots, x_n))^f$ in $\mathcal{M}$ iff $\alpha \notin v_{\mathcal{M}}(\forall x L(x, x_1, \ldots, x_n))$. By Lemma 1 this happens iff $v_{\mathcal{I}_{x/d}}(L(x, x_1, \ldots, x_n)) \not\geq a$ for some instantiation d of a, depending on the values of the other free variables in L.

$(\exists, t)$, $(\exists, f)$ follow analogously. □

After this translation, from any formula ϕ we obtain a formula Φ in clause form, containing literals of the form $\boxed{\alpha}$ L^t and $\boxed{\alpha}$ L^f where L is an atom and $\alpha \in D(S_{n^2})$.

Theorem 3. *ϕ is a theorem iff Φ is unsatisfiable.*

Proof: Follows from Theorem 2, Proposition 1 and Proposition 2. □

Proposition 3. *The number of clauses generated from a given formula ϕ is in $\mathcal{O}(n^2 l)$, where l is the number of subformulae of ϕ, and n^2 the number of truth values. If the formula ϕ does not contain the connectives $\Rightarrow$ and $\neg$, then the number of clauses generated from ϕ is in $\mathcal{O}(nl)$.*

Proof: *(Sketch)* It is easy to see that for every $\alpha \in D(A)$ the split degree of the rules in Proposition 1 and Proposition 2 is 3 in case of $\vee$ and $\wedge$; 2 for

$S_1, \ldots, S_{n-1}$, $\sim$, and $\forall, \exists$; and in $\mathcal{O}(n)$ for $\neg$ and $\Rightarrow$. The maximal number of clauses is generated by the subformulae of the form $\psi = \psi_1 \Rightarrow \psi_2$. In this case, for every $\alpha \in D(S_{n^2})$ the number of clauses generated by ($\boxed{\alpha}\ P^f_\psi \vee \boxed{\alpha}\ \psi^t$) and ($\boxed{\alpha}\ P^t_\psi \vee \boxed{\alpha}\ \psi^f$) is bounded by $2|\{\beta \mid \beta \geq \alpha\}| + 1$. Thus, the number of clauses generated from a formula ϕ has as upper bound $1 + 2 \cdot l \cdot \Sigma_{i=1}^{n-1}(2i+1) = 1 + 2 \cdot l \cdot (n^2 - 1)$, hence is (in the worst case) in $\mathcal{O}(n^2 l)$. The estimations for formulae not containing $\Rightarrow$ or $\neg$ follow from the fact that the branching factor is constant for $\sim$, $S_1, \ldots, S_{n-1}$, $\vee, \wedge, \exists, \forall$. $\square$

4.1 Further Improvements

The structure of $D(S_{n^2})$ can be used in order to further reduce the number of clauses[1]. For this, we use the fact that $D(S_{n^2})$ consists of two branches and that the transformation rules for the operations in $\{\vee, \wedge, \neg, \Rightarrow\}$ preserve the branch of $D(S_{n^2})$. For formulae that do not contain the De Morgan negation $\sim$, all the clauses generated by the renaming of subformulae only contain signs in one of the branches of $D(S_{n^2})$. It is sufficient to give a refutation for the clauses corresponding to one of the branches of $D(S_{n^2})$. For the other branch a similar refutation can be constructed by simply renaming the nodes, and they can be then combined to a refutation by resolution for the clause form of ϕ.

The set of signed clauses that would be generated in this case corresponds to the following conjunction of formulae:

$$\boxed{\uparrow(1,0)}\ P^f_\phi \text{ in } \mathcal{M},$$

$$(\boxed{\uparrow(i,0)}\ P_\psi(x_1,\ldots,x_n)^t \vee \boxed{\uparrow(i,0)}\ \sigma(P_{\psi_1},\ldots,P_{\psi_m})^f)$$
$$(\boxed{\uparrow(i,0)}\ P_\psi(x_1,\ldots,x_n)^f \vee \boxed{\uparrow(i,0)}\ \sigma(P_{\psi_1},\ldots,P_{\psi_m})^t)$$

in $\mathcal{M}$; for every $i = 1, \ldots, n-1$, for all subformulae $\psi = \sigma(\psi_1, \ldots, \psi_m)$ of ϕ and all instantiations in D of the free variables $x_1, \ldots, x_n$ of ψ,

$$(\boxed{\uparrow(i,0)}\ P_\psi(x_1,\ldots,x_n)^t \vee \boxed{\uparrow(i,0)}\ (Qx)P_{\psi_1}(x,x_1,\ldots,x_n)^f)$$
$$(\boxed{\uparrow(i,0)}\ P_\psi(x_1,\ldots,x_n)^f \vee \boxed{\uparrow(i,0)}\ (Qx)P_{\psi_1}(x,x_1,\ldots,x_n)^t)$$

in $\mathcal{M}$; for every $i = 1, \ldots, n-1$, for all subformulae $\psi = (Qx)\psi_1(x, x_1, \ldots, x_n)$ of ϕ and all instantiations in D of the free variables $x_1, \ldots, x_n$ of ψ.

5 Automated Theorem Proving

In [SS98], where we focus on theorem proving for sets of signed clauses, we note that the translation to clause form described above is a translation to (many-sorted) classical logic ($\boxed{\alpha}\ L^t$ stands for $\mathsf{holds}(L, \alpha)$, and $\boxed{\alpha}\ L^f$ for $\neg\mathsf{holds}(L, \alpha)$).

[1] We thank Luisa Iturrioz who suggested that it may be possible to further improve the efficiency of automated theorem proving for SH_n-logics by exploiting the structure of $D(S_{n^2})$; the remarks below show that this is possible; a more thorough research, also for more general logics, is planned for future work.

This also explains the fact that the polarity of formulae can be used to further reduce the number of clauses generated in the translation to clause form.

Therefore, checking the satisfiability of the sets of signed clauses obtained after the clause form transformation described in Section 4 does not present a problem. For instance, as shown in [SS98], the validity of ϕ can be checked by applying classical resolution to the set Φ^c of classical clauses obtained from the signed CNF of ϕ by replacing $\boxed{\alpha}\ L^t$ with $\mathsf{holds}(L, \alpha)$, and $\boxed{\alpha}\ L^f$ with $\neg\mathsf{holds}(L, \alpha)$, to which the set of clauses $\mathsf{Her} = \{\{\neg\mathsf{holds}(x, \alpha), \mathsf{holds}(x, \beta)\} \mid \alpha \leq \beta\}$, expressing the heredity of truth, is adjoined.

Alternatively, versions of *signed resolution* can be used, which generalize existing signed resolution rules for regular logics [Häh96]. We illustrate these ideas by presenting a version of negative hyperresolution for signed clauses, inspired by the method for regular clauses in [Häh96].

Negative Hyperresolution

$$\frac{\left\{\boxed{x_1}\ p_1^f\right\} \cup D_1, \ldots, \left\{\boxed{x_n}\ p_n^f\right\} \cup D_n, \left\{\boxed{y_1}\ p_1^t, \ldots, \boxed{y_n}\ p_n^t\right\} \cup E}{D_1 \cup \cdots \cup D_n \cup E}$$

provided that $n \geq 1$, $y_i \leq x_i$ for all $i = 1, \ldots, n$ and $D_1, \ldots, D_n, E$ are negative.

Proposition 4. *A set Φ of ground signed clauses is unsatisfiable if and only if $\Box$ can be derived from Φ by a finite number of applications of many-valued negative hyperresolution.*

Proof: *(Sketch)* It is easy to see that if $\Box$ can be derived from Φ by a finite number of applications of many-valued negative hyperresolution then Φ is unsatisfiable (this follows from the fact that if $\mathcal{M}$ is a model for the negative clauses $C_1, \ldots C_n$ and for the positive clause C then $\mathcal{M}$ is a model of any of their resolvents). The proof of completeness closely follows the proof in [Häh96] or [AB70]. Let $nl(\Phi)$ be the total number of literals in Φ and $nc(\Phi)$ the total number of clauses in Φ. It is obvious that $nl(\Phi) \geq nc(\Phi)$. We will proceed by induction on the difference $k(\Phi) = nl(\Phi) - nc(\Phi)$. If $\Box \in \Phi$ then the conclusion is obvious. Therefore in what follows we will assume that $\Box \notin \Phi$.

Case 1. $k(\Phi) = 0$: In this case $nl(\Phi) = nc(\Phi)$. Since $\Box \notin \Phi$, Φ must consist only of unit clauses. Since Φ is unsatisfiable, there must exist two clauses $\{\boxed{\alpha}\ p^t\}$ and $\{\boxed{\beta}\ p^f\}$ in Φ such that $\alpha \leq \beta$. Then $\Box$ can be derived from the clauses $\{\boxed{\alpha}\ p^t\}$ and $\{\boxed{\beta}\ p^f\}$ where $\alpha \leq \beta$ by negative hyperresolution.

Case 2. $k(\Phi) > 0$ (i.e. $nl(\Phi) > nc(\Phi)$).

Subcase 2a: Assume that all non-positive clauses consist of one literal. Then it follows that all negative literals in Φ appear in unit clauses. Since Φ is unsatisfiable, there is a positive clause in Φ which immediately produces the empty clause with suitable negative unit clauses.

Subcase 2b: There is a non-positive non-unit clause $C = \{\boxed{\beta}\ p^f\} \cup D \in \Phi$ with $D \neq \Box$. Let $\Phi' = \Phi \backslash \{C\}$, $\Phi_1 = \Phi' \cup D$, and $\Phi_2 = \Phi' \cup \{\{\boxed{\beta}\ p^f\}\}$. Since

Φ is unsatisfiable it follows that both Φ_1, Φ_2 are unsatisfiable. Moreover, Φ_1 and Φ_2 contain the same number of clauses as Φ, but they have fewer literals. Hence, $k(\Phi_1) < k(\Phi)$ and $k(\Phi_2) < k(\Phi)$. Since Φ_1 and Φ_2 are both unsatisfiable, by the induction hypothesis, $\Box$ can be deduced from Φ_1 and $\Box$ can be deduced from Φ_2 by hyperresolution. Consider a hyperresolution deduction of $\Box$ from Φ_1. If we replace each occurrence of D by C in this proof then we obtain a valid hyperresolution deduction with last clause $\Box$ or $\{ \boxed{\beta}\, p^f \}$. If the last clause is $\Box$, we have already a hyperresolution deduction of $\Box$ from Φ. If the last clause is $\{ \boxed{\beta}\, p^f \}$, then its deduction from Φ can be extended to a deduction of $\Box$ from Φ using the fact that there is a deduction of $\Box$ from Φ_2. $\Box$

The completeness theorem (for the non-ground case) uses an extension of the lifting lemma to signed literals (for details cf. e.g. [SS97]).

It may be that translation to classical logic combined with the use of classical resolution is simpler and more satisfactory for automated theorem proving in this kind of logics than devising specialized signed resolution schemes. In [GSS99] the use of techniques from classical logic such as superposition and ordered chaining in automated theorem proving in many-valued logics is studied.

6 Comparison with Other Methods

We now briefly compare the method for translation to clause form described here with other existing methods. Consider first the very general structure-preserving methods for translation to clause form that use the algebra of truth values given in [BF95]. The split degree of rules of the type $(\Box, v)^+$ induced by a k-ary operator $\Box$, given a truth value v, is at most $|W|^{k-1}$, if W is the set of truth values. Since in a structure-preserving translation to clause form such rules have to be considered for every truth value v, the clause form of a formula with n occurrences of at most r-ary operators and m occurrences of quantifiers contains no more than $n|W|^r + m2^{|W|} + 1$ clauses if optimal rules are used (cf. [BF95]). In the presence of operators that are at most binary, and if the only quantifiers are $\forall$ and $\exists$, the number of clauses generated this way is in the worst case quadratic in the number of truth values, hence, for SH_n-logics it would generate $\mathcal{O}(ln^4)$ clauses for formulae containing at least one binary operator. (This upper bound is actually reached if the very general rules in [BF95] are used as presented there.) Additional improvements may be achieved by special minimization techniques, as done for instance in [Sal96]. The method of Salzer starts with an arbitrary conjunctive normal form (e.g. constructed from the truth table, as in [BF95]), saturates it under sets-as-signs resolution, and selects a minimal subset of the saturated set of clauses by any covering-set-algorithm. The results in [Sal96] show that the conjunctive normal forms obtained this way are optimal. However, the method does not bring much information about the general form of the conjunctive normal forms, or on the kind of signs actually needed in such conjunctive normal forms for whole classes of logics.

One important advantage of the method we presented here is that only elements of the Priestley dual of the set of truth values are used as signs, thus fewer signs have to be taken into account in the process of translation to clause form. Our method is especially efficient in situations when the difference between the number of elements of the algebra of truth values and the number of elements of its Priestley dual is large. In the case of SH_n-logics the number of elements of the algebra of truth values S_{n^2} is n^2, whereas the number of elements of $D(S_{n^2})$ is $2(n-1)$. Even for linearly-ordered sets of truth values the set of clauses introduced by the Heyting negation (determined by a technique similar to that used in Proposition 1) is the same as that obtained with Salzer's algorithm [Sal96], i.e. linear in the number of truth values.

Moreover, the signed formulae we use, namely $\boxed{\alpha}\ \phi^t$ and $\boxed{\alpha}\ \phi^f$, are very similar to the "positive and negative regular formulae" of the form $\boxed{\geq i}\ \phi$ resp. $\boxed{\leq i}\ \phi$ introduced in [Häh96] for regular logics. The only difference is that in [Häh96] totally ordered sets are considered, whereas we consider duals of finite distributive lattices[2]. In the particular case of totally ordered lattices of truth values, Hähnle's notions of positive and negative literal are recovered: $\boxed{\geq i}\ \phi$ corresponds to $\boxed{\alpha}\ \phi^t$ and $\boxed{\leq i-1}\ \phi$ to $\boxed{\alpha}\ \phi^f$, where $\alpha = \uparrow i$, which justifies the terminology "literal with positive (negative) polarity" in [Häh96].

7 Conclusions

In this paper we illustrated by one example, namely SH_n-logics, an efficient transformation procedure to a signed clause form, and a refutation procedure based on negative hyperresolution for many-valued logics based on distributive lattices with operators. This method extends in a natural way the work of Hähnle [Häh96,Häh98] for regular logics, and, we think, will help in making automated theorem proving in logics based on distributive lattices with operators more efficient. A detailed presentation of these ideas for SH_n-logics, an extension to a more general framework, and the description of a Prolog implementation can be found in [SS97]. The detailed presentation of a general method based on these ideas is the subject of an extended paper, [SS99a].

Acknowledgments. We gratefully acknowledge the support from MEDLAR II (ESPRIT BRP 6471; financed for Austria by FWF) during our stay at RISC-Linz, COST Action 15, and a postdoctoral fellowship at MPII. We thank M. Baaz, R. Hähnle, L. Iturrioz, E. Orłowska, J. Pfalzgraf, and G. Salzer for stimulating discussions and for their papers which inspired our own work. We also thank the referees for their helpful comments.

---

[2] For the linearly-ordered case, the negation of "$\boxed{\geq i}\ \phi$ is true" is "$\boxed{\leq i-1}\ \phi$ is true", in cases when the set of truth values is not linearly ordered this does not necessarily hold.

References

[AB70] R. Anderson and W. Bledsoe. A linear format for resolution with merging and a new technique for establishing completeness. *Journal of the ACM*, 17:525–534, 1970.

[BF95] M. Baaz and C.G. Fermüller. Resolution-based theorem proving for many-valued logics. *Journal of Symbolic Computation*, 19:353–391, 1995.

[DP90] B.A. Davey and H.A. Priestley. *Introduction to Lattices and Order*. Cambridge University Press, 1990.

[GSS99] H. Ganzinger and V. Sofronie-Stokkermans. Chaining calculi and resolution-based theorem proving in many-valued logic. In preparation, 1999.

[Häh94] R. Hähnle. Short conjunctive normal forms in finitely valued logics. *Journal of Logic and Computation*, 4(6):905–927, 1994.

[Häh96] R. Hähnle. Exploiting data dependencies in many-valued logics. *Journal of Applied Non-Classical Logics*, 6(1):49–69, 1996.

[Häh98] R. Hähnle. Commodious axiomatization of quantifiers in multiple-valued logic. *Studia Logica*, 61(1):101–121, 1998.

[IO96] L. Iturrioz and E. Orłowska. A Kripke-style and relational semantics for logics based on Łukasiewicz algebras. Conference in honour of J. Lukasiewicz, Dublin, 1996.

[Itu82] L. Iturrioz. Modal operators on symmetrical Heyting algebras. In T. Traczyk, editor, *Universal Algebra and Applications*, Banach Center Publications, Vol. 9, pages 289–303. PWN-Polish Scientific Publishers, 1982.

[Itu83] L. Iturrioz. Symmetrical Heyting algebras with operators. *Zeitschrift f. math. Logik und Grundlagen d. Mathematik*, 29:33–70, 1983.

[Sal96] G. Salzer. Optimal axiomatizations for multiple-valued operators and quantifiers based on semilattices. In M. McRobbie and J. Slaney, editors, *Proc. 13th Conference on Automated Deduction, New Brunswick/NJ, USA*, LNCS 1104, pages 688–702. Springer Verlag, 1996.

[Sco73] D.S. Scott. Background to formalization. In H. Leblanc, editor, *Truth, Syntax and Modality. Proceedings of the Temple University Conference on Alternative Semantics*, Studies in Logic and the Foundations of Mathematics, Vol. 68, pages 244–273, 1973.

[SS97] V. Sofronie-Stokkermans. *Fibered Structures and Applications to Automated Theorem Proving in Certain Classes of Finitely-Valued Logics and to Modeling Interacting Systems*. PhD thesis, RISC-Linz, J.Kepler University Linz, Austria, 1997.

[SS98] V. Sofronie-Stokkermans. On translation of finitely-valued logics to classical first-order logic. In H. Prade, editor, *Proceedings of ECAI 98*, pages 410–411. John Wiley & Sons, 1998.

[SS99a] V. Sofronie-Stokkermans. Automated theorem proving by resolution for finitely-valued logics based on distributive lattices with operators. Submitted, 1999.

[SS99b] V. Sofronie-Stokkermans. Priestley duality for SHn-algebras and applications to the study of Kripke-style models for SHn-logics. Multiple-Valued Logic – An International Journal, To appear, 1999.

Full First-Order Sequent and Tableau Calculi with Preservation of Solutions and the Liberalized δ-Rule but without Skolemization

Claus-Peter Wirth

Informatik 5, Universität Dortmund, D-44221, Germany
wirth@LS5.cs.uni-dortmund.de

Abstract. We present a combination of raising, explicit variable dependency representation, the liberalized δ-rule, and preservation of solutions for first-order deductive theorem proving. Our main motivation is to provide the foundation for our work on inductive theorem proving.

1 Introduction

1.1 Without Skolemization

We discuss how to analytically prove first-order theorems in contexts where Skolemization is not appropriate. It has at least three problematic aspects.

1. Skolemization enrichs the signature or introduces higher-order variables. Unless special care is taken, this may introduce objects into empty universes and change the notion of term-generatedness or Herbrand models. Above that, the Skolem functions occur in answers to goals or solutions of constraints which in general cannot be translated into the original signature. For a detailed discussion of these problems cf. Miller (1992).
2. Skolemization results in the following simplified quantification structure: "For all Skolem functions $\vec{u}$ there are solutions to the free existential variables $\vec{e}$ (i.e. the free variables of Fitting (1996)) such that the quantifier-free theorem $T(\vec{e}, \vec{u})$ is valid. Short: $\forall \vec{u}\colon\ \exists \vec{e}\colon\ T(\vec{e}, \vec{u})$." Since the state of a proof attempt is often represented as the conjunction of the branches of a tree (e.g. in sequent or (dual) tableau calculi), the free existential variables become "rigid" or "global", i.e. a solution for a free existential variable must solve all occurrences of this variable in the whole proof tree. This is because, for $B_0, \ldots, B_n$ denoting the branches of the proof tree,
$$\forall \vec{u}\colon\ \exists \vec{e}\colon\ (\ B_0 \wedge \ldots \wedge B_n\ )$$
is logically strictly stronger than
$$\forall \vec{u}\colon\ (\ \exists \vec{e}\colon\ B_0\ \wedge\ \ldots\ \wedge\ \exists \vec{e}\colon\ B_n\ ).$$
Moreover, with this quantification structure it does not seem to be possible to do inductive theorem proving (*ITP*) by finding, for each assumed counterexample, another counterexample that is strictly smaller in some wellfounded ordering.[1] The reason for this is the following. When we have some counterexample $\vec{u}$ for $T(\vec{e}, \vec{u})$ (i.e. there is no $\vec{e}$ such that $T(\vec{e}, \vec{u})$ is valid) then for

[1] While this paradigm of ITP was already used by the Greeks, Pierre de Fermat

R. Caferra, G. Salzer (Eds.): Automated Deduction, LNAI 1761, pp. 282-297, 2000.

different $\vec{e}$ different branches B_i in the proof tree may cause the invalidity of the conjunction. If we have applied induction hypotheses in more than one branch, for different $\vec{e}$ we get different smaller counterexamples. What we would need, however, is one single smaller counterexample for all $\vec{e}$.

3. Skolemization increases the size of the formulas. (Note that in most calculi the only relevant part of Skolem terms is the top symbol and the set of occurring variables.)

The 1st and 2nd problematic aspects disappear when one uses *raising* (cf. Miller (1992)) instead of Skolemization. Raising is a dual of Skolemization and simplifies the quantification structure to something like: "There are raising functions $\vec{e}$ such that for all possible values of the free universal variables $\vec{u}$ (i.e. the nullary constants or "parameters") the quantifier-free theorem $T(\vec{e},\vec{u})$ is valid. Short: $\exists\vec{e}\colon \forall\vec{u}\colon T(\vec{e},\vec{u})$." Note that due to the two duality switches "unsatisfiability/validity" and "Skolemization/raising", in this paper raising will look much like Skolemization in refutational theorem proving. The inverted order of universal and existential quantification of raising (compared to Skolemization) is advantageous because now $\exists\vec{e}\colon \forall\vec{u}\colon (\ B_0 \wedge \ldots \wedge B_n\ )$ is indeed logically equivalent to $\exists\vec{e}\colon (\ \forall\vec{u}\colon B_0\ \wedge\ \ldots\ \wedge\ \forall\vec{u}\colon B_n\ )$. Furthermore, ITP works well: When, for some $\vec{e}$, we have some counterexample $\vec{u}$ for $T(\vec{e},\vec{u})$ (i.e. $T(\vec{e},\vec{u})$ is invalid) then one branch B_i in the proof tree must cause the invalidity of the conjunction. If this branch is closed, then it contains the application of an induction hypothesis that is invalid for this $\vec{e}$ and the $\vec{u}'$ resulting from the instantiation of the hypothesis. Thus, $\vec{u}'$ together with the induction hypothesis provides the strictly smaller counterexample we are searching for for this $\vec{e}$. The 3rd problematic aspect disappears when the dependency of variables is explicitly represented in a *variable-condition*, cf. Kohlhase (1995). This idea actually has a long history, cf. Prawitz (1960), Kanger (1963), Bibel (1987). Moreover, the use of variable-conditions admits the free existential variables to be first-order.

1.2 Sequent and Tableau Calculi

In Smullyan (1968), rules for analytic theorem proving are classified as α-, β-, γ-, and δ-rules independently from a concrete calculus. *α-rules* describe the simple and the *β-rules* the case-splitting propositional proof steps. *γ-rules* show existential properties, either by exhibiting a term witnessing to the existence or else by introducing a special kind of variable, called "dummy" in Prawitz (1960) and Kanger (1963), and "free variable" in footnote 11 of Prawitz (1960) and in Fitting (1996). We will call these variables *free existential variables*. With free existential variables we can delay the choice of a witnessing term until the state of the proof attempt gives us more information which choice is likely to result in a successful proof. It is the important addition of free existential variables that makes the major difference between the free variable calculi of Fitting (1996) and the calculi of Smullyan (1968). Since there use to be infinitely many

(1601-1665) rediscovered it under the name "descente infinie", and in our time it is sometimes called "implicit induction", cf. Wirth & Becker (1995), Wirth (1997).

possibly witnessing terms (and different branches may need different ones), the γ-rules (under assistance of the β-rules) often destroy the possibility to decide validity because they enable infinitely many γ-rule applications to the same formula. *δ-rules* show universal properties simply with the help of a new symbol, called a "parameter", about which nothing is known. Since the present free existential variables must not be instantiated with this new parameter, in the standard framework of Skolemization and unification the parameter is given the present free existential variables as arguments. In this paper, however, we will use nullary parameters, which we call *free universal variables*. These variables are not free in the sense that they may be chosen freely, but in the sense that they are not bound by any quantifier. Our free universal variables are similar to the parameters of Kanger (1963) because a free existential variable may not be instantiated with all of them. We will store the information on the dependency between free existential variables and free universal variables in *variable-conditions*.

1.3 Preservation of Solutions

Users even of pure Prolog are not so much interested in theorem proving as they are in answer computation. The theorem they want to prove usually contains some free existential variables that are instantiated during a proof attempt. When the proof attempt is successful, not only the input theorem is known to be valid but also the instance of the theorem with the substitution built-up during the proof. Since the knowledge of mere existence is much less useful than the knowledge of a term that witnesses to this existence (unless this term is a only free existential variable), theorem proving should—if possible—always provide these witnessing terms. Answer computation is no problem in Prolog's Horn logic, but also for the more difficult clausal logic, answer computation is possible: Cf. e.g. Baumgartner & al. (1997), where tableau calculi are used for answer computation in clausal logic. Answer computation becomes even harder when we consider full first-order logic instead of clausal logic. When δ-steps occur in a proof, the introduced free universal variables may provide no information on what kind of object they denote. Their excuse may be that they cannot do this in terms of computability or λ-terms. Nevertheless, they can provide this information in form of Hilbert's ε-terms, and the strong versions of our calculi will do so. When full first-order logic is considered, one should focus on *preservation of solutions* instead of computing answers. By this we mean at least the following property: "All solutions that transform a proof attempt for a proposition into a closed proof (i.e. the closing substitutions for the free existential variables) are also solutions of the original proposition." This is again closely related to ITP: Suppose that we finally have shown that for the reduced form $R(\vec{e},\vec{u})$ (i.e. the state of the proof attempt) of the original theorem $T(\vec{e},\vec{u})$ there is some solution $\vec{e}$ such that for each counterexample $\vec{u}$ of $R(\vec{e},\vec{u})$ there is a counterexample $\vec{u}'$ for the original theorem that is strictly smaller than $\vec{u}$ in some wellfounded ordering. In this case we have proved $T(\vec{e},\vec{u})$ only if the solution $\vec{e}$ for the reduced form $\forall\vec{u}\colon\ R(\vec{e},\vec{u})$ is also a solution for the original theorem $\forall\vec{u}\colon\ T(\vec{e},\vec{u})$.

1.4 The Liberalized δ-Rule

We use '$\uplus$' for the union of disjoint classes and 'id' for the identity function. For a class R we define *domain*, *range*, and *restriction to* and *image* and *reverse-image of a class A* by $\mathrm{dom}(R) := \{\, a \mid \exists b\colon\ (a,b) \in R \,\}$; $\mathrm{ran}(R) := \{\, b \mid \exists a\colon\ (a,b) \in R \,\}$; ${}_{A}|R := \{\, (a,b) \in R \mid a \in A \}$; $\langle A \rangle R := \{\, b \mid \exists a \in A\colon (a,b) \in R \}$; $R\langle B \rangle := \{\, a \mid \exists b \in B\colon\ (a,b) \in R \}$. We define a *sequent* to be a list of formulas. The *conjugate* of a formula A (written: $\overline{A}$) is the formula B if A is of the form $\neg B$, and the formula $\neg A$ otherwise. In the tradition of Gentzen (1935) we assume the symbols for *free existential variables*, *free universal variables*, *bound variables* (i.e. variables for quantified use only), and the *constants* (i.e. the function and predicate symbols from the signature) to come from four disjoint sets $\mathrm{V}_\exists$, $\mathrm{V}_\forall$, $\mathrm{V}_{\mathrm{bound}}$, and Σ. We assume each of $\mathrm{V}_\exists$, $\mathrm{V}_\forall$, $\mathrm{V}_{\mathrm{bound}}$ to be infinite and set $\mathrm{V}_{\mathrm{free}} := \mathrm{V}_\exists \uplus \mathrm{V}_\forall$. Due to the possibility to rename bound variables w.l.o.g., we do not permit quantification on variables that occur already bound in a formula; i.e. e.g. $\forall x\colon A$ is only a formula in our sense if A does not contain a quantifier on x like $\forall x$ or $\exists x$. The simple effect is that our γ- and δ-rules can simply replace *all* occurrences of x. For a term, formula, sequent Γ etc., '$\mathcal{V}_\exists(\Gamma)$', '$\mathcal{V}_\forall(\Gamma)$', '$\mathcal{V}_{\mathrm{bound}}(\Gamma)$', '$\mathcal{V}_{\mathrm{free}}(\Gamma)$' denote the sets of variables from $\mathrm{V}_\exists$, $\mathrm{V}_\forall$, $\mathrm{V}_{\mathrm{bound}}$, $\mathrm{V}_{\mathrm{free}}$ occurring in Γ, resp.. For a substitution σ we denote with '$\Gamma\sigma$' the result of replacing in Γ each variable x in $\mathrm{dom}(\sigma)$ with $\sigma(x)$. We tacitly assume that each substitution σ satisfies $\mathcal{V}_{\mathrm{bound}}(\mathrm{dom}(\sigma) \cup \mathrm{ran}(\sigma)) = \emptyset$, such that no bound variables can be replaced and no additional variables become bound (i.e. captured) when applying σ.

A *variable-condition* R is a subset of $\mathrm{V}_\exists \times \mathrm{V}_\forall$. Roughly speaking, $(x^\exists, y^\forall) \in R$ says that $x^\exists$ is older than $y^\forall$, so that we must not instantiate the free existential variable $x^\exists$ with a term containing $y^\forall$. While the benefit of the introduction of free existential variables in γ-rules is to delay the choice of a witnessing term, it is sometimes unsound to instantiate such a free existential variable $x^\exists$ with a term containing a free universal variable $y^\forall$ that was introduced later than $x^\exists$:

Example 1.1 $\exists x\colon\ \forall y\colon\ (x = y)$ is not deductively valid. We can start a proof attempt via: γ-step: $\forall y\colon\ (x^\exists = y)$. δ-step: $(x^\exists = y^\forall)$. Now, if we were allowed to substitute the free existential variable $x^\exists$ with the free universal variable $y^\forall$, we would get the tautology $(y^\forall = y^\forall)$, i.e. we would have proved an invalid formula. In order to prevent this, the δ-step has to record $(x^\exists, y^\forall)$ in the variable-condition, which disallows the instantiation step.

In order to restrict the possible instantiations as little as possible, we should keep our variable-conditions as small as possible. Kanger (1963) and Bibel (1987) are quite generous in that they let their variable-conditions become quite big:

Example 1.2 $\exists x\colon\ (\mathsf{P}(x) \lor \forall y\colon \neg\mathsf{P}(y))$ can be proved the following way: γ-step: $(\mathsf{P}(x^\exists) \lor \forall y\colon \neg\mathsf{P}(y))$. α-step: $\mathsf{P}(x^\exists)$, $\forall y\colon \neg\mathsf{P}(y)$. δ-step: $\mathsf{P}(x^\exists)$, $\neg\mathsf{P}(y^\forall)$. Instantiation step: $\mathsf{P}(y^\forall)$, $\neg\mathsf{P}(y^\forall)$. The last step is not allowed in the above citations, so that another γ-step must be applied to the original formula in order to prove it. Our instantiation step, however, is perfectly sound: Since $x^\exists$ does not occur in $\forall y\colon \neg\mathsf{P}(y)$, the free variables $x^\exists$ and $y^\forall$ do not depend on each other and there is no reason to insist on $x^\exists$ being older than $y^{\forall}$. Note that moving-in the existential quantifier transforms the original formula into the logically equivalent formula $\exists x\colon \mathsf{P}(x) \lor \forall y\colon \neg\mathsf{P}(y)$, which enables the δ-step introducing $y^{\forall}$ to come before the γ-step introducing $x^{\exists}$.

Keeping small the variable-conditions generated by the δ-rule results in non-elementary reduction of the size of smallest proofs. This "liberalization of the δ-rule" has a history ranging from Smullyan (1968) over Hähnle & Schmitt (1994) to Baaz & Fermüller (1995). While the liberalized δ-rule of Smullyan (1968) is already able to prove the formula of Ex. 1.2 with a single γ-step, it is much more restrictive than the more liberalized δ-rule of Baaz & Fermüller (1995). Note that liberalization of the δ-rule is not simple because it easily results in unsound calculi, cf. Kohlhase (1995) w.r.t. our Ex. 1.3 and Kohlhase (1998) w.r.t. our Ex. 4.12. The difficulty lies with instantiation steps that relate previously unrelated variables:

Example 1.3 $\exists x\colon \forall y\colon \mathsf{Q}(x,y) \lor \exists u\colon \forall v\colon \neg\mathsf{Q}(v,u)$ is not deductively valid (to wit, let Q be the identity relation on a non-trivial universe). Proof attempt: One α-, two γ-, and two liberalized δ-steps result in

$$\mathsf{Q}(x^{\exists},y^{\forall}),\ \neg\mathsf{Q}(v^{\forall},u^{\exists}) \qquad (*)$$

with variable-condition

$$R := \{(x^{\exists},y^{\forall}),\ (u^{\exists},v^{\forall})\}. \qquad (\#)$$

(Note that the non-liberalized δ-rule would additionally have produced $(x^{\exists},v^{\forall})$ or $(u^{\exists},y^{\forall})$ or both, depending on the order of the proof steps.)
When we now instantiate $x^{\exists}$ with $v^{\forall}$, we relate the previously unrelated variables $u^{\exists}$ and $y^{\forall}$. Thus, our new goal $\mathsf{Q}(v^{\forall},y^{\forall}),\ \neg\mathsf{Q}(v^{\forall},u^{\exists})$ must be equipped with the new variable-condition $\{(u^{\exists},y^{\forall})\}$. Otherwise we could instantiate $u^{\exists}$ with $y^{\forall}$, resulting in the tautology $\mathsf{Q}(v^{\forall},y^{\forall}),\ \neg\mathsf{Q}(v^{\forall},y^{\forall})$.
Note that in the Skolemization framework, this new variable-condition is automatically generated by the occur-check of unification:
When we instantiate $x^{\exists}$ with $v^{\forall}(u^{\exists})$ in $\mathsf{Q}(x^{\exists},y^{\forall}(x^{\exists})),\ \neg\mathsf{Q}(v^{\forall}(u^{\exists}),u^{\exists})$ we get $\mathsf{Q}(v^{\forall}(u^{\exists}),y^{\forall}(v^{\forall}(u^{\exists}))),\ \neg\mathsf{Q}(v^{\forall}(u^{\exists}),u^{\exists})$, which cannot be reduced to a tautology because $y^{\forall}(v^{\forall}(u^{\exists}))$ and $u^{\exists}$ cannot be unified.
When we instantiate the variables $x^{\exists}$ and $u^{\exists}$ in the sequence $(*)$ in parallel via

$$\sigma := \{x^{\exists}{\mapsto}v^{\forall},\ u^{\exists}{\mapsto}y^{\forall}\}, \qquad (\$)$$

we have to check whether the newly imposed variable-conditions are consistent with the substitution itself. In particular, a cycle as given (for the R of $(\#)$) by $y^{\forall}\ \sigma^{-1}\ u^{\exists}\ R\ v^{\forall}\ \sigma^{-1}\ x^{\exists}\ R\ y^{\forall}$ must not exist.

We make use of "[...]" for stating two definitions, lemmas, theorems etc. in one, where the parts between '[' and ']' are optional and are meant to be all included or all omitted. '$\mathbb{N}$' denotes the set of and '$\prec$' the ordering on natural numbers.

Validity is expected to be given with respect to some Σ-structure (Σ-algebra) $\mathcal{A}$, assigning a universe and an appropriate function to each symbol in Σ. For $\mathrm{X} \subseteq \mathrm{V}_{\mathrm{free}}$ we denote the set of total $\mathcal{A}$-valuations of X (i.e. functions mapping free variables to objects of the universe of $\mathcal{A}$) with $\mathrm{X} \to \mathcal{A}$ and the set of (possibly) partial $\mathcal{A}$-valuations of X with $\mathrm{X} \leadsto \mathcal{A}$. For $\pi \in \mathrm{X} \to \mathcal{A}$ we denote with '$\mathcal{A}{\uplus}\pi$' the extension of $\mathcal{A}$ to the variables of X which are then treated as nullary constants. More precisely, we assume the existence of some evaluation function 'eval' such that eval($\mathcal{A}\uplus\pi$) maps any term over $\Sigma\uplus X$ into the universe of $\mathcal{A}$ such that for all $x \in X$: $\mathrm{eval}(\mathcal{A}\uplus\pi)(x) = \pi(x)$. Moreover, eval($\mathcal{A}\uplus\pi$) maps any formula B over $\Sigma\uplus X$ to TRUE or FALSE, such that B is valid in $\mathcal{A}\uplus\pi$ iff $\mathrm{eval}(\mathcal{A}\uplus\pi)(B) = \mathsf{TRUE}$. We assume that the *Substitution-Lemma* holds in the sense that, for any substitution σ, Σ-structure $\mathcal{A}$, and valuation $\pi \in \mathrm{V}_{\mathrm{free}} \to \mathcal{A}$, validity of a formula B in $\mathcal{A} \uplus ((\sigma \uplus {}_{\mathrm{V}_{\mathrm{free}}\setminus\mathrm{dom}(\sigma)}|\mathrm{id}) \circ \mathrm{eval}(\mathcal{A}\uplus\pi))$ is logically equivalent to validity of $B\sigma$ in $\mathcal{A}\uplus\pi$. Finally, we assume that the value of the evaluation function on a term or formula B does not depend on the free variables that do not occur in B: $\mathrm{eval}(\mathcal{A}\uplus\pi)(B) = \mathrm{eval}(\mathcal{A} \uplus {}_{\mathcal{V}_{\mathrm{free}}(B)}|\pi)(B)$. Further properties of validity or evaluation are definitely not needed.

2 Two Versions of Variable-Conditions

We now describe two possible choices for the formal treatment of variable-conditions. The *weak* version works well with the non-liberalized δ-rule. The *strong* version is a little more difficult but can also be used for the liberalized versions. Several binary relations on free variables will be introduced. The overall idea is that when (x, y) occurs in such a relation this means something like "x is older than y" or "the value of y depends on or is described in terms of x".

Definition 2.1 (E_σ, U_σ, [Strong] Existential R-Substitution)
For a substitution σ with $\mathrm{dom}(\sigma) = \mathrm{V}_\exists$ we define the *existential relation* to be $E_\sigma := \{\, (x', x) \mid x' \in \mathcal{V}_\exists(\sigma(x)) \wedge x \in \mathrm{V}_\exists \,\}$ and the *universal relation* to be $U_\sigma := \{\, (y, x) \mid y \in \mathcal{V}_\forall(\sigma(x)) \wedge x \in \mathrm{V}_\exists \,\}$. Let R be a variable-condition. σ is an *existential R-substitution* if σ is a substitution with $\mathrm{dom}(\sigma) = \mathrm{V}_\exists$ for which $U_\sigma \circ R$ is irreflexive. σ is a *strong existential R-substitution* if σ is a substitution with $\mathrm{dom}(\sigma) = \mathrm{V}_\exists$ for which $(U_\sigma \circ R)^+$ is a wellfounded ordering.

Note that, regarding syntax, $(x^\exists, y^\forall) \in R$ is intended to mean that an existential R-substitution σ may not replace $x^\exists$ with a term in which $y^\forall$ occurs, i.e. $(y^\forall, x^\exists) \in U_\sigma$ must be disallowed, i.e. $U_\sigma \circ R$ must be irreflexive. Thus, the definition of a (weak) existential R-substitution is quite straightforward. The definition of a *strong* existential R-substitution requires an additional transitive closure because the strong version then admits a smaller R. To see this, take from Ex. 1.3 the variable-condition R of (#) and the σ of ($). As explained there, σ must not be a strong existential R-valuation due to the cycle $y^\forall\ U_\sigma\ u^\exists\ R\ v^\forall\ U_\sigma\ x^\exists\ R\ y^\forall$ which just contradicts the irreflexivity of $U_\sigma \circ R \circ U_\sigma \circ R$. Note that in practice w.l.o.g. U_σ and R can always be chosen to be finite, so that irreflexivity of $(U_\sigma \circ R)^+$ is then equivalent to $(U_\sigma \circ R)^+$ being a wellfounded ordering.

After application of a [strong] existential R-substitution σ, in case of $(x^\exists, y^\forall) \in R$, we have to ensure that $x^\exists$ is not replaced with $y^\forall$ via a future application of another [strong] existential R-substitution that replaces a free existential variable $u^\exists$ occurring in $\sigma(x^\exists)$ with $y^\forall$. In this case, the new variable-condition has to contain $(u^\exists, y^\forall)$. This means that $E_\sigma \circ R$ must be a subset of the updated variable-condition. For the weak version this is already enough. For the strong version we have to add an arbitrary number of steps with $U_\sigma \circ R$ again.

Definition 2.2 ([Strong] σ-Update)
Let R be a variable-condition and σ be an [strong] existential R-substitution. The [*strong*] *σ-update of* R is $E_\sigma{\circ}R\ [\circ\ (U_\sigma{\circ}R)^*]$.

Example 2.3 In the proof attempt of Ex. 1.3 we applied the strong existential R-substitution $\sigma' := \{x^\exists \mapsto v^\forall\} \uplus {}_{\mathrm{V}_\exists \setminus \{x^\exists\}}|\mathrm{id}$ where $R = \{(x^\exists, y^\forall),\ (u^\exists, v^\forall)\}$. Note that $U_{\sigma'} = \{(v^\forall, x^\exists)\}$ and $E_{\sigma'} = {}_{\mathrm{V}_\exists \setminus \{x^\exists\}}|\mathrm{id}$. Thus: $E_{\sigma'}{\circ}R = \{(u^\exists, v^\forall)\}$; $E_{\sigma'}{\circ}R \circ U_{\sigma'}{\circ}R = \{(u^\exists, y^\forall)\}$; and $E_{\sigma'}{\circ}R \circ U_{\sigma'}{\circ}R \circ U_{\sigma'}{\circ}R = \emptyset$. The strong σ'-update of R is then the new variable-condition $\{(u^\exists, v^\forall),\ (u^\exists, y^\forall)\}$.

Let $\mathcal{A}$ be some Σ-structure. We now define a semantic counterpart of our existential R-substitutions, which we call "existential $(\mathcal{A}, R)$-valuation". Suppose that e maps each free existential variable not directly to an object of $\mathcal{A}$, but can additionally read the values of some free universal variables under an $\mathcal{A}$-valuation $\pi \in \mathrm{V}_\forall \to \mathcal{A}$, i.e. e gets some $\pi' \in \mathrm{V}_\forall \rightsquigarrow \mathcal{A}$ with $\pi' \subseteq \pi$ as a second argument; short: $e\colon \mathrm{V}_\exists \to ((\mathrm{V}_\forall \rightsquigarrow \mathcal{A}) \to \mathcal{A})$. Moreover, for each free existential variable x, we require the set of read free universal variables (i.e. $\mathrm{dom}(\pi')$) to be identical for all π; i.e. there has to be some "semantic relation" $S_e \subseteq \mathrm{V}_\forall \times \mathrm{V}_\exists$ such that for all $x \in \mathrm{V}_\exists$: $e(x)\colon (S_e\langle\{x\}\rangle \to \mathcal{A}) \to \mathcal{A}$. Note that, for each e, at most one semantic relation exists, namely $S_e := \{\ (y, x) \mid y \in \mathrm{dom}(\bigcup(\mathrm{dom}(e(x)))) \wedge x \in \mathrm{V}_\exists\ \}$.

Definition 2.4 (S_e, [Strong] Existential $(\mathcal{A}, R)$-Valuation, ϵ)
Let R be a variable-condition, $\mathcal{A}$ a Σ-structure, and $e\colon \mathrm{V}_\exists \to ((\mathrm{V}_\forall \rightsquigarrow \mathcal{A}) \to \mathcal{A})$. The *semantic relation of* e is $S_e := \{\ (y, x) \mid y \in \mathrm{dom}(\bigcup(\mathrm{dom}(e(x)))) \wedge x \in \mathrm{V}_\exists\ \}$. e is an *existential* $(\mathcal{A}, R)$*-valuation* if $S_e{\circ}R$ is irreflexive and, for all $x \in \mathrm{V}_\exists$, $e(x)\colon (S_e\langle\{x\}\rangle \to \mathcal{A}) \to \mathcal{A}$. e is a *strong existential* $(\mathcal{A}, R)$*-valuation* if $(S_e \circ R)^+$ is a wellfounded ordering and, for all $x \in \mathrm{V}_\exists$, $e(x)\colon (S_e\langle\{x\}\rangle \to \mathcal{A}) \to \mathcal{A}$.
For applying [strong] existential $(\mathcal{A}, R)$-valuations in a uniform manner, we define the function

$$\epsilon\colon (\mathrm{V}_\exists \to ((\mathrm{V}_\forall \rightsquigarrow \mathcal{A}) \to \mathcal{A})) \to ((\mathrm{V}_\forall \to \mathcal{A}) \to (\mathrm{V}_\exists \to \mathcal{A}))$$

by $(e \in \mathrm{V}_\exists \to ((\mathrm{V}_\forall \rightsquigarrow \mathcal{A}) \to \mathcal{A}),\ \pi \in \mathrm{V}_\forall \to \mathcal{A},\ x \in \mathrm{V}_\exists)$

$$\epsilon(e)(\pi)(x) := e(x)({}_{S_e\langle\{x\}\rangle}|\pi).$$

3 The Weak Version

We define R-validity of a set of sequents with free variables, in terms of validity of a formula (where the free variables are treated as nullary constants).

Definition 3.1 (Validity) Let R be a variable-condition, $\mathcal{A}$ a Σ-structure, and G a set of sequents. G is *R-valid in $\mathcal{A}$* if there is an existential $(\mathcal{A}, R)$-valuation e such that G is $(e, \mathcal{A})$-valid. G is $(e, \mathcal{A})$*-valid* if G is $(\pi, e, \mathcal{A})$-valid for all $\pi \in \mathrm{V}_\forall \to \mathcal{A}$. G is $(\pi, e, \mathcal{A})$*-valid* if G is valid in $\mathcal{A} \uplus \epsilon(e)(\pi) \uplus \pi$. G is *valid in $\mathcal{A}$* if Γ is valid in $\mathcal{A}$ for all $\Gamma \in G$. A sequent Γ is *valid in $\mathcal{A}$* if there is some formula listed in Γ that is valid in $\mathcal{A}$.
Validity in a class of Σ-structures is understood as validity in each of the Σ-structures of that class. If we omit the reference to a special Σ-structure we

mean validity (or reduction, cf. below) in some fixed class K of Σ-structures, e.g. the class of all Σ-structures (Σ-algebras) or the class of Herbrand Σ-structures (term-generated Σ-algebras), cf. Wirth (1997), Wirth & Gramlich (1994) for more interesting classes for establishing inductive validities.

Example 3.2 (Validity) For $x^{\exists} \in \mathrm{V}_{\exists}$, $y^{\forall} \in \mathrm{V}_{\forall}$, the sequent $x^{\exists}{=}y^{\forall}$ is $\emptyset$-valid in any $\mathcal{A}$ because we can choose $S_e := \mathrm{V}_{\forall}\times\mathrm{V}_{\exists}$ and $e(x^{\exists})(\pi) := \pi(y^{\forall})$ resulting in $\epsilon(e)(\pi)(x^{\exists}) = e(x^{\exists})({}_{S_e\langle\{x^{\exists}\}\rangle}|\pi) = e(x^{\exists})({}_{\mathrm{V}_{\forall}}|\pi) = \pi(y^{\forall})$. This means that $\emptyset$-validity of $x^{\exists}{=}y^{\forall}$ is the same as validity of $\forall y\colon \exists x\colon x{=}y$. Moreover, note that $\epsilon(e)(\pi)$ has access to the π-value of $y^{\forall}$ just as a raising function f for x in the raised (i.e. dually Skolemized) version $f(y^{\forall}){=}y^{\forall}$ of $\forall y\colon \exists x\colon x{=}y$. Contrary to this, for $R := \mathrm{V}_{\exists}\times\mathrm{V}_{\forall}$, the same formula $x^{\exists}{=}y^{\forall}$ is not R-valid in general because then the required irreflexivity of $S_e{\circ}R$ implies $S_e = \emptyset$, and $e(x^{\exists})({}_{S_e\langle\{x^{\exists}\}\rangle}|\pi) = e(x^{\exists})({}_{\emptyset}|\pi) = e(x^{\exists})(\emptyset)$ cannot depend on $\pi(y^{\forall})$ anymore. This means that $(\mathrm{V}_{\exists}\times\mathrm{V}_{\forall})$-validity of $x^{\exists}{=}y^{\forall}$ is the same as validity of $\exists x\colon \forall y\colon x{=}y$. Moreover, note that $\epsilon(e)(\pi)$ has no access to the π-value of $y^{\forall}$ just as a raising function c for x in the raised version $c{=}y^{\forall}$ of $\exists x\colon \forall y\colon x{=}y$.
For a more general example let $G = \{\ A_{i,0}\ldots A_{i,n_i-1} \mid i{\in}I\ \}$, where for $i \in I$ and $j \prec n_i$ the $A_{i,j}$ are formulas with free existential variables from $\vec{x}$ and free universal variables from $\vec{y}$. Then $(\mathrm{V}_{\exists}\times\mathrm{V}_{\forall})$-validity of G means validity of

$$\exists\vec{x}\colon \forall\vec{y}\colon \forall i{\in}I\colon \exists j{\prec}n_i\colon A_{i,j};$$

whereas $\emptyset$-validity of G means validity of

$$\forall\vec{y}\colon \exists\vec{x}\colon \forall i{\in}I\colon \exists j{\prec}n_i\colon A_{i,j}.$$

Besides the notion of validity we need the notion of reduction. Roughly speaking, a set G_0 of sequents reduces to a set G_1 of sequents if validity of G_1 implies validity of G_0. This, however, is too weak for our purposes here because we are not only interested in validity but also in preserving the solutions for the free existential variables: For ITP, answer computation, and constraint solving it becomes important that the solutions of G_1 are also solutions of G_0.

Definition 3.3 (Reduction)
G_0 *R-reduces to* G_1 *in* $\mathcal{A}$ if for all existential $(\mathcal{A}, R)$-valuations e:

if G_1 is $(e, \mathcal{A})$-valid then G_0 is $(e, \mathcal{A})$-valid, too.

Now we are going to abstractly describe deductive sequent and tableau calculi. We will later show that the usual deductive first-order calculi are instances of our abstract calculi. The benefit of the abstract version is that every instance is automatically sound. Due to the small number of inference rules in deductive first-order calculi and the locality of soundness, this abstract version is not really necessary. For inductive calculi, however, due to a bigger number of inference rules that usually have to be improved now and then and the globality of soundness, such an abstract version is very helpful, cf. Wirth & Becker (1995), Wirth (1997).

Definition 3.4 (Proof Forest)
A *(deductive) proof forest in a sequent* (or else: *tableau*) *calculus* is a pair (F, R) where R is a variable-condition and F is a set of pairs (Γ, t), where Γ is a sequent and t is a tree whose nodes are labeled with sequents (or else: formulas).

Note that the tree t is intended to represent a proof attempt for Γ. The nodes of t are labeled with formulas in a tableau calculus and with sequents in a sequent calculus. While the sequents at the nodes of a tree in a sequent calculus stand for themselves, in a tableau calculus all the ancestors have to be included to make up a sequent and, moreover, the formulas at the labels are in negated form:

Definition 3.5 (Goals(), $\mathcal{AX}$, Closedness)
'Goals(T)' denotes the set of sequents labeling the leaves of the trees in the set T (or else: the set of sequents resulting from listing the conjugates of the formulas labeling a branch from a leaf to the root in a tree in T).
We assume $\mathcal{AX}$ to be some set of *axioms*. By this we mean that $\mathcal{AX}$ is $\mathrm{V}_\exists\times\mathrm{V}_\forall$-valid. (Cf. the last sentence in Def. 3.1.)
The tree t is *closed* if Goals$(\{t\})\subseteq\mathcal{AX}$.

The readers may ask themselves why we consider a forest instead of a single tree only. The possibility to have an empty forest provides a nicer starting point. Besides that, if we have trees (Γ,t), $(\Gamma',t')\in F$ we can apply Γ as a lemma in the tree t' of Γ', provided that the lemma application relation is acyclic. For deductive theorem proving the availability of lemma application is not really necessary. For ITP, however, lemma and induction hypothesis application of this form becomes necessary.

Definition 3.6 (Invariant Condition) The *invariant condition on* (F,R) is that $\{\Gamma\}$ R-reduces to Goals$(\{t\})$ for all $(\Gamma,t)\in F$.

Theorem 3.7 *Let the proof forest (F,R) satisfy the above invariant condition. Let $(\Gamma,t)\in F$. If t is closed, then Γ is R-valid.*

Theorem 3.8 *The above invariant condition is always satisfied when we start with an empty proof forest $(F,R):=(\emptyset,\emptyset)$ and then iterate only the following kinds of modifications of (F,R) (resulting in (F',R')):*

Hypothesizing: *Let R' be a variable-condition with $R\subseteq R'$. Let Γ be a sequent. Let t be the tree with a single node only, which is labeled with Γ (or else: with a single branch only, such that Γ is the list of the conjugates of the formulas labeling the branch from the leaf to the root). Then we may set $F':=F\cup\{(\Gamma,t)\}$.*

Expansion: *Let $(\Gamma,t)\in F$. Let R' be a variable-condition with $R\subseteq R'$. Let l be a leaf in t. Let Δ be the label of l (or else: result from listing the conjugates of the formulas labeling the branch from l to the root of t). Let G be a finite set of sequents. Now if $\{\Delta\}$ R'-reduces to G (or else: $\{\,\Lambda\Delta\mid\Lambda\in G\,\}$), then we may set $F':=(F\backslash\{(\Gamma,t)\})\cup\{(\Gamma,t')\}$ where t' results from t by adding to the former leaf l, exactly for each sequent Λ in G, a new child node labeled with Λ (or else: a new child branch such that Λ is the list of the conjugates of the formulas labeling the branch from the leaf to the new child node of l).*

Instantiation: *Let σ be an existential R-substitution. Let R' be the σ-update of R. Then we may set $F':=F\sigma$.*

While Hypothesizing and Instantiation steps are self-explanatory, Expansion steps are parameterized by a sequent Δ and a set of sequents G such that $\{\Delta\}$ R'-reduces to G. For tableau calculi, however, this set of sequents must actually have the form $\{\ \Lambda\Delta \mid \Lambda \in G\ \}$ because an Expansion step cannot remove formulas from ancestor nodes. This is because these formulas are also part of the goals associated with other leaves in the proof tree. Therefore, although tableau calculi may save repetition of formulas, sequent calculi have substantial advantages: Rewriting of formulas in place is always possible, and we can remove formulas that are redundant w.r.t. the other formulas in a sequent. But this is not our subject here. For the below examples of α-, β-, γ-, and δ-rules we will use the sequent calculi presentation because it is a little more explicit. When we write $\frac{\Delta}{\Pi_0 \ldots \Pi_{n-1}}\ R''$ we want to denote a sub-rule of the Expansion rule which is given by $G := \{\Pi_0, \ldots, \Pi_{n-1}\}$ and $R' := R \cup R''$. This means that for this rule really being a sub-rule of the Expansion rule we have to show that $\{\Delta\}$ R'-reduces to G. Moreover, note that in old times when trees grew upwards, Gerhard Gentzen would have written $\Pi_0 \ldots \Pi_{n-1}$ above the line and Δ below, such that passing the line meant implication. In our case, passing the line means reduction.

Let A and B be formulas, Γ and Π sequents, $x \in \mathrm{V}_{\mathrm{bound}}$, $x^{\exists} \in \mathrm{V}_{\exists} \setminus \mathcal{V}_{\exists}(A\Gamma\Pi)$, and $x^{\forall} \in \mathrm{V}_{\forall} \setminus \mathcal{V}_{\forall}(A\Gamma\Pi)$.

α-rules: $\quad \dfrac{\Gamma\ \ (A\vee B)\ \ \Pi}{A\ \ B\ \ \Gamma\ \ \Pi}\ \emptyset \qquad \dfrac{\Gamma\ \ \neg(A\wedge B)\ \ \Pi}{\overline{A}\ \ \overline{B}\ \ \Gamma\ \ \Pi}\ \emptyset \qquad \dfrac{\Gamma\ \ \neg\neg A\ \ \Pi}{A\ \ \Gamma\ \ \Pi}\ \emptyset$

β-rules: $\quad \dfrac{\Gamma\ \ (A\wedge B)\ \ \Pi}{A\ \ \Gamma\ \ \Pi \qquad\qquad B\ \ \Gamma\ \ \Pi}\ \emptyset \qquad \dfrac{\Gamma\ \ \neg(A\vee B)\ \ \Pi}{\overline{A}\ \ \Gamma\ \ \Pi \qquad\qquad \overline{B}\ \ \Gamma\ \ \Pi}\ \emptyset$

γ-rules: $\quad \dfrac{\Gamma\ \ \exists x\colon A\ \ \Pi}{A\{x\mapsto x^{\exists}\}\ \ \Gamma\ \ \exists x\colon A\ \ \Pi}\ \emptyset \qquad \dfrac{\Gamma\ \ \neg\forall x\colon A\ \ \Pi}{\overline{A\{x\mapsto x^{\exists}\}}\ \ \Gamma\ \ \neg\forall x\colon A\ \ \Pi}\ \emptyset$

δ-rules: $\quad \dfrac{\Gamma\ \ \forall x\colon A\ \ \Pi}{A\{x\mapsto x^{\forall}\}\ \ \Gamma\ \ \Pi}\ \mathcal{V}_{\exists}(A\Gamma\Pi)\times\{x^{\forall}\} \qquad \dfrac{\Gamma\ \ \neg\exists x\colon A\ \ \Pi}{\overline{A\{x\mapsto x^{\forall}\}}\ \ \Gamma\ \ \Pi}\ \mathcal{V}_{\exists}(A\Gamma\Pi)\times\{x^{\forall}\}$

Theorem 3.9 *The above examples of α-, β-, γ-, and δ-rules are all sub-rules of the Expansion rule of the sequent calculus of Th. 3.8.*

4 The Strong Version

The additional solutions (or existential substitutions) of the strong version (which admit additional proofs compared to the weak version) do not add much difficulty when one is interested in validity only, cf. e.g. Hähnle & Schmitt (1994). When also the preservation of solutions is required, however, the additional substitutions pose some problems because the new solutions may tear some free universal variables out of their contexts:

Example 4.1 In Ex. 1.2 a liberalized δ-step reduced $\mathsf{P}(x^{\exists}),\ \ \forall y\colon \neg\mathsf{P}(y)$ to $\mathsf{P}(x^{\exists}),\ \neg\mathsf{P}(y^{\forall})$ with empty variable-condition $R{:=}\emptyset$. The latter sequent is $(e,\mathcal{A})$-valid for the strong existential $(\mathcal{A},R)$-valuation e given by $e(x^{\exists})(\pi) := \pi(y^{\forall})$. The former sequent, however, is not $(e,\mathcal{A})$-valid when $\mathsf{P}^{\mathcal{A}}(a)$ is true and $\mathsf{P}^{\mathcal{A}}(b)$ is false for some a, b from the universe of $\mathcal{A}$. To wit, take some π with $\pi(y^{\forall}) := b$.

How can we solve the problem exhibited in Ex. 4.1? I.e. how can we change the notion of reduction such that the liberalized δ-step becomes a reduction step?

Definition 4.2 (Choice-Condition and Compatibility)
C is a $(R,<)$-*choice-condition* if C is a (possibly) partial function from $V_\forall$ to formulas, R is a variable-condition, $<$ is a wellfounded ordering on $V_\forall$ with $(R \circ <) \subseteq R$, and, for all $y^\forall \in \mathrm{dom}(C)$: $z^\forall < y^\forall$ for all $z^\forall \in \mathcal{V}_\forall(C(y^\forall)) \setminus \{y^\forall\}$ and $u^\exists \; R \; y^\forall$ for all $u^\exists \in \mathcal{V}_\exists(C(y^\forall))$.
Let C be a $(R,<)$-choice-condition, $\mathcal{A}$ a Σ-structure, and e a strong existential $(\mathcal{A},R)$-valuation. We say that π is $(e,\mathcal{A})$-*compatible with* C if $\pi \in V_\forall \to \mathcal{A}$ and for each $y^\forall \in \mathrm{dom}(C)$: If $C(y^\forall)$ is $(\pi,e,\mathcal{A})$-valid, then $C(y^\forall)$ is $({}_{V_\forall \setminus \{y^\forall\}}|\pi \uplus \eta, e, \mathcal{A})$-valid for all $\eta \in \{y^\forall\} \to \mathcal{A}$.

Note that $(e,\mathcal{A})$-compatibility of π with $\{(y^\forall, B)\}$ means that a different choice for the π-value of $y^\forall$ does not destroy the validity of the formula B in $\mathcal{A} \uplus \epsilon(e)(\pi) \uplus \pi$, or that $\pi(y^\forall)$ is chosen such that B becomes invalid if such a choice is possible, which is closely related to Hilbert's ε-operator ($y^\forall = \varepsilon y\colon (\neg B\{y^\forall \mapsto y\})$). Moreover, note that $\emptyset$ is a $(R,\emptyset)$-choice-condition for any variable-condition R.

Definition 4.3 (Extended Strong σ-Update) Let C be a $(R,<)$-choice-condition and σ a strong existential R-substitution. The *extended strong σ-update* $(C',R',<')$ *of* $(C,R,<)$ is given by $C' := \{\, (x, B\sigma) \mid (x,B) \in C \,\}$, R' is the strong σ-update of R, $<' := < \circ (U_\sigma \circ R)^* \cup (U_\sigma \circ R)^+$.

We are now going to proceed like in the previous section, but using the strong versions instead of the weak ones. The tableau version is omitted because it differs from the sequent version just like before.

Definition 4.4 (Strong Validity) Let C be a $(R,<)$-choice-condition, $\mathcal{A}$ a Σ-structure, and G a set of sequents. G is C-*strongly* R-*valid in* $\mathcal{A}$ if there is a strong existential $(\mathcal{A},R)$-valuation e such that G is C-strongly $(e,\mathcal{A})$-valid. G is C-*strongly* $(e,\mathcal{A})$-*valid* if G is $(\pi,e,\mathcal{A})$-valid for each π that is $(e,\mathcal{A})$-compatible with C. The rest is given by Def. 3.1.

Example 4.5 (Strong Validity) Note that $\emptyset$-validity does not differ from $\emptyset$-strong $\emptyset$-validity and that $V_\exists \times V_\forall$-validity does not differ from $\emptyset$-strong $V_\exists \times V_\forall$-validity. This is because the notions of weak and strong existential valuations do not differ in these cases. Therefore, Ex. 3.2 is also an example for strong validity. Although $\emptyset$-strong R-validity always implies (weak) R-validity (because each strong existential $(\mathcal{A},R)$-valuation is a (weak) existential $(\mathcal{A},R)$-valuation), for R not being one of the extremes $\emptyset$ and $V_\exists \times V_\forall$, (weak) R-validity and $\emptyset$-strong R-validity differ from each other. E.g. the sequent $(*)$ in Ex. 1.3 is (weakly) R-valid but not $\emptyset$-strongly R-valid for the R of $(\#)$: For $S_e := \{(y^\forall, u^\exists),\ (v^\forall, x^\exists)\}$ we get $S_e \circ R = \{(y^\forall, v^\forall),\ (v^\forall, y^\forall)\}$, which is irreflexive. Since the sequent $(*)$ is $(e,\mathcal{A})$-valid for the (weak) existential $(\mathcal{A},R)$-valuation e given by $e(x^\exists)({}_{S_e\langle\{x^\exists\}\rangle}|\pi) = \pi(v^\forall)$ and $e(u^\exists)({}_{S_e\langle\{u^\exists\}\rangle}|\pi) = \pi(y^\forall)$, the sequent $(*)$ is (weakly) R-valid in $\mathcal{A}$. But $S_e \circ R \circ S_e \circ R$ is not irreflexive, so that this e is no *strong* existential $(\mathcal{A},R)$-valuation, which means that the sequent $(*)$ cannot be $\emptyset$-strongly R-valid in general.

Definition 4.6 (Strong Reduction)
Let C be a $(R,<)$-choice-condition, $\mathcal{A}$ a Σ-structure, and G_0, G_1 sets of sequents. G_0 *strongly* (R,C)*-reduces to* G_1 *in* $\mathcal{A}$ if for each strong existential $(\mathcal{A},R)$-valuation e and each π that is $(e,\mathcal{A})$-compatible with C:

if G_1 is $(\pi,e,\mathcal{A})$-valid, then G_0 is $(\pi,e,\mathcal{A})$-valid.

Definition 4.7 (Strong Proof Forest)
A *strong proof forest in a sequent calculus* is a quadruple $(F,C,R,<)$ where C is a $(R,<)$-choice-condition and F is a set of pairs (Γ,t), where Γ is a sequent and t is a tree whose nodes are labeled with sequents.

The notions of Goals(), $\mathcal{AX}$, and closedness of Def. 3.5 are not changed. Note, however, that the $\mathrm{V}_\exists\times\mathrm{V}_\forall$-validity of $\mathcal{AX}$ immediately implies the $\emptyset$-strong $\mathrm{V}_\exists\times\mathrm{V}_\forall$-validity of $\mathcal{AX}$, i.e. the logically strongest kind of C-strong R-validity.

Definition 4.8 (Strong Invariant Condition)
The *strong invariant condition on* $(F,C,R,<)$ is that $\{\Gamma\}$ strongly (R,C)-reduces to Goals($\{t\}$) for all $(\Gamma,t)\in F$.

Theorem 4.9 *Let the strong proof forest* $(F,C,R,<)$ *satisfy the above strong invariant condition. Let* $(\Gamma,t)\in F$ *and* t *be closed. Now:* Γ *is* C*-strongly* R*-valid and, for any injective* $\varsigma\in(\mathcal{V}_\forall(\Gamma)\cap\mathrm{dom}(C))\to(\mathrm{V}_\exists\backslash\mathcal{V}_\exists(\Gamma))$, $\Gamma\varsigma$ *is* $\emptyset$*-strongly* ${}_{\mathrm{V}_\exists\backslash\mathrm{ran}(\varsigma)}|R$*-valid and even* $\emptyset$*-strongly* R'*-valid for*
$R' := {}_{\mathrm{V}_\exists\backslash\mathrm{ran}(\varsigma)}|R \;\cup\; \bigcup_{y\in\mathrm{ran}(\varsigma)} \{y\}\times\langle\!\{\varsigma^{-1}(y)\}\!\rangle{<} \;\cup\; \mathrm{V}_\exists\times\mathrm{dom}(C)$.

Theorem 4.10
The above strong invariant condition is always satisfied when we start with an empty strong proof forest $(F,C,R,<) := (\emptyset,\emptyset,\emptyset,\emptyset)$ *and then iterate only the following kinds of modifications of* $(F,C,R,<)$ *(resulting in* $(F',C',R',<')$*):*

Hypothesizing: *Let* $R' := R\cup R''$ *be a variable-condition with* $(R''\circ<)\subseteq R'$. *Set* $C' := C$ *and* $<' := <$. *Let* Γ *be a sequent. Let* t *be the tree with a single node only, which is labeled with* Γ. *Then we may set* $F' := F\cup\{(\Gamma,t)\}$.

Expansion: *Let* C' *be a* $(R',<')$*-choice-condition with* $C\subseteq C'$ *and* $R\subseteq R'$. *Let* $(\Gamma,t)\in F$. *Let* l *be a leaf in* t. *Let* Δ *be the label of* l. *Let* G *be a finite set of sequents. Now if* $\{\Delta\}$ *strongly* (R',C')*-reduces to* G, *then we may set* $F' := (F\backslash\{(\Gamma,t)\})\cup\{(\Gamma,t')\}$ *where* t' *results from* t *by adding to the former leaf* l, *exactly for each sequent* Λ *in* G, *a new child node labeled with* Λ.

Instantiation: *Let* σ *be a strong existential* R*-substitution. Let* $(C',R',<')$ *be the extended strong* σ*-update of* $(C,R,<)$. *Then we may set* $F' := F\sigma$.

When we write $\dfrac{\Delta}{\Pi_0\ldots\Pi_{n-1}}\;\begin{matrix}C''\\R''\\<''\end{matrix}$ we want to denote a sub-rule of the Expansion rule which is given by $G := \{\Pi_0,\ldots,\Pi_{n-1}\}$, $C' := C\cup C''$, $R' := R\cup R''$, and $<' := <\cup<''$. This means that for this rule really being a sub-rule of the Expansion rule we have to show that C' is a $(R',<')$-choice-condition and that $\{\Delta\}$ strongly (R',C')-reduces to G.

Let A and B be formulas, Γ and Π sequents, $x \in \mathrm{V_{bound}}$, $x^{\exists} \in \mathrm{V}_{\exists} \setminus \mathcal{V}_{\exists}(A\Gamma\Pi)$, and $x^{\forall} \in \mathrm{V}_{\forall} \setminus (\mathcal{V}_{\forall}(A\Gamma\Pi) \cup \mathrm{dom}(<) \cup \mathrm{dom}(C))$. The α-, β-, and γ-rules differ from those of the weak version only in a triple instead of single $\emptyset$-annotation. Liberalized δ-rules:

$$\frac{\Gamma \quad \forall x\colon A \quad \Pi}{A\{x \mapsto x^{\forall}\} \quad \Gamma \quad \Pi} \begin{array}{l} \{(x^{\forall}, A\{x \mapsto x^{\forall}\})\} \\ (\mathcal{V}_{\exists}(A) \cup R\langle \mathcal{V}_{\forall}(A)\rangle) \times \{x^{\forall}\} \\ \leq\langle \mathcal{V}_{\forall}(A)\rangle \times \{x^{\forall}\} \end{array} \qquad \frac{\Gamma \quad \neg\exists x\colon A \quad \Pi}{\overline{A\{x \mapsto x^{\forall}\}} \quad \Gamma \quad \Pi} \begin{array}{l} \{(x^{\forall}, \overline{A\{x \mapsto x^{\forall}\}})\} \\ (\mathcal{V}_{\exists}(A) \cup R\langle \mathcal{V}_{\forall}(A)\rangle) \times \{x^{\forall}\} \\ \leq\langle \mathcal{V}_{\forall}(A)\rangle \times \{x^{\forall}\} \end{array}$$

Theorem 4.11 *The above examples of α-, β-, γ-, and liberalized δ-rules are all sub-rules of the Expansion rule of the sequent calculus of Th. 4.10.*

The following example shows that R'' of the above liberalized δ-rule must indeed contain $R\langle \mathcal{V}_{\forall}(A)\rangle \times \{x^{\forall}\}$.

Example 4.12 $\exists y\colon \forall x\colon (\neg \mathsf{Q}(x, y) \vee \forall z\colon \mathsf{Q}(x, z))$ is not deductively valid (to wit, let Q be the identity relation on a non-trivial universe). γ-step: $\forall x\colon (\neg \mathsf{Q}(x, y^{\exists}) \vee \forall z\colon \mathsf{Q}(x, z))$. Liberalized δ-step: $(\neg \mathsf{Q}(x^{\forall}, y^{\exists}) \vee \forall z\colon \mathsf{Q}(x^{\forall}, z))$ with choice-condition $(x^{\forall}, (\neg \mathsf{Q}(x^{\forall}, y^{\exists}) \vee \forall z\colon \mathsf{Q}(x^{\forall}, z)))$ and variable-condition $(y^{\exists}, x^{\forall})$. α-step: $\neg \mathsf{Q}(x^{\forall}, y^{\exists})$, $\forall z\colon \mathsf{Q}(x^{\forall}, z)$. Liberalized δ-step: $\neg \mathsf{Q}(x^{\forall}, y^{\exists})$, $\mathsf{Q}(x^{\forall}, z^{\forall})$ with additional choice-condition $(z^{\forall}, \mathsf{Q}(x^{\forall}, z^{\forall}))$ and additional variable-condition $(y^{\exists}, z^{\forall})$. Note that the additional variable-condition arises although $y^{\exists}$ does not appear in $\mathsf{Q}(x^{\forall}, z)$. The reason for the additional variable-condition is $y^{\exists} \ R \ x^{\forall} \in \mathcal{V}_{\forall}(\mathsf{Q}(x^{\forall}, z))$. The variable-condition $(y^{\exists}, z^{\forall})$ is, however, essential for soundness, because without it we could complete the proof attempt by application of the strong existential $\{(y^{\exists}, x^{\forall})\}$-substitution $\sigma := \{y^{\exists} \mapsto z^{\forall}\} \uplus {}_{\mathrm{V}_{\exists} \setminus \{y^{\exists}\}}|\mathrm{id}$.

Another interesting point is that now that we have achieved our goal of liberalizing our δ-rule and strictly increasing our proving possibilities, we must not use our original non-liberalized δ-rule of section 3 anymore. This sounds quite strange on the first view, but is simply due to our changed notion of reduction: There is a fundamental difference related to the occurrence of the universal quantification on π between the notion of (weak) reduction

$$\ldots(\forall \pi\colon G_1 \ (\pi, e, \mathcal{A})\text{-valid}) \Rightarrow (\forall \pi\colon G_0 \ (\pi, e, \mathcal{A})\text{-valid}) \ldots$$

and the notion of strong reduction

$$\ldots \forall \pi\colon (G_1 \ (\pi, e, \mathcal{A})\text{-valid} \Rightarrow G_0 \ (\pi, e, \mathcal{A})\text{-valid}) \ldots.$$

This difference in the nature of reduction renders the weak version applicable in areas where the strong version is not. For this reason (and for the sake of stepwise presentation) we have included the weak version in this paper although the strong version will turn out to be superior in all aspects of the calculus of Th. 4.11 treated in this paper. For a more detailed discussion of this difference in the nature of reduction and its essentiality, cf. Wirth (1998).

Moreover, note that (as far as Th. 4.11 is concerned) the choice-conditions do not have any influence on our proofs and may be discarded. We could, however, use them for the following purposes:

1. We could use the choice-conditions in order to weaken our requirements for our set of axioms $\mathcal{AX}$: Instead of $\emptyset$-strong $\mathrm{V}_{\exists} \times \mathrm{V}_{\forall}$-validity of $\mathcal{AX}$ the weaker C-strong $\mathrm{V}_{\exists} \times \mathrm{V}_{\forall}$-validity of $\mathcal{AX}$ is sufficient for Th. 4.9.

2. If we add a functional behavior to a choice-condition C, i.e. if we require that for $(x^{\forall}, A) \in C$ the value for $x^{\forall}$ is not just an arbitrary one from the set of values that make A invalid, but a unique element of this set given by some choice-function, then we can use the choice-conditions for simulating the behavior of the δ^{++}-rule of Beckert & al. (1993) by using the same free universal variable for the same C-value and by later equating free universal variables whose C-values become equal during the proof.
3. Moreover, the choice-conditions may be used to get more interesting answers:

   Example 4.13 Starting with the empty proof tree and hypothesizing
   $$\forall x\colon \mathsf{Q}(x,x),\ \exists y\colon \left(\neg\mathsf{Q}(y,y) \wedge \neg\mathsf{P}(y)\right),\ \mathsf{P}(z^{\exists})$$
   with the above rules we can produce a proof tree with the leaves
   $$\neg\mathsf{Q}(y^{\exists},y^{\exists}),\ \mathsf{Q}(x^{\forall},x^{\forall}),\ \exists y\colon \left(\neg\mathsf{Q}(y,y) \wedge \neg\mathsf{P}(y)\right),\ \mathsf{P}(z^{\exists})$$
   and $$\neg\mathsf{P}(y^{\exists}),\ \mathsf{Q}(x^{\forall},x^{\forall}),\ \exists y\colon \left(\neg\mathsf{Q}(y,y) \wedge \neg\mathsf{P}(y)\right),\ \mathsf{P}(z^{\exists})$$
   and the $(\emptyset,\emptyset)$-choice-condition $\{(x^{\forall}, \mathsf{Q}(x^{\forall},x^{\forall}))\}$.
   The strong existential $\emptyset$-substitution $\{y^{\exists}\mapsto x^{\forall},\ z^{\exists}\mapsto x^{\forall}\} \uplus {}_{V_{\exists}\setminus\{y^{\exists},z^{\exists}\}}|\mathrm{id}$ closes the proof tree via an Instantiation step. The answer $x^{\forall}$ for our query variable $z^{\exists}$ is not very interesting unless we note that the choice-condition tells us to choose $x^{\forall}$ in such a way that $\mathsf{Q}(x^{\forall},x^{\forall})$ becomes false.
   The rules of our weak version of section 3 are not only unable to provide any information on free universal variables, but also unable to prove the hypothesized sequent, because they can only show
   $$\forall x\colon \mathsf{Q}(x,x),\ \exists y\colon \left(\neg\mathsf{Q}(y,y) \wedge \neg\mathsf{P}(y)\right),\ \exists z\colon \mathsf{P}(z)$$
   instead.

   Thus it is obvious that the calculus of Th. 4.11 is not only superior to the calculus of Th. 3.9 w.r.t. proving but also w.r.t. answer "computation".

Finally, note that (w.r.t. the calculus of Th. 4.11) the ordering $<$ is not needed at all when in the liberalized δ-steps we always choose a completely new free universal variable $x^{\forall}$ that does not occur elsewhere and when in the Hypothesizing steps we guarantee that $\mathrm{ran}(R'')$ contains only new free universal variables that have not occurred before. The former is reasonable anyhow, because the free universal variables introduced by previous liberalized δ-steps cannot be used because they are in $\mathrm{dom}(C)$ and the use of a free universal variable from the input hypothesis deteriorates the result of our proof by giving this free universal variable an existential meaning (because it puts it into $\mathrm{dom}(C)$) as explained in Th. 4.9. The latter does not seem to be restrictive for any reasonable application.

All in all, when interested in proving only, the (compared to the weak version) additional choice-condition and ordering of the strong version do not produce any overhead because they can simply be omitted. This is interesting because choice-conditions or Hilbert's ε-expressions are sometimes considered to make proofs quite complicated. When interested in answer "computation", however, they could turn out to be useful.

W.r.t. the calculus of Th. 4.11 we thus may conclude that the strong version is generally better than the weak version and the only overhead seems to be that we have to compute transitive closures when checking whether a substitution σ

is really a strong existential R-substitution and when computing the strong σ-update of R. But we actually do not have to compute the transitive closure at all, because the only essential thing is the circularity-check which can be done on a bipartite graph generating the transitive closures. This checking is in the worst case linear in $|R| + \sum_\sigma (|U_\sigma| + |E_\sigma|)$ and is expected to perform at least as well as an optimally integrated version (i.e. one without conversion of term-representation) of the linear unification algorithm of Paterson & Wegman (1978) in the standard framework of Skolemization and unification. Note, however, that the checking for strong existential R-substitutions can also be implemented with any other unification algorithm.

Not really computing the transitive closure enables another refinement that allows us to go even beyond the fascinating *strong Skolemization* of Nonnengart (1996), whose basic idea can be translated into our framework in the following simplified way. Instead of proving $\forall x\colon (A \vee B)$ it may be advantageous to prove the stronger $\forall x\colon A \vee \forall x\colon B$, because after applications of α- and liberalized δ-rules to $\forall x\colon A \vee \forall x\colon B$, resulting in $A\{x \mapsto x^{\curlyvee}_A\}$, $B\{x \mapsto x^{\curlyvee}_B\}$, the variable-conditions introduced for $x^{\curlyvee}_A$ and $x^{\curlyvee}_B$ may be smaller than the variable-condition introduced for $y^{\curlyvee}$ after applying these rules to $\forall x\colon (A \vee B)$, resulting in $A\{x \mapsto y^{\curlyvee}\}$, $B\{x \mapsto y^{\curlyvee}\}$, i.e. $R\langle\{x^{\curlyvee}_A\}\rangle$ and $R\langle\{x^{\curlyvee}_B\}\rangle$ may be *proper* subsets of $R\langle\{y^{\curlyvee}\}\rangle$. Therefore the proof of $\forall x\colon A \vee \forall x\colon B$ may be simpler than the proof of $\forall x\colon (A \vee B)$. The nice aspect of Nonnengart (1996) is that the proofs of $\forall x\colon A$ and $\forall x\colon (A \vee B)$ can be done in parallel without extra costs, such that the bigger variable-condition becomes active only if we decide that the smaller variable-condition is not enough to prove $\forall x\colon A$ and we had better prove the weaker $\forall x\colon (A \vee B)$. The disadvantage of the strong Skolemization approach, however, is that we have to decide whether to prove either $\forall x\colon A$ or else $\forall x\colon B$ in parallel to $\forall x\colon (A \vee B)$. In terms of Hilbert's ε-operator, this asymmetry can be understood from the argumentation of Nonnengart (1996), which, for some new variable $z \in \mathrm{V}_{\mathrm{bound}}$ and t denoting the term $\varepsilon z\colon (\neg A\{x \mapsto z\} \wedge (A \vee x{=}z))$, employs the logical equivalence of $\forall x\colon (A \vee B)$ with $\forall x\colon A \vee \forall x\colon (B\{x \mapsto t\})$ and of $\forall x\colon A$ with $\exists x\colon (A\{x \mapsto t\})$. Now, if we do not really compute the transitive closures in our strong version, we can prove $A\{x \mapsto x^{\curlyvee}_A\}$, $B\{x \mapsto x^{\curlyvee}_B\}$ in parallel and may later decide to prove the stronger $A\{x \mapsto y^{\curlyvee}\}$, $B\{x \mapsto y^{\curlyvee}\}$ instead, simply by merging the nodes for $x^{\curlyvee}_A$ and $x^{\curlyvee}_B$ and substituting $x^{\curlyvee}_A$ and $x^{\curlyvee}_B$ with $y^{\curlyvee}$.

5 Conclusion

All in all, we have presented a combination of raising, explicit variable dependency representation, the liberalized δ-rule, and preservation of solutions for first-order deductive theorem proving. Our main motivation was to provide the foundation for our work on inductive theorem proving (cf. Wirth (1999)) where the preservation of solutions is indispensable.

To our knowledge we have presented on the one hand the first sound combination of explicit variable dependency representation and the liberalized δ-rule and on the other hand the first framework for preservation of solutions in full first-order logic.

References

Matthias Baaz, Christian G. Fermüller (1995). *Non-elementary Speedups between Different Versions of Tableaux.* 4th TABLEAUX 1995, LNAI 918, pp. 217-230, Springer.

Peter Baumgartner, Ulrich Furbach, Frieder Stolzenburg (1997). *Computing Answers with Model Elimination.* Artificial Intelligence **90**, pp. 135-176.

Bernhard Beckert, Reiner Hähnle, Peter H. Schmitt (1993). *The Even More Liberalized δ-Rule in Free Variable Semantic Tableaux.* Kurt Gödel Colloquium, LNCS 713, pp. 108-119, Springer.

Wolfgang Bibel (1987). *Automated Theorem Proving.* 2nd rev.ed., Vieweg, Braunschweig.

Wolfgang Bibel, Peter H. Schmitt (eds.) (1998). *Automated Deduction — A Basis for Applications.* Kluwer Acad. Publ..

Melvin Fitting (1996). *First-Order Logic and Automated Theorem Proving.* 2nd extd. ed., Springer.

Gerhard Gentzen (1935). *Untersuchungen über das logische Schließen.* Mathematische Zeitschrift **39**, pp. 176-210, 405-431.

Reiner Hähnle, Peter H. Schmitt (1994). *The Liberalized δ-Rule in Free Variable Semantic Tableaux.* J. Automated Reasoning **13**, pp. 211-221, Kluwer Acad. Publ..

S. Kanger (1963). *A Simplified Proof Method for Elementary Logic.* In: Siekmann & Wrightson (1983), Vol. 1, pp. 364-371.

Michaël Kohlhase (1995). *Higher-Order Tableaux.* 4th TABLEAUX 1995, LNAI 918, pp. 294-309, Springer. Revised version is: Kohlhase (1998).

Michaël Kohlhase (1998). *Higher-Order Automated Theorem Proving.* In: Bibel & Schmitt (1998), Vol. 1, pp. 431-462.

Dale Miller (1992). *Unification under a Mixed Prefix.* J. Symbolic Computation **14**, pp. 321-358.

Andreas Nonnengart (1996). *Strong Skolemization.* MPI–I–96–2–010, Max-Planck-Institut für Informatik, Saarbrücken.

Michael S. Paterson, Mark N. Wegman (1978). *Linear Unification.* J. Computer and System Sci. **16**, pp. 158-167, Academic Press.

Dag Prawitz (1960). *An Improved Proof Procedure.* In: Siekmann & Wrightson (1983), Vol. 1, pp. 159-199.

Jörg Siekmann, G. Wrightson (eds.) (1983). *Automation of Reasoning.* Springer.

Raymond M. Smullyan (1968). *First-Order Logic.* Springer.

Claus-Peter Wirth (1997). *Positive/Negative-Conditional Equations: A Constructor-Based Framework for Specification and Inductive Theorem Proving.* Dissertation (Ph.D. thesis), Verlag Dr. Kovač, Hamburg.

Claus-Peter Wirth (1998). *Full First-Order Sequent and Tableau Calculi With Preservation of Solutions and the Liberalized δ-Rule but Without Skolemization.* Report 698/1998, FB Informatik, Univ. Dortmund. `http://LS5.cs.uni-dortmund.de/~wirth/publications/gr698/all.ps.gz`.

Claus-Peter Wirth (1999). *Full First-Order Free Variable Sequents and Tableaux in Implicit Induction.* 8th TABLEAUX 1999, LNAI, Springer, to appear.

Claus-Peter Wirth, Klaus Becker (1995). *Abstract Notions and Inference Systems for Proofs by Mathematical Induction.* 4th CTRS 1994, LNCS 968, pp. 353-373, Springer.

Claus-Peter Wirth, Bernhard Gramlich (1994). *On Notions of Inductive Validity for First-Order Equational Clauses.* 12th CADE 1994, LNAI 814, pp. 162-176, Springer.

Acknowledgements: I would like to thank Ulrich Furbach and his whole group for all they taught me on tableau calculi. Furthermore, I would like to thank Michaël Kohlhase for his encouragement to drop Skolemization, and Peter Padawitz for the possibility to finish this work. Finally, I am indebted to an anonymous referee for his careful reading of an earlier version of this paper and his most useful remarks.

Editorial Remark: Wirth (1998) is a long version of this paper including all proofs.

References

Author Index

Lecture Notes in Artificial Intelligence (LNAI)

Vol. 1620: W. Horn, Y. Shahar, G. Lindberg, S. Andreassen, J. Wyatt (Eds.), Artificial Intelligence in Medicine. Proceedings, 1999. XIII, 454 pages. 1999.

Vol. 1621: D. Fensel, R. Studer (Eds.), Knowledge Acquisition Modeling and Management. Proceedings, 1999. XI, 404 pages. 1999.

Vol. 1623: T. Reinartz, Focusing Solutions for Data Mining. XV, 309 pages. 1999.

Vol. 1624: J. A. Padget (Ed.), Collaboration between Human and Artificial Societies. XIV, 301 pages. 1999.

Vol. 1630: M. M. Huntbach, G. A. Ringwood, Agent-Oriented Programming. XIV, 386 pages. 1999.

Vol. 1632: H. Ganzinger (Ed.), Automated Deduction – CADE-16. Proceedings, 1999. XIV, 429 pages. 1999.

Vol. 1634: S. Džeroski, P. Flach (Eds.), Inductive Logic Programming. Proceedings, 1999. VIII, 303 pages. 1999.

Vol. 1637: J.P. Walser, Integer Optimization by Local Search. XIX, 137 pages. 1999.

Vol. 1638: A. Hunter, S. Parsons (Eds.), Symbolic and Quantitative Approaches to Reasoning and Uncertainty. Proceedings, 1999. IX, 397 pages. 1999.

Vol. 1640: W. Tepfenhart, W. Cyre (Eds.), Conceptual Structures: Standards and Practices. Proceedings, 1999. XII, 515 pages. 1999.

Vol. 1647: F.J. Garijo, M. Boman (Eds.), Multi-Agent System Engineering. Proceedings, 1999. X, 233 pages. 1999.

Vol. 1650: K.-D. Althoff, R. Bergmann, L.K. Branting (Eds.), Case-Based Reasoning Research and Development. Proceedings, 1999. XII, 598 pages. 1999.

Vol. 1652: M. Klusch, O.M. Shehory, G. Weiss (Eds.), Cooperative Information Agents III. Proceedings, 1999. XI, 404 pages. 1999.

Vol. 1669: X.-S. Gao, D. Wang, L. Yang (Eds.), Automated Deduction in Geometry. Proceedings, 1998. VII, 287 pages. 1999.

Vol. 1674: D. Floreano, J.-D. Nicoud, F. Mondada (Eds.), Advances in Artificial Life. Proceedings, 1999. XVI, 737 pages. 1999.

Vol. 1688: P. Bouquet, L. Serafini, P. Brézillon, M. Benerecetti, F. Castellani (Eds.), Modeling and Using Context. Proceedings, 1999. XII, 528 pages. 1999.

Vol. 1692: V. Matoušek, P. Mautner, J. Ocelíková, P. Sojka (Eds.), Text, Speech, and Dialogue. Proceedings, 1999. XI, 396 pages. 1999.

Vol. 1695: P. Barahona, J.J. Alferes (Eds.), Progress in Artificial Intelligence. Proceedings, 1999. XI, 385 pages. 1999.

Vol. 1699: S. Albayrak (Ed.), Intelligent Agents for Telecommunication Applications. Proceedings, 1999. IX, 191 pages. 1999.

Vol. 1701: W. Burgard, T. Christaller, A.B. Cremers (Eds.), KI-99: Advances in Artificial Intelligence. Proceedings, 1999. XI, 311 pages. 1999.

Vol. 1704: Jan M. Żytkow, J. Rauch (Eds.), Principles of Data Mining and Knowledge Discovery. Proceedings, 1999. XIV, 593 pages. 1999.

Vol. 1705: H. Ganzinger, D. McAllester, A. Voronkov (Eds.), Logic for Programming and Automated Reasoning. Proceedings, 1999. XII, 397 pages. 1999.

Vol. 1711: N. Zhong, A. Skowron, S. Ohsuga (Eds.), New Directions in Rough Sets, Data Mining, and Granular-Soft Computing. Proceedings, 1999. XIV, 558 pages. 1999.

Vol. 1712: H. Boley, A Tight, Practical Integration of Relations and Functions. XI, 169 pages. 1999.

Vol. 1714: M.T. Pazienza (Eds.), Information Extraction. IX, 165 pages. 1999.

Vol. 1715: P. Perner, M. Petrou (Eds.), Machine Learning and Data Mining in Pattern Recognition. Proceedings, 1999. VIII, 217 pages. 1999.

Vol. 1720: O. Watanabe, T. Yokomori (Eds.), Algorithmic Learning Theory. Proceedings, 1999. XI, 365 pages. 1999.

Vol. 1721: S. Arikawa, K. Furukawa (Eds.), Discovery Science. Proceedings, 1999. XI, 374 pages. 1999.

Vol. 1730: M. Gelfond, N. Leone, G. Pfeifer (Eds.), Logic Programming and Nonmonotonic Reasoning. Proceedings, 1999. XI, 391 pages. 1999.

Vol. 1733: H. Nakashima, C. Zhang (Eds.), Approaches to Intelligent Agents. Proceedings, 1999. XII, 241 pages. 1999.

Vol. 1735: J.W. Amtrup, Incremental Speech Translation. XV, 200 pages. 1999.

Vol. 1739: A. Braffort, R. Gherbi, S. Gibet, J. Richardson, D. Teil (Eds.), Gesture-Based Communication in Human-Computer Interaction. Proceedings, 1999. XI, 333 pages. 1999.

Vol. 1744: S. Staab, Grading Knowledge: Extracting Degree Information from Texts. X, 187 pages. 1999.

Vol. 1747: N. Foo (Ed.), Adavanced Topics in Artificial Intelligence. Proceedings, 1999. XV, 500 pages. 1999.

Vol. 1760: J.-J. Ch. Meyer, P.-Y. Schobbens (Eds.), Formal Models of Agents. Poceedings. VIII, 253 pages. 1999.

Vol. 1761: R. Caferra, G. Salzer (Eds.), Automated Deduction in Classical and Non-Classical Logics. Proceedings. VIII, 299 pages. 2000.

Lecture Notes in Computer Science

Vol. 1734: H. Hellwagner, A. Reinefeld (Eds.), SCI: Scalable Coherent Interface. XXI, 490 pages. 1999.

Vol. 1564: M. Vazirgiannis, Interactive Multimedia Documents. XIII, 161 pages. 1999.

Vol. 1591: D.J. Duke, I. Herman, M.S. Marshall, PREMO: A Framework for Multimedia Middleware. XII, 254 pages. 1999.

Vol. 1624: J. A. Padget (Ed.), Collaboration between Human and Artificial Societies. XIV, 301 pages. 1999. (Subseries LNAI).

Vol. 1635: X. Tu, Artificial Animals for Computer Animation. XIV, 172 pages. 1999.

Vol. 1646: B. Westfechtel, Models and Tools for Managing Development Processes. XIV, 418 pages. 1999.

Vol. 1735: J.W. Amtrup, Incremental Speech Translation. XV, 200 pages. 1999. (Subseries LNAI).

Vol. 1736: L. Rizzo, S. Fdida (Eds.): Networked Group Communication. Proceedings, 1999. XIII, 339 pages. 1999.

Vol. 1737: P. Agouris, A. Stefanidis (Eds.), Integrated Spatial Databases. Proceedings, 1999. X, 317 pages. 1999.

Vol. 1738: C. Pandu Rangan, V. Raman, R. Ramanujam (Eds.), Foundations of Software Technology and Theoretical Computer Science. Proceedings, 1999. XII, 452 pages. 1999.

Vol. 1739: A. Braffort, R. Gherbi, S. Gibet, J. Richardson, D. Teil (Eds.), Gesture-Based Communication in Human-Computer Interaction. Proceedings, 1999. XI, 333 pages. 1999. (Subseries LNAI).

Vol. 1740: R. Baumgart (Ed.): Secure Networking – CQRE [Secure] '99. Proceedings, 1999. IX, 261 pages. 1999.

Vol. 1741: A. Aggarwal, C. Pandu Rangan (Eds.), Algorithms and Computation. Proceedings, 1999. XIII, 448 pages. 1999.

Vol. 1742: P.S. Thiagarajan, R. Yap (Eds.), Advances in Computing Science – ASIAN'99. Proceedings, 1999. XI, 397 pages. 1999.

Vol. 1743: A. Moreira, S. Demeyer (Eds.), Object-Oriented Technology. Proceedings, 1999. XVII, 389 pages. 1999.

Vol. 1744: S. Staab, Grading Knowledge: Extracting Degree Information from Texts. X, 187 pages. 1999. (Subseries LNAI).

Vol. 1745: P. Banerjee, V.K. Prasanna, B.P. Sinha (Eds.), High Performance Computing – HiPC'99. Proceedings, 1999. XXII, 412 pages. 1999.

Vol. 1746: M. Walker (Ed.), Cryptography and Coding. Proceedings, 1999. IX, 313 pages. 1999.

Vol. 1747: N. Foo (Ed.), Adavanced Topics in Artificial Intelligence. Proceedings, 1999. XV, 500 pages. 1999. (Subseries LNAI).

Vol. 1748: H.V. Leong, W.-C. Lee, B. Li, L. Yin (Eds.), Mobile Data Access. Proceedings, 1999. X, 245 pages. 1999.

Vol. 1749: L. C.-K. Hui, D.L. Lee (Eds.), Internet Applications. Proceedings, 1999. XX, 518 pages. 1999.

Vol. 1750: D.E. Knuth, MMIXware. VIII, 550 pages. 1999.

Vol. 1751: H. Imai, Y. Zheng (Eds.), Public Key Cryptography. Proceedings, 2000. XI, 485 pages. 2000.

Vol. 1753: E. Pontelli, V. Santos Costa (Eds.), Practical Aspects of Declarative Languages. Proceedings, 2000. X, 327 pages. 2000.

Vol. 1754: J. Väänänen (Ed.), Generalized Quantifiers and Computation. Proceedings, 1997. VII, 139 pages. 1999.

Vol. 1755: D. Bjørner, M. Broy, A.V. Zamulin (Eds.), Perspectives of System Informatics. Proceedings, 1999. XII, 540 pages. 2000.

Vol. 1758: H. Heys, C. Adams (Eds.), Selected Areas in Cryptography. Proceedings, 1999. VIII, 243 pages. 2000.

Vol. 1760: J.-J. Ch. Meyer, P.-Y. Schobbens (Eds.), Formal Models of Agents. Poceedings. VIII, 253 pages. 1999. (Subseries LNAI).

Vol. 1761: R. Caferra, G. Salzer (Eds.), Automated Deduction in Classical and Non-Classical Logics. Proceedings. VIII, 299 pages. 2000. (Subseries LNAI).

Vol. 1762: K.-D. Schewe, B. Thalheim (Eds.), Foundations of Information and Knowledge Systems. Proceedings, 2000. X, 305 pages. 2000.

Vol. 1763: J. Akiyama, M. Kano, M. Urabe (Eds.), Discrete and Computational Geometry. Proceedings, 1998. VIII, 333 pages. 2000.

Vol. 1767: G. Bongiovanni, G. Gambosi, R. Petreschi (Eds.), Algorithms and Complexity. Proceedings, 2000. VIII, 317 pages. 2000.

Vol. 1768: A. Pfitzmann (Ed.), Information Hidig. Proceedings, 1999. IX, 492 pages. 2000.

Vol. 1769: G. Haring, C. Lindemann, M. Reiser (Eds.), Performance Evaluation: Origins and Directions. X, 529 pages. 2000.

Vol. 1770: H. Reichel, S. Tison (Eds.), STACS 2000. Proceedings, 2000. XIV, 662 pages. 2000.

Vol. 1774: J. Delgado, G.D. Stamoulis, A. Mullery, D. Prevedourou, K. Start (Eds.), Telecommunications and IT Convergence Towards Service E-volution. Proceedings, 2000. XIII, 350 pages. 2000.

Vol. 1780: R. Conradi (Ed.), Software Process Technology. Proceedings, 2000. IX, 249 pages. 2000.